LEO TOLSTOY
and the
CANADIAN DOUKHOBORS

LEO TOLSTOY
and the
CANADIAN DOUKHOBORS

A Study in Historic Relationships

by
Andrew Donskov

Expanded and Revised Edition

UNIVERSITY OF OTTAWA PRESS
2019

The University of Ottawa Press (UOP) is proud to be the oldest of the francophone university presses in Canada and the only bilingual university publisher in North America. Since 1936, UOP has been "enriching intellectual and cultural discourse" by producing peer-reviewed and award-winning books in the humanities and social sciences, in French or in English.

Library and Archives Canada Cataloguing in Publication

Title: Leo Tolstoy and the Canadian Doukhobors : a study in historic relationships / Andrew Donskov.

Names: Donskov, Andrew, 1939- author.

Description: Expanded and revised edition. | Includes bibliographical references and index.

Identifiers: Canadiana (print) 20190166630 | Canadiana (ebook) 20190166649 | ISBN 9780776628509 (softcover) | ISBN 9780776628516 (PDF) | ISBN 9780776628523 (EPUB) | ISBN 9780776628530 (Kindle)

Subjects: LCSH: Tolstoy, Leo, graf, 1828-1910—Political and social views. | LCSH: Tolstoy, Leo, graf, 1828-1910—Correspondence. | LCSH: Dukhobors—Canada, Western—History—19th century. | LCSH: Dukhobors—Canada—History. | LCSH: Immigrants—Canada—History—19th century.

Classification: LCC PG3385 .D65 2019 | DDC 971.0088/2899—dc23

Legal Deposit: Fourth Quarter 2019
Library and Archives Canada

Copy editing	Robbie McCaw
Proofreading	Robert Ferguson
Typesetting	Édiscript enr.
Cover design	John van der Woude and Elizabeth Schwaiger
Cover image	Valentin Fëdorovich Bulgakov (*left*), Vladimir Grigor'evich Chetkov (*standing*), Lev Nikolaevich Tolstoy. Photo by Vladimir Chertkov

The University of Ottawa Press gratefully acknowledges the support extended to its publishing list by Canadian Heritage through the Canada Book Fund, by the Canada Council for the Arts, by the Ontario Arts Council, by the Federation for the Humanities and Social Sciences through the Awards to Scholarly Publications Program, and by the University of Ottawa.

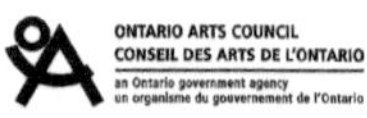

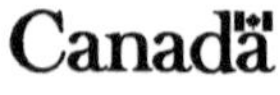

To the memory of
two outstanding individuals
scholars and teachers
Lidija D. Gromova
1925–2003
and
Eli A. Popoff
1921–2014

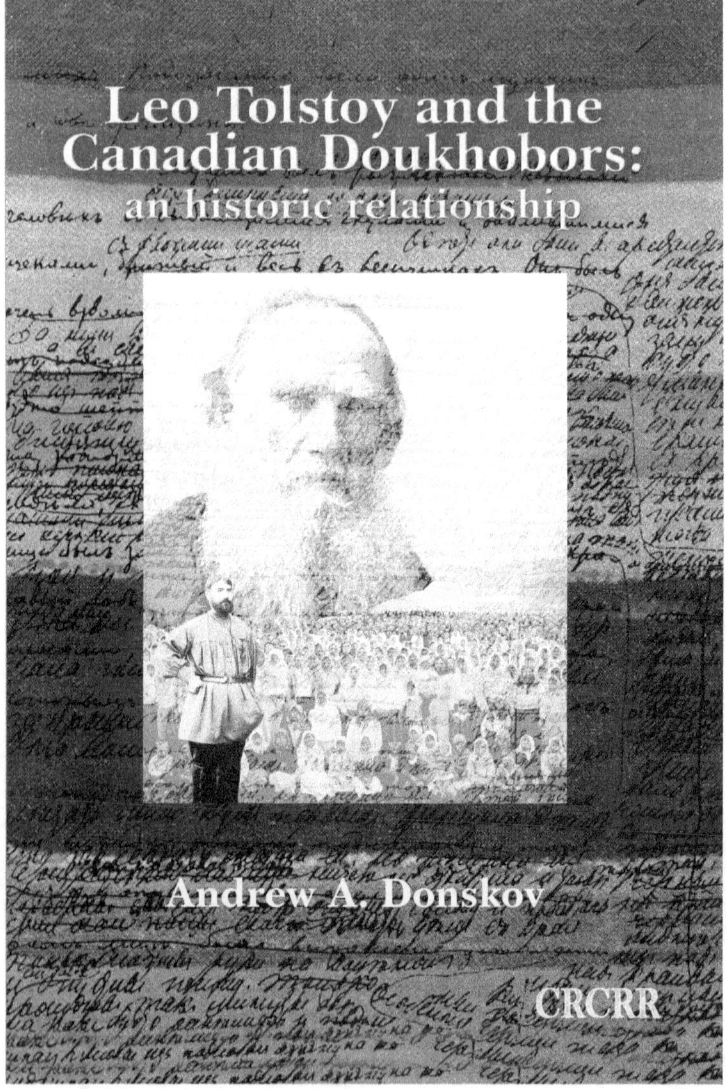

This collage, created by Jan Kabatoff and Pierre Bertrand for the first edition, features Leo (Lev Nikolaevich) Tolstoy (above) and Doukhobor leader Peter (Pëtr Vasil'evich) Verigin, integrated into a background photo of Doukhobors assembled for prayer [*molenie*]. The writing on the cover shows Tolstoy's corrections to a draft of his novel *Resurrection*, which he was prompted to complete in order to help finance the Doukhobors' emigration to Canada in 1899. The whole design is woven into a Doukhobor ornamental tapestry known as a *palás*.

TABLE OF CONTENTS

ACKNOWLEDGEMENTS TO THE FIRST EDITION

THE PRESENT PUBLICATION owes its appearance to many individuals and institutions in both Canada and Russia.

My first debt of gratitude is owed the State L.N. Tolstoy State Museum in Moscow in particular, its director, Professor Vitalij Borisovich Remizov for allowing me access to its treasure house of archival documents, as well as his able colleagues, senior researchers Natalija Kalinina and, especially, Tat'jana Nikiforova for their most valued input. With no less enthusiasm I thank Vladimir Il'ich Tolstoy (great-great-grandson to Leo Tolstoy and current director of the Yasnaya Polyana Tolstoy Museum Estate) and this museum's head of research Dr. Galina Alexeeva for their consultation and advice regarding materials on the Doukhobors contained in Tolstoy's library at Yasnaya Polyana. Still in Russia, my great appreciation is due Dr. Marina Shcherbakova, Head of Classical Literature at the Russian Academy of Sciences' Institute of World Literature, as well as to her colleague Liudmila Gladkova, for their valuable assistance in facilitating access to some rare documentary materials.

On the Canadian side of the Atlantic, I gratefully acknowledge the assistance of the following: Dr. J. Laurence Black, Director of Carleton University/ Laurentian University's Centre for Research on Canadian-Russian Relations, for providing me access to hundreds of archival documents on the Doukhobors in his Centre's extensive collection; Mary Stevens, former Head of the Petro Jacyk Resource Centre at the University of Toronto's Robarts Library, for her assistance with the James Mavor Archive; [the late[1]] Jack McIntosh, formerly of Special Collections at the University of British Columbia's Main Library — surely the most thorough bibliographer of Doukhobor sources — for his help

1 John Duncan 'Jack' McIntosh passed away in May 2019 at the age of 79.

in locating pertinent rare documents on Tolstoy; and the staff of the Library and Archives Canada in Ottawa for their assistance in this project.

I am most grateful to artist Jan Kabatoff, not only for her superb cover illustration [to the first edition; see p. vi of the present volume] but also for her essay on the meaning of Tolstoy in her life and work. Corresponding accounts have been graciously provided by two of the most prominent writers on Doukhobor history and culture — [the late[2]] senior Doukhobor historian and writer Eli Popoff and well-known Doukhobor ethnographer Koozma Tarasoff. Mr. Tarasoff has, in addition, kindly allowed me to reproduce some of his maps and photographs.

Appreciation is also due Jason Harshenin, former editor of the Doukhobor journal *Iskra,* for publishing my "Questionnaire for the Doukhobors on L. N. Tolstoy" *(Iskra,* N° 1905, March 2001) along with the many readers who responded thereto, and his successor, Lisa Poznikoff, for permission to print texts and photos from various editions of *Iskra.* And a note of thanks goes to the students of my University of Ottawa course on Tolstoy (between 1997 and 2004) who, from a fresh point of view, helped me clarify certain aspects of the Tolstoy–Verigin correspondence, as well as to my former student, Jacqueline Bélisle, and Stéphane McGirr, for their work on the index.

I should like to express my heartfelt gratitude to two colleagues, both members of the Slavic Research Group at the University of Ottawa John Woodsworth and Arkadi Klioutchanski for their unstinting and most valuable input from the inception to the completion of this project. I am especially grateful to John Woodsworth for his translation of many texts from Russian into English.

The financial assistance received from the Social Sciences and Humanities Research Council of Canada, as well as the moral and financial support on the part of the University of Ottawa, is most gratefully acknowledged.

Portions of this book have appeared (in different forms) in various journal articles *Russkaja literatura* (St. Petersburg), *Novyj zhurnal* (New York), *Russian Literature* (Amsterdam), *Canadian Ethnic Studies* (Calgary) as well as in the following books: *L.N. Tolstoj i M.P. Novikov: Perepiska* (Tolstoy–Novikov correspondence) and *L.N. Tolstoj i T.M. Bondarev: Perepiska* (Tolstoy–Bondarev correspondence; both published in Munich by Otto Sagner, 1996) and three publications of the Slavic Research Croup at the University of Ottawa: *Sergej Tolstoy and the Doukhobors: a journey to Canada* (1998); *L.N. Tolstoj i F.A. Zheltov: Perepiska* (Tolstoy–Zheltov correspondence, 1999) both co-published by the L.N. Tolstoy State Museum in Moscow, which later appeared in English translation (2001) under the editorship of Ethel Dunn; *Edinenie ljudej v tvorchestve L. N. Tolstogo/The Unity of people in Leo Tolstoy's works* (2002), co-published by the Russian Academy

2 Eli A. Popoff passed away in the summer of 2014 at age 93.

of Sciences' Institute of Russian Literature in St. Petersburg and Institute of World Literature in Moscow.

Finally, my most sincere and fervent gratitude is humbly offered to my close friend, that legendary Tolstoy scholar Dr. Lidija Dmitrievna Gromova (1925–2003), who so willingly shared her lively interest in and considerable knowledge of the Tolstoy–Doukhobor connection. Indeed, she herself had a close connection with Canada both as an Honorary Member of the Slavic Research Group at the University of Ottawa and as the recipient of a medal recognizing her "outstanding scholarly contribution" to the University of Ottawa in 1999. I shall be ever thankful for her constant encouragement, direction and guidance, always with a never-disappearing cheerful smile — all of which I terribly miss.

November 2005 A. Donskov
University of Ottawa

PREFACE TO THE SECOND EDITION

THE PRESENT VOLUME, *Leo Tolstoy and the Canadian Doukhobors: A Study in Historic Relationships*, constitutes a second, expanded edition of a volume first published in 2005 by Carleton University's Centre for Research on Canadian-Russian Relationships, albeit with a very small circulation.

This new edition includes important updates in references and in the Bibliography, an extended timeline, brief biographies of six Doukhobor scholars, a filial tribute to the late Doukhobor historian Eli A. Popoff, and the addition of new supplementary Russian-sourced archival materials (which are becoming ever more difficult to secure), along with some additional facts and some typographical corrections. All-in-all, the present edition has been expanded by several hundred pages.

An especially significant addition is the inclusion of the complete correspondence between Tolstoy and the Doukhobor leader Pëtr Vasil'evich Verigin, who in 1902 was released from exile in Siberia to join the majority of his flock newly arrived on the Canadian prairies. It is a remarkable, tangible record of two kindred spirits, both striving to unite people in love, peace, and mutual respect by living according to the rule of conscience and moral ethics, as opposed to government edicts.

This renewed publication is especially timely and applicable to a world fraught with conflict, distemper, and belligerence on many sides. The issues it deals with are relevant not only to the Doukhobors living today in Canada, Russia, and elsewhere, but to mainstream society's day-to-day relationships with any identifiable groups marked by ethnic, cultural, religious, or simply geographical distinctiveness.

In addition to providing certain correctives for existing studies on Tolstoy and the Doukhobors, it will also mean that future research on the subject

— by historians, ethnographers, theologians, literary critics, sociologists or political scientists, as well as by Doukhobor laity — will rest on a more complete documentation.

Furthermore, it concerns an area of Tolstoy studies, both literary and sociological, that remains relatively under-investigated in both Russia and the West — namely, his philosophical identification with the ideals of Doukhobor and similar 'spiritual' movements and his occasional active (even financial) support of their causes.

Before proceeding to thank those involved with this new edition, I must acknowledge my indebtedness to Dr. J. Laurence (Larry) Black, director of the Centre for Research on Canadian-Russian Relations (which is now based at Laurentian University in Sudbury, Ontario), for permission to reproduce, almost in full, the 2005 edition of Tolstoy and the Canadian Doukhobors. A similar note of thanks goes to Leonardo Sbrocchi and his Legas Press for allowing me to include the Tolstoy–Verigin correspondence in John Woodsworth's English translation from their bilingual (Russian-English) 1995 publication under my editorship.

My acknowledgements in the earlier edition of this present volume mentioned a number of individuals and institutions to which I still owe a debt of gratitude, but of course that list needs to be updated here. In the first place, the whole concept of this expanded edition arose from the long-term publishing plans of the University of Ottawa Press, Canada's oldest French-language university press and the only bilingual university press in North America — plans which envisage a whole series of books on Tolstoy. Three of these have already been published — viz., Sofia Andreevna's autobiographical memoir *My Life* (2010), *Tolstoy and Tolstaya: A Portrait of a Life in Letters* (2017), *Leo Tolstoy in Conversation with Four Peasant Sectarian Writers: The Complete Correspondence* (2019).

Specifically I am grateful to its Director, Lara Mainville, along with her exceptional team of professionals: Managing Editor Elizabeth Schwaiger, Acquisitions Editor Caroline Boudreau, Marketing Coordinator François Lavigne and Digital Production Coordinator Mireille Piché.

Similarly, this volume could not have come about without the involvement of a second group of people — namely, prominent representatives of the Doukhobors themselves, dedicated to the continued preservation of Doukhobor ideology, customs and heritage, who either contributed directly to the book or provided consultation and answers to vital questions from (most importantly) an insider's point of view. In particular, I am thankful to:

- writer-actor-producer-musician-lecturer Larry Ewashen, who served for many years as Curator of the Doukhobor Discovery Museum Centre in Castlegar, B.C., and has contributed photos to the current volume;

- journalist-writer-historian Dmitri (Jim) Popoff, a former editor of the Doukhobor magazine Iskra in Grand Forks, B.C. — Dmitri and his legendary historian-father Eli Popoff (whose essay is reproduced posthumously in this edition) have been prominent exponents of the Doukhobor identity and the preservation of the Russian language among their people (a largely successful undertaking);
- journalist-photographer-ethnographer Koozma Tarasoff of Ottawa, who has authored an on-line blog as well as produced a number of seminal books and photo-exhibits on Doukhobor life — he has kindly provided many of the illustrations in this volume;
- visual artist Jan Kabatoff, who has undertaken — with the collaboration of Pierre Bertrand — to illustrate the Doukhobor experience in multi-media art (see an example on p. vi of this volume) — like Eli Popoff, Jan Kabatoff and Koozma Tarasoff have also contributed essays to our book;
- the current Executive Director of the Union of Spiritual Communities of Christ (USCC) John J. Verigin Jr., whose late father John J. Verigin Sr. was for sixty years de facto leader of the Doukhobor community in British Columbia and was awarded both the Order of Canada and the Order of British Columbia;
- the husband-and-wife team and current co-editors of *Iskra*, Barry Verigin and Stephanie Swetlishoff-Verigin, whose monthly publication continues to provide (in both English and Russian) ongoing opportunities for the sharing of Doukhobor culture and ideas today.

Appreciation is also due Andrei Conovaloff, an American researcher and editor of the on-line blog *Molokans in America*, who has taken a lively interest in communicating with the Molokans' kindred spirits, the Doukhobors, and who has provided me with many excellent suggestions.

A special note of gratitude to my friend, colleague, and translator John Woodsworth, who has collaborated with me in producing both this new edition of Tolstoy and the Canadian Doukhobors and its 2005 predecessor.

I also hereby acknowledge the support received from the Social Sciences and Humanities Research Council of Canada, as well as from the Faculty of Arts at the University of Ottawa.

My greatest debt of all is to my wife, Natalia Smirnoff-Donskov, for much helpful advice and constant moral support.

December 2018

Andrew Donskov, F.R.S.C.
Distinguished University Professor
University of Ottawa

INTRODUCTION

ON 20 JANUARY 1899,[1] Canada witnessed the beginning of its largest mass immigration in its history when a group of some 7,500 Doukhobors began arriving from the Russian Caucasus and settling, under the auspices of a Canadian government initiative, as collective homesteaders on the Canadian prairies. This was a group that had suffered considerable persecution, by church and state authorities in Russia, for their pacifist and other non-Orthodox beliefs. Intensified enforcement of a law requiring all citizens to swear an oath of allegiance to the tsar, Alexander III, and perform compulsory military service had dealt a major blow against the sect. In 1895, the Doukhobors responded by burning all the weapons they possessed in a mass protest; this, in turn, led to increased persecution — including police surveillance, incarceration, and torture.

The Doukhobors' 1899 emigration to Canada was supported, both morally and financially, by Leo Tolstoy, who saw in their manifest pacifism and simple Christian approach to life a practical embodiment of his own ideals. Tolstoy, in fact, requested his eldest son, Sergej L'vovich, to accompany one of the four boatloads of Doukhobors to Canada, right to their new homestead sites on the prairies. Sergej L'vovich concluded his diary of the trip as follows:

1 Or 8 January by the Old Style (OS), Julian calendar. Before February 1918 Russia operated on the Julian calendar (still used in the Russian Orthodox Church); by that time most Western countries had adopted the New Style (NS), Gregorian calendar, proclaimed in 1582, abolishing the leap year for those centenary years not divisible exactly by 400. By the nineteenth century the OS calendar was twelve days behind the NS (thirteen days in the twentieth century); e.g., Christmas Day (25 December) 1898 OS was 6 January 1899 NS, while New Year's Day 1899 in Russia was 13 January in the West.

> I am happy that I have spent almost six months with them and have come to know them. And not only do I not regret having participated in their emigration, but I am proud to have had at least a small part in bringing it about. It is a pity that these good people have left Russia, but their emigration was unavoidable. Naturally, the first years of their life in Canada will be very difficult, but their future is assured. (Donskov 1998: 350–51)[2]

The story of the Doukhobors[3] in Russia is largely the story of persecution, exile, suffering, banishment — and the remarkable resilience of the human spirit. It was their rejection of violence and their simple peasant lifestyle that originally brought their plight to the attention of Leo Tolstoy in the early 1890s, who by this time had already written the majority of his principal theoretical works on social and religions questions. The intensive persecution that followed the Doukhobors' 'Burning of Arms' in the Caucasus in June 1895 was a direct challenge to Tolstoy's philosophy of non-violence, his rejection of organized religion, and of private property and privilege based on social class and elitist authority. This persecution, set against the background of the nationalism and militarism of the times, led Tolstoy to stress all the more the doctrine of non-violent resistance to evil as a fundamental tenet of Christian doctrine.

Tolstoy's eventual intervention in support of the Doukhobors, and of their endeavour to escape persecution by emigrating, represented nothing new. Time and again he had spoken out against the persecution of various religious sects,[4] including the Quakers, Mennonites, and other Christian pacifists. In an age of near-universal conscription in Russia and Europe, Tolstoy had pleaded more than once on behalf of pacifists, but never with such burning interest and fervent action as with the Doukhobors. For one thing, the persecution affected a far greater number of Doukhobors than of other Christian sects in the past (e.g., the Molokans, the Stundists); also, the intense persecution following the 'Burning of Arms' threatened their very lives.

It was the Doukhobors' lifestyle, however, and its closeness to the ideals of Tolstoy's own philosophy, that was no doubt the strongest attraction

2 Works are cited by the author's name and date of publication; page numbers, where relevant, follow the colon. Publication details are provided in the Bibliography.

3 The term *dukhobortsy* (a.k.a. *dukhobory* — Doukhobors, which literally means 'spirit-wrestlers') is usually ascribed to Archbishop Ambrosius of Ekaterinoslav, who used it derogatorily in reference to strugglers *against* the Spirit. The sect members themselves adopted the term in its positive sense, of people struggling *for* the Spirit. It should be noted, however, that according to ethnographer Svetlana Inikova (1999: 2n6) the term was "first encountered in a report by the Slovenian Archbishop Nikifor to the synod in March of 1786. In November of the same year the Slovenian eparchy was transformed into the Ekaterinoslav eparchy, headed by Archbishop Ambrosius."

4 The Doukhobors rejected the label *sectarians* [*sektanty*] imposed on them by the state and religious officialdom, for they believed themselves to be the true Christians. While some Doukhobors today find the term *sect* inappropriate, it is used throughout this volume simply in its historical sense as designating a minority religious group.

for the writer. He constantly received reports from his followers (known as *Tolstoyans)* recounting the Doukhobors' honest toil on the land; their communal sharing; the love of God they cherished within themselves; their absolute rejection of war, killing, and violence; and, not least, their willingness to suffer persecution for the sake of truth. In all of this Tolstoy saw the practical embodiment of virtually everything he himself aspired to and promoted in his own works.

Furthermore, Tolstoy the pragmatist was never content to confine his creative output to the purely philosophical plane; he was constantly searching for practical examples to illustrate his theories, especially among the Russian peasantry. Here in the Doukhobors he felt he had found his prime example, particularly insofar as this group, more than any other, combined a peasant lifestyle with a strong endeavour to put Christ's teachings to practical, everyday use — in daily living rather than through organized religion — exemplifying an ideal coming together of the spiritual and the practical.

It was during a momentous period of his life — the profound emotional and spiritual 'crisis' that had begun after his completion of *Anna Karenina* in 1877 — that Tolstoy first learned of the sect. The subsequent impact of the Doukhobors' ideas on his thought at this time is evident in his writings (especially his treatises) of the 1890s in his advocacy of principles such as *unity of people, the kingdom of God within*, the advantages of a *simple peasant life* based on manual labour and mutual sharing, removed from the evils of urban corruption. Like the Doukhobors, he too rejected official church orthodoxy and shared their absolute rejection of violence, including of violent resistance to evil. It was in part this doctrine, found in Tolstoy's writings following his spiritual crisis, that later came to be known as *Tolstoyism.*

Even more than Tolstoy himself, his followers — the Tolstoyans — tended to see in the Doukhobors the highest embodiment of the Christian ideals that they themselves had only professed in words. It was the Tolstoyans who were largely instrumental in the decision to choose Canada as the Doukhobors' destination and in arranging for them to be taken there. The two Doukhobor representatives who embarked on an exploratory trip to Canada in the spring of 1898 were accompanied by members of a Tolstoyan community in England. It was the Tolstoyans who conducted negotiations with Canadian government officials concerning the emigration. And, along with Quakers, Russian landowners and Leo Tolstoy himself (through royalties from his novel *Resurrection*), they were among the principal contributors to its financing.

It was also the Tolstoyans (with the encouragement of their mentor) who largely took upon themselves the task of escorting the boatloads of Doukhobors to Canada and seeing to their establishment there, some of whom stayed months, even years, to help the emigrants settle in their new homeland.

Many outside Russia championed the Doukhobor cause as well. First and foremost among these was Vladimir Chertkov, who was then living in exile in England. Others included John K. Van der Veer in the Netherlands, Eugen Heinrich Schmitt in Germany, Jonas Stadling in Sweden, John Kenworthy in England, and James Mavor in Canada,[5] as well as many Quakers (particularly in Britain and America). Through the publication of pleas for help in pamphlets and articles, these individuals and groups drew the sympathy of the Western world to the Doukhobors' plight; a number of them even travelled to Russia to gain first-hand knowledge of the sect.[6]

While a number of studies exist on the subject of Tolstoy and the Doukhobors, no one has systematically investigated their relationship (not to mention the involvement of other Tolstoy family members) from its beginning in the 1880s to Tolstoy's death in 1910 or included in their study the views of current Doukhobors on the subject.

In this work, my objectives are to provide a sustained and detailed study of how both parties (including Tolstoy's family) viewed the other, and how each drew upon the other's ideas and activities; to investigate the extent and nature of the involvement of Tolstoy and his family in the Doukhobors' affairs; and to examine the consequences of their actions and the personal sense of fulfilment they derived from their involvement.

My investigation is based on a study of (a) a half dozen of Tolstoy's articles on the Doukhobors, (b) more than 500 of his letters to or concerning the Doukhobors, (c) letters written to Tolstoy (both published and unpublished) by or concerning Doukhobors, (d) the complete correspondence of Tolstoy and Pëtr V. Verigin, (e) state and church reports and accounts, and (f) the Doukhobor journal *Iskra*. I shall also seek to explain the Doukhobors' role in at least two of Tolstoy's fiction works — namely, the novel *Resurrection* (begun in 1889, published in 1899) and the play *And the Light Shineth in Darkness* (unfinished, begun in the late 1880s, published in 1911).

In *Resurrection,* one can see not only the Doukhobors' indirect influence (in that the 1895 Burning of Arms and their subsequent pressing need for emigration provided Tolstoy with the much-needed stimulus to finish the novel), but also the role of sectarians in clarifying [*ujasnit'*] protagonist Prince Dmitrij Nekhljudov's (and, by extension, the writer's own) thoughts and ideas in his pursuit of moral regeneration — views on persecution and punishment, for example, which occupied Tolstoy so intensely, especially after 1895.

5 See Mavor's extensive correspondence regarding resettlement of the Doukhobors in Canada, and his continued interest in this group, in Signori 1989. See also Alexeeva 2000.

6 For example, at the end of 1897 the Englishman Arthur St. John, in the company of Tolstoy's close friend (and Moscow Art Theatre actor) Leopol'd Sulerzhitskij, paid a visit to Doukhobor leaders in the Caucasus, bringing them letters and funds collected by American Quakers. It was these funds that helped more than a thousand Doukhobors settle in Cyprus — a move which proved disastrous. In April 1899 this party relocated to Canada.

While the sectarians in the novel were in fact Molokans (who broke away from the Doukhobors primarily because they did not wish to abandon the printed Bible), it may be argued that it was mainly the Doukhobors who were guiding the author's pen in *Resurrection* — an idea which is supported by a close reading of both Tolstoy's correspondence and his diary entries. It was after the Burning of Arms that Tolstoy introduced peasant sectarians into the novel (then in its sixth redaction) — and, most significantly, these were drawn from native Russian sectarians and not imported evangelicals, such as Lord Radstock, who had so fascinated a great many of Tolstoy's contemporaries among the Russian aristocracy.

Questions of persecution and punishment, conscientious objectors, and the correct way to live also dominate Tolstoy's unfinished play *And the Light Shineth in Darkness* (referred to repeatedly by its author as "my drama"). The play's protagonist propagates what is essentially Doukhobor philosophy: belief in God within the heart; an honest, peaceful, and collective lifestyle, free of either government intervention or subjugation to the church; universal brotherhood. The protagonist's disciple, a young conscript, refuses to swear the oath of allegiance to the tsar and pays a heavy price for his new-found convictions. After incarceration and unsuccessful attempts to persuade him to return to the Orthodox fold, the conscript is first threatened with punishment in a disciplinary battalion (as in fact happened with many Doukhobor recruits) and then sent to an insane asylum. At the same time, another character, a member of the Orthodox clergy, is moved to leave the church and join the Doukhobors. In the play, as in the novel, however, the Doukhobors are neither psychologically nor artistically developed; they function more as an abstraction to elucidate or *clarify* (again, *ujasnit'*) ideas pertaining to the inner conflict of the aristocratic protagonist.

Tolstoy's support of and interest in the Doukhobors met with mixed reaction in Russia. His attitude and actions were perceived by some of his contemporaries as those of a "continually repentant nobleman" — to compensate for past injustices toward the peasantry on the part of the aristocratic class (to which Count Tolstoy belonged by virtue of birth). The Doukhobors were seen by ecclesiastical critics as undermining the foundations of the Russian Orthodox Church, which finally led to Tolstoy's excommunication in 1901. The state perceived the Doukhobors as characteristic of *anarchism*, undermining the established institutions of the tsarist regime. There was little in the way of a balanced assessment.

I am not aware of any significant and sustained discussion of Tolstoy on the part of Soviet literary critics or historians, who were prevented by official policy from examining (at least publicly) the religious aspects of the writings and philosophy of this essentially religious writer. Soviet printed material on the Doukhobors is equally insufficient — they were written about only as dictated by political agenda. In the early stages of Soviet power, for example, certain party activists (in particular, Vladimir Bonch-Bruevich) found them useful as a potential illustration of a communal lifestyle, while later their religious practices made them more of a thorn in the Communists' side.

In more recent times there has appeared valuable material (though not directly dealing with the subject at hand) in two books by A. I. Klibanov: *Istorija religioznogo sektantstva v Rossii (60-e gody XIX v. – 1917 g.)* [History of religious sectarianism in Russia (1860s–1917)] and *Religioznoe sektantstvo i sovremennost' (sotsiologicheskie i istoricheskie ocherki)* [Religious sectarianism and the present time (sociological and historical outlines)], published in Moscow in 1965 and 1969, repectively; these deal mainly with the issue of pacifism among religious sectarians and Tolstoyans, and their conscientious objection to military service. Excellent archival work on the Doukhobors is currently being carried out in Russia by Svetlana Inikova, an ethnographer with the Russian Academy of Sciences' Institute of Ethnology and Anthropology, and currently the foremost authority on the Doukhobors, as well as by Galina Alexeeva, head of academic research at the Tolstoy Museum Estate at Yasnaya Polyana.

In terms of Western criticism, mention should be made of a useful volume by J. W. Bienstock, *Tolstoï et les doukhobors: faits historiques réunis et traduis du russe* (1902) — largely, however, an anthology of Tolstoy's writings on the Doukhobors — which includes a brief historical sketch of the sect. A more important work is *A Peculiar People: The Doukhobors* (1904) by Aylmer Maude, Tolstoy's English translator (and, for a time, a Tolstoyan), in particular its chapter on Tolstoy's tenet of non-violent resistance to evil, which the Doukhobors shared. Mention must also be made of Michael Holman (retired of Leeds University) and his studies of British Tolstoyans and their role in Doukhobor emigration (see, e.g., Holman 2000).

A thoroughly balanced, scholarly view of the same subject is offered in Chapter 12 ("Russian sectarian pacifism: The Tolstoyans") of Canadian Peter Brock's *Pacifism in Europe to 1914* (1972), which details a number of reasons for the close ties between the writer and the sect. And one can by no means overlook George Woodcock and Ivan Avakumovic's book *The Doukhobors* (1968), which was a landmark contribution in its day, especially their chapter on P. V. Verigin. Also worthy of note are Nina and James Kolesnikoff's article "Leo Tolstoy and the Doukhobors" in *Canadian Slavonic Papers* (1978), and Viktor Buyniak's "Tolstoy and the Doukhobors" in the *Chelsea Journal* (1978).

In a well-argued paper, "Pacifist politics and peasant politics: Tolstoy and the Doukhobors, 1895–1899," Josh Sanborn (1995) maintains that the Doukhobors' Burning of Arms in 1895 was a carefully orchestrated political act, calculated to portray themselves as ideal peasants in order to secure Tolstoy's help, while Tolstoy in turn benefited from the Doukhobors' example in his own political struggle with European pacifists and militarists. Indeed, Tolstoy saw the Burning of Arms as betokening a new movement in Russian history — a movement toward a higher concept of life, and as a priceless opportunity to win over public opinion to the support of such a movement.

The year 1995 also saw the publication (in Russian, with English translation) of correspondence between Tolstoy and the Doukhobor leader Pëtr Vasil'evich Verigin (Donskov 1995a), whose letters were inaccessible until then. Shortly thereafter, John Woodsworth (1997) compiled a catalogue of 1,660 pages of documents on the Doukhobors from imperial Russian archival files, photocopies of which are held by Carleton/Laurentian Universities' Centre for Research on Canadian-Russian Relations (CRCRR). Some two hundred of these documents were translated by the catalogue's compiler into English and published in 1999 as Volume 1 of the Canada-Russia series under the joint sponsorship of the CRCRR and the University of Ottawa's Slavic Research Group (Woodsworth 1999a). Woodsworth also compiled a comprehensive description online of the portrayal of Doukhobors, entitled "Canadian Doukhobors on the Web: An Annotated Guide" (2002). Jack McIntosh of the University of British Columbia Library did the same for print materials with an exhaustive bibliography of publications (see, e.g., McIntosh 1995a, 1995b).

At least two dissertations on Tolstoy and the Doukhobors appeared around the turn of the twenty-first century. Jennifer Anderson (1997) wrote a master's thesis at Carleton University on the role of Tolstoy, Pëtr Kropotkin, and James Mavor in the Doukhobor emigration. And, four years later, American researcher April Bumgardner (2001) did a M.Phil. dissertation at the University of Glasgow on Doukhobor history and ideology as reflected in the relationship between Tolstoy and Verigin, in which she drew significantly upon their personal correspondence, as published in Donskov (1995a).

These and other comparable works call for a re-examination of many aspects of Doukhobor history.

With a few notable exceptions, writings on some aspects of the subject by Doukhobors themselves tend to focus on the more positive aspects of their relationship to Tolstoy — the traditional view of him as their *dedushka* [grandfather], benefactor, mentor, and kindred spirit — rather than his evident disagreements with certain areas of mainstream Doukhoborism[7] or his changing attitudes toward the movement over time. His exchange of letters with Pëtr V. Verigin (though, in fairness, this became available to most Doukhobors and scholars only after its 1995 publication), reveals a marked difference of opinion on a number of issues, and an attitude that can only be characterized as something less than 'brotherly' affinity and mutual love. (The same can be said of Tolstoy's correspondence with other sectarians — e.g., the Skoptsy, Shakers, etc.)

7 For example, on the issue of communal land holdings, Tolstoy was more in agreement with the radical Sons of Freedom splinter group than with the majority of Doukhobors. On this see two excellent articles: Inikova 2002 and Kolesnikoff 2000.

One of the exceptions to be noted is the prolific Doukhobor historian, ethnographer, and writer Koozma J. Tarasoff, who does not refrain from discussing the more controversial aspects of the sect, including Tolstoy's criticism of them — see, for example, his guest essay in this volume. In another guest essay, Jan Kabatoff, a well-known and respected Doukhobor artist, offers a candid, balanced assessment of Tolstoy's views on art and its significance in her career.

It may be said that Doukhobor writers in general have made a significant contribution to an understanding of this symbiotic relationship, including echoes of Tolstoy's thought in their pacifist tenets and philosophy of non-violent resistance to evil. See, especially in this connection, an article by John J. Verigin Sr. (1978) — written with the assistance of Eli and Jim (D. I.) Popoff — which could be considered to represent the closest possible approximation to a collective Doukhobor position on Tolstoy. Another salient example is Larry Ewashen's (1996b) "Tolstoy and the Doukhobors today," an address given at the closing banquet of a major international conference on Lev Tolstoy and the Concept of Brotherhood at the University of Ottawa, in February 1996.

Eli Popoff (author of the third guest essay in the present volume) was featured, along with Svetlana Inikova, as a keynote speaker at a 1999 Doukhobor centenary conference.[8] Much valuable material on the Doukhobors' relation to Tolstoy was presented at that conference, in particular at the session devoted to "The role of Tolstoy and his followers" in Doukhobor emigration to Canada. This session featured papers by Holman (2000), Alexeeva (2000), Gromova-Opul'skaja (2000), and Klioutchanski (2000).

What is puzzling, on the other hand, is the outright absence of Doukhobors from some otherwise superb studies on Tolstoy, even on such Doukhobor-related questions as his attitude to non-violence — particularly three works by brilliant Tolstoy specialists: Galina Galagan's *Khudozhestvenno-èticheskie iskanija L.N. Tolstogo* [L.N. Tolstoy's artistic and ethical seekings] (1981), Richard F. Gustafson's *Leo Tolstoy, Resident and Stranger: A Study in Fiction and Theology* (1986), and Rimvydas Silbajoris's *Tolstoy's Æsthetics and his Art* (1990).

The present study should serve as a corrective to these lacunæ, as well as to currently held views and scholarly writings based on inadequate documentation — especially as regards the Tolstoyans, Pëtr V. Verigin's correspondence, Sergej Tolstoy's journey to Canada, and Sofia Andreevna Tolstaya's diary and correspondence with her son. (Indeed, studies of Tolstoyana cannot be considered complete without taking archival documents such as these into account.) Possibly the greatest practical import of this publication will be the

8 The full title of the conference, as well as its proceedings, was *The Doukhobor Centenary in Canada: A Multi-Disciplinary Perspective on Their Unity and Diversity* (Donskov, Woodsworth, and Gaffield 2000). It was organized jointly by the University of Ottawa's Slavic Research Group and Institute of Canadian Studies.

comprehensive description of the historical and literary relationship between Tolstoy (including his family) and the Doukhobors — an analysis based, in good part, on previously unavailable archival documents or little-known materials.

In Chapter 1, I offer a brief outline of Doukhobor history and philosophy in order to elucidate both the parallels and differences with Tolstoy's views on religion and government.

Chapter 2 discusses Tolstoy's intense search for the meaning of life, for moral renewal and the ideal life, including the practical application of his ideals of universal unity — the unity of human beings both with nature and among themselves, without national or religious distinctions.

In Chapter 3, I examine the nature and extent of church and state opposition to Tolstoy and his followers, drawing on both published and unpublished government and police surveillance reports as a manifestation of official wrath against not only various sectarian movements (including the Doukhobors and 'anarchist' factions), but especially against Tolstoy and his adherents for spreading such ideas from one sect to another and stirring up the populace at large with feelings antagonistic to the authorities. In particular, I make a detailed survey of the attacks on Tolstoy found in the Russian Orthodox Church's quasi-official journal, *Missionerskoe obozrenie [Missionary Review], founded in* 1896 with the aim of counteracting the increasing popular spread of Tolstoy's teachings. These attacks were greatly disturbing both to himself and to members of his household.

Chapter 4 focuses on the specific involvement of Tolstoy and his family (especially his eldest son, Sergej L'vovich, and his wife, Sofia Andreevna) in the Doukhobors' emigration to Canada — choosing the final destination, making the practical preparations, escorting the various parties of Doukhobors, and overseeing their establishment on the Canadian prairies.

Chapter 5 is based on Tolstoy's writings about the Doukhobors (including literary works, treatises, and articles), as well some correspondence (more than 500 letters he wrote) on the subject.

Chapter 6 reproduces the complete correspondence between Tolstoy and the Pëtr V. Verigin, including extensive annotations.

While the principal part of my investigation concludes with the death of Tolstoy in 1910, I have added a seventh chapter, offering a glimpse into the legacy of the Tolstoy–Doukhobor relationship for Canadian Doukhobors today. This chapter examines how the latter regard the writer from a modern perspective, based in part on questionnaires returned from more than 140 Doukhobors over the course of several years.

The theme of the final chapter is carried over into three guest essays by prominent contemporary Doukhobors — an artist, an historian-cum-storyteller, and a writer-ethnographer. These essays offer a timely 'view from within,' complementing the otherwise external, scholarly perspective of the book.

I also considered it important for the reader's benefit to include a number of archival documents. First, there are two chapters of Sergej Tolstoy's diary describing (a) the preparations for the Doukhobor emigration from the Caucasus, and (b) his journey in Canada, escorting the Doukhobors by train from Halifax to Winnipeg, along with his 'Conclusion,' summing up his experience with the Doukhobors.[9] Next come excerpts from Sofia Andreevna Tolstaya's memoirs and diaries (some of the latter published here for the first time, others for the first time in English). These are followed by thirty-two archival letters (mostly hitherto unpublished) by Sofia Andreevna and various other individuals dealing with Doukhobor emigration — all arranged in chronological order. Both the documents and letters are provided with extensive annotations.

Finally, there is a five-part appendix, comprising the following:

(1) a timeline of significant events in Doukhobor history, from its earliest beginnings in the seventeenth century to September 2018;
(2) a filial tribute to the late Doukhobor historian Eli A. Popoff;
(3) a chronology of Tolstoy's letters concerning the Doukhobor (1891–1910);
(4) a list of publications by Sergej L'vovich Tolstoy; and
(5) a copy of the bilingual questionnaire sent to Canadian Doukhobors as discussed in Chapter 7.

In sum, this volume presents a significant number of manuscript texts and documents, as well as letters written to Tolstoy by Doukhobors in both the Caucasus and Canada, for further study — not only by literary specialists but by scholars and students in a variety of disciplines and in many parts of the world, as well as by members of the Doukhobor community. And Tolstoy's ideas on religious sectarianism, pacifism, and communal sharing, as reflected in the Doukhobors' practical experience, should be of considerable interest to those concerned with contemporary social problems in religious, philosophical, sociological, and historical studies.

9 Reproduced from Donskov 1998a: 237–70, 317–21, 349–51.

PART I

THE DOUKHOBORS AND TOLSTOY

CHAPTER 1

The Doukhobors: An Outline of Their History and Beliefs

THE REFORMS initiated in the early 1650s in the Russian Orthodox Church by Patriarch Nikon[1] provoked major resistance among believers, ending in the *Raskol*, or great schism, which reverberates through Russian religious life even today. Over time it led to a profusion of dissident sects.[2]

Studies of the Doukhobors have not yet succeeded in clarifying the exact origins of this pacifist sect,[3] a sect with no formal organization or internal canons and little in the way of their own historical records; there

1 These reforms resulted from internal divisions within the church, as well as from external pressure from both the state and Western religious institutions. One salient example was Nikon's 1653 decree that the sign of the cross should henceforth be made with three fingers instead of two. Other examples involved modifications to sacred texts and liturgy. The Old Believers (or Old Ritualists), i.e., those who did not accept Patriarch Nikon's reforms, were later divided into the *popovtsy* [priestists], who were willing to accept repentant Nikonian priests, and the *bespopovtsy* [priestless], who conducted their services and performed sacraments without clergy, holding that the reforms and the deaths of Old Believer bishops and priests made any further ordination impossible.

2 Official statistics of 1863 indicate that the Russian nonconformists numbered 8,220,000, not including the Old Believers, who, historically, ought not to be considered sectarians. See Bolshakoff 1950: 15–16; Miljukov 1972: 114–16; Heier 1970: 16–21; *Missionerskoe obozrenie* 1896: 1 (January): 31–44.

3 Settlements in the Caucasus were distributed in four regional locations: (a) Mokrye gory [Wet Mountains], in the Akhalkalak Uezd of Tiflis Gubernia in what is now Georgia; (b) Elizavetpol', 250 km east of Tiflis in what is now Azerbajdzhan; (c) Kars (including the villages of Terpenie, Spasovka, and Gorelovka), in what is now Turkey; (d) Bashkichetskij, a small settlement in what is now Armenia.

is no overall consensus, either among Doukhobor or non-Doukhobor historians.[4]

There is, however, a general agreement that a contributing factor in the establishment of the sect was the appearance of several strong leaders, such as Siluan Kolesnikov, who, having established a major centre for the movement in his native Ekaterinoslav Gubernia [Ekaterinoslav Province] of Russia, in the middle of the eighteenth century, proceeded to persuade a rich merchant from Tambov Gubernia to set up a 'Doukhobor' community there.

The basis of Doukhobor faith is the belief that the spirit of God resides in every human being, and that to violate a human being in any way is to defile the spirit of God in him; hence their pacifism and their firm belief in the equality of all human beings, regardless of one's station in life. Since both the Russian state and the Russian Orthodox Church not only tolerated but even condoned warfare, the Doukhobors strongly resisted both conscription and church rituals. In the Doukhobor concept of the Trinity, each of the three 'persons' is associated, respectively, with (a) a spiritual essence, (b) a spatial dimension, and (c) a particular channel through which individual assimilation with the Divine is effected: God the Father, with (a) light, (b) height, and (c) memory; God the Son, with (a) life, (b) breadth, and (c) understanding; God the Holy Ghost, with (a) peace, (b) depth, and (c) will. God, in turn, is defined as "the power of love, the power of life which is the Source of all that exists."

Doukhobors believe in Christ, not as God in the flesh but as the son of God, just as they hold themselves and all others to be God's children. With a strong conviction of what is morally right and wrong, they reject nearly all formal aspects of religion — icons, feasts, religious holidays — but still bow to each other as a sign of respecting God within each individual, and still offer guests the traditional Russian symbols of hospitality: bread, salt, and water, placed in the centre of the table, symbolizing the basic staples of human existence. They reject the Bible as a written document, although they admit the value of some of its teachings.

The Doukhobors adhere to the belief that heaven and hell are concepts, or states of mind. They reject any mediation (i.e., by a priest) between a person and God, and see no need for a creed,[5] for church sacraments such as baptism,

4 Much excellent archival work on this question is being done in Russia by Svetlana Inikova, an ethnographer with the Russian Academy of Sciences' Institute of Ethnology and Anthropology. See her superb article "Spiritual origins and the beginnings of Doukhobor history," presented as a keynote address at the Doukhobor Centenary conference at the University of Ottawa (Inikova 2000), and Eli Popoff's companion keynote address (Popoff 2000).

5 In response to the question as to what the Doukhobors believe or, more specifically, as to what their creed is, sect members are wont to say that they have none — i.e., no formal, codified canon of officially formulated beliefs. In his pioneer work *Christian Martyrdom in Russia*, published in London (in English translation) in 1900, Vladimir Chertkov begins his section on "Their teachings" by stating: "The chief article in the Doukhobors' profession of faith is the

marriage or funeral ceremonies — or, indeed, written records of any kind,[6] including scripture.

One exception to written records is the *Zhivotnaja kniga dukhobortsev* [Living Book of the Doukhobors], compiled and published in St. Petersburg in 1909[7] by Vladimir Dmitrievich Bonch-Bruevich, who shared some of Tolstoy's ideas.[8] Comprising the body of Doukhobor psalms and hymns, the book aimed to inspire the right kind of life and, at the same time, emphasize the nature of change in the group's experience over its turbulent history. Indeed, a significant element of the Doukhobor religion is a cappella music, thus with no instrumental accompaniment or written scores but, as Woodcock and Avakumovic note,

> interpreted as outflowing from the divinely inspired spirit within each of the singers.... And the psalms and hymns (containing the major tenets of their religion) that are set to it are the authentic expression of the Doukhobor people, of their beliefs and history, recorded mainly by anonymous folk bands and welded into tradition by the very method of oral transmission that rendered written religious literature unnecessary to a peasant people living in a rural society where literacy was rare.[9]

There have indeed been a number of formulations of Doukhobor beliefs published over the years.[10] One of the most concise was drafted by Doukhobor leader Pëtr V. Verigin, in the form of "a Doukhobor psalm"; it is given here in Eli Popoff's English translation (see Popoff 1982: 26).

service and worship of God in the spirit and in truth." He then goes on to say, "They know no creed, and only say of themselves that they are of the faith of Jesus."

6 Refusal to keep records of births and deaths, along with their rejection of any source of religious teaching other than their own inner conscience, inevitably brought them into conflict not only with Russian church and government authorities, but also with their Caucasus neighbours, and, later, with legislative authorities and a misunderstanding public in Canada.

7 This was a revised and expanded version of Bonch-Bruevich's *Spisok psalmov, pisem, rasskazov i drugikh rukopisej po issledovaniju uchenija zhizni i pereselenija v Kanadu zakavkazskikh dukhobortsev* [List of psalms, letters, stories, and other research manuscripts on the Transcaucasian Doukhobors' teachings of life and resettlement in Canada], published through the Geneva branch of Chertkov's *Svobodnoe slovo* [Free Word; Chertkov also published a journal of the same name] publishing house in 1900, soon after his return to Europe from living with the Doukhobors during their first year in Canada (see Woodsworth 1999a: 5).

8 See Bonch-Bruevich 1909. One of many Doukhobor proverbs he recorded reads: *Napishite vo serdtsakh, vozvestite vo ustakh* [Write it in your heart, proclaim it with your mouth].

9 Woodcock and Avakumovic 1977: 21, 22. See also Mealing 1995. On the importance of song in Doukhobor life see Perry 1999.

10 For example, Novitskij's seminal book *Dukhobortsy: ikh istorija* i *verouchenie* (1882); Maude's *A Peculiar People* (1970: 12–20, 79–105); Chertkov's *Christian Martyrdom in Russia* (1900); an outline by an anonymous representative of the imperial Department of Police, published in English translation in Woodsworth 1999a: 26–28; an article in the Russian Orthodox Encyclopedia ("Dukhoborchestvo — russkaja sekta" 1913); a summary in the chapter "The people of God" in Woodcock and Avakumovic (1968: 17–34); a summary by Treadgold (1968: 89–91); and by many Doukhobor writers published in *Iskra* and elsewhere (see the Bibliography).

1. The members of the Community revere and love God as the source of all being.
2. They respect the dignity of man both in themselves and in their fellow men.
3. The members of the Community regard everything that exists with love and admiration, and they try to bring up their children in the same tendency.
4. By the word *God* they understand the power of love, the power of life which is the Source of all that exists.
5. Life is systematic progress ahead, and everything strives toward perfection, and through this process strives to unite with its original Source of life, as if from the seeds received to give returns in the form of ripe fruit.
6. In everything that exists in our world we see consecutive stages toward perfection — thus, beginning with a stone, it passes over to plants; then come animals, the fullest development of which is man, regarding him from the point of view of life and in the sense of a conscious being.
7. The members of the Community hold that to destroy or hurt any living thing is blameworthy. In every separate being there is life and hence God, especially in a human being. To deprive a man of life is not permissible under any circumstances whatsoever.
8. In their beliefs, the members of the Community accord full freedom to all living things, and more so to the life of man. Therefore any organization founded on violence they regard as unlawful.
9. The basis of man's existence is the power of thought, or reason. Basic food for his physical existence are air, water, fruits and vegetables.
10. It is recognized that the life of mankind is essentially a communal life based on the moral law, which has as its rule: "What I do not wish for myself, that I must not wish for anyone else."

Certain Doukhobor beliefs, for obvious reasons, aroused suspicion on the part of church and state authorities. On 13 July 1897, Caucasus governor Prince Grigorij Sergeevich Golitsyn summed up official views on such beliefs and attitudes in a memo to the imperial Department of Police.[11]

On the authorities

- There is one tsar, in heaven, there should be no tsar on earth [...].
- Does the emperor have a mark on his body that you call him the anointed one? What extra thing has God given him — an [extra] finger or an eye? Why is he tsar, and not you or I or someone else? [...] We hear that there is an

11 Case N°1053 Part 1, Sheets 517, 520, and 521, listed in Woodsworth 1997 as Document #1897-07-13b. Also published (in translation) in Donskov 1995c: 254. A fuller analysis of official reaction to Tolstoy's teachings and Doukhobor beliefs will be presented in Chap. 3.

emperor in Russia, but we do not know his name, we are not interested — we do not concern ourselves with that.

- In England, they say, the son of a cobbler is tsar; whoever is chosen by the people is the one who must reign.
- The unblemished tsar is Jesus of Nazareth. Who wanted to kill Christ — wasn't it Herod? Wasn't it the royal governor Pilate that crucified the Saviour? In the same way, they crucify verity and truth, and us. [...]
- Civil servants and the tsar are all brethren, they should be equal; let them all set their hand to the plough, just like everyone else [...].
- Rulers and robbers, they're all the same, 'craftsmen' — only the latter rob at night, while the others (the rulers) attack and rob the people day and night. [...]

On land

- The land is God's, it is created for all equally. Possession is robbery.
- The princes and the landowners have robbed the people, seizing so much land. There should be no partition of land: everyone should have as much land as he needs to feed himself. [...]

On the fatherland

- We do not recognize a fatherland on earth, all people are our compatriots. We are 'members of the Christian community of universal brotherhood.'
- We are pilgrims, we are striving (to reach) our heavenly fatherland, and we do not cherish or wish to defend an earthly [fatherland].
- Military service [is something] we absolutely reject, just as before, when it was not accepted by all our Doukhobors, according to the commandment "Thou shalt not kill."
- Criminals and robbers should be judged by the Lord Himself, not by people who are just as sinful.
- Prisons should not exist. We rejoice with those who are in prison, and grieve over those who put people there. [...]

The rejection of the supreme authority of the tsar was a particular sticking-point with the authorities, one the latter were quick to attribute to the harmful influence of the Tolstoyans on the Doukhobors.[12]

During the reign of Catherine the Great (1762–1796), the sect experienced an unobstructed growth in numbers. Partly because of the influence of their teaching upon their neighbours, however, as well as the discord that had arisen within their own ranks, the Doukhobors began to suffer persecution in 1793, when the government ordered the resettlement of those living in the Ekaterinoslav and Khar'kov Gubernias to an area known as Molochnye vody [Milky Waters] in the Melitopol' district of the Tauride Gubernia (now the Crimea).

The persecution was somewhat mitigated with the ascension of Alexander I to the throne in 1801. Known for his tolerance of religious ideas, he showed

12 Golitsyn noted (see Woodsworth 1997, Sheet 517), e.g., that "this harmful and dangerous movement is not based on any enactments of governmental authorities provoking the Doukhobors' displeasure but is deeply rooted in their sectarian views inculcated in them by the enemies of our political system."

a special fondness for the Doukhobors by offering them generous land grants and additional financial assistance. In 1804 the Doukhobors of Tambov and Voronezh Gubernias were allowed to join their brethren under a similar arrangement. The local authorities were instructed to keep the Doukhobors together and not mix them with neighbouring populations; to offer them official protection and not oppress them, but to forbid any proselytization on their part. In 1818, the tsar himself paid a visit to the Doukhobor settlements and left with a favourable impression.

However, Nicholas I, who succeeded Alexander in 1825, saw danger in the Doukhobors' teaching and, ten years later, struck a commission to investigate. In the meantime, local authorities had begun to take a noticeably more hostile attitude toward the sect. In 1839, the tsar's commission recommended that the Doukhobors be resettled in the Caucasus, specifically to the Akhalkalak and Elizavetpol' regions, where a group of Doukhobors had already been relocated from the Don River area in 1821. The move took four years to complete (1841 to 1845). The new area was mountainous (some 1,500 metres in elevation) and required a shift in occupation from grain farming to cattle raising, to which the sect members managed to adapt with remarkable speed.

The Doukhobors worked their new large parcels of land with their customary industriousness and managerial efficiency, and, with modest needs, quickly prospered. Their so-called golden period of Doukhobor prosperity (1864–1886) was presided over by their capable and charismatic leader, Luker'ja Vasil'evna Kalmykova. Enjoying the complete confidence and respect of her followers, Kalmykova was an absolute leader, stern but fair, a mediator in internal conflicts, a solution finder, one who sought to live in peace with the local authorities, at the same time managing to prevent them from encroaching upon the sect's internal and economic life. She succeeded in organizing the internal structure of the community in such a way that, up until her death, it was said that the Doukhobors knew no trouble, terror, or financial need. They functioned, in fact, as a virtual 'state within a state.'[13]

Trouble began for the Doukhobors, however, following Kalmykova's death in 1886, when the community divided over the question of her successor. The faction known as the Large Party [*Bol'shaja partija*], led by Pëtr Vasil'evich Verigin,[14] whom Kalmykova had personally groomed for the leadership, triumphed in the end over the so-called Smaller Party [*Malaja partija*]. By 1892, possibly under the influence of Lev Tolstoy, though mainly out of their personal conviction that it was wrong to harm any living being, Verigin and

13 Right from the days of their settlement in Molochnye vody, in the early nineteenth century, Doukhobor leaders governed from a residential complex known as *Sirotskij dom* (lit., 'Orphan House') — see Department of Police archival documents in Woodsworth 1999a: 30, 35.

14 *Pëtr Vasil'evich Verigin* (1859–1924).

his immediate supporters had become vegetarians, but not all members of the Large Party were willing to take this step. Those who did were known as *postniki* [fasters], while those who resisted were called *mjasniki* [meat-eaters].

In 1887, a new source of trouble arose when compulsory military service was introduced in the Caucasus, and by 1894 all Russian citizens were obliged to take an oath of allegiance to the tsar. Verigin's call to refuse to take the oath[15] was viewed with alarm by the authorities, who had already come to look upon the Doukhobors as a socio-political movement with communist leanings, for which their religious doctrine served mainly as a deceptive veneer. Contributing to the climate of suspicion was the assassination of Alexander II in 1881, after several years of unsuccessful attempts on his life.

Increased proselytizing among the Doukhobors on the part of a number of Tolstoyans only increased official suspicion. An official account of this proselytizing is contained in the "Confidential note of Prince Shervashidze, Governor of Tiflis, to the Commander-in-Chief of the Civilian Sector in the Caucasus S. A. Sheremetev," dated 4 October 1895. The following is Prince Shervashidze's own résumé of a lengthy account, entitled "On the Criminal brotherhood of sectarian *Doukhobors*, whose aim is insubordination to the higher authorities":[16]

> **Sheets 99v.–101:** The conversion to the Tolstoyans that has taken place among a significant part of the Large Party must be looked upon as an undesirable phenomenon, and more regrettable than the continuation of the Doukhobor sect in the form it had in the Caucasus.... The teaching of the Tolstoyans, on the other hand, based on the broadest possible cosmopolitanism, preaches only personal help, which, in combination with the requirement of everybody's religious concentration on themselves (*The Kingdom of God is Within You*) and the denial of family principles as well as the citizen's duty to the state, destroys any element of community, and therefore country, and imprisons the human being in the narrow selfishness of living one's life. Such teachings must undoubtedly be considered to be most harmful, and the sectarianism resulting therefrom to be the least tolerable in the nation; furthermore, should the resettled fasting group continue to live together with other members of the Large Party, it is to be expected that the teachings of the fasters will inevitably be adopted by the larger group, especially in view of Pëtr Verigin's support of these teachings.
>
> **Sheet 104:** According to the information I have received, the exiled sect members are verbally and even actively promulgating their teachings to which end, apart from persuading people verbally of the futility and sinfulness of military

15 At the same time, Verigin, recently exiled to Siberia, enjoined his followers to abstain from the use of alcohol and tobacco.

16 GARF [State Archives of the Russian Federation], Department of Police, 6th Case File, Collection 102, Inventory 192, Case N° 163. Extensive excerpts from this document are included in Donskov 1995c.

service and paying taxes, they do not hire themselves out to landowners, but offer financial aid and help through their physical labour to poor families of the peasant population, for which they seek no remuneration, or they restrict themselves to receiving the most pitiful compensation for tilling the ground, thereby indicating that all people should live in such brotherly unity. Such a sermon is very enticing for the dark masses of the peasantry, hence one should always be wary lest the local population become attracted by it and its harmful teachings begin to take root among them.

Sheet 105: In view of the above, I suggest it would be advisable to send the Doukhobor fasters out of the province altogether, it would be best of all to send them out of the country into neighbouring Turkey, where, according to rumours, they have been trying to go [themselves].[17]

This is one of the earliest official records hinting at the Doukhobors' possible emigration. The involvement of other sources is pointed out in the same official report:

Sheet 537: According to rumours circulated among the 'dark' Doukhobors, England and America are now vying for the 'privilege' of having the Doukhobors; L. N. Tolstoy, they say, is ready to send all Doukhobors abroad at his own expense. Under the influence of such stories, the Doukhobors sent a deputation to Count Tolstoy at Yasnaya Polyana, where they received whole trunkfuls of books. [...] There is some basis for supposing that Chertkov in London and Princess Nakashidze — a fervent disciple of Tolstoy's ideas and Doukhobor patron who recently left Tiflis — have been traipsing abroad on this business [the Doukhobor emigration].

The possibility of mass Doukhobor emigration must have been discussed most seriously by the authorities shortly after the Burning of Arms in 1895, when the tension culminated in a mass demonstration and burning of weapons in three separate districts of the Caucasus. More surveillance and

17 Governor Shervashidze's notes contain a detailed account of the Doukhobor agitations at the end of May and the eve of the Burning of Arms, which provoked even more stringent measures:

Sheet 544v–545r: In terms of political convictions, the majority of the Doukhobors from Elizavetpol' belong to the class of moderate fasters, who are willing to make compromises with the ruling authorities, except as regards military service.

Sheet 546v: The Kars Doukhobors, by comparison with others, are in all respects the most rebellious and dangerous source of anarchist anti-government ferment.

Sheet 547: The Kars Doukhobors, more radically than others, have adopted the teachings of anarchy and Tolstoyism, and are therefore the most convinced and stubborn followers of the criminal anarchist community. In every Doukhobor settlement there are several leading spokesmen who come out with terse explanations justifying the anarchist way of thinking and the criminal conduct of their comrades, sometimes literally citing passages from the underground writings of Count L. Tolstoy. The mood everywhere is one of triumph, provocation and insolence.

repressive measures followed, undoubtedly constituting the most severe persecution experienced in their history.[18]

Examples of these repressive measures are detailed in a secret report by Sergeant Major Efim Mamotov to the Department of Police on 18 September 1895,[19] outlining six specific instances where Doukhobor women were raped by Cossack soldiers with the approval of their *Esaul* (Commander) Praga, and the refusal of local authorities to investigate, citing as grounds the Doukhobors' reluctance to co-operate with the Russian government.

As will be seen in greater detail in Chapter 4, the decision on an appropriate place of emigration involved a number of factors: the Doukhobors' refusal to swear allegiance to authority, to bear arms, or to send their children to public school; their need for freedom to practise their religion and communal way of life unhindered by hostile or jealous neighbours. Possible destinations then included Chinese Turkestan, Mongolia, Manchuria, the American state of Texas, the Hawaiian Islands (formally annexed by the United States in 1898), and Cyprus (which had been under British rule since 1878).[20]

Tolstoy was initially enthusiastic about Mongolia (suggested by the editor of *Sankt-Peterburgskie vedomosti,* Prince Èsper Ukhtomskij, but promptly rejected),[21] then about Hawaii (which was soon dismissed as inappropriate to the Doukhobors' experience). Over Tolstoy's objections, it was decided to follow the Quakers' suggestion and send the Doukhobors to Cyprus, and in August 1898 some 1,100 of them arrived in two boatloads at the Cypriot port of Larnaca. The hot climate and unfamiliar local conditions proved a disastrous mix, however, and an unusually large number of them died from illness.[22]

Canada was first suggested as a possibility by the Russian anarchist Prince Pëtr Kropotkin, who had travelled across Canada in 1897 and observed the ordered and successful Mennonite settlements on the prairies. Kropotkin had come to know the Doukhobors in the 1860s on the Amur River in Siberia

18 Adding to the atmosphere of suspicion and repression was the negative attitude of the senior procurator of the Holy Synod, Konstantin Pobedonostsev (a particularly harsh opponent of Russian sectarianism), who was the leading instigator of Tolstoy's excommunication from the Russian Orthodox Church, effected in 1901.

19 Case 1053, Sheets 68–73r, listed in Woodsworth (1997) as Document #1895-0916d. Published (in Russian) as part of Donskov's 1996(e) article in *Novyj zhurnal,* "Sozhzhenie ognestrel'nogo oruzhija (1895 g.) i ego posledstvija" [The Burning of Arms (1895) and its consequences]. See also the report by Major General Surovtsev and Colonel Grebenshchikov in Woodsworth 1999a: 64–66.

20 See Report of Dept. of General Affairs, Ministry of Internal Affairs, Division 5, entitled *Istorija dukhoborcheskogo obshchenija* [History of the Doukhobor communion] (n.d.: 41v), summarized in Woodsworth 1997: C5, D9.

21 See letter from Caucasus Governor Prince Golitsyn to the Minister of External Affairs Count M. N. Murav'ëv of 24 April 1898, translated in Donskov 1995c: 259–60.

22 The remaining emigrants were eventually brought to Canada on a third boatload, which arrived at Quebec City in May 1899 (see Chap. 4).

(where some were exiled) and was favourably impressed with their way of life. He and Chertkov contacted James Mavor, a political-economy professor at the University of Toronto who was himself interested in the phenomenon of communal living. At their request, Mavor approached the Canadian government about accepting the Doukhobors as immigrants.[23]

An accord was reached 5 October 1898. Tolstoy asked his friend Leopol'd Sulerzhitskij to accompany the first boatload of Doukhobors to Canada.[24] The second boatload he entrusted to his eldest son, Sergej L'vovich Tolstoy. Thus it was that Sergej L'vovich sailed from Batoum on 4 January 1899 (22 December 1898 OS) aboard the *SS Lake Superior*, accompanying more than 2,000 Doukhobors to their promised new land, to fulfil their hopes for a new life unencumbered by the surveillance, persecution, and indignities of the past.

Summarizing his impressions of the Doukhobors on their journey to Canada, Sergej Tolstoy ends his diary account with the following:[25]

> In conclusion I should like to share my impressions of the Doukhobors. The Doukhobors by their piousness stand above the average level of both Russians and Canadians. One need not share their sense of exclusivity, their conviction that they are a special people — a community of universal brotherhood, or their worship, even the deification of their leader Pëtr Verigin, or their indifferent attitude (to the point of denial) of European culture and science. But one cannot deny their loyalty to the tenets of their faith, their perseverance in actually living their faith and their readiness to suffer for it. This they have proved by their actions. If there are among them some self-seeking people or those who depart from Doukhoborism, they are the rare exceptions. They are honest, sober, industrious, courteous and clean-living. They lack the three vices from which, it must be admitted, the Russian people suffer: drunkenness, cursing and thievishness. I am happy that I have spent almost six months with them and have come to know them. And not only do I not regret having participated in their emigration, but I am proud to have had a least a small part in bringing it about. It is a pity that these good people have left Russia, but their emigration was unavoidable. Naturally, the first years of their life in Canada will be very difficult, but their future is assured.

That their future was indeed assured may be seen in the swelling of their numbers in Canada, to some 30,000 strong today.[26] Their development over

23 See Woodcock 1995 and Anderson 1996; also Alexeeva 1998.

24 The SS *Lake Huron* left Batoum 22 December (10 December OS) 1898. The preparations for this first departure are described in the chapter from Sergej Tolstoy's diary "Resolving questions of emigration," see p. 259.

25 Published in Donskov 1998a: 350–51. The full text of Sergej Tolstoy's concluding chapter is reproduced here in Part III.

26 A higher estimate, 40,000, is given in Tarasoff 2002: ix. According to census figures provided by Eli Popoff (1983: 117), 12,300 Doukhobors are currently living in British Columbia, 8,000 in Saskatchewan, 3,000 in Alberta, and the rest in other provinces. After their arrival in Canada,

the intervening hundred-plus years, however, has by no means been an easy course.

In a letter to Tolstoy of 16 August 1898[27] Verigin declared himself to share Tolstoy's opposition to the idea of emigration in principle; he was, however, resigned to it if no better option should prove forthcoming. His followers were given permission to emigrate toward the end of that year, but their leader was not allowed to join them until July 1902, when his final term of exile came to an end.

On his way to Canada, Verigin first stopped to see Tolstoy at Yasnaya Polyana, and then for a visit with Vladimir Chertkov in England. Chertkov arranged for Verigin to give a lecture on Doukhobor philosophy in London. His audience was impressed by both his sharp mind and his striking physical appearance.

The months preceding his arrival in Canada in December 1902 were marked by a troublesome incident in the fledgling Doukhobor community in Canada, among a radical splinter group who referred to themselves as "Svobodniki" — later known as the Freedomites or, as popularized in the press, the Sons of Freedom.[28] Members of this sect, adopting an extreme interpretation of Verigin's call to self-renunciation, had taken it upon themselves to turn their farm animals loose and destroy or give away virtually all their personal possessions. More than a thousand of their number set off on a pilgrimage to find a place where they could live unencumbered by external constraints.

All attempts by Canadian authorities to resolve the situation proved fruitless. On 15 December 1902, Tolstoyan Ivan Tregubov wrote to a friend: "Perhaps his presence among the Doukhobors will help them find themselves more quickly and work out a lifestyle that more closely corresponds to their spiritual make-up."[29]

This prediction turned out be accurate. A month later, Verigin related to Tolstoy how he diffused the trouble by telling the radicals:[30]

the Doukhobors established sixty-one villages in Saskatchewan and Assiniboia (in an area later absorbed into Saskatchewan) — see Ewashen and Tarasoff 1994: 17–18.

27 Reproduced in Chapter 6 (Letter Nº 6).

28 For some recent, detailed studies of this group, see the series of eight papers by Jim E. Popoff (1987, 1988) entitled "What were the main historical reasons and causes for the rise of the splinter movement known as the Sons of Freedom?"; Kolesnikoff 2000; Inikova 2002. Doukhobors today are divided into three groups: Independents (stemming from those who sought accommodation with Canadian government regulations and became independent farmers), Community Doukhobors (from those who followed Verigin to British Columbia in 1908 to preserve their communal lifestyle), and the Sons of Freedom (an offshoot of the latter, who took the communal way of living to the extreme). The latter two groups are concentrated mainly in British Columbia, while most of the Independents still live in Saskatchewan and Alberta. For more information on each of these factions, see Frantz 1961: 47–52.

29 In Woodsworth 1999a: 217–19.

30 In Donskov 1995a: 54.

> Your motives of self-sacrifice for the common good of human life are legitimate and precious ones, but there is no need to let the children go hungry and cold, so for the time being why not remain with all the rest of the brethren and teach them? Those with families took this explanation, too, as a revelation from God.

Verigin's arrival in Winnipeg is described in a number of contemporary newspaper accounts. The following excerpt, from the *Manitoba Free Press*, is typical:[31]

> Physically, Verigin is a splendid type of his race. Tall and strongly built, and of erect and graceful carriage, he would attract attention among hundreds of good-looking men.

His followers in Canada, emphasizing what they perceived as his spiritual strength, reprised the title *Gospodnij* (i.e., 'the Godly' or 'belonging to the Lord,' though often mistranslated as 'the Lordly'), which had originally been granted him by Luker'ja Kalmykova.

As indicated above, the leader's presence among his flock as they adjusted to their new homeland had an overall calming effect on their communal life as a whole. He gave the Doukhobors a new collective name, calling them the Christian Community of Universal Brotherhood (CCUB). He became their spokesman in negotiating questions of his followers' rights and responsibilities vis-à-vis the Canadian government.

The issue of land ownership and registration was a particularly thorny one. The government had originally allowed the Doukhobors the privilege of collective ownership, but, in 1905, withdrew this exemption and began demanding registration of homesteads on an individual basis — a procedure which, in 1908, entailed swearing an oath of allegiance to the Crown, thereby obligating sect members to military service if Canada should ever go to war.

Disenchanted with changing official attitudes, in 1905 Verigin sent his lieutenant Ivan Konkin to Siberia to dissuade a party of Doukhobors newly released from exile from emigrating to Canada. His advice went unheeded, however, and the new arrivals faced a less-than-friendly welcome.

The following year, continuing with this protest, he went to Moscow along with several trusted followers to enquire into the feasibility of relocating the Doukhobors en masse back to Russia. Receiving no positive reaction from tsarist officials and, more importantly, no guarantee sect members would be exempted from military service, he was obliged to abandon the idea and returned to Canada to pursue other options.

In the summer of 1907, Verigin discovered orchard lands in British Columbia that the Doukhobors could purchase communally, with no oath-of-allegiance

31 *Manitoba Free Press*, 22 December 1902; quoted in Ewashen 2001. For more on Verigin's life and activities in Canada, see Donskov's (2005) article in the *Dictionary of Canadian Biography*.

requirement. The following year, a good four-fifths of his flock followed their leader to new settlements in British Columbia's Kootenay region, mainly in the Castlegar and Grand Forks areas. Historian Carl Tracie (2002) speculates that Verigin may have deliberately settled certain Doukhobors in small, scattered communities around Castlegar to prevent further fragmentation of the sect, at the same time keeping them largely isolated from the surrounding English-Canadian society — a scheme that actually ended up precipitating the dissolution it was intended to prevent.

Indeed, some Doukhobors, contrary to Verigin's advice, had already accommodated themselves to official demands and registered their homesteads, either taking the oath of allegiance or claiming an exemption that had earlier been granted to the Mennonites. These 'Independent' Doukhobors, remaining on the prairies as individual farmers, assimilated more quickly to Canadian ways than did their 'Community' brethren in British Columbia. Verigin himself discouraged any contact with the Independents, and even opposed (unsuccessfully) their exemption from military service during the First World War.

He and his Community followers, however, while finding orchard farming in British Columbia more compatible with their vegetarian philosophy than cattle raising on the prairies, were by no means freed from conflict with officialdom over land, education, and the registration of vital statistics. Nevertheless, under his guidance (summed up in his motto, *Toil and Peaceful Life*), the British Columbia Doukhobors prospered, while the CCUB expanded into other enterprises, including sawmills and brick factories.

Verigin's dictatorial insistence on enforcing radical moral standards, however, not only provoked conflict with Canadian officials but also caused some members of his own flock to leave the fold. On the other hand, what steps he did take to compromise with the authorities — permitting public schooling[32] and tax paying in return for continued exemption from military service, for example — did not sit well with the more radical Sons of Freedom, who resorted to acts of public nudity and arson against the Community Doukhobors' homes, businesses, and schools.

In October 1924 the hatred directed against Verigin from both sides led to tragedy, when a bomb exploded in the train carriage he was riding from Castlegar to Grand Forks, killing Verigin. While it was generally viewed as an assassination, the culprit was never found, and Pëtr V. Verigin has continued to live on in Doukhobor memory as something of a martyr to the community's ideal of living a Christian life free of violence, and with no requirement to obey any authority other than God.

His exalted stature, even today, among members of an otherwise egalitarian sect may be explained at least in part by that most Doukhobors have

32 By 1922, there were so many Doukhobors in the Grand Forks area that a new public school was opened primarily for sect members' children.

traditionally considered their leaders to be divinely chosen incarnations of God on earth. This naturally made Verigin a unique and controversial figure, especially in the Canadian context. He was evidently endowed with a natural ability which fitted him for the role, far surpassing his sectarian brethren both in intellectual capacity and in the development of the philosophical underpinnings of Doukhobor faith, yet at the same time remaining 'one of them' in spirit and community purpose. He embodied the ideal combination of individual prowess and communal bonding, which was only strengthened by his taking on the role of their leader.

His intellectual prowess has been widely noted by both contemporary and more recent commentators — Doukhobor and non-Doukhobor alike. Woodcock and Avakumovic (1977: 185), for example, described him as "a powerful personality with a mind that was quick, subtle, and capable, even if it was not profound." He wrote a number of sermons and original psalms that the Doukhobors still hold as a part of their religious creed, along with a series of morally instructive dialogues and stories (e.g., "A Fantasy"[33] — a fable condemning drinking, carousing, and gambling). Those that are not published are to be found mainly in the archives of Vladimir D. Bonch-Bruevich (a Soviet official who collected Doukhobor lore). One especially interesting unpublished piece, entitled simply "Some thoughts" (written in 1914 in the form of a dialogue), discusses the controversial issue of Doukhobor education and relations with the Canadian government.[34]

Perhaps the single most important element behind Verigin's successful leadership was his remarkable capacity for *pragmatism* — he was constantly aware of the need to balance his idealism against what was feasible in life.[35] This strikes one as a quality that goes beyond the purely intellectual — rather, it appears to be an innate feeling of moderation that allowed Verigin not to give in to superfluous emotion, either when moving forward toward his ideal or when undertaking a necessary temporary retreat out of practical considerations. Verigin showed truly exceptional leadership in this regard.

It was this capacity for a realistic evaluation of any situation that allowed him, even at a relatively young age, to correctly understand and fully embrace

33 Published, together with John Woodsworth's English translation, in Donskov 1995a: 34–36, see p. 156.

34 State Museum of the History of Religion, St. Petersburg, folio 2, inv. 7, folio 491. Another sermon, composed in 1922, entitled "The mysteries of world laws: How the universe is kept together," takes the form of an allegory on the organization of the world and man's place in it (folio 951).

35 For example, after expressing his sorrow over the number of Doukhobors departing from the sect's principles into carnivory, alcohol and tobacco consumption, and condoning violence, he still, as a compromise, offered thanks to God "that for the preservation of Christ's teaching there will be a party of Doukhobors in number even one thousand persons who shall eat no meat, drink no whisky, smoke no tobacco and refuse the murder of people — wars. One thousand persons is quite a large party in which it will be possible for Christ to dwell" (James Mavor archive, University of Toronto, MG29, C16).

the Doukhobor concept of rejection of violence. The Burning of Arms in the Caucasus in 1895 had a practical as well as a symbolic significance. One Soviet commentator on the Doukhobors aptly noted that "the class struggle in their midst was taking on an ever-sharper focus," and went so far as to condemn Verigin for "physically disarming the Doukhobors."[36] In fact, of course, Verigin made entirely the right choice, albeit a difficult one. He preferred repression against his followers to either a bloody internal quarrel or a prolonged active conflict with authorities, which would be doomed to failure. His spirited correspondence with Tolstoy[37] bears testament to this.

Verigin's 'special talent' became even more noticeable in Canada, where, from the moment of his arrival in 1902, he endeavoured to smooth the Doukhobors' transition to their new homeland, combining the duties of a spiritual leader of a major sectarian community with the extremely fruitful task of managing this community's financial and social development. His capacity for common sense guided him in searching out compromises with Canadian authorities (the examples of this are too numerous and widely known to detail here).

It may be pointed out, however, that this common sense also helped Verigin cope with events on an immeasurably broader scale. He was well aware, for example, of what any revolution entailed, and as early as 30 April 1917, when as yet hardly anybody in Canada knew anything about the Bolsheviks, he initiated a letter from the Doukhobors to the Russian Provisional Government of 1917, requesting a guarantee that the lives of the tsar and the imperial family would be spared.

No less an important component of Verigin's character was his desire and ability to *learn*, endowing him with a significant breadth of vision, which in tum allowed him to function rather effectively outside the Doukhobor community. He was able to draw from the outside world whatever might be beneficial to the Doukhobors and put it to practical use. This may be seen, for example, in his relationship with Tolstoy and the writer's followers, as well as in the Doukhobors' use of the latest farm machinery machinery.[38] He also had a great desire for constant inner development and a striving for moral and spiritual self-perfection. In a letter to Tolstoy of 3 May 1909 (Letter N° 34 in Chapter 6), for example, he writes of his "goal to free myself from the desire for power."

Verigin, of course, was not successful in every undertaking, and not all his failures can be attributed simply to the effect of unfavourable external circumstances. Some of them were due to his own human weaknesses, such as

36 Klibanov 1965: 111, 113.

37 See Chapter 6 of the present volume.

38 Because of their collective purchasing power, the Doukhobors were in a much better position than individual homesteaders to afford the latest mechanized equipment — an advantage that provoked jealousy on the part of their English-Canadian neighbours (see Woodsworth 1999a: 7).

conflicts with his wife and his son. His son, Pëtr Petrovich Verigin, came to Canada twice during his father's lifetime, with the intention of settling here but, failing to find common understanding with his father, returned to Russia each time.

Verigin also had particular difficulty coming to terms with the Society of Independent Doukhobors, formed in 1916. In his attempts to counter their activities he even enlisted the aid of the Canadian authorities, which, of course, went directly against the sect's moral principles.[39]

The observer of today cannot help feeling some discomfort at the way Verigin carried out his duties as leader, using methods that can only be termed authoritarian — a trait early noticed and criticized by Tolstoy. In evaluating this aspect of his career, one must remember that Doukhobor leaders, starting long before Verigin, customarily enjoyed absolute authority, so one cannot simply fault Verigin for accepting the status quo. A Doukhobor leader was also entrusted with setting a moral example for his followers, and Verigin carried out this task significantly better than many of his predecessors.

Some scholars have legitimately questioned Verigin's sincerity. As noted in the Introduction, for example, Josh Sanborn speculated that Verigin called for the Doukhobors' arms burning in 1895 specifically to elicit a favourable reaction from Tolstoy. We have evidence, too, that most of Verigin's letters to Tolstoy were meticulously crafted, even copied from preliminary drafts. After all, as pointed out earlier, Verigin benefited significantly from Tolstoy's reputation in support of the Doukhobors, just as Tolstoy found in the Doukhobors a practical example of his theories opposing the state (especially state religion) and in favour of non-violent resistance to evil.[40]

It is also worth noting the reaction of the Sons of Freedom to Verigin's attempts to reconcile the practical with the ideal. They concluded that what he said in public (i.e., for the benefit of English-Canadian society) was not what he actually intended for his followers. This confirms the observation that the concept of honesty for the Doukhobors was inextricably linked to their us-versus-them view of the world, in which sincerity in regard to outsiders was not an absolute requirement in a leader. It is quite likely that Verigin himself did not make an exemption in the case of his own followers — witness his earlier mentioned "A Fantasy," which he wrote specifically "for the simple people," without regard to their religious sensibilities, likely considering manipulation of them an entirely acceptable practice.

Verigin will most probably continue to be remembered as a leader who went a long way toward uniting the two approaches — the practical and the ideal — established, respectively, by the original eighteenth-century Doukhobor

39 See Woodcock and Avakumovic 1977: 241–42.

40 At one point, Tolstoy, in a letter to two of his daughters (Tat'jana L'vovna and Marija L'vovna), called the Doukhobors "the people of the 25th century" (*PSS* 71: 497). (*PSS* = Tolstoy's *Polnoe sobranie sochinenij* [Complete collected works].)

leaders: Siluan Kolesnikov and his successor, Ilarion Pobirokhin. Kolesnikov counselled his followers to keep a low profile and not quarrel with the dominant state religion, no matter in which society they lived, while Pobirokhin, Kolesnikov's idealistic and temperamental successor, paid far less attention to the requirements of objective reality and introduced the first known ideological schism into the sect. It was Verigin's efforts to balance these two contrary approaches that unwittingly served as the catalyst for the ultimate fragmentation and dissolution of the sect's organizational structure in Canada.

It is important to note that the viewpoint of the modern researcher is only one possible variant of the many perspectives that could be selected in evaluating the life and career of Pëtr Vasil'evich Verigin. It is by no means the one which Verigin himself would have been concerned with or have attempted to respond to. In the eyes of his erstwhile Doukhobor followers, the man was a prophet, if not a living deity — the embodiment of the 'Spirit,' in fact — and this was the only criterion which bestowed authority in the eyes of many Doukhobors.

An objective analysis of the man would require examining how he came to terms with his unique, assigned role in all its many variants — and this would be a major study on its own. It is impossible to evaluate Verigin's career on the basis of one or two instances of success or failure. The discipline of history has still not come up with satisfactory scientific norms for evaluating the lives of those considered prophets by their followers and contemporaries. Further archival study of the Doukhobors and their leaders, however, is one promising step in the right direction.

The period following the death of Pëtr V. Verigin up to the end of the 1930s is usually seen as a period of decline in Doukhobor history. A number of profitable co-operative enterprises, including their flagship firm, the CCUB, fell victim to the Great Depression and closed their doors, resulting in a general malaise in the community as a whole. In 1938, the British Columbia government began to foreclose on Doukhobor properties, although they were eventually able to buy them back.

In 1927, Pëtr Vasil'evich Verigin's long-estranged son, Pëtr Petrovich Verigin,[41] arrived from Russia to take his father's place as Doukhobor leader. A number of factors, however, including his evident moral weaknesses, led to the new leader's premature demise, in 1939. Not long before his death he and his leadership colleagues dissolved the CCUB, replacing it with the Union of Spiritual Communities of Christ (USCC), which exists to this day.

There were many trials and tribulations, lasting well into the 1960s, largely stemming from the discrepancy between Doukhobor beliefs and the accepted traditions of their host country, Canada. Distrust on the part of Canadian authorities was aroused in part by the Doukhobors' refusal to swear an oath of

41 See Inikova 1999: 98–104.

allegiance to the monarch or to serve in the armed forces (the latter a particularly sore point among many returning First and Second World War veterans). In the early 1950s, the refusal of the Sons of Freedom members to send their children to provincially run public schools led to the BC government's forcibly removing Doukhobor children from their parents' care, incarcerating them in a fenced school compound at New Denver; parental visits were permitted only occasionally and only through the wire fence.[42] Despite all these challenges (or, perhaps, because of them) the Doukhobors continued to feel united in their commonly held beliefs — notably, an unflagging pacifism, a staunch condemnation of any manifestation of man's inhumanity to man, and respect for the inviolability of the human being as representing the image of God.

The death of Pëtr Petrovich Verigin in 1939 marked the start of a gradual overall assimilation of the Doukhobors into the majority Canadian culture, especially after the 1957 agreement with the Sons of Freedom to end the New Denver incarceration of children by having their children educated in public schools. Because of the concentration of their numbers in the Castlegar and Grand Forks districts of the Kootenays, the Doukhobors have, in turn, had a marked effect on public education in these centres, which have now incorporated Russian-language instruction into their regular school programmes, available to the town's general population. And, since the 1960s, a significant number of Canadian Doukhobors have had the opportunity to spend periods of study in Russia under the auspices of the Rodina (lit. 'Motherland') Society in Russia. Many of these students took the opportunity to visit Yasnaya Polyana (Tolstoy's ancestral estate) during their study visit.

Education about their Russian origins, including the support they received from Tolstoy, has indeed been a prominent feature of Canadian Doukhobor education, especially in the latter half of the twentieth century. It was a prominent feature of the journal *Iskra* [The Spark], which began publication in Grand Forks in 1943 as a weekly and continues today as a monthly illustrated bilingual periodical, with articles, poems, letters, and announcements in English and Russian (see Chap. 7). A parallel magazine in Saskatchewan, known as *The Inquirer*, was published during the 1950s, with a focus on Doukhobors, Quakers, and Mennonites, among others. A Russian-language radio programme ran for more than twenty years in Grand Forks, and coverage of Doukhobor activities has been featured on local television.

42 Today those who were so incarcerated are still seeking redress from the BC government for their suffering. In Saskatchewan, by contrast, conflicts over education were minimal, given that province's devolution of most educational decisions to local control and the fact that the vast majority of Doukhobors living there were Independents, rather than Community or Sons of Freedom members. In fact, one of the leaders of the Independents, Peter G. Makaroff, became the first Slavic law graduate at the University of Saskatchewan in 1918; his achievement in turn stimulated further public (including post-secondary) education among Independent Doukhobors. For more on Makaroff, see Bumgardner 2001: 34, 90–91; Tarasoff 2002: 296–99.

Russian heritage is an inescapable feature of the annual Doukhobor youth festivals in the Kootenays, as well as in a number of other celebratory events held throughout the year in Doukhobor communities throughout Western Canada. Almost all of these events involve choral singing of Doukhobor psalms and hymns, passed down in oral tradition from generation to generation from their ancestors in Russia. These choirs have given countless performances, not only for their own brethren but in public concerts in a number of cities in Canada and abroad, including Russia and at the United Nations headquarters, in New York, and today the psalms are sung not only in Russian but in English and French as well.

In 1987 the Rodina Society presented two Doukhobor communities in Veregin (Saskatchewan) and Castlegar (BC) with life-size statues of Tolstoy, the work of Russian sculptor Jurij Chernov.[43]

In describing the unveiling of the monument in the village of Veregin, Saskatchewan, in a 1987 issue of *Iskra,* Il'ja Tolstoj (great-grandson to Leo Tolstoy) wrote poignantly (see I. V. Tolstoj 1987):

> Before erecting any monument, sculptors and architects make a study and select a suitable architectural-landscape milieu. This is a very important part of the creative process. I think there is another side that is equally important — the human milieu in which a person's sculptural likeness is destined to live. Will this monument's life be among people who are active, express vitality and enrich the soul, or who turn out to be a cold and unresponsive part of artistically organized space?
>
> I have the feeling that, out among the Doukhobors in Saskatchewan and British Columbia, Tolstoy will live. For many years now, an inner dialogue has been taking place between Tolstoy and the Doukhobors. In the beginning Tolstoy entered their lives as a part of their outlook on life — a peasant, sectarian outlook. But over the years this same Tolstoy has helped them sail out onto the vast ocean of universal human ideas.

Very much in keeping with the Tolstoyan tradition, the Doukhobors in Canada have also joined with other like-minded groups[44] in opposing the expansion of military activities, including chemical, biological, and nuclear warfare. Beyond that, however, they continue to see their role as bridge builders between peoples; they are frequently involved in exchanges of Russian and Canadian artists, writers, scholars, filmmakers, and such.[45] Witness the

43 Jurij Chernov was born in Moscow in 1935; he graduated from the prestigious V. I. Surikov State Art Institute in Moscow and has had numerous exhibits in Russia and abroad. Among his works are monuments to the writer Maksim Gorky and to the first human in space, Jurij Gagarin.

44 Such groups include the Quakers, Mennonites, Molokans, the Canadian Peace Alliance, the UN Association in Canada, the World Federalists, and the Coalition to Oppose the Arms Trade.

45 Their role as 'bridge builders,' among other contributions, has been acknowledged by the honours bestowed upon their leader during most of the latter half of the twentieth century, John J. Verigin Sr., by authorities in both countries. In 1977 he was awarded the Order of Canada,

description of this aim in the 1980 USCC "Report on the future" (USCC 1980: 22):

> Such a bridge of understanding is vitally necessary if a violent confrontation between the two 'superpowers' is to be averted. It is a legitimate and integral part of our Doukhobor purpose to do our best to nurture such understanding and friendlier relations, in the interest of world peace and the universal brotherhood of mankind.

The Tolstoyan ideal (shared by the Doukhobors) of fostering unity among the world's peoples — particularly as seen through Tolstoy's fiction and his correspondence with prominent sectarians — is the subject of the next chapter.[46]

followed by the Order of British Columbia in 1996. In 1989, then Soviet President Mikhail Gorbachëv presented him with the Order of Peoples' Friendship.

46 Tolstoy's correspondence with Pëtr V. Verigin is the subject of Chap. 6. Other specific Doukhobor links to Tolstoy relating to the period from 1924 to the present are discussed in Chap. 7. For a brief outline of Doukhobor history in twentieth-century Canada, see Tarasoff 1995: 14–17.

CHAPTER 2

The 'Unity of People' as Tolstoy's Lifelong Aim[1]

IN THE NINETEENTH and twentieth centuries, the search for the ideal world was reinforced by Russian Christians and Marxist philosophies, accompanied by an increase in the number of treatises on the subject — utopias and dystopias. By the early nineteenth century the idea of *unity of people* had already taken on the status of a prominent objective among Russian philosophers.

Significant contributions to this ideal were made by three outstanding thinkers: (a) Nikolaj Fëdorovich Fëdorov (1828–1903), who proposed a *total unity* [*vseedinstvo*] of the dead and the living; (b) Vladimir Solov'ëv (1853–1900), who envisaged a state of world harmony based on the principles of *Godmanhood* [*Bogochelovechestvo*] in addition to the universal feminine principle of love *Sophia* [*Sofija*] and reconciliation among human beings; and (c) Semën Ljudvigovich Frank (1877–1950), who also promoted *total unity* as a dominant philosophical concept.[2]

1 Much useful material concerning the 'unity of people' in Tolstoy's works was presented at a 1996 international conference at the University of Ottawa entitled Lev Tolstoy and the Concept of Brotherhood (for the proceedings, see Donskov and Woodsworth 1996), where prominent Tolstoy scholars from various countries examined the concept in the context of his major novels, moral treatises, and lesser-known works. The conference included an open forum on "Tolstoy at the threshold of the twenty-first century," exploring the relevance of his ideas on brotherhood to the current generation of readers, as well as a closing speech by Doukhobor Village Museum curator Larry Ewashen (1996b), "Tolstoy and the Doukhobors today." A significant part of this chapter is drawn from Donskov, Galagan, and Gromova 2002).

2 See Josef Metzele's (1996) illuminating paper "The concept of 'brotherly love' in Tolstoy's late prose."

Most prominent among the unity promoters, however, were Dostoevsky and Tolstoy. The latter, especially, laid great emphasis on the love of goodness, of the *other* rather than the *self*. The supremacy of truth and non-violent resistance to evil, discernible even in his early fiction, grew in intensity throughout his literary works, both fiction and treatises. As early as 1855, his proclamation "to work *consciously* for the unification of people through religion" (*PSS* 47:37–38) situated the idea of "unity of people" within the spiritual and Christian context.

Tolstoy also read widely in the major Western and Eastern philosophies. In the Christian Scriptures, Jesus' Sermon on the Mount was particularly meaningful to him, inculcating in him the idea that life should be a process of moral self-perfection. His treatise *On Life* [*O zhizni*] (1886–1888) picked up on the biblical dictum (1 John 4:8) of God as *love* and love as the only rational activity, along with the concomitant notion of the fundamental opposition between *good* and *evil*.[3]

Tolstoy's very first published work appeared in print more than 165 years ago — the narrative *Childhood* [*Detstvo*] (1852), which would come to be hailed as the writer's first masterpiece, initiating a trilogy describing the 'stages of life' experienced by every growing human being: childhood, adolescence, and youth.

At the same time, Tolstoy was coming to grips with a fundamental question: Why do people write? [*Dlja chego pishut ljudi?*].[4] And, over time, a response began to take shape. From the very beginning he attached a high degree of responsibility to the writing profession: literary creativity was imbued with intense moral and philosophical seekings.[5] His creative activity

3 In his major religious treatise *V chëm moja vera* [*What I Believe*] (1884), Tolstoy sets forth five 'commandments' in summary of his creed: (1) do not be angry, (2) do not lust, (3) do not swear, (4) do not resist evil with violence, (5) love all people without distinction. See *PSS* 23:348–65.

4 This is an early recognition on Tolstoy's part that people want to be happy, but since "the only way of finding happiness is through virtue, then it is wise to read only...those books which teach virtue" (*PSS* 1:246). He further specified which books one should indeed read: "those which are dogmatic, speculative and founded on principles of reason — others are excluded by common sense." This attitude remained consistent throughout Tolstoy's life.

5 Writing, Tolstoy believed, was an excellent vehicle for propagating the concept of unity among people. This is attested in both his literary works and his extensive correspondence with, in particular, Russian sectarians (see below). In his letters to Pëtr Verigin, he made numerous attempts to convince the Doukhobor leader of the value of books (which Verigin rejected on the grounds that Jesus taught only by the spoken word). Tolstoy argued that a good book had a spiritually unifying power, especially for readers in far-off places — witness these excerpts from his letter of 14 October 1896 (Donskov 1995a: 22, 24):

"God leads people to himself to do His will in all sorts of ways: both conscious, when people try to do His will, and unconscious, when they are doing what they think is their own will. To do God's will, to establish His kingdom on earth, people must be united among themselves, so that all may be one, as Christ recognised himself as one with the Father. To reach this kind of unity one must follow first, the inner path — the knowledge and clear expression of truth, as Christ showed us, which unites all people, and secondly, the external path of spreading this message of

was governed by an over-riding concern for *good,* which he turned into his literary compositions.

Tolstoy's profound psychological analysis, focused as it was on the depths of the human soul, not only uncovered the true content of feelings, thoughts, and actions, but penetrated the nuclei which harboured in themselves the seeds of moral growth and development. The extreme sincerity which Tolstoy held to be a law of the creative process (which he himself attributed to Jean-Jacques Rousseau) was what led to further discoveries, such as in the chapter "Grief" ["Gore"] in *Childhood.* The hero, Nikolen'ka, at his mother's deathbed, is able to experience genuine sorrow only for a brief moment, and condemns himself for the insincerity of his feelings, which wandered from one thing to another during his viewing of her dead body (*PSS* 1:85–86):

> [I]t makes me ashamed when I think back on this sadness, because there was always some sort of selfishness mixed in with it: either the desire to show that I was grieving more than the rest, or the impression I was making on other people, or the aimless curiosity that provoked me to make observations on Mimi's cap and the faces of those present. I condemned myself for not experiencing a feeling of sorrow all by itself, and tried to hide all the rest; consequently, my grief was insincere and unnatural.

Immediately a comparison follows with the old housekeeper Natal'ja Savishna, who bore the deepest and sincerest suffering of all, living at the behest of a tradition uniting her with all people.[6] As Ol'ga Slivitskaja (1988: 74) notes,

truth, which is effected in all sorts of various ways: by trade and conquests, by travels on foot and by rail, by telegraph and telephone, and by books, as well as many other means of communication. Some of the latter — conquests, for example — I am obliged to reject, but others, such as books and quick communication devices I have no right to reject, and cannot help using if I do not wish to deny myself a handy tool whereby to serve God."

"[M]an's task at the present time is not dreaming about what people once were and how to make them again that way, but in providing for the well-being of people who are living today. And the well-being of people who are living today requires them not to torture or oppress others, not to deprive them of the fruits of their labours, not to force them to work [to produce] things they don't need or cannot use, but most importantly, not to consider it possible or legitimate — in the name of some cause or material success — to destroy the life and well-being of one's neighbour, or, what is the other side of the coin, to violate love. Once people realize that the purpose of mankind is not material progress, that this progress is inevitable growth, and that there is only one purpose — the well-being of *all* people, that this purpose is higher than any material purpose people can set for themselves, then everything will be in its proper place. And it is to this [end] that people of our time must direct their whole effort."

One may also find a number of references to writing in Tolstoy's fiction works, e.g., Levin's writing on private property in *Anna Karenina*, Nekhljudov in *Resurrection* [*Voskresenie*], or Fedja Protasov in *The Living Corpse* [*Zhivoj trup*].

[6] "Her soul aspired to God, she entreated Him for her [the protagonist's mother] and for herself, she trusted and honoured His will. Here was someone who truly loved and understood her, I thought, and I was ashamed of myself" — translated from Tolstoy, *Detstvo* (iz pervoj redaktsii, gl. 24, ruk. 4) [*Childhood*], reproduced in Donskov, Galagan, and Gromova 2002: 93.

Nikolen'ka experiences "an indissoluble feeling of suffering from the insincerity attached to his suffering." But his recognition of this — and recognition invariably signifies change — leads to *self-awareness* [*samopoznanie*], a step toward *self-perfection* [*samousovershenstvovanie*].

The themes of *sincerity* [*iskrennost'*] and *falsehood* [*lozhnost'*] permeate the trilogy and continue as important subjects in all Tolstoy's major fiction and publicistic works.

Having passed through "the desert of adolescence," Nikolaj Irten'ev seeks out new paths of moral development and, concomitantly, unity with others. A spiritual friendship with other young people furnishes strength for his own progress and a firm stand against one's surroundings. The impulsion of youth opens the way to the freedom to part from them. Here is the leading thought of *The Cossacks* [*Kazaki*]. It is interesting that in Tolstoy's final extant manuscript, "The Cossacks" appears in place of the crossed-out title "Youth (The Caucasus, 1853)."[7] Tolstoy had initially conceived this work, in effect, as the concluding part of what he saw as the "four stages of development."

The Cossack camp where Tolstoy's hero ends up (in the manuscripts he bears the name of Rzhavskij) is a peasant world, albeit one with no serf law, oppression, or want, and therefore with a greater degree of freedom. And yet it has a military atmosphere, inasmuch as it borders on a neighbouring community of aggressive mountain dwellers with warlike tendencies. The perception of this world in its ideal embodiment is expressed by the old woodsman Eroshka leading the sophisticate, Olenin, into the woods to catch a momentary glimpse of total unity with all living things. As is known, the character of Eroshka was modelled after Epifan Sekhin, in whose hut Tolstoy was quartered while serving at the Starogladkov camp. Epifan's stories and precepts found their way into Tolstoy's diary, and subsequently onto the pages of his manuscripts and the published narrative.

One might say that this constitutes a spontaneous philosophy of universal unity of human beings with Nature, and among human beings themselves, without national or religious distinctions:

> The way I see it, everything is of one piece, everything God did He did for the joy of humanity. Take the beasts, for example: they live in the Tatar's swamps just as in ours and, wherever they go, there is the home that God gave them, and that is where they find their food. But our people say that you'll go to hell if you eat cream on Wednesdays. I have eaten horsemeat on Wednesdays, and nothing happened — I think it's all just a pile of lies.[8]

7 *Junost' (Kavkaz 1853 g.)*. Cf. Zhdanov 1955: 82.

8 Translated from Tolstoy, *Kazaki* (iz pervoj redaktsii "Kavkazskogo romana," ruk. 14), reproduced in Donskov, Galagan, and Gromova 2002: 100.

Such a philosophy is capable of saving a moth flying into a flame, pitying a slain Chechen, and having compassion on Olenin, whom "the girls do not love."

Olenin leaves the camp misunderstood and unloved, without understanding or accepting the laws of such a centripetal world. No unity takes place, although as Edward Wasiolek has shown — in a sacramental scene in the stag's lair — Olenin experiences, albeit for a brief moment, oneness with Nature and the world about him. The blissful condition soon fades as "reflection distorts what he experiences."[9]

But Tolstoy in this instance does not condemn: both sides are right, both must continue to exist — the people's side, so that it may, in holding fast to its righteousness, be imbued with Christianity; the other side, that it may seek out new paths of self-perfection and unity and recognize its guilt before the people. But that will happen only later.

These are the same questions that concerned Tolstoy in his three major novels (*War and Peace*, *Anna Karenina*, *Resurrection*).

War and Peace is set in Russia and Europe at the beginning of the nineteenth century. In the 1860s, when the novel was written, this was already history. But much more than a historical novel, it is first and foremost a philosophical work about peoples, at any time, in any place.

National unity for the purposes of repulsing a foreign invader is something natural and joyful, in spite of all the sufferings and losses. All the main characters of the book go through these trials, and thereby achieve unity ("we must get together," Pierre Bezukhov tells himself). In one such scene, from Part 1 of Volume 3,[10] Natasha Rostova, who has been fasting after refusing Andrej Bolkonskij because of her nervous tension, finds herself at the church service not long before the French occupation of Moscow. She prays there together with everyone and for everyone, solemnly placing herself in God's hands. One Tolstoy draft includes the following description: "'O Lord, take me!' she said in tears, losing herself in all the complexity of these joyful impressions."

In Tolstoy's epic everything is brought together and reflected in each other: history and people's private lives; the good of unity and the evil of disunity. Napoleon plays the same criminal role in the lives of nations as Anatol' Kuragin plays in Natasha's fate. Her attraction for Anatolij, according to Tolstoy, is what constitutes "the hub of the novel." Yes, a person may be free in their private life (as distinct from historical personages, who are subject

9 See Wasiolek's (1978) perceptive study of the so-called sacramental scenes in Tolstoy's works, where his major characters, necessarily seekers of truth and a meaning of life indestructible by death, are depersonalized and brought to a point where they realize that they are indeed part of a unified whole, together with myriad other elements equally important in this unity. See especially Wasiolek's chapters discussing *Childhood*, *The Cossacks*, *War and Peace*, and *Anna Karenina*.
10 The draft of this scene is reproduced in Donskov, Galagan, and Gromova (2002: 166–67), from which the quotation at the end of this paragraph is translated.

to the unfathomable laws of existence), but this freedom is not limitless, in view of the existence of the moral ideal. Natasha almost perishes on the path of limitless freedom — an event which is the focus of almost the entire second volume of *War and Peace*. After suffering through history with Anatolij, Natasha will later tell Pierre that she has become better; she has become a good person.

Within the framework of unity prevailing in *War and Peace*, the powers of evil are doomed to defeat. This does not happen in the novel *Anna Karenina*, set in another era, where everything is "mixed up" and "turned upside down." The heroine's gloomy thoughts just before her suicide to a large extent reflect what Tolstoy himself experienced and then described in *Confession [Ispoved']* (begun in 1875 and not completed until the early 1880s). Here we may note his acknowledgement that he hid the rope to keep from hanging himself and did not take his hunting rifle lest he might use it as an easy means to ending his life. During the time he was writing *Anna Karenina*, Tolstoy was sometimes inclined to agree with nineteenth-century German "philosopher of pessimism" Arthur Schopenhauer.

But Tolstoy's healthy genius, his own constant striving for unity with the world, pointed the way out of the crisis. New sources of moral support appeared. In *Anna Karenina* this positive potential is evident in certain apparently quite unexpected scenes.

First, we see Karenin at his dying wife's bedside. He is returning from Petersburg to Moscow, where he was consulting with a divorce lawyer, believing Anna's death to be the best way out. And suddenly all is forgiven: he weeps, kisses her hands, obeys her request to offer a hand of reconciliation to her lover. A miracle occurs, which overwhelmed even Dostoevsky, that great master of tales of the unexpected. There will be no salvation: all three will be punished for Anna's violation of the moral law. And salvation, according to Tolstoy, is something that can be hoped for only through the path of good, the path of unity.

Another characteristic episode is Levin's wedding. It is known that there is a strong autobiographical component in these chapters. It is unlikely, however, that when Tolstoy married Sofia Andreevna Bers, in 1862, he was so deeply affected by the wedding ceremony or took the priest's admonitions so to heart. As recounted in *Confession* (1884), at this time, while remaining an Orthodox believer, he had long become indifferent to this aspect of religion. But, working on the novel and addressing himself to its readers, he made a conscious effort to rise above his own doubts and to point out such a path to the unity of people, one within the framework of ecclesiastical faith.

It is worth mentioning that, at the time he was completing the novel, Tolstoy claimed he was making a concerted effort to observe church rules (attending services and confession, fasting), hoping to achieve thereby a kind of unity with the beliefs of the majority of people. Presently, however, he became disappointed with these outward manifestations of religious feeling and he rejected them in favour of preserving an *inner faith.* The moment of harmonious reconciliation and understanding was embodied in *Anna Karenina.*

In the final chapters of the novel, Levin does find an actual way out. It consists in *living by God.* It means rejecting any form of selfish pride, including family pride (i.e., exclusive love of one's own family) and looking upon *all* people as one's brethren. An impossible dream — utopian, perhaps — but this is what was preached two thousand years ago by one nailed to a cross.

During the last thirty years of his literary career Tolstoy was ever concerned with the idea of renewal of life, of a sudden and inevitable transformation, or 'resurrection.' The novel that bears this name was written in the 1890s, at a time when manifestations of enmity and uprisings in all walks of life in Russia and throughout the world had intensified to extremes. Tolstoy, of course, witnessed all this, and responded to much of it with a passion. And at the same time, he persisted even more forcefully in his search for salvation, as well as a reconciliation of contradictions in applying his beliefs to practice.

As if returning to the source of his creativity — and to the stage of his youth, similar to the episode with Katjusha Maslova and Dmitrij Nekhljudov in the novel — Tolstoy insists in *Resurrection* on an inner repentance, moral purification, and growth in soul as the basis for collective living. No matter how gloomy and difficult the scene in the prison cell where Maslova finds herself, no matter how cruel and unjust the sentence meted out to her, no matter how complex her current relations with Nekhljudov, resurrection is possible for her — and for him — on the basis of Christian truths contained in the Gospels.

The open references to the Scriptures are an indispensable element of all Tolstoy's writings of this period. Christianity and its commandments, above all the law of universal love, serve to counter the evil enemy forces — particularly the hopes of revolutionaries (as also depicted in *Resurrection*) to change the world by violence, replacing the outward forms of societal existence. From Tolstoy's point of view, there was only one thing needed — a social order based "on free agreement and mutual love" (*To Political Activists [K politicheskim dejateljam]). It* was in the name of this love that he protested against the punishment of peasants who were trying to attain, through their "disorders," only one thing (albeit necessary for them) — namely, *land* — and was devastated that peaceful, kind Russian peasants were learning so quickly to "make revolution."

The truths he discovered after *Confession* not only saved Tolstoy from despair but infused his whole writing activity with considerable new meaning. His sharp criticism of the anti-Christian structure of society led to a confrontation with the whole power of the state, with the church, and with his own family. The latter conflict was aroused by his outline for the autobiographical drama *And the Light Shineth in Darkness* (as noted, begun in the 1890s but not published until 1911), which Tolstoy repeatedly called 'my drama,' and resulted in his leaving Yasnaya Polyana. As to his argument with the official church, his 'falling away' from it led in part to a rupture with the majority of his beloved peasantry of Russia, who traditionally adhered to Orthodoxy, although it did bring him closer to the Doukhobors.

The critical pathos evident in Tolstoy's works strengthened the Protestant, disuniting mood in the country, which was marching irrevocably toward revolution, in spite of the postulate of 'non-violent resistance to evil' and the conviction that evil could be conquered not through violence but simply through refusal to participate in evil actions. Hence his ardent support of all sorts of sectarians,[11] even while realizing the limitations and disuniting influences inherent in each of them.

It seems appropriate at this point to turn our attention to Tolstoy's relationship with the peasantry, as well as religious dissidents, whose members either coincided with or influenced his philosophy and who were used by Tolstoy in his literary works and social treatises both to complement the characters of nobility and to serve as examples of the possibility of achieving unity among humankind. Especially noteworthy are his exchanges of letters with Sabbatarian Timofej M. Bondarev (Donskov 1996c), Molokan writer Fëdor Zheltov (Donskov 2001), and radical dissident Mikhail Novikov (Donskov 1996a).

The text of Tolstoy's treatise *Tak chto zhe nam delat'?* [*What Then Must Be Done?*] (1886) suggests two powerful role models for his (and, by extension, others') moral regeneration. He wrote (*PSS* 25:386),

> Over my whole lifetime two Russian thinkers had a profound moral influence on me; they enriched my thought and clarified my worldview. These people were not Russian poets, scholars or preachers — they were two remarkable men who are still alive today, having lived their whole lives by the sweat of their brow — the peasants Sjutaev and Bondarev.

This paragraph reveals several important features in Tolstoy's thought. It begins with a reference to his lifelong preoccupation with moral questions. It suggests the exclusion of any contribution from his own class or from the clergy to his *Weltanschauung*, which drew upon the solid moral fibre of ordinary Russian peasants, whose life derived its meaning from working "by the sweat of their brow." They had not only enriched, but actually *clarified* [*ujasnili*] his thought for him. This was an extremely important point for him in his so-called post-conversion period (following the completion of *Anna Karenina* in the late 1870s) and is of utmost importance in any discussion of Tolstoy and the peasantry.

11 See Edmund Heier 1970, especially Chap. 1, "Social and religious disillusionment of the age (1850–1900)": 1–29.

It is also significant that the two peasants mentioned were both sectarians. Vasilij K. Sjutaev (1820–1892) was well known to Tolstoy and contemporary writers, while Bondarev (1820–1898), a Sabbatarian (a splinter group of the Molokans, they had earlier broken away from the Doukhobors), carried on an extensive correspondence with Tolstoy from 1885 until his death.[12]

The word *ujasnit'* [to clarify, make more comprehensible] may be seen here as a key to understanding the development of Tolstoy's thought. It suggests the confirmation of an idea — in this case, the writer's moral stance. Elsewhere in the same treatise he writes:[13]

> *The moral laws already exist,* mankind has only to clarify them for itself.... This clarification [*ujasnenie*] of the moral law is not only the most important, but is the only cause for all mankind [to espouse].

In this connection, the image and function of the Doukhobors is similar to that of other peasants, both in his life and in his works, taking the form of a catalyst in the regeneration of his aristocratic heroes — compare with the function of the peasant Karataev in the regeneration of Pierre in *War and Peace,*[14] Levin and the peasant Platon in *Anna Karenina,* Nekhljudov and the peasant sectarian in *Resurrection.* Levin was transformed by the story he heard from a peasant about the just and meaningful life of another peasant, and he comes around full circle to the 'truth' that already lies within him: "I've discovered nothing. I've simply learnt about what I knew already," he says at the end of the novel.

It is significant, however, that his mentor was a peasant, free of the burdensome layers of civilization. Tolstoy realized that the questions of 'how to live' (and die) which tantalized his characters of station (and himself) could not be answered through moral-intellectual discourse;[15] the questions are 'answered,' however, on a deeper, more organic level through the 'truth' as perceived both by himself and by his characters of station (which are the

12 Regarding Bondarev's writings on religious utopias, see Donskov (1996b: 115). For more on Bondarev and Sjutaev, see Bondarev (1890, 1906); Donskov (1996b, 1997); Gastev (1912); Kosovanov (1958); Shesterikov (1928); "Unknown author" (1913).

13 *PSS* 25:226; italics added.

14 In *War and Peace* the peasant Karataev also serves as an embodiment of peasant 'collectivist thinking' (as does the peasant Gerasim in *The Death of Ivan Il'ich*) in contrast to Pierre's individualism; calmness and steadfastness in contrast to moral perplexity; rural simplicity and sincerity in contrast to the artificiality and decorum of the aristocracy. In order to find any kind of solid foundation, Pierre must be complemented by someone who reflects the spirit of all people and not just one of its individual components. Pierre, whose very name represents the foreign-influenced nobility, must become *Pëtr* (*Pjotr*) — free, as much as possible, from the layers of 'civilization' (see Ovsjaniko-Kulikovskij 1905: 90). For him, Karataev signifies the whole of which Pierre seeks to become a part. He is especially attracted to Karataev's *roundness* (Tolstoy uses this term and its many derivatives to describe him) — an image which, like the circle, from ancient times symbolized completeness and was often used in reference to deity [*bozhestvo*] and theophany [*bogojavlenie*].

15 See Rimvydas Silbajoris's (1996) "The brotherhood and solitude of death in Tolstoy."

almost exclusive focus of his major works) through their association with peasants.

Tolstoy's "new-found" faith integrated the ideal of brotherly love and other Christian virtues into different genres — drama, story-drama, folk tales [*narodnye rasskazy*] — where Tolstoy placed considerable emphasis on mankind's moral obligations.[16] In contrast to his works prior to *Confession*, where the main emphasis was on the regeneration and moral awakening of his characters of station — where they could and did learn from the peasants the virtues of simplicity, sincerity and naturalness — in Tolstoy's later writings the peasants themselves learnt from their peers and, in fact, from Tolstoy's own ideas (see Donskov 1979).

Vlast' t'my [*The Power of Darkness*] (1886), almost entirely made up of peasant characters, is a case in point. Although many critics see the power of money as the chief evil entering the villages from the corrupt cities, "the power of darkness" is greater. Darkness is in everything where there is no God. Light — in a religious sense, it must be there, too — is conscience. Conscience is alive as long as there is acceptance of God. In this play, as in many other of his writings, Tolstoy does not deal with a world in which there are no moral laws; rather, he sets the action in a world in which moral laws have been violated.

The central character, Nikita, wedged between his evil mother Matriona and his saintly father Akim, commits a number of crimes — the result (as it becomes clear) of his departure from the peasant way of life and his going off to work in the city. He will be redeemed when he awakens morally and returns to the simple ways of peasant life. Here, as in *Khozjain i rabotnik* [*Master and Man*] (1895), Tolstoy adds a new dimension to the portrayal of peasants and, consequently, to the ideas they represent: truth is attained by both Nikita and Vasilij through spiritual insight rather than through the intellectual reasoning that is mainly responsible for bringing about Nekhljudov's conversion in *Resurrection*. Nikita's words at the end, "Papa, forgive me, damned as I am. You told me from the start, when I went astray," reveal that, by a full realization of his sins, he has seen the truth so characteristic of his father, the simple peasant, whose moral feelings cannot be separated from his religious beliefs.

In 1884 Tolstoy, along with Vladimir Chertkov and Pavel Birjukov, started his own publishing house, which he aptly named *Posrednik* (lit., 'Intermediary'), where he edited and published stories not only *about* peasants, but also *by* and *for* peasants. He next turned his attention to the idea of creating a theatre for the illiterate, with the thought of advancing not only their literary appreciation but, more importantly, their moral education — to point out where and how to find a higher truth. His first effort along this

16 See Lidija Gromova-Opul'skaja's (1996) essay "The philosophy and æsthetics of brotherhood in Tolstoy's fiction," and Galina Galagan's (1996) "The idea of world renewal."

line was a dramatization of two stories: *Haggai* [*Aggej*] (1886) and *Peter the Publican* [*Pëtr Khlebnik*] (1884–1894).

Tolstoy also wrote a number of original story-legends — for example, *What [Do] Men Live By?* [*Chem ljudi zhivy?*] (1885) and *The Power of Childhood* [*Sila detstva*] (1908). The story-drama form easily lends itself to the propagation of moral beliefs and the raising and solving of socio-ethical questions — especially in view of his intended target audience, for whom the traditional dramatic form would be cumbersome and archaic.

Tolstoy's story-dramas are replete with wise old men, anchorites, and pilgrims, all of whom, while understanding and sympathetic to human weaknesses and frailties, manage to attain an inner freedom and spiritual poise through exploring the themes of self-denial, meditation on God, good and evil, and selfless service to one's neighbour.

These story-dramas emphasize a number of themes of Tolstoy's moral philosophy, including sin's origin in the human mind and the urgency of moral self-perfection, both pointing to the importance of the act of repentance. Tolstoy embodies these concepts in two ideal characters, both repentant sinners, one of whom renounces and withdraws from mankind in order to save himself, while the other expiates his sin by actively working for the well-being of those around him. Both meekly accept their fate, though Tolstoy makes clear his strong preference for the latter — witness his comment about Father Sergius, the eponymous hero of a posthumously published (1911) short story: "Woe to those who live by the labour of others!"

Critic Boris Sushkov comments on Tolstoy's story-dramas as follows:

> Man is cruel, morally dead until such time as he thinks and feels himself to be the only sinless and irreplaceable centre of the universe. His moral awakening begins when he likens himself to some other human being — "crawls into his skin." Especially into the skin of one's 'enemy,' changes places with him. And then one begins to understand one's identification (likeness, sameness) with the other person, one's equality with him on the plane of human right to life — and this means killing another is tantamount to killing one's self. Only after one has been in the skin of the enemy he planned to execute does the hero of the tale "Assirijskij tsar' Asarkhadon" [Asarkhadon the Assyrian King] experience moral awakening.
>
> In the second tale-in-miniature, *Trud, smert' i bolezn'* [Labour, death and disease], the whole history of mankind is covered in the space of two-and-a-half pages — the history of people's tortuous search for the true humanitarian paths, for true human happiness. And in *Tri voprosa* [Three questions] — the third tale in this 'triptych' — the king learnt from a holy hermit the answers to three most complex questions: "How much time should I spend reflecting and not miss [the opportunity to act], so that I shan't have to repent later?" "What people are the most needful to me, and so which ones should I have the most and the least to do with?" "What activities are the most important and, consequently, which ones should I do before others?"

> Here is another 'triptych' from Tolstoy's folk tales: *What Do Men Live By?* [*Chem ljudi zhivy?*], *Where Love Is, There Too Is God* [*Gde ljubov', tam i Bog*] and *A Grain the Size of a Chicken-Egg* [*Zerno s kurinoe jajtso*]. They are all written on Gospel themes and teach moral truths, which are just as incontrovertible as mathematical truths.[17]

A detailed discussion of Tolstoy's *narodnye rasskazy* is offered by both Gary Jahn and Josef Metzele in the framework of Tolstoy's concept of brotherhood and its role in achieving unity of people.[18] This discussion highlights two significant models, adherence to which, Tolstoy firmly believed, would lead to self-perfection and the unity of people — namely, "toil on the land" (both in his articles and his letters, especially in his correspondence with peasants) and "the wisdom of children." These themes are also reflected in Tolstoy's relationship with the Doukhobors.

Tolstoy had a lifelong interest in the question of land and its importance to the peasants. He wrote several articles on this topic, and once poeticized the land in the famous hay-cutting scene with Levin in *Anna Karenina*.[19] It can be seen to permeate his play *Plody prosveshchenija* [*Fruits of Enlightenment*] (1890), witness the third peasant's plea: "Have mercy, Father. Our land is small, there's no place to pasture any cattle, or even chickens. *(bows)* Do not sin, my Father! *(bows)*."

Tolstoy referred to this "Do not sin" and the importance of the peasant land question in a letter to Bondarev of 23 June 1894, in a discussion of the popular American reformer and economist Henry George's plan to liberate the land "from its invaders, or rather, the liberation of workers from the slavery arising from the ownership of land by those who do not till it."

SECTARIAN TIMOFEJ BONDAREV

Throughout his correspondence with Bondarev (see Donskov 1996b, 2019), Tolstoy applied a religious perspective to the question of landless peasants. The letters are marked with frequent repetitions of his tenet that physical, land-tilling labour is a necessary precondition for a moral, happy, and joyful life on earth. Bondarev, for his part, kept insisting that field labour is a fundamental *religious* law of life. Bondarev comes across as a colourful figure, a Russian peasant who, though unshakeable in his convictions, is not at one

17 Quoted from Sushkov 1991: 16–17. For more on these themes, see my two articles on Peter the Publican (Donskov 1996c, 1996d).

18 See Jahn 1996; Metzele 1996.

19 On the religious motifs permeating this episode and their role in the unity of people, see Gustafson 1986: 420–27. According to Grodetskaja (2000b: 222), 'peasant labour,' along with what Levin learns from observing the peasants, "eliminates the contradiction between the individual and society...and also eliminates the contradiction between the corporeal, carnal, 'animal' (natural) and the spiritual (divine)."

with his milieu because of the penetrating insight of his sharp analytical mind and the logic of his conclusions.

In his correspondence with Bondarev, Tolstoy makes particular reference to Bondarev's work *Torzhestvo zemledel'tsa, ili Trudoljubie i Tunejadstvo* (hereinafter referred to as *The Triumph of the Land-tiller, or Industry and Idleness*) — a work Tolstoy helped get published. Written in the late 1870s and early 1880s, it is largely based on the biblical decree in Genesis (3:19): "In the sweat of thy face shalt thou eat bread, till thou return unto the ground; for out of it was thou taken." Bondarev argues that people sin because they do not obey this rule, which he takes literally. Tolstoy shared Bondarev's criticism of militarism and the noble classes, as well as his condemnation not only of the corruption rampant in the civil service but also the narrowness and intolerance of the church hierarchy.

Over and over again in his subsequent works Tolstoy returns to Bondarev's ideas.[20] In working out his *Cycle of Readings* in 1904, he included in the "Monthly readings" section an excerpt from Bondarev's book, with an accompanying article he had penned in 1895. He also mentions Bondarev in a diary entry in 1906 (*PSS* 55:212):

> It has become quite clear to me of late that the life of the land-tiller is not just one of the various types of life, but is life itself, just as the Bible is life itself, the only life of mankind, and it is only through such a life that the higher human qualities can be manifested. The chief mistake in the organization of human societies — a mistake that removes the opportunity for any kind of intelligent life-structure — is that people wish to set up their society either without any land-tilling activity or whereby such activity is only one — and the most demeaning — way of life. How right is Bondarev!

All this testifies to the existence of a complementary or even symbiotic relationship between society and the tilling of the land, a hypothesis confirmed in Tolstoy's letter to Bondarev of 26 March 1886:

> I read your long manuscript and addendum. Both are very good and true.... I am in agreement with everything said in the manuscript and shall only mention a couple of points where I see things differently. The first law is "In the sweat of

20 Abbreviated variants of Bondarev's work are known to us from their publication in the weekly *Russkoe Delo* (1888, N° 12–13), with an afterword by Tolstoy. In 1890, thanks to Tolstoy's co-operation, a French translation was published, *Léon Tolstoï et Timothé Bondareff: Le travail*, translated from the Russian by V. Tseytline and A. Pagès. Interestingly, an English version, published the same year, was based not on the Russian but on the French translation — for both editions see Bondarev 1890. Bondarev repeatedly complained both to Tolstoy and to G. I. Uspenskij about the poor translation of his work (a reverse translation into Russian was done by a local translator at his request), as well as about the many abridgements. The manuscript ran approximately 200 sheets. *The Triumph of the Land-tiller, or Industry and Idleness* was also published in condensed form by Posrednik in 1906 (see Bondarev 1906).

> thy face shalt thou eat bread," but in order for this law to avoid being violated, one must also obey a second law: "Resist not evil."[21]

And later on Tolstoy frankly acknowledges: "I have found in you a strong helper in this cause. I hope you have found a helper in me. Our cause is one and the same" (Donskov 1996b: 34).

It is worth noting that Bondarev's work proved very timely for Tolstoy, appearing at the very moment when the latter was particularly concerned over questions of the peasantry (especially the suffering and maltreatment experienced by the Doukhobors), hard labour, the simplicity of peasant life, and so on. Such questions grew out of the deep dissatisfaction the writer felt toward his social class, and even more toward himself. Bondarev's ideas were a source of enrichment to Tolstoy's own views on life and gave a religious perspective to the whole issue of peasant labour that was a lifetime concern of Tolstoy's.

SECTARIAN FËDOR ZHELTOV AND THE MOLOKANS

In the early 1880s Tolstoy made the acquaintance of a Molokan named Fëdor Alekseevich Zheltov,[22] from the village of Bogorodskoe (near Nizhnij Novgorod).[23]

The Molokans, who called themselves 'Spiritual Christians,' were a group of Russian peasants who (like most other sects) had broken with the official Russian church, in their case more than three hundred years ago. They were subjected to cruel persecutions and were sent en masse to Transcaucasia, where they managed to live out several generations in relative security. The persecutions resumed, however, with the outbreak of the Russo-Japanese War. As committed pacifists, they refused to bear arms or even to perform non-combatant army service. In anticipation of further persecutions, about 5,000 Molokans emigrated to America in 1905–1907, seeking freedom of conscience.

In contrast to the Doukhobors, from whom they separated approximately at the end of the eighteenth century, the Molokans acknowledge the Scriptures as a source of knowledge of the truth, although they interpret them rather freely.[24] They reject the doctrine of the Trinity and the saints; their concept

21 Donskov 1996b: 33–34. Tolstoy concluded the letter by reaffirming the importance of physical labour: "I shall soon be 60 years old and have had millions of torments, but over the past few years I have been both reaping and ploughing, and hope to do so again this year. And joy and health and inner peace I find most of all in this work."

22 The following discussion on Zheltov is drawn in part from my introduction to the English translation of the Tolstoy–Zheltov correspondence (Donskov 2001: 1–22), edited by Ethel Dunn.

23 Tolstoy had actually made his first contact with Molokans back in 1871, in Samara, where his family owned an estate. He often met with representatives of the local population, for whom he had great respect. Dunn (1995: 166) presents a table compiled by I. Morozov for 1925, which shows that Molokans were to be found in every region of the then Soviet Union.

24 The relations between the Molokans and the Doukhobors today are positive. The majority of Molokans emigrated to America (principally California) rather than Canada, although this has not prevented the two groups from celebrating common holidays together and maintaining a

of church amounts to accepting a society of believers in which all are equal; they reject an ordained, paid clergy, along with icons and the sacraments; and, according to the Ten Commandments, refuse to swear oaths of allegiance or to bear arms (their mystic and ascetic tendencies are evident in their belief that the Holy Spirit descends upon them and reveals the Lord's power to them).

With a few exceptions, their ideas correspond to the tenets Tolstoy postulated, following his so-called religious conversion, as the most significant. While the topic 'Tolstoy and the Molokans' is naturally not as extensive as 'Tolstoy and the Doukhobors,' its importance derives from both his active involvement in the Molokans' destiny and their considerable usefulness to him in working out his personal philosophy in the 1880s and especially in the 1890s.

Various questions relating to aspects of the Molokans' life, character, and beliefs are noticeably reflected in Tolstoy's letters, diaries, articles, and involvement in civic affairs, as well as (to a lesser extent) in his literary works — notably his novel *Resurrection* and his writings in the memoir genre.

Let us briefly examine a number of documents in which Tolstoy's overall favourable attitude toward the Molokans is clear. Tolstoy respected them (as he did sectarians in general) for their freedom of thought, their disagreement with the official church, their boldness in confronting the authorities, and for their inner purity and simplicity. In a letter to his wife, Sofia Andreevna, written 19 July 1881 from Patrovka (Samara Gubernia), where he was undergoing a program of *kumys* [fermented mare's milk] treatments, Tolstoy wrote: "I have just...spent a whole day in Patrovka, attending a Molokan meeting and dinner, as well as a district court session where an innocent Molokan was on trial, and later at another Molokan meeting.... The meeting included a discussion of the Gospels. They are clever people and remarkably bold" (*PSS* 83:293–94).

He continues the description of these people a few days later, in a letter to his wife of 22–23 July (*PSS* 83:296):

> They are shy about their poverty, being scarcely aware of it. The Molokans are extremely interesting people. I attended their prayer service, observed their interpretation of the Gospels, and participated, and then they came to me and asked me to interpret them from my own understanding; and I read to them excerpts from my outline [of the Gospels]. The seriousness, interest and clear common sense of these semi-literate people is astonishing.

In a letter to P. V. Velikanov (17 December 1896), Tolstoy emphasizes the intensity of their faith (*PSS* 69:222):

good working relationship. Friendly relations between the two groups were prevalent even back in the Caucasus. For an example of how the Molokans helped the Doukhobors in an extremely difficult situation, see the Slavjanka Doukhobors' letter to Tregubov, Document #1896-02-27c, in Woodsworth 1999a: 76–77.

> The impression you received from the Siberian Molokans is the same one I remember receiving from the Samara Molokans upon my first acquaintance with them. I was expecting too much of them, and I gather you did too. But upon becoming more closely acquainted with them, I discovered among these protesters, both young and old, an active movement and a growing religious feeling.

After being informed that certain Molokan children had been taken away from their parents and sent to various monasteries and nunneries with the aim of breaking the Molokans' will and to punish them for confessing their own faith, Tolstoy wrote two letters of concern to Tsar Nicholas II, condemning such actions. At the same time these letters served as a passionate call for freedom of religion; the first was dated 10 May 1897 (*PSS* 70:74), the second 19 September 1897 (*PSS* 70:140–41):[25]

> You have only to send an impartial, righteous person to the places where those persecuted for their faith have been exiled to Siberia, or the Caucasus, or the Olonets region, and to the places where they have been imprisoned, and you would see from this person's report the frightful deeds that are being committed in your name.

On 18 September 1897, an announcement sent "to the English papers" informed readers of the violence being committed against the Molokans in Russia, with special emphasis on the fact that the Molokan children abducted from their parents had been languishing in monasteries and nunneries for four months already (see *PSS* 70:138). It is known that Tolstoy frequently helped famine victims in poor harvest years. His letter "To the Editor of *Russkie vedomosti*" testifies to his ongoing interest in and assistance to the Molokans (see his letter of 28 February 1898 in *PSS* 72:79–80).

After learning that those Molokans who wanted to leave Russia and join the Doukhobors in Canada would not take his advice and stay in Russia, and

25 In 1897 there was a report circulating through the Nikolaev and Buzuluk Uezds that local police superintendents and officers were abducting children from their parents' homes at night. It turned out that these children were being sent to various monasteries and nunneries throughout Samara Gubernia. Such ill-conceived actions on the part of the authorities were to some degree facilitated by the proposals adopted at the Kazan' missionary conference that took place in August 1897, where, along with other measures to counteract dissident sects, it had been decided to petition for the adoption of a law allowing children to be removed from parents and sent to diocesan shelters. It was not long before this measure was applied to Molokan children. After reading an account of the conference in the newspaper *Russkie vedomosti*, Tolstoy noted in his diary: "A disturbing account of the missionary conference in Kazan'" (*PSS* 53:150). In spite of both verbal and written protests by lawyers and other well-wishers, the authorities relented only when Tolstoy, with his characteristic resourcefulness and power of persuasion, succeeded in attracting the attention of both the Russian and foreign press, which condemned such actions. Tolstoy's daughter Tat'jana L'vovna also petitioned on their behalf before the procurator of the Holy Synod, Konstantin Petrovich Pobedonostsev. The children were returned to their parents only in February 1898. See Chertkov 1918: 20–24.

being persuaded that they would not go back on their decision to flee persecution, Tolstoy offered them moral and financial help — see his letter to Aleksandr Nikiforovich Dunaev of 9–11 September 1900 (*PSS* 72:450), as well his reply to Aleksandr Bodjanskij of 2 October 1900 (*PSS* 72:465–66), who had written from Canada on 21 August 1900 describing the arrival of three Molokans who had come to enquire into the possibility of resettling their brethren there.

A. S. Prugavin's account, "Lev Tolstoy and the Samara Molokans," gives an impression of the warm human relations between Tolstoy and the Molokans, without any hint of criticism. Prugavin met with Tolstoy in the summer of 1881 "in the wilds of the Samara steppes" (as he put it), in the village of Patrovka, Buzuluk Uezd, at a Molokan meeting. Prugavin emphasizes that, following the Samara famine of 1873–74, when Tolstoy did so much for the Samara peasantry, he began to enjoy an exceptional popularity and trust, not only among the population of Patrovka but also in the neighbouring regions. Even if the Molokans were not followers of his teachings, they considered him a kindred spirit, a true friend, and patron (see Prugavin 1911a).

Indeed, Tolstoy maintained contact with the Molokans, Doukhobors, and other sectarians to the end of his life. He was sympathetic to their plight, shared their dismay at the authorities' cruel treatment of nonconformists, but still insisted that these persecutions would have a positive outcome.[26]

Highly significant in this respect is the correspondence between Zheltov and Tolstoy,[27] which, lasting from 1887 until 1909, is permeated with a feeling of mutual respect on the part of these two remarkable people. The closing expressions speak for themselves: "With brotherly love," "Your loyal brother," "With sincere love and faithfulness with all my heart."[28] And in his diary of 14 February 1890, Tolstoy noted (*PSS* 51:18):

> Zheltov and his wife, sister and brother-in-law were here today. Most original people. He is very bright and free-spirited. He will have a great influence.

26 However, when certain sectarian rituals contradicted the laws of nature (or, frequently, his own concepts), Tolstoy was by no means a model of patience. For example, the Skoptsy (lit., 'castrates') were a sect that practised asceticism, including castration of both men and women. In a letter to one of their members, G. P. Men'shin, of 31 December 1897 (*PSS* 70:225), offering his opinion on the sect and the foundations of their teachings, he wrote: "Forcible or even *voluntary* castration is counter to the whole spirit of Christian teachings." He further reminded him of the delicacy needed in interpreting Jesus' words regarding castration (Matt. 19:12) with the following admonition, "even if the interpretation of the letter should seem unconvincing to you, one must remember that it is the spirit alone that quickeneth."

27 A total of fifty-one extant letters, published for the first time in English translation in Donskov 2001.

28 In spite of this closeness and close spiritual kinship between two (one may say) preachers, since their written dialogue was one *among equals*, there are a few letters where notes of disagreement may be heard, where the authors stand by their own views.

A week later he wrote to Dmitrij Khilkov[29] (*PSS* 65:29):

> Among the many people I have come across, I am especially delighted by the Molokans of the Nizhegorod village of Bogorodskoe. They have a 30-year-old leader named Zheltov. He visited us the other day (though I have known him for some time). He is one of the Molokans who is completely free from dogmatism and superficiality; he is most sincere and genuine, bright and talented.

The fundamental content of their letters is the discussion of religious questions, along with a wide array of burning social problems. Zheltov's religious beliefs, which in many respects coincided with the views of Tolstoy, are discussed in some detail in a letter dated 15 October 1889, along with the tenets of the Molokan faith. The content of this letter, as well as of several other of Zheltov's letters which are so extensive as to approximate detailed critical articles or treatises, gives a picture of their author as an extremely intelligent person and a personable figure. On the one hand, this Russian peasant sectarian remains unshaken in his convictions as a thinker, while on the other he stands out, like Bondarev and Novikov, as a stranger to his own milieu by virtue of his sharply penetrating analytical mind, the breadth of his reading, and the logic of his arguments.

Zheltov's letters to Tolstoy are fraught with a multitude of interwoven themes. These include educational issues (especially relating to child raising), the true meaning of literature, marriage, prayer (should it be in a group or in solitude? "Only in solitude," replies Tolstoy), the person of Jesus Christ, famine, drunkenness, and useful books for the people to read.

In most cases Tolstoy agrees with Zheltov's point of view. In a number of his letters he offers advice, as a veteran to a novice; in some he gently criticizes the inflexibility common to the majority of sectarians. Both correspondents decry the corruption of government agencies, both are critical of the upper classes and the limited and intolerant attitudes of the ecclesiastical authorities, and take a strong stand against militarism.

29 *Prince Dmitrij Aleksandrovich Khilkov* (1858–1914) — a graduate of the Page Corps (an elite military academy for the aristocracy in pre-Revolutionary St. Petersburg) and a veteran of the Russo-Turkish war (1877–1878). Upon retiring from the service he took up residence on a farmstead he owned near the village of Pavlovka in the Sumy district of Khar'kov Gubernia, where he worked together with the peasants. Influenced by Lev Tolstoy's ideas, Khilkov sold all his land to the peasants for the price of their annual rent (i.e., for next to nothing) and farmed seven *desjatina* (just over seven ha.) allotted to him by the peasants. In 1890, Khilkov was accused of promoting sectarianism among the peasants and was exiled for five years to Transcaucasia, where he became closely acquainted with the Doukhobors. Khilkov was allowed to go abroad in 1898, and he went with the first group of Doukhobors to Canada, where he stayed until the summer of 1899. Later he changed his views and went back to Russian Orthodoxy. At the very beginning of the First World War, Khilkov enlisted as a volunteer on active duty and perished in battle in Galicia in 1914.

Tolstoy and Zheltov are also linked by their common concern about the problems of the landless peasants.[30] The letters frequently mention the need for physical labour on the land as one of the conditions for a moral, happy, and joyous life on earth.

SECTARIAN MIKHAIL NOVIKOV

Another prominent sectarian with whom Tolstoy was in frequent correspondence was the radical dissident Mikhail Novikov (1871–1939),[31] who ruthlessly condemned Russian Orthodox sacraments and rituals, maintaining what he professed to be true religion (as set forth in his treatises *Staraja vera* [1908; The old faith] and *Novaja vera* [1909; The new faith). Even earlier, in 1906, while aware of Novikov's tenuous status as an educated man in a largely peasant community, Tolstoy had expressed disagreement with his requests to the local bishop (Donskov 2004: 59):

1) that the church, as represented by the priests, leave my life and that of my family alone;
2) that the children born to me be registered without any prayers or rituals, and only on the basis of my declaration;
3) that any marriages my children may enter into be registered without wedding ceremonies and recognized in the legal sense on an equal basis with others;
4) that the land allotted to me and my family not be subject to any taxes by the church.

To Tolstoy, this kind of reasoning represented nothing more than a distraction from more important spiritual concerns. In a letter dated 4 September 1907 he responded to Novikov as follows (Donskov 1996a: 99):

> To bury your children without the services of the clergy, not to fast and not to go to church — that is not faith: you have rejected the superstitions of the old faith, but you have no faith yourself. It is in this, in the fact that you do not believe in a spiritual principle of life and its requirements, that your

30 For example, in a letter dated 27 December 1900 (Donskov 2001: 140), Zheltov conveys the thanks of a landless peasant, named A. A. Antipin, for Tolstoy's "compassion in his endeavour to bring his complaint to court" along with his own "deep, heartfelt gratitude...as I had hoped that you would set this fellow on the right path and afford him whatever help he needed." Antipin was an Old Believer, from the village of Vorsma, sentenced to exile in Transcaucasia for his outspoken remarks on the Eucharist. Tolstoy appealed to the jurist Anatolij Fëdorovich Koni for help, and the Moscow district court commuted his exile to a three-month prison term. In September 1918, however, Antipin was executed by the Bolsheviks after being accused of counter-revolutionary activity. On the proselytizing of Molokan beliefs by brothers Ivan and Aleksandr Prokhanov, and their peculiar interpretation of the gospels, see Shcherbakova 2000b.

31 The thirty-two extant letters between Tolstoy and Novikov were published for the first time in Donskov 1996a.

> misfortune lies, and not at all in the lack of land and the unfairness of the economic structure.

Tolstoy was firmly opposed to citing external influence on one's inner soul as an excuse for one's own inaction. He frequently reminded his correspondents of Sjutaev's dictum: "It's all in you, it's all in you."

Yet Tolstoy evidently felt a strong attraction to Novikov on the personal and intellectual level; witness Tolstoy's repeated attempts to secure the publication of Novikov's manuscripts in a number of journals. Most significant of all is Tolstoy's expressed desire to take refuge with Novikov and his family upon fleeing Yasnaya Polyana in the autumn of 1910, shortly before his death. On 20 October 1910 Novikov came to see Tolstoy at Yasnaya and had a long and serious conversation with him.[32] Four days later, on 24 October, he wrote Novikov as follows (Donskov 1996a: 116):

> In connection with our conversation just before you left, I am turning to you with the following request: if it should turn out that I actually come to your place, perhaps you could find for me some small, warm cabin, all by itself, so as not to impose upon you and your family for any length of time.

Perhaps it is only natural that in his time of greatest need Tolstoy sought refuge not with a member of his family, or even one of his many avowed followers, but with someone from the Russian peasant class — a dissident at that — with whom he had had more than his share of disagreements on principles of faith, and yet to whom he evidently felt closer in spirit than to anyone else at that point. Novikov replied to Tolstoy a few days later, offering to put a room in his own home at the writer's disposal for as long as desired, yet at the same time expressing his concern that abandoning his customary surroundings at Yasnaya might not only be bad for Tolstoy's health but would run counter to his avowed moral precepts. The following extract from his reply is significant (Donskov 1996a: 117):

> The time for you to change the outward conditions of your life for the good of the cause and by virtue of the awakening consciousness within you has passed, and there is no longer any point in changing them for good. Your life is drawing to its close (in the temporal sense), but it is still dear both to me and all who are near to you in spirit, and we all desire only one thing — that it last as long as possible, and that is feasible only in the conditions to which you have been accustomed, in which you have been living all your eighty-three [*sic*] years. As much as I would like to see you set free among all the simple folk, for the sake of preserving your life in such an ageing body [and] maintaining the opportunity for communication with you which everyone cherishes — I cannot seriously hope for this. My only hope is that the remains of your earthly days are not

32 According to Tolstoy's diary entry for that date (*PSS* 50:121).

> imposed upon by arrangements for communication with those who love you. On the other hand, if you would like a temporary visit with your friends for a day, a week or so, or a month, my cabin is very convenient.... That is how I feel, but if you feel otherwise, it shall be according to your wishes, and not mine, and if so, my room will be available to you for as long as you want.

It may indeed be seen as a cruel 'irony of fate' that Tolstoy's intended final sojourn with his friend Novikov never came to pass, and that he was obliged to spend his final hours at the isolated Astapovo railway station rather than in the company of those closest to him in spirit. It was one more bitter confirmation of a truth that had haunted Tolstoy over many years — the ideal which was so clear to him in thought yet difficult, if not impossible, to reach. In this case the difficulty, at least, in 'simplifying himself' [*oprostit'sja*], in becoming closer to Tolstoy the peasant rather than Tolstoy the nobleman, had been recognized by Novikov.

It was a difficulty that was constantly faced both by Tolstoy himself and the characters of station that populated his novels.

OTHER SECTARIANS

It will be noted that the beliefs underlying Novikov's requests to the bishop bear evident similarities to the Doukhobors' desire to live their lives free from bureaucratic interference. That Tolstoy did not dismiss their beliefs and practices as readily as in the case of Novikov suggests that he found in the Doukhobors a sounder spiritual basis underlying these beliefs and practices — a greater manifestation of the divine spark, which attracted him to their cause. This is all the more significant in view of his well-known preference for coming to the aid of individual sectarians rather than sectarian movements en masse.

Various Russian sects figure prominently not only in Tolstoy's publicistic writings but also in his fiction works and correspondence. In *Resurrection*, as previously noted, it is sectarians who are assigned to 'clarify' Nekhljudov's (and, by implication, Tolstoy's own) thoughts and concepts in his search for moral rebirth; scenes depicting the repression and punishment of the sectarians were introduced into the novel (then in its sixth revision) in 1895, following their burning of arms. Although, as mentioned, Tolstoy described his sectarians as Molokans rather than Doukhobors.

It is noteworthy that Tolstoy's sectarians were Russian,[33] in contrast to many of his contemporaries, who were more attracted to the depiction of foreign evangelists (e.g., Lord Radstock in England or his Russian disciples, such as Vasilij Aleksandrovich Pashkov).[34] He was attracted, however, by certain ideals of non-Russian sects — for example, the innovatory nature of the

33 On Tolstoy's interest in the Pavlovtsy (lit. 'Paulites'), e.g., see Camfield 1990.

34 On Tolstoy's negative opinion of foreign evangelists proselytizing in Russia, see Heier 1970, especially Chap. 3 (82–102); also Heier 1962.

Shakers, their communal farms, their strong adherence to the doctrine of chastity, their rejection of church authority, their belief in the moral benefit of physical labour.[35]

Russian sects provided a formal expression for social protest in the context of historical circumstances. While some sects dated from the time of the schism in the 1650s, many saw the peak of their activity during the late nineteenth century, following the emancipation of serfs in 1861. Progressive elements in Russian society were unable to find any spiritual connection with the people as a whole — witness the failure of the 1870s 'going to the people' [*khozhdenie v narod*] movement, which attempted to enlighten the peasantry through various educational projects. But such projects only resulted in increasing the gap between the educated classes and the peasants and caused a feeling of devastation among the latter — as seen in a number of literary works of the period, such as Gleb Uspenskij's novel *Vlast' zemli* [1882; *The Power of Land*].

CHILDREN AND ART

The assassination of Alexander II in 1881 by young radicals marked a hardening of government attitudes toward any kind of protest. Similar repressive measures were taken against the many (from both higher and lower classes) who dared voice their disenchantment with the Russian Orthodox Church and affiliate themselves with one of the foreign Christian preachers recently arrived in Russia in search of new converts. It was against this political and social background that Tolstoy, after completing *Anna Karenina*, took his search for meaning in life into new directions. A period of spiritual crisis led to the embracing of a 'new-found' faith-philosophy, based on a harmonization of his own views with the simple approach to life he observed among those who tilled the land. He pleaded with the peasants to persevere in the face of persecution by church and state authorities — witness his advice to Prince Dmitrij Khilkov,[36] in the summer of 1896 (*PSS* 69:140–41):

> persecution is not only an inescapable condition of establishing truth, but it is a compulsory condition thereof. Don't be concerned about the friction — if there is no friction, I can tell you right from the start that there will be no progress.

His affinity for and financial assistance to the sectarians[37] notwithstanding, Tolstoy persistently rejected one of their principal tenets — namely, the

35 On other points he disagreed with the Shakers (e.g., the claim that one of their number, Ann Lee, was the incarnation of Christ in female form). It might be noted that some of the early Doukhobor leaders considered themselves to be an embodiment of Christ (see, e.g., Document #1895-11-01c in Woodsworth 1999a: 22–23). For more on Tolstoy and the Shakers, see Haugh 1978 and Fersen 1970. On Tolstoy and the English Quakers, see Greenwood 1975.

36 For a police profile of Khilkov, see Document #1900-3KH-b in Woodsworth 1999a: 199–201.

37 It should be noted that the term *sectarian* was frequently used by Tolstoy with a negative connotation. In his letter to Pëtr V. Verigin of 14 October 1896, e.g., Tolstoy criticizes Verigin's

importance of group identity (i.e., the sense of belonging *to their own faith*), which inherently signified disunity and separation from those of other faiths. On the contrary, in both his correspondence and his works he insisted on subjugating such identity to the overarching concept of the *unity of people*, which alone could provide a true motive power for the moral and spiritual uplifting of mankind.

Finally (in chronological terms), Tolstoy's struggle for unity of people is distinctly evident in a set of dialogues on various subjects, written shortly before his death under the overall title *Detskaja mudrost'* [1909–1910; *Wisdom of Children*]. Specific topics included religion, war, the fatherland, the empire, taxes, harsh judgements, kindness, remuneration of labour, drunkenness, capital punishment, prisons, wealth, loving those who insult you, printing, remorse, art, science, civil-law courts, criminal law, property, children, and education.[38]

In these one- and two-page dialogues, Tolstoy dealt with subjects that had acquired for him a particular significance, especially after *Anna Karenina*. They all have a moral purport and unmistakably reflect Tolstoy's world view. They provide a thematic summary of Tolstoy's five moral imperatives, their corollaries and effects (drawn, as noted, from the Sermon on the Mount), but the form in which the material unfolds is fresh. Important issues, broader problems, the so-called cursed questions that plagued Tolstoy all his life, and which turned most of his major protagonists into seekers after truth, are now discussed in dialogue form between adults and children, or between older and younger children. The "wisdom of children," as revealed from the dialogues, confirms the truth of the Psalm (8:2): "Out of the mouth of babes and sucklings hast thou ordained strength." The children (largely from the peasantry) taking part in these exchanges call into question accepted notions, only to be met by answers which may seem nonsensical, perverse, criminal, or inhuman.

Childhood and childlikeness had a special meaning for Tolstoy, and he often chose children as active participants in raising important questions or supplying answers to the gnawing problems plaguing his major characters (who are, as a rule, unable to fully resolve them). This may best be explained through his elaboration of Jesus' dictum on children (Matt. 19:13–14): "Then were there brought unto him little children, that he should put his hands on them, and pray: and the disciples rebuked them. But Jesus said, Suffer little children, and forbid them not, to come unto me: for of such is the kingdom of heaven." In his *Uchenie Khrista, izlozhennoe dlja detej* [1908; *Christ's Teachings Explained for Children*], he rendered this passage in his own words, listing

condemnation of books as follows: "To tell you the truth, your stubborn resistance to books seemed merely a sectarian habit of defending a position once it has been adopted and declared" (Donskov 1995a: 22).

38 For a discussion of the theme of *unity* and the stylistic nature of these dialogues, see Donskov 1989.

the qualities of children as he thought Christ must have seen them and as he himself saw them (*PSS* 57:115):

> Once some children were brought to Jesus. The disciples started to chase the children away. Jesus saw it and said:
>
> "It isn't right to chase the children away. Children should not be chased away, but rather learnt from, because they are closer than adults are to God's kingdom. Children do not curse, do not bear malice, do not fornicate, do not swear, do not take anyone to court, do not know any difference between their own people and others. Children are closer than adults to the Kingdom of Heaven. Children should not be chased away, but looked after so that they are not led into temptation."

One must keep in mind that Tolstoy waged even his severest criticism against the establishment *for a good purpose.* He might have been mistaken in the means by which the good purpose could be achieved, but he was always striving for one thing — justice and the unity of people. History does not always listen to wise men, though there are exceptions (such as Mahatma Gandhi). But the further one reads, the clearer it becomes that violence as a principle of life must be overcome by people's rational efforts, as supported by Tolstoy's works.

During the final years of his career Tolstoy wrote a great deal about art — his forewords to the translated writings of Guy de Maupassant and to Sergej Semenov's *Krest'janskie* rasskazy [1894; Peasant Stories], his article "On Shakespeare and Drama" ["*O Shekspire i o drame*"; 1904–1906], his afterword (in 1905) to Anton Chekhov's story "Darling" ["Dushechka"], among others. All this is well known. Less known is his remarkable article that accompanied the publication in Russia of the *Journal intime* of the Swiss Henri-Frédérique Amiel.[39] Far beyond all the other writings of this poet, æsthetic, and philosopher, Tolstoy was enamoured with his strikingly sincere journal, not intended for publication, which embodied the doubts, hesitations, and *seekings* for truth inherent in every thinking individual.

Tolstoy's own principal theoretical composition was his treatise *What is Art?* (1897–1898). Possibly his words from the article on Amiel also apply here, at least in part. Granted, there are livelier, dearer pronouncements on art to be found in Tolstoy's short articles, diaries, letters, and oral utterances as recorded by contemporaries. But the main idea of the treatise will remain forever paramount: here, as nowhere else, Tolstoy explicitly states his concept that art must be based on an ethical system, the highest aim of which is the unity of people in a worldwide brotherhood. Art must be not only accessible,

39 The two-volume *Fragments d'un journal intime* appeared in print in 1883–1884. Selected excerpts were translated from French into Russian some ten years later by Tolstoy's daughter Marija L'vovna, and Tolstoy wrote in his foreword thereto: "While it is possible to find more graceful and eloquent expressions of religious feeling than those of Amiel, it is difficult to find any more sincere and heart-wrenching" (*PSS* 29:211).

but also 'infectious,' in order to exert a salutary influence on the majority of people and draw them together instead of dividing them. The treatise points to *religious art* as the highest expression of art itself.[40]

Tolstoy's outwardly restricting views on art initially caused a great deal of soul-searching for one young Canadian Doukhobor artist in particular, until she, not unlike the early Doukhobors' reaction to being characterized as 'spirit-wrestlers,' turned an apparent negative label into a positive opportunity by exploring what she discovered as the manifestations of art — not in what Tolstoy *said* about art but in his whole career as a writer and religious philosopher. In her guest essay in this volume, Jan Kabatoff draws the inference that it was the Doukhobors' very "appeal for humanitarian assistance" that "resurrected the creative 'urge' in him," spurring him on to complete his third major novel, *Resurrection,* which she sees as most fully embodying his threefold nature as artist, philosopher, and humanitarian.

More than anyone else, perhaps, it was the Doukhobors who reawakened in Tolstoy his humanitarian concerns — the great desire to see his philosophy, hitherto expressed primarily in his literary art, embodied in people's everyday lives. This is acutely evident in his letter to the Doukhbors in the Caucasus, dated 20–21 August 1897. Promising financial help, he asked in return for their continuing "spiritual help," explaining (*PSS* 70:126–27),

> this help lies in your taking the lead in following Christ's path; it is easier to walk behind than out in front. You are taking the lead, and many are grateful to you for that.... There is so much I would like to tell you and so much to learn from you.

This particular letter points out a genuine symbiotic relationship between Tolstoy and the Doukhobors: their example satisfied his need to prove the practicability of his philosophy, and, in return, he was able to satisfy their need for a strong public advocate, as well as for financial assistance. They presented one possible answer to the vital questions obsessing him during this period: How was mankind to overcome its disunity, the violence and bloodshed leading it down the path of doom? Where could one find the life-creating principles capable of transforming the world's moral state? The Doukhobors, he concluded, were heading in the right direction through their faith in a God of Love, thereby excluding any kind of coercion or violence, and upholding universal brotherhood as a fundamental law for mankind. The love for God

40 For a detailed study on this subject, see Heier 1979: 324–36. Gustafson's (1986) study also sees art as serving a religious function, pointing to Tolstoy's view of the æsthetic experience as a form of religious experience and of the concomitant realization that we belong to each other right here, right now. Amy Mandelker (1996) defines one aspect of Tolstoy's æsthetics as *eucharistic* — i.e., relating to the experience of communion or brotherhood resulting from exposure to Christian art. Caryl Emerson's (1996) essay "What is infection and what is expression in *What is Art?*" argues in defence of Tolstoy's position on these two major aspects of his theory of art.

which they cherished within themselves, their honest toil on the land, their communal sharing, their absolute rejection of war, killing, and violence — all this was something Tolstoy insisted was worth preserving and supporting in whatever way he could.

The stand against militarism which Tolstoy shared with the Doukhobors is particularly evident in his 1898 article *Dve vojny* [*Two Wars*], devoted to the Spanish-American wars for Cuba and the Philippines, as will be seen in Chapter 5. Tolstoy contrasted this cruel unjust war with the ongoing 'war' of the Doukhobors against all wars, their refusal to carry out military service, to kill, or to prepare for killing (which soon led to the resettlement of large numbers of Russian and Ukrainian peasants to Canada).

More pacifist now than ever before — mainly, perhaps, through his association with the Doukhobors — Tolstoy actively and unreservedly began to propagate their common views, with the unstinting support of his followers. This joint campaign was met with extreme countermeasures on the part of the government and its close ally, the Russian Orthodox Church, expressed in both widespread censorship and strictures in church-sponsored publications — including *Missionerskoe obozrenie* — which form the basis of discussion in the next chapter.

CHAPTER 3

Tolstoy and the Tolstoyans: State and Church Opposition

DURING THE 1880S AND 1890S Tolstoy wrote a number of works which reveal his religious, socio-political, agrarian, and artistic ideas that comprise what can be called *Tolstoyism.* These ideas, broad as they were and simple as they seemed, included a strong belief in God (minus an ecclesiastical hierarchy), Jesus Christ as the greatest human teacher,[1] and the Sermon on the Mount as the greatest source of inspiration and influence on him. Equally important was his strong conviction in the power of love, in a simple life and the unity of people (regardless of their religious and social distinctions), and, as the central core of his teaching, non-violent resistance to evil. As Haugh (1978: 232) notes:

> Tolstoy was profoundly impressed by Edward Bellamy's *Looking Backwards* (1888), a novel which takes place in Boston in 2000 when the U.S. is under socialism. According to Bellamy's novel, one works only until age 45, there is no poverty, and everyone is motivated by honor. Tolstoy was also deeply impressed by Adin Ballou's *Christian Non-Resistance Catechism.* His letter of June 30, 1890 to Ballou reads in part: "The non-resistant catechism I have translated and will circulate it among our friends... I quite agree with you that Christianity will never enter its promised land till the divine truth on the non-resistance principle shall be recognized, but not the nominal church will recognize it. I am fully convinced that the churches are and have always been the worst enemies

1 But not Jesus Christ as 'God in the flesh.'

> of Christ's work. They have always led humanity not in the way of Christ, but out of it ..." [2]

Peter Brock devoted a chapter of his 1972 monograph on European pacifism to Tolstoy's followers, known, as mentioned, as Tolstoyans. He traces the birth of Tolstoyism to the Russian intelligentsia of the late 1870s (1972: 454, 465), describing as its principal tenet the rejection of violent resistance to evil. A few years earlier, William Edgerton (1968: 66–67) had noted that "Tolstoy himself considered the heart of Tolstoyism to be the doctrine of non-resistance to evil through violence," stemming from his renewed faith in basic Christian teachings (69–70). In his recent dissertation on Tolstoyan ethics, Aleksandr Kashirin (2002: 8) took note of Tolstoyism's "ideological striving for the ideal of integrity" as "one of the traditions of Russian religious culture."

Tolstoy forthrightly claimed that when Jesus told his followers "resist not evil" (Matt. 5:39)[3] he meant it literally. With the publication of his *Confession* in 1879, signalling his break with the Russian Orthodox Church, along with treatises outlining his ideas on religion, especially *An Examination of Dogmatic Theology* (1880) and *What I Believe* (1884), Tolstoy and his followers (whose numbers were steadily increasing) initiated a powerful movement against both secular and religious authorities.

According to Ivan Avakumovic (1978: 2), the movement amounted to something resembling a 'Tolstoy International.'

The Tolstoyans who were either sent or went of their own accord to live among the Doukhobors in the Caucasus and write about their situation were by no means a homogeneous lot. Some, such as Vladimir Chertkov, Prince Dmitrij Khilkov, and Aleksandr Bodjanskij, belonged to the nobility, while others were of more humble extraction. Tolstoy's followers also included a number of foreigners then resident in Russia — e.g., the Russophile Paul Boulanger from France, or Tolstoy's friend and valued English translator, Aylmer Maude. It should be noted that the Tolstoyans tended to regard the Doukhobors as the virtually perfect embodiment of the Christian ideal — the living realization of what they themselves had only verbally professed. Like the *narodniki* [populists] before them, who venerated and idealized the simple Russian peasant, the Tolstoyans felt obliged to offer sympathy and help to the unjustly persecuted Doukhobors, even to the point of changing their own lifestyles and customs to resemble those of the sect (insofar as this was possible in the light of their class and educational background).

The Tolstoyans considered their primary goals to be (a) the dissemination of their revered teacher's ideas and (b) the encouragement of others to

2 The Tolstoy quotation here is taken from *PSS* 65:113; see also 65:34–36. See also Hugh McLean's (1994) illuminating paper "Tolstoy and Jesus," and Pål Kolstø's (1991) "Leo Tolstoy, a church critic influenced by Orthodox thought."

3 The Russian New Testament reads "*ne protiv'sja zlomu*" [resist not the evil one].

lead the kind of life advocated in his post-conversion writings. These writings, permeated as they were with Tolstoy's doctrine of non-violent resistance to evil, as well as his condemnation of officialdom (i.e., government, church, and legal hierarchies — especially the prevailing laws on private property), naturally aroused the suspicion and wrath of authorities not particularly known for their tolerance of contrary views. But the Tolstoyans' efforts succeeded in increasing the writer's popularity among the populace at large.[4] One Tolstoyan, A. S. Suvorin, went so far as to say, "We have two tsars — Nicholas II and Lev Tolstoy."

Even though the Christian doctrine of non-violence lay at the centre of Tolstoyism, the movement encompassed a broad range of related secular interests — ideological, social, and political.[5] And while acknowledging its religious roots, Kashirin (2002: 1) calls Tolstoyism "a phenomenon of Russian culture," and further defines it as "not just an *experiment* but also a *type of world-view*." Edgerton (1968: 85) pinpoints some of Tolstoy's specific secular ideas embraced by Tolstoyans as follows:

> [W]holesale rejection of the state and all its institutions, his vegetarianism, his passionate advocacy of [radical American economist] Henry George's single-tax system as the basis of all economics, his wrong-headed rejection of most of the Western world's greatest art on the grounds of narrow utilitarianism, his dogmatic opposition to birth control and wet-nurses, his sternly puritanical attitude toward sex, his abstinence from alcohol and tobacco, his hostility to science and technology, and all the other passionately argued opinions that can be found in his writings.

The Tolstoyans went beyond theoretical discussion and attempted to put what they saw as Tolstoy's ideas into practice in various ways. Many of them were politically active — either as uncompromising pacifists or as non-violent opponents of the existing social, political, and religious order. Like other populists, they recognized the importance of persuading the common Russian people of the need for change. In a recent article on the influence of Tolstoyism on the Caucasus Doukhobors in the 1890s, a leading Russian ethnographer, Svetlana Inikova (2002: 53–54) described the approach of one particular Tolstoyan, Ivan Tregubov, to this question as follows:

> Tregubov considered *tolstovshchina* (a less frequently used term for Tolstoyism) as he himself referred to Tolstoy's teachings, a lever by which one could "turn life around." But in order for Tolstoyism to become this lever, it must be spread among the people: without the people there could be no thought of overturning

4 On the Tolstoyans' influence on the Svobodniki (Sons of Freedom) Doukhobor movement, see Inikova 2002.

5 According to Edgerton (1968: 67), the various reasons for rejection of violence could be "classified in two general categories: religious and secular."

> anything. But the spread of Tolstoy's ideas among the people can only be successfully carried out in rationalistic sects such as the Doukhobors, the Molokans and especially the Stundists.

One of the Tolstoyans' attempts to spread their mentor's ideas among the people involved setting up 'Tolstoyan colonies' along the principles of Tolstoy's teachings. In this the Tolstoyans were strongly influenced by the examples they had seen in already existing peasant sectarian communities such as the Doukhobors. The Tolstoyans, however, tended to romanticize the sectarians they encountered — as Inikova (1999b: 76) put it, "they saw in the Doukhobors only what they wanted to see," and effectively blinded themselves to the reality of the situation.

Tolstoy himself was more insightful than his followers on this point. Indeed, he took pains to distinguish himself from them; witness his famous saying: "*Ja Tolstoj, no ja ne tolstovets*" [I am Tolstoy, but I am not a Tolstoyan]. Ever the realist,[6] he recognized that his own teachings could well set a standard that was too difficult for the vast majority of mankind to attain (see Edgerton 1968: 70). His own tempered realism tended to be conveniently "overlooked or ignored," as Edgerton points out, "both by Tolstoj's [*sic*] critics and opponents and by his followers" (71).

REACTION ON THE PART OF GOVERNMENT AUTHORITIES

Government authorities, especially, considered Tolstoy's teaching extremely anarchical and employed various means of combatting what they perceived as Tolstoy's undermining of the very foundation of the tsarist system. Measures included rigorous surveillance of Tolstoy's activities, basically tracking the writer's every move, including his visits to others and others' visits to him; ruthless interventions in the lives of his family and friends; merciless censorship and censure of his work — both his literary and publicistic writings, beginning with the early 1880s.[7] And as much as they were suspicious of Tolstoy, they were even more suspicious of Tolstoyans, who had taken it upon themselves to promote Tolstoy's ideas (sometimes with their own more radical interpretation) among the Russian populace at large — including the Doukhobors and other sects already under surveillance.

The following excerpts from an unpublished government report by V. M. Skvortsov (editor of *Missionerskoe obozrenie* — see below) bear testimony to the extent of official concern:

6 According to Brock (1972: 464), "not all his followers succeeded in matching the tempered realism of their master."

7 See Donskov 1995b. On the basis of police-intercepted correspondence, one government memo, of 21 July 1897, recommended that extreme measures be taken to prevent Tolstoy and members of his family, as well as Boulanger and other Tolstoyans, from meeting with Doukhobor delegations who were to come to Moscow for just such a purpose (Semjakin 1897).

The criminals in this story are [first:] Count Tolstoy, as an anarchist and founder of a heretical sect, whose false teachings, spreading unhindered throughout the intelligentsia and seeping into the populace, portend great troubles in the future; then Prince Khilkov, as the initiator and steward of the criminal false teaching which has been adopted by the [Doukhobor] Fasters.... The third criminal, even more harmful and clever than Khilkov, is [A. M.] Bodjanskij, and after him come a company of Doukhobor agitators: [P. V.] Verigin, [Ivan] Konkin, Verigin's brothers, the Vereshchagins, etc. (Skvortsov 1896: 20–21)

The Kars Doukhobors have most closely assimilated the teachings of anarchy and Tolstoyism and consequently are the most persuaded and stubborn followers of the criminal anarchical fellowship. In each Doukhobor settlement there are several ringleader-spokesmen, sounding forth with brash explanations in justification of the anarchical way of thinking and the criminal behaviour of like-minded persons, sometimes quoting word-for-word the underground writings of Count L. Tolstoy. Everywhere the mood is somehow triumphant, provocative and insolent. (Golitsyn 1897: 547)

It is not a difficult task for the administration to deal with local agitators, i.e., among the Doukhobors themselves, inasmuch as the ringleaders and the most fanatical among them have already been sent out of the region, and therefore presumably rendered incapable of harming their fellow Doukhobors. But it is not as easy a matter to deal with the underground agitation of the Tolstoyans, who to this day will not let the Doukhobors alone with their pernicious influence. (Assistant prosecutor of Elisavetpol' regional court, as quoted in Woodsworth 1999a: 96)

This tense situation in the Doukhobor communities, fed by emigration stirrings among the Doukhobor-Fasters, is undoubtedly attributable to the relentless harmful influence on these sectarians on the part of *Tolstoyan agitators, who were the initiators of the proposal to send the Doukhobors abroad,* as is evident from intercepted sectarian correspondence.... In conjunction with their like-minded counterparts in England (the Quakers) they have proposed resettling the Doukhobors abroad in the English dominions, and without first securing the English government's consent to such resettlement, have persuaded [the Doukhobors] to leave their places of residence — a decision which has led to the financial ruin of many Doukhobors. Such actions by the Tolstoyans, which have paralysed all our Government's efforts to make the Doukhobors they have bewildered listen to reason, are evidently based solely on these agitators' fanatical attempts to make the Doukhobors a prime example of Tolstoy's ideas — to prove, whatever the cost, that their ephemeral sociopolitical utopia can become a reality. (Golitsyn 1898, as translated in Woodsworth 1999a: 100, 102)

The Veriginite Doukhobors, left to their own devices, rancorous to the point of insanity, carried away in a rapturous frenzy, provided extremely fertile soil for all sorts of anti-government propaganda, which has surfaced in the form of the Tolstoyans who were sent to the Caucasus as administrative exiles....

> Tolstoyism has led the majority of the Large Veriginite [P]arty of Doukhobors completely astray and has served as a source for the latest anarchical disruptions. (Skvortsov 1896: 1)

Skvortsov concluded his report with the following recommendations:

> In view of the general facts set forth I would recommend: before anything else, and as quickly as possible:
>
> 1) adopt, as deemed feasible by the government, suppressive measures against Count Tolstoy in relation to his 'troops' who are agitating unhindered, preaching anarchical sectarianism among the Orthodox and sectarian populace;
> 2) send Prince Khilkov and Bodjanskij out of the country;
> 3) imprison Verigin and Konkin; otherwise their association with their Doukhobor followers, who have now managed to get through to him in Siberia, will never cease;
> 4) punish other criminal agitators of anarchical propaganda with administrative exile.

Three years later, after the first two boatloads of Doukhobors had left for Canada, Skvortsov had further recommendations to prevent members of other Doukhobor parties from following them:

> I would venture to say that it is in the government's interest not to allow this new group of four to six thousand Doukhobors to move away from the area. They have, moreover, a flourishing economy and up unto now have behaved themselves lawfully in all respects. To prevent the malicious agitation by local Tolstoyans and the American [*sic*] Doukhobor Fasters from again leading the quiet faction of Doukhobors down the path of anarchy, it would seem wise, at the present time, to take measures to cut off the written provocations through official seizure of correspondence addressed to the Transcaucasian Doukhobor leaders, as well as to refuse categorically Verigin's request to go to America. It would also be very useful to circulate information among the Transcaucasian Veriginite Doukhobors.
>
> On the basis of my personal observations, I would say that if Verigin is allowed to emigrate to America, then all the Doukhobors, with the possible exception of the Goreloe (i.e., the Third) Party will be lost to Russia. (Skvortsov 1899, as translated in Woodsworth 1999a: 113)

Such government actions, however, could almost be considered as 'mild' compared to the condemnation of Tolstoy and Tolstoyans on the part of the official church. After all, Tolstoy had taken it upon himself to deny not only ecclesiastical authority but, even more significantly, what was (in the church's eyes) the underlying metaphysical principles of Christianity — the church's sacraments and dogmas, its hierarchy, biblical miracles, even the divinity of Jesus Christ — and substitute his own moral interpretation of these principles, outlining his views in his religious treatises and other post-conversion writings. In his book *Religija i kul'tura,* originally published in 1899, contemporary critic V. V. Rozanov (1990: 357) described Tolstoy's relationship to the Russian Orthodox Church as follows:

> They did not understand each other, did not even know each other. And they went their separate ways — to condemnation on the one hand (Tolstoy's excommunication from the church) to utter disdain on the other (Tolstoy's attitude to the church).

The act of excommunication followed a long period of personal attacks by church officials on Tolstoy and his teachings. The condemnation was most vociferously expressed in a journal known as *Missionerskoe obozrenie.*

MISSIONERSKOE OBOZRENIE 1896–1901[8]

The Orthodox journal *Missionerskoe obozrenie* [Missionary Review, hereinafter *MR*] was founded in 1896 at least in part for the purpose of counteracting the widespread popularity enjoyed by Tolstoy's teachings, and to deal with questions relating to the church's internal, anti-sectarian mission, its struggle against 'rationalistic' and 'mystic' sects[9] existing among the Orthodox population.

> By the mid-1890s the church had taken upon itself the mission of active opposition to the sectarian movement, which it considered a spurious heresy and "a sad and painful phenomenon in the life of the church and society," one as dangerous to the state as to the church itself.[10]

8 I have selected these first five years of *Missionerskoe* obozrenie (under several headings) as the most representative example of the stand of the Russian Orthodox Church vis-à-vis not only Tolstoy but also his followers, and, indeed, the Doukhobor and other sectarian movements in Russia in the period of their most fervent activity. I should like to thank both Lidija Gromova and Marina Shcherbakova for their assistance in researching *Missionerskoe obozrenie.*

9 These included both old established sects such as the Jews, the Doukhobors, and the Molokans, along with newly formed groups — e.g., the Baptists, and their offshoot, the Stundists (an evangelical movement of German Baptists in Ukraine, named for the *Bibelstunden* [Bible study groups] they organized); the Pashkovites (named after its founder, a retired colonel, Vasilij Pashkov in St. Petersburg, uncle to V. G. Chertkov, who had become enamoured with the ideas of Lord Radstock); and the Tolstoyans. Still other groups — e.g., the Khlysts (a group practising self-flagellation, otherwise known as the Khrists), the Shaloputians (lit. 'ne'er-do-wells'), the Mormons, and the Skoptsy — were classified as 'secret sects.'

10 *MR* January 1896: vi–vii (hereafter all references to *MR* in this chapter will be designated by date and page alone.) Witness the following paragraph from that same, first issue of *MR* (viii): "History and contemporary observations show that forms of religious vacillation and free-thinking conceal and sometimes deliberately serve as a cover for social free-thinking, while religious belief and profession today are so closely connected with political sympathies that there is no way politically one can close one's eyes to the religious sectarianism and ecclesiastical anarchy popular in Society."

As a result of the analysis and classification of the sectarian movement, as approved by the Second [All-Russian] Missionary Conference, held in Moscow in 1891, under the direction of V. K. Sabler, head of the synod's chancellery, the most dangerous sects were determined to be the Doukhobors, Molokans, Stundobaptists, and Pashkovites. "This is also the category where *Tolstoyism* belongs; it was not discussed by the Conference as it was only later that it was determined to be a sect all on its own with clearly expressed anti-ecclesiastical, atheistic and socialistic characteristics" (January 1896: 5).

THE INTELLIGENTSIA

The 1860s and 1870s, in the view of many *MR* writers, saw the culmination of the Russian intelligentsia's estrangement from the Russian people and their turning to the West for inspiration, spurred on by Alexander II's reforms.[11]

Noting that the common people were now more susceptible to influence by 'rationalist' sects than before, Archbishop Ambrosius of Khar'kov denounced what he saw as the "spirit of rejection in respect to Christian doctrines and the practical institutions of the Orthodox Church," which was inevitably fostering a general desire for "independence from all authority, including the Church's." He is particularly concerned about the susceptibility of the young.

The journal expresses a specific concern in regard to the alleged attempt of *educated* sectarians (i.e., members of the intelligentsia) to control sectarianism in the public at large [*narodnoe sektantstvo*] — not just in religious matters but on the political and societal level, under the guise of religion.[12] In this category, the Tolstoyans were frequently the targets of specific condemnation.

> Stundo-Baptist propaganda has been going on among the Molokans for many years now, and in recent times Doukhoborism has been driven crazy by Tolstoyism, which has found in this sect compatible ground and is enjoying considerable success. (January 1896: 73)

The "News and Notes" column in the October 1898 issue of *MR* reported on a Tolstoyan colony in England, reproducing (in Russian translation) a description by Maurice Muret in *Le Journal des débats* of 14 August 1898. Similar

11 See the article by Father I. Fudel', "The basis for the struggle with sectarianism" (January 1896: 18–19): "These [reforms] resulted on the one hand in a great mental turbulence, on the other in a turbulence in the nation's economic well-being, social structure, in its religious and moral attitudes... [the people] had to come face to face with principles practised by the intelligentsia that were contrary to their own world view."

12 For one thing, the church saw as its mission a struggle not just against "popular darkness" [*t'ma narodnaja*] but with "the darkness of the evil spirits of the educated sectarians" [*t'my dukhov zloby intelligentskogo sektantstva*] (January 1897: 49–50).

reports were published on other Tolstoyan colonies, especially those that suffered a demise.[13]

The following May, *MR* featured an opinion piece by K. Popov, a priest of the Penza diocese, entitled "The fruits of Count Tolstoy's teachings" ["Plody uchenija grafa Tolstogo"], in which he describes his encounter with the elderly father of a young Tolstoyan at the gates of the Nikol'skij Monastery in Moscow:

> For a long time I thought about this hapless old fellow, abandoned by his son in old age without anything to live on. For a long time I could not forget about my meeting with him, his tears, his mental anguish, for which Count Tolstoy and his teachings were to blame. "And what if this old man is not alone, but one of many left hapless and penniless by Count Tolstoy?" I thought. "How will Tolstoy answer before the Lord God for troubling the souls of inexperienced people with his anti-Gospel teachings, leading them astray from "the true path" and ruining the happiness of so many families?" (May 1899: 571)

HISTORY OF SECTARIANISM

The essence of Russian sectarianism was described in *MR* by F. Titov as "*an independent attempt* — granted, a false one and occasionally even downright ugly — *an attempt on the part of our people to find the path to salvation apart from the guidance of the Orthodox Church, independently of its* teachings and traditions" (January 1896: 31). The 'rationalistic' sects, influenced by the liberalism of the 1860s–1880s, were considered especially dangerous. These specifically included the Doukhobors, Molokans, and above all the Tolstoyans.[14] The Tolstoyans were described as the "chief instigators of this movement, so

13 For a thorough discussion of Tolstoyan activities in England, see Holman 1978; for Vladimir Chertkov's Tolstoyan activities after his exile in England, see Holman 1988. On the demise of Tolstoyan colonies in Russia, England, the Netherlands, and America, see Buyniak 1969.

14 According to the Khar'kov diocesan conference, "Tolstoyan sectarianism...has the potential to become the dominant form [of sectarianism], bringing our unstable, diversified, rationalistic sects together. And this is understandable: in comparison with the others, the teachings of this sect include a lot of things of actual practical interest, tempting to the errant masses: in regard to questions of faith, the Tolstoy doctrine rouses devout people's religious feelings and offers a solution to issues of a particular community life. In doing so it unleashes and feeds the beast of political passion dormant in every crowd — passion, which over the past millennium has been controlled and held in check by the benevolent power of Orthodoxy, which has fostered in the Russian people their inherent feelings of ideal citizenship, a world-renowned sense of selfless loyalty and obedience to authority" (January 1897: 47). And on the following page: "Tolstoy's numerous agents began applying particular zeal and energy to *merging all the various teachings of rational sectarianism with those of its own heretical teacher.... Sectarian heresies are gradually losing their uniqueness and originality as they unite with Tolstoy's heresy....* Sectarians are cooling to purely religious issues *and are approaching socialist and nihilist grounds....* Molokans, Khlysts and ne'er-do-wells have recently been lured by various itinerants into Tolstoyism and, *forsaking religion, are giving themselves over to more societal ambitions.*" It should be pointed out, however, that not all scholars include the Tolstoyans in the category of 'rationalistic sects' (see Inikova 2002).

unfortunate for the Doukhobors," as they were "luring a peaceful population into criminal anarchy" (January 1900: 131).

By the summer of 1897 the sectarian question had become a topic of some prominence in the Russian and foreign press (even the 'heavy' literary journals such as *Vestnik Evropy* [*Herald of Europe*] and newspaper giants like *The Times* of London), especially in regard to their coverage of the Third All-Russian Missionary Conference, held in Kazan' that August. *MR*'s editor, V. M. Skvortsov,[15] parodied their tone:

> And indeed: here was a conference of some kind of priests and parish school teachers daring to pronounce their condemnation "on the religious-philosophical views" of Count L. N. Tolstoy, consigning this idol of liberal society to the slums of dissident sectarianism, casting a shadow on the tinsel glint of Tolstoy-worship and its cult which have blinded the false wise men of the close of our century! (September 1897: 738–39)

MR contributors were of varying opinions regarding the degree to which the origin and development of Russian sectarianism could be attributed to external causes. F. Titov, for example, considered them less significant than the Russian people's own fundamental ignorance of their own faith — an ignorance which made them susceptible to harmful religious influences (see January 1896: 41–42). That Tolstoyan ideas had been observed among south-Russian Stundists gave grounds for speculating that Tolstoyism had built strong nests among the Orthodox peasant population of the Khar'kov Gubernia and was here displaying its socialist-communist tendencies — a consequence of what *MR* saw as its evident "anti-Christian" character.[16]

Toward the end of the decade, *MR* was once more taking notice of a tremendous well of support for Tolstoyan and sectarian ideas on the part of the press, both at home and abroad — resulting from "agitation on behalf of supposedly repressed sectarians by the liberal-progressive sector of our society, including all the devotees and followers of the sectarian teacher of Yasnaya Polyana" (January 1899: 137).[17]

15 According to his biographer, I. S. Prokhanov, Skvortsov was "one of the most zealous missionaries" of the Orthodox Church of the time, and notorious in the foreign press as comparable to the Grand Inquisitor, though foreign sectarian publications dared not say a word against him (see November 1898: 1499). The name *Skvortsov* is derived from the Russian word for *starling*, and this was the code name sectarians used to designate Skvortsov's agents in their correspondence (see Prokhanov 1992: 84).

16 This designation was evidently based on the Tolstoyan (and general sectarian) perception of Christ not as a God figure but "a mere mortal, albeit a great philosopher and moralist (Tolstoy, however, rated higher in the eyes of the Tolstoyans!)" (February 1897: 178).

17 Singled out for particular criticism were a handful of Tolstoyans in Britain: Vladimir Chertkov, Dmitrij Khilkov, Pavel Birjukov, and Ivan Tregubov, who had started both a publishing firm and a modest periodical, *Bratskij listok* [The Brotherhood Page], to, as *MR* put it, slander "both the Orthodox Church and government authority" (January 1899: 137).

The church's fears were strongly expressed in Skvortsov's report to the opening of the Tauride missionary conference, in May 1899, "On old events and new phenomena in the sphere of sectarianism and the missionary cause."

> Intelligentsia apostates...are attempting to join themselves to popular sectarianism with the aim of becoming their leaders or, as they see it, *the front line of the popular forces on the road to progress both in their religious* and especially in their societal views.... The societal and anti-Christian religious views of the Tolstoyans have been more accepted by the hearts and minds of both old and new sectarians than Pashkovism. Tolstoyism is beginning to penetrate more and more into the populace. The Tolstoyans' destructive influence on the Doukhobors is already known. It has also found its way both into the new Stundism and into the old Molokanism. (October 1899: 307–08)

Skvortsov went on to depict Tolstoy's humanizing of the Christ figure as undermining the only 'restraining wall' keeping sectarians from falling into outright socialism — namely, "faith in the divine inspiration of the Scriptures and in Christ as the Redeemer and Saviour" (October 1899: 310). Citing the "Rules of the Society of Educated Molokans,"[18] he warned that such heresy was the fruit of a union between popular sectarianism and the 'sectophile intelligentsia,' which was already leading to a state of popular nihilism and godlessness in Russia. In other words, what the church hierarchy had predicted several years earlier was coming to pass.[19]

18 These included the following tenets:

- *Unification* of educated sectarianism on the basis of a worldview that would exclude any contradiction between religion and science, and would lead to a state of mutual harmony between them.
- *Transformation of traditional* (i.e., popular) *sectarianism* through the help of such a world view.
- Membership in the society is open to *all people* sympathetic to its goals and wishing to act according to its spirit ("And just how many sectarianism sympathizers are there among the intelligentsia or even among people in public and government jobs?!" Skvortsov asks).
- In order to promote the ideas of the sect (religious scientific, moral, economic), each member of the society must be in the closest possible contact with the sectarians — go to their meetings, hold discussions, organize local self-educational circles, set up lectures and courses on various subjects, establish libraries, etc.
- Moral and financial encouragement and support for any tendency among sectarians for primary, secondary or higher education.
- Preparation and distribution among sectarians of various mimeographed educational brochures.
- An accumulation of capital by the society on the basis of membership fees and voluntary contributions to offer financial aid to novice sectarians and for various other expenses. (See October 1899: 310–11)

19 For example, the Doukhobors' successful emigration prompted a group of Stundobaptists in the Pavlovka region of Khar'kov Gubernia to apply for exit permits, this time to the United States. However, according to *MR*, reports on the hardships experienced by the Canadian Doukhobors caused them to have second thoughts, fearing conditions in America might be equally difficult. Just as the Tolstoyans had taken control of the Doukhobors in the Caucasus, the Stundobaptists,

L. N. TOLSTOY AND HIS TEACHINGS

At the Third All-Russian Missionary Conference in Kazan' (1897), it was established that Tolstoyism as a sect had begun developing and promoting its teachings among the Orthodox populace and mystic sectarianism around the end of the 1880s. Its branding by the church as the "deceitful enemy not only of Orthodoxy, but also of Christianity as a whole" was based on Tolstoyism's practical application to the ideas and the life of ordinary people.

Tolstoy himself was accused by the *MR* of creating "his own made-up Christianity...with his own gospel, commandments and other blasphemous caprices of a wild religious fantasy, unrestrained by the laws of the Divine mind or by obedience to the authority of the Church" (January 1896: 60). Tolstoy's mistaken view of God (in the church's eyes) as people-dependent is elaborated in an article by S. Kokhomskij in the second January 1896 issue of *MR*, entitled "The made-up teachings of Count L. Tolstoy and his arbitrary interpretation of the beginning of the Gospel of John."

Two years later Kokhomskij followed up with a scathing attack on Tolstoy's *Khristianskij katekhizis* [1877; *Christian Catechism*], pointing out what he saw as inexplicable contradictions in the writer's philosophy of a man-based God (May 1898: 738),[20] although he admits that "Tolstoy himself in certain places, out of necessity, leans toward the true concept of God as the Supreme Being, the Creator, and the Lawgiver of mankind" (738).

Tolstoy's socialist tendencies were further analyzed by N. I. Ivanovskij, a respected theologian and distinguished professor of the Kazan' Seminary, who went so far as to say, "Count Tolstoy is by no means a theologian and no interpreter of the Holy Scriptures, but an outright socialist" aiming to "reconstruct the social order" (February 1896: 89).[21]

in the journal's view, were continuing to win over their cousins the Molokans in southern Russia. This new attraction was considered especially dangerous: even though the Molokans had departed further from the letter and spirit of Gospel teachings than the Stundobaptists, they were still perceived as constituting a lesser threat to the established socio-political order and to the dominance of the Orthodox Church.

20 Kokhomskij specifically accused Tolstoy of confusing love for God with love for one's fellow man, thereby limiting God to whatever love one can find in man — a confusion he saw most strongly in the treatise *What Men Live By* and confirmed in *Where Love Is, There Too Is God* (see July–August 1896: 9). The critic had a more favourable opinion of a third Tolstoy treatise, *Two Elders* (July–August 1896: 13), but he took the writer to task for focusing too much attention on God's love and not enough on His wrath.

21 His accusations against "the most typical representative of modern socialism" (February 1896: 11) went further: "[Tolstoy], therefore, only used the Gospel texts as means of applying his personal ideal of a moral Christian life to the conditions of societal life; he wished to incarnate the kingdom not of this world in an earthly kingdom.... This has led to a confusion between personal moral Christian ideals and the demands of the public State.... To counter Tolstoy...one need only point out and thoroughly explain that it is impossible to apply [Gospel commandments] to the conditions of an earthly kingdom, until we have come unto the perfect man, unto the measure of the stature of the fulness of Christ (Eph. 4:13)" (February 1896: 8–9).

Ivanovskij noted further that though not an organized sect, Tolstoy's followers are to be found everywhere, and observed that "the same spirit of socialism has permeated other sects of the Molokan-Doukhobor type," and that "exposing all this will be a service not only to the Church but to society as well" (February 1896: 11).

In an 1897 reprint from *Moskovskie vedomosti* [lit. *Moscow News*], L. A. Tikhomirov carried the accusations further in his "Episodes from the history of Tolstoyism," in which he called Tolstoy's teachings "too crazy to be widely accepted," and singled out Prince Dmitrij Khilkov, reporting extensively on his proselytizing activities in the Khar'kov Gubernia (see January 1897: 51).

At the Kazan' conference, Archpriest T. V. Butkevich, a professor at Khar'kov University, gave a report outlining the situation in the Pavlovka area of the Sumsk district of the Khar'kov diocese, which for several years already "had been a hotbed of the destructive influence of the false teachings of Tolstoyism," especially as promulgated by Tolstoyan Prince Dmitrij Khilkov (see September 1897: 807–11).[22]

According to Butkevich, the essence of the violently anti-church doctrines of Tolstoyism was summed up in Tolstoy's *Christian Catechism*, which, he says, exposes not only Tolstoy's (and his followers') "obvious departure from the Orthodox Church, but also their heresy, including their denial of all the main tenets of Christianity and the Church with its structure, sacraments and rituals" (September 1897: 828–29). This document — one designed to popularize Tolstoy's teachings among the common and less-educated populace — used a religious format to convey a fundamentally socio-political and anarchical message. Hence the danger of Tolstoyism lay especially in its claim to societal and political ambitions.[23]

22 Part of the report reads: "No matter how hard the Tolstoyans, led by Prince Khilkov, try to spread the new teachings, his metaphysics will never be accessible to the peasants; it appeals to them from a religious point of view, since it offers salvation without any striving or moral effort on the individual's part, requiring neither prayer nor fasting nor observing of rituals, nor holding of sacraments or other forms of worship. But especially attractive and tempting to the uncultured minds of the peasants are the socialist-anarchist teachings of Tolstoyism, as promulgated in Pavlovka. No paying of taxes, no surrendering of one's children to military service, taking away lands from their owners, getting rich without toil, having nothing to do with the police and courts, not bowing to anyone, not obeying anyone, not carrying out any laws or government decrees, always and everywhere being the complete and utter master of one's self, without a single material need!... Surely that must be paradise on earth for a peasant!" (September 1897: 811).

23 Tolstoyism came in for another round of severe criticism at the Tauride missionary conference, in May 1899, in which Nikolaj, bishop of Tauride, called the movement "the denial not only of the Church but also the government — a terrible doctrine, aimed at the overthrow of all the foundations of human well-being, of everything people have lived by heretofore. Tolstoyism has recently begun spreading everywhere, like a gangrene — not only among the upper classes of Russian society (the so-called intelligentsia), but even among our good country people. I know about the activities of this party in Khar'kov Gubernia and among the Doukhobors in the Caucasus, as well as in many other places. After Stundism, it is the most dangerous phenomenon in our life today" (September 1899: 265).

TOLSTOY'S TEACHINGS THROUGH THE EYES OF M. V. GNEVUSHEV

A series of articles by M. V. Gnevushev, entitled "The true sense and meaning of the teachings of Count L. N. Tolstoy," endeavoured to achieve an objective presentation of two competing points of view on the part of the intelligentsia: those who aimed to discredit his teachings, exposing them as deceitful, empty and dangerous, and those who eagerly heeded "the *new* words about the *new* life and spread them throughout the world, thereby enhancing the teachings themselves" (February 1898: 191).

As the most prominent Tolstoy apologist, Gnevushev singled out Nikolaj Strakhov, author of the article "Talks on Count L. N. Tolstoy" in *Voprosy filosofii* [Problems of philosophy]. Gnevushev concludes,

> This defence harnesses every effort to portray Tolstoy's personality and his sermon in the best possible light: his sermons are founded on the highest Christian moral principles, he is active among the worst (in all aspects) of society, his self-sacrifice is incomparable, and so forth. If all this is to be condemned, then it is apparent that the condemners have no proper understanding of the tremendous phenomenon Tolstoy presents in the religious and moral life of the world. (196)

Gnevushev went on to observe, on the other hand, that "Tolstoy himself, his whole doctrine, his whole life at present, is nothing but the direct result of those very evils he has taken it upon himself to heal" (197).

Strakhov's contention that Tolstoy possessed "a sensitive soul, a strong mind and an extremely extraordinary imagination" (198) is compelling indeed, as is his observation that everything that happened in Russia in the second half of the nineteenth century made a strong impression on the writer. Tolstoy's attempt to stand, as it were, apart from the literary circles of his time by no means protected him from the influence of life itself; this attempt, in fact, is seen as largely a result of his comparative lack of sophistication.

Far from denigrating Tolstoy's talent, Gnevushev took pains to point out that it was his very talent that fuelled the writer's highly developed imagination and gave enhanced relief and colour to everything he expressed. He explained that this imagination aggravated Tolstoy's disappointment with the moral decay he saw all around him and with the lack of any real idealism to feed his soul. This in turn drove the writer onto a mutual wavelength with the intelligentsia, many of whom were seeking meaning in life in secular rather than ecclesiastical pursuits, and so "stood far apart from the true light" (199–200). Hence, as Gnevushev later stated in his concluding article, Tolstoy's teachings were 'Christian' in name only, constituting a 'new Christianity' or a 'new Gospel,' which was more human and earthly than Divine or Christly in character (June 1898: 808).[24]

24 Since the strength of moral values are in direct proportion to their grounding in religious faith, Gnevushev argued, Tolstoy's moral teachings were made weaker and less effective by their

The result, according to the critic, could only be increased moral complexities and soul-rending hardships for the people so influenced — and he cited as prime examples the Stundists in southern Russia and the Doukhobors in the Caucasus, who, he felt, had been bitterly deceived by the false hopes offered to them by the Tolstoyans (see June 1898: 824).

COUNTERING TOLSTOY'S INFLUENCE ON CONTEMPORARY SOCIETY

The analytical articles in *MR* were specifically aimed at countering the influence of Tolstoy's ideas on the minds of his contemporaries and on the members of other, hitherto less troublesome (in the church's eyes) sectarian groups — an influence whose rapid growth was all too obvious in any current literature that reflected public opinion. They were designed to expose the basic tenets underlying Tolstoyism, many of which Tolstoy himself did not understand, as incapable of offering a true and complete solution to the burning religious questions of life — questions which could be satisfactorily answered only by the teachings of Orthodoxy.

In an evident endeavour to enhance the appeal of its own presentation, *MR* presented in its January 1899 issue an "open letter to an intelligentsia friend who has been attracted by the teachings of L. N. Tolstoy," anonymously authored by someone identified only as "Amicus." The 'letter' began by quoting, as it were, an appeal for help by a young person 'caught in the crossfire' between Tolstoy's teachings and the opposing views of relatives, friends, and church doctrine — a confusion which, it is claimed, had already driven him close to insanity and even suicide (January 1899: 72).

After stating his unqualified praise for Tolstoy's skill as a writer and a recognition of his services, as a seeker of truth, in pointing out the moral deficiencies of surrounding society, Amicus went on to observe:

> When, instead of limiting himself to this, Tolstoy tries to treat contemporary ills and takes on the role of a reformer of public life, he very clearly reveals his Achilles' heel. His vivid picture of sad, contemporary reality, so masterfully sketched by the skilled and experienced hand of the artist, gives way to a strange, grandiosely designed but weakly executed, utterly fantastical portrayal in *The Kingdom of God is Within You*. Here, against an overall foggy backdrop, rife with indistinct outlines of Western European pantheism and East Asian Buddhism,

lack of a divine foundation to support them. Gnevushev further reasoned: "Demanding from people a high degree of moral perfection, Tolstoy encumbers them with a heavy and uncomfortable yoke, for he makes them rely upon their own forces and does not provide an adequate motivation to bring goodness to perfection, to attain the ideals of life he sets out for them.... The weight of the Tolstoyan yoke on the lives of his followers is seen and will continue to be seen in the disappointment which has befallen and will befall all who are caught up in his teachings. Having lost faith in everything, they are naturally looking for a real self-renewal in the Tolstoyan fold, and expecting to find in his doctrine a sense of spiritual satisfaction — and how are they to feel when they discover that it is just as false as their former pursuits, as false, indeed, as all other new-fangled philosophical and theosophical systems?" (June 1898: 812).

> the amazed spectator is greeted by the sharply delineated dirty and tasteless spots of crude caricatures and worthless blasphemies. (January 1899: 74)

He portrays the writer as one exhausted by his searches for answers to the problems of the world — to the point where he is content with the mere *search* for truth and uses this activity to justify all sorts of contradictions and paradoxes he encounters in this search.[25]

In continuation pieces in the summer and autumn issues of *MR*, Amicus described Tolstoy's principal mistake (and that of others in a similar position) as falsely extrapolating from the part to the whole — blaming the church as a whole for the deficiencies of its individual members. He also denied there was anything new about Tolstoy's heresies: it was only that Tolstoy had managed to "take this kind of heresy farther than before, present it in a more illustrious form and, worst of all, mask it artificially as the teachings of Christ Himself, thereby luring many young and unsuspecting hearts into temptation" (September 1899: 212). In fact, many, according to Amicus, did confuse Tolstoy's teachings with those of Christ, especially when they learned about the latter primarily through the former.

TESTIMONY FROM FORMER TOLSTOYANS

From time to time, *MR* also published open letters from former Tolstoyans who had 'repented' and returned to the Orthodox fold. These, too, reveal their own particular perception of the writer's views.

One of these apostates was a Ukrainian by the name of Mikhail Sopots'ko, who, identifying himself at first only by his initials, wrote in the February 1897 issue (148–49) that "Tolstoy's teachings on violence, the courts and Christianity without Christ are a sermon on the most bloodthirsty anarchy." Two-and-a-half years later he maintained that "the lie needs to be burnt and routed out of thoughts and hearts *not without bloodshed*" (October 1899: 358). In a lengthy "Confession of a repentant Tolstoyan," published in the November 1899 *MR*, Sopots'ko expresses serious concern that young people, "our future leaders of the Orthodox population: pastors, teachers, professors, directors,

25 According to Amicus, Tolstoy came the closest to finding the truth he was searching for when he, like his character Levin in *Anna Karenina*, attempted to probe the mysteries of the spirit of the Russian people and discovered that faith in God was capable of saving him from suicide. But because he did not have a sufficiently rich experience in dealing with 'the inner, spiritual life,' "Tolstoy could not penetrate the soul of the populace as deeply as could the genius Dostoevsky," and was therefore incapable of finding the true Christ that was central to the suffering hearts of the true followers of Russian Orthodoxy (see January 1899: 75–76). Hence his approach to the church did not go much beyond ritual. The writer's worldly background prevented him from penetrating beyond the external appearance to see "the inner link that existed between the members of the living organism of the Church as the body of Christ" (76). Tolstoy attacked the functions of the church on the basis of a superficial acquaintance with its teachings, from a standpoint "where everything is beheld through the prism of a self-deceived, self-conceited mind which is not submissive to Christly faith" (76).

administrators" (November 1899: 504), will be led astray by Tolstoyism from learning the commandments and the Gospel teachings and fulfilling them sufficiently to achieve salvation from hell. He recommends that immediate attention be paid to every single potential future leader to keep them from falling under Tolstoy's influence (505).[26]

Commenting specifically on Tolstoy's recently published treatise *The Kingdom of God is Within You*, Sopots'ko remarked that the writer's heresy made it sound more as if "the kingdom of *Satan* is within us, and is revealed in our relationships with our neighbours" (November 1899: 715). He accused Tolstoy of a superficial approach to Christianity in place of a deep and heartfelt sympathy with the crucified Christ — one such as Tolstoy himself portrayed in his character of Natasha Rostova in *War and Peace* (this had provoked Sopots'ko to tears when he read the novel as a youth). He advised Tolstoy to follow the example of the prodigal son in the Bible (Luke 15:11–32) and heed the call back to the mother church, assuring him of the great concern of many Orthodox members for the salvation not only of Tolstoy but for all those who have put their own salvation at risk by following his false teachings.

TOLSTOY'S SOCIO-LITERARY ACTIVITY

A number of not unfounded accusations were levelled at Tolstoy by Orthodox critics — even though many of them recognized his significant contribution to Russian literature. Several examples are outlined below:

- An especially critical piece was V. V. Rozanov's article, published in the October 1896 issue of *Russkoe obozrenie* [Russian Review] and reviewed in *MR* March–April 1897 (328–29). Provoked by Tolstoy's letter to an American sympathizer, Ernest Crosby, it urged readers to strive more persistently for the true sense of the Gospel passages taken out of context by Tolstoy to support his own heresies.
- Particular criticism was directed at the publishing firm Posrednik, which Vladimir Chertkov had founded with Tolstoy's blessing and which had issued a number of Tolstoy's works.[27]

26 In December 1899, when Tolstoy was seriously ill, Mikhall Sopots'ko addressed him with another open letter in *MR*, paying his respects but making his own position unmistakably clear: "I will say that you, Lev Nikolaevich, are closer and more comprehensible with your inner peace to us who have opened our eyes, have been many times tempted, than to all the other blind, untempted followers which we ourselves once were.... It is clear to me now that [God] desired and still desires to draw you close to Himself with His grace, meekness, longsuffering and love that gave the Father's Beloved Son into the hands of sinners to be crucified. Why will you not heed the still small voice of God's love?" (December 1899: 713–14).

27 *MR* noted, e.g., that Posrednik publications were particularly popular with sectarians, even with the Doukhobors who were otherwise known for their general antipathy to books of any kind; in addition, whole workshops had been organized in the Russian south, as well as in the

- The September 1897 issue of *MR* featured a critical response, authored by V. M. Skvortsov, to Tolstoy's open letter on the Samara Molokans being separated from their children, as published in the *Sankt-Peterburgskie vedomosti* [St. Petersburg News]. Skvortsov accused Tolstoy of misleading the public by overgeneralizing an incident which, he said, was clearly an exception, by stating that the church had removed children from the homes of "many, many sectarians and dissidents" (September 1897: 786).
- In 1898, P. T. Degtjarev accused Tolstoy of misusing his reputation as a novelist to put before the public any number of worthless articles, leaflets, and even books (see October 1898: 1362).
- In its April 1899 issue, in what was perhaps the most stinging attack of all in its early annals, *MR* reprinted a letter (from *Russkij list*) from someone, identified only as "a foreigner," accusing Tolstoy of loving only himself and his own popularity, and of having no love for Russia or the people he purported to be writing for. "If Pushkin can be compared with a doctor," observed the letter writer, "then Tolstoy is a surgeon, for whom Russia is an interesting subject for scientific research. But the great surgeon himself is sick with his striving for popularity and with his love of self, and for this reason his operations are not always successful" (April 1899: 512).

APPRAISAL OF *THE KINGDOM OF GOD IS WITHIN YOU*

A detailed evaluation of Tolstoy's treatise *The Kingdom of God is Within You* from the Orthodox perspective appeared in a brochure by Archimandrite Antonius, published in Kazan' in 1896, and was reviewed by P. Kozitskij in the September 1896 issue of *MR*. Antonius strongly criticizes Tolstoy's attempt to identify his own teachings with Christianity, observing that even his sense of morality is founded much more "on pantheism and materialistic atheism" than on Gospel or church teachings.[28]

In examining both the external and internal motivation for Tolstoy's doctrine of non-resistance to evil, Antonius saw the writer's highest goals as

Caucasus, to distribute Tolstoy's "high-and-mighty gospel" to sectarians (see February 1896: 41–42).

28 Tolstoy's doctrine of 'non-resistance to evil,' which is central to this particular treatise, Antonius describes as "the Gordian knot in Tolstoy's morality" (September 1896: 182), which is not given a proper philosophical grounding in the treatise. Instead, he says, "Christian teachings on morality are higher than those of Tolstoy, for they demand of the individual not just a superficial minimum of good behaviour, like Tolstoy with his five commandments and in particular his commandment of non-resistance, but moral purity and an inner love; if non-resistance to violence is to be endorsed, it can only be a non-resistance that can destroy evil with spiritual power. In cases where there is no possibility of overcoming evil through spiritual power, Christianity allows resistance and compels the individual to bitterly admit that his deed is not one of pure goodness, but only a lesser evil by comparison with non-resistance. Hence the Church only suffers war as a lesser evil, but does not condone it" (September 1896: 180–84).

enjoyment and suffering, rather than good and evil, which were presented only from a utilitarian — and hence, crudely materialistic — standpoint. He summed up his criticism as follows:

> Tolstoy's moral teachings are devoid not only of all psychological persuasion, but, as constituting a fixed materialistic outlook on the human soul, they have no logical possibility of acting on the mind and will of their adherents. In their theoretical definitions, which make no absolute distinction between good and evil, defining these concepts instead as variant forms of advantage and harm, they are not moral teachings but eudemonic — dead. (September 1896: 64)

Antonius' analysis met with full approval by the *MR* reviewer, who found it useful not only in exposing Tolstoy's heresies but also in resolving the question of not offering violent resistance to evil.

THE DOUKHOBORS IN THE CAUCASUS: 1895–1898

The Third All-Russian Missionary Conference, in 1897, opened with an address by V. M. Skvortsov entitled: "O tserkovno-obshchestvennom i gosudarstvennom znachenii missionerstva" [On the meaning of missionary activity to the church, the public, and the state], which dealt in particular with the question of the Caucasus Doukhobors. His remarks bear quoting at some length.

> Does not the Transcaucasian Doukhobor epic, which is causing so much fuss both here in Russia and abroad, hold a goodly number of lessons for taking stock and being on guard in respect to our sectarian communities?
>
> [O]ver the past fifty years there had not been a single police station with as many as five cases of Doukhobor crime, and not one complaint came from this peaceful population.... The Doukhobors were recognized by the local administration as a most reliable colonizing element for the frontier.
>
> And what has happened now? The celebrated Doukhobors have always thought of themselves as a 'special nation'...
>
> [A]s it turns out, in Doukhoborism we have not so much a religious as a societal sect which, like all our rationalist sects, represents 'combustible material,' capable of erupting into a fearful blaze at the first spark it encounters — and here the spark was provided by anarchistic propaganda among the Doukhobors.... And here we are now, witnesses to a mess of political trouble unprecedented in history: as many as eight thousand sectarians are not only openly and insolently declaring to each and everyone but actually showing in action their utter disregard of citizenship and their refusal to recognize the holy authority of God's Anointed Monarch, saying they have "one Heavenly King, and do not recognize any earthly King, and there should be none such."
>
> Quite a transformation indeed has occurred over the past two or three years amidst the most celebrated part of the Russian sectarian populace! There is a serious danger that such an infection of anarchy can touch the neighbouring Molokan and Prygun [Jumper] populations. Is it conceivable that something similar could happen not only in the masses, but even with individuals among

> Orthodox people, slandered as a 'drunken crowd' by the liberal camp of sectophiles? (August 1897: 629–30)

According to *MR*, Tolstoyans with their propaganda easily took advantage of the Doukhobors' annoyance at the government's rejection of their persistent pleas to return their leader Pëtr Vasil'evich Verigin from exile in the Far North (see October 1896: 297), influencing (in Verigin's name) not only the Doukhobor population in the Caucasus but also Verigin himself — it is reported that the exiled leader was especially taken with Tolstoy's treatise *The Kingdom of God is Within You.*

Again, as per *MR*, it was the Tolstoyan influence that made the Doukhobors into a "criminal anarchical confederation (the Fasters' party), which is unwilling to recognize the supreme authority of the Tsar or obey the government agencies authorized by him, and disregards government institutions, laws, property rights etc." (January 1897: 46). On the basis of Skvortsov's report, the missionary conference declared the Doukhobors (specifically the fasters) a "particularly harmful and extremely dangerous sect — dangerous both to the Church and to the State" (November 1897: 1044–45).[29]

The danger was exacerbated in the Doukhobors' case by their strategic geographical location on the frontier, the Russian Empire's first line of defence against any military advance from Turkey, and the effect of the Tolstoyan influence called into question their reliability as a colonizing element.

> Those settled in the Kars Oblast as the vanguard of the Russian campaign on the Turkish border have almost all turned out to be traitors to the Tsar and the fatherland. They have openly refused to recognize any authority, laws or civil duties to the State, including military service. It would naturally be impossible for this formerly praiseworthy but now rebellious anarchical population to remain at a frontier outpost of the Russian territory. The greatest mistake of the theory, prevalent until just recently, of colonizing the Russian frontier with sectarians and German aliens was rooted in a purely utilitarian, political-economic, one-sided view which did not take into account either spiritual interests or the fundamental roots of the life of the Russian State — i.e., Orthodoxy.

MR was quick to dismiss the counter-arguments of the liberal press (both Russian and foreign) — to the effect that the Doukhobors were suffering from official persecution, not to mention poverty, hunger, disease, and even fatalities among the exiled fasters, stating emphatically that such rumours were false, having been fabricated by the Tolstoyans themselves (see June 1898: 833). Such judgements were made, claimed *MR*, on the basis of the journal's own research (deemed more objective than that of the devious Tolstoyans), not only among the fasters but also Doukhobors of other parties, neighbouring

29 In October of 1897, an article by Tolstoy had appeared in the *Stockholm Tagblatt* suggesting the Nobel Peace Prize be awarded not to himself but to the Doukhobors.

Terpenie village, first official Doukhobor settlement in the Milky Waters region of Tavrida Gubernia, Russia, ca 1817.

Leo Tolstoy in 1868, a few years prior to his “spiritual awakening”.
Professional photograph.

The historic “Burning of arms” in Transcaucasia, 28–29 June 1895. Rendition by Doukhobor artist Bill Perehudoff.

Five young Doukhobor men from Kars who took part in the “Burning of Arms” in June 1895. Left to right: Ivan Ivanovich Planidin, Pëtr Ivanovich Dorofeev, Grigorij Vasil’evich Verigin, Pavel Vasil’evich Planidin, Semën Efimovich Chernov.

First page of Tolstoy's letter to Pëtr Vasil'evich Verigin, 14 October 1896 (Letter N° 3).

Vladimir Grigor'evich Chertkov (1854–1936), a close associate of Tolstoy's, who helped expose the persecution and suffering of the Doukhobors.

Sir Clifford Sifton, Canadian Minister of the Interior, whose vigorous immigration policy paved the way for the acceptance of the Russian Doukhobors in Canada in 1899.

On board the *S.S. Lake Huron*, the first shipload of Doukhobors en route to Canada, January 1899.

James A. Smart, Canadian Deputy Minister of the Interior, who officially met the first shipload of Doukhobors arriving in Halifax in January 1899.

On board the S.S. *Lake Superior*, the fourth and final shipload of Doukhobors en route to Canada. Left to right: Dr Mercer, Captain Taylor, Leopol'd Antonovich Sulerzhitskij.

Doukhobor women and girls knitting and mending clothes on board the *S.S. Lake Superior* en route to Canada, 1899.

Three medical assistants on board the *S.S. Lake Superior* (1899).
Left to right: Anna de Carousa, Anna Robetz, Elizaveta Markova.

Sergej L'vovich Tolstoy (L. N. Tolstoy's eldest son), who accompanied the second boatload of Doukhobors to Canada in the winter of 1899.
Photo by V. Chekhovskij

Six participants in accompanying the second boatload of Doukhobors to Canada. Left to right – standing: D. A. Khilkov, L. A. Sulerzhitskij, S. L. Tolstoy; sitting: M. A. Sats, E. D. Khirjakova, M. A. Chekhovich. *Photo by J. F. Mitchell, Winnipeg, 1899.*

Doukhobor children in quarantine on Lawlor's Island near Halifax, 1899.

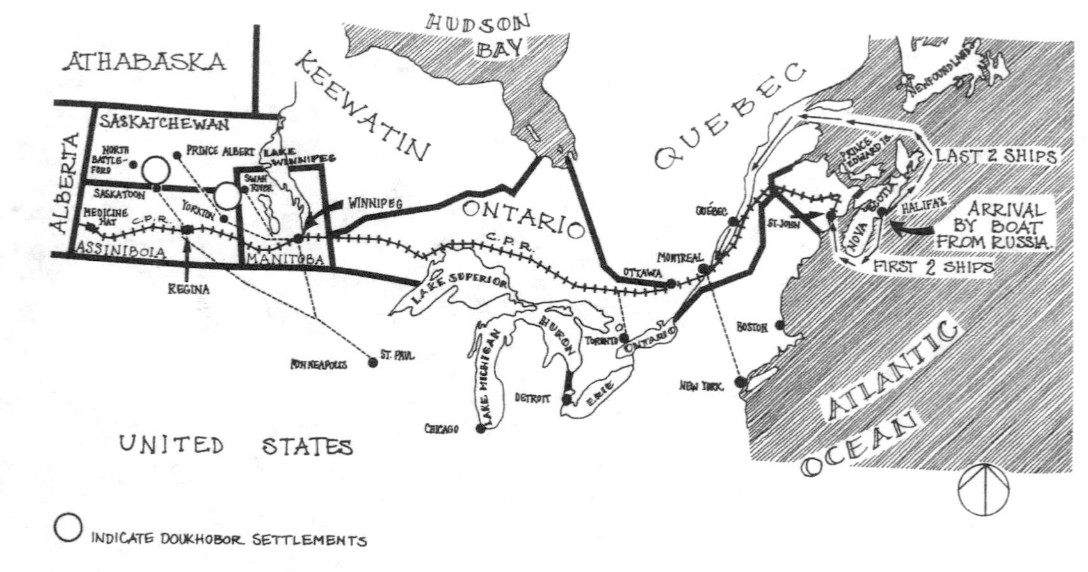

Map of Doukhobor migration routes within Canada, 1899, tracing the routes taken by the four parties of Doukhobors from Halifax or Québec to Saskatchewan and Assiniboia on the Canadian prairies.

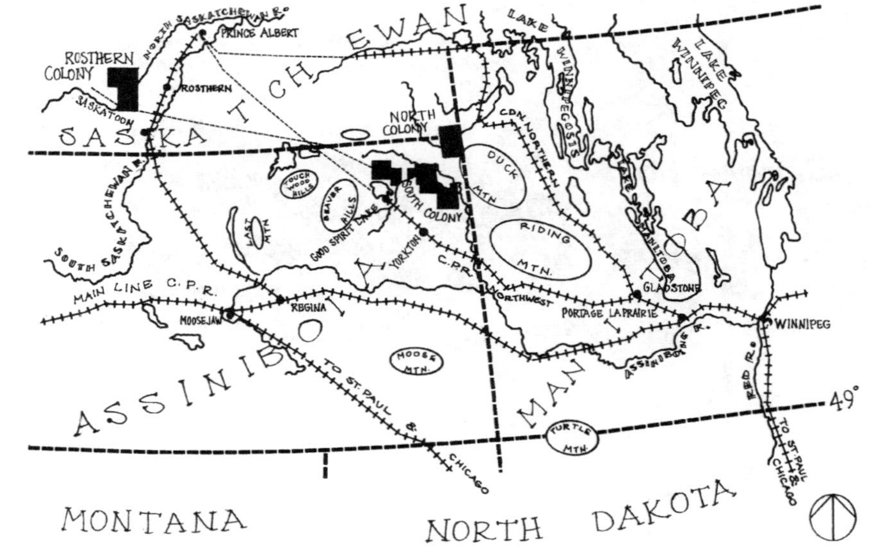

Map of early Doukhobor settlements in Saskatchewan, Assiniboia (now part of Saskatchewan) and Manitoba, 1899.

Doukhobor women pulling a plough on the Canadian prairies, May 1899.

Vladimir Dmitrievich Bonch-Bruevich (1873–1955) — politician (later Lenin's personal secretary) who accompanied the fourth boatload of Doukhobors to Canada in May 1899.

August the 4/16.
1899

Dear Sir

In answer to your kind letter, I send you these photos, which will remind you the whole company, and the few days that we all have had the pleasure of spending with you. Every one asked me to send their compliments to you, and we hope that you will come once again to visit your russian friends.

Yours truly

Css S. Tolstoy

Note written (in English) by Sofia Andreevna Tolstaya to University of Toronto professor James Mavor in August 1899.

Two young Canadian Doukhobor couples:
Tatyana and Michael Saprikin (*left*); Maria and Ivan Pereverzoff (*right*).

Doukhobor village near the town of Veregin, Saskatchewan, ca 1900.

The village of Voznesenie, North Colony, Saskatchewan, ca 1901.
This common village plan was copied from Doukhobor villages in the Caucasus.

Pëtr Vasil'evich Verigin (1859–1924), shown during a stopover with the Chertkovs in Christchurch, England, in November 1902, on his journey from Siberian exile to join his fellow-Doukhobors already settled on the Canadian prairies. *Photo by V. G. Hooper.*

Stundists and Molokans, Armenian and Tatar residents of the area, and local administrative and judicial offices (see June 1898: 839–40).

The journal's 'research' was undoubtedly carried out by Skvortsov, who travelled to the Caucasus in December 1895 on a fact-finding mission at the behest of Konstantin Pobedonostsev, senior procurator of the Holy Synod. After a week or so in Tiflis, studying archival case history on Doukhoborism, Skvortsov spent the month of January surveying Doukhobor communities (see February 1896: 59). Some of his findings were published in a letter in *Moskovskie vedomosti* of 28 January 1896, noting the tremendous popularity of Tolstoyism among the intelligentsia of the Caucasus (especially the women), and suggested Tolstoyan propaganda might be responsible for the unrest among the Doukhobors.

MR also attempted to correct what it saw as Tolstoy's misperception — oft repeated by his followers — that the Tolstoyans were simply "*helping* the Doukhobors who *were suffering for their faith*":

> The respected count himself is mistaken, and is misleading others. The Doukhobors are in no way being punished *for their faith* or religious convictions, but for their political wilfulness and excesses, for their outrageous disregard for the laws of the empire and mocking the supreme authority of our land — something that is not justified by any faith in the world except anarchy. (February 1896: 845)

MR further emphasized that the exiling of the Doukhobor fasters from their settlements was at best a *necessary evil*, a measure adopted as a last resort only after all other options had been exhausted (see February 1896: 848). Even in exile, *MR* faulted the Doukhobors for maintaining a haughty attitude and refusing to co-operate with their host landowners, who took pains to accommodate them and often offered them the opportunity for work, which the Doukhobors declined. When they did agree to work, they would overcharge for their services and abuse their host's land and possessions. In doing so they soon became unpopular and disliked by the local population, and gained a reputation as stubborn and miserly anarchists, a picture completely the opposite of that painted by the Tolstoyans (see February 1896: 854).

THE DOUKHOBOR EMIGRATION TO CANADA: 1898–1899

One of the first reactions on the part of the Orthodox press to the possibility of Doukhobor emigration from Russia is to be found in an article by Skvortsov, published in the May 1898 issue of *MR*, entitled "Nedorazumenie v obshchestve i pechati, po povodu pereselenija zagranitsu zakavkazskikh «dukhoborov-postnikov», oni zhe i «khristiane vsemirnogo bratstva»" ["Misunderstanding in society and the press in respect to the resettlement abroad of the Transcaucasian 'Doukhobor Fasters,' or the 'Christians of the universal brotherhood'"]. Here Skvortsov admitted, almost apologetically:

> As an unwilling sacrifice of getting blindly carried away with *Tolstoyism,* the dark masses of Doukhobors are unfortunate and deserve our pity. After trying all possible measures, however, given the crazed mass movement of a politically unreliable, unruly and dangerous element [of society], the government was left with no alternative but to willingly permit the fasters to resettle abroad. This is the only true way of dealing with the tangled issue. Let the dirty scum flee, which all told counts for less than half of the entire Doukhobor population. At least the intelligent part of the Doukhobor sect will free itself from the crazed, unruly, anarchical element. So we can only wish the Doukhobor Fasters Godspeed, and the Tolstoyans the success they desire in fulfilling their thankless mission. (May 1898: 710–11)

Almost a year later, following the departure of the first two boatloads of Doukhobors to Canada, Skvortsov was still blaming the Tolstoyans for what he saw as the sect members' inevitable "economic and moral sufferings" (March 1899: 323).

Skvortsov's article in this issue of *MR* also outlined a number of details concerning the Doukhobors' emigration to date — specifically, the significant role played by the English Quakers, who were seen as saving the venture financially following a quarrel between two of the Russian Tolstoyans, Chertkov and Prince Khilkov; the disastrous failure of the Cyprus resettlement because of unfavourable climatic conditions (forty-five of the 1,126 who went there died of fever); and the uncooperative attitude on the part of the British authorities on the island. He went so far as to recommend that, in their own interests, no more Doukhobors be allowed to leave Russia, citing the fear that

> the American [*sic*] Fasters[30] and our intelligentsia Tolstoyans enraged at the [Russian] government will undoubtedly try everything they can to lure the largest possible number of their wealthy Doukhobor brethren to Canada, to make their colony there more populous, richer and stronger, so there may be a greater opportunity of carrying on anarchical and communist experiments. (March 1899: 330)

In its December 1898 issue, *MR* took issue with an article that appeared in the English paper the *Levant Herald,* which, based on an account in the journal *The Nineteenth Century* by Prince Pëtr Kropotkin, portrayed the Doukhobors as fleeing persecution by the Russian government and establishing a flourishing colony in the Canadian province of Manitoba.[31] *MR* wonders aloud why

30 None of the Doukhobors at this time actually settled in America, though a few Tolstoyans (notably A. M. Bodjanskij and P. Demens) tried unsuccessfully to attract the Doukhobors there instead of Canada. Russian sources of the day, however, sometimes conflated *America* with the North American continent as a whole.

31 The Doukhobor settlements, as reported by Prince Dmitrij Khilkov in an article in *Juzhnoe obozrenie* of 22 December 1899, were actually located "along the Western boundary of Manitoba in the territories of Assiniboia and Saskatchewan" (Woodsworth 1999a: 130).

the British press, which had shown itself so indifferent to the plight of its own "genuinely persecuted and ill-treated fellow citizens — the Irish in England, for example — are particularly generous in their sympathy to the supposedly wretched situation" of dissident Russian sects (December 1898: 1645).

The *MR* counter-article brings up three points in particular:

(1) The Russian government's allowance of German colonies on its territory, even near its Western borders with Austria and Germany, "without regard for the religious or political make-up of the colonists" (1646), should be questioned.
(2) In referring to the wealthy Mennonite sectarian settlements in Canada, the *Herald* should also take into account that their counterparts back in Russia are equally well-off, thanks to the generosity of the Russian government, which granted them special privileges over many years, such as exemption from certain duties toward the State.
(3) The *Herald* should question whether it is fair for the Russian government to maintain special privileges for a few sects who do not even care to defend it when necessary, at the expense of the vast majority of its citizens "who believe rightly and act rightly." (1647)

In the *Herald*'s position the *MR* critic sees a stereotypical Anglo-Saxon world view — whereby spiritual development and nobility of character are subordinated to the worship of material wealth, and even the slightest legal demand of a nation upon its citizens is equated with persecution for one's faith.

In the autumn following the Doukhobor emigration, *MR* reprinted a later-famous letter written by one of the Doukhobor settlers, Ivan Goncharov, from Canada, which, it points out, only confirms the correctness of the journal's earlier prediction that "this venture will mean only a new tightening of the Tolstoyan noose around the neck of the unfortunate sectarians" (October 1899: 424).

THE DOUKHOBORS IN CANADA AND AMERICA: 1900–1901

In its January 1900 issue *MR* noted the Doukhobors' situation in Canada was portrayed far more "rosily" in the Russian press than in American papers. One of the latter is quoted describing the potential exploitation of Doukhobor emigrants by the Southern Pacific Railroad, which was attempting "to sell them at a profit several unsaleable plots of wilderness land, which the railway company had received gratis from the [American] government, and *intends to settle the Doukhobors in a place where it can collect payment from them for transporting every pound* [of goods] which they bought or sold" (January 1900: 178). It accused the railway company of taking advantage of the Doukhobors' lack of English and of showing them only its own lands, and the company agent of standing to collect a "fat fee" should the Doukhobors accept the deal.[32]

MR then turns to a comment on the above in the Russian paper *Novoe vremja*. One of its correspondents, identified only as "Sigma,"[33] notes that, should the Doukhobors accept the deal, they would risk becoming the slaves of the American railway company instead of the Canadian Pacific Railway. *MR* continues:

> It seems to me, notes Mr. Sigma, that those writers who lure Russians to Canada and America by their lies and tempting descriptions are careless writers; and it seems to me that the tempting descriptions of American charms is in essence *pulling innocent people into an unprofitable deal.* And the Russian press should be more careful about spreading the information for which they rightly condemn and chastise emigration agents. (January 1900: 178)

MR further notes Sigma's advice to the Doukhobors to emigrate to China instead, along with the Doukhobors' reply that the Russians could easily conquer China and impose their will once more upon the sect. The journal concludes its review with the sentiment: "Now for this hatred towards Russia the Doukhobors are being cruelly punished by God."

In its March issue of the same year, *MR* marked the death of Aleksej Zubkov in the Akhalkalak district of the Caucasus, the popular leader of the non-Veriginite Doukhobors, whom the journal described as "the last of the Mohicans of old, traditional Doukhoborism" (March 1900: 481), citing his resemblance, not only in looks but also in terms of standing among his people, to the German chancellor Otto von Bismarck. Most significantly from the Orthodox viewpoint, Zubkov was celebrated for his moderate stance vis-à-vis the Russian Church and his willingness to co-operate with state authorities instead of working against them. *MR* observes that Zubkov might have been decorated by the state for his service as a Doukhobor elder had he not, like a true Doukhobor, refused to wear state medals. It describes his burial in the most sacred of Doukhobor cemeteries, alongside their former revered leader, Luker'ja Kalmykova (see March 1900: 487).

By the end of the year new reports were arriving from Canada on the Doukhobors' difficulties in coping with their new situation — particularly in respect to Canadian government authorities and the private Canadian Pacific Railway. The latter was attempting to take away the settlers' lands on a technicality.

32 The reference is to a delegation of Doukhobors and Tolstoyans from Canada brought to California by a P. A. Demens with the aim of encouraging them to resettle in America. The Doukhobors, however, were unimpressed. The venture is described in two documents (#1899-12-31c and #1900-IJO-j) in Woodsworth 1999a: 115–17, 160–64.

33 *Sigma* (S. N. Syromjatnikov) — see Note 8, page 318, in Letter N° 3 in Part IV.

> The fact that Prince Khilkoff and all his associates were absolutely incapable of taking any practical steps gave the Canadian Pacific [Railway] the opportunity to rip off the unfortunate Doukhobors. It is difficult to see how this whole tragic Doukhobor venture will end. (December 1900: 839–40)

MR's next issue reported that the "American" (i.e., Canadian) authorities were now demanding from the Doukhobors full compliance with all local laws, including registration of births, deaths, and marriages,[34] causing younger Doukhobors to blame their elders for bringing them to Canada, and giving occasion for *MR* to point to the ignorance on the part of Canadian authorities of "the Russian kindly attitude toward sectarians" (January 1901: 147).

Such reports only seemed to confirm an earlier, twenty-page analysis (by a critic identified only as "E. Ja.") published in the November 1900 issue of *MR*, outlining what it saw as the chain of events leading up to the 'disastrous' emigration venture and, particularly, the role of Tolstoy and his followers therein. The analysis included the following points:

(1) In contrast to foreign press reports, the Doukhobors were not *expelled* from Russia for their religious convictions but left *of their own free will* because they were reluctant to obey authorities and fulfill their duties as citizens of the Russian Empire (see November 1900: 522).

(2) In contrast to rumours spread by the Tolstoyans, the Doukhobors were not suffering from poverty and starvation, but even those exiled in 1897 possessed significant financial reserves, amounting to thousands of roubles; in fact, they were better off than many of the central Russian Orthodox population (see 522–23).

(3) The Tolstoyan intelligentsia urged the Doukhobors to continue their passive "struggle with violence"; that is, with authority, assuring them that even if the Russian government did not grant them a place to live undisturbed, they would be welcomed as desired settlers just about anywhere else in the world, and promised they would be reunited with their Siberian-exiled leader, Pëtr Vasil'evich Verigin (see 524).

(4) The Russian government patiently bided its time in the hope that the radical Doukhobors' agitation would be smothered by the example of their more moderate brethren.

> Thus it would have been, if it hadn't been for the agitation among the Doukhobors on the part of the intelligentsia Tolstoyans, who cherished the anarchical Doukhobor religious movement as a unique experiment unprecedented in our sectarian history, as the embodiment in action, in the lives of a whole mass of people, of the Tolstoyans' own crazy dreams; heads full of diseased ambition wanted to experiment and show to the world, through the

34 For further discussion on this question and its resolution, see Woodsworth 1999a: 156–58.

> Doukhobor masses, the Tolstoyan Kingdom of God on earth life on the basis of non-violence and the religious-socialist commune, without the services offered by citizenship or civilization. (526)

Another factor in the Tolstoyans' mindset was their hatred toward the government, which was evident in their attempts to deprive Russia of "thousands of useful workers" (see 526) — a hatred they passed on to the Doukhobor leaders.

(5) The two Doukhobors led by Prince Khilkov on a tour to scout out new lands in Canada, not knowing English or anything about local conditions, were mere "automatons" in the hands of Khilkov.[35] The prince himself was the victim of zealous Canadian railway agents, who showed him the lands in winter when it was most difficult to appraise their real quality. The railway's desire to settle undesirable wilderness areas coincided with the Tolstoyans' efforts to keep the Doukhobors as isolated as possible from urban temptations (see 528).

(6) It is hoped that the "struggle for survival and [their] instinct for self-preservation" in Canada will "sober the more sensible among the Doukhobor masses away from the intoxication of Tolstoyan fantasies" and "weaken the sectarians' blind fascination with the anarchical and communist principle of falsehood and life" (see 526). Reports that this had indeed been taking place and that the Doukhobors were beginning to think of themselves and their families ahead of others had been extremely disappointing, not only to the Tolstoyans but also to Tolstoy himself.

> Tolstoy's irritation and sorrow in view of the metamorphosis away from communal living and, consequently, in the Doukhobors' views, are fully understandable: after all, so many of his brightest hopes as an arch-heretic were pinned on the Doukhobor movement, it had cost so many sacrifices — indeed, so many lives — to resurrect and maintain this movement, and suddenly at the first onrush of one of life's storms, the Doukhobor temple, erected according to the Tolstoyans' detailed plan, turned out to be built on sand, without firm foundations, and is now beginning to crumble at its very foundations, on its communal side! (526)

Tolstoy's appeal to the Doukhobors to "keep the faith," written and signed in his own hand in February 1899 (and reprinted with critical annotations as part of the current article), had all the markings of the "pharisaical rantings of a fanatic who is set in his erroneous ways," "demanding from his slaves blind

35 For a full account of Khilkov's exploratory tour with the Doukhobor scouts, see his series of articles from *Juzhnoe obozrenie* in English translation in Woodsworth 1999a: 121–64. For a perceptive study of Khilkov's relationship with Tolstoy, see Ershova 2001.

obedience to his morality"; such an appeal reveals Tolstoy "unmasked, as a true teacher of heresy and a diehard communist revolutionary" (526).

The article concludes with the stinging question as to whether it might be "simply too easy for the new intellectuals to catch the poor Russian peasant in their trap for their criminal experiments," pointing to this "psychopathic pursuit of Tolstoy's" and the evident apathy toward it on the part of society and the press as a "dangerous omen of our time" (542).

It is little wonder that with such venomous attacks from the official church, not to mention the dozens of books denigrating Tolstoy and his teaching that appeared within the period discussed here (1896–1900), and avidly reviewed in *Missionerskoe obozrenie* (obviously by hand-picked reviewers), and with the government unflinchingly behind them, the church, in 1901, excommunicated Tolstoy.[36]

Tolstoy persevered, however. No issue so deeply preoccupied him (or his family) during the two years prior to the Doukhobor departure to Canada in 1899 than the well-being of these people, as will be seen in Chapter 4.

36 The same year, *MR* published a booklet entitled *Dukhobory v Amerike i graf L. N. Tolstoj* [Doukhobors in America and Count L. N. Tolstoy).

CHAPTER 4

The Doukhobors' Journey to Canada in the Tolstoy Family's Correspondence

THE DOUKHOBORS' JOURNEY TO CANADA, which began in December 1898 and continued through four boatloads until May of the following year, is well documented in a vast exchange of letters on the subject between the Tolstoy family and a number of correspondents around the world, including letters among family members themselves. Three figures are of particular note and will be discussed in greater detail: Sergej L'vovich Tolstoy and Sofia Andreevna Tolstaya in this chapter and Pëtr Vasil'evich Verigin in Chapter 6, wich also contains 38 letters between Tolstoy and Verigin.

The very first known reference to the Doukhobors in Tolstoy's correspondence dates from 8 May 1891 (#1891-05-20),[1] in a letter received from one of his followers, Vladimir Chertkov, about the refusal of five Doukhobors to serve in the military (see note to #1891-05-20). At the time, Tolstoy was working on his treatise *The Kingdom of God is Within You*, and subsequently included a reference to this incident in the final manuscript.

The next year another follower, Prince Dmitrij Khilkov,[2] was exiled to the Caucasus, where he came into close personal contact with the Doukhobors — see Tolstoy's letters to and about Khilkov of 1892 (#1892-04-16, #1892-05-07, #1892-09-26). In a letter to Khilkov of 9(?) December 1892 (#1892-12-20),

1 Letters are cited according to the index number assigned in the Chronology (see Appendix), which is based on the NS calendar. Dates of letters given in the text reflect the original, OS dating; NS dates appear in square brackets.

2 See Chap. 2, Note 29.

Tolstoy tells Khilkov of his just-completed meeting with two English Quakers (John T. Bellows and Joseph J. Neave), who were on their way to visit Khilkov and the Doukhobors in the Caucasus.[3]

Two years later, on 9 December 1894 (#1894-12-21), in a letter to N. N. Ivanov, Tolstoy describes his first face-to-face contact (of that same day) with Doukhobor representatives at his Moscow home. These were Vasilij Ob"edkov, Vasilij V. Verigin,[4] and Vasilij Vereshchagin, who were escorting their leader, Pëtr Vasil'evich Verigin, from his place of exile in Arkhangel'sk to the town of Obdorsk, in Siberia. During the stopover in Moscow, the Doukhobor leader was held in Moscow's Butyr Prison and denied permission to receive any visitors, including Tolstoy.

Then, in a letter to Eugen Heinrich Schmitt of 27 March 1895 (#1895-04-08), Tolstoy specifically mentions the Doukhobors (along with the Neo-Stundists) among the ranks of Russian sectarians — about whom he is ready to share with Schmitt pertinent information in his possession.[5]

The summer of 1895 brought news about the events in the Caucasus in letters (to which Tolstoy responded) from Chertkov (see #1895-06-20), Khilkov (#1895-08-10), and Molokan writer Fëdor Zheltov (#1895-08-31). In two letters written 4 September 1895 — one to M. V. Alekhin (#1895-09-16a), the other to his son Lev L'vovich (#1895-09-16b) — Tolstoy tells of an exploratory trip to the Caucasus undertaken by another of his followers, Pavel Birjukov, to observe the Doukhobor situation there and report back. Birjukov subsequently writes and publishes an appeal, entitled *Help!* [*Pomogite!*], along with Chertkov and Ivan Tregubov, accompanied by an afterword by Tolstoy (#1895-09-22).

At this stage we already see in the correspondence Tolstoy's characteristic meticulous approach to the question in his insistence on obtaining accurate and objective information about the Doukhobors. Of particular note is Tolstoy's letter to Khilkov of 29 July 1895 (#1895-08-10), rejecting the notion of a political pamphlet on the subject. Tolstoy's scrupulous caution may also be seen in his remarks concerning additions to Birjukov's article in December of that year (#1895-12-30b).

This was also the time he initiated correspondence with the Doukhobor leader P. V. Verigin (see #1895-11-06a, #1895-11-26, #1895-12-03).[6]

Tolstoy still had his doubts, however, as evidenced in the same letter to Khilkov (#1895-08-10). Perhaps he was concerned lest a public polemic over the Doukhobors be turned into a boisterous anti-government campaign and drown out whatever sympathy there might be for the actual persecution

3 They would also be paying a visit to the Stundist sect in southern Russia (see Neave 1910).

4 Pëtr V. Verigin's brother.

5 See also two subsequent letters to Schmitt, written in September and October 1895 (#1895-09-27, #1895-10-11).

6 See Chapter 6.

victims. Moreover, one cannot exclude the possibility that Tolstoy was still unsure as to whether the Doukhobors actually deserved all the publicity they were being shown by people close to him — see, for example, his letter to Chertkov of 1 December 1895 (#1895-12-13).

Another example is his letter to Tolstoyan Aleksandr Bodjanskij of 2 October 1895 (#1895-10-14), in which he for the first time approaches the idea, raised by Bodjanskij in an earlier letter, of resettling the Doukhobors abroad. Rejecting his correspondent's proposal that the Doukhobors should leave Russia, he adds, "if even some, or even all of the Doukhobors, weakened from persecution, should renounce their faith, this would show that they lack this unique support and joy the consciousness of doing God's will, and so they are left with nothing to hold on to and they are perforce obliged to give up" (*PSS* 68:195).

Further on he sets out his own position quite succinctly:

> The only help that lies within my power is to summon sympathy for God's cause among the greatest number of people.... This is exactly what I have tried to do to the best of my ability by writing an article about it and sending it to the English and German papers. I would very much like to express my own sympathy and love directly to the Doukhobors, but I don't know how to do that. (*PSS* 68:196)

Tolstoy's hesitation cannot simply be dismissed as ephemeral or insignificant, since it did continue for some time. Even after six months, Tolstoy still could not think of any means of helping the Doukhobors. On 12 March 1896 he wrote to M. A. Schmidt: "After all, the crux of it is that there is nothing we can do, there is no way we can help these sufferers" (#1896-03-24).

Tolstoy was by no means shying away from the topic. Though the references are rare (#1895-10-17a, #1895-12-30a), they still figured in his correspondence — for example, in two letters penned in February 1896 to Chertkov (#1896-02-25) and John Kenworthy (#1896-03-10a) — certainly in the context of the overall sectarian movement in Russia (cf. #1896-03-05, #1896-03-10b). He is indeed delighted at his friends' attempts to become better acquainted with the Doukhobors. To Evgenij Ivanovich Popov's query in March 1896 as to whether to agree to Verigin's proposal to go to the Caucasus, he responds: "I cannot give any advice, but I can't help saying that I would be very much delighted at such a proposal" (#1896-03-27). A few days later he admits to Khilkov: "Many things in life concern me and seem to call for my participation — above all, the Doukhobor cause" (#1896-04-01), at the same time encouraging his followers to take up the cause not just for the Doukhobors' benefit but for their own as well (#1896-04-01).

As the year 1896 advanced, however, Tolstoy gradually became more and more directly involved in Doukhobor affairs. At the end of October, for example, he wrote a letter to the head of the disciplinary battalion (#1896-11-12a; see also his letter about this to Chertkov, #1896-11-14), which back in March he had refused to do, in spite of Schmidt's request (#1896-03-24) — basing his plea for clemency toward the Doukhobors on ethical and moral concerns. While it is hardly possible to fully reconstruct the change in his thinking process between these two letters, some hint can be gained from his laconic remark in a May 1896 letter to A. A. Shkarvan (#1896-05-14): "In spite of the persecutions and their consequences, our Doukhobors just keep on growing in spirit."

It was in the summer of 1896, according to the correspondence chronology, that Tolstoy made his first appeal for financial aid to the Doukhobors, in a letter of 30 July to V. A. Morozova (#1896-08-11). At the same time he expressed concern over how information on the persecution should be brought to the public's attention — compare this with his polemic with Khilkov in a letter written in the summer of 1896 (#1896-08-15). Still, this and other letters (e.g., #1896-11-12b) point to his deep conviction that nothing short of persecution was really capable of advancing the Doukhobors' quest for spiritual development.[7] Indeed, his chief motivating factor throughout this period was always his sympathy for the persecuted and his desire to help them as best he could. In contrast to many other sympathizers, including even those who were fairly close to him, this, rather than attacking the persecutors, was Tolstoy's priority.

On the other hand, it is evident right from the start that the Doukhobors meant something more to Tolstoy than simply people needing sympathy and assistance. He was able to discern in them the concrete embodiment of his ideals of earthly life. However, experienced realist that he was, not given to excessive excitement or hasty conclusions, he was in no hurry to accept his initial impressions as final. He felt the need, one might say, to put these Doukhobors to the test. But anyone who dared take such a task upon one's self, especially someone like Tolstoy, needed significant grounds to do so.

By the time Pavel Birjukov, Ivan Tregubov and Vladimir Chertkov had drafted their *Help!* appeal, Tolstoy was ready to play an active role in publicizing the Doukhobors' plight — see his letters to Chertkov (#1895-12-13) and Tregubov (#1896-11-29). And even though he might not have erased all doubts in his mind about what help he could really be to the cause, he actively pursued this interest all through 1897 (see #1897-01-23), even at some personal risk. In a letter of 18 May 1897, for example, he implored A. S. Suvorin, the editor of *Novoe vremja,* to publish Paul Boulanger's article about the plight of the Caucasus Doukhobors (#1897-05-30a). While the article in question had already appeared in *Russkie vedomosti* — on 20 March 1897 [1 April], *Novoe vremja* declined Tolstoy's request. It should be emphasized again, however, that Tolstoy' s primary interest was in alleviating suffering rather than taking countermeasures against those responsible — this is most evident in his

7 It should be pointed out that in writing about sectarians and their refusal of military service, Tolstoy does not always mention the Doukhobors by name (see, e.g., #1896-11-24).

letters written in 1897 and 1898 to Sokrat Byrdin (#1897-03-02), Paul Boulanger (#1897-03-06a, #1898-06-03), and Birjukov (#1898-05-02, #1898-05-13).

At one point, in fact, Tolstoy even felt the need of justifying his participation in the appeal — specifically, in his letter to P. N. Gastev of 26 February 1897 (#1897-03-10). This might explain his motivation behind a warning to Tregubov on 26–28(?) February 1897 (after announcing his intention to work more actively in the cause against persecutions): "Don't look for sufferings or persecutions — I know that temptation. It is not good because it encourages a poor attitude toward people" (#1897-03-12).

Here is the crux of all Tolstoy's doubts in a nutshell. In his October 1895 letter to Bodjanskij (#1895-10-14), cited earlier, Tolstoy had spoken confidently and at length about the value of persecution for Christians. Now he also saw possible negative consequences of persecution for the souls of the persecuted. It does not mean simply that Tolstoy had had less sympathy for the Doukhobors earlier, when he did not know them as well, and more sympathy for them once he got to know and love them. Nor does it mean that he suddenly started seeing the persecution simply as a contributing factor in the hardening of the victims' attitudes. No, it means Tolstoy was obliged to thoroughly re-examine his fundamental views on life, and this was not an easy task for him. Even as he was helping work out the practical arrangements for the Doukhobors' resettlement in Canada, he confessed to Birjukov in a letter of 18 September 1898 (#1898-09-30a): "Sometimes I think that this emigration is a weakness and a sin."[8] It may well be that his February 1897 letters to Gastev and Tregubov mark the turning point of Tolstoy's changing attitude toward the Doukhobor emigration.

Tolstoy was constantly giving heed to the effectiveness and consequences of proposed actions. Even after deciding that a broad information campaign was necessary, he confided in his letter to Gastev (#1897-03-10) his lingering doubts about the wisdom of collecting funds for the Doukhobors, and on 2 March 1897 confessed to Eugen Schmitt (#1897-03-14) that "I don't put any stock in subscriptions and financial aid."

This whole waiting period, characterized by an ambivalent attitude betokening his ongoing mental searchings, continued for several months. Finally, on 13 August 1897, he wrote Birjukov: "Let's try not to forget, let's try to feel their sufferings and try to help them. How, I don't know yet, but I hope life will show us" (#1897-08-25a). But there was never any question of his underlying attraction to them. In letters of 17 December 1896 (#1896-12-29) and 30 May 1897 (#1897-06-11a) he told how busy he was with the Doukhobor cause.

Beginning in early 1897, references to specific issues begin cropping up in the correspondence — for example, collections of funds (#1897-03-30, #1897-07-28a, #1897-08-27, #1897-10-08, #1898-03-09b), the Doukhobors exiled

8 Later, in January 1900 (#1900-01-19), he would advise the Pavlovka Stundists *not* to follow the Doukhobors' example of emigration to Canada.

to Siberia (#1897-03-06b, #1897-04-08, #1897-07-02a, #1897-07-02c, #1898-01-12), the notion of nominating the Doukhobors for the Nobel Peace Prize (#1897-09-15, #1897-09-24, #1897-10-05) — and his appeals to the Doukhobors themselves grow more frequent (#1896-11-12b, #1897-07-02b, #1897-07-28b, #1897-09-02, #1898-01-06). He shows a more positive attitude toward the Doukhobors (e.g., #1897-01-18, #1897-08-25b, #1897-09-02, #1897-10-29). At the end of a letter written 13 August 1897 (#1897-08-25b) he expresses his joy over increasing world interest in the doctrine of non-violence, adding, "The Doukhobor situation, unfortunately, remains unchanged, but all the sufferings they have endured have not, so far, shaken their resolve." That little phrase "so far" is significant, in light of his earlier doubts. A few months later, in a letter of 17 October, he states more confidently: "[T]here is no need to worry about people like the Doukhobors" (#1897-10-29).

As may be seen from later correspondence, this marked the beginning of a relatively brief in-between period, after the old doubts had been resolved and before new grounds for a more negative view appeared. It was a period when Tolstoy looked upon the Doukhobors with a great deal of admiration and idealization. Perhaps the idealization was only natural, directed as it was toward a people he initially doubted, then found faith in and devoted his energies to helping.

It was at this period that the question of emigration reappeared, almost unexpectedly, and before long took the forefront. In a letter to J. Gibson of 9 March 1898 (#1898-03-21), Tolstoy referred to the Doukhobors' plan to "set out for England or America" as a *fait accompli*,[9] and thereupon plunged himself headlong into the business of organizing their emigration. This endeavour involved several specific tasks (as defined by Tolstoy himself): selection of a location for resettlement, collection of funds, and organizing the actual resettlement process (#1898-03-29a, #1898-03-31b).

And here, on the surface at least, a paradox presents itself. At the very moment when Tolstoy was the most confident in the Doukhobors' spiritual resources, he accepted not just the possibility but the inevitability of their emigration to a less troubled part of the world. Yet we have noted the complexity of his reflections and the different directions his thought could be taking simultaneously. On the one hand, the Doukhobors had indeed turned out to be a people whose capacity and readiness to endure suffering he could no longer doubt. On the other hand, his whole attitude toward the nature of suffering itself had undergone a sea change: he now saw suffering as a "temptation" — something that could adversely affect the Doukhobors in their progress from materialism to spirituality.

The first question, naturally, was where the Doukhobors should go. In an open letter to the sect of 19 March 1898 (#1898-03-31c), Tolstoy suggested four

9 This is echoed in several other letters of this period; e.g., #1898-03-20, #1898-03-30.

possibilities: the American state of Texas, Cyprus (still a British dominion at the time), Chinese Manchuria, or Chinese Turkestan. The second alternative was raised by Chertkov, the latter two by Prince Èsper Ukhtomskij (cf. #1898-03-29c).

Tolstoy at first favoured the Manchuria option (#1898-03-31c, #1898-04-10b, #1898-04-10c) in view of its proximity to the Chinese Eastern Railway (known by its Russian acronym KVZhD) line, which was under construction at the time. At the same time, through a friend, he sent an enquiry to Texas, to which he refers in a letter to Chertkov of 29 March 1898 (#1898-04-10c).[10] The same day, he wrote Paul Boulanger that "the Doukhobor cause has entered a new phase and is demanding our complete attention" (#1898-04-10a).

A few days earlier, on 26 March [7 April], Ukhtomskij had approached the Russian Minister of Foreign Affairs proposing Mongolia, but this was eventually turned down (cf. #1898-04-10b). As the search continued over the next several months, new possibilities were proposed, including Serbia and Turkey (which he rejected) and Hawaii (which he rather favoured).[11]

By August 1898, after receiving reports of the Doukhobor delegation's visit to Western Canada (#1898-08-29b), which included Khilkov and Tolstoy's English translator Aylmer Maude, as well as of James Mavor's[12] enquiries with the Canadian government (#1898-08-24b), Tolstoy was convinced that Canada was the most logical choice. The Russian government's approval of this destination was confirmed by Tolstoy in his letters to Birjukov and Sulerzhitskij of 30 September 1898 (#1898-10-12c, #1898-10-12d). But by this time, one boatload of 1,126 Doukhobors had already embarked for Cyprus (only to be obliged to continue on to Canada the following spring).[13]

Next arose the inevitable question of financing. Tolstoy had raised the matter of collecting funds for the Doukhobors the previous year — in his letters to K. T. Soldatenkov (#1897-08-27) and A. N. Dunaev (#1897-10-08), for example — but had not followed through. Now he obtained a list of wealthy potential donors from Dunaev (#1898-07-28) and started sending out personal appeals to the names on the list (##1898-08-17a–e, ##1898-09-29d–e, ##1898-09-30c–1898-10-12b, ##1898-10-18a–c and ##1898-10-24a–c). Even more significant was his letter to his publisher, Aleksej Suvorin, of 12 October 1898, in which Tolstoy declared his readiness to accept some royalties from

10 See also his letter to the Doukhobors of 19 March 1898 (#1898-03-31c).

11 See, e.g., his letter to Sulerzhitskij of 20 October 1898 (#1898-11-10a). For further information, see Klioutchanski 2000.

12 Mavor, a University of Toronto professor, was in contact with Prince Pëtr Kropotkin, a Tolstoyan who had spent some time in Canada. On 12 August 1898, Tolstoy wrote Chertkov that if Cyprus did not prove suitable for the Doukhobors, they should probably take up Mavor's proposal and move en masse to Canada (#1898-08-24b). Mavor also had correspondence with Sofia Andreevna Tolstaya. See also Ewashen 2001b.

13 Cf. Note 3 (*PSS* 71:424) to Tolstoy's letter of August 1898.

his new novel, *Resurrection*, to help finance the Doukhobors' emigration (#1898-10-24d).[14]

Tolstoy involved himself in all the minutiæ of the emigration process (see, e.g., #1898-07-25b, #1898-08-24a), especially the selection of escorts. This was no ordinary detail. It was not simply a question of finding a large number of his followers to help in the move. His aim, rather, was to put together a 'team' of a select few he knew he could count on. The importance he attached to the selection process may be seen in excerpts from his letters, for example, to V. F. Orlov of 17(?) September 1898: "[I]t is very difficult for people of our world to be helpful to the Doukhobors. I for one could only benefit from any kind of spiritual good they exude" (#1898-09-29b), and to Chertkov of 12 December:

> I am shocked by the number of people trying to join up with the Doukhobors. People want to dry out in their presence. But they do so at the expense of providing needed moisture to the Doukhobors. Will they somehow survive this onslaught? Still, it is apparent that so it must be. Everybody has to live and help each other. (#1898-12-24c)

Of special significance, as will be shown later in some detail, is the participation of the writer's son, Sergej L'vovich Tolstoy, with whom he could be especially frank and whose perceptions and observations he had high regard for.[15] The day after leaving the Black Sea port of Batoum on the *Lake Superior* on 24 December 1898, Sergej L'vovich wrote a letter to his father expressing his own doubts about the emigration and the wisdom of assisting the Doukhobors.[16] A few weeks later, however, while Sergej was still with the Doukhobors in Canada, his father wrote him on 15 February, referring to British Tolstoyan Arthur St. John: "I think that our brother's involvement with them will be helpful (it could very well be harmful) in that their own principles are becoming better clarified" (#1899-02-27f).

Sergej L'vovich was one of two people entrusted by Tolstoy with the task of rounding up the first emigrating Doukhobor parties in the Russian Caucasus and escorting them to Canada (his role will be described in greater detail later in this chapter). The other was Moscow Art Theatre actor Leopold Sulerzhitskij, whose own refusal of military service on religious grounds in 1895 had already brought him into conflict with the authorities (see Tolstoy's

14 Initially, Tolstoy was ready to devote all royalties, not only from *Resurrection* but also from *Father Sergius* [*Otets Sergij*] to the Doukhobor cause (see #1898-07-28), but later limited it to 'first-publication' royalties from *Resurrection*.

15 See, e.g., Tolstoy's letters to his son of 17(?) September 1898 (#1898-09-29a) and 4 January 1899 (#1899-01-16). Tolstoy also refers to his son's mission to the Caucasus in a letter to Ukhtomskij of 12 November 1898 (#1898-11-24).

16 Sergej L'vovich's letter is reproduced in English translation in Donskov (1998a: 355), as well as in the present volume (Letter N° 10 in Part IV). Sergej L'vovich's doubts were later resolved (see Donskov 1998a).

letter to E. I. Popov of 30 November 1895 [#1895-12-12]),[17] and Tolstoy was repeatedly obliged to write to Prince Grigorij Golitsyn, chief of civil affairs in the Caucasus, to plead for permission for Sulerzhitskij to carry out his appointed task.[18]

There were other difficulties, too. There were financial disagreements with Chertkov[19] and Maude refused to translate *Resurrection* because the proceeds were tied to the Doukhobor cause.[20] In the meantime, Tolstoy complained about the lack of unity among those offering assistance.[21]

Events, nevertheless, moved ahead. On 5 December, Tolstoy let Khilkov know about the finalization of plans for the eventual resettlement of the Doukhobors in Canada (#1898-12-17e), and, on the same day, as the first ship was preparing to set sail, Tolstoy confided to Maude that "for the most part, we're over the summit and it's all downhill from here on in" (#1898-12-17f). In early January, Tolstoy happily informed Birjukov that departures from Batoum had begun (#1899-01-12).

But it was far from over yet. There was still the matter of the 1,100-plus Doukhobors on Cyprus, who were not thriving. On 24 January, Tolstoy wrote Birjukov: "I want to help the Cyprus people, but to date I don't see any possibility" (#1899-02-05a). While Tolstoy had already decided to allot certain royalties from *Resurrection* to help the Doukhobors, Maude's refusal to undertake the translation (#1899-01-24b) was still a problem. The upshot was that the whole process, which had occupied a great deal of Tolstoy's time and thought for the latter half of 1898,[22] dragged on for two or three more years, well after the actual resettlement had taken place.

In the meantime, we learn from his continuing correspondence that Tolstoy's own attitude to the Doukhobors was undergoing yet another change. The enthusiastic confidence which had replaced his earlier doubts was now giving way in turn to a more objective evaluation — he was now expressing his concern over the absence of "shadows" in the more or less black-and-white descriptions he had read of them. In a letter of 15 February 1899 to Arthur St. John, who was then looking after the party of Doukhobors on Cyprus, he wrote, "It is strange to say, but I was happy to learn of the Doukhobors' failings. In the portrait people draw of them there are no shadows, and so they don't seem alive" (#1899-02-27d). He further elaborated this theme in a

17 Cf. also his letter to his son Lev L'vovich of 18 December 1895 (#1895-12-30a). After his 1895 arrest, Sulerzhitskij was later persuaded to join the army after a temporary incarceration in an insane asylum. This incident may have contributed in part to Tolstoy's writing of *I svet vo t'me svetit* [*And the Light Shineth in Darkness*].

18 See, e.g., #1898-07-26a, #1898-08-19, #1898-11-20.

19 See Tolstoy's letters to Chertkov written in October and November 1898 (#1898-10-27, #1898-10-28d, #1898-11-01b, #1898-11-10b, #1898-11-12).

20 See Tolstoy's letter to Maude of 12 January 1899 (#1899-01-24b.)

21 See, e.g., his letter to M. L. Obolenskaja of 26(?) February 1899 (#1899-03-11).

22 Tolstoy admitted as much in his letter to A. Järnefelt of 16 December 1898 (#1898-12-28b)

letter to Sergej L'vovich the same day (#1899-02-27f). In contrast to his earlier expressed confidence that here was a people one need have no concern about (see #1897-10-29), it had finally dawned on him that they were vulnerable human beings after all.

It is very likely that his earlier pronouncements, however, had been sincere — for example, when he wrote to them on 21 August 1897: "[Y]ou are the first to set an example of walking in Christ's path" (#1897-09-02), or even earlier, in January 1897, in his letter to Tregubov, calling the Doukhobors "a model of non-violent structure and government which the enemies of Christianity accuse us of lacking" (#1897-01-18). Yet eight years later, on 26 October 1905, he would write to the very same Tregubov: "We know too little about the Doukhobors, and they can hardly serve as a model for Christian life" (#1905-11-08). The intervening years of alternate stages of doubt, enthusiastic confidence, and disenchantment evidenced two of Tolstoy's remarkable characteristics: his capacity to cease from an earlier idealization and his ability to reconcile himself with people who did not measure up to an anticipated ideal.

Tolstoy had good reason to be concerned about people wishing simply to "dry out" in the Doukhobors' presence. At first he was delighted by all the attention being paid to them and his friends' desire to join their cause — see his letters along this line to Popov in March 1896 (#1896-0327),[23] Tregubov in March 1898 (#1898-04-01), and Bodjanskij in September 1898 (#1898-09-21).

In a letter to foreign newspapers of 19 March 1898 (#1898-03-31) he even offered to act as an intermediary for those wishing to help. In contrast, by the end of 1898 he had begun discouraging such contact; his negative advice to V. I. Skorokhodov of 11 December 1898 (#1898-12-23) was only the first of many such dissuasions. To the Pavlovka Stundists, in particular, he wrote a letter, in January 1900 (#1900-01-19), advising them *not* to go join the Doukhobors in Canada, and four years later, in a letter to Ivan Matveevich Sergeev of 22 January 1904 (#1904-02-04), offered similar advice to Doukhobor exiles in the Irkutsk area.[24] It is evident, moreover, that this particular brand of

23 In this letter to Popov (quoted earlier in the chapter), Tolstoy further advised caution on the question of accepting Verigin's proposal to visit the Doukhobors in the Caucasus: "I feel a difference between us and them — something that causes divisions that we both tend to cover up in our cherishing of our mutual affection and our fear of rupturing it. But there is a falsity in this cover-up. And this falsity, if it exists, must be destroyed.... And if [it tums out that] there is nothing dividing us, or what there is can be easily smoothed out and explained, then the more will be our joy. The question is: How do you feel in the depths of your heart? — and give yourself a good questioning on this point. If you feel yourself fully ready and joyful about going there, then go, but if there is any doubt or hesitation, then hold back."

24 To Russians who wrote enquiring about helping the Doukhobors in Canada, Tolstoy would supply the appropriate Canadian address, but would unfailingly discourage them from going — e.g.: #1905-02-25 (P. P. Rajskij, February 1905), #1906-02-13 (Pavel Molchanov, late January 1906), #1907-07-20 (P. A. Kuznetsov, July 1907), #1908-02-11 (A. I. Bejlin, late January 1908), #1909-01-27 (P. V. Jablonskij-Sokolovskij, January 1909), #1910-09-26 (M. Egoshin, September 1910).

'heroism' was beginning to annoy Tolstoy. He began responding to such letters more and more often through his secretaries (in later years, of course, this was necessitated by his increasingly constant fatigue).

It is hardly likely that Tolstoy was simply concerned about foreign influences on the Doukhobors. He realized that neither they nor any other role model could substitute for an individual's own inner moral struggles. Virtually all his responses in this direction were along the lines of these excerpts from two letters of early 1909: "[T]he improvement of one's life takes place all by itself and no change of place is needed for this to happen" (#1909-02-11, to P. E. Eremeev); "Changing external conditions is a fruitless waste of one's energies, which should be directed at inner mental toil" (#1909-05-07, to P. V. Jablonskij-Sokolovskij).

Tolstoy became more and more persuaded that such toil was needed by the Doukhobors themselves. He would occasionally receive news from Canada that disturbed and annoyed him, as, for example, the "illusory temptation of private property" they were exposed to,[25] or a plan to resettle the Doukhobors from Canada to the American state of California, which he warned against in his letter to the émigrés of 7 March 1900 (#1900-03-20a).[26] His comments on the sect grew less and less optimistic — note his letter to Verigin's son-in-law Ivan Konkin of 24 February 1901: "I fear they are becoming rich only in terms of material sufficiency, and are growing spiritually poor. There are few who are strong in spirit left among them, and the temptations are many" (#1901-03-09). His letter to the Canadian Doukhobors themselves, of 30 May 1901, put it somewhat more gently: "If only we don't close our eyes to our sins and don't stop trying to make ourselves at least a little better, wiser and more loving, everything will be all right in our lives, both here and beyond the grave" (#1901-06-12).

It should be emphasized that this did not mean Tolstoy was still casting doubt on the emigration itself. At the time of the move, he responded to the doubts experienced by his son Sergej L'vovich by writing him, in January 1899, "I do share your fears and doubts, but not in regard to Canada" (#1899-01-16).[27] And in spite of his general discouraging of others to follow them, he did make efforts to facilitate the release of the remaining Doukhobors from Siberian exile so that they could join their brethren in Canada (see #1900-11-18 to P. N. Sokol'nikov, #1903-11-06c to Grand Prince Nikolaj Mikhajlovich, #1904-01-15c to Prince Grigorij Golitsyn) and offered financial assistance to those that remained (#1904-06-14a to P. Orlov and S. Usachëv).

But Tolstoy still could not close his eyes to the danger of the persecutions, nor indeed to the subtle inclinations of some sectarians to give into the

25 As described in his letter to Chertkov of 2 January 1900 (#1900-01-14).

26 See also his letter to Chertkov of the same date (#1900-03-20b).

27 Response to Sergej L'vovich's letter of 24 December 1898 [5 January 1899], reproduced in Part IV (Letter N° 10); cf. Note 16 above.

'temptation' of achieving martyr status in their own and others' eyes, against which he had warned Tregubov in a letter back at the end of February 1897 (#1897-03-12). In a letter to Evgenij Ivanovich Popov in Canada, written in the summer of 1908 (#1908-07-08), he took care to advise the sect members not to judge each other on the basis of ritual observances.

Nor does it mean that Tolstoy felt any less warmly toward the Doukhobors. This was not the motivation behind his remark to the Maudes, in March 1901, that the Doukhobors were now self-sufficient and needed no further financial support (#1901-03-21, #1901-04-04). It is more likely that he simply felt the time had come for them to make their own way in life. This might also explain his blunt discouragements addressed to the would-be Doukhobor helpers noted above. The wisdom of this position may be seen in his argument with Chertkov over whether the Doukhobors should compromise with the Canadian government over the demand to register individual landholdings as well as births and deaths in their communities: Tolstoy, unlike Chertkov, favoured a more flexible approach in this case.[28]

On the matter of the radical Sons of Freedom Doukhobors, who turned their cattle loose and set out on a 'pilgrimage trek' (later to be returned home under Royal Canadian Mounted Police [RCMP] escort after a meeting with the newly-arrived Verigin), Tolstoy wrote to Tregubov on 20 August 1902 (#1902-09-02):

> You ask my opinion about the Doukhobors' actions. The feeling I had while thinking about this is similar to what I would feel if I saw someone climbing up a mountain I was going to climb myself — who had already climbed up high and grasped hold of an overhang or branch, which either could be used to push him even higher or could break off and cause him to fall to the bottom. I'm afraid for him, but I can't say anything to him, since I don't know his strength, but I'm delighted by the fact that he is attempting it.

The breadth of Tolstoy's epistolary exchanges on the Doukhobor question deserves particular mention. His correspondents ranged from persecuted Doukhobors to government officials responsible for the persecutions, from his own friends and followers to wealthy landowners of the noble classes, from exiled political prisoners to the tsar himself. And it must not be forgotten that his 500 or so letters on the Doukhobors constituted but a tiny fraction of the vast range of Tolstoy's overall correspondence during these years.

Equally broad were the horizons (as revealed through his correspondence on the Doukhobors) of Tolstoy's benevolent yet objective outlook on the world as a whole, which enabled him to see this remarkable group of people from more than one point of view — both as representatives of Russian

28 See his letter to Canadian Doukhobors V. Potapov and I. Ponomarëv of 18 January 1901 (#1901-01-31), as well as his letter to Chertkov of 22 April 1902 (#1902-05-05).

sectarians and as ambassadors of a growing international antiwar movement, both as victims of persecution in need of financial help and victims of their own temptations in need of spiritual advice, both as an ideal embodiment of his own dearly held philosophies and as human beings who, like everyone else, did not always measure up to this ideal.

SERGEJ L'VOVICH TOLSTOY

Tolstoy's eldest son, Sergej L'vovich, played an active role in the Doukhobors' actual journey to Canada, escorting one of the four boatloads that would take some 7,500 Doukhobors, with Tolstoy's support and blessing, to the New World, to Canada — witness the following accounts.[29]

1. On 22 December (10 December OS) 1898 the SS *Lake Huron* left the port of Batoum on the Black Sea for Canada with 2,140 exiled Doukhobors aboard. After encountering fierce storms en route, it finally arrived just outside Halifax, Nova Scotia, a month later, on 20 January 1899. Ten people died during the crossing, and one was born. After a quarantine inspection at Lawlor's Island, Halifax Harbour, the ship proceeded to Saint John, New Brunswick, where seven trains were waiting to take the new immigrants to the Canadian prairies.
2. On 4 January 1899 (10 December 1898 OS) the *SS Lake Superior* left Batoum bound for Canada with approximately 2,300 Doukhobors on board (some 1,600 of them from Elizavetpol' and the remainder from Kars). This crossing took only twenty-three days, but it was followed by a twenty-seven-day quarantine on Lawlor's Island because of a case of smallpox on board. Six people had died en route.
3. On 18 April 1899 the *Lake Superior* picked up just over a thousand Kars Doukhobors from Larnaca, Cyprus, where they had made an unsuccessful attempt to settle. This time there was one death and one birth during the voyage, which ended 9 May in Quebec City.
4. At the beginning of May 1899 the *Lake Huron* made one additional voyage, crossing from Batoum to Quebec with 2,286 Doukhobors aboard. Four people died en route and, again, an outbreak of smallpox meant almost a month's quarantine, this time on Grosse-Île in the Gulf of St. Lawrence, before the immigrants could leave for the west.

Behind these dry, journalistic accounts lies one of the truly significant episodes in the history of both Russia and Canada — a mass exodus from the Old World at the turn of the century, and resettlement in the New, involving some 7,000 people.

29 These accounts, along with parts of the subsequent text of this chapter, are drawn from my introduction to *Sergej Tolstoy and the Doukhobors: A Journey to Canada* (Donskov 1998a: 1–23).

After an accord was reached with the Canadian government, on 5 October 1898, accepting the Doukhobors as immigrants, Tolstoy (as indicated above) asked a family friend, Leopol'd Sulerzhitskij, to accompany the first boatload of Doukhobors to Canada.[30] The second boatload he entrusted to his own eldest son, Sergej L'vovich Tolstoy.[31]

Thus it was that Sergej L'vovich sailed from Batoum on 4 January 1899 aboard the *SS Lake Superior*, accompanying more than 2,000 Doukhobors to their promised new land, to fulfil their hopes for a new life, unencumbered by the surveillance, persecution, and indignity of the past. Sergej L'vovich kept a detailed diary of his journey. In addition to its primary purpose of recording events and impressions, this unique narrative presents tangible evidence of the involvement of Tolstoy's family in the Doukhobor cause. It comprises an objective, judicious description of the Doukhobors' plight — a perception that is indeed confirmed by a closer study of the text. Whether this is due to his highly specialized technical background or to his natural sense of impartiality, Sergej L'vovich's account constitutes a measured — and therefore all the more significant — portrayal of these people. He seems to walk a middle line between the customary idealization of the Doukhobors by their supporters on the one hand and outright censure from their critics on the other, between his father's often unequivocal praise for the sect and their official condemnation by the Russian church and state.

The diary, which takes the reader from "Resolving questions of emigration" through the transatlantic crossing described in "At sea" to the "Visit to homestead sites" in Canada, portrays the daily events of the journey as they occurred, but also includes material subsequently added from the perspective of hindsight. A historical introduction was added to take account of the considerable period of time elapsed between the completion of the journey at the

30 Sulerzhitskij also accompanied the third party in April. The fourth boatload was escorted by Vladimir Bonch-Bruevich (1873–1955) and Dr. Vera Mikhajlovna Velichkina (1868–1918), who would later become Bonch-Bruevich's wife.

31 Sergej L'vovich Tolstoy (1863–1947) spent the early part of his life at Yasnaya Polyana, where he was home-schooled by his parents. He showed an above-average aptitude for music, which he was later able to explore during his student days in Moscow. By 1886 he had completed a candidate's degree (equivalent to a PhD) in chemistry at Moscow University, and he was fluent in English, French, and German. In the early 1890s he was involved in municipal politics in the Chern district of Tula Gubernia, where his personal estate (Nikol'skoeVjazemskoe) was located. An unhappy marriage to Marija Konstantinovna Rachinskaja (daughter of the director of an agricultural academy near Moscow) ended with his wife's untimely passing in 1900, but not before the birth of their son, Sergej Sergeevich. His second marriage, in 1906 to Countess Marija Nikolaevna Zubovaja, was happier, though it produced no offspring. Following his father's death in 1910, Sergej L'vovich took an active part in organizing the Tolstoy Museum in Moscow and later became one of the editors of the Jubilee Edition of Tolstoy's complete works, launched in 1928. He was honoured by the Soviet government on the occasion of his eightieth birthday, in July 1943.

end of the century and the publication of the diary in 1949.[32] Sergej L'vovich's meticulous preparation of the manuscript, with its many corrections and revisions, shows the care he took to achieve factual and stylistic accuracy.

In many respects Sergej L'vovich's account is a broad panorama (often found in literature on travel), focusing not only on the Doukhobors but also on the writer's total experience. He describes Russian government officials, shipping clerks, and the British consular representative in Batoum, along with many features that would simply not have come to the attention of the Doukhobors themselves: his brief but sensitive feelings of nature, his first visit to a Canadian city (Halifax), his initial impressions of the Canadian prairies, and his encounters with various Canadians involved in the settlement process.

As far as his relationship with the Doukhobors is concerned, a reading of his diary and other pertinent materials gives one the impression that Sergej L'vovich never seems to think without feeling, nor to feel without thinking. The characters who fill his pages are neither ideal nor idealized, but his sincere interest in them is never in doubt. He is not judgemental, but rather lets the Doukhobors' stories tell themselves, seldom intruding with his personal commentary: witness the impressions left on the Doukhobors by the luxurious office of Prince Golitsyn, Vasilij Popov's farewell speech to the Batoum authorities, or his account of one Doukhobor man who abandoned his young wife who had taken ill.[33] In reporting the elders' complaint about some youths who helped themselves to extra potatoes, he acknowledges the legitimacy of the elders' point of view but hastens to add that "neither are the *starichki* [elders] altogether right" — they needed to bake more bread and potatoes to satisfy healthy young appetites.[34]

There are other examples where Sergej L'vovich shows his skill at understanding and bringing peace to a situation without belabouring the problem.

32 Only a small part of the diary was actually published at the time, and that posthumously; see "Moe uchastie v èmigratsii dukhoborov v Kanadu" [My participation in the Doukhobor's emigration to Canada] in S. L. Tolstoy 1949. The diary contrasts with Leopol'd Sulerzhitskij's 'fresher' account, published in 1905 by L. N. Tolstoy's Posrednik, entitled *V Ameriku s dukhobortsami* [To America with the Doukhobors], which begins *in medias res* (see Sulerzhitskij 1905). Sulerzhitskij was evidently identifying 'America' with the continent rather than with the nation of America. While there are naturally many factual correspondences between the two diaries, Sulerzhitskij's account includes more in the way of dialogue — Doukhobors talking to him and to each other — in contrast to Sergej L'vovich's more analytical, descriptive approach.

The decision to postpone the publication of his own diary may have been at least partly due to his desire to avoid competing with Sulerzhitskij. But Sergej L'vovich may have also been waiting to reach a later generation of readers whose own memories of the event from the news of the day might benefit from a fresh reminder. Such a hope was only fully realized in 1998 with the joint Russian-Canadian publication of the complete diary (Donskov 1998a).

33 See Sergej Tolstoy's diary in Donskov 1998a; entries for 15 [27] November 1898, 10 [22] December 1898, and 29 December 1898 [10 January 1899], respectively. The second of these entries is reproduced in the present volume (see p. 288). Unless otherwise noted, all subsequent references are to be found only in Donskov 1998a.

34 See entry for 9 [21] January 1899.

He also indicates that problem-solving in such a large group might have been much more difficult had he been dealing with someone other than the Doukhobors. He describes his fellow passengers aboard the *Lake Superior* as human beings rather than as sect members, and his descriptions frequently come across as laconic even where it seems that more compassion might have been called for (witness his description of the burial at sea, 9 [21] January 1899); however, this may very well have been a deliberate measure to avoid false sentimentality. There is very little mention of the Doukhobors' faith or doctrine; the diarist seems less interested in their ideas than in the human characteristics they embody.

The objectivity of Sergej L'vovich's account is further enhanced by his allowing others to voice their opinions (both positive and negative) of the sect. He tells us, for example, of *Kavkaz* [Caucasus] editor Jurij Miljutin's criticism of both the Doukhobors and the authorities, and of the sympathies for the group held by the wealthy Molokan Tret'jakov, who shared his lodgings with the Doukhobors in Batoum.[35] Other examples are Captain Taylor of the *Lake Superior*, who during the crossing grew to respect his Doukhobor passengers, and the Canadian doctors Jones and Montizambert, the first of whom reacted to the new immigrants critically to start, the other more tolerantly, during the difficult quarantine experience at Lawlor's Island.[36]

Another notable feature of the diary is that Sergej L'vovich himself is one of the characters in the saga (as, again, one often finds in travel literature). First there is the process of discovering the 'self': as the son of an aristocrat, Sergej L'vovich is well aware of both the historical and personal gulf that separates him from the peasants. But even more important is the symbolic mental journey, a search for ultimate meaning in life, his considerable doubt (at first) about the wisdom of the Doukhobors' emigration, and his own personal motivation in helping them in their quest for a new life in a new land. In the closing paragraph of his diary, the personal perspective (the 'I') is very prominent:[37]

> I am happy that I have spent almost six months with them and have come to know them. And not only do I not regret having participated in their emigration, but I am proud to have had a least a small part in bringing it about.

The chance to observe a unique group of people for so long and in so many different situations in the Caucasus, in their gathering at Batoum, in cramped conditions at sea, in a long and irritating quarantine, and in their final adaptation to the challenging new natural and cultural surroundings in a winter on the Canadian prairies was a rare opportunity indeed. Furthermore, the

35 See entries for 14 [26] November (see p. 279 below) and 11 [23] December 1898, respectively.

36 Entries of 24 January [5 February] 1899 and 4 [16] February 1899, respectively.

37 See "Conclusion" to Sergej Tolstoy's diary in Part III, p. 294.

exceedingly large group of emigrants under his charge was extremely diverse in their experience of persecution, their financial status, and degree of adherence to their religious principles in practice.

Sergej L'vovich responds to each situation on either a collective or an individual basis with the characteristic detachment of an observer. For example, in a letter to his father describing the Doukhobors waiting for their ship at Batoum, he describes their patience, their courtesy, and respect for each other.[38]

> The Doukhobors are indeed a special people: during the whole time of their trip and their stay here — and the first party has been here five days already — there has not been a single sharp word or complaint; everything is proceeding calmly and in an orderly fashion.

On occasion, his observations are reinforced with vivid descriptive images, especially in his entries while crossing the Atlantic, when amid unavoidably poor sanitary conditions and cramped quarters, amid sickness, pain, and death, Sergej L'vovich suffered with them. During the above-mentioned burial at sea, the writer did not let his observer's impartiality keep him from conveying the pleas of family members to lower the body slowly into the sea in place of the unceremonious dumping from a plank, and the jarring interruption of the Doukhobors' psalm singing by a young boy's cry of alarm: "They've tossed her into the sea!"[39] But there are also more joyous pictures, as when, for example, both old and young rushed out on deck to marvel at a passing school of dolphins.[40]

On occasion, too, the serious tone of Sergej L'vovich's diary is interrupted by a humorous illustration, as in the story of the young Doukhobor male facing conscription who managed to board ship dressed as a girl who had recently died, and so evade the authorities;[41] the contradictory views of making *kvas* (a fermented beverage made from rye bread) on the ship (the Doukhobors claimed it improved their digestion, while the English captain considered 'that damned stuff' a danger to the health of his crew and personally saw to its removal);[42] or the amazement of the *angliki* (as the Doukhobors' referred to English-Canadians) at the Doukhobors' resourcefulness in building their own Russian *banja* [bath house],[43] returned only by the Doukhobors' own astonishment at the Canadians' pioneering skills in setting up plain canvas tents in -20 degrees Celsius conditions, and insulating them with snow,[44] and

38 See entry of 3 [15] December 1898 (see p. 281).
39 Entry of 9 [21] January 1899.
40 See entry of 1 [13] January 1899.
41 See entry of 22 December 1898 [3 January 1899].
42 See entry of 10 [22] January 1899.
43 See entry of 5 [17] March 1899 (last paragraph).
44 See entry of 5 [17] March 1899 (third paragraph).

at an Indigenous man's success in lassoing a horse after his English-Canadian counterpart had failed in a similar attempt.[45]

One has the impression from reading his diary, his correspondence with others, and letters written about him that Sergej L'vovich Tolstoy was indeed a highly moral, kind, and responsible individual.

He seems to have possessed good organizational skills (in spite of his own repeated praise of Sulerzhitskij's superior abilities in this area), an excellent knowledge of the workings of the imperial government, and a firm resolve to carry out his decisions, as seen, for example, in his conduct with Golitsyn's assistant Justin Mitskevich and with the guard at Richner's,[46] as well as in his dealings with other officials in the Caucasus, with medical and ship's personnel during the quarantine, and with the immigration officials in Winnipeg (see his chapters 3, 5, and 7).

As indicated above, Sergej Tolstoy manifests a quality of objectivity in his writings; a seemingly innate quality, which must have been nurtured during his formative years at home and reinforced in his professional scientific pursuits.[47] He does not divide people according to their good or bad, seeing both as natural characteristics of humankind.

In a letter to his mother, for example, he describes Prince Dmitrij Khilkov as "not an altogether tactful person," yet as one who is "able to put things into the proper perspective, without getting distracted by details and trifles," and concludes that he (Sergej Tolstoy) "could not really take his place" in helping the Doukhobors in their resettlement in Canada.[48]

With respect to the Doukhobors themselves, Sergej L'vovich at times tempers his generally high opinion of them with descriptives like *medlitel'nyj* [sluggish], Although his perception may have been coloured by his acknowledged state of exhaustion during the crossing and the enormous weight of responsibility he felt for these people, to whom he was both a deliverer and a sounding board for their complaints. Like any other human being, he admitted to certain preferences; for example, he mentions several times in his diary and letters how he favoured the Kars Doukhobors over those from Elizavetpol', finding them more eager to help each other, to work and share in a collective structure.[49]

Sergej L'vovich's character should also be viewed against the background of his membership in the Russian nobility. No feelings of superiority over other people, no matter who they might be, are noticeable and, quite possibly, were simply not part of his nature — meaning he was an aristocrat in the true

45 See entry of 6 [18] March 1899 (third paragraph).

46 See entries of 15 [27] November and 20 November [2 December] 1898 (see p. 274).

47 Consult the Appendix for a selected list of Sergej Tolstoy's publications.

48 Letter of 23–24 February [7–8 March] 1899 (Letter N° 18 in Part IV).

49 See, e.g., his diary entry of 29 January [10 February 1899] and his letter to his sister of 3 [15] February 1899.

sense of the word. His sense of equality is evident not only in his dealings with the Doukhobors (with whom he obviously sympathized) but even more so in conflict situations, particularly with officials, over the course of the journey. It is not surprising that Sergej L'vovich did not feel at home, to say the least, with the self-conceit of Prince Golitsyn, whose conduct he found all the more distasteful given that they belonged to the same social class. It is not surprising that he found in the Doukhobors a condition of "indifference to the grandeur surrounding the prince."[50]

Nevertheless, Sergej Tolstoy, like his father, could not free himself entirely of the class consciousness of his birth and his upbringing. In the chapter "Visit to homestead sites," for example, he describes a barely livable hut, the residence of a certain Mrs. Harley, which to his amazement contained

> a decent piano along with the compositions of Chopin and Beethoven. Having been deprived of music since leaving Yasnaya Polyana, I took exceptional pleasure in having a go at this instrument.[51]

His residual class consciousness is further illustrated in the moving letter he wrote to his father from the *SS Lake Superior* en route to Canada:[52]

> Sitting in this cabin and knowing that for the next 22–25 days I shall not have contact with anyone in the outside world, I feel extremely lonely. The English on the one hand, and the Doukhobors on the other. I never can feel completely at home with the Doukhobors — they are too withdrawn into their community.

As though sympathizing with his son, Lev Nikolaevich Tolstoy insisted in his letter to his son of 15 February 1899 (#1899-02-27):

> On your return journey to Russia, when you are in New York make sure you go to see Crosby. I have already written to him about you. He is a very kind and serious person and *will open the doors for you to the New York literary circles.*[53]

Such revelations of Sergej L'vovich's underlying feelings must be balanced against his overall rejection of class distinctions. He repeatedly emphasizes the awkwardness he feels when these distinctions come to his attention — for example, when he is assigned a first-class cabin aboard the ship, while most of his fellow passengers, some of them sick and dying, are housed in cramped and uncomfortable quarters.[54]

50 Entry of 25 November [7 December] 1898 (see p. 278).
51 Entry of 3 [15] March 1899 (last paragraph).
52 Letter of 24–25 December 1898 [5–6 January 1899] (Letter N° 10 in Part IV).
53 *PSS* 92:72–74; italics added.
54 See, e.g., entries of 27 Dec. 1898 [8 Jan. 1899] and 8 [20] January 1899.

Sergej L'vovich further endears himself to the reader by his all-too-human fears and doubts, and, above all, by his honesty. In the above-mentioned 'confessional' letter to his father he calls into question his participation in the Doukhobor emigration. He begins by casting doubt on the wisdom of their move, on his ability to conduct it, on his possible ulterior motives for agreeing to participate (to help forget his troubled marriage, to please his father and thereby mitigate the recent tension between them, to attain a degree of purification through self-sacrifice).[55]

That Sergej L'vovich's relationship to the Doukhobors represented something far greater than personal self-gratification is quite clear in his correspondence with people involved in the emigration (government officials, Quakers, and especially Sulerzhitskij and Herbert Archer). Unfortunately, none of Sergej L'vovich's letters to Archer or the Khudjakov family have ever been discovered, but their letters to him reveal their profound respect and admiration for him. The Khudjakovs call him, endearingly, by the diminutives *Serëzha* and *Sergunja*. In an unpublished letter to Lev Tolstoy, written 20 February 1899, shortly after arriving in Canada, Savelij Khudjakov wrote the following (OR GMT):

> First of all we send you our gratitude for your love and compassion for us. May God save you for encouraging your son Sergej L'vovich to come with us; the help he gave we can never repay. May God send him all good. He did not rest during our whole crossing, he was all the time helping take care of everything, especially when the ship was rolling heavily; you see, our people don't have much experience, and because of this many of us left ourselves open to all sorts of sufferings.

Sergej L'vovich was concerned not only about the Doukhobors' physical well-being but also about their level of literacy and culture. Especially disturbed by their lack of access to Russian books in their new land, he took it upon himself, in December 1899, to order a number of books from a Moscow dealer (N. P. Karbasnikov) to be shipped to them in Canada, including one hundred copies each of the Russian New Testament and the Christian Gospels.

For many years after his return to Russia, Sergej L'vovich maintained his correspondence with the Doukhobors[56] and afforded assistance to those who

55 The elder Tolstoy was evidently moved by his son's 'confession.' In a return letter of 4 [16] January 1899 (#1899-01-16), he responded as follows (*PSS* 72:6–8): "I have just received your letter, Serëzha, of the 25th, sent from Constantinople. And I felt sorry for you, and afraid for you, and warmed by your relationship to me. I am weak when it comes to holding back tears, and began weeping.... The whole life of any individual is a constant loosening and untying of knots.... My advice: to every demand life presents to you respond according to the highest indications of your conscience.... You condemn yourself for having gone partly for my sake. But this is something precious to me, something which moves me to tears."

56 See, e.g., Nikolaj Khudjakov's letters to him in Donskov 1998a: 215–29; two of them are reproduced in English translation in the Part IV (see Letters N° 27 and N° 32).

remained in Yakutsk, frequently acting on their behalf in their dealings with the authorities.[57]

He also found himself defending the Doukhobors' decision to emigrate in the face of continued criticism. As late as 1904, Prince Èsper Ukhtomskij, writing from Canada, described the Doukhobors' living conditions as "repulsive," declaring that "their settlement in Canada is altogether a poor farce, an experiment with living beings who did not deserve to be cast overboard, as has happened."[58] Sergej L'vovich's strongly worded, emotional retort in defence of the emigration emphasized that the situation was quite the opposite: the Doukhobors were prospering financially in Canada, much more so than they would have had they stayed in the Caucasus. He suggested that the Russian government "was afraid that the Doukhobors remaining in Russia would mount a campaign to go to America, and at one time the government prohibited any publication of anything from Canada it judged disadvantageous to itself," and that rumours to the contrary were fostered by "radicals and revolutionaries" who were "unhappy to see the departure from this part of Russia by what they considered to be a revolutionary element."[59]

SOFIA ANDREEVNA TOLSTAYA

Direct written comments on the Doukhobors by Leo Tolstoy's wife, Sofia Andreevna Tolstaya, are limited to some dozen pages, though many more references may be found scattered throughout her letters. Her concerns over the time and resources her husband devoted to their cause (at the expense of what she saw as more important work and family activity) were frequently exaggerated by critics (including those among the Doukhobors themselves) and associated with an image of a "coarse," "domineering," or "hysterical" woman, with no attempt to seek the reasons behind her often negative pronouncements in their regard. In contrast to such stereotypes (which persist even today[60]), Sofia Andreevna was a highly intelligent woman. In addition to her roles as a caring wife and exemplary mother of thirteen children, she also served as editor and publisher of a number of collections of her husband's works, as well as a translator and author (however modest) in her own right.

Her negative remarks on the Doukhobors may be attributed to her constant worry over her husband's health and the detrimental effect thereon, which she

57 See Sergej L'vovich's extensive correspondence with authorities in Russia, Britain, and Canada, along with various individuals in *Sergej Tolstoy and the Doukhobors: A Journey to Canada* (Donskov 1998a: 161–227); note especially his long letters written to family members describing the Doukhobors and their initial settlement in Canada (353–69). The Appendix to Donskov 1998a also includes a number of additional documents from his archive pertinent to the Tolstoy family's involvement in the Doukhobor cause.

58 See Letter N° 29 in Part IV.

59 See Letter N° 30 in Part IV.

60 Witness the negative image of Sofia Andreevna in Canadian Frank Moher's (1997) play *Tolstoy's Wife*, centred on her attitude to the Doukhobors and to her husband's involvement with them.

associated with his obsessive preoccupation with controversial issues — in this case, with a people whom she saw as rejecting their duty to defend their fatherland by arms if necessary, and bent on leaving it for somewhere else. She was particularly disturbed by her husband's frequent clandestine meetings with Tolstoyans and Doukhobors at the family estate, and the constant police surveillance of their lives which such contacts inevitably provoked.

In her diary (Tolstaja 1978) she noted, on 13 September 1898:

> I can't find any pity in my heart for people who refuse military service and thereby cause impoverished peasants to become soldiers in their place and at the same time demand a million roubles to take them out of Russia.

Incidentally, such opinion is shared even today by a number of critics of the Doukhobors in both Russia and Canada.

In the same 1898 diary entry she defended her stance by expressing her "sympathy for [Tolstoy's] efforts to help the famine victims in 1891 and 1892, and even today," further noting how she herself had "worked and assisted and given money." She continued:

> And now, if anyone is to be helped financially, it should be only the humble peasants who are dying of starvation, and not the proud Doukhobor revolutionaries.[61]

Another flashpoint for her annoyance was Tolstoy's decision to break his own longstanding rule and devote the royalties from his novel *Resurrection* to the Doukhobor emigration.[62] Her well-known dislike for this work was compounded by her antipathy toward its irreverent content — particularly its ridicule of the sacraments of the Russian Orthodox Church. In October 1895, not long after Tolstoy had become consciously aware of the Doukhobors and their plight, she stated (quite astutely) in a letter to her husband:

> I received your little letter[63] just before I left. It is brief, but again one that lets me feel the whole of you very close to me, and reachable, and kind, and understandable. Besides, I feel quite ashamed and sorry to tell you this, but for some reason I find joy in the fact that you have become disenchanted with your narrative.[64] I've felt all along that it was *contrived*, and that it did not well up from the depths of your heart and talent. It was something you *composed*, but did

61 For the full context of these quotes, see her 13 September 1898 diary entry in Part III.

62 In the early 1890s Tolstoy had declared that he would not accept royalties on any of his work published after 1880, and that all royalties on works published prior to that date would go to his wife and family; see also Note 14 above.

63 A letter dated 28 October 1895 (*PSS* 84:243).

64 In his letter of 28 October, Tolstoy wrote: "Today, the 28th, I did some good thinking, some writing, and finally abandoned the narrative I started. A wretched piece" (*PSS* 84:243). The work in question was an early draft of *Resurrection*, which he laid aside temporarily.

> not *live*. I would like something from you in which I can rejoice approvingly at every word of your piece, the way Akim delights in the confession and repentance of his son.[65]

In spite of her anxieties, she nonetheless continued to assist her husband in his work both on the Doukhobor cause and on the novel which their need for financial support prompted him to finish.[66] And her expressions of concern over her son Sergej's safety during his trip to Canada (see her letters to him reproduced here in Part IV) betray far more than a mother's worry over her son's physical well-being: they testify to a deeper understanding of the cause for which he has joined his own efforts to those of his father, a sense of pride in his accomplishments in this direction, an encouragement of his unwavering perseverance in continuing his efforts therein. Witness the following examples:

> Dear Serëzha. We have been reading and rereading your last letter from Batoum[67] many times. For the first time I felt a wrench in my heart and got very worried about you, even though the whole time I have been very understanding and sympathetic toward the cause you are currently involved in. (Letter [N° 11] of 27 December 1898])

> Dear Serëzha, the papers today [are reporting] that there is a huge storm in London, and we are all despairing for you and your fellow travellers. We too have been having a lot of storms all over and terrible winds, but no frost and almost no snow. Your letter is very bleak; I can imagine that things are pretty challenging, difficult and complicated for you. One comfort — no efforts and no labours are ever in vain, and they will always have their reward. I remember how Papa often doubted during the famine years[68] as to whether help was really needed, were they doing the right thing? But things turned out all right in the end, and everyone was left with splendid memories. (Letter [N° 12] of 5 [17] January 1899)

> At long last, dear Serëzha, we received a letter from you today. It took from the 17th of January to the 3rd of February to get here. Now a lot more time has gone by and the quarantine has probably ended. How unexpected and bothersome

65 This letter may be found in English as Letter N° 182 in Donskov 2017. *Akim* — a character in *The Power of Darkness*.

66 Witness her comment in her letter to her son Sergej of 23 January 1899 (Letter N° 14 in Part IV), which he received upon his arrival with the second boatload of Doukhobors in Canada, to the effect that her husband was "continuing to work zealously on *Resurrection* — the copying is being done for him by Aleksandr Petrovich [Ivanov], and Marusja, and Tanja, and me — we're all helping."

67 *Last letter from Batoum* — Sergej L'vovich sailed from Batoum on the *Lake Superior* on 10 December [22 December] 1898.

68 *The famine years* — The reference is to 1891–92, when Tolstoy helped organize a relief campaign for famine victims near Tolstoy's estate in Samara Gubernia. The entire family took an active part in alleviating the victims' plight.

> that was! You've gone through a lot of suffering this past while! And you don't write anything about your health. Still, there's a lot of interesting things — things that will never be erased from memory our whole lives and will be so pleasant to think back upon later, eh? (Letter [N° 16] of 3 [15] February 1899)

Finally, mention must be made of one more aspect of Sofia Andreevna's legacy of letters,[69] diaries, and reminiscences in regard to the Doukhobors — namely, their strong indication of the depth and significance, not only of Tolstoy's personal involvement in the Doukhobor cause but of its relationship to other events in his family life and writing career. The novel *Resurrection* offers a prime example of such interrelationships. First, as indicated, it was the need to support the Doukhobors in their emigration that prompted him to finish the novel in the first place, and then to make a flagrant exception to his own royalty rule. The Doukhobors' influence extended to the *content* of the novel, for, even though its peasant characters were identified as Molokans, there is reason to conclude that they were more likely based on the Doukhobors (rather than the Molokans) Tolstoy was acquainted with. This influence will be discussed at some length in the next chapter.

Further, as we have already seen, the novel — including both its content and the distribution of the proceeds therefrom — served as a major flashpoint in the ongoing difference of opinion between Tolstoy and his wife in regard to his obsession with controversial causes and its distracting effect on his home and family life. Sofia Andreevna's input on the Doukhobors and her husband's involvement in their affairs thus offers invaluable insights for anyone seeking a more complete picture of Tolstoy the writer, philosopher, social activist, and benefactor, not to mention Tolstoy the human being and family man, in the context of turn-of-the-century Russian society.

69 For example, her correspondence on the Doukhobors with Professor James Mavor.

CHAPTER 5

The Doukhobors in Tolstoy's Writings

(1) Composition of family, place of residence, names [of family members].
(2) Childhood. How you[1] lived before.
(3) Court case over [Orphan] House. How it began.
(4) Death of [Luker'ja] Kalmykova. How Verigin took her place.
(5) Verigin's previous life.
(6) Renewal. How you stopped drinking, smoking...
(7) How you shared money. Was it everyone [sharing] or just [the people in] Gorijsk? In as much detail as possible.
(8) How farm animals were shared.
(9) Exile of the elders and Verigin. When?
(10) How you decided to refuse military service.
(11) Burning of arms (less detail, as this is known). Executions, beatings, rapings (in detail).
(12) Expulsion [from settlement], devastation.
(13) Refusal [of military service] by new recruits.
(14) Refusal [of military service] by those issued draft cards.
(15) Disciplinary battalion.
(16) Gorijsk and Tiflis Prisons.
(17) Exile to Siberia.

As much as possible (biographical) [information] about what you saw or participated in.

THE ABOVE SKETCH IS TAKEN from unattributed notes held by the Tolstoy Museum in Moscow (published in Golinenko 1994: 195), written on the

1 The term *you* is collective in this document, referring to the Doukhobors as a whole.

reverse side of a letter dated 8–12 October 1898, which Tolstoy received from I. M. Vinogradov (caretaker in the home of Vladimir Chertkov's mother). According to Golinenko, it most likely represented an outline for an article to be written by a Doukhobor named Vasilij Nikolaevich Pozdnjakov, who had been exiled to Yakutsk Oblast' in 1895 for refusing military service. Pozdnjakov met with Tolstoy on a number of occasions, and his account "Pravda o dukhoborakh v Zakavkaz'e i v Sibiri" [The truth about the Doukhobors in the Transcaucasus and Siberia] was published by Chertkov in 1914 in his *Ezhemesjachnyj zhurnal literatury, nauki* i *obshchestvennoj zhizni* [Monthly journal of literature, science and societal life],[2] although Golinenko admits discrepancies between it and the plan outlined above.

It does not seem to me too far-fetched to speculate that Tolstoy himself may have had in mind writing a longer work of historical fiction in which the Doukhobors would be given a central role. The first few questions above are highly reminiscent of Tolstoy's autobiographical works, the best example being *Confession.* In fact, the comprehensiveness of the outline suggests a work larger than an article.

This was a time when Tolstoy was intensely involved both in the Doukhobor cause[3] and in writing his last major novel, *Resurrection* [*Voskresenie*].

As things stand, however, Tolstoy's works do not contain a sustained artistic portrayal of the Doukhobors, either as individuals or as a group. But there are significant references, both explicit and implicit — not only in *Resurrection* but also in his play (which remained unfinished) *And the Light Shineth in Darkness* [*I svet vo t'me svetit*],[4] and in the following articles and article-length letters (all to be discussed in some detail below):

- *Tsarstvo Bozh'e vnutri vas* [*The Kingdom of God is Within You*] (1890–93), *PSS* 28 (entire volume).
- Pis'mo v inostrannye gazety po povodu gonenij na kavkazskikh dukhoborov (1895) [Letter to foreign newspapers on the persecution of the Caucasus Doukhobors], *PSS* 39:209–15 (Letter #1895-08-14).
- Posleslovie k stat'e P. I. Birjukova «Gonenie na khristian v Rossii v 1895 g.» (1896) [Afterword to article by P. l. Birjukov, "Persecution of Christians in Russia in 1895"], *PSS* 39:99–105.
- Posleslovie k vozvaniju «Pomogite!» (1897) [Afterword to the appeal *Help!*], *PSS* 39:192–96.
- Redaktoru gazety «Stockholms Dagblad» (1897) [To the editor of the newspaper *Stockholms Dagblad*], *PSS* 70:148–54 (Letter #1897-10-05).

2 Pozdnjakov 1914; see also Brock 1964–65.

3 On 24 March 1898 (Letter #1898-04-05e) he wrote Tregubov: "The Doukhobor emigration is taking up all my attention at the moment."

4 *PSS* 31:113–83. Tolstoy worked on the play in the latter half of the 1890s.

- "Po povodu kongressa o mire: Pis'mo k shvedam" [On the peace congress: Letter to the Swedes] (1899), *PSS* 90:60–66.
- *Dve vojny* (1898) [*Two Wars*], *PSS* 31:97–101.
- Pis'mo k pereselivshimsja v Kanadu dukhoboram (15/27 fevralja 1900 g.) (1900) [Letter to the Doukhobors who emigrated to Canada (15/27 February 1900)] (see L. N. Tolstoj 1900 in the Bibliography; Letter #1900-02-27).

THE KINGDOM OF GOD IS WITHIN YOU (1890–1893)

Even though *The Kingdom of God is Within You* makes only a brief reference to the Doukhobors per se, there is no question that it was they, along with the other sects mentioned (e.g., Quakers, Mennonites, Molokans), who served as an impetus for Tolstoy to write this treatise. The whole work comprises a denunciation of civil and ecclesiastical authorities and their divisive effects on ordinary people, their sanctioning of war and military service, the incarceration of those refusing military service, and their opposition (including, sometimes, persecution) of those actively pursuing the Christian path of brotherly love and non-violent resistance to evil.

As the title suggests, the solution to the world's evils requires inner transformation of the individual, beginning with refusal to submit to any government policies requiring conscience-violating use of force. In the early part of the treatise, Tolstoy sets forth what he believes to be a logical foundation for his pacifist beliefs, drawn from the works of American pacifists such as William Lloyd Garrison and Adin Ballou,[5] as well as the doctrines of some pacifist sects; for example (*PSS* 28:22):

> There are people — there are hundreds of thousands of Quakers, there are Mennonites, there are our own Doukhobors, Molokans and people not belonging to any particular sect, who believe that violence and, consequently, military service is incompatible with Christianity, and that is why every year here in Russia a number of recruits refuse military service on the basis of their religious convictions. How does the government react? Does it release them? No. Does it force them to go and, in case of refusal, punish them? No. In 1818 the government acted as follows. Hardly anybody in Russia knows of what Nik[olaj] Nik[olaevich] Muravëv-Karskij[6] wrote in his diary, as it did not pass the censor.

5 In the summer of 1889 Lewis G. Wilson, a colleague of the American pastor Adin Ballou (1803–90), sent Tolstoy a copy of Ballou's book *Christian Non-Resistance.* Tolstoy commissioned poet Anna Pavlovna Barykova to translate the book for a Russian edition. It was Tolstoy's foreword to this edition that eventually grew into the treatise *The Kingdom of God is Within You.*

6 *Nikolaj Nikolaevich Muravëv-Karskij* (1794–1866) — Russian general who participated in a number of conflicts, from the War of 1812 to the Crimean War in the 1850s. He published a number of accounts of his experiences.

Tolstoy then proceeds to quote Muravëv's description of a group of forcibly relocated peasants who might possibly have been Doukhobors.

> *2 October 1818. Tiflis.*
> In the morning the commandant told me that five of a landowner's peasants in Tambov Gubernia were recently sent to Georgia. These people were recruited into the army, but did not wish to serve. They have already been whipped a number of times and made to run the gauntlet, but they willingly submit to the most cruel torture, and even death, to avoid service. "Release us," they say, "and leave us alone, and we shall not bother anyone. All people are equal, and the tsar is just as much a human being as we are; why should we pay tribute to him? Why should I put my life in danger to kill in war someone who has done me no wrong? You can tear us to pieces, but we shall never change our thoughts, put on uniforms and eat military rations. People who sympathize with us will offer us charity, but government [handouts] are something we have never had and do not want." These are the words of peasants who claim there are many more like them in Russia. Four times they were brought before a ministerial committee and they finally decided to petition the tsar, who ordered them to be sent, as a correctional measure, to Georgia, and ordered the commandant to forward him monthly reports of gradual success in bringing these peasants back to a normal way of thinking.[7]

A few paragraphs later, Tolstoy notes that "all available violent measures of our times are being employed for the 'correction' of those who refused, bringing them around 'to genuine thoughts' and keeping the whole affair in strictest secrecy." He describes the ordeal suffered by a typical unwilling recruit as follows:

> It usually begins with the refusing recruit being sent to the priests, who, to their shame, always administer an admonishment. But since this admonishment, given in Christ's name, to reject Christ (i.e., Christ's teachings on non-violence) is almost always unsuccessful, he is passed on to the gendarmerie. The gendarmes, as a rule, finding no political [fault] in him, return him, whereupon he is sent along to scientists, doctors and a mental hospital.... This person is either exiled to some distant outpost or brought before a court on charges of insubordination, convicted of disciplinary infractions and imprisoned in a 'disciplinary battalion.'

It goes without saying that Tolstoy hoped his treatise would arouse public sentiment against what he saw as unfair and anti-Christian practices on the part of the government and the official church. Both the work and the hopes pinned on it by its author were naturally very much in line with the views held by the Doukhobors and their post-1886 leader, Pëtr Vasil'evich Verigin.

Whether Verigin actually read *The Kingdom of God is Within You* in the year or two following its appearance in 1893 is a matter of some dispute. The

7 This and the following quotation are translated from *PSS* 28:22–24.

historian Josh Sanborn insists that Verigin had read it by the spring of 1895, and that its strongly pacifist message was a motivating factor behind Verigin's call to the Burning of Arms in the summer of 1895.[8] Erstwhile Tolstoyan Bonch-Bruevich (1901: xxii–xxiv),[9] on the other hand, maintained that, while Verigin may indeed have read some of Tolstoy's writings prior to 1895, *The Kingdom of God is Within You* was not among them; this is the view taken by the majority of scholars.

Sanborn's contention is based on a letter of Verigin's (undated, a fact contributing to the confusion) headed "To all Doukhobors of the Large Party" ["Ko vsem dukhobortsam Bol'shoj partii"], which is considered by the Doukhobors to contain the essence of their beliefs (and which is still used in their prayer services). Sanborn (1995: 61) writes,

> The first incontrovertible signal that Verigin had read *The Kingdom of God is within you* was a rather blatant one: he repeated word for word, without naming its source, a lengthy section of the book in a letter to his followers in the Transcaucaus.

The 'repetition' mentioned by Sanborn refers to the translation of the "Declaration of Sentiments" written by William Lloyd Garrison (1838) and delivered to a Boston peace convention, which Tolstoy cited in his treatise as a description of non-violent resistance.

It cannot be denied that the ideas expressed in *The Kingdom of God is Within You,* including its quotations from Garrison, would naturally have appealed to Verigin, and furnished him momentary inspiration, possibly even a catalyst for his implementation of his principle of non-violence in calling for the Burning of Arms. But an examination of the whole history of the Doukhobors — their longstanding beliefs in the inviolability of human life and persistent pacifism, combined with the cruel treatment they had already received at the hands of officialdom[10] — suggests strongly that Verigin would have proceeded as he did with or without the prior influence of Tolstoy's treatise.

A closer look is warranted at Verigin's actual letter to the Doukhobors, which Sanborn claims was quoted "word for word" from Tolstoy's treatise. The similarities are evident but there are also differences, both significant and minor, which tend to be overlooked by scholars on both sides of the question.

The question posed by Verigin at the beginning of the letter, literally translatable as "In what does your faith consist?" [*V chëm zakljuchaetsja tvoja*

8 On the Burning of Arms, see Note 18 in Chap. 1.

9 On Bonch-Bruevich's involvement in the Doukhobor emigration, see Note 7 in Chap. 1.

10 It is evident that the authorities (both church and state) were convinced that Tolstoy and his followers were actively involved in the Burning of Arms, as amply evidenced by the extensive surveillance and barrage of criticism described in Chap. 3. See also Note 18 in Chap. 1, where Governor Shervashidze's report (Sheet 547) includes a reference to the Doukhobors' "citing passages from the underground writings of Count L. Tolstoy."

vera?], echoes the very first line of Tolstoy's tract "In 1884 I wrote a book entitled *What I Believe*."[11]

Next, Tolstoy opens his treatise with three biblical epigraphs:

> Ye shall know the truth, and the truth shall make you free. — John 8:32
>
> [F]ear not them which kill the body, but are not able to kill the soul: but rather fear him which is able to destroy both soul and body in hell. — Matt. 10:28
>
> Ye are bought with a price; be not ye the servants of men. — 1 Cor.7:23

Verigin uses the first and third of these (in reverse order) in his own letter. He then proceeds to copy the last two paragraphs of Garrison's "Declaration" (the first in part, the second in its entirety), just as Tolstoy quoted it in his treatise (*PSS* 28:7–8). He further uses three excerpts from Tolstoy's own text, albeit with changes in sequencing and the ideas expressed therein, as well as putting greater emphasis on *his own* creed.

There is not sufficient space here to discuss all the similarities and differences between the two pieces. However, the general conclusion may be drawn that while Verigin's letter to the Doukhobors does indicate a strong possibility that he had read *The Kingdom of God is Within You*, Sanborn's contention that he "repeated word for word, without naming its source, a lengthy section of the book"[12] may be considered an exaggeration. On the contrary, Verigin's editing, his stylistic elucidation of the text, and his selection of only those passages he deemed appropriate (assuming that he had indeed read Tolstoy's piece in advance), mean that he must have made a critical examination of the text before penning his letter to his followers.

LETTER TO FOREIGN NEWSPAPERS ON THE PERSECUTION OF THE CAUCASUS DOUKHOBORS (1895)

In a letter to Tolstoy of 14 July 1895, Prince Dmitrij Khilkov[13] describes the punishment meted out to the Doukhobors following the Burning of Arms on 28–29 June, based on an eyewitness account, and asked the writer to have it published in Russian and foreign newspapers. Tolstoy was vehement in his rejection of Khilkov's request, stating that the account in its present form was utterly lacking in credibility. On 29 July, he wrote in reply (*PSS* 68:132):

> [T]his account is written very poorly — poorly not because it is lacking in literary merit. On the contrary, it is lacking in simplicity, accuracy, definition and

11 Note that in Russian this is *V chëm moja vera?* — literally, "In what [is] my faith?"— to which Verigin's question *V chëm zakljuchaetsja tvoja vera?* is almost identical.

12 Incidentally, on a good number of occasions Tolstoy himself borrowed from other sources without attribution.

13 On Khilkov, see Chap. 2, Note 29.

> truthfulness, and the overall tone is not good — somehow ironic, humorous not the kind of tone that should be used in talking about such terrible matters.... in order for the article to have an influence on those whom it ought to, it must be written with strict veracity, attention to detail, and accuracy.

Nevertheless, as a consequence of this exchange, Tolstoy asked another follower, Pavel Birjukov, to go to the Caucasus and investigate the situation for himself. His resulting report was entitled "Persecution of the Christians in Russia in 1895," to which Tolstoy originally intended to write a foreword,[14] but then decided against it. The article itself remained unpublished during Tolstoy's lifetime. It appeared for the first time in 1938 in *Letopisi Gosudarstvennogo literaturnogo muzeja* [Chronicles of the State Literary Museum] (see Birjukov 1938).

However, in September 1895 Tolstoy reworked the foreword he had begun into a letter on the same subject designed to be published in foreign newspapers. He sent it to a British Tolstoyan named John Kenworthy, who translated it into English and published it in *The Times* of London, in its issue N° 34715 of 23 October 1895.[15]

In his foreword, Tolstoy acknowledges his familiarity with the Doukhobors' plight, comparing their sufferings to those of Christians under the persecutions of the Roman emperor Diocletian during the years 284–286 CE (*PSS* 39:209):

> At this very moment in the Caucasus persecution is going on against the Christian Doukhobors. It seems to be quite true that their tormentors are just as cruel and deaf to their victims' sufferings as those in the times of Diocletian, and the victims just as firm and courageous. One cannot remain silent, knowing what is taking place there. I have close knowledge of the situation and cannot help but do everything within my power to alleviate the victims' plight and, especially, the sin of their tormentors who, as always, know not what they do.

Tolstoy goes on to point out that the only effective means of helping both the persecutors and the persecuted anywhere in the world, including Russia, was through the "light of truth" [*svet istiny*], appealing to the higher nature of those "who in their error, persecuting and aggrieving the followers of Christ, think that they are doing this as a favour to God" (209).

In a complete contradiction of official pronouncements, Tolstoy sees the Doukhobors' non-violent resistance to the authorities' heavy-handed

14 Cf. Tolstoy's diary entry for 8 September 1895, upon hearing Birjukov's report (*PSS* 53:53): "Must write a foreword."

15 See *PSS* 39:237–38; also L. N. Tolstoj 1895. In his 'letter' he explained: "Truly and undoubtedly the most important thing described in this note is this: that in various places the Doukhobors have been again and again cruelly tortured, that a large number of them have been incarcerated and that more than 450 families have been completely devastated and turned out of their homes" (L. N. Tolstoj 1895: 475).

measures — including their refusal to undertake military service and swear loyalty to the tsar — as a direct result of their adherence to Christ's teachings on respect for the sanctity of human life, their Christian-inspired work ethic, their endeavour to live a simple, honest, sober life in a communal spirit. Ironically, this also led in turn to a significant increase in their material prosperity, whenever they were left alone to practise their principles — a prosperity which provoked both admiration and envy, the latter sometimes accompanied by threats from neighbouring local tribes. The foreword also indicates Tolstoy's appreciation of their outward appearance as strong, stalwart, and handsome people.

Yet, with his customary objectivity, he does not refrain from pointing out that the Doukhobors were not immune to the elements of dissension and disunity which plagued all sects that tend to be closed within themselves. While noting the evident link between growth in material prosperity and a decline in religious consciousness, he feels there has been some improvement along this line under the "highly religious Pëtr Verigin" (210) and his immediate predecessor, Luker'ja Kalmykova.

Tolstoy then goes on to voice his regret at not being able to see Verigin during the latter's stopover at a Moscow prison on his way to a second exile in Siberia in 1895. He also notes how impressed he was by both the appearance of, and the thoughts expressed by, Verigin's brother and the two others whom he did see at that time. Here is an excerpt from Tolstoy's description (211):

> These people have the appearance of ordinary educated people. They wear European dress: frock coats, overcoats, they are clean-shaven, except for a moustache, with a well-groomed appearance. When they greet you they are unbelievably meek and polite, and rather formal. With the exception of Verigin's friend who lives with him, they are all extremely strong, stalwart people. One of them is an old fellow, uncommonly well-preserved, as happens only with people who lead a hard-working, moral life. My conversations with these people have convinced me that the Doukhobors' beliefs were shared by all people who have since the time of its [first] preaching confessed Christianity and not the imitation teachings promulgated by the Church in the place of Christ. These beliefs are that man is the son of God, bound to carry out the will of his Father, and the will of his Father consists in establishing God's kingdom. And God's kingdom is established through the recognition of the brotherhood of all people and the destruction of enmity and violence and the establishing of love and harmony. Thus, in doing the will of God, man thereby also attains his own salvation and his highest good. And so the Doukhobors, like all true Christians, reject both violence and corporal punishment, wars, the killing of animals, and even the right to use violence in self-defence.

Tolstoy recommends the newspaper send its own correspondent to verify the events he describes, both on account of the urgency of the situation and the looming threat of even greater persecutions. He acknowledges his "even greater" concern with saving the authorities, "from the tsar to the Cossack," from participation in and responsibility for the persecutions. Moreover, he sees the current situation with the Doukhobors as yet another manifestation of the oft-repeated, age-old conflict (*PSS* 39:214):

> [T]he inevitable clash of the violence-oriented lifestyle which professes itself to be Christian with the genuinely Christian conduct of people who by no perverted twist of thought can be considered unchristian — a people whom one not only cannot disapprove of but cannot help being excited about. Because one cannot help but recognize that people who act that way do so in the name of the highest qualities of the human soul, and if mankind falls to recognize these heights it falls to the level of an animal existence.

As a prime manifestation of this clash he points to the refusal to participate in military service, not only by Doukhobors but also by other groups such as the Russian Stundists and the Austrian Nazarenes. In urging an investigation of the matter by independent sources, he issues a poignant challenge to what he terms "Christian governments" (214–15):

> It is high time for Christian governments to stop hiding their head like an ostrich in the face of their rising denunciator — the Christian spirit infusing the people of our time — and give a clear and direct answer to this spirit's demands: either renounce violence, i.e., renounce one's self as the government, or renounce Christ, i.e., the good and truth that serve as the only justification for a government's existence. ... the more light that is thrown upon this subject, the better.

AFTERWORD TO ARTICLE BY P. I. BIRJUKOV, "PERSECUTION OF CHRISTIANS IN RUSSIA IN 1895" (1896)

In 1896, a version of Birjukov's article "Persecution of Christians in Russia in 1895" was published for the first time, together with an afterword [*posleslovie*] by Tolstoy, by a Russian émigré named M. K. Èlpidin.[16] Tolstoy's afterword, while significantly reworked from his original foreword, expresses similar sentiments and contains one or two passages with an almost identical wording.[17] In the afterword, he takes great pains to point out why the government, in effect, had no other choice but to act the way it did toward these people

16 *Mikhall Konstantinovich Èlpidin* (1835–1908) — a radical dissident who had escaped from confinement and fled to Switzerland in 1865. The following year he opened his own Russian-language printing house in Geneva, publishing more than 200 titles before his death in 1909, including a number of Tolstoy's treatises.

17 For example, compare the following fragment of the original foreword cited above (*PSS* 39:214) with the following, almost identical excerpt from the 1896 afterword (*PSS* 39:102–03): "By no perverted twist of thought can one consider the actions of these people bad or unchristian — a people whom one not only cannot disapprove of but cannot help but be excited about. Because one cannot help but recognize that people who act that way do so in the name of the highest qualities of the human soul, and if it fails to recognize these heights, mankind falls to the level of an animal existence."

whom it considered — quite legitimately so — as a threat to its very existence. After all, they were protesting against what Tolstoy saw as the government's hypocritical reliance on violence as a means of maintaining public order (in contradiction to the teachings on non-violence inherent in the very Christianity it outwardly professed). The only logical consequence of allowing such protests would be the undermining of the government itself by popular opinion — and popular opinion was joining the sectarian protesters in ever increasing numbers.[18] (*PSS* 39:101):

> The tragedy lies in the fact that governments are obliged to rule over Christian peoples, even if they are not yet fully enlightened, but with every passing day and hour are becoming more and more enlightened by Christ's teachings. All governments from the time of Constantine have known and felt this, and instinctively have done everything within their power to darken the true sense of Christianity and suppress its spirit. They knew that once people adopted this spirit there would be an annihilation not only of violence but of the government itself, and so the governments have taken their own measures, setting up their own government departments, piling up laws and institutions one after the other in the hopes of burying beneath them that undying spirit of Christ which has been incubated in people's hearts.

Not only that, but Tolstoy goes even further, claiming that such an inevitable destruction of the existing order of things can be seen as divinely ordained, a manifestation of the divine will. To the question: "But what will happen if the government is overthrown?" Tolstoy responds as follows (104):

> The answer to this question is always the same. There will be what ought to be, whatever is pleasing to God, whatever is consistent with what He has inculcated in our hearts and the law He has revealed to our minds. ...the overthrow of the government that is now taking place is taking place not because some individual or some people deliberately wanted to overthrow it, but because it is inconsistent with God's will, revealed to our minds and incubated in our hearts.

He goes on to reinforce his thought with an appeal to the conscience of those responsible for the immediate situation faced by the Doukhobors (104):

> One who refuses to incarcerate his brethren or to kill them has no designs on the overthrow of the government; all he wants is not to go against God's will, to refrain from doing what not only he but all people who have risen above an animal state undoubtedly recognize as evil. If, in the course of this, the government

18 Already, Tolstoy notes (*PSS* 39:102), a number of Orthodox believers had begun to follow the Doukhobors' example of rejecting militarism. Declaring supporters of the cause worldwide to be in the millions, he foresaw the mqvement spreading not only to other Russian Christian sects (e.g., Molokans, Stundists, Khlysts) but even further, to Muslim groups such as the Harijits (a radical Muslim sect formed in the seventh century who favoured equality and the election of imams) and Babists (a liberal Muslim sect formed in 1844, the forerunner of Baha'i).

> is overthrown, this means only that the government was demanding the contrary of God's will — i.e., evil — and because the government, therefore, is evil and so must be overthrown.

Toward the end of the afterword Tolstoy ties his arguments into Jesus' pithy saying from St. John's Gospel (16:33), which he uses as an initial epigraph: "In the world ye shall have tribulation: but be of good cheer; I have overcome the world."

AFTERWORD TO THE APPEAL *HELP!* (1897)

The continued persecutions of the Doukhobors throughout 1896 prompted three prominent Tolstoyans — Pavel Ivanovich Birjukov, Ivan Mikhajlovich Tregubov, and Vladimir Grigor'evich Chertkov — to draft an appeal to the public, both in Russia and abroad, to apprise them of the sect members' plight and, hopefully, to enlist some kind of aid (financial, political, diplomatic) toward alleviating that plight. In early November 1896, Tolstoy did some major editing on the awkward draft of the appeal Chertkov had sent him, which in turn was reworked by the authors. Tolstoy still found fault with their new draft, saying it had a feeling of "coldness" and "exaggeration," and advised the authors to append their signatures. On 11 (or possibly 12) December, Chertkov came to Moscow to discuss it with Tolstoy in person, and on 14 December the final draft was approved, to which Tolstoy penned his afterword.

A few weeks later Chertkov (with Tolstoy's approval) returned to St. Petersburg, where he tried in vain to bring the appeal to the notice of Tsar Nicholas II. But the large number of typewritten copies which had been circulating in the meantime prompted the authorities to sentence its three authors to exile. While Birjukov and Tregubov were sent to Kurland Gubernia (now part of Latvia), Chertkov was exiled to England, where in 1897 he published the appeal with the authors' appended signatures and Tolstoy's afterword.[19]

The first task Tolstoy set himself in his contribution was to vouch for the authenticity of the appeal, citing the meticulous editing process to eliminate anything that might, even if it were true, smack of "exaggeration," so that "everything now reported in this appeal is the genuine, undoubted truth" (*PSS* 39:192).

Tolstoy then deals squarely with potential counter-arguments to the appeal — the tendency simply to dismiss the Doukhobors as fanatics and social nuisances — before outlining the basis for his own support of them. He compares the circumstances underlying the appeal to the "still small voice" in which Elijah discerned God's presence, in contrast to the more conspicuous appearance of the wind, earthquake, and fire.[20] According to Tolstoy, nearly

19 See *PSS* 39:248–49.

20 See 1 Kings 19:11–12. In the Russian Bible, the Hebrew words rendered "still small voice" in the Authorized Version are translated by the equivalent of "the fluttering of a quiet breeze" [*vejanie tikhogo vetra*].

all the questions of politics and diplomacy being discussed at the time by the world's parliaments pale in importance by comparison with the situation now unfolding among the Caucasus Doukhobors — a situation calling mankind to examine the whole nature of how one lives one's faith in God, going so far as to compare the Doukhobors in certain respects to Jesus' own disciples. In a poignant paragraph, Tolstoy writes (*PSS* 39:194):

> It was possible, after all, that neither Pilate nor Herod understood the reason that the Galilean [i.e., Jesus] causing trouble in their jurisdiction had been brought to them for judgement. They did not even see fit to investigate what his doctrine consisted in. And if they had known it, they might be forgiven for thinking that it would come to nought (as Gamaliel has said).[21] But we, on the other hand, cannot help but know of this same doctrine, or of the fact that it has not disappeared over the course of 1,800 years, and will not disappear until it has come to fruition. And if we know that, then we cannot, despite the fact that the Doukhobors are insignificant, uneducated and unknown, help but see the whole significance of what is happening with them. After all, Christ's disciples were just as insignificant, unrefined and unknown people. Christ's disciples could not, indeed, be otherwise. After all, it is not something new that is happening with the Doukhobors — or, rather, with the universal brotherhood of Christians, as they now call themselves — but only the growth of that seed planted by Christ 1,800 years ago — the resurrection of Christ himself.

In the spirit of avoiding the "exaggeration" he had referred to earlier, Tolstoy freely admits that the Doukhobors have managed to only partially manifest the Christ ideal; still, he suggests, their success in achieving what they have accomplished to date by far surpasses the wildest dreams of the average Christian. He also notes that, sooner or later, the whole significance of the Doukhobor movement would indeed "break through to the light, overthrow its oppressors and take over the world. It is only a question of time" (*PSS* 39:195–96). And he points to the acute contrast between "the cruelty and blindness of the Russian government" and "the amazing meekness and tenacity with which the new Christian martyrs are bearing these persecutions" (*PSS* 39:196) as a sign that such a realization will come sooner rather than later.

TO THE EDITOR OF THE NEWSPAPER *STOCKHOLMS DAGBLAD* (1897)

On 27 November 1895 Swedish industrialist and philanthropist Alfred Nobel signed his last will and testament, establishing the Nobel Prizes in physics, chemistry, medicine, economics, literature, and peace. Unlike the others, the peace prize was to be administered by a committee appointed by the Storting,

21 See Acts 5:34–39. A Pharisee scholar, Gamaliel advised the persecutors of Jesus' apostles: "Refrain from these men, and let them alone: for if this counsel of this work be of men, it will come to nought: but if it be of God, ye cannot overthrow it; lest haply ye be found even to fight against God" (Acts 5:38–39).

the Norwegian parliament. The Storting approved the arrangement in April 1897, following Nobel's passing in December 1896, and the Swedish scholarly institutions entrusted with administering the other prizes followed suit with their approvals a year later.[22] The prizes received royal proclamation in 1900, and were first awarded in 1901.

With the Storting's approval of the peace prize, in 1897, rumours began circulating as to who the first recipient might be. Upon learning that his name was being touted among the potential candidates, in early October 1897 Tolstoy took advantage of a visiting Swede, Voldemar Langlet, to write an open letter on the subject to the editor of the *Stockholms Dagblad*, which Langlet translated into Swedish on the spot.[23]

In his letter Tolstoy declines nomination in favour of a group of people who, he insists, not only eminently deserved the prize but were in great need of the funds that came with it. He begins making his case for the Doukhobors as follows (*PSS* 70:149):

> I would say that the terms of Nobel's will concerning individuals who have done the most to serve the cause of peace are extremely difficult to fulfil. People who really serve the cause of peace do so because they serve God, and so they do not need monetary rewards and will not accept them. But I would say that the terms of the will would be amply fulfilled if the prize money were to go to the needy families of those who serve the cause of peace. I am talking about the Caucasus Doukhobors. No one in our time has served or is continuing to serve the cause of peace more effectively and earnestly than these people.

At this point he proceeds to describe the Doukhobors' situation in some detail, telling about the punishments they were subjected to for their refusal to swear an oath of allegiance to the tsar and undertake military service. He then makes a sharp contrast between people who live in peace and those who merely talk about peace (149):

> These people say: "We are Christians and therefore cannot agree to be killers. You can torture us, you can even kill us. We cannot prevent that, but we cannot subject ourselves to you, because we confess the same Christ that you recognize." These words are very simple, and by no means new, to the point that it seems strange even to repeat them. But in the meantime these words, spoken in our time and under the conditions the Doukhobors find themselves in, have great significance.
>
> In our time everyone talks about peace and about the means of achieving it. Those who talk about peace are professors, writers, members of parliament and

22 Norway was politically joined to Sweden until 1905. The Nobel Committee of the Storting was renamed the Norwegian Nobel Committee in 1977.

23 In a cover letter to the editor, written in French, Tolstoy expressed his concern over the potentially poor quality of the Swedish translation, explaining it was written and translated in some haste, but hoped it would be publishable nevertheless.

> peace societies, yet those same professors, writers, members of parliament and peace societies, on occasion, express feelings of patriotism; when it comes their turn, they quietly take their place in the ranks of the military, assuming that war will be stopped not by their own efforts but by somebody else's, and not in their time but some time later.

After blaming priests and pastors for failing to point out the incompatibility of war with Christianity, and politicians for losing no opportunity to talk pompously about peace in public, even in front of the very troops that they may send into war, he points to the Doukhobors as an example of a real service to the cause of peace (150–51):

> And so, amidst this general falsehood, the actions of the Doukhobors, who do not talk about peace, but only talk about how they do not want to be killers, take on a special importance, because they show the world that age-old, simple, indisputable and only means of establishing peace, which was already revealed to people long ago by Christ, but which in times past people have been so far from that it did not seem applicable, though in our time it has become so natural that many can only wonder why it has not yet been applied by all the people of the Christian world.

Then, after elaborating in turn on the simplicity, indisputability, and uniqueness of this solution as the only one possible, and enumerating other historical and contemporary examples of refusal of military service, Tolstoy comes to the main point of his discourse: namely, that all war is a deception perpetrated by authorities for their own self-interest, and that the Doukhobors have done the greatest service in the cause of peace by exposing this grand deception (152–53):

> So, if peace has not yet come, it is not because there is no general desire among people for it, or because there is no love of it, but only because of an insidious deception by which people have believed and maintain that peace is impossible and war unavoidable. And so in order to establish peace among people, especially among Christians, and to overthrow war, there is nothing new that needs to be incubated in people. They need only be freed from the deception by which they have been indoctrinated to act against their common will...
>
> The actions of the Doukhobors are tearing the last coverings off the deception concealing the truth from the people. And the Russian government knows this and is trying with all its might to keep maintaining that deception, at least for a time.... And this liberation from deception and, consequently, an approximation to the establishment of real peace on the earth — this is the real achievement of the Doukhobors. Thus I would say that nobody has served the cause of peace better than they. The terrible circumstances in which their families are now living (you can learn about them in an article published in the June 1897 issue of *Humanitas*) mean that nobody more than they deserve to be awarded the money which Nobel bequeathed to people serving the cause of peace.

The letter was published, but Tolstoy's recommendation to award the first peace prize to the Doukhobors was not heeded. Nor was his expressed desire not to be a candidate himself: in fact, his name was on the short list for the first Nobel Prizes in both peace and literature. In both cases, however, there was a controversy about whether he had been properly nominated,[24] and the nomination documents showed little acquaintance with either his literary or peace activities. Then, after Tolstoy was properly nominated for the literature prize the following year, the secretary of the Swedish academy that administered the prize dismissed the nomination on the grounds that Tolstoy had "denounced all forms of civilization," "rewritten the New Testament," and "denied the right of both individuals and nations to self-defence." Not only that, but "Tolstoy was opposed to prizes anyway and would not accept one" (Abrams 2001: 42).

In light of Tolstoy's comments on the Doukhobors and their exposition of the "deception" of war, it is interesting to take note of the comments by the advisor to the Norwegian committee for the 1909 peace prize, when Tolstoy's name was once more on the short list, this time nominated by five members of the Storting. As reported by Irwin Abrams (2001) in his book *The Nobel Peace Prize and the Laureates: An Illustrated Biographical History, 1901–2001*,

> The adviser wrote a strong positive report of thirteen pages, showing great familiarity with Tolstoy's writings and his doctrine of nonresistance. He discussed the attacks on patriotism, militarism, and the state and Tolstoy's advocacy of refusal to do military service; he summarized the hostile opinions and concluded that Tolstoy's inadequacies and exaggerations would be forgotten. What would be remembered was that he had placed humanity face-to-face with its own conscience.

However, as Abrams notes, the committee did not accept the advisor's recommendation and Tolstoy was once again passed over, this time in favour of two peace-minded politicians. How well the 1909 laureates managed to escape the negative image Tolstoy had earlier painted of 'peace-minded politicians' in his nomination of the Doukhobors for the first peace prize is for history to judge.

ON THE PEACE CONGRESS: LETTER TO THE SWEDES (1899)

A year and a half after writing his letter to the *Stockholms Dagblad* Tolstoy was presented with another occasion to address the Swedes on the subject of peace and the Doukhobors. A European peace congress had been called (at the initiation of none other than Tsar Nicholas II), to take place in The Hague in May 1899. A group of concerned Swedish intellectuals wrote to Tolstoy early in the year, asking him to advise the tsar, his ministers, and the Russian public at large of the potential contribution to peace that could be made by

24 According to Abrams (2001: 42), more than forty Swedish writers and artists signed a tribute to Tolstoy as a token of their protest against his potential disqualification.

governments removing the penalty for refusing military service or making provision for some sort of alternative service that did not require the bearing of arms. As reported by the editors of *PSS* (90:367), the Swedish scholars wrote as follows:

> The assembled government representatives must give a hearing to our declaration, since, in the interests of basic humanity, the very goal of the congress will not allow such an important dedaration to go unheeded.

By 12 January 1899 Tolstoy had penned a letter in reply, this time sending it to Swedish writer/translator Jonas Stadling for translation and publication in Swedish and other languages. Stadling carried out both tasks with such speed that Tolstoy missed the opportunity to include his revisions to the letter before Stadling's publication of it — in three countries in three languages: in Swedish in *Aftonbladet,* in English in the *Daily Chronicle*, and in German in the [*Berliner*] *Lokal-Anzeiger.* Later in the year Chertkov's *Svobodnoe slovo* journal published the revised version in England.[25]

Tolstoy begins his reply by describing the Swedish scholars' plan of universal disarmament through individuals' refusal of military service as not only "completely reasonable" [*sovershenno spravedlivo*] but, in fact, the *only* practicable means to this end. At the same time, he warns his addressees, in the strongest possible language, not to expect real reform either from the congress or from its sponsoring governments, citing the Russian government's treatment of the Doukhobors as an example:

> The conference will have as its goal not the establishment of peace, but the concealment from people of the only means of liberating them from the disasters of war, which is the refusal of individuals to take part in military killing, and hence there is no way the conference can take this subject under discussion.
>
> Any government will always deal with conscientious objectors to military service the same way as the Russian government has dealt with the Doukhobors. At the same time as it was proclaiming to the world its supposed peace-loving intentions, it was covering up the fact that it was torturing, devastating, and persecuting the most peace-loving people in Russia — simply on account of the fact that they were peace-loving not in word but in deed and therefore refused military service. All European governments have acted in exactly the same way, though less crudely, perhaps, in cases of refusal of military service. This is how the governments of Austria, Prussia, France, Sweden, Switzerland and Holland have acted and they are incapable of acting otherwise.[26]

Tolstoy reinforces his warning with an equally frank prediction that governments "will never openly permit people to refuse military service or refuse

25 This is the version reproduced in *PSS* 90:60–66, quoted here.

26 *PSS* 90:63.

to pay tax in support of military service (which amounts to the same thing), because they know that such refusals expose the government's deception and undermine its authority" (*PSS* 90:64). He also states that the need for armed troops will be reduced or eliminated "only when public opinion puts a label of shame on people who sell their freedom out of fear or for profit and join the ranks of the murderers called troops" — an outcome that will be followed by "a new era in the life of mankind" (65).

"TWO WARS" (1898)

The brief article "Two Wars,"[27] dated 15 August 1898 (written during the period when Tolstoy was most heavily involved in writing *Resurrection*), expresses the writer's vehement condemnation of the Hispano-American war, especially the United States of America as the aggressor, which seized not only Puerto Rico in the Caribbean but also the Spanish-held islands of Guam and the Philippines in the Pacific. The article was originally penned in response to a request from an American woman, Jessie L. Gladwin,[28] in Pueblo, Colorado, asking him to write a few words describing his feelings and thoughts on the noble role of the American nation and the heroism of its soldiers and sailors in the ongoing conflict.[29]

Contrary to his correspondent's expectations, Tolstoy dismisses the Hispano-American war as "obsolete, vain, stupid and cruel, inopportune, backward [and] barbarous...which through the killing of one group of people attempted to decide the question of how and by whom another group of people should be governed" (*PSS* 31:97). After noting that the particular war in question had now ended, Tolstoy then proceeds to speak of "another war," which, he says "is still going on and will end only when there is an end to all wars" (*PSS* 90:65). This war the writer sees as totally different from the first one:

> [T]his is a new, self-sacrificing, holy war, based on love and reason alone — a war against war itself, which has already been declared by the better, leading part of Christian humanity against the other, crude and wild, part of this same humanity, and which has been waged in recent times by a handful of Christian people, the Caucasus Doukhobors, against the mighty Russian government. (65)

27 *Dve vojny* (L. N. Tolstoy 1898a), first published in Chertkov's *Listki svobodnogo slova* in 1898, may be found in *PSS* 31:97–101. For excerpts from the first and third redactions of this work, see Donskov, Galagan, and Gromova 2002: 251–56.

28 In his reply article, Tolstoy erroneously refers to a certain "gentleman" in Colorado named "Jesse Gladwin" (*PSS* 31:97). See the Russian translation of Gladwin's letter in Gladwin (1898) 1965: 474.

29 Gladwin had apparently sent similar appeals to some 500 public figures, Tolstoy being N° 440 on his list. She planned to exhibit the responses and contribute the revenue from the exhibit to the American Red Cross for their assistance to sick and wounded American soldiers.

In contrast to the 'first war,' which was currently occupying the minds of the Christian world, Tolstoy bemoans the fact that the 'second war' is hardly even perceived, let alone talked about, by the public at large. He then launches into his familiar critique of the government's subversion of its own citizens merely to exercise its own authority. He pictures this government deceptively addressing its citizens as follows (*PSS* 31:98):

> I demand that you yourselves join the organizations which I have set up, where you will be turned into unthinking cogs of one huge machine — the army, under my control. Once in this army, you will cease being people with your own will and do everything according to my wish. First and foremost I wish to exercise authority; the means I use to exercise this authority is killing, and therefore I shall teach you to kill.

The government's counter-argument, that such tactics were required to defend itself from external enemies, and thereby achieve peace, Tolstoy dismisses as an outright lie. He puts his own justification for this into the mouths of the Doukhobors themselves (with some legitimacy, given the extreme closeness of their worldview to his own):

> And then there come people who say:
>
> What you say about the danger threatening us and your concern about protecting us from it is a deception. All states claim to want peace, yet at the same time they arm themselves against each other. Besides, according to that very law which you recognize, all people are brethren, and there is no difference in belonging to any particular state, and thus the attacks on us by other states which you threaten us with are not something that terrifies us; they are meaningless to us. The main point is that under that very law which is given to us by God and which you, too, recognize — even as you demand we participate in killing — there is a prohibition not only against killing but against any form of violence, and therefore we cannot and will not take part in your preparations for killing, we will not contribute money toward it and we will not join the regiments you have set up, where they pervert people's minds and consciences, turning them into tools of violence, subject to any evil person who takes such a tool in hand. (99)

Such a plea, Tolstoy believes, lies at the very core of the 'second war' — waged on behalf of true Christian beliefs, against the Russian government's attempts to combat these beliefs with all the means at its disposal: police arrests (including house arrests), prohibition of correspondence, interception of letters, spying, the forbidding of any public airing of the Doukhobors' plight in the press, disinformation concerning the Doukhobors' situation, beatings, imprisonment, exile, family separations. Against all this, he says, "the Doukhobors have set forth their one religious weapon: meek logic and patient persistence, and they say: 'We should not subject ourselves to people more than to God, and no matter what you do to us, we cannot and will not subject ourselves to you'" (99).

As the article proceeds, Tolstoy's tone grows more impassioned in defence of his unsung heroes, "who, unseen and unheard by anyone, have been dying and continue to die from their beatings or in stinking jail cells, or in arduous exile, yet still to their last breath remain faithful to goodness and truth" (99–100). It reaches its highest pitch when he talks about the incarceration of four innocent peasants — Evdokim Drozhzhin, Nikolaj Izjumchenko, Pëtr Ol'khovik, and Kirill Sereda[30] — in the infamous 'disciplinary battalions.'[31] They, like their Doukhobor counterparts (according to Tolstoy), should not be regarded as 'useless victims' but as martyrs equal in significance to the early Christian martyrs, for their power to open the eyes of millions of people to the injustice now being perpetrated against them. Toward the end of *Two Wars* he writes, cuttingly,

> I know hundreds of people, soldiers both old and young, who have begun to doubt the legitimacy of their actions in the light of the persecutions against these meek, hard-working Doukhobors. I know people who for the first time have begun thinking about life and the meaning of Christianity after seeing and hearing about the life of these people and the persecutions they have been subjected to.
>
> And the government, with millions of people under its control, knows this and feels that it has been wounded to its very core. (101)

In other words, as he expressed in a letter written about the same time (5 December 1898)[32] to two of his daughters, he indeed saw the Doukhobors as "people of the 25th century," far ahead of their time. This represents the

30 *Evdokim Nikitich Drozhzhin* — a village teacher, he was incarcerated in 1891 in a Voronezh prison for refusal to serve in the army, and died in captivity three years later. His biography by Evgenij Popov (1898) was published in England under the title *Zhizn' i smert' Evdokima Nikiticha Drozhzhina, 1866–1894* (an earlier edition with a preface by Tolstoy had appeared in Berlin in 1895). Like Drozhzhin, with whom he corresponded, *Nikolaj Trofimovich Izjumchenko* refused military service and in 1892 was sentenced to two years in a disciplinary battalion, followed by an additional three-year exile in Siberia. His story is presented in Brock and Keep 2003. *Pëtr Ol'khovik* and *Kirill Sereda* served their sentences in the lrkutsk disciplinary battalion; their cases are mentioned in a letter Tolstoy wrote to Sabbatarian Timofej Bondarev (see Donskov 1996b: 112–13). (The Sabbatarians [Subbotniki] were an offshoot of the Molokans, who had earlier broken away from the Doukhobors. See Chap. 2).

31 These 'disciplinary' or penal battalions are described in a footnote in Peter Brock and John Keep's (2001: xii) introduction to *Life in a Penal Battalion of the Imperial Russian Army: The Tolstoyan N.T. Iziumchenko's Story*: "Penal battalions were introduced in 1878 to replace the penal companies that had existed earlier. The number of inmates declined from over 5,000 in the late 1870s to over 3000 in the late 1880s. On 1 January 1888 the figure was 3691; another 2395 men were posted to them and 2656 discharged, of whom 120 had died. Most inmates served sentences of two to three years. About one-third were sentenced for desertion. One-third were illiterate.... Flogging (up to one hundred strokes) was permitted only on those categorized as '[previously] punished' (*shtrafovannye*) and in the event of aggravating circumstances."

32 Letter #1898-12-17a (*PSS* 71:497).

height of Tolstoy's conviction that in the Doukhobors' way of life he finally found a practical example of his own firm belief in the possibility of attaining here on earth a higher form of truth and some semblance of the 'meaning of life.' To him, the Doukhobors were indeed a 'light shining in darkness' (as indicated in his play, further discussed below), a light which must be kept lit, in the face of all government, church, and domestic obstacles, including, indeed, his own doubting self.

AND THE LIGHT SHINETH IN DARKNESS (UNFINISHED)

This play Tolstoy referred to as "my drama,"[33] a designation that in no small part prompted scores of critics to see in its chief protagonist, Saryntsev, none other than Tolstoy himself.[34] "In this drama," he commented at the end of 1893, "I wish to set forth my personal confession, my struggles, my religion and sufferings in a word, all that is dear to my heart.... But believe me, I shall die before I finish my desired task."[35]

Indeed, the play remained unfinished and was published posthumously in 1911, though it had occupied Tolstoy's mind for more than two decades. The earliest known specific mention of the play in writing, hinting broadly at its subject, is an entry in Tolstoy's diary of 5 February 1890 (*PSS* 51:17):

> I have thought of a drama about life: the despair of one who has seen the light and takes this light into the gloom of life with the hope and confidence of illuminating this gloom, when suddenly the gloom becomes even darker.

One cannot help but be struck by the strong echoes of the writer's own domestic conflict with his wife, Sofia Andreevna, concerning both his conversion and his determination, over her vehement objections, to share his property and wealth with the long-oppressed peasants. What is central to the drama, however, is not a struggle between two concepts of the world — there is, in fact, only one world view presented, that of Saryntsev — but the hero's own internal conflict, pitting his newly acquired Tolstoyan ethics (as discussed in Chapter 3) against his incessant doubts as to the rightness of these ethics.

Of particular interest to the Doukhobor question is another character named Boris Cheremshanov, a disciple of Saryntsev, who follows to the end the lessons he has learned from his mentor. To the latter's question "How am I to live without suffering from internal discord?" the disciple replies that (in keeping with his literal adherence to the Gospels) "It stands to reason, there is just one way: don't take part" (*PSS* 31:147).

33 The most complete, penultimate variant of the first act was published for the first time in Donskov, Galagan, and Gromova 2002: 222–36.

34 A number of sources deal with the autobiographical nature of the play, dating its beginning in the latter half of the 1880s. See Dolgov 1917; Sreznevskij 1920; Gashkene-Chervinskene 1960.

35 *Sbornik vospominanij o L. N. Tolstom* (Moscow, 1911): 69, quoted in Donskov, Galagan, and Gromova 2002: 236.

This principle of non-violent resistance to evil, vehemently opposed by the government, its military establishment, the land-owning class, and the official church, is portrayed mainly through the episodes dealing with Cheremshanov's refusal to enter the army when called up as a conscript. Tolstoy has endowed him with sensitivity, a logical mind, sincerity, bravery, and the desire for active involvement. He breaks his engagement to the girl he loves, giving up the wealth he would have acquired through the marriage. As an only son, his actions bring no end of grief to his mother. Despite all this, let alone the bitter criticism and admonishments directed against him, provoking both physical and mental stress, along with the threat of being sent either to the disciplinary battalion or to the lunatic asylum, Cheremshanov refuses to submit to those who loudly profess to be Christians even as they force him (in his words) to reject Christ and his teachings.

A good part of *And the Light Shineth in Darkness* was written during 1896 and 1897, at the very time when the writer was (as indicated above) preoccupied with finding a solution to the Doukhobors' plight. Even though Cheremshanov is of noble blood, his avowed reasons for his stand as a conscientious objector echo in good measure the reported motivations of the Doukhobors on this question.

In Act 3, Scene 2, for example, the young recruit's answers to official questions, as read by an adjutant, bear a remarkable resemblance to the Doukhobors' own replies to such questions (*PSS* 31:159–60):

> GENERAL *(handing the paper to the adjutant).* Read this, please.
> ADJUTANT *(reads).* "To the questions posed to me concerning (1) why I will not take the oath of allegiance and (2) why I am refusing to fulfil the demands, and what prompted me to utter words insulting not only to the military class but to the supreme authorities as a whole, to the first question I reply: I will not take the oath because I confess the teachings of Christ. In Christ's teachings taking an oath is directly and specifically forbidden, as in the Gospel of Matthew 5: 33–38, also in James 5:12."
> GENERAL. They are still rationalizing, interpreting it in their own way.
> ADJUTANT *(continues reading).* "In the Gospel it is written: 'Swear not at all. But let your communication be, Yea, yea; Nay, nay: for whatsoever is more than these cometh of evil.' In the Epistle of James: 'But above all things, my brethren, swear not, neither by heaven, neither by the earth, neither by any other oath: but let your yea be yea; and your nay, nay; lest ye fall into condemnation.' But never mind the fact that the Gospel gives a direct indication that one should not swear. Even if it didn't, I still could not swear that I would carry out the will of men, since under Christian law I am bound to always carry out the will of God, which may be incompatible with the will of men."
> GENERAL. Still rationalizing. If only they'd listened to me, none of this would have happened.
> ADJUTANT *(reads).* "I am refusing to carry out the demands of the people known as the government because..."

> GENERAL. What insolence!
> ADJUTANT. "...because these demands are criminal, evil. They require of me that I join the army and learn to kill and prepare to kill, whereas I am forbidden to do this by both the Old and New Testaments and, above all, by my conscience. As to the third question.... As to the third question, as to what has prompted me to insult people to their face, I reply that I was prompted to do this by my desire to serve God and expose the deception which is being perpetrated in His name. I hope to hold to this desire until the day I die. And so..."

In his article, V. I. Sreznevskij (1920: 155) refers to an unnamed person who may have had some influence in Tolstoy's mind on the creation of Cheremshanov:

> This occurred in 1865 and evidently gave only the basic features of Boris's character. Then, with new revisions of the drama these features were supplemented by what was given by other people who held views close to the type Tolstoy wanted to create. So perhaps in the portrayal of Boris one can find a certain similarity not only in terms of his views and convictions, but even of his living conditions with one of Lev Nikolaevich's friends, B., who in his time also suffered for his convictions, and even up to the present is continuing to put the Master's legacy into practice.[36]

While this is, of course, possible, it is evident that the primary source of the character Boris Cheremshanov, revealing in dramatic form the continuation — indeed, the confirmation — of the ideas and faith expounded in *The Kingdom of God is Within You* was the Doukhobor sect, whose destiny Tolstoy had become so involved in, including the beliefs he and they shared in common.

Another case closely related to the Doukhobors' was that of Tolstoyan Leopol'd Antonovich Sulerzhitskij. This Moscow Art Theatre actor was very close to the Tolstoy household and, at Tolstoy's request, accompanied two of the four boatloads of Doukhobors to Canada. Like Cheremshanov, Sulerzhitskij was arrested (in 1896) for his refusal to be conscripted, but because of family pressures and resulting depression, he eventually consented to serve in the navy. Interestingly, both Tolstoy and his protagonist Saryntsev expressed a total, uncritical understanding of those who, for whatever reason, changed their minds and obeyed the summons to join the army.

While Saryntsev's and Cheremshanov's criticism of official orthodoxy is much the same as in his other works already mentioned — and needs little in the way of further discussion here — it might be worthwhile to draw attention to a few interesting points which often escapes critical notice. One of these is Tolstoy's courage in including three Orthodox priests among his *dramatis personæ,* since at that time there was an official prohibition against showing priests on stage.

36 For a thorough study of Tolstoy's familiarity with and knowledge of conscientious objectors, see Brock 2003.

The first priest, Vasilij Nikanorovich, is young and likeable, but inexperienced, and not persuasive in his defence of the official church in his encounters with the sharp-tongued dissident Saryntsev. The second, a Father Gerasim, is older and more experienced in his dry, business-like approach, and proves a more challenging opponent for Tolstoy's protagonist. The third priest (unnamed) appears only briefly, attempting to persuade Cheremshanov to recant his dissidence and return to the fold; his pleas and admonitions, however, are rejected by the unwilling recruit as tantamount to the official position of the government.

It is Vasilij Nikanorovich who is persuaded by Saryntsev's teaching to leave the church and join the dissident movement. Note the following exchange from Act 3, Scene 3 (*PSS* 31:157):

> MAR'JA IVANOVNA [Saryntsev's wife]. Our priest has arrived, our Vasilij Nikanorovich. He's going to the Bishop. He's leaving the parish.
> NIKOLAJ IVANOVICH [Saryntsev]. Really!

In Scene 5 of the same act, Saryntsev himself enquires about the priest's decision (158):

> NIKOLAJ IVANOVICH. Have you really quit?
> PRIEST. I couldn't take it anymore.
> NIKOLAJ IVANOVICH. I didn't expect this so soon.
> PRIEST. I couldn't go on. In our way of life one cannot be indifferent. We are obliged to take confession and give communion, but when I found out it wasn't genuine...
> NIKOLAJ IVANOVICH. So what are you going to do now?
> PRIEST. Now I am going to see the bishop to be tried. I'm afraid they'll send me to the Solovetsky Islands.[37] I thought at one point of fleeing abroad, of asking you, but then I reconsidered: that would be cowardice. You see, there's my wife.
> NIKOLAJ IVANOVICH. Where is she?
> PRIEST. She's gone to her father's. Her mother was with us and took our little boy. It was very painful. I felt very much like... *(stops, trying to hold back tears).*

In Act 4, Scene 3, which takes place a year later, Saryntsev, informed by his wife that "Vasilij Nikanorovich has repented and returned to the fold," sadly responds, "that is unfortunate." (178). It is not evident, however, just where the priest has been in the meantime. The hint of incarceration or exile in the passage quoted above may possibly suggest a wish to join the Doukhobors in Canada (where by this time they have already settled).

37 *Solovetsky Islands* — a group of islands in the White Sea in Russia's Far North. Tolstoy's priest is most probably referring to the Solovetsky Monastery there, which later (during Soviet times) became a notorious concentration camp for political dissidents. The islands are now a popular destination for eco-tourists.

This supposition is given some credence at the very end of the play, in Act 5, which we have only in Tolstoy's skeleton outline, amounting to barely more than a single page (184). After showing Cheremshanov serving his sentence in a disciplinary battalion, there is a quick change of scene to the tsar's official quarters, where the prisoner's mother pleads (unsuccessfully) for the release of her son. She once more puts the blame on Saryntsev and again threatens to kill him. Just before she carries out her threat, Saryntsev is shown as saying: "I've achieved nothing. I've ruined Boris, and Vasilij Nikanorovich has recanted." Directly Saryntsev is shot by Cheremshanov's mother, and in walks the priest in the company of "Doukhobors." Tolstoy's last cue reads as follows: "He (Saryntsev) dies, delighting in the fact that the church's deception has now been exposed and his life once again has meaning." Not only from this, but also on the basis of Tolstoy's many diary entries, letters, and articles, the implication is clear that Vasilij Nikanorovich, having left the official church once again, has now joined the Doukhobors, and that it is they who are responsible for exposing the church's deception.

RESURRECTION (1899)

"16 December 1899" is the date the author put to his printed text of the novel *Resurrection*. His work on *Resurrection* had been going on intermittently since 1889. No other work by Tolstoy in the last two decades of his literary activity was subjected to so many corrections and redactions, and the corrections themselves required multiple editing. Add to that the pressure for haste felt by the author to raise the funds (through royalties from the novel) needed for the Doukhobors' emigration. His diaries of the period, as well as the multitude of letters (see "Chronology of Letters" in this volume), are replete with comments on the work as being "No good," "Not sufficiently corrected," "Too hasty!"[38] One can only imagine the writer's pain (for he was an incorrigible corrector of his own works) at having to compromise his principles in order to hasten the novel's publication (with a view to facilitating an earlier departure of the Doukhobors for Canada). Not only that, but the novel owes its very existence as a published work to the Doukhobors. At the Doukhobor centenary conference in Ottawa, in 1999, Lidija Gromova declared her conviction that "the novel *Resurrection* would have remained unfinished and unpublished if there had not been the need for funds to help relocate a persecuted people."[39] And elsewhere she writes (Gromova-Opul'skaja 1998: 354):

38 On Tolstoy's feverish work on *Resurrection* to raise the necessary funds for the Doukhobors' emigration, see the chapter "Obshchestvennaja dejatel'nost' Tolstogo. «Voskresenie» dlja dukhoborov" [Tolstoy's social activism: *Resurrection* for the Doukhobors] in A. L. Tolstaja 1953: 205–11.

39 Gromova-Opul'skaja 2000: 168. She goes on to quote a comment attributed to Tolstoy in conversation with the publisher Adolph Marks: "If it hadn't been for that [accepting royalties to assist the Doukhobor cause], I would never have finished writing *Resurrection*."

> On a number of occasions Tolstoy would do the proofreading over again so radically that the whole thing had to be recopied with the corrections, then corrected again, then recopied again, and so forth, until it was once more typeset from the author's manuscript and then several additional typesettings might be required after that.

It was during these seemingly endless corrections that the sixth redaction of the novel was composed, introducing several new personages along with a number of sectarians, and it is this redaction that is of principal interest to our study on Tolstoy and the Doukhobors.

In keeping with many of Tolstoy's later literary works, *Resurrection* deals with the moral regeneration of its chief protagonist, Nekhljudov. His attempts to correct his past life take him through several stages, especially his decision to marry the girl Katjusha, whom he has wronged. Renouncing his wealth and the high position secured for him by his aristocratic background, he follows Katjusha to Siberia, where she has been exiled on account of an unjust conviction at the hands of the hated courts.

Like Levin in *Anna Karenina*, Nekhljudov discovers that the most important thing in life is *living by God* and viewing all people as one's brethren. As we saw in Chapter 2 above, this truth is already espoused by Tolstoy's characters of higher social status, but to bring about their regeneration they must be brought into contact with simple Russian peasants, who instinctively know what is important in life. Examples of such pairings may be found in all of Tolstoy's major works: Pierre Bezukhov and Karataev in *War and Peace*, Levin and Platon (along with other peasants) in *Anna Karenina*, Ivan Il'ich and Gerasim in *The Death of Ivan Il'ich*, and now Nekhljudov and various peasant sectarians[40] he encounters in both prison and exile in *Resurrection*.

A few comments are also in order on the *fourth* redaction of the novel. It is here for the first time that Tolstoy introduces the Molokan sectarians, whose plight becomes of increasing concern to Nekhljudov as his moral regeneration proceeds, and he begins to intercede on their behalf with the Russian government.[41]

Again, it is in the fourth redaction that Tolstoy brings in an Old Believer,[42] but he has a change of heart and omits this character from the fifth draft.

40 For further information on these sectarians, see N. K. Gudzij's commentary on the novel in *PSS* 33:368–70, 390.

41 This episode may well be based on Tolstoy's own efforts on behalf of the Samara Molokan parents whose children were taken away from them to be educated in Orthodox institutions, and on whose behalf Tolstoy twice petitioned the tsar, Nicholas II (see Chap. 2, p. 38). For more information on the Molokans, see Note 23 and Note 24 in Chap. 2.

42 *Old Believers* [Starovery] — also known as Old Ritualists [Staroobrjadtsy] — those who did not accept the Orthodox Church reforms under the Patriarch Nikon in the seventeenth century,

Instead, in the sixth redaction, Nekhljudov meets a peasant who, like the Doukhobors, rejects all authority, secular and ecclesiastical, and believes that God dwells in each human being regardless of religious classification.[43]

While none of the sectarians depicted in *Resurrection* is actually labelled a 'Doukhobor,' it is evident from a host of other sources (letters, articles, diary entries[44] made not only by him but also by members of his family, reminiscences of acquaintances), as well as from his concurrent involvement (beginning in 1895) with the Doukhobors' plight and emigration, that the Doukhobors were the motivating factor behind not only Tolstoy's decision to finish the book but also the prominent role of peasant sectarians in the novel, including their function as a catalyst in bringing about the moral regeneration of a member of a higher social class.

There are several indications that Tolstoy had even thought of writing a sequel to *Resurrection,* focusing on the new peasant life of his reborn hero, Nekhljudov. I would venture to suggest that this might have been the 'longer work of historical fiction' referred to earlier in this chapter (see p. 102 above), for which the series of questions addressed to a Doukhobor at the very beginning of the chapter might well have served as an outline.

Tolstoy left the door open for a sequel when he concluded the published text of *Resurrection* with these words:

> From that night began an entirely new life for Nekhlujdov, not so much on account of his new living conditions, but because everything that had happened to him up to that point had taken on a completely new meaning. Where this new stage of his life will end up, only the future will tell (*PSS* 32:445).

Note also Tolstoy's diary entries of 23 June 1900: "I terribly want to write a fictional — not a dramatic, but an epic — sequel to *Resurrection*: the peasant life of Nekhljudov," and 28 November 1900: "Yesterday I read Novikov's article,[45] which gave me the distinct impression of recalling what I had forgotten — the life of the ordinary people: their needs, their humiliation and our guilt. Oh, if only God had ordained me to express everything I feel in this piece."[46]

but insisted on maintaining traditional forms of ritual. This led to what is known as the Raskol, the great schism, when not only Old Believers, but also dissidents who wanted to be free from ritual (like the Doukhobors), broke away from the official Church.

43 According to Gudzij (*PSS* 33:390), Tolstoy based this character on a peasant of the Wanderers [Beguny] sect, named Andrej Vasil'evich Vlasov, who wrote Tolstoy in mid-October 1899, describing several episodes from his own life. See also *PSS* 72:221–25.

44 For a sample of his diary during the writing of *Resurrection*, see Part III, p. 298.

45 See Donskov 1996a. Tolstoy is referring to Mikhail Novikov's article "Voice of the peasant" ["Golos krest'janina"], a powerful indictment against both church and state, and dealing precisely with the above concerns. Tolstoy received a copy of it in December 1900 and facilitated its publication in Chertkov's *Svobodnoe slovo* (Novikov 1904).

46 *PSS* 54:65. See also Gromova-Opul'skaja 1998: 368.

Had he written such a sequel, it is hard not to suppose that the Doukhobors, their way of life, respect for all life, pacifist convictions, and work ethics would have formed its basic content.

LETTER TO CANADIAN DOUKHBORS (1900)

Over the course of 1899 the Doukhobors had settled into three main geographical 'colonies': (a) the 'Northern Colony,' at Swan River, where the so-called 'Cold Mountain' Doukhobors from the first boatload (accompanied by Leopol'd Antonovich Sulerzhitskij) had settled; (b) the 'South[ern] Colony,' near Dead Horse Creek and White Sand, settled mainly by the Kars and Elisavetpol' Doukhobors from the second boatload (accompanied by Sergej L'vovich Tolstoy), along with the Cold Mountain Doukhobors on the third boatload from Cyprus (also escorted by Sulerzhitskij) and some from the fourth boatload (escorted by Vladimir Dmitrievich Bonch-Bruevich and his fiancée, Dr. Vera Mikhajlovna Velichkina; (c) a newer settlement, near Prince Albert, on the Saskatchewan River, home to some of the wealthier Doukhobors from the fourth boatload.

The differences in financial position among the various colonies, even among individual Doukhobors, were signficant.[47] Those with greater financial resources began acquiring farm tools and household goods as personal property (possibly under the influence of the English-speaking majority of Canadians surrounding them); many, in time, broke away from the community and began living as independent homesteaders. Even in their first year in Canada, the community spirit (by which most possessions were held in common) that had been so strong back in Russia showed signs of weakening, and reports on this trend from a variety of eyewitnesses soon reached Tolstoy. These reports are summarized in the commentary in *PSS* (72:316) as follows:

> In their letters to Tolstoy they did not hide their disillusionment and, perhaps, did not always give an objective description of the situation, occasionally contradicting each other, but all the accounts basically boiled down to one thing: the spiritual attitude among the majority of Doukhobors was declining, and the new ways of life were a far cry from Doukhobor ideals.

Tolstoy himself was even blunter in his own summary, which he outlined early on in the same letter, dramatically putting it into the mouths of "the enemies of Christianity" (*PSS* 72:305–06).

> "There they are, your Doukhobors," the enemies of Christianity now say, "no sooner did they emigrate to Canada, a free country, than they started living like

47 For a comparison table, see the commentary on Tolstoy's letter in *PSS* 72:314–16.

everyone else, each one amassing property for himself and not only refusing to share it with his brethren, but trying to grab as much for himself as he can."[48]

After Tolstoy began composing his letter (#1900-02-27, found in two redactions in *PSS* 72:305–14[49]) at the end of December 1899, he wrote to Chertkov[50] in England (*PSS* 72:316).

> I've started writing, but it's not coming. I very much want to show the young people who are getting distracted what kind of subtle and crude deception the desire for property and security is.

The desire for property and the striving for security, in fact, are the two major themes running through both drafts of the letter, which Tolstoy ties in first with Christian teachings in the Gospels[51] and then specifically with the overriding Doukhobor principle of non-violence. He approaches the link to non-violence by first citing a common argument Christians use in justifying their holding of personal property — namely, that there is nothing wrong with the practice as long as they share their surplus with the poor. "But," says Tolstoy (306),

> this is false. After all, personal property means that what I consider my own I will not only refuse to give to anyone who wants to take it from me, but I will protect it from him. There is no way you can protect what you consider your own other than through violence — i.e., by fighting, duelling or even murder, as necessary. If there weren't any of this violence and murder, then nobody could hold personal property.

And just in case any readers of his letter thought they could keep holding personal property and still maintain a convincing stand on non-violence, Tolstoy

48 In his earlier draft Tolstoy had prefaced this accusatory summary by an even stronger condemnation, again from the "enemies of Christianity" (311): "'We said all along,' the enemies of Christianity now cry and write in the papers, 'that it is impossible to live a Christian life without violence, without an army, and that is just how it has turned out, in our opinion. Your Doukhobors are nothing but restless, crude people, no different from anybody else.'"

49 Second redaction: 305–10; first redaction: 310–14.

50 As the intermediary to whom Tolstoy entrusted his letter, finally completed on 15 February 1900, Chertkov printed about two thousand copies and circulated them among the Doukhobor settlements in Canada.

51 Citing Jesus' dictum from the Sermon on the Mount, "Ye cannot serve God and mammon" (Matt. 6:24/Luke 16:13), Tolstoy identifies personal property squarely with "mammon," stating over and over again (with variations) that personal property is incompatible with Christianity — e.g., "After all, it only *seems* to us that one can be a Christian and still hold personal property and keep from sharing it with other people, but that is impossible. Once let people admit that, and very soon there will be nothing left of Christianity but words — and, unfortunately, insincere and hypocritical words at that" (*PSS* 72:306). Similarly, in the case of security, Tolstoy resorts once more to Jesus' sermon, "seek ye first the kingdom of God, and his righteousness; and all these things shall be added unto you" (Matt. 6:33), and further draws the lesson from the parable of the rich man (Luke 12: 16–21) that looking for security in material things is a fruitless and endless task.

not once but twice reminds the Doukhobors that "Christian teachings cannot be taken piecemeal: it is either all or nothing" (307, repeated 308). He also ties in the prohibition against property and material security to the Christian work ethic, which he phrases as "working as much as possible and contenting one's self with as little as possible" (308).

On two occasions Tolstoy admits the difficulty (though not the impossibility) of adhering to such an ethic. Near the beginning of the letter he takes account of the specific temptations involved in living "amongst alien people" and then of "living in a community" (306). Later on he recognizes how hard it is (a) to have nothing of one's own; (b) to share with anyone who asks; (c) to accept the decisions of elected community leaders, especially when they seem unfair; (d) to put up with each other's deficiencies; and (e) to withstand the temptations of luxury and abstain from meat, tobacco, and wine (309).

Yet despite the acknowledged difficulty, he does appear to be directing a specific appeal to the Doukhobors' own conscience, instilling in them a sense of guilt over their evident departures from their long-held principles and a sense of danger of losing all that they had suffered so much for in the past, in the hope that this will goad them, if not downright shame them, into returning, individually and collectively, to their former path of strict adherence to Christian requirements.

But he also points out the benefits of such adherence — he lists six of them, in fact, telling the Doukhobors how much more advantageous it is to live that way,

> ...first, because, in not providing for the future, you will not be spending useless energy on [trying to accomplish] something impossible for mortal man providing for himself and his family;
> ...second, you will not be wasting energy on fighting with others to hold back every piece of property you own from those around you;
> ...third, because you will be earning and acquiring incomparably more working as a community than you would working every man for himself;
> ...fourth, because, in living together as a community, you will be spending less on yourselves than you would if each were to live separately;
> ...fifth, because, in living a Christian way of life, instead of envy and ill feeling, you will attract to yourselves love, respect and perhaps even imitation on the part of the people around you;
> ...sixth, because you will not be ruining the work which you began before and which has brought shame to your enemies and joy to the friends of Christ.[52]

52 *PSS* 72:308–09. In the earlier redaction Tolstoy listed just three 'benefits' to the Christian way of life: the first two were similar to the sixth and first points, respectively, in the final draft, while the third, for some reason, was dropped in the later version — namely, "you will be acting advantageously for your soul in that you will save it, improve it and draw it closer to the God it is supposed to go to" (314).

Following the correspondence of Tolstoy and Pëtr V. Verigin in Chapter 6, the seventh chapter will examine the modern-day fruits of Tolstoy's efforts in a profile of the Canadian Doukhobors today, including a look (at least in part) on the ways (if any) in which the admonitions he sets forth in the above letter still resonate among the descendants of his 'kindred spirits' in twenty-first-century Canada.

CHAPTER 6

Tolstoy's Correspondence with Pëtr Vasil'evich Verigin

PËTR VASIL'EVICH VERIGIN

TOLSTOY'S EXCHANGE OF LETTERS with Doukhobor leader Pëtr V. Verigin[1] (published in full in Donskov 1995a) comprises one of the most noteworthy parts of his overall correspondence on the Doukhobors — a remarkable summary of the philosophies of what appear as two equally powerful intellects, revealing their points of commonality as well as frequently acute differences. It spans nearly fifteen years (November 1895 to May 1910), and while it broaches a broad variety of subjects, it is fundamentally an exchange of thoughts on the meaning of life, man's relationship to God, and the purpose of human existence.

The thirty-eight extant letters included in this volume (see also Donskov 1995a and 2019) do not represent the full extent of the correspondence. Because of the confiscation of mail by the imperial Department of Police at the time, a good number of letters are still missing, especially for the year 1897. Still, what has been published reveals a remarkable and fascinating relationship between two 'giants' — one a nobleman with a worldwide reputation as a stellar novelist, sixty-seven years old at the outset of their correspondence, the other a thirty-six-year-old peasant who had already spent eight years in exile for holding views that bore a striking similarity to Tolstoy's own.

As indicated, the correspondence deals less with the practical questions of emigration than with the ideas germane to Tolstoy and Verigin as thinkers, and hence, while this exchange has already been discussed in a variety of

1 For details on Pëtr V. Verigin's life, please see Chap. 1 (esp. the second half of the chapter).

scholarly articles,[2] it may be appropriate at this juncture to elaborate to some degree on the commonalities and differences in views expressed in the letters.

Of particular interest is the fact that, even though Verigin began the correspondence with a great deal of respect for the writer, and even a feeling of kinship, he was quite confirmed in his own views on life; moreover, he did not hesitate to express them or defend his strongly held convictions. His arguments about the irrelevance of literacy and books in general, for example, are forcefully (albeit one-sidedly) presented.[3] Tolstoy, in turn, despite the discrepancy in such views, as well as the obvious differences in age and professional reputation, was prepared to treat Verigin more or less as an equal.

The letters deal with a broad range of topics. In the first half of the exchange (while the Doukhobor leader was still in Siberian exile, in Obdorsk), we find, for example, Verigin's criticism of both secular and ecclesiastical authorities in Russia, whereas his letters written from Canada are characterized more by what seemed to Tolstoy to be an inordinate attention to the material welfare of his flock.

Still, there is no lack of discussion of spiritual matters: man's relationship to God, faith, love of humanity, the meaning of human life (which Verigin in one letter[4] defined as "to keep one's heart from evil"). Another commonality of views is found in the theme of the *unity of people*, which runs like a leitmotif through Verigin's letters, with Tolstoy's responses nodding approval. In contrast to laws and restrictions imposed by government and church authorities, both Verigin and Tolstoy saw a need for all humankind to live according to the God-consciousness within each individual, united in kindness, love, and respect for everything living, regardless of human categorizations.

The chief difference between the two thinkers may be seen in their approaches to the world and humanity's quest for spiritual truth. In contrast to Verigin's more extreme points of view, Tolstoy seems better able to come to terms with mankind's evident flaws and find a way around them.[5] His letters reveal a greater philosophical and intellectual bent, despite his evident sincerity in his quest for spiritual enlightenment. But he has no hesitation

2 See Gromova-Opul'skaja 1995, 2000; Woodsworth 1995; Bumgardner 2001.

3 In this argument, near the beginning of their correspondence (see, e.g., Letter N° 2 below), Verigin emphasizes the power of the spoken "living word," which Christ gave his disciples direct orders to spread — as opposed to a written piece that is open to many interpretations, including misinterpretation. He accordingly acknowledges his greater fascination with Tolstoy's life than his writings, and, when it comes to the latter, his preference for Tolstoy's treatises over his fiction.

4 Letter 32, dated 2 February 1909.

5 In his letter to Verigin of 14 October 1896 (Letter N° 3) — e.g., in discussing the problem of whether the end necessarily justifies the means — Tolstoy rejects the notion that material and spiritual progress are mutually exclusive. Toward the end of the letter he also takes note of the discrepancy between his philosophical ideas and his born-into-nobility lifestyle, claiming to be "surrounded...by all sorts of luxuries which I hate but have not the strength to extricate myself from," and acknowledges the moral support he derives from Verigin's example.

in examining his own (and humanity's) conception of God, acknowledging that it may be all too coloured by a misguided attempt to define a perfect spiritual concept on the basis of imperfect physical human experience.[6] This subjectivity in perceiving God provoked a serious inner struggle in Tolstoy. At the same time, he rejected what he saw as the Doukhobors' tendency to take the perception of God beyond the rational into the realm of the mystical and superstitious.[7]

A close reading of the letters indicates that, over the period of their correspondence, Tolstoy exerted a significant influence on the Doukhobor leader, even if (initially, at least), Verigin's powerful intellect was unprepared to accept Tolstoy's views when they contradicted his own.[8] Moreover, through Verigin, the influence of a number of Tolstoy's ideas was felt throughout the whole Doukhobor movement.[9]

There was undoubtedly a significant influence in the opposite direction as well.[10] By the time of their first meeting, in 1902, when Verigin was on his way to Canada, a fair number of letters had already been exchanged. In addition, Tolstoy had been made aware of the Doukhobor leader's vigorous intellect by a great number of reports forwarded to him by common acquaintances. That Verigin had come from a peasant milieu, a people in whom Tolstoy for so many decades had sought and, at least partially, found a meaning of life that

6 See, e.g., Letter N° 8, where Tolstoy writes: "This misconception of God comes mainly from our inculcated beliefs about the creation of the world, about our knowledge of how the world was created and who created it.... We do not see the frightening absurdity of such a conception only because we are too accustomed to it."

7 See, e.g., Letter N° 10, in which Tolstoy urges that "such a superstition...should not be encouraged, as I am sure you fully agree, and that if such a superstition exists, it exists against your will."

8 The gradual 'softening' of Verigin's attitude toward his acceptance of Tolstoy's ideas, along with his resultant character transformation, is extensively examined in Woodsworth 1995.

9 Noted Doukhobor historian Eli Popoff (author of a guest essay in this volume), however, points out that more of this influence may have actually come through Verigin's son, Pëtr Petrovich Verigin (1881–1939), than through Verigin himself. Pëtr Petrovich, whose adopted surname *Chistjakov* literally signifies 'the Cleanser,' was invited by the Doukhobors to come to Canada to succeed his father as leader, after the latter's death in a railway explosion. In a personal communication, Popoff (2001) wrote: "One thing that I wished to mention to you is about something that has been continually overlooked by researchers on Doukhobor philosophy as it is presently espoused. And that is that although we have on record the correspondence of Peter V. Verigin and Leo Tolstoy, and other historical data pointing to the influence of Tolstoyan philosophy, via Peter V. Verigin, on Doukhobor thought, in my researches and study of the development of modern Doukhobor thought I find that Peter P. Verigin-Chistiakov the son of Peter Lordly, brought in as much if not more Tolstoyan philosophy into modern Doukhobor ideology than did his illustrious father. Whether because he knew of the close contacts his father had with Leo Tolstoy, or whether he did this entirely of his own volition, it is known that from a very young age Peter Chistiakov made a very thorough study of all of Leo Tolstoy's writings." Note: *Lordly* is a common mistranslation of the Russian *Gospodnij*, which means in fact 'belonging to the Lord.'

10 This aspect of influence is frequently pointed out (and occasionally exaggerated) by Doukhobors today — cf. the section on "Doukhobor perceptions of Tolstoy's ideas" (as well as the third sample letter under "Doukhobors' comments on Tolstoy") in Chap. 7.

would endure beyond death, further endeared him to the writer, both on a personal level and as a model for the subsequent portrayal of peasants in his works.[11] Tolstoy's perception of their mutual influence can be summed up in his aforementioned letter to E. I. Popov (#1896-03-27):

> We need closer communication [with the Doukhobors], whereby we can borrow a good deal from them — in looking at them we can discover our own weaknesses — and they can borrow something from us.

11 For more on this influence, see Chap. 5 above.

TOLSTOY AND VERIGIN: LETTERS 1895–1910

1. L. N. TOLSTOY ❧ P. V. VERIGIN
21 November 1895. Moscow.

Dear Brother!

Ivan Mikhajlovich Tregubov[12] has sent me your letter to him,[13] and I was very glad to read it, glad to learn of you and to hear your voice, as it were, and understand what you are thinking about, and how you think and what you live by. I see from your letter that you live in a spiritual world and concern yourself with spiritual questions. That is vital for the good of mankind, for only in the spirit is man free, and only through the spirit is God's work done, and only in the spirit does man feel himself at one with God, since "God is spirit."[14]

The thoughts you express in your letter about the superiority of live communication over dead books greatly appealed to me, and I share them. I write books and therefore I know all the harm that they cause; I know how people who are unwilling to accept truth know how not to read or not understand anything that goes against the grain and exposes them, how they reinterpret and distort, how they have reinterpreted the Gospel.

I know all that, yet all the same I think that *in our time* books are unavoidable. I say 'in our time' — in contrast to the gospel times, when there was no printing of books, there were simply no books, and the means of communicating thoughts was purely oral. Back then it was possible to get by without books, because neither did the enemies of truth have books; but now we cannot let just the enemy have this powerful tool to use for deceit and not use it for truth. Not to use books or letters for communicating one's thoughts and to receive thoughts of other people is tantamount to not using the power of your own voice to communicate instantly to many people what you wish to say, or not to use your hearing to understand what another person is saying out loud, but to admit that thoughts can be communicated and received only one on one or through whispering.

Letters and print have simply increased by thousands — by hundreds of thousands — the numbers of people capable of hearing one express one's

12 *Ivan Mikhajlovich Tregubov* (1858–1931) — an Orthodox priest's son who rejected Orthodoxy in favour of Tolstoy's teachings. As an avid Tolstoyan he collected and studied materials on peasant sectarians and publicly defended them in the face of official persecution.

13 Letter from P. V. Verigin to I. M. Tregubov, 5 August 1895, published in Bonch-Bruevich 1901: 14–16. In 1893 Tregubov left the Moscow Seminary to work at the Posrednik publishing house. Thanking Tregubov for the books sent to Obdorsk, Verigin added: "Books help a lot in working things out, but can sometimes be a big hindrance as well. Whereas our own voice of appeal will never deceive you, as long as our desires are sincere, that is, as long as the soul is fully present." Later, Tregubov continued sending Tolstoy letters from Verigin and other Doukhobors.

14 John 4:24.

thoughts, but the relationship between the communicator and the receiver remains the same; just as in oral conversation the listener can delve into and understand what he is hearing, or can let what is being said to him go in one ear and out the other, the same is true with print: just as it is possible for the reader to misinterpret a book he is reading, so can one who listens with his ears; just as one can — as we see — write nonsense or write too much, so is it possible to talk that way. There is a difference, but the difference is sometimes in favour of oral, sometimes written communication.

The advantage of oral communication is that the listener feels the soul of the speaker, but here too is the disadvantage that quite often empty-headed chatterers — lawyers, for example — endowed with the gift of the gab, attract people not by the reasonableness of their words but by their oratorical mastery, which doesn't happen with books; another advantage of oral communication is that the person who doesn't understand can ask for clarification, and yet there is the disadvantage that people who don't understand, often on purpose, can ask unnecessary questions and break the train of thought, which also does not happen with books.

The disadvantages of books are, first, that paper will tolerate anything and you can print all kinds of nonsense, at the cost of enormous efforts on the part of paper and typography workers, which would be impossible in oral communication, since people don't bother listening to nonsense; secondly, the fact that they (books) are multiplying in huge quantities and the good ones are lost in a sea of stupid, meaningless and harmful books.

Nevertheless, the advantages of books are also considerable, consisting mainly in the fact that the circle of one's listeners is expanded by hundreds of thousands compared to people listening to oral communication. And this expansion of the circle of listeners is important not simply because there are a lot of them, but because among the millions of people of various nations and social status who have access to a book, 'kindred spirits' turn up all by themselves; people living tens of thousands of versts[15] from each other, people who don't even know each other, are united into one and live by a single soul and derive spiritual joy and courage from the realization that they are not alone. This is the kind of communion I now have with you and with many, many people of other nations who have never seen me, but who are closer to me than my blood sons and brothers.

But the chief argument in favour of books is the fact that, given a certain degree of development in the outward standard of living, books — and print in general — have become people's means of communication with each other and therefore we cannot afford to neglect this means. So many harmful books have been written and circulated that this harm can be counteracted only by books. You fight fire with fire. Christ said: "What ye hear in the ear, that

15 *verst* = 1.07 km.

preach ye upon the housetops."[16] Well, this preaching upon the housetops is the printed word. The printed word is the very same language, only very far-reaching, and therefore everything said about language applies to the printed word as well: we use language to bless God and to curse people created in God's likeness; and so you can never be careful enough about what you say and hear, just as about what you print and read.

I am writing all this not because I thought that you think differently (I see from your letter that you understand this the same way), but because these thoughts have come to me and I wanted to share them with you. I was especially touched by what you said in your letter to the effect that *"if we preserved what was already given to us from above, we should be perfectly happy. And whatever is necessary and lawful must inevitably be in each one of us, and comes directly from above or from within ourselves."* This is quite right, and that is my concept of man too.

Everyone would undoubtedly know God's truth, know all they needed to know to accomplish what God wants from them in this life, as long as this truth that has been revealed to man is not clouded by false human interpretations. And for that reason to know God's truth man needs first of all to reject all false interpretations and all worldly temptations that would lead him to accept these interpretations, and then the truth alone will remain, the truth which is available to babes, since it is innate to the human soul. The big challenge is in throwing out the lie without throwing out some of the truth with it, as well as, in the process of explaining the truth, to avoid introducing new errors.

I thank you, dear brother, for the greetings you sent me. Write to me in Moscow, if there is nothing stopping you, at the Tolstoy house in Khamovniki Lane. Is there anything I can do for you? You will make me very happy if you give me something to do.

I embrace you as a brother.

Lev Tolstoy

21 November 1895

2. P. V. VERIGIN ❧ L. N. TOLSTOY
1 August 1896. Obdorsk.

I contradict myself.
— P. Verigin

My Kind and Dear Friend Lev Nikolaevich!

I thank you wholeheartedly for the attention expressed in your letter to me of 21 November 1895. — I received it just a few days ago. The simplicity of your

16 Matth. 10:27.

discussion speaks of the clarity and the straightforwardness of your heart, hence: "out of the abundance of the heart the mouth speaketh."[17]

Your arguments about literacy are correct through and through — especially in regard to the present time. — As you yourself say. But I sometimes allow myself — to idealize my thought in general terms, not taking account of time or circumstance. — Forsaking literacy in our day — even for a brief time, i.e., for a moment, would be tantamount to depriving everybody of shoes, or depriving contemporary women of their hats, all decked out with lace and bird feathers. That would unquestionably lead to a state of considerable bewilderment. Just the scandalous image of shoeless and hatless people would be a revolting sight. In spite of the fact that if you look at it seriously, people might still behave lawfully even without entangling their feet in boots and shoes or distorting the natural appearance of the head. I would suppose, as regards the highest cult of emancipated women, that if they didn't wear hats, their brains and thoughts would not suffer in the least.

So too with literacy, it's a kind of 'fashion of the times.' As you yourself argue, literacy is needed as a means of communication for the time. Someone who is literate sees in this manner his own self — even his thoughts, but generally the image is not correct. Being literate is like having fine clothes (though obtained through someone else's labour), but even an illiterate can be a human being, in the larger sense of the word.

I have often had the occasion to witness such scenes — people spending several hours in conversation and instinctively drawing closer together, through the union of the Spirit-thought, and then suddenly parting, cutting off their conversation in the middle of a word, once they find that a third party to the conversation, as it turns out, is completely illiterate. In reply to the question "And which *lycée* did you attend?," the answer is received that he did not attend school at all. — You will completely agree that the judgement of these two (by their own admission) literate people is out and out wrong: if they hadn't found out about the illiteracy, all three would have parted friends.

Just so, a contemporary lady with a hat and veil will not offer her hand to a tanned and bare-headed Tyrolian woman, failing to understand that a hat, or a fancy dress with a ribbon and stars, is only a 'passing fad' which does not enhance the intellect in the least. One can be literate and not understand anything, or *feel* anything, and, vice-versa, be illiterate and yet have a clear comprehension of what is going on around one. Literacy should not be considered a lever for people's mental development, especially their basic spiritual progress. — At the end of this letter I am attaching an excerpt from my diary, about the basic motive-force behind our evolution.

Now I shall answer your specific arguments as to the legitimacy of literacy. — In the first place you say: "How often people do not read and do not want

17 Matth. 12:34.

to comprehend what goes against their habits!" This is because for a patient who has finally given in to a disease, who cannot get up and take his medicine, it isn't enough to supply him with flasks filled with prescribed remedies, or send them to him by post; what is needed is the personal presence of the doctor, his advice, as well as his healthy, cheerful countenance — this is what inspires people. — This is why, as far as I can tell, the more genuine thinkers about truth have gone and helped sick people personally, instead of just offering them medicines.

And Christ did not command his followers to sow the living word just because there was no book-publishing then — there had been publishing for several thousand years before Christ, only in different forms — but because he found the living word a more accurate means of communication, not only because of its simplicity but also the opposite, because of its complexity. One can read and copy what someone else has written, but one can really think and speak only one's own thoughts.

Literacy has caused people to fall into a major blunder: often they take and read the Psalms when they have nothing in common with them, and so it is no wonder that the word is not inculcated in the listeners, "they say and do not."[18] — A writer or reader can be compared to a pharmacist who reads prescriptions and uses them to prepare medicines, one who often does not believe in his own actions but carries out his duties for material gain — for pay. I personally compare the thinker or speaker to the doctor, whose healthy countenance in front of the patient and charming words testify to his faith in the medicine he offers. And what if the patient should challenge the doctor, — as you say: "People who don't understand, often on purpose, can ask unnecessary questions and break the train of thought," which is only natural. But this very criticism will incite the doctor to even more detailed and convincing arguments. — Just like the oral preachers of a proper life did, which would be impossible in the case of books. Just as the pharmacist cannot add one word to the prescription, because he doesn't understand anything. The countenance of the pharmacist who doesn't believe in the medicines only makes the patient feel uneasy; he unconsciously thinks: "Why aren't you completely healthy yourself, if this medicine is so effective?"

When I give out or read humanitarian booklets, people often remark to me: "Why don't you yourself live what you read to us about?" I reply frankly: "I am reading or offering to you what someone else has written." The situation, as you can see, is rather awkward. Asking others to do what you don't believe in yourself. So it is with writing.

To tell the truth, how many writers do we have that write their own ideas? And not just transcribe what has been written for thousands of years?

Just think, is it necessary to write on paper about the danger of murder,

18 Matth. 23:3.

when an inner voice within us calls us to show mercy? — Is it absolutely necessary to write about equality, when the seed of Unity and Brotherhood has been planted in each one of us? — Is it necessary to write in the press about freedom, when the Spirit which lives within us and supports our life is a free entity? There is no need to write about this, the need is to go and live according to what our inner voice tells us. — The voice of justice, not of animality, which we can learn with the help of reason even without being literate.

People who through violent means impose slavery on their fellow brethren do so not because they are illiterate but because they have not been educated spiritually — they are unwilling to submit to the inner call, the voice of conscience. And as far as the usurper is concerned, no book is going to be of any help if he himself has not been made to understand the futility of his despotic inhuman stand. — If there is to be any mediating influence, it will be the example of a living humble person, and not a dead book lying on the despot's desk.

Bear in mind what happened with the Gospel when people copied it on paper instead of the living heartfelt truth, as Christ commanded: "Lo I have written my law in your hearts and will put the word in your mouths, go and preach good will."[19]

Was Christ the only one to say this? — The Spirit dwelling within us is constantly calling us to the law of God, but we are reluctant to trust ourselves to such an elementary simple truth, but think up artificial fetters to encumber our progress toward a free existence. — Tell me, please, would it be reasonable for me to devote whole volumes to the subject of freedom to write, taking no account of the fact that by this very writing I am keeping millions of people in underground mines extracting the wherewithal to realize the goal of literacy? Or as in ancient times to have slaves hew out whole poems on stones (or tablets, as they were called)? In the middle ages they tore skins from animals (parchments) and wrote on them — I consider all that highly unlawful. But without such paraphernalia literacy would not be realizable.

The advantage of literacy is an imaginary one — a misleading one. If you agree that books have been the means by which so much evil has come into human existence, then why must you too bend over backward using books to destroy this evil, citing the not entirely logical saying: *Fight fire with fire*? — If you admit that a dagger is dangerous, why must you try to destroy the dagger by means of another dagger? It is possible to wash away a body of water — a pond for example — by a much stronger stream of water from above, but I submit that it is possible to dry out the place by another means, namely, the gradual lowering of the level of water in the pond, and in time the area will grow over with luxuriant grass.

19 Cf. Jer. 31:33, which, in the Authorized Version, reads: "But this shall be the covenant that I will make with the house of Israel; After those days, saith the Lord, I will put my law in their inward parts, and write it in their hearts; and will be their God, and they shall be my people." For Jesus' commandment "Go and preach," see Mark 16:15.

Christ's saying "What ye hear in the ear, that preach ye upon the housetops"[20] I don't take to mean writing. It must be taken in its literal sense: preach, but preach freely, openly, not being concerned about the circumstances. — For Christ to speak quietly — "in the ear," as he expressed it, meant that he was imparting the teaching of love in a concentrated form, as if in an embryo, and sometimes secret conversation was a necessary measure in the circle of His listeners, at least half of whom were already his followers, until this teaching had gone from one person, i.e., Christ, to many people and had become stronger, so that it could be preached openly, preached "from the housetops," with no fear of being arrested or wiped out by the opponents of truth. Christ was here saying that "when you feel the power of the calling, as well as multiply in numbers, then go and preach openly what you have heard in secret." The most important thing is the example of your life. — I tell you honestly, my esteemed friend, Lev Nikolaevich, out of your whole life, as far as I understand you, it is not your writings, in the form of literary compositions, that appeal to me, but rather your life, your actions, the way you left an artificial life for a natural human one. — If you had simply presented an idealized view of equality/brotherhood with the lowest levels of the populace, as you thought at the time when you were living in Moscow, and hadn't gone into this brotherly people's own milieu, not actually mingled with them in real life, you would not, to tell the truth, have deserved the high authority and reputation you have now. I think this opinion is shared by many who know you. To write the way you have written — well, that could have been done in Moscow, but to live the way you are now living, in the country — in Moscow would be impossible.

You say that "through literacy you can communicate with many, including me." I don't know about other people, but as regards to me, that is not quite correct. I can honestly say that I loved you and knew you even before you wrote to me. — To put it clearly I will say it this way: I love all good people and strive to draw closer to them with all my heart, and somehow it turns out that I share a common life with them, regardless of who they are, where they may be, what their name is, and whether there are a lot of them or not. I believe only in an unlimited number of good people, that is, in the power of good, and if you are good, only then do I sincerely love you. Of course your letter serves as a report or communication of what is already an established fact (according to accepted opinion), but I repeat: for me the greater reality is the Spirit, the power of thought — the power of spiritual love, rather than love of things. — Such communication, as you see, is only possible through true spiritual love, where deception is impossible. If, however, one believes in the power of literacy, the power of paper, it is quite often possible to be deceived.

---

20 Matth. 10:27.

In their press reports about the latest movement in our community in the Caucasus, correspondents are somewhat mistaken when they say the Christians of this community refuse to obey the government, as the main tenet of our convictions is not to disobey but to avoid giving orders to people in any form, especially when it comes to using forcible means. The government knows that we refuse military service, inasmuch as we have simply decided not to violate the rights of any, so to speak, living creature, especially human beings. By refusing to carry out their duties, our elders and community law enforcers have stated that they are not in a position to govern their districts, i.e., people like themselves, not that they would disobey their elders. — In principle, according to our convictions, elders must always be obeyed; it is only that *we must not be elders ourselves.*

I thank you most heartily for your wish to help me with any need. Nothing is needed at the moment. My warmest wishes to you for all blessings from the Lord God. — I am healthy, thank God, in spirit and body. Summer in Obdorsk this year has been very warm and spring came early: even the month of May was warm, which almost never happens here. I am spending the summer doing a little manual work besides. In the spring I began unloading wood from the rafts. Our artel was made up of three people. For tossing the wood out of the water and making fires on the shore they pay 20 kopeks a *sazhen'*.[21] Then we rolled out the logs. This kind of work pays 60–80 kopeks a day.

I have worked alongside a stonemason building stoves; for a simple Russian stove they pay 15–20 roubles, up to 30 roubles for a Dutch stove. — I have gone haying a couple of times, helping widows mow hay.

A small inconvenience is that I am under strict orders not to leave the settlement. Last winter, for example, I went a couple of times to the outskirts of Obdorsk to get wood, and this raised such a fuss that an official came out from Berezov to look into it and collect depositions. Even on such silly questions as "What would Verigin need wood for?" The official lives in the Berezov District, where it gets down to minus forty or fifty; but in spite of all that, there are still people who don't know why people collect wood from the forest.

When I arrived in Obdorsk, I soon found a small hut to rent (it used to be a smithy), remodelled it and began living there. The police authorities wouldn't allow it, they told to me to rent a 'residential' apartment, and made me pay 6 roubles a month instead of 1½. — I suppose it was just an expression of the high-handed rudeness of the local police, which I am indifferent to.

I was put on official notice that I must under no circumstances leave Obdorsk (meaning the boundary of the populated settlement). I can live with this, since according to my convictions I feed myself from plants; I don't feel it is right to fish. But the region here lives exclusively off the fishing industry. I don't have to leave the settlement to get bread; if only I can get some work,

21 *sazhen'* — a unit of length equivalent to a little more than two metres.

one can earn one's living here in the settlement doing day-labour. — But for an ordinary person such a restriction would be quite intolerable. As I said, the region lives off fish and they won't even let you travel three or four versts to set your nets.

I still hope they will give me a place to live where I can grow my own bread, or do some kind of agricultural work, which I have the talent for. And I am not in the least surprised by such condescension on the part of the government: after all, it will soon be ten years (in 1897) that I have been deprived of real physical activity, which of course has a bad effect on one's moral disposition.

Anyway, being in exile I have learnt a lot of useful things, for example, I have studied almost the whole northern land, in all its aspects. Most importantly, since I have had nothing to do, I have been examining myself, and even though I haven't learnt everything yet, my study is progressing gradually — something it's quite an effort to do when you're involved in organized, unvarying physical labour.

So far people at home have been sending me money, but in my latest letters I have been telling them not to do that. I think it's quite shameful if a physically healthy person like myself can't earn my own living. Especially since the arrests in our community are continuing, which means the family's finances are getting shaky. Lately they've begun imprisoning the women too.

The question of 'non-violent resistance to evil' is completely answered to my mind, for which I offer you, on behalf of the whole community, our sincere and heartfelt gratitude. You, dear brother Lev Nikolaevich, have personally done a great deal for our age. — I completely agree with your opinion — no matter how you look at it, no good deed was done.

Warmest greetings to everyone I know, and I wish you in brotherhood all blessings from God.

Pëtr Verigin

P.S. Write to me, if you would be so kind. — I did not receive from you any letter in the mail.

Yours, Pëtr

1st Aug. '96
Village of Obdorsk.

Diary excerpt

All that is visible to our eyes is the imprint of the Creator, the supreme will. Through visible images, as through a prism, comes the majesty — the will — of the Creator, imprinted in our mind. Like the shadow of a person on a photographic plate. — In other words, we can see God in His creations.

Mind, thought, will — that is the ideal, and all the image-forms seen by our thought — that is the real. When the mind or will comes into contact with the real — that is, with actual matter, harmony obtains: the harmony of reason, of report, and hence of reality as well. Without matter thought would lose itself in space (if it is possible to imagine such a thing), and have no support. — Idealism, or the will, is a bird, while reality, or matter, is a tree. The bird, no matter how easily and quickly it flies in the air, must still alight and rest.

The Divine Will and the human mind are of similar origin, and so we involuntarily pay attention to every form, to every manifestation of matter — that is a Divine secret, a universal law. In considering a prism, we try to penetrate and examine what lies behind it; by the same token we strive to unite with an entity similar to ourselves, or at least to know it. Our brain, as I indicated, is a glass plate, on which are imprinted the shadows of visible objects, and we distinguish clearly the image of what we wish to see.

The more visible images there are, the greater the exhilaration (in us), and the greater our curiosity and inquisitiveness, which also uplifts our soul.

In every object that exists there is the presence of God, since God is life, and what exists also lives. — The Sophists strive in vain to re-create God (in their opinion), calling Him Nature. — Nature is God too.

If our earth should be destroyed because of old age, it cannot be supposed that the existence of God would thereby end as well, since there are still *masses* of worlds in which He will continue to exist. Even if all existing worlds should die, in their place new ones would arise, hence God is eternal.

To believe in God means believing in life. I believe and I live. To truly believe in God — to believe in life — means striving for eternal life. While everything lives and hence everything believes in God, that is, in life, the distinct ideal of the immortality of life belongs to a more rational entity, for example, man. — The desire for eternal life depends entirely on us, on our faith in life, our faith in God. A small example of the meaning of faith, of the desire to live, may be seen in the following: an animal that happens to fall into the water vigorously begins to struggle, thereby expressing faith, the desire to live, and doesn't drown. — The animal is saved by faith in life.

The embryo of faith in life has been planted in us to serve as a proof that we live. — But developing this faith in life, faith in God, as I have said, depends entirely on us, on our desire. If we desire eternal life, to merge with the Divine principle, which Christ calls Father, we shall indeed live — live eternally; if we do not desire this, we shall die; meaning that what we ourselves desire will actually come to pass. — A lack of desire to live leads to destruction, and we lose even that talent which was given to us as an embryo and which we have held fruitlessly without using it.

The thought of faith is a fine-honed arrow of an abstract mental trait. — Like an arrow shot from a bow, or a leaden bullet, it reaches its target as desired by the marksman, so does serious thought concentrated on a known object — an animate one, of course, and will not remain without significance as long as it does not take any kind of distances into account.

It is from this that very often arises, so to speak, extraordinary mutual love. The pair upon meeting almost cry aloud, not to mention the fact that they have been struck with one another spiritually.

Such instances can be explained by the influence of the love exuded by the most delicate fibres of the spirit. — People create for themselves their most adorable ideal and finally begin to deify it, and if this ideal but exists, the spirit of desire, worship or supremacy will find it and cause mutual attraction. — The person — either a man or a woman (sometimes both of the same gender) — unaccountably begins to feel some kind of attraction and finally power taking over. The actual meeting then only complements an already--existing closeness. And if the love or mutual feeling should arise after the usual encounters and getting acquainted, this influence is simplified to the point of clarity.

It follows that age very often is not significant. Young girls may fall in love with old men (I am talking about true love, not about money) because the old man's desire has subjugated this girl many years his younger, or vice-versa. Such an influence is possible only in the case of true spiritual love, not in the play of fantasy.

There is a lot of evidence showing that a horse led out of the stable for the first time will neigh and submit to the approaching rider, while not letting other people get near him, even if they are physically stronger. The horseman's confidence and resolute desire to possess such a horse restrains and overcomes the animal's obstinacy. — Communication with animals helps them draw the animals closer and they begin to love the person communicating with them; here a similar factor is at work, the power of love, of thought or spirit.

If you agree with all this, then you can completely accept the veracity of stories about wilderness-dwellers frequently taming lions and bears.

P. Verigin

Obdorsk
1896

3. L. N. TOLSTOY ❧ P. V. VERIGIN
14 October 1896. Yasnaya Polyana.

Dear Friend,

I received your letter[22] yesterday and hasten to reply. Letters both to you and from you take a long time, and I have not that long to live. There is much that is just and witty in your arguments against books — the comparison with

22 The reference is to Letter N° 2 above.

the pharmacist and the doctor — but they are all groundless, mainly because you compare books with live communication as if books excluded live communication. In fact one does not exclude the other, they help each other. To tell you the truth, your stubborn resistance to books seemed merely a sectarian habit of defending a position once it has been adopted and declared. But this exclusivity does not fit the picture I have drawn of your intellect, especially of your cordiality and sincerity.

God leads people to Himself to do His will in all sorts of ways: both conscious, when people try to do His will, and unconscious, when they are doing what they think is their own will. To do God's will, to establish His kingdom on earth, people must be united among themselves, so that all may be one, as Christ recognized himself as one with the Father.

To reach this kind of unity one must follow first, the inner path — the knowledge and clear expression of truth, as Christ showed us, which unites all people, and secondly, the external path of spreading this message of truth, which is effected in all sorts of various ways: by trade and conquests, by travels on foot and by rail, by telegraph and telephone, and by books, as well as many other means of communication. Some of the latter — conquests, for example — I am obliged to reject, but others, such as books and quick communication devices I have no right to reject, and cannot help using if I do not wish to deny myself a handy tool whereby to serve God.

The same objection you make in regard to books and the railway, about having to go underground for minerals and process them in a blast-furnace, the same could be said about making ploughshares, spades and scythes. And there is nothing wrong with going underground for minerals or working with blast-furnaces, and when I was young, or as any young man today will gladly crawl boldly underground and dig out the ore, just as long as it is not forced upon him and does not continue ten hours a day his whole life long and he is provided with all the comforts people have thought up, as long as everybody works, and not just hired slaves.

Well, let's not talk any more about that, but do believe me that in writing this to you, I am not writing simply because I have written many books and am still writing them — I agree with you that the simplest good life is worth more than the finest books — and not even just because books have made it possible for me to make contact — this autumn, for example — with a Hindu who completely shares our Christian outlook and who sent me an English book written by a compatriot[23] of his, explaining the doctrines of the Brahmans which coincide with the essence of Christ's teachings, as well as to

23 In his diary of 14 September 1896, Tolstoy noted: "During this time there was a letter from the Hindu Tod and a marvellous book on Indian wisdom, *Joga's Philosophy*" (*PSS* 53:106). The book Tod sent was Swami Vivekananda's *Yoga Philosophy: Lectures Delivered in New York, Winter of 1895-6 by Swami Vivekananda on Râja Yoga, or Conquering the Internal Nature* (New York: Longman Green, 1896).

contact some Japanese people who confess and preach pure Christian morality, two of whom came to visit me a few days ago.[24]

This is not what leads me to disagree with you and refuse to reject the printing of books, along with the railway, the telephone, etc., but something else: when I look at an anthill in a meadow, I cannot bring myself to suppose that the ants were mistaken in ploughing up this anthill and doing everything they do in it. Just the same, when I look at everything people have done materially, I cannot suppose that they have done everything by mistake.

As a person (and not an ant) I see deficiencies in the human hill which I cannot help wanting to correct — hence I participate in the general work — but I don't want to destroy the whole hill of human labour, I only want to rearrange whatever has been arranged improperly therein. And there is a great deal that has been improperly arranged in the human hill, which I have written and continue to write about, which I have been and still am concerned about, and try as best I can to change.

What is wrong in our life, first and foremost, is that the means has been established as a goal, while what ought to be a goal — the well-being of one's neighbour — has been established as a means, i.e., that one's well-being — indeed one's very life — is sacrificed for the production of equipment, which is sometimes necessary for everyone, but at other times only to satisfy the whim of a single individual, when human lives are lost for the production of what is needed only by a few, and sometimes even of harmful things, which no one needs. It is wrong that people forget, have forgotten, or do not know that in producing not only something like a mirror, but even the most needed and important objects like a ploughshare or a scythe, there should be no loss either of life or of the happiness of the single most insignificant-looking human being, because the meaning of human life lies only in the well-being of all people. To destroy the life and well-being of any individual for the sake of everyone's well-being is like cutting off an animal's limb for the sake of its well-being.

This is the terrible mistake of our time: not the fact that we have book-printing, railways, etc., but that people consider it permissible to sacrifice the well-being of even a single individual for the achievement of a particular cause, whatever it might be. Once people lose the sense and purpose of what they do (there is only one purpose: the well-being of one's neighbour), once

24 At Yasnaya Polyana at the end of September 1896, Tolstoy received a visit from the Japanese writer and editor of the journal *Kokumin no tomo* [Friend of the People], Tokutomi Sohō, and a colleague from the journal named Fukai. They were recommended to Tolstoy by another Japanese man, Konishi Masutari, who had accepted the Russian Orthodox faith and was studying at the Kiev Seminary. Konishi became acquainted with Tolstoy in 1892 and, upon returning to his homeland, began translating Tolstoy's writings into Japanese. The Japanese seemed to Tolstoy "very enlightened and liberated in their views on people" (*PSS* 69:153). Later, however, Tolstoy befriended Sohō's younger brother, Tokutomi Roka, and fell out with the elder brother because of his nationalistic, militaristic views.

they decide that they can sacrifice the life and well-being of some old man or even an idiot whose life is a burden to everyone, then it is possible to sacrifice someone who is not quite as old or not quite as stupid, and there is nowhere to draw the line, anyone can be sacrificed for a cause. This is wrong, and must be fought against.

People must realize that no matter how useful and important book-printing, railways, ploughs or scythes seem to be, we do not really need them and they can just as well disappear until we learn how to make them without destroying people's lives and happiness. This is the crux of the matter, which people tend to skirt around on one side or the other and get confused.

Some say you want to destroy everything mankind has worked so hard to achieve, you want to take us back to the days of barbarism in the name of some sort of moral law, that moral law is wrong if it is inimical to the state of well-being mankind has achieved through its progress. Others say — and I fear you may be of this opinion, and it is one people ascribe to me — that since all material improvements in life contradict the moral law, all these improvements are in and of themselves false and so must be rejected. To the first group of critics I reply that we don't need to destroy anything, we only need not to forget that mankind's purpose in life is the well-being of all and therefore, if some improvement denies even a single individual's well-being, then that improvement must be thrown out and not introduced again until we find some means of producing and using it without violating even a single individual's well-being. And I think that such an approach to life would eliminate a great many of the useless and harmful products, while ways would be found very soon to produce the useful ones without violating people's well-being.

To the second group of critics I reply that in progressing from the stone age to the bronze age, the iron age, and eventually reaching its present material state, mankind could not possibly have been mistaken, but has been following an immutable law of self-perfection, and that turning back the clock is neither desirable nor possible, any more than is returning to apehood; moreover, man's task at the present time is not dreaming about what people once were and how to make them again that way, but in providing for the well-being of people who are living today. And the well-being of people who are living today requires them not to torture or oppress others, not to deprive them of the fruits of their labours, not to force them to work to produce things they don't need or cannot use, but most importantly, not to consider it possible or legitimate in the name of some cause or material success to destroy the life and well-being of one's neighbour, or, what is the other side of the coin, to violate love.

Once people realize the purpose of mankind is not material progress, that this progress is inevitable growth, and that there is only one purpose — the well-being of *all* people, that this purpose is higher than any material purpose people can set for themselves, then everything will be in its proper place. And it is to this end that people of our time must direct their whole effort.

Whining about the fact that people today can't live without tools, like wild animals, living off fruits, is like me, an old man, whining about the fact that I no longer have teeth or dark hair, or the strength I had in my youth. What I need to do is not to put in teeth or dye my hair or do physical exercise, but rather to try to live the way an old man should, giving priority not to worldly matters but to God's business — that is, to unity and love, to accept worldly matters only insofar that they do not interfere with God's business.

This is what mankind too needs to do at its present time of life. To say that railways, gas, electricity and printing of books are harmful since people's lives are lost because of them is like saying that ploughing and sowing are harmful simply because I didn't get the field ploughed in time, but allowed it to grow over and then sowed without ploughing, i.e., I did first what I should have done later.

I was so glad to read what you write about your life and about how, by applying to it the teachings you confess, you manage to eke out a living for yourself even in the difficult conditions in which you find yourself. There is nothing like this to show how sincere a person really is. I have become rather poor at doing this, surrounded as I am by all sorts of luxuries which I hate but have not the strength to extricate myself from. Hence your example is a support to me, and I keep on trying.

Thank you for sending the excerpt from your diary. In regard to the thoughts you express there, I should like to share with you some of my own ideas along this line. I shall do so at another time.

Farewell for now, and please don't let any bad feeling rise up against me for criticizing the thoughts you expressed, not only in your letter to me but also in the one you wrote to Evgenij Ivanovich.[25] You are very dear to me and I am trying to be as frank with you as possible, in a brotherly way.

Your loving friend, Lev Tolstoy

14 Oct. 1896

4. P. V. VERIGIN ❧ L. N. TOLSTOY
2 September 1897. Obdorsk.

2nd September '97, Village of Obdorsk.

Esteemed Lev Nikolaevich!

The bearer of this letter is a science student at St. Petersburg University, who along with a companion spent the summer searching out flora and fauna along the banks of the River Ob. They were in Obdorsk as well, and

25 Verigin's letter to Tolstoyan Evgenij Ivanovich Popov (1864–1938).

I spent quite a happy time with them. We fell to talking about a lot of things, including you personally. Upon departure the bearer of this letter expressed a sincere desire to see you, and thus I took the opportunity of writing you.

I can't really say anything in particular about myself. By God's grace I live safe and sound. On the 29th of July of this year my official period of exile came to an end. Now they've given [me] another five years. I have now served ten years altogether as follows: I was first sent away for *five* years, after which they added another *three* years, and on being transferred to the Berezov district they tacked on another *two* years, and now another *five*. A game like this is virtually inexplicable.

But I am more disturbed by the frightfully arbitrary treatment of Christians in the Caucasus. You are probably aware that many are being sent to the Yakutsk and Irkutsk regions, and even in the Caucasus itself the [authorities] are dispersing them among the local population, [specifically] selecting places with cruder morals. And typically they are not allowing wives and children to go with their husbands. But I think it is just a question of time before the people settled in the Yakutsk and Irkutsk regions manage to get permission for their wives to come, if [the authorities] are so inclined.

In Moscow, too, it seems, a lot of arrests have been made. For a long time now I have not been getting any letters from Moscow. The last letter I wrote you was on the 10th of March of this year. Another one was addressed to you care of I. M. Tregubov, dated 4th March. Did you receive them?[26]

The most dangerous element in the Christian movement, from the point of view of the established order, is the refusal to kill a human being. As I said, this is the most important, fundamental point both for Christians and the opposing side. I would say it is possible (and essential) to go to all the imperial courts [of the world] and propose that this idea — the idea of humanity and humanitarianism — be enshrined in law — not just as a matter of principle, but so that anyone wishing to live Christianity in any country not be subject to oppression.

As far as drawing up a petition is concerned, let me suggest the following to you, my esteemed Lev Nikolaevich! *You could* write to all Christian communities in America and Europe, who would send some of their members to some place in Europe, and a kind of conference would be held which you could also attend. After working out a plan of action, [a delegation] of no more than two or three Christian people could be selected from all the communities, who would personally visit all the leaders of the established order. I think that such a plan would not be without result.

26 The whereabouts of these letters are unknown. We know that Tolstoy sent one of them in July of 1897 to Paul Boulanger (known in Russian as Pavel Bulanzhe), who was in charge of organizing aid to the Caucasus Doukhobors.

I sincerely wish you, my esteemed Lev Nikolaevich, all blessings from the Lord God. Please give my heartfelt greetings to all my friends. Your brother in Christ,

P. Verigin

5. L. N. TOLSTOY ❧ P. V. VERIGIN
24 June 1898. Yasnaya Polyana.

24 June.

Dear Brother Pëtr Vasil'evich.

All your friends are upset that communication with you has been cut off.

I am sending you this note just to find out if this route is reliable. If this letter reaches you, send me a reply to Moscow care of His Excellency Aleksandr Andreevich Bers,[27] at the Poljakov house on Tverskoj Boulevard. As far as I know, your parents are alive and well. [Ivan] Ivin and Pëtr Mukhortov have gone abroad to see our friends and brothers in England. Nothing has been decided yet about where to emigrate. There have been some good proposals from America.

I shall write you about everything in detail if communication is established.

I send you brotherly greetings. I ask you not to lose heart and remember not only that many, many brothers are thinking about you and love you, but also that God is thinking about us and loves us in the measure that we do His will and help bring about His kingdom in our hearts and in the world.

Your loving brother,

Lev Tolstoy

6. P. V. VERIGIN ❧ L. N. TOLSTOY
16 August 1898. Obdorsk.

16th Aug. '98, Village of Obdorsk.

Esteemed Lev Nikolaevich!

I am taking advantage of a wayfarer to send you this letter with my heartfelt greetings and my wish that you receive all good from God. Thank God I am healthy and safe.

After a period of uninterrupted correspondence I wrote you two or three more letters which the 'censor' has probably not sent on to your address, since I have not received any letters from you either.

So much has accumulated to talk to you about heart to heart that I shall have to restrain myself, otherwise I fear the letter will be a long one.

27 *A. A. Bers* (1845–1918) — brother of Tolstoy's wife, Sofia Andreevna; served in the Moscow Land Bank on Tverskoj Boulevard.

I recently read your account in *Rus'* about the famine.[28] This chronic famine is indeed a sorry state for a people, but even sorrier is the authorities' refusal to give bread to starving people, while taking away their daily bread is openly tolerated, even encouraged by all possible means!

Dispiritedness — or rather, the lack of development of the spirit in the life of a people — is unquestionably the root cause of all a people's ills, but the lowering or raising of a people's spirits largely depends on the material conditions of human life. When you talk of spiritual aid to a people, I presume you mean their total liberation from outside interference by anyone offering 'aid.' Otherwise, wouldn't it mean that Nature, God and life itself were unjust to every living thing, including man, holding man in a state of spiritual backwardness?

It seems to me that what has led to this sorry state of the masses is man's artificial attempt to help his fellow man — especially in respect to his spiritual development. People who have been falsely taught, wanting to protect their fellow man from the cold — not noticing that they themselves are very weak — and gradually covering his body, have piled up such a weight (on top of it) that it only serves to stifle him! This is how all educational accumulations grow in modern life. We must forsake, as much as possible, all artificially developed 'chimeras' — which themselves, as you rightly believe, live off the resources of the people — and give people room to breathe freely, and then the people will strengthen themselves and develop and advance under the influence of the universal evolution of life! All we have to do is not interfere with this movement. Because of our limited strength, we of course cannot really interfere with or stop this evolutionary movement, but we are retarding and disfiguring our own lives.

As an example I would cite the following: it came to people's consciousness a long time ago, as you know, that God is life (Christ's words). But some people, teachers, would have us see God in figures made by craftsmen, figures often sitting on thrones and wearing royal crowns! And this new-fangled teaching, which has held mankind for thousands of years in the chains of ignorance, etc., etc., is called *education.* What people in Russia are thirsting for now is not education but *liberation* in the broad sense of the word, the total liberation of the individual from being watched over by other human beings.

Cannot those who have taken upon themselves the task of educating the masses see and admit the simple fact that all their artificially worked out

28 In his article *Famine or Not?*, which appeared in the newspaper *Rus'* of 2–3 July 1898, Tolstoy wrote: "If by famine is meant not enough to eat, not what people are dying from at the moment but rather what people live off of, but live poorly, dying prematurely, becoming disfigured, degenerating and failing to procreate, then such famine has existed about twenty years already for most of the centre of the black-earth region, and is especially strong this year" (*PSS* 29:221). For running the article, the paper received a warning from the Ministry of Internal Affairs (which could be followed by suspension or closure).

educational plans are a burden of oppression on the already weakened back of the working man?

Last winter the Governor of Tobol'sk was here. He invited me to his quarters and was extremely kind and polite toward me. We talked for over three hours, it was over high tea, and with him were three members of his 'entourage,' who also took part in the conversation. He questioned me with some interest on how I had become acquainted with you. When I replied that I had got to know you simply by correspondence, they were really surprised that people could get to know each other so well through correspondence!

I attach a copy of the petition we sent to the Ministry of Internal Affairs.[29] I wanted to know your opinion, dear Lev Nikolaevich, on the matter of sending the Doukhobors abroad. Personally, I am *almost* positively *against* emigration. You see, the members of our community are in need of self--improvement, and so, wherever we went, we would take our weaknesses with us; and even though an individual can generally live more freely abroad, I don't think the difference would be all that great. People are the same everywhere.

If it comes right down to emigration, then I foresee the following conditions: the government must return all the resettled Doukhobors to their families, and give a two- to three-year grace period for emigration. The community could send three or four trustworthy people to look over the place proposed for us. Then there is also the question as to whether there are places free in America for us, so that the local population would have no objection to our settling there. Finally, we could hire two or three American ships and go at once.

Please write and tell me, dear Lev Nikolaevich, whether you are in touch with any American acquaintances regarding the emigration of the Doukhobor Community. [Write to me care of:]

Aleksej Ivanovich Stepanov
Village of Zaval'naja (suburb)
City of Tobol'sk

Once he has received your letter, he will forward it to me by some traveller. If you have any papers to send me, address them to Stepanov; he is a good friend of mine — and of yours.

The police do not give me any letters at all, and do not send out any of mine. I am allowed to write — as the Governor warned me — to my parents, and my letters should not contain any 'philosophical arguments' (the Governor's

29 The Doukhobors' application for permission to emigrate was originally addressed to the Empress Aleksandra Fëdorovna; she passed it on to the senate, from where it was sent to the commanding officer in the Caucasus, G. S. Golitsyn. Permission was forthcoming only for those who were not in exile or subject to military conscription. Later, Tolstoy wrote to Russian and foreign newspapers, and, on behalf of the Doukhobors, to Tsar Nicholas II. A copy of Verigin's application to the Ministry of Internal Affairs is preserved in the Tolstoy archives.

expression). There is a Russian Orthodox Church mission in Obdorsk, this year two monks have come out to run it — one from St. Petersburg, and they have preached sermons in church over and over again about the Doukhobor community, about its evil, its danger to the State, etc. I warned the monks that if they continued doing so I would be compelled to remind them of certain unjust misrepresentations about our community. One Sunday they allowed me to speak in church. A heated debate ensued, but a lot of the people here accepted my point of view on world issues.

The priests asked about our rejection of icons. I explained that we worship God, to whom everything that exists is subject, not only the earth and everything on it, but everything in the universe too. God is *life* and is present in all that exists, and is equally present to protect man, for example, as the smallest bird or insect, and therefore, I said: God, whom we worship, is immeasurably vast and great, and it is impossible to put Him in any kind of frame, let alone to represent Him pictorially; we can feel God only in our heart and soul, and express His quality of Love to all living things around us.

There were six priests there; one of them spoke with me, but by and by they all started talking; I drew their attention to the noise they were making, and some of the people who were listening agreed with me. The priests got into such a state of excitement that one of them said: Show us your God, or Love! Some of the people even laughed at such a question. I replied: You are repeating the words of the Pharisees which were addressed to Christ; but I am sure you understand what love means, only you aren't willing to confess it, moreover, you are holding the people in darkness for the sake of material advantage.

Before this confrontation the priests had promised to ask questions and hold discussions periodically on Sundays, but this did not happen more than once. The elder priest among them made a trip to talk to the Bishop about the discussion. He recently returned, but what he came back with I have no idea.

Recently someone came to see me on behalf of my relatives. He managed to come into the apartment and was here no more than *five* minutes when the police came and arrested him. Half an hour later they sent him off in a convoy. He didn't have a passport.[30] They don't give out passports to Doukhobors. Last year, too, some people tried to come and visit me, but they never got here. There was another person too, Mikhajlo Androsov, I think he was at your place.[31] I find such trips quite superfluous. But my old mother is extremely

30 *passport* — here referring to an internal identification document required for travel within the Russian empire.

31 Mikhajlo Androsov, along with other Doukhobors, visited Verigin in Obdorsk in 1895. In December 1896 he tried again to see Verigin, but thirty kilometres from Obdorsk he was arrested and sent home in a convoy. On 13 January 1897 he stopped to see Tolstoy on his way through Moscow. In replying to Androsov's story of his life after his return, Tolstoy wrote him in July of the same year: "Give my greetings and love to all the brethren. I have not seen anyone except

concerned and doesn't even trust letters saying I am alive. Even though this person is travelling in a convoy and won't get there quickly, at least he'll tell her he saw me.

I don't receive any mail from those sent to the Yakutsk region, no correspondence is permitted.

In the magazine *Mir Bozhij* [God's World] there was an account of a conference of missionary priests at Kazan'. The question they raised was typical, about taking children away from sect members! Only it turned out after that that there was nowhere to put them! Any discussion of this matter is superfluous![32]

The magazine *Mir Bozhij* [God's World] is available in Obdorsk. I then sent a letter to the editor regarding the conference. I am sending you a copy. It is quite probable that the police did not forward it.[33]

The conference thought your writings extremely dangerous! To tell the truth, you have uncovered a lot of lies lately. The priests are especially angry at you, and with some justification, for you with your "Little Pamphlets" won't let them hide any more in their sheep's clothing, when in fact they are Wolves.

The summer here has been quite warm and relatively long. There are a lot of berries growing here: cloudberries, bilberries, bog whortleberries, *kljazhitsa,* mountain cranberries, there are a few red currants and I have spent almost the whole summer in the field gathering berries. Moreover, I have procured myself a joiner's bench and some tools; I also have a lathe and am working little by little on that. Come winter I thought I would start making boots, even set up a cobbler's shop, since there are no boots here and people are in great need of them. I think the disadvantage of a cobbler's trade is that you have to sit for longer periods than normal, and that is harmful. In general I do not get regular physical exercise; but in any case I prefer work in the open air, for example, this summer I took great delight in mowing and gathering hay. Haying is also quite profitable here; they don't set up hayfields, everyone mows where he wishes. There are not that many haymakers here, since almost everybody goes off fishing for a living.

you, but all of you are closer to me than people I have spent my whole life with, because I see in your lives the manifestation of the God I live by.... More and more brethren who share our spirit are cropping up all over Russia and abroad. I believe that the kingdom of God is drawing closer. Write to me." (*PSS* 70:107)

32 On the Kazan' missionary conference (August 1897), see Note 25 on p. 38 above. Among other steps taken in the struggle with dissident sects, it was decided to petition for a law which would allow children to be taken from their parents and brought up in diocesan orphanages. Shortly thereafter, this measure was applied to the children of the Molokans. After reading an account of the conference in the newspaper *Russkie vedomosti,* Tolstoy noted in his diary: "A disturbing account of a missionary conference in Kazan" (*PSS* 53:150).

33 The whereabouts of both the original sent to the magazine and the copy sent to Tolstoy are unknown.

Last summer there were two students here from St. Petersburg University collecting flora and fauna.

One of them very much wanted to see you, and so I sent a letter with him — did you receive it or not?[34]

Recently some ships passed through Obdorsk, travelling down the river to Ob Province. This is the second time they were carrying bread to exchange for foreign goods, mainly things made of iron. I don't think such trade is particularly profitable. While sending more and more crops away, Russia is going hungry herself; besides, all the soil is becoming depleted because it isn't getting enrichment in the form of crop waste, and so forth. Russians are starting to produce crops more easily, but it's sad that the producers themselves don't get to eat them, trading them instead for various foreign improvements.

Give my sincere greetings to all the Brothers and Sisters in Spirit. I wish you all the best.

Pëtr Verigin

I am sending you "A Fantasy" — an idea that came together last winter. The bishop was here, and I wrote it in honour of his visit. When I met him I presented it to him, but he didn't take it, explaining that he receives all documents through the Consistory. If possible, see if you can make a small pamphlet out of this idea; I think it will be useful for the simple folk!

A Fantasy

This booklet describes how in Russia the Virgin Mary recently appeared to a peasant-fellow.

The peasant returned home later than usual from the forest with his load of wood. His wife asked him why he was so late. As he excitedly unharnessed the horses, he told his wife to call all the people in the village to come at once, and he would recount a miracle. And when the people, both men and women, had gathered, this is what he told them:

"Here I am on my way home, brothers and sisters, carting my load of wood and with the Lord's Prayer running through my mind, and I think to myself: Now when will the Kingdom of God come on earth as it is in heaven?

"'Nightfall was a-comin' on, but I could already see our village not too far away, just over the second brook. And now, my friends, my heart's a-jumpin,' not so much for joy or as if I were afraid. Yeah, here I am tryin' to get ol' Pegasus to get a move on, when all of a sudden, what do I see, just a few *sazhen'* away, but someone — a woman — comin' towards me, an' it looks like Anna Trofimovna Potapova. An' even before I get close I cry out: 'Trofimovna! Where're you off to for the night?' — In the meanwhile Pegasus,

34 See Letter N° 4.

without me noticin' him, has gone off the road and stopped in the soft snow. So now Trofimovna's come up to me, an' she turns to me and says: 'Peace be with you, good man!' An' then I noticed it wasn't Trofimovna, but I couldn't move, somehow a joy too great for words spread right through me. This woman stood there on road on the trodden snow much taller than me, an' I was somehow looking up.

"'I've been wanting to meet you for a long time, my dear fellow,' she began again. 'Listen, remember, go and tell everyone in your village from the smallest to the greatest, tell everyone you meet in your life.

"'You people often turn in prayer to the Lord God, and this is almost pointless, since right after you pray you go and do more wickedness. And still the Lord is [so] merciful that He is patient and waits for the Kingdom of God to be accepted by people, because people in their foolishness do a lot of bad things. Tell everyone that people have now fallen under the influence of three serious vices: vodka, tobacco and card-games. If people do not forsake these vices they will perish, because from these three vices come a whole multitude of sins: poverty, envy, murder, covetousness, and so on.

"'Just think how much you, simple people of God, suffer from vodka and other fermented drinks. You know it's not long now till the Great holiday of the whole Universe, Christmastide, and in the days leading up to it I always come down to earth to comfort the hearts of people who call upon the Lord. But when the day comes to celebrate Christmas, how do people celebrate it? When people call upon the Lord for help in their infirmities, the Lord sends me to the sorrowing and it is good for me to treat the wounds of those who are repentant; but even if a drunkard starts swearing and cursing, mentioning the word *mother,* I must still come to earth and abide in man's world, because they, people, call upon me.'

"I wanted, dear brothers and sisters, to fall upon my face to the earth and ask forgiveness for the whole human race, but the Virgin stopped me by raising her hand and saying: 'Do not do that, but remember most distinctly what I say. When you drink vodka, people's insides gradually decay and it causes harm to the blood — especially when women drink vodka, their children are born already diseased. Besides, when someone squanders his money on vodka, there is not enough to take care of his household, and this leads little by little to resentment in the family, and just think, what kind of a Christian life is that! In fact it would be better for people who drink vodka not to call themselves Christians. After all, Christ was sent by God to proclaim peace and a good life, but when people go and drink vodka there is no room for peace in the family. Tobacco is harmful because smoke infects the blood and makes a person irritable, causing even more quarrels to break out in the family. People who smoke bear children who are diseased, nervous and malicious. Tobacco smoke breathed in by people in their homes, especially by children, is very harmful to the lungs and the brain, and gives rise to frequent headaches. Think again, people, of how much bread is destroyed in vodka distilleries! Truly I tell you that it was Satan who helped man think up vodka distilleries, to drive people deeper into sin. And how much of the best land is ploughed up for tobacco, when something useful could be grown on it.

"'Card-games are bad for mankind because they distract people's minds from thinking about useful things: how the world was created and formed, and what is the best way for people to live — [these are things] they should gather to talk about after [completing] necessary daily chores. Even a country dweller can lose all his property, and again [this gives rise to] unpleasant situations and quarrels in the family.

"'Vodka, tobacco and card-games cause even more harm for rich people. They hold expensive feasts, replete with costly fermented drinks in great quantities, and when the feasts are over, where do they turn to compensate for what has been lost? Like it or not, they have to get it by all sorts of bad and devious ways, since people who drink wine, smoke tobacco and play cards are used to living an idle and luxurious life. And it often happens that rich people lose their whole fortune at cards and the final result is a ruined life and [possibly] even suicide.

"'City people, including civil servants, merchants, priests and all the rich people of this world, who get drunk on vodka, smoke tobacco and play cards, will all meet a most tragic end, because their behaviour is a temptation for the common people; but you, simple country folk, stay away from the cities, because in them is corruption and death for human souls.

"'I say again to you, good man, remember and tell everyone that if people forsake drinking vodka and anything fermented, smoking tobacco and playing cards, they will be saved, and there will reign peace on earth and good will toward men!'

"At these words a bright circle formed around the Virgin and in her arms I saw a child of unspeakable beauty, who said: 'All that my Mother said is verity and truth: I, Christ, confirm this. Go and preach to all who believe in the Spirit of Truth.' Then the bright circle began to get bigger, and the Blessed Virgin and Christ began rising higher and higher until they were hidden in the heavenly clouds..."

7. L. N. TOLSTOY ❧ P. V. VERIGIN
1 November 1898. Yasnaya Polyana.

1 November. Yasnaya Polyana.

Dear Brother Pëtr Vasil'evich.

I was so delighted to receive your letter. The only news I have had about you is the letter you sent with the students. I answered it and sent you another long letter, describing everything that has been happening with the brethren lately. I sent this letter under special circumstances, but I fear that it too did not reach you.[35]

I am now sending you an account of everything that has been done and is being done to date. The ship that is to carry the first migrants (around 2,000 people) is to arrive for them in Batumi on the 4th of December. When the second ship will set sail is still unknown.[36] I was so happy to read in your letter your idea of God in the conversation with the missionaries; but I was especially happy to read your ideas on the resettlement. I share your opinion completely — namely that it is not the place where we live that is important, or the conditions surrounding us, but our inner mental state. Ye shall know the truth and the truth shall make you free[37] — everywhere, no matter where you are.

You write that you are almost against resettlement, and I am too, but living in hardship and exile, you are in a position to tell the suffering people that they should keep on suffering and hold out to the end, whereas I who live in freedom and under all the best conditions find it awkward to tell people who are suffering: keep on suffering, keep holding on. And it is sad that we (Russians) are parting with those who are close to us in spirit (I take comfort in telling myself that our brethren are to be found everywhere), and it is sad, too, that people have not held on to the end and thereby helped other people know the truth, since nothing testifies to the truth more than the sufferings that one must bear for it.

I was very glad to hear about your life and the life of the exiles in Yakutsk. We shall try to have them reunited with their wives.

Your letter to the Minister of Internal Affairs is unlikely to produce any action. But I am almost certain that once all the migrants are settled in Canada, they will release you and the Yakutsk people as well.[38]

I have just received some good news: 300 people scattered around various villages have been given permission to return and are being issued passports.

I doubt your "Fantasy" will ever be published, even though it would be useful. I shall send it to Posrednik.[39]

35 The whereabouts of these letters of Tolstoy's are unknown.

36 The second ship, the *SS Lake Superior*, set sail from Batoum 3 January 1899 (23 December 1898 by the old-style calendar), carrying approximately 2,300 Doukhobors and escorted by Tolstoy's eldest son, Sergej L'vovich Tolstoy. For a full account of the Doukhobor emigration to Canada, see Sergej Tolstoy's diary reproduced (in English translation) in Donskov 1998a: 231–352: see excerpts in Part III below.

37 See John 8:32.

38 Verigin was able to go to Canada in 1902, the Yakutsk exiles in 1905. See Verigin's letter to Tolstoy from England en route (Letter N° 12) and his letter from Yorkton, Saskatchewan (Letter N° 23).

39 "A Fantasy" was never published by Posrednik. It was published for the first time in its original (along with an English translation) in Donskov 1995a: 34–36 (see pp. 156–158 above).

Don't condemn the account if you find it not that well written. It was compiled by our friend from some English articles (thank God we have a lot of friends).[40] Farewell. I embrace you in brotherhood.

Lev Tolstoy

8. L. N. TOLSTOY ❧ P. V. VERIGIN[41]
20 November 1898 (approx.). Yasnaya Polyana.

Your letter greatly delighted me, dear Brother Pëtr Vasil'evich.[42] I wrote to you at the address you know about, and I am now writing another letter to send with the sisters who are going your way.[43] I'm sending along Khilkov's letter about the situation in Canada,[44] they will tell you about the situation in the Caucasus.

Everything is going well. But what you wrote to us can never be repeated often enough — that it is not the place where we live that is important, but our relation to God and to mankind, whether we believe that life is in the spirit rather than the flesh, and whether we are prepared, remembering this every time we are faced with a choice between our spiritual and corporeal welfare, to sacrifice all our worldly, temporal affairs for the sake of preserving our eternal soul. In all probability I do not have long to live, and there is so much I want to say that seems clear and important to me, yet overlooked by mankind.

Lately I have been preoccupied by the thought that a great many of our troubles come from our misconception of God, and our resulting lack of faith in Him. This misconception of God comes mainly from our inculcated beliefs about the creation of the world, about our knowledge of how the world was created and who created it. From this superstition comes a misconception of a God who, like man, is either resting quietly or setting out to do what he fancies, along with an even greater misconception as to the beginning of the world and of mankind, and therefore about the end of the world and of human life. We do not see the frightening absurdity of such a conception only because we are too accustomed to it.

40 The account was compiled by Aylmer Maude, the English translator of Tolstoy's novel *Resurrection*, who took an active part in the cause of the Doukhobors' resettlement.

41 This letter was published in *PSS* 71:500–02, dated 5(?) December 1898. The date was changed: the letter was sent with Vasilij Pozdnjakov and the Doukhobor wives who were going to see their husbands in Yakutsk, who all visited Tolstoy at Yasnaya Polyana around 20 November. In a letter to his son Sergej, actually dated 5 December 1898, Tolstoy specifically mentioned that "they passed through safely with Pozdnjakov about two weeks ago" (*PSS* 71:499).

42 Tolstoy is responding a second time to Verigin's letter of 16 August 1898 (Letter N° 6 above).

43 As a precautionary measure, Tolstoy does not mention Pozdnjakov, who was exiled to the Yakutsk area.

44 A letter from Prince Dmitrij Khilkov, written from Montréal, dated 13 November 1898 (25 November, new style), with a detailed description of the future home of the Doukhobors. Khilkov also wrote that Aylmer Maude was planning to go to Ottawa to discuss all the issues with the Canadian Ministry of the Interior.

In actuality, however, for anyone who is not bound by these absurd superstitions, the question of the origin and the end of the world never arises. Such a person sees himself alive in the world in both time and space, he sees neither ahead of him nor behind him an end to either time or space, and having realized this, is concerned only with how to understand the laws of the world, especially the law of his life, as expressed in Christianity — the will of the Father of life. A free and rational person tries only to understand and fulfil in this world the law of his life, which like the world has no beginning or end, to carry out the will of God, that God whom he acknowledges as being behind His laws and whom he cannot formulate any concept of for himself. He knows only that the being who established these laws exists, but he (a rational person) does not attempt to understand this being and his purposes, realizing that he as a limited part cannot comprehend the whole. All he can understand is that the nature of this God of life, manifest in his soul, is love, that is, the triumph of unity over disunity.

In the Judæo-ecclesiastical understanding man has formulated for himself a concept of God, of His attributes, of His activity (creation, redemption, etc.) and does not pay attention to His laws, to His will, which man is called upon to carry out and which is revealed to him in his heart — through reason and love. Yet given a rational, simple understanding of life, without the superstition of a creation, it is clear that man knows only the law of God, His will, and directs all his efforts toward clarifying it (the law) for himself and following it; about God he knows nothing except that He exists and has given man His law to carry out.

At first glance it seems that both the world and mankind began and therefore must end, and death and the end of the world become frightening things; but at a second, rational glance, just as the world never began and will never end, so has our life never begun and will never end, and therefore there can be no end of the world, and death is not something frightening, since it is only a change more acute than all the changes that occur in our temporal life. There are no rewards or punishments, but only what is here already — namely, the fact that the good one does always leads to a common good, while the evil one does leads to a common evil, and good is joyous, whereas evil is tormenting. Good is unity, i.e., love. Evil is disunity, hate.

What do you think about all this?

Embracing you in brotherhood,

L. Tolstoy

9. P. V. VERIGIN ❧ L. N. TOLSTOY[45]
1 February 1899. Obdorsk.

1st Feb. '99. Village of Obdorsk.

My esteemed Lev Nikolaevich, after such a long silence I have been meaning to write you at least a couple of lines. I shall begin right away with the question that is preoccupying my thought at the moment — about the resettlement of the Caucasus Christians to America [*sic*].[46] As far as emigration in general is concerned, I held no prior assumptions, although even back in the homeland some reasoned that if the government still refused to let us live according to our convictions, we would be forced to ask them to let us go abroad. Which in fact has happened.

I have great hopes — once our emigrating brethren are safely across the ocean and settled in their places, they should be able to begin a good life there. Unquestionably a lot of effort will be required to adapt to their new situation. I have to say that over the past ten years the people of our community have been severely shaken in their basic view of the world; they are like a flock of partridges into which several shots are fired, and after some of them fall down dead on the spot, the frightened remainder instinctively all fly off, mostly in different directions. It is possible to collect them together again, but to get the flock back to a normal state requires a certain period of time.

The analogy between people and partridges is flawed only in the fact that *people do not have to lose their self-control,* but this is true only of those with very strong natures; and in a crowd there is always a certain degree of failure. I say this because our brethren in the Caucasus, as a result of going through a *fundamental change in their lives,* moving to a new place, may go against the accepted rule of solidarity. I am not saying our people, having settled in America, should necessarily submit to some kind of *arbitrary regime;* this is my conviction: no matter what may be the communal life of any group of people, first and foremost there must be full freedom of thought for every individual. In communal living people can be united only by their vital material interests, something that requires a sense of community in and of itself.

How I would like to be at this very moment with those who have gone to America! I think some agriculture could be arranged quite properly in the early days. I know that some good people are looking after the resettlement there,

45 Tolstoy did not receive this letter until January 1902 (see Letter No 11 below). In the archives there is an accompanying note dated 15 November 1901, signed *Chelovek* [A Person] (this was A. I. Stepanov), explaining that Verigin's letter had been all this time going back and forth between Tobol'sk and Obdorsk, waiting for someone who could take it to its destination.

46 It is evident that Verigin is here using *America* in reference to the whole North American continent, rather than the United States of America.

but it is very important to arrange things properly, as their future life depends on it. I would support an agreement whereby villages were constructed as they usually are, i.e., the houses built in rows according to the lie of the land, but even if built by common efforts and using common standards, the little houses would each have room only for a single family. As for space for storing purely communal things like grain, etc., a separate barn should be built for grain. Later, facilities like repair shops, creameries and mills, could be built by each village for their common interest and through their collective efforts. As long as the ground yields fruit, essential agricultural equipment could be purchased on credit from local factories, and even such things as are needed to set up a mill, for example, state-of-the art turbines, etc. This could all be worked out over a period of several years, although getting into debt up to one's ears is not by itself a right thing to do.

The settlements should comprise no more than fifty households each; this is important for convenience in cultivating the fields. The disadvantage of a large village is that the fields are a long ways out. Fifty households must be considered a large settlement when you think of the offspring being multiplied. — But of course then they could move away to new villages.

Teaching literacy to the children, including the girls, must be considered a priority right at the start. The only literacy I consider essential is the *ability to read and write,* without attributing to literacy any positive signification for bringing up children. Ideally, literacy should be taught by the child's father, or an older brother or sister, just like the mending of clothes and shoes, the knitting of stockings, the binding of harrow chains, etc. Only you have to watch out that the child doesn't become a 'professional' cobbler, or a girl become a hosiery-maker, like many people who become 'professors of literacy' but remain perfect ignoramuses in other departments of life, ending up, for the most part, in the position of 'Shchedrin's generals.'[47]

I am in touch with the brethren in Yakutsk. Their life there may not be all that easy, but they write me cheerful letters all the same. They have already tried sowing grain and planting a few choice vegetables, and the results have been satisfactory. Only the tilling of the soil was typical: the first summer they had but one horse to plough with, so they harnessed ten men to the other wooden plough and they ploughed too! I read that in issue N° 51 of *Nedelja,* it was reprinted from some newspaper their Yakutsk reporter had.

I sent them a clipping of that story and asked them to tell me whether they really ploughed the ground harnessed up that way! I don't suppose there's anything special in it, but still it is typical of their determination as regards the land, i.e., to get their 'daily bread' directly from the land, by whatever means necessary.

47 The reference is to the generals of a fictional account by the Russian satirist Mikhail Evgrafovich Saltykov-Shchedrin.

You are probably aware that there are altogether seventy-three of our brethren in Yakutsk. They are settled on the Notora River. Some have had their wives come to be with them. Some serious thought must be given to the plight of the exiles and I have come to the following conclusion: petition the government to let all of us (exiles) go abroad — I already sent a request to the Minister of Internal Affairs, which I asked to be presented to the Emperor for consideration. The only failing of my requests is that they look more like directives rather than the positive requests favoured by the authorities on the whole. In the statement I forwarded to them I indicated that "the government won't lose anything by letting all the resettled Christians of our community go abroad. It will only be ridding itself of people who are a danger to it."

This is my basic belief, namely that all of us exiles should go to our brethren in America (it is worth mentioning here that some of the exile's wives have already gone abroad in the hope that their husbands will win their release by petition); however, if the government positively refuses to let us leave Russia, we should try to adjust to making ourselves at home here, and try as best we can to set up our farming on the right footing. As the experiment has shown, it is possible to grow grain on the Notora; this already gives us some hope for making a living by farming; in that case I shall ask them to transfer me to the brethren at Yakutsk. Three of my blood brothers were settled separately several hundred versts from all the rest, on the river Maja. They were settled separately as the main 'rowdies.'

I only recently received the letter which was written at your place last year by the three Caucasus brethren who were with you, along with your attached note. It turns out they had actually brought it several times to Obdorsk, but couldn't give it to me for fear of the police. During the whole time of my stay here people have been very frightened, and according to one policeman, a person can almost get sent into exile just for one meeting with me, not to mention the possibility of close friendship. The church is especially 'ardent' in warning people against getting close to me. They quite often preach sermons openly mentioning me by name. This is being done by the missionary Church; the one here includes three clergymen, two of them monks. I have pointed out to them several times upon meeting — we have got to know each other through visits — that such an openly hostile attitude goes against even the simplest courtesy, let alone downright politeness. They reply that "current circumstances compel them to act that way" — ?

Last year, or possibly back in '97, in the fall, I got their agreement on my right of reply in the church, in the interests of accuracy in their reports to the people on the nature of our community, — since they are trying to blacken the whole life of our community.[48] Naturally this debate turned out to have a 'scandalous' effect, even today they regret they ever gave me permission to

48 Cf. Letter N° 6.

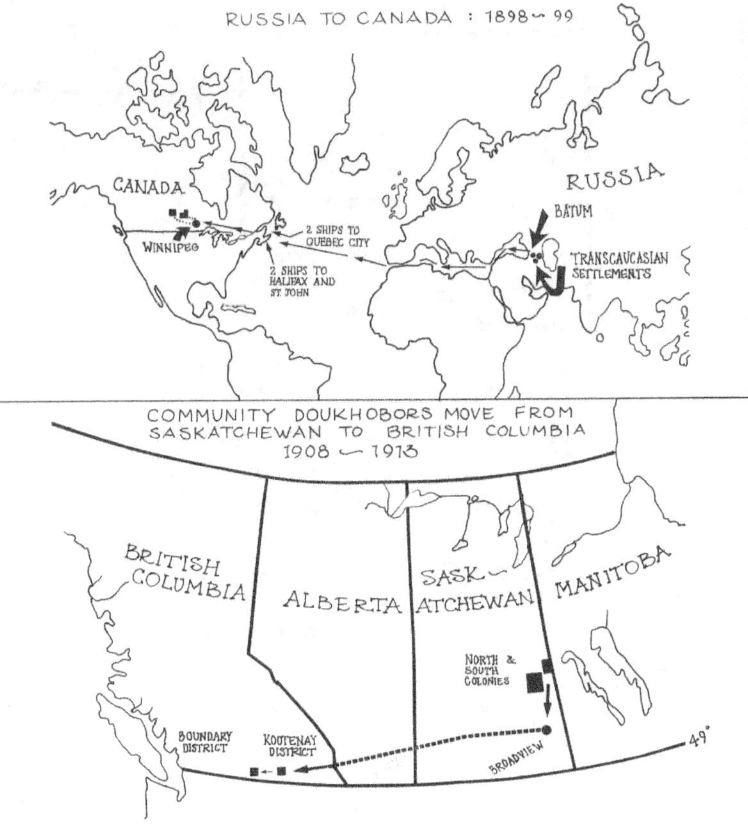

Geographic movements of the Doukhobors 1898–1913.

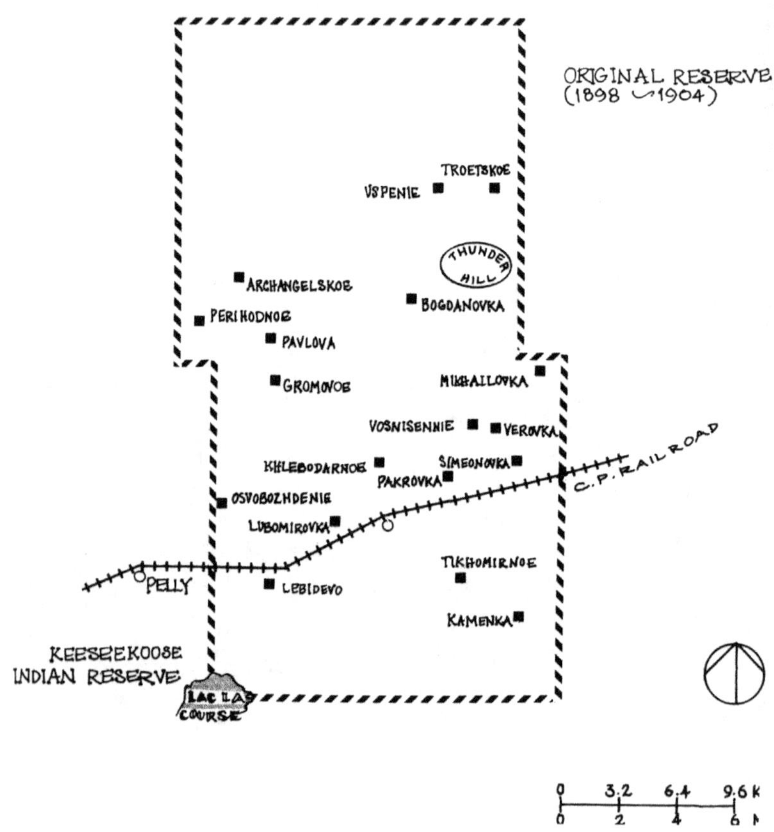

Map showing Doukhobor villages in the North Colony (Swan River) in northeastern Saskatchewan, 1907.

Lev Nikolaevich Tolstoy, 1908. *Photo by V. G. Chertkov.*

Relocation from Saskatchewan to British Columbia, 1909. A wagon caravan moves people and supplies from Doukhobor villages on the prairies to this railway embarkation point at Broadview, Saskatchewan, from where they would travel by train to their new home in the British Columbia interior.

Postcard portrait of Lev Nikolaevich Tolstoy (*front*), January 1902.
Photo by Scherer, Nabholz & Co., Moscow.

Postcard of L. N. Tolstoy (*back*), postmarked in St. Petersburg, 12 January 1902.

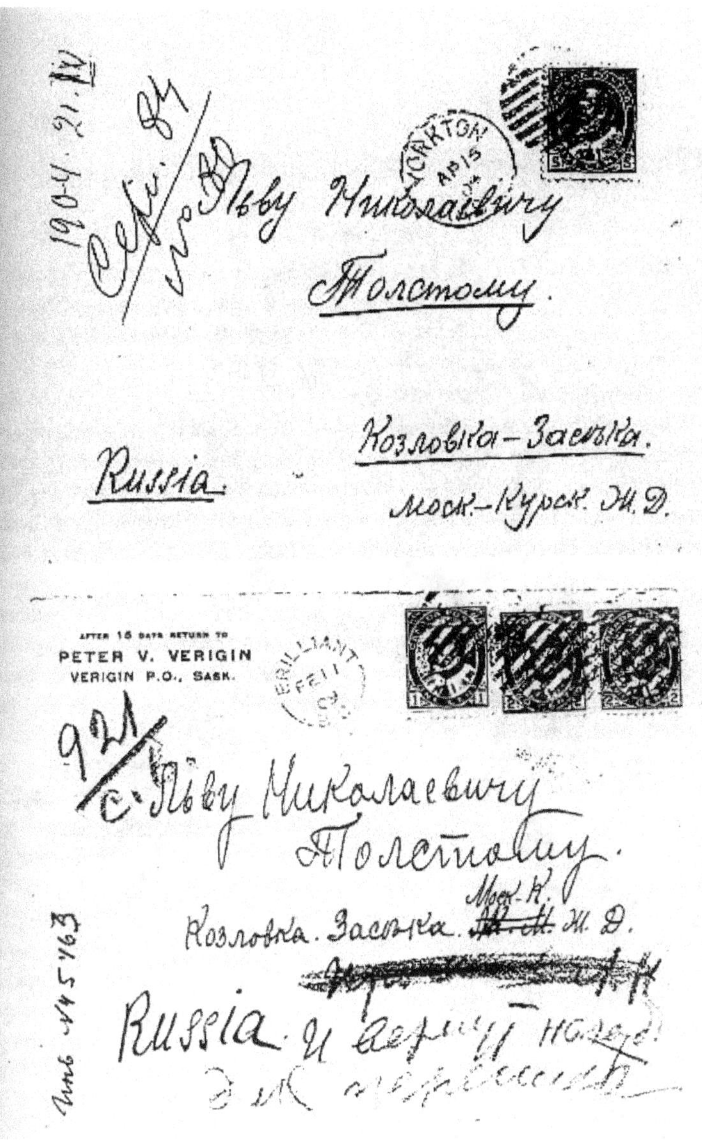

Envelopes for two letters sent by Pëtr Vasil'evich Verigin to Tolstoy from Canada — the first dated 12 April 1904 (Letter N° 20), postmarked at Yorkton (Assiniboia, now Saskatchewan), the second dated 2 February 1909 (Letter N° 32), postmarked at the Doukhobor community of Brilliant (British Columbia), though the return address reflects Verigin's former residence in Verigin, Saskatchewan.

Pëtr Vasil'evich Verigin (1859–1924). *Photo by V. G. Hooper.*

Left to right: Valentin Fëdorovich Bulgakov, Vladimir Grigor'evich Chertkov, Lev Nikolaevich Tolstoy, 1910. *Photo by Tomas Tapsell.*

L. N. Tolstoy Museum, Povarskaja Street, Moscow.
Tolstoy Exhibition, Hall N° 1 (1911–20).

L. N. Tolstoy Museum, Povarskaja Street, Moscow.
Tolstoy Exhibition, Hall N° 2 (1911–20).

Tolstoy's youngest daughter Aleksandra at the Chertkovs' home in Teljatinki, in 1911. Left to right, standing: Aleksandr Modestovich Khirjakov, Vladimir Grigor'evich Chertkov; Seated: Marija Nikolaevna Tolstaja, Aleksandra L'vovna Tolstaja, Anna Konstantinova Chertkova. *Photo by Tomas Tapsell.*

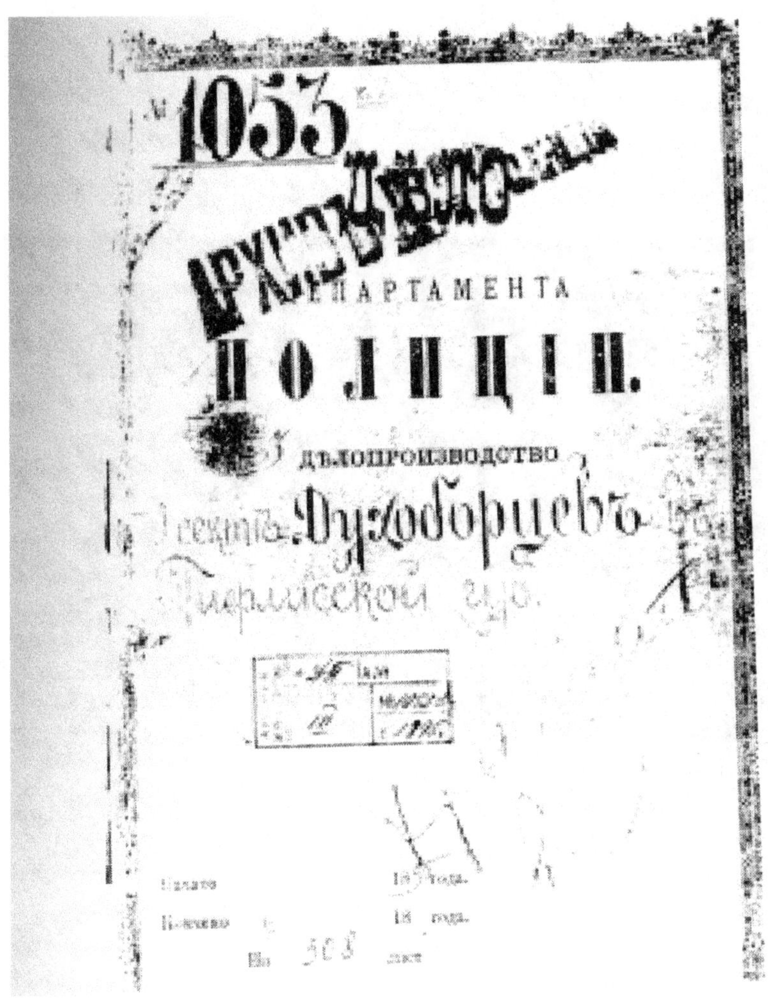

№ 1053

ДЕПАРТАМЕНТА

ПОЛИЦІИ.

ДѢЛОПРОИЗВОДСТВО

секты Духоборцевъ

Report cover of case file (Delo 1053) on the Doukhobors
from the Department of Police. See Woodsworth 1999a: xxii.

Trial of the ‘Tolstoyans’ at the Moscow Military Circuit Court, 25 March 1916. Tolstoy’s last secretary, Valentin Fëdorovich Bulgakov, is seated at the far left in the second row.

Doukhobor children in the village of Otradnoe, Saskatchewan, ca 1918.

A Doukhobor *sobranie* (community gathering) held 24 September 1924 on an island in the Kootenay River near the Doukhobor settlement of Brilliant, B.C., close to Castlegar and the present site of Selkirk College. (See photo extension on facing page) Five weeks later, on 29 October, Pëtr Vasil'evich Verigin (shown here standing at a desk, *centre-right*) would be killed in a railway explosion.

Funeral of Pëtr Vasil'evich Verigin at Brilliant, B.C., 2 November 1924, attended by more than 7,000 people (including 500 non-Doukhobors).

Doukhobor community members take a rest from threshing rye at Brilliant (B.C.), August 1932.

Mikhail Vasilievich Soukeroff and his wife Maria Larionovna stand in the kitchen of their communal village home in Brilliant, B.C., in 1932. At the height of the community enterprise, each such kitchen fed 40–50 people per meal.

Eli A. Popoff (1921–2014) was a recognized authority on Doukhobor history, philosophy and folklore. Here he is at work transcribing and translating traditional Doukhobor psalms.

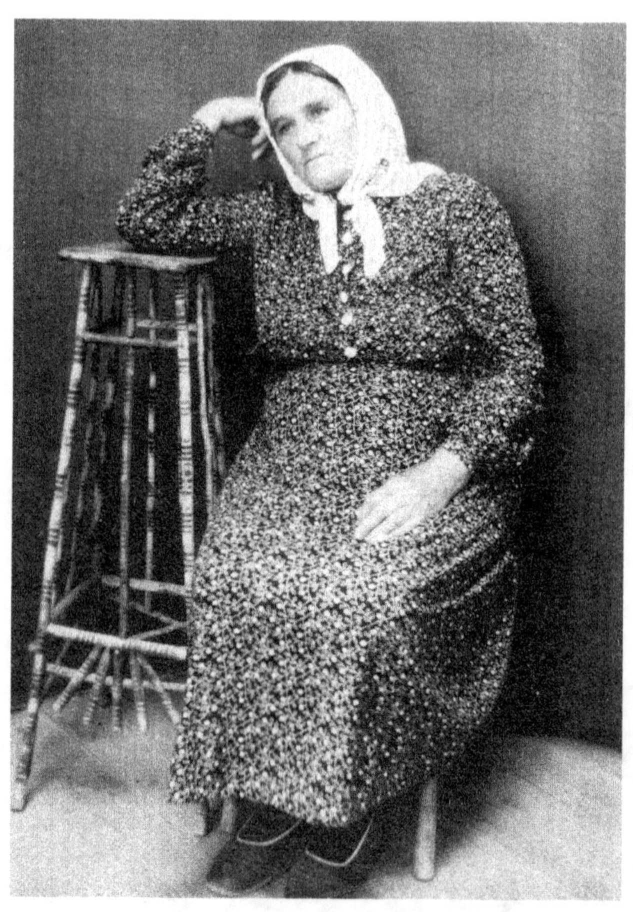

Anna Petrovna Markova (1902–1978), who was released from Siberian exile only in the mid-1950s (this photo was taken soon afterward), was a prominent woman pioneer in Canadian Doukhobor history.

Russian historian Aleksandr Il'ich Klibanov (*right*) talks with Doukhobor ethnographer Koozma J. Tarasoff in July 1977.

Doukhobors of Slavjanka village in Azerbaijan greet Canadian Doukhobor visitors during an historic tour of ancestral settlements in the Soviet Union, July 1977.

A reunion of Tolstoy's descendants at Yasnaya Polyana on 1 June 1991, including his two surviving (at the time) grandchildren: Sergej Mikhajlovich and Vera Il'inichna (*seated front centre*). A number of Doukhobor delegates had also been invited to participate, in view of their close relationship to their "Dedushka Tolstoy". Seated at the far left in the photo is Tolstoy's great-grandson Il'ja Vladimirovich Tolstoj, who first made contact with a Doukhobor leader, John J. Verigin Sr (*seated centre-right*), the great-grandson of Pëtr Vasil'evich Verigin: they met in Moscow in 1980. Seated at Vera Il'inichna's left is Nikolaj Pavlovich Puzin, Honorary Director of Yasnaya Polyana and compiler of the Tolstoy genealogy.

Iskra cover of Issue #1905 (25 March 2001), which incluced the Slavic Group's survey questionnaire to determine the perception of Tolstoy among Canadian Doukhobors today. (See also the reproduction of the questionnaire in Appendix 5 of this volume). The cover features a photo of Tolstoy on the farmlands of Yasnaya Polyana.

John J. Verigin Sr, (1921–2008), great-grandson of Pëtr Vasil'evich Verigin, Honorary Chairman of the Union of Spiritual Communities of Christ (USCC) until his passing in 2008. Awarded the Order of Canada in 1977 and the Order of British Columbia in 1996. Presented with the Order of Peoples' Friendship by Mikhail Gorbachev in 1989.

Andrei I. Conovaloff – prominent writer and ethnographer

Koozma J. Tarasoff (right) on the occasion of receiving his Friends for Peace Award in September 2012; shown here with his wife Kristina (*centre*) and daughter Tamara (left).

Koozma J. Tarasoff, Doukhobor historian and ethnographer in Ottawa.

Larry (Larion) Ewashen delivering a lecture at the Convention of BC Museums Association in May 2009.

John J. Verigin Jr, great-great-grandson of Pëtr Vasil'evich Verigin, Executive Director, Union of Spiritual Communities of Christ (USCC).

Jim (Dmitri Il'ich) Popoff, Editor of the Doukhobor journal *Iskra* (1986–1992; 1997–2000).

Eli (Il'ja Alekseevich) Popoff (1921–2014; *seated, left*) with his wife Dorothy (Avdot'ja Ivanovna, *née* Rilkova; 1927–; *seated, right*). Standing behind them are three of their children (*from left to right*): Elena Il'inichna, Jim (Dmitri Il'ich), and Natalia Il'inichna. Both daughters now reside in Russia: Elena in Moscow and Natalia at Yasnaya Polyana.

Jan Kabatoff – Doukhobor artist

speak. Not only had a certain church regulation been broken, but they were placed in a serious and awkward situation vis-à-vis the people — thus the church was packed to overflowing; after I outlined a brief but well-reasoned account of our community's views and our efforts to live as much as possible the Christian way of life, the people looked at the priests' perturbed faces with great astonishment. When I pointed out that the priesthood through their organized ecclesiastical position were only hiding the real truth from the life of the people and consequently the people were being held in bondage, the priests literally revolted. My talk was already drawing to a close, and the debate ended. It was rumoured that the Archbishop of Tobol'sk gave them a severe reprimand for such 'permissiveness.'

In the latest post I received a telegram, saying that my father died on the 15th of January. His death was natural — my father was already well past eighty. His clothing was quite worn out!

A few words about my life at the moment: I occupy a room six *arshins* square;[49] a joiner's bench and a lathe have been set up against one wall; various tools are arranged on the wall itself; by the opposite wall there is a bed and a clothes tree, and beside the bed a table three *arshins* along, with bookshelves at one end. I use this table for eating, taking tea and writing. The room is quite comfy and bright, there are four windows, all facing the north-east sun.

I wish you, Lev Nikolaevich, all good from God, and give my regards to all the people I know; I am healthy, thank God.

P. Verigin

No correspondence is permitted, except with family.

Address: Aleksej Nikitich Chuprov, Obdorsk

10. L. N. TOLSTOY ❧ P. V. VERIGIN
20 January 1901. Moscow.

20 January 1901. Moscow.

Dear Brother Pëtr Vasil'evich.

At Bodjanskij's request I am sending along his letter to you, concerning you as well as the brethren living in Canada.[50] I quite agree with him that if

49 *arshin* — a unit of measurement of length equivalent to seven-tenths of a metre. Note: "six *arshins*" is, no doubt, an allusion to the amount of land needed for one's burial in Tolstoy's story *How Much Land Does A Man Need?* (1886).

50 *Aleksandr Mikhajlovich Bodjanskij* (1842–1916) — a landowner in the Ekaterinoslav and Khar'kov Gubernias who gave up his land to the peasants. In 1892, because of his contacts with the Doukhobors, he was arrested and sent to the Caucasus. Seven years later he emigrated to Canada, where he lived among the Doukhobors, returning to Russia in 1905. The whereabouts

the Doukhobors indeed harbour a personal superstition, ascribing a supernatural significance to your personality, in spite of any advantage which might ensue from such a superstition, such as exercising a beneficial influence on the weaker ones, it should not be encouraged, as I am sure you fully agree, and that if such a superstition exists, it exists against your will.

The only point on which I differ with Bodjanskij is that he would allow an exception in the case of certain individuals' influence. I don't think that's right; I believe that in a Christian society all are equal and that everybody learns from each other: the old from the young, the educated from the uneducated, the clever from the dull-minded, and even the virtuous from the reprobate. Everybody learns from each other, depending on through whom and at what time the spirit of God speaks.

There are no special people: all are sinful and all may be saints. From what I hear from those who have been in Canada, the information he (Bodjanskij) gives about the life of the brethren there is correct, but I think he is too harsh on them and that the spark of religious service to God is not being extinguished in them. If and when it should be dimmed for a while, it will no doubt flare up again with renewed strength. I am sending along to you another letter written to me by Ponomarëv and Potapov, from which you will see what they are concerned about at the moment.[51]

I am very sorry not to have heard any news from you for a long time. I have been writing, but apparently the channels by which I have sent the letters are not reliable. Our friends and I are thinking of you, and I, at least, have not ceased trying to persuade the government to let you and the other exiles leave. I made another attempt just the other day, with a letter on this subject to the Tsar.[52] I have no idea what will come of it. Quite possibly nothing. But I shall try again. Farewell. My best brotherly wishes to you.

Lev Tolstoy

I am enclosing the brothers' letter to you.

of Bodjanskij's letter to Verigin are unknown. Bodjanskij is the author of "The Doukhobors. Collection of stories, letters, documents and articles on religious questions" (Bodjanskij 1907).

51 Ivan Ponomarëv and Vasilij Potapov wrote to Tolstoy from Canada on 31 December 1900 about disagreements with the Canadian government on questions of land ownership and registration of vital statistics. In his reply of 18 January 1901 (*PSS* 73:17–18), Tolstoy considered the first point very important, but thought an agreement with the authorities possible on the registration of births, marriages and deaths.

52 The reference is to Tolstoy's letter to Tsar Nicholas II dated 7 December 1900 (*PSS* 72:514–16), with an appeal to cease religious persecution, along with a request to allow the wives and mothers of those sent to the Yakutsk area to return to central Russia.

11. L. N. TOLSTOY ❧ P. V. VERIGIN

17 January 1902. Gaspra.

Dear Brother Pëtr Vasil'evich, I have only now received your letter of February 1899. Some stranger passed it along to me.[53] You probably know from other sources about the life of your brethren and mine in Canada; I shall tell you only briefly that, according to the latest reports, their material needs are being well supplied; not only have they no further need of help, but they are helping others. I only hope they are also prospering spiritually. And I believe they will, in spite of the fact that outwardly many of them seem to have somehow been weakened at present: they have forsaken the communal life and given in to temptation.[54] I think such a departure from the appearance of Christian life will not harm them and will lead them on toward the perfection all living beings strive for and are moving toward. The Christian leaven in them is so strong that, having tasted worldly life, they cannot help but wish to return to the Christian life. And if they return, they will do so consciously, and not simply out of a feeling of gregariousness or submission to authority, as is the case with many of them now.

There is something else I should like to tell you, namely, that I am most unhappy about their refusal to accept personal ownership of land. Such a refusal would be meaningful if they were perfect in everything else. But in the more important things they are departing from the requirements of a Christian life, while here all at once they are wrecking their lives over a formal acknowledgement of land ownership (once they have received the land as personal property, they can always make use of it on a communal basis). The same is true of their refusal to register births and marriages. There will still be questions on which they will have to stand up for their Christian beliefs — or, rather, their Christian life — such as, for example, the question of war, or the courts, and so on — then is the time to stand firm with all their might.

I haven't heard anything about you for a long time. Write to me about yourself, your feelings, thoughts and plans. I am keeping this letter short as I fear it may not reach you, and besides, I have been ill for a long time and I feel I am quickly drawing closer to death, or rather to the transition into another form of life, and I am writing in bed. Perhaps that will serve as an excuse for my poor handwriting.

Embracing you in brotherhood,
Your Brother, Lev Tolstoy

17 Jan. 1902

53 See Letter N° 9, Note 45.

54 Tolstoy wrote about this in February of 1900 in his missive "To the Doukhobors who have emigrated to Canada" (*PSS* 72:305–10).

12. P. V. VERIGIN ❧ L. N. TOLSTOY
15 November 1902. Christchurch.

15th November 1902. England.

Dear Friend Lev Nikolaevich!

Forgive me for not informing you for such a long time on the progress of my trip. I send you my heartfelt greeting, and ask you to pass along my regards to Sofia Andreevna.[55] God give you health and prosperity.[56]

I have been staying for over a week now with the dear Chertkov family.[57] I arrived here on the 5th of the month. On the 20th I plan to leave for America [*sic*]. I have been here rather long; I should have gone straight to see my elderly mother. I was at a meeting in London. I wasn't going to go, but Vladimir Grigor'evich persuaded me that I must show myself to the English community. It still turned out that I presented myself a bit like a Russian 'polar bear,' since I don't understand a word of English. Vladimir Grigor'evich read a rather well-written account he had prepared about the Doukhobors in general and especially about the latest movement,[58] attempting to explain this movement, which grew out of more or less respectable motives, while for the most part it has been rather crudely condemned in the press.

The audience listened attentively, and later I was asked [to explain] the Doukhobor views on several issues. Vladimir Grigor'evich interpreted.

There does not seem to be much practical sense in the new movement, but, God willing, everything will turn out all right.

I shall write you in detail when I get to Canada.

I wish you all good from God. I am in good health.

Pëtr Verigin

55 *Sofia Andreevna* — Tolstoy's wife, Sofia Andreevna Tolstaya.

56 Verigin was in Yasnaya Polyana 30–31 October 1902, on his way from exile to Canada.

57 Vladimir Chertkov was sent abroad in 1897 "for propaganda and illegal interference in sectarian affairs." He lived in England, where he published works by Tolstoy that had been banned in Russia. The Chertkov family was able to return to Russia in the summer of 1907.

58 The reference is to the 'pilgrimage movement' — see Letter N° 13 below.

13. P. V. VERIGIN ❧ L. N. TOLSTOY
12 January 1903. Poterpevshee.

12th Jan. 1903. Village of Poterpevshee.[59]

To Lev Nikolaevich Tolstoy

Forgive me, dear Friend, Lev Nikolaevich, that I have not so far written you a detailed letter about my trip. On the way, of course, I could have written several letters, but I am not a very regular correspondent. Even though I very much wanted to send you a telegram once I had crossed the border, I couldn't, I was afraid I might get left behind by the train, and so I hardly stepped outside the carriage right until we reached London, where Vladimir Grigor'evich Chertkov greeted me with open arms. I spent two weeks with this dear family, hardly noticing the time. Though Anna Konstantinovna[60] is physically ill, she is cheerful and strong in spirit.

Vladimir Grigor'evich went with me to Liverpool and saw me aboard ship. The crossing was quite stormy. All the passengers had to wait four days on the ship in the harbour at Saint John for medical inspection; it turned out there was one person on board with symptoms of smallpox.

Three Doukhobors came to meet me in Saint John along with someone sent by the Minister from Ottawa, who told me that if I had the time free, the Minister would like to see me in Ottawa. I agreed and went to see him. I declined to talk about the matter of the Doukhobor emigration, and advised the Minister that I was still like a guest in Canada. The Minister was very kind to me.

Just three days later I was with the Doukhobors. You can imagine, my dear Lev Nikolaevich, how my soul was overflowing with ecstasy and feelings of joy upon arriving at the first Doukhobor village — that was the village of Blagodarnoe.[61] The second village was the one where my mother is living; I found her extremely cheerful and quite healthy for her years.

I should now like to touch upon a more important question in the Doukhobors' life — their recent 'pilgrimage movement.' The place and time of writing this letter do not allow me to go into detail as to my own opinion on this movement — or rather, on the true significance of what amounts to an accomplished fact. At the bottom of it there are three mixed feelings which prompted some fifteen hundred Doukhobors to leave the place where they were living and set out on the road without any particular direction.

Neither the representatives of the Canadian Government nor the Doukhobor people who have been looking after their liberation from their

59 *Poterpevshee* (pron. *po-ter-PEF-she-yeh*) — lit. 'Enduring' — the name given to one of the Doukhobor settlements in Canada.

60 *Anna Konstantinovna Chertkova* (*née* Diterikhs)— wife of Vladimir Grigor'evich Chertkov. For more on Verigin's stay with the Chertkovs, see Letter N° 12 above.

61 *Blagodarnoe* (pron. *bla-go-DAR-no-yeh*) — lit. 'Grateful.'

sorry plight, beginning in the Caucasus right up to now, have explained accurately or in detail what the political as well as the territorial and economic obligations of the Doukhobors would be should they decide to stay and live in Canada. This state of uncertainty has delayed the acceptance of land, and has led to one opinion among the Doukhobors that the government's conditions are too strict, and so some Doukhobors have decided they should leave the land that was offered to them, saying *Let us go and search of truth,* i.e., in search of a more humane attitude toward the settlers on the Government's part.

Others in this group of three 'feelings' declared that the Canadian climate is too cold and that as vegetarians they would never get used to a climate like this; *let's go and find a milder climate,* they said.

According to a third opinion: "The land is fruitful here, and the climate, even though cold, is still a very healthy one; we shall prosper living here, while out there in the world — in humanity world-wide — there are many poor people, our brothers and sisters; let us go and tell everyone along the way that people must stop smoking tobacco, drinking vodka and quarrelling, put an end to military organizations and the violent oppression of people who are their brethren — people working in the mines, for example, or in other types of community labour." This was the literal explanation given me by those who belonged to the third group of the 'three feelings' — the so-called preachers of Christ's teachings.

My own personal opinion about all those fifteen hundred people, as far as I can tell, is that all these people seem very solid and reasonable members of the community, including the women and girls, many of whom tell me they have decided not to get married but to live and work spiritually for Christ, i.e., for the equalization of human rights in community life.

That is all I know about this movement so far. As a deep-thinking psychologist, Lev Nikolaevich, you will be able to understand this phenomenon that has arisen among the Doukhobors for yourself, in general and in the particular. I shall add my own opinion: I cannot seem to distinguish this movement from the overall question of injustice in life that is vexing mankind.

The whole party was recommended by the government to turn back at Menidos, a hundred and thirty miles [= 210 km] from the Doukhobor settlements. All the Doukhobors behaved very meekly in front of the police and there was no violence. They are now living in their own houses, they have plenty to eat, and since the day I arrived have not accepted government aid.[62]

I might compare this movement to Abraham's actions in bringing his son as an offering to God, and when Abraham took up the knife to slay his son, God's angel stayed his hand — or rather, Abraham himself came to the realization that he did not have to slay his son, and God told him to take his son, go home and live a life of praise to God.[63] I voiced this opinion to almost all

62 See Letter Nº 21.

63 See Gen. 22:12–17.

the Doukhobors who were walking, having left their whole way of life behind them, and said: "Your motives of self-sacrifice for the common good of human life are legitimate and precious ones, but there is no need to let the children go hungry and cold, so for the time being why not remain with all the rest of the brethren and teach them?" Those with families took this explanation too as a revelation from God.

I embrace you and pray to God for your family's well-being.

P. Verigin

P.S. There will soon be a meeting to discuss acceptance of land.

14. L. N. TOLSTOY ❧ P. V. VERIGIN[64]
9–13? February 1903. Yasnaya Polyana.

Dear Pëtr Vasil'evich,

I have not replied to you for some time as I have been ill. I am slowly approaching death and am afraid lest the remaining days of my life be poorly spent and yield no benefit to mankind. This is the great advantage of old age and disease, outweighing by a hundredfold the disadvantages of disease and old age.

The account you have given me of the Doukhobors and your explanation of the recent movement seem quite in order. May God help you, dear friend, in that position of responsibility where you exercise considerable influence on people, not to sin against them by giving them wrong direction.

My advice, which I have thought through before God and offer to you in my love for you and the Doukhobor brethren, is to get yourself personally as much out of the way as possible, not taking sides on current issues but encouraging the brethren in only one thing: to act as God desires his children to act, and most importantly, not to violate the love among themselves in the name of this or that understanding of God's will. God's will is the same for all: to love Him and love each other, and in order to be in a position to love Him and love each other, they must deny self and serve one another in everything. The most fearsome evil is the enmity which arises among people out of their differing concepts of man's duties toward God. So I ask you to use all your influence to combat this.

If only those who reject the use of animal labour and those who are content to stay in one place and till the soil would consider love and unity between them an actual possibility, regardless of differences of opinion, if they would only love and help others as well as their own, and put this love above all else, everything would be good, and in one way or another a unity of views would be achieved.

64 Handwritten by Tolstoy's daughter M. L. Obolenskaja. Signed in Tolstoy's own hand.

In a word, the longer I live, and the closer I come to the end, the more obvious it is to me that only one thing is needed: the establishment of God's kingdom, which comes about through people's love for each other. But this love does not come all by itself; we must make an effort to draw it close to us, the same effort by which God's kingdom is revealed.

I think you are aware of all this, and that you feel and act in this spirit, and I am glad of it.

Thank you for writing me; please do write again, and if possible, tell me in detail about how the different Doukhobor settlements are progressing and whether there is harmony among them.

Farewell, and may God grant you and all the Doukhobor brethren the highest possible good in the world — unity and love among yourselves.

Lovingly, Lev Tolstoy

15. L. N. TOLSTOY ❧ P. V. VERIGIN[65]

24 October/6 November [new style] 1903. Yasnaya Polyana.

Dear Pëtr Vasil'evich,

Yesterday I had a visit from old Aleksej Aleksandrovich Fofanov, who was released from the Yakutsk area. As you know, he, Novokshonov and Shcherbakov arrived in the Caucasus, preparing to go to Canada to be re-united with their families. But besides not being granted foreign passports, [another] misfortune has befallen them, which Fofanov himself will write you about: they had all their money stolen from them, so that now they have no means of getting to Canada. I am petitioning for foreign passports to be issued to them, and I hope to be successful in this. But in any case, because of this misfortune, they need money. If the community is willing to give them enough money for their living and their passage, you can send it to me, or to save time you can telegraph me how much you are sending and I shall see the amount gets to these old people.

I was very glad to hear the news that your life and that of your family and our brethren have been progressing and are continuing to get better and better, closer and closer to Christ's precepts.

I am not writing to you with my own hand, as I am not feeling entirely well these days. But my overall health is as it should be for one quickly approaching a change in one's form of life. I shall be happy to hear from you. Farewell, and brotherly greetings.

Lovingly, Lev Tolstoy

6 November 1903.

65 Handwritten by Ju. I. Igumnova, an artist and friend of Tolstoy's daughter Tat'jana Tolstaja. She lived at Yasnaya Polyana for several years, helping take care of correspondence and copying manuscripts. The signature is in Tolstoy's own hand. A note from Aleksej Fofanov was attached.

16. P. V. VERIGIN ❧ L. N. TOLSTOY
1 December 1903. Otradnoe.[66]

Dear Lev Nikolaevich!

My heartfelt thanks for letting me know how you are getting on. May the Lord save you! Please give my best regards to your whole family, with my wishes for all good to you from God.

I received your letter along with the attached note from Alësha Fofanov,[67] and now I am hastening to send you two hundred dollars, which I would ask you to give to the old ones who turned to you for help. Address it to *Vasilij Shcherbakov.*

We are sending this rather small amount for the living expenses of Fofanov, Shcherbakov and Novokshonov, wherever they happen to be staying for the time being. If they are able to come to Canada, we might be able to offer some further help.

How hard you work! Dear, kind Lev Nikolaevich, it seems that wherever we turn you are expending your depleting bodily forces. Happy is the man whose frail body has not yet been forsaken by Soul or Mind and is that much more able to struggle with circumstances around him.

I'm not about to give you [at this time] a whole account of myself and my surroundings since coming to Canada. The main reason is not to overburden your attention.

As for how the Doukhobors are settling in to community life here, I cannot say that things are getting 'better and better' as you suggest, but as far as is humanly possible, especially for a large group of people, to adopt good character traits, the community is coming along well, thank God.

In a brief letter I cannot go into all the pros and cons of the people's community life, except to say that here in Canada the Doukhobors have been faced with a number of good reasons to unite in their community life. There is a great lack of resources and agricultural equipment and under Canadian regulations one can make a fairly good living off the land, but homestead plots are too unequal to [profitably] work the land individually. This summer, though, thanks to collective labour in working the land, the Doukhobors have managed to plough and prepare for spring sowing more than ten thousand acres of land. In addition, since I arrived they have bought about four hundred work horses. They have acquired — as major purchases, very important to them, eight steam threshers: six 18-h.p. machines drawn by horses and two 20-h.p. self-propelled vehicles. The grain and vegetable harvest was fairly good and these eight machines proved extremely efficient in

66 *Otradnoe* (pron. *ot-RAD-no-yeh*) — lit. 'Delightful' — the name of another Doukhobor village in Saskatchewan.

67 *Alësha* (pron. *al-YO-sha*) — diminutive form of the name Aleksej.

the threshing. The six [stationary] threshers have now been set up in various plots of land as mills, they grind the grain and process fibres for cooking oil, while the two vehicles have gone into the forest where they will be set up to saw lumber. In the spring we are planning to manufacture bricks and tiling, using steam power. The Canadians are beginning to be quite amazed: on the one hand there are Doukhobors walking around stark naked, wanting to abandon physical labour altogether, while on the other hand they are acquiring the most up-to-date agricultural equipment and are starting to work in a very business-like fashion so as to protect their equipment from the bankers. Among useful acquisitions I might mention are over a hundred grain scythes, which work very cleanly and quickly. Now each forty-family village has nine pair of work horses, fifteen cows, and a few sheep, and all summer long we have been buying more things. Carts, sleighs, ploughs, harrows, etc. have been bought according to the number of horses. We have also bought some thoroughbred horses and are planning to raise our own acclimatised horses, as they are quite expensive to buy.

We shall be preparing a detailed account of our farming activities over the summer; maybe we shall send you a copy, at least the young people around you might be interested in it.

As to the Yakutsk brethren and their emigration to Canada, if they will permit, I have come up with a plan: to set up a bank account in Yakutsk so that those who are emigrating can draw out money for passage, and another account in Moscow or Batumi, so that travellers who get that far can provide themselves with the means to proceed further. Our whole community has sent notice about this to Yakutsk, also five hundred dollars has been sent to help support — *in that location* — old people like Fofanov, Shcherbakov and Novokshonov, and people who are ill. The community advised them by letter that should a need arise, they could send a request by telegram and we would be sure to send them money, but only if the requests come in the name of all the exiles together. This [past] summer I collected the names of all the people in Siberia and sent them to the English [*sic*] Government, which has promised to intervene with the Russian authorities about releasing them from Yakutsk — we have even set aside some land here for that number of people. But if our brethren in Yakutsk have no patience, if you look at it objectively, it seems nobody is to blame. In the heat of the moment I feel extremely angry even toward such old people as Fofanov and Shcherbakov, whom I have nothing but contempt for. They are looking for they know not what, and consequently misfortune and trouble await these older people, when instead they should quietly eat their daily bread and praise the Lord. Well, never mind! Nothing in this world is ever useless; all that is being done is being done for the better.

I embrace you in thought and wish you again all good from God.

Lovingly,
Peter Verigin

1 Dec. '03
Village of Otradnoe. Yorkton [Saskatchewan].

17. L. N. TOLSTOY ❧ P. V. VERIGIN
2 January 1904. Yasnaya Polyana.

Dear Brother Pëtr Vasil'evich,

I received your letter with the cheques and have sent the money to the old people. I was surprised by your harsh attitude toward them. I don't think they deserve it. They received five hundred roubles from Maude and write that they now have enough money. The question of passports has not yet been resolved, though they are promising to issue them.[68]

I am enclosing Murav'ëv's letter about the Pavlovka villagers who were exiled to labour [camps] with their families.[69] These are deeply religious people, suffering on account of a momentary distraction, who not only have not asked for anything to date, but have even refused the help [that was offered]. Now, it seems, they are in dire need, and I was thinking: if your community agreed to return to Maude the five hundred roubles he sent, I would send this money to the Pavlovka people. I hope that the community of universal brotherhood will not turn this down. Please reply. The news I have of you through Tan[70] and from your kind letter is a delight both to me and to everyone who shares a kindred spirit with your community. You will forgive me if I as an old man take the liberty of giving advice to you and those around you. In all probability you know yourself what I am about to tell you, but it doesn't hurt to repeat an idea if it is a right one. Don't get carried away, dear friend, by the material success of the community. Remember that this success is based on the unity stemming from the religious consciousness which brings everyone together. Thus religious feeling is the basic capital underlying even material well-being, [while the latter] by itself is not only unimportant, but oftentimes destructive, undermining the very source from which it flows. "In this rejoice not, that the spirits are subject unto you; but rather rejoice, because your

68 Tolstoy applied to Grand Prince Nikolaj Mikhajlovich and the head of the civil sector in the Caucasus, Prince Grigorij Golitsyn, with a request to issue foreign-travel passports to Fofanov, Shcherbakov and Novokshonov.

69 In 1901, the peasant sectarians from the village of Pavlovka in Sumy County (Ukraine), under the strong influence of Prince Dmitrij Khilkov, destroyed a local church. A trial took place January–February 1902, where they were represented by lawyer N. K. Murav'ëv (1870–1936). In spite of twelve people testifying in their defence, severe sentences were handed down: four were given prison terms, while forty-five were exiled to hard labour for periods of up to fifteen years.

70 *V. G. Bogoraz-Tan* (1865–1936) — writer, ethnographer, member of the *Narodnaya Volya* [People's Will] party, visited the Doukhobors in Canada in the summer of 1903. His accounts were published in the newspaper *Russkie vedomosti* — it was these Tolstoy was referring to; he did not come to know Tan (Bogoraz's pseudonym) personally until early in 1905.

names are written in heaven."[71] And so I feel that the most important thing is to protect, arouse and support that religious feeling, which is needed not just for one's material well-being but for the genuine happiness of all. So no matter how absurd the movement for animal liberation and Heavenly Life might seem, it is more important than all the steam threshers, scythes, harvesters, etc., just as steam in the engine is more important than all the cars with freight attached to it. If steam senselessly escapes outside, then all one needs to do is to make it work productively. The same goes for the Heavenly Life Party. They have the vital element that brings genuine good to one's self and others, while those who despise their motives and set up marvellous useful machines and see in them the meaning of life have nothing to offer themselves or others but certain destruction. I am sure you know this and feel and act this way, but I wanted to say this to you.

Your loving brother, Lev Tolstoy

2 Jan. 1904

18. P. V. VERIGIN ❧ L. N. TOLSTOY
20 February 1904. Otradnoe.

Village of Otradnoe. — Canada.
1904 20th February (n. s.)

To Lev Nikolaevich Tolstoy
[from] Pëtr Verigin.

My dear Lev Nikolaevich, forgive me for offending you with my crude comments regarding the old people. It is the fault of an evil that is common to all of us. For all your pains may the Lord send you physical health and peace of mind.

As far as the Pavlovka villagers are concerned, in response to your request for 500 roubles I am sending you three hundred dollars to do with as you please. And as for Maude, if he has sent 500 roubles to the old people, as you say, we shall reimburse him.

With you, my esteemed Lev Nikolaevich, I should like to be even more open than is customary. Which means at the moment I presume the Doukhobors' financial accounts and expenses should be as accurate as possible.

Maude has written me twice now that he has money set aside for loans to the Doukhobors for travel from Yakutsk to Canada. Just how much money there is Maude doesn't say, only that the money is to be used and repaid, but without interest.

On the 28th of this current month of February there is to be a conference with two people attending from each village. I shall raise Maude's proposal among other issues. Since the Doukhobors have accepted a great deal of help

71 See Luke 10:20.

from friends over the last twenty years I don't suppose they will decline this offer. (I am enclosing a brief statement of income and expenses over the past year, which will show that the Doukhobors' financial affairs are not exactly rosy.)

Proper travel arrangements from Yakutsk should be made insofar as possible. For example, there should be at least a small sum of money — an account — available in Yakutsk, a second source in Moscow and a third in England or on the American [*sic*] side. They should select the shortest and cheapest possible route. I came by Moscow, London and Saint John, and found it very convenient. I'm speaking about those who want to emigrate directly from Yakutsk to Canada. This systematic arrangement doesn't apply to those who go [back] to Russia upon being released, these can only be offered some private aid to get by on, as much as people can afford. We are not sending any money now for my sister and brother-and-law. We don't have it.

I am sincerely grateful to you, Lev Nikolaevich, and may the Lord bless you for your warning against getting too strongly carried away by material concerns; I am afraid of that myself, but right now we only wish to have our daily bread, something we really want to earn, since the Doukhobors have a great many children. As it happens, at the moment the Doukhobors are involved in discussions regarding becoming subjects of the English king. The majority do not want to hear about taking out citizenship; they reason that this would violate Christ's basic teaching about the equality of all people. Taking out citizenship would mean observing a formal order: everyone receiving a 160-acre plot of land would have to sign a form pledging an oath of full allegiance to "Edward," to defend his honour and so forth and to live in Canada for ever. If I may express an opinion, apart from violating the principle of equality of all people, I cannot guarantee that I will stay living in Canada for a long period of time, as the climate in the place where the Doukhobors are settled now is rather cold and we have to struggle to sow our grain and to make sure it is not killed by the frost. There are many good reasons for this: almost every year now the grain has had a hard time escaping autumn frosts, since the land has not been tilled properly. The earth should definitely be steam-ploughed for two years running, and wheat sown only in the third year. All that is possible with specialized equipment. (We are considering buying a 25-horsepower steam plough to try out this spring; one that could drive eight ploughs over virgin soil, or ten or eleven over soft soil.) If we fulfil, more or less, all the requirements for dividing the land and sowing the grain and still don't come up with a good yield, then it stands to reason we can't keep on living here forever, and so the question of citizenship I would say is rather premature. We don't know what explanations the English [*sic*] government will accept; that is something only time will tell.

This experiment will take at least three to four years, over which time the Doukhobors, one would assume, will manage to save up at least some money, and if the government should decide to make life miserable for the Doukhobors over some question of citizenship, we shall be willing to agree to it. It will only prove for the umpteenth time that all monarchical governments have outlived their time and are tolerable only as an evil in human life in general.

My love to you, yours ever faithfully,

Peter Verigin

Statement of Expenses and Income for 1903
of the Doukhobor community in Canada

			$	¢
1.	Purchased	35 horses in Winnipeg	6,719	.50
	»	5 colts	3,150	.00
	»	323 horses from Rain & Feirce [?]	25,696	.00
	»	7 horses from Bikyanin and 2 from Plaksin	1,200	.00
	Transport and delivery expenses for all horses, purchase of various items for horse herds and guides:		906	.05
		Total	37,671	.55
	Agricultural equipment			
2.	Purchased	4 horse-drawn steam engines with threshers	9,250	.00
	»	2 self-propelled steam engines with threshers	6,000	.00
	»	2 stationary machine saws	900	.00
	»	Grease for steam engines, [payments] to Inspector and food on journey	142	.24
	Paid for Prince Albert steam engines		2,000	.00
	Supplies for steam engines, engine operators' expenses		1,100	.00
	50 scythes, 32 hay-cutters and 20 000 pounds of threads		10,309	.00
	45 cutters 20 sowers 16 wagons 109 ploughs 234 triple harrows 12 grain-cleaners and 152 sleighs		14,092	.55
			43,793	.79
3.	Purchased	Fabric materials total	29,338	.29
4.	Land accepted from the government and purchased by Pëtr Vasil'evich		36,250	.00
5.	Purchased	wheat, oats and flour	9,720	.20
6.	»	Horse collars and footwear supplies	13,445	.22
7.	»	Winter boots for men and women	4,913	.58
8.	»	Iron, Dishes, implements, etc.	5,901	.11
9.	»	Salt, Kerosene and [?]	2,653	.08
10.	»	Sugar, Tea and lard	2,294	.87
11.	»	Woollens	1,505	.00
12.	»	Soap	1,707	.00
13.	»	Mill equipment and millers' expenses	868	.63
		Total	108,656	.98
		Total for this page	190,122	.32

			$	¢
		[Balance] forward	190,122	.32
14.	Purchased	sheep	1,461	.00
15.	"	Oil and containers for it	1,765	.72
16.	Goods transport by rail		1,530	.75
17.	Money sent to Siberia, Maude and other places		3,086	.00
18.	Railway trips and food on journey		852	.15
19.	Liman School		745	.85
20.	Government Office in Yorkton		303	.60
21.	To Iosif Konstantinovich		300	.00
22.	Vasja Golubov's expenditures on steam engines and threshers		364	.60
23.	Stationery expenses, paper for correspondence and typewriter		284	.35
24.	Paid to Egor Majer (Blacksmith)		255	.00
25.	Given to Archer at different times		157	.50
26.	Loaned to Mifodij		125	.00
27.	Paid for repair of all equipment		142	.00
28.	Sawmill expenses, etc.		155	.00
29.	Ivan Pod.'s expenditures on himself and the workers in Yorkton		41	.46
30.	Fees [?] for wood, bank interest, stable fees, and post-office box in Yorkton		83	.10
	Total		201,775	.40
31.	Petty-cash purchases for all 47 villages		13,769	.52
	Total		215,544	.92
32.	Agricultural income for all 47 villages		152,474	.24
	Outstanding debt		63,070	.68

Payment of debt to be made at the depots in the City of Winnipeg in the autumn of 1904. Without interest.

19. L. N. TOLSTOY ❧ P. V. VERIGIN

3/15 March 1904. Yasnaya Polyana.

I received your letter, dear Pëtr Vasil'evich, with the statement of the community's income and expenses, which I found most interesting, along with a cheque for £61.

Maude didn't wait for the reimbursement of the money he sent to the old people, but sent another 500 roubles for the Pavlovka villagers, which I sent along to them. So your money (£61) remains unused. I shall put it into the bank and await your reply as to what should be done with it. Yesterday I received a letter from Konkin saying that he is waiting for money from you to take him and his daughter to Canada, since he is now released and hopes to emigrate in May.[72] Should I send him the £61? Let me know. So much for business matters.

I quite understand the difficulty and even the impossibility of Christians recognizing the authority of the king and pledging him allegiance. It appears there is no place left on earth where Christians can live without being persecuted. I think this should spur Christians even more to do God's will and live a Christian life, which worldly people are so far removed from. What will come out of this it is impossible to say, but one thing is certain: nothing but good can result from doing God's will, for those who do it as well as for all the people of the world.

I was so glad to hear from you that the material well-being of the community is not keeping you from seeing the need to strive for spiritual perfection, and I hope that this striving for spiritual perfection, which is the sole purpose of each individual, is going on among you without let-up.

Thank you for your good wishes. I am getting along very nicely. I work as much as I can, unfortunately at the easiest task and the one of most doubtful benefit — writing. Right now I am writing about war,[73] about the senselessness of it all, and about how we can be saved from it not by Christ's words, but by practising his teachings, and I am enjoying undeserved happiness, and the love of those good people who are so dear to me.

Farewell. I embrace you in brotherhood and wish you Godspeed in that activity which you never need repent of and constantly draws you nearer to God.

Lovingly, Lev Tolstoy

Write to me about yourself and the brethren at least occasionally.

3 [old style]/15 [new style] March 1904

20. P. V. VERIGIN ❧ L. N. TOLSTOY
12 April 1904. Otradnoe.

Canada. — Yorkton. Village of Otradnoe. 12 Apr. 1904.

My dear Lev Nikolaevich, I am happy to inform you that we are all alive and well, especially in the Spirit, thank God. Now that spring has come, my mother has begun to recover from a serious winter illness — no doubt like everything in nature. — She sends you and your whole family her warmest regards and her deep gratitude for your attentions to her relatives and everyone else. She

72 Ivan Konkin's letter dated 2 February 1904 is on file in the Tolstoy archives. Tolstoy's reply is in *PSS* 75:58.

73 The reference is to Tolstoy's article *Bethink Yourselves!* [*Odumajtes'!*] concerning the Russo--Japanese war.

asks us to read each of your letters several times to her, and we — Grigorij and I, her children — are happy to do so. You, my esteemed Lev Nikolaevich, are so exceedingly kind and good to me to write so often. I, of course, have a deep appreciation for the Spirit of Peace within you, as do all the Doukhobors; it is just that they cannot so freely express their feelings in words. — I am talking about the true Doukhobors. — No doubt this is an exclusively Christian trait — not to talk a lot. To me even Christ seems to represent more a silent human observer and an exemplary practical life.

Your last letter of 3/15 March has arrived. My heartfelt thanks — and those of all my Doukhobor friends — to you for all you are doing for all the suffering people. Don't send the £61 you have on hand to Konkin just yet. The Doukhobors have sent him two hundred dollars — not for coming to Canada, mind you, but for improving living conditions for him and his sick daughter. Konkin's family may soon be coming to Moscow to see you — I beg you to help them, dear Lev Nikolaevich, to have your friends arrange things for his sick daughter, for example — see if the doctors can't help with this illness.[74] If you still have the £61 on hand, you can spend as much of it as is necessary on this case.

The winter here has been a long one with lots of snow. Now, God be thanked, spring is opening up. All the children in the Doukhobor villages are singing their greeting to spring: "*prishla Vesna k nam molodaya*" [Spring has come to us young and fair]! And really, she is eternally young! How marvellously the world is constructed! How fervently I wish, dear Lev Nikolaevich, that you could be here in the Doukhobor villages and see these 8- to 10-year old children singing their songs of spring — many of them memorized out of good contemporary song-books. I feel such images — these groups of children — would prove a significant reward for your long labours as a fighter for truth.

There are about thirty or forty children in each settlement, some have as many as fifty around ten years of age, of both sexes. I am most excited about the children in our Doukhobor milieu — they are a strong bond between me and the Doukhobors. For example, when the children sing "all our faces look happy," they really do have a little smile on their face at that time. How innocent and carefree the children are in their young souls! They have little use for 'conflicts,' even among the very highest powers in the world.

I embrace you as a son, and in brotherhood.

Lovingly,
Pëtr Verigin

74 Konkin's daughter was mentally ill.

21. P. V. VERIGIN ❧ L. N. TOLSTOY
1 April 1905. Toronto.

1 April 1905. City of Toronto.

Esteemed Lev Nikolaevich!

At the moment I have come along with two Community representatives from our settlements to the cities of southern Canada. We had a small matter to take up with the Canadian Government, whose headquarters is located in Ottawa.

The situation is this: when the Doukhobors settled at Assiniboia and Swan River (the places take their names from rivers), they were told to settle in villages and divide the land up according to their cattle herds, and not by individual homesteads as is customary in Canada. This was granted by the former Minister of Internal Affairs [Clifford] Sifton, who has since retired. But now that the Doukhobors are organized, so to speak, and have begun to till the land that happens to lie close by, leaving most of the homesteads untouched, the government sees this as a violation of official custom and the English-speaking residents have started riding around the fields assigned to us, selecting the good unploughed lands for themselves. They have begun applying to the local department offices to have these homesteads transferred to their name as free homesteads.

The official custom in Canada is that someone who has registered a homestead (160 acres) and lets three years go by without ploughing it forfeits the right to that land. It is indeed a logical system: the land can only be enjoyed by those who work it. Of course, in Canada there are many imperfections and misappropriations of land and greedy hands out only after money. But I am speaking of the so-called Crown lands — which are only given to migrants — every male 18 or over is given a plot free, on a one-time-only basis. It is for this reason that we have come to Ottawa and now the government is once again confirming its promise and is sending notice to the department offices closest to our villages, so that the Doukhobors won't lose their lands to someone else. Still, they consider such a 'privilege' to be a violation of official custom.

The local residents, especially, are beginning to regard the Doukhobors with some degree of envy, since the Doukhobors through their community organization are able to raise their standard of living more quickly and so get ahead of the English. For example, the Doukhobors already have twenty sets of steam threshers (a 'set' consisting of a steam engine and a thresher), up to two hundred scythes, cutters and other state-of-the-art equipment. The wheat is ground at home, they have bought wood-cutting machines, along with ten steam engines for ploughing this summer — last summer we experimented with just one.

Of course all this setting up angers the English speakers in the neighbourhood — they are a self-loving race, and even after twenty years individual homesteaders still can't afford to buy a steam thresher. No wonder, since a steam thresher costs $3,000, and three thousand dollars is not something a person living off wheat or oats can easily come by. The English would love the Doukhobors to break up into small farms and serve out a 'bondage' of individual indebtedness to the banks.

A farmer's life in Canada isn't all that enviable; with the rare exception, farmers each owe five or six hundred or even a thousand dollars; I'm talking about the ordinary have-not immigrants who need to borrow that much at first to get started. And once a person is obliged to fall into a state of indebtedness, this makes his situation extremely difficult, as almost all his income must go to pay interest on the loan. The local 'spider' banks have no hesitation in charging ten or twelve or even twenty percent. And so the Doukhobors with their community organization try not to fall under the 'spiders'' control. The English-speaking farmers who all live on individual homesteads are upset because their own enterprises might fall behind, while the capitalists are upset because they don't get goods or money from the Doukhobors for interest.

The spiritual life of the Doukhobors, dear Lev Nikolaevich, is moving along at its usual pace. After all, these were not highly moral people to begin with and it is impossible to demand they start living an 'angelic' life all at once.

Many find the climate too cold, as they would like to get by without any help at all from cows and work cattle. With this in mind we plan to go this summer and have a look at British Columbia and California; if there is any possibility at all of moving, the ones who want to work with fruit-growing will go.

The Doukhobors are not averse to sending representatives even to Australia; to this end we are in correspondence with a former Doukhobor friend living in Australia. Of course, all of this is not a search for Spiritual Truth but only for a comfortable place to live. But the so-called Sons of Freedom Doukhobors[75] abstract life to the extreme and say that a person living in a cold, harsh climate who exploits animals is that much further from the Truth.

During this trip we went to see a Russian Consul named [Nikolaj Berngardovich] Struve in Montréal, as the Kars Doukhobors were paid for their houses and we had to get the money from him. Struve is a rather likeable fellow. In Toronto we are visiting textile factories to get fabrics and other manufactured goods first-hand for the community. There is a Professor Mavor[76]

75 For more on the Sons of Freedom, see Chap. 1 above (p. 13).

76 James Mavor, a political-science professor, first went to see Tolstoy in 1889. He helped the Doukhobors resettle in Canada; his letters and Tolstoy's replies have been preserved. Tolstoy's son Sergej L'vovich Tolstoy recalled that the proposal to emigrate to Canada originated with Mavor's friend Pëtr Kropotkin: "Mavor started a publicity campaign about the desirability of having the Doukhobors as immigrants, as they were people who had suffered for their faith, hard-working and on the whole quite respectable, and he began to lobby the Canadian government to let them

in Toronto — a good friend of ours; he and I have agreed to go pay you a visit some time, my esteemed Lev Nikolaevich. We are spending a couple of days together. Last night we went to the theatre, where there was playing a comedy-drama, so to speak. You might even be familiar with it: 'Bourgeois' is warned by a Martian not to misuse his position of wealth; in the end the Martian brings on thundering and deprives the earthling of his wealth, turning him into a beggar. The comedy made quite an impression on my companions — Semën Vereshchagin and Semën Rybin; upon returning to the hotel we talked for a long time about the injustices in our life.

Recently I sent a letter to [Aleksej Ivanovich] Stepanov care of you. If you receive it, please pass it on to him.

Give my heartfelt greetings to all our friends. I wish you all blessings from the Lord God.

I'm keeping healthy.

Pëtr Verigin

22. L. N. TOLSTOY ❧ P. V. VERIGIN
28 May 1905. Yasnaya Polyana.

Dearest brother Pëtr Vasil'evich,

I received your kind and interesting letter[77] some time ago now and was so glad both that you remember me and that the financial affairs of your community are coming along well. God grant only that material success does not mean a weakening of spiritual effort and striving for perfection. It often happens that way, just like with a balance: as one goes up, the other goes down. You have to try to raise the level of the fulcrum, but if the balance has to swing one way or another, it is better to let people be materially poor so long as they are enriching themselves spiritually. I think, and I hope, and I wish that this is how it will be with the Doukhobors. The spiritual life in your community is so much aflame that it should not go out, but only keep on flaming.

I am happy that the Yakutsk people have returned. My brotherly greetings to you and all those who know me.

Lev Tolstoy

28 May 1905

into Canada" (see S. L. Tolstoj 1949: 188). Mavor visited Yasnaya Polyana in the summer of 1910, during his travels through China, Japan and Russia.

77 Tolstoy noted, with some sadness, that in a number of his letters Verigin seemed to be overly concerned with the material well-being of the Doukhobors. Hence his urging them to strive more for spiritual goals and less for material ones.

23. P. V. VERIGIN ❧ L. N. TOLSTOY
3 July 1905. Otradnoe.

Christian Community of Universal Brotherhood

The Doukhobors in Canada

3rd July '05. Village of Otradnoe
Yorkton. — Canada.

To Lev Nikolaevich Tolstoy
[from] Pëtr Verigin.

Dear Friend Lev Nikolaevich, I have received your letter and it has been a very big help to me. The word 'Dear' where you are concerned has become simply the kindest word, since you, kind Lev Nikolaevich, are truly a dear person to me. Every one of your words overflows with simplicity and sincerity, and that is something dear to us all, if only people would treat each other more simply and sincerely.

Your fears for the Doukhobors' future in Canada are valid and understandable. But I cannot refuse to accept people's close participation in building material progress — since in many respects the spiritual does not depend upon us, it is something that touches each one individually. — For example, I can give someone a heifer, a horse, a hundred roubles and so on, but I can't give him a soul, and insofar as I am able to observe human life, it strikes me as an impossible task. — There is a special place for that, where the spirit of life and understanding originates. The Spirit "bloweth where it listeth"[78] and where it goes we do not know. Although Christ says: the world knoweth me not, but you know me.[79] Of course, this 'knowledge' should be interpreted as unity of the spirit.

You are aware, dear Lev Nikolaevich, that the Doukhobors came to Canada materially poor and possibly, according to your understanding, therein lies their advantage. Our material insufficiency has probably drawn their hearts closer together and led them to God — since God is manifested in the unity of human hearts.

It seems to me that the whole world was created and exists for good, so why should material wealth — as we deem it — serve us for evil? When someone begins to misuse his wealth or sets the acquisition of wealth as his goal in life, then that is quite a different story. The Doukhobors think a lot about the

78 See John 3:8.
79 See John 14:17.

growth of the soul and it seems to me that they are even doing a lot of work in this direction, and this is their sense of good for the time being, while ahead of them stands the God of mercy — I am saying that we should become more merciful — and this is a person's goal in life.

I must say that the material conditions of our community life are basically in good order, but there is no strong growth yet. Do you think it is easy to get started in a desert place? We had to build more than sixty villages, with housing for each individual family. The climate is too cold to stay in the open air. Even in a desert place each household needs food to eat: what would you have done? — probably not just clasped your hands together and looked up to the sky expecting manna to fall, as the Israelites did.[80] The Doukhobors have a great many children, and I still notice that the children are not yet receiving enough nourishment from their mothers' milk and no wonder, since what the mothers have to eat is meagre indeed.

Would it have been rational for me to walk about the neighbourhoods, comforting the mothers who might lose their children because of malnutrition? As if the spirit which inspires our hearts and the bread which feeds our bodies did not come from the one God and Father?! Unfortunately the people up to now have made a distinction between the spiritual food and the material.

This summer in our community we have ten steam engines doing the ploughing, 25 horsepower each. It is easy for such powerful machines to pull eight ploughs each; that was the way we did it last year experimenting with just one engine. Now we hitch four [ploughs] together along with another machine called a cutter, which trails along behind and breaks up the earth, the way women cut cabbage. Such a tool is extremely useful simply because it reduces the burden on the horses, since [normally] after ploughing you have to go over it two or three more times to break it up, but this cutter is quite a heavy machine. — You probably know: it consists of twenty-inch discs or larger, very sharp, in a row of fourteen or more; with a team of four good horses, if you lower it to full depth it is too hard on the horses. That's where the steam engine has the advantage: you can lower the cutter to full depth right off, and then go over it just one more time cross-wise, and that's enough.

On the 30th of June we got a bank draft from the Yorkton bank to send to Moscow in the name of Aleksandr Nikiforovich Dunaev[81] — ten thousand dollars to bring the Yakutsk brethren over. I asked Aleksandr Nikiforovich to get our Moscow Friends to arrange the tickets to be sent. Konkin too will probably be in Moscow by that time.

I told him that you, Dear Lev Nikolaevich, should not be disturbed [on this matter]; I think such affairs can be looked after by slightly younger people.

80 See Ps. 78:23–24.

81 *Aleksandr Dunaev* (1850–1920) — a friend of Tolstoy's, who at one time shared his views; he was one of the directors of the Moscow Commercial Bank.

I wish your whole family complete health. And may the Lord send you, Dear Lev Nikolaevich, many more years of a healthy life.

I am keeping healthy myself. Your brother in Christ,

Pëtr Verigin

24. P. V. VERIGIN ❧ L. N. TOLSTOY
24 November 1906. Moscow.

24 November, Moscow.

Esteemed Lev Nikolaevich,

Six of us have come from the Doukhobor society in Canada with the express purpose of seeing you.

Yesterday your son Sergej L'vovich dropped by and told us some people in your house are sick.[82] Please let us know by telegram whether we can come to see you now.

On the trip here we agreed we might take an apartment in the village near your place, get settled in and then see you when it is possible.

With heartfelt respect for you,

Pëtr Verigin

Address:
'Taku' Rooming House
Ostozhenka
Moscow

25. L. N. TOLSTOY ❧ P. V. VERIGIN
30 November 1906. Yasnaya Polyana.

I did not reply to you by telegram, dear Pëtr Vasil'evich, as your letter arrived during the time of my daughter's illness. — I shall be most happy to see you and your friends.[83]

Lev Tolstoy

30 November 1906

82 At Yasnaya Polyana, Tolstoy's daughter Marija L'vovna Obolenskaja was gravely ill. She died 27 November 1906.

83 Verigin and five other Doukhobors (Ivan Faddeevich Makhortov, Pavel Planidin, D. N. Gridchin, Anastasija Golubëva, Marfa Dymovskaja) visited Yasnaya Polyana 6–10 December 1906. The doctor Dushan Makovitskij noted in his diary (1979–81: 2:322–27):

Everyone was very attentive to the Doukhobors. They were most pleasant and interesting… Ivan Faddeevich [Makhortov] brought L. N. [Lev Nikolaevich] a teacup from Canada. L. N. thanked him and said, "When I have a cup, I shall remember." Nastas'ja [Anastasija Golubëva] brought Aleksandra L'vovna [another of Tolstoy's daughters] an Indian needle cushion. Ivan

26. P. V. VERIGIN ❧ L. N. TOLSTOY
10 December 1906. Kozlovka-Zaseka Station.

10th Dec. '06. Zaseka Station.

Deeply esteemed Lev Nikolaevich,

Our whole group, headed by Grandfather Makhortov,[84] is sincerely grateful to you and your whole family for your warm welcome; may the Lord bless you for such hospitality. I did want to see you again today, but was not bold enough to do so. Perhaps we shall see each other again some time, the Lord willing.

Farewell.

Your brother in God,

Pëtr Verigin

27. P. V. VERIGIN ❧ L. N. TOLSTOY
12 January 1907. Sofia, Bulgaria.

12 Jan. (old style) '07. City of Sofia.

Esteemed Lev Nikolaevich,

At the moment we are at the railway terminal waiting for our train to Budapest. After leaving your place we stopped at Khar'kov to see Bodjanskij, and visited Sevastopol' and Yalta.

Bodjanskij recommended we have a look at the Black Sea coast — the western side.

From Sevastopol' we sailed directly to Constantinople and from there by steamship to Burgas.

Not far from Burgas there is some land for sale at 30 roubles per *desjatina.*[85]

If it were necessary, I think we could move a small colony of about 500 people here and set up good orchards.

We are all in good health, thank God, and send our heartfelt greetings to you and your whole family. Our 'Grandfather' is especially lively and keeps us entertained throughout the trip.

Faddeevich, Nastja and Mavrusha [Marfa Dymovskaja] all addressed L. N. using the word *ty* [the familiar form of address]: *"A ty, dedushka..."* [You, Grandpa...]

Ivan Faddeevich had served in the Sevastopol' campaign. In reminiscing about it he asked L. N. where he had been sent there.

L. N. recounted:

"But, thank God, I didn't have to fire even once. There was an order to fire case-shot during an attack, but I wasn't there..."

Pleasant conversations with the Doukhobors; they prayed silently, standing up, both before and after meals. They do that in hotels too, in Chicago for example. And they would sing a psalm (sitting down).

84 Ivan Faddeevich Makhortov was eighty-six years old at the time.

85 *desjatina* — a unit of land equivalent to slightly more than 1 hectare.

Iosif Konstantinovich[86] is with us — he came to help us inspect the location near Burgas, and now wants to go see the sisters in England as well.

Snow has fallen here and the temperature is minus 20°.

We have had to spend an extra three days in Burgas because of snow-covered roads. Now we are hurrying to get through to our friends in Geneva, and then home as quickly as possible. Forgive me for not writing to you sooner.

Pëtr Verigin

28. P. V. VERIGIN ❧ L. N. TOLSTOY
9 March 1907. Otradnoe.

9th March '07. Village of "Otradnoe."
Verigin, Sask.
Canada.

Dear Friend Lev Nikolaevich,

Here we are, thank God, back home safe and sound. Everyone's fine. 'Grandfather' stayed calm and cheerful the whole way home. All my companions have now gone off to their own relations, but they asked me, if I should be writing to you, to be sure to send you their heartfelt greetings and gratitude for your warm hospitality.

The route we chose for the whole trip turned out most successfully, as nowhere in our travels did we meet serious cold spells, and we saw a lot of cities and places. When we passed through Russia in the autumn, winter had not yet set in, and as it approached we were already heading further south and so, returning through central Europe, we managed to avoid severe winter conditions. Throughout the trip I kept jotting down information — at least brief notes — about the life of different ethnic groups, and about the land too, in case we should acquire some land in a warm climate for the brethren of the Doukhobor community. After we left you we went to Khar'kov, Sevastopol', Constantinople, Budapest, Vienna, Geneva and Paris, as well as to see our friends the Chertkovs [in England]. Favourable living conditions are to be found on the west side of the Black Sea in Bulgaria; we could also have plots of land in Switzerland and probably in Italy as well, since the people there do not feel like tilling the ground — the rich classes who own the land are happy to give it away [to be tilled]. There are some free fruit-growing lands near New York. I am talking about these lands in particular because many of the Doukhobors are inclined toward this type of activity. I am planning in the near future to go out

86 *Iosif Konstantinovich Diterikhs* (1868–1932) — brother to Anna Konstantinovna Chertkova (V. G. Chertkov's wife) as well as to Ol'ga Konstantinovna Tolstaja (Andrej L'vovich Tolstoj's wife until 1903). Until 1897 he lived in the Caucasus as 'superintendent of the mountain tribes.' His sympathy for the Doukhobors led to his being exiled from the Caucasus. He took an active part in all their affairs.

and gather information about acquiring lands for fruit-growing on the Pacific coast. I should tell you that we are prepared to resettle in small colonies in different parts of the world. — At least that is how I personally see it.

Upon my return to Canada I was greeted by some big news in the Doukhobor community: all the lands registered in the Doukhobors' name have been declared 'free,' and now they are inviting people who agree to accept British Citizenship and to live and work on the land on an individual basis to register their homesteads afresh. All the rest of the community, including women and children, will only get 15 acres apiece.

Quite a touchy question, isn't it? I wonder what 'devices' the Government will resort to, and how the Doukhobors will react: will they accept Citizenship or prefer to live in an indeterminate situation? Or rather, be in a more determinate position without Citizenship. The Government has cast the die, so to speak; whether it can win or not, only time will tell.

I'm quite satisfied that the Doukhobors have accepted this proposal with quiet equanimity, probably because the majority of them already decided the question of Citizenship about three or four years back — in the negative.

There have been 'whisperings' abroad in the country that such actions by the Government amount to 'dirty tricks.' People have been diligently ploughing and sowing grain, they've been tilling the land in a fairly acceptable manner, and now this land is being taken from them without just cause.

The Doukhobors on the whole are enjoying full health and prosperity.

For me personally the trip was very beneficial. I saw many people who far surpass me in moral perfection, and I have learnt a great deal. Seeing your living example has given me moral support. I am more and more convinced that one's salvation, or the meaning of life, is in this: namely, *to keep one's heart from evil.* This is our highest task — adoption by God the Father.

I have told our brothers and sisters about the hunger in Russia; they will no doubt respond with at least a small contribution of money. We shall leave its disposition up to you.

I wish you, Esteemed Lev Nikolaevich and all your family and friends all blessings from the Lord. I keep healthy,

Pëtr Verigin

29. L. N. TOLSTOY ❧ P. V. VERIGIN*10*
August 1907. Yasnaya Polyana.

Most kind Pëtr Vasil'evich!

I have endeavoured to distribute your community's donation of 10,000 roubles to the famine victims as best I could, in the province of Samara.[87]

87 An imperial Russian province on the middle Volga, southeast of Moscow. During the Soviet period, the city of Samara was known as Kujbyshev.

I was helped in this by my young friends — religious people — Sutkova, Kolesnichenko and Rjabov. They've gone now, and I still have 2,800 roubles left undistributed. Another 800 roubles will probably be given out now in the same Samara province, but that still leaves 2,000, and I would appreciate some guidance from the donors. There is great need everywhere; the money could be given out again in Samara, where the harvest has been extremely poor, or here, where there are many needy unemployed. Please let me know.

I have received word that your community, in spite of being deprived of their land, is coming along well, thanks to their good life of brotherhood,[88] and I am so happy to receive this practical confirmation of the truth that people's well-being depends on them themselves, on their fulfilling or not fulfilling the law of God. I send brotherly greetings to you and all the brethren who remember me.

Lev Tolstoy

10 Aug. 1907

30. P. V. VERIGIN ❧ L. N. TOLSTOY
15 September 1907. Otradnoe.

V. A. POTAPOFF,
Manager

TRADING STORE OF THE DOUKHOBOR SOCIETY
Dry Goods, Hardware, Groceries, Crockery, Etc.
WHOLESALE AND RETAIL

Verigin, Sask., 15 Sept. (new style) 1907
CAN. NOR. RY.

Esteemed Lev Nikolaevich, I received your letter of 10th Aug. I am most grateful to learn that you are alive and well. My heartfelt greetings to you and all your family and friends.

We are all in good health, thank God.

As regards the money — the donation — I spoke with several of the brethren — they say "They (i.e., you) should do whatever seems best."

I wish you all good. Your brother in Christ,

Pëtr Verigin

88 V. A. Makaseev and Pavel Planidin wrote from Canada in the spring of 1907. Their letters, along with Tolstoy's replies, have been preserved in the Tolstoy archives (see *PSS* 77:109, 111).

31. P. V. VERIGIN ❧ L. N. TOLSTOY
13 June 1908. Otradnoe.

OFFICE OF THE
PETER V. VERIGIN
REPRESENTATIVE
OF THE DOUKHOBOR SOCIETY

VERIGIN, SASK. 13 June 1908
Canada
from Pëtr Verigin

Much esteemed Lev Nikolaevich,

I hasten to inform you that this spring the Doukhobor community purchased some 2,700 acres of land in British Columbia for growing fruit trees. The land is not far from the city of Nelson, at the confluence of two rivers — the Kootenay and the Columbia. The place is characterized by fresh air, clean fresh water and a rather mild climate, where we can grow apples, plums, and a delicious and abundant variety of sweet cherries — right on the banks of the Columbia River, which is one of the most beautiful rivers I have ever seen. The colour of the water, for example, is equal to that of the river in Geneva.

At the moment ninety people are clearing the land for fruit-trees and about 600 young trees were planted in the spring. The move will take place gradually over the next five or six years, since we still have a lot of ploughed land here and harvest time has just arrived.

Next spring we are planning to send out another two or three hundred people to prepare the land for habitation, while our farming activities will gradually decrease in the old place until final termination.

We are living well, thank God. Last year our wheat was killed by the frost, but since the autumn we tried to buy enough for the whole year and for the sowing and now, thank God, we are enjoying good, pure bread. The prospects are good for this summer's harvest and a rather large amount of grain has been sown.

The move to [British] Columbia should mean a rather significant change in our community's farming activities. The basic activity should be the growing of fruits and vegetables, but we also propose to set up a dairy industry through controlled cultivation of hay and vegetables for fodder.

We should also like to acquire a small plot of land in a warmer place for those without livestock.

My warmest greetings to you and your whole family. Your brother in Christ,

Pëtr

32. P. V. VERIGIN ❧ L. N. TOLSTOY
2 February 1909. Brilliant.

OFFICE OF THE
PETER V. VERIGIN
REPRESENTATIVE
OF THE DOUKHOBOR SOCIETY

VERIGIN, SASK. 2nd Feb. 1909

To Lev Nikolaevich Tolstoy
[from] Pëtr Verigin.1

Deeply esteemed Lev Nikolaevich, I hasten to inform you of our community's joy. We recently acquired a bit of land in [British] Columbia to experiment with growing fruit-trees. It seems I have already told you about that. But it turns out that the people who have been living there almost a year now are extremely happy with the place. And it is important that a person should be happy with at least something in life. True happiness leads to true prayer on our part to our Heavenly Father.

This is now my fourth visit to [British] Columbia. I was out here on business last summer, but this time I came expressly to see and observe the winter. The climate is remarkably mild and healthful. I have had many conversations with my brothers and sisters here, and they all want me to ask you to come and stay with us, perhaps to live out the remaining of your precious days here in peace. I say this in all sincerity, because I am quite certain that you would be very happy living among the Doukhobors. Especially in the past while the Doukhobors have been drawing closer and closer in their behaviour and understanding to the Kingdom of God on Earth. Maybe you have heard rumours that many of the Doukhobors are falling away from the community life — but this in no way stops the rest — or even the ones departing — from being good Christian people. Recently we adopted the motto: *Keep your heart from evil.* I cannot deny that I was the one who proposed this now (for a long time) fundamental tenet, but it was as if an electric shock-wave had gone through each of the Doukhobors, and each one asked himself the question: What am I to do from now on? Since all the former rituals, even the little ones, are changing, the only thing we have to observe is: *Keep your heart from evil.* I understand this in its simplest everyday sense, namely, use your mind to keep your heart from getting agitated; at the least loss of equanimity — our basic human characteristic: being calm — the blood starts rushing and everyone knows the rest of the story. I think that all the churches in the world might have been founded by mankind to attain this goal — to be at peace for at least a little while. There is no church where anger and violence are accepted as being right. And since the building of temples to pray in has long been abolished by the Doukhobors, we are now faced with an insurmountable barrier: how to get into the Kingdom of God without praying? A sincere investigation of Christ's teachings makes it clear that Christ preached a fundamental commandment: Mercy. Probably not the kind of mercy that consists in going to church once a week and being merciful for an hour or two, then devoting one's self completely to evil intents the rest of the time. The Doukhobors used to do that often. Now there is nothing to be done — even reciting or reading the psalms you were so enthusiastic about in your conversation with Pavel Planidin. (He told me about that.[89]) But if you want to be a Doukhobor, there's only one thing necessary: keep your heart from evil. Wherever a person may be, whether in church or marching behind a plough, the requirement is the same.

I also want to share with you some spiritual joy about myself. I have become kinder of heart. I feel this is the highest degree of joy and virtue man can experience on earth. In your writings you often say that man has not and cannot have a purpose on earth. I think, I feel, that keeping one's self from evil can constitute a purpose and that this purpose is achievable, offering the highest complete human satisfaction, since it draws me toward Divine truth. From what I understand of Christ, it is only through Mercy that he too became one with our common Father. — The creative power is Mercy. — Evil is destructive wherever it appears. By nature man must be good — we can set this as a goal for ourselves, and it will be good and true.

I wish you and your whole family all good from the Lord. Your loving brother in Christ,

P. Verigin

My address is now:
P. Verigin.
Brilliant, B.C.,
Canada.

33. L. N. TOLSTOY ❧ P. V. VERIGIN[90]
18 March 1909. Yasnaya Polyana.

Yasnaya Polyana. 18 March 1909.

I was happy to receive news of you, dear Pëtr Vasil'evich, and good news at that. I have the highest sympathy for your decision to free yourselves from all

89 Pavel Planidin visited Yasnaya Polyana in December 1906 (see Letter N° 25 above) and once accompanied Tolstoy on his daily walk. Dr. Makovitskij noted in his diary for 9 December: "[…] Planidin marvelled how the old man could walk: he got tired [keeping up] with him."
90 Only an unsigned typewritten copy of this letter has been preserved in the Tolstoy archives. The whereabouts of the signed copy sent to Verigin are unknown.

outward forms of worship, replacing them with works of life. But I think that such a decision, if it is to be a lasting one, must flow from the consciousness of each individual. I am not saying that this is unquestionably right, but it is my opinion based on my personal experience. I have only found that to be lasting which I have attained through my own inner struggles.

Please do keep sending me details about you and your community, about the results of your decision to move, and so forth.

Lovingly, Lev Tolstoy

P.S. Forgive me for not writing sooner, but I have been constantly ill the past while.

34. P. V. VERIGIN ❧ L. N. TOLSTOY
3 May 1909. Brilliant.

OFFICE OF THE
PETER V. VERIGIN
REPRESENTATIVE
OF THE DOUKHOBOR SOCIETY

Brilliant, B.C.

VERIGIN, SASK. 3 May 1909

"Dolina Utesheniya."[91]

The letter I received from you, kind Lev Nikolaevich, was precious to me. It was precious because the few words of your letter expressed the sincerity of your heart. This is indeed the essence of its benefit for others in every respect.

I have noticed many times with myself, when I am writing or conversing from the sincerity of my understanding, only then is it beneficial either for me or for my listener.

I should explain to you that I was the one in our community who proposed exchanging ritualism for contriteness of heart. I can only say and express this for myself, and that's how I put it to all the Doukhobors. The only compulsory rule I make for myself is to keep myself from evil; everything else, even though useful, I may or may not do. But to make myself a better person is for me a must.

All the rest of the people in our community are free to observe their old rules, if they wish.

I myself often attend meetings where they read psalms and sing. But these meetings have now taken on a freer form, rather than a strict one, as before.

91 *Dolina Utesheniya* — lit. 'Valley of Consolation' — the name given by the Doukhobors to their new settlement in British Columbia.

I have now made it a goal to free myself from the desire for power, and that is possible when I free myself from evil.

We have almost finished planting the orchards at our new place. We have planted basic types of trees: apple, plum, sweet-cherry, pear, peach, about fifteen thousand altogether, also lots of small bushes, and 6,000 grape vines.

We've made a good beginning for our first year, thank God.

I am very sorry to hear that you are continuing ill. I really wanted to come and see you once more — even to spend two or three weeks near your home at Yasnaya.

If you should happen to run into her, please give my regards to the elderly lady whose house we roomed at.[92] She was quite annoyed that I paid her so little for the flat. If I come to Yasnaya again, I'll make it up to her.

Greetings to your whole family. With deep respect,

P. Verigin

Brilliant, B.C.,
Canada.

35. P. V. VERIGIN ☙ L. N. TOLSTOY
26 September 1909. Otradnoe.

P. Verigin
Verigin, Sask.
Canada.

26 Sept. '09.
Village of "Otradnoe"

To Lev Nikolaevich Tolstoy
[from] Pëtr Verigin.

Esteemed Lev Nikolaevich, I have been meaning to write you a few lines about things going on in our life.

Today is Sunday: Christ is Risen![93] This year our whole life shows great prosperity, both in our material and Spiritual affairs. People in our community have begun to consciously relate to their situation. It is amazing how God can gradually bring people to the consciousness of Nature around them as well as to the adoption of the eternal laws of spiritual understanding. I have observed this in the Doukhobors and feel it in myself.

Beginning in the Caucasus, it was there they learnt to perform good deeds in terms of physical actions, such as rejection of military service and abstention from wine, smoking and the killing of animals. Those are all good

92 From 6 to 10 December 1906, Verigin, along with five other Doukhobors from Canada, visited Tolstoy at Yasnaya Polyana. See Letter Nº 25 above.

93 The Russian word for 'Sunday' [*voskresen'e*] is taken from the word for 'resurrection' [*voskresenie*].

deeds, but they are all concerned with corporeal morality. Now we come to the awareness of the need to strive to perfect our spiritual understanding as well. God has truly done a marvellous job of arranging the universe and putting man into the world to gradually strive for perfection!

We have had an abundant harvest of everything here in Saskatchewan, where we have been growing grain. And our life in B.C. is off to a good start too. We could not ask anything more of the Lord, and we can only offer praise and thanksgiving for the course our life has taken over the past thirty years. Glory to God and thanksgiving to all good people.

I am sending along my letter to our community. This is an example of how I communicate with the Doukhobors, whenever I have something to say to them.

The results of the harvest are in: around 500,000 bushels of oats, a hundred thousand or so of wheat and around a hundred thousand of barley.

We don't sow too much wheat, since the last two years it was killed by the frost and we decided to sow only for our own needs. The oats and barley, except for our own needs — for the year — we sell. Our earnings from this summer are expected to be around 150,000 dollars. — It is too bad that so far we haven't been able to get by without additional earnings. — And now there's the move on top of that. But it is all turning out for the better, thank God!

This summer the wheat has done exceedingly well, but we do not regret having sown so little of it, since per acre oats have proved to be no less profitable than the very best wheat. For example, on an acre of land we can grow twenty-five bushels of wheat [selling] at 70 cents a bushel — $17.50, while oats yields eighty bushels at 28 cents — $20.40 [*sic*], and besides, the oats are a sure crop, while wheat quite often fails in these parts.

The move to B.C. is significant as it means we will require several times less acreage for fruit- and vegetable-growing than here on the prairies. When we did nothing but grow grain and raise cattle we were using more than 300,000 acres, while at the moment, it looks like if we have 15,000 acres in B.C. suitable for fruit- and vegetable-growing it will be more than enough. So we are thinking more about growing fruits and vegetables under the best conditions possible. We have already managed to purchase 7,000 acres of good-quality land, for orchards, vegetable gardens and meadow-lands. Bees do well [out there]. This autumn we already have good, sweet-scented honey — home--made. Only in small quantities. Amazing people, the English: for a thousand miles around we managed to find only twenty beehives, which we bought to get started. The swarming has been good.

I can tell you, esteemed Lev Nikolaevich, that the Doukhobors in their experience of seeking the truth are a unique example meriting serious attention. Suffice it to say that over the past ten years of living in Canada — under rather dreadful conditions, to start with — there haven't been any serious quarrels leading to violence, as happens all the time in Russian villages. Or another remarkable phenomenon: in our forty villages there has not been a single fire. Many houses and barns are roofed over with bog-rushes. I put this down to a more sober life-style and abstinence from tobacco; it often happens that someone will light a cigarette and toss the burning match away just anywhere. And how many kids hide from their elders to have a smoke and set the thatch on fire. In Russia whole villages have burnt down that way. And we are but simple Russian peasants. But the Lord has led us into the light of understanding. Praise be to you too, dear Lev Nikolaevich, for showing people the harm that comes from smoking and vodka.

We are planning on installing an underground system of tubes and taps to provide good irrigation for our orchards in B.C. About 30,000 feet of various sizes of tubing have been delivered for installation this autumn.

If all goes well, in five or six years I imagine some of the Doukhobors ought to be moving back to Russia. With such useful experience they should be quite valuable there.

I embrace you in love and wish you all blessings from the Lord.

Yours, P. Verigin

Christian Community of Universal Brotherhood

The Doukhobors in Canada

24 September 1909
Letter to the Christian Community of Universal Brotherhood
from Pëtr Verigin.

Glory to the Lord.

1. I hasten to inform you, Brothers and Sisters, that I have come here to see how your life is getting on, and all the brothers and sisters living in Dolina Utesheniya have asked me to give you their heartfelt greetings. Life here in Dolina Utesheniya has got off to a good start in all respects, thank the Lord.
2. As you know, on the 20th of this month we held a conference in the village of Otradnoe. The first item on the agenda was an account of the expenses involved in the move to B.C. Secondly it was decided that all the villages should pay off their debts, since we must settle our debts in Winnipeg and other cities. Thirdly, the question was raised about new expenses anticipated in connection with the move, as a result of which it was decided to collect one hundred dollars from each wage-earner in every village.
3. I did propose at the conference that each village should take care of its own grain sales individually, without my participation. However, in

view of the rather low prices offered by the elevator operators — I found out for certain that the Canora elevators are allowing only 23 cents a bushel for oats, and 24 cents in Kamsack — I have decided to recommend that we all ship our oats this fall to Port Arthur[94] [and sell] at their prices. Port Arthur is now offering 35 cents a bushel for N° 2 oats; with freight charges at 6 cents, that gives us 29 cents, and even if there are some extra shipping costs involved, we still get at least 28 cents a bushel, a big difference compared with 23 or 24 cents. All those willing I invite to take their oats to the nearest depot and load the hopper-cars for shipment to Port Arthur. Anyone who can sell for at least 28 cents a bushel here on the spot is free to do so.

Misha Kazakov and Sëma Rybin are in charge of shipping. They are the ones to see about hopper-car assignments.

I invite all the villages closest to our Station to bring their oats to the elevator; the cars will be loaded from there.

4. We have temporarily stopped all purchases of goods; as soon as all the villages have paid off their old debts, I shall ask all villages to come to a conference for consultation and the appointment of new people to look after the purchase and delivery of goods, since Vasja Potapov and Sëma Rybin have asked to be relieved. And I think we shall be able to deliver [new] goods soon and we shall all be clothed and shod through the grace of God. Praise the Lord for good harvests in everything and our earnings this year.
5. I suggest, Brothers and Sisters, that you give your sincere attention to the move. This is not the time to raise extraneous issues, since a lot of expenses will be involved in the move. At the moment everything is going well for us in setting things up in B.C. The little gardens are coming along nicely, and I shall make sure everything is in good order.
6. I would ask the brothers and sisters of the Bogdanovo and Kirilovo villages in the Prince Albert area to hold back any extra wheat they may have to supply our needs in B.C. I suggest they contribute the hundred-dollar levy from this summer's income, and we will pay them for the wheat. It will be fairer that way.
7. We hope to have a large flour-mill in operation shortly, and anyone wanting to grind white flour for themselves may do so. In addition, any village that wishes to can bring at least a hundred bushels of fine wheat to the elevator at the mill, which will be used to grind white flour to take out to B.C.; part of it will be required for community needs. Anyone who wishes can also bring oats for making oatmeal. We plan to make oatmeal for B.C. out of the community harvest oats.

94 *Port Arthur* — a grain port on Lake Superior, which in 1970 amalgamated with the city of Fort William and two smaller townships to form the city of Thunder Bay, Ontario. Canora and Kamsack are small prairie towns on the Canadian National Railway line in central Saskatchewan.

8. I would like to remind you that a carload of various vegetables, beetroot, onions, hops and peas, is being sent to Dolina Uteshenіya. They don't need any potatoes, as they have managed to grow their own there, thank the Lord.
9. All those who can should take their oats now to the elevator at the Station, where each village's shipment will be weighed precisely. The other villages should start loading very shortly, as soon as you know where the cars are assigned, so as not to miss the boats at Port Arthur. The oats should be clean, as if you were going to use them yourselves, so that they can fetch a good price.
10. I strongly urge you to pay off all your debts this autumn, since our Office is preparing our accounts for the move to B.C. and replacing the brothers who have been working in our offices up to now.

With my whole heart I praise and thank the Lord for our current life and well-being, and I call upon all of you as brothers and sisters to praise the Lord as well.

Your loving brother in Christ,

Pëtr

36. L. N. TOLSTOY ❧ P. V. VERIGIN
4 October 1909. Yasnaya Polyana.

4th October '09.

I thank you, kind brother Pëtr, for your letter and joyful news of your brethren, especially about the striving for spiritual perfection you wrote about. Whatever good there is in our life is found in the soul, in its drawing nearer to God. Concern over physical things for the most part only detracts from the inner workings of the soul. May God help you and the brethren succeed in the "one thing [that] is needful."[95] Give my love to the brethren, along with my regret that I am physically separated from them and from you. I am sending you several books. I would like them to be approved by the brethren.

Lovingly, Lev Tolstoy

95 See Luke 10:42.

37. P. V. VERIGIN ❧ L. N. TOLSTOY
4 February 1910. Otradnoe.

OFFICE OF THE
PETER V. VERIGIN
REPRESENTATIVE
OF THE DOUKHOBOR SOCIETY
VERIGIN, SASK. 4 Feb. 1910

To Lev Nikolaevich Tolstoy
[from] Pëtr Verigin.

Esteemed Lev Nikolaevich, I received your letter some time ago and am only now getting around to a reply.

I am sending you an account of our community's last conference.

Last summer we had a good harvest of everything. We collected a million bushels of grain all told. Vegetables were also in abundance.

We are having a nice, warm winter.

The community life is coming along well, thank the Lord. I shall soon be going to B.C. for the garden planting.

I wish you and all your family and friends all blessings from the Lord.

Lovingly,

P. Verigin

I am keeping healthy.

38. P. V. VERIGIN ❧ L. N. TOLSTOY
15–17 May 1910. Otradnoe.

Canada
P. Verigin
Verigin, Sask.
Canada.

15 May 1910.
Village of "Otradnoe"

To[1] Lev Nikolaevich Tolstoy
[from] Pëtr Verigin.

Ask one of the young people to read this to you.

Esteemed Lev Nikolaevich, even though it's been a long time since I heard from you, I hasten to pen my greetings to you.

You are in need of quiet now, and so the less you have to write the better.

I recently got back from B.C. The garden planting was all finished there before the first of May. Here too in Saskatchewan the sowing is completely done. We are sowing more oats here, as wheat is sometimes killed by the frost. We have sown more than last year.

We are all getting along well, thank the Lord. Lately I have been thinking about the possibility of man's immortality.

Immortality is a definite possibility if man himself desires it. Christ calls this desire *faith*. "If ye have faith as a grain of mustard seed, ye shall say unto this mountain, Remove hence to yonder place; and it shall remove."[96] The same with immortality — if someone desires it — if he believes, it will come to pass. It is an area that is entirely spiritual.

Physical birth marks the beginning of the existence of one's personality. In becoming acquainted with his environment, man can develop within himself spiritual understanding as well. This brings him closer to the consciousness of eternal life. So I'm starting to believe absolutely that if I were able, if I desired, to make the effort to develop within myself an understanding of the value of eternal life and wanted to enter into it, then that, too, would come to pass. It would happen just like with the mountain Christ speaks of in his parable.

My body will be buried in the ground, but my consciousness of and desire for eternal life will remain immortal. And it is only after the death of this body that genuine conscious life begins. We shall not be born again physically, but by the power of the Spirit we shall enter into immortality, and we shall only be regenerated, perfecting ourselves more and more. It is extremely important for man to work out and attain the consciousness of his immortality here, and maintain his faith in immortality within himself, for when man dies physically, this consciousness will not die along with the body but will go on to eternal life. This will in fact be man's resurrection — or rather, the consolidation of his consciousness of eternal life.

Following my physical death and my first spiritual regeneration my faith in immortality will be strengthened a thousandfold; at the moment I have only a mortal awareness of it. Just running this through my mind, I might say that the basis of my life originated here in the body, without my will, while spiritual consciousness is something I must work out of my own free will. If I desire it, I shall indeed enter into immortality — into eternal life. Whereas if I don't want to work it out or decide to leave this question unresolved, I will live only a physical life and will die and nothing will be left of me but fertilizer for the ground.

17th May.

We have got ourselves a small contract to build an embankment along the railway line not far from the villages. And now people are coming together

96 See Matth. 17:20.

from all the villages for this communal work. The plan of action is this: during sowing time all the people and horses were home busy with the sowing. Now that is finished and they are out on contract work. We aim to finish this by the 15th of August and return home for the grain harvest. The [contract] work is 10 to 15 miles from the nearest villages. We should get about sixty thousand dollars altogether for the job. We consider this as household income, as we provide our own meals and tools.

I am on the road with the group, and have taken some paper along to write you this letter.

I would like to again bring up a question which deeply concerns me — the question of man's immortality.

Everything that has appeared cannot be destroyed, but only changed in form — to our observation. For example, luxuriant couch-grass is now thriving where potatoes once grew, and so forth.

There is no way I can believe that I can simply disappear without a trace. If so, I would not be endowed with such a broad range of thought. As Descartes rightly says: "I think, and therefore I am convinced that I exist."[97] Thought within me leads me to believe that I can, through thought — the greatest tool on the human plane of existence — go on to immortality. This thought shows me that the spirit lives outside of time and space. What pleasure it gives me, esteemed Lev Nikolaevich, to remember the times I met with you and we could converse at least briefly. And this memory is re-born within me quite often. Truly I can say: "The Spirit bloweth where it listeth, and whence it cometh, and whither it goeth no man knoweth."[98] In conclusion let me say: Everything depends on man's will, or desire. Our Heavenly Father has given full [freedom of] will to his son, man; as he desires, so he can act; all desires can be fulfilled.

Oh how I wish I could see you now and talk with you face to face!

I wish you all blessings from the Lord. Give my heartfelt greetings to all your family and friends. Lovingly,

P. Verigin

97 A variant of French philosopher René Descartes' (1596–1650) famous saying *Cogito, ergo sum* [I think, therefore I am].

98 See John 3:8. The Greek word *pneuma*, translated as 'wind' in the Authorized Version, is rendered *Dukh* [Spirit] in the Russian Synodal Bible.

CHAPTER 7

Tolstoy and the Canadian Doukhobors Today

> There are believers whose custom it is to bow low before every person with whom they come into contact. They say they do this because in every individual dwells the Spirit of God. No matter how strange this custom may seem, it is based on a profound truth.[1]

THE ABOVE STATEMENT, which refers (though not explicitly) to the Doukhobors, is significant in several ways. First, it is one of Tolstoy's personal observations included in the collection of his beloved maxims, *Cycle of Readings*. It was made in the twilight of the writer's life, after almost twenty years of familiarity, interest, and involvement in the Doukhobor movement. Despite his acknowledged preference for individual sectarians (e.g., Sjutaev, Bondarev, Novikov, Zheltov) — in contrast to sects as collectives — the piece in which this statement appears indeed refers to a collective. Above all, it shows a reverence for the truth that it contains regarding the relationship of human beings to each other and to God.

Perhaps the greatest token of the Doukhobors' respect for and homage to Tolstoy is their acceptance of a gift of two statues of their beloved *dedushka* — their "grandfather" — from the Rodina heritage society in the former Soviet Union, in 1987, the work of sculptor Jurij Chernov.[2] Their willingness to receive these statues and allow their erection in two of their Canadian communities (Veregin, Saskatchewan, and Castlegar, British Columbia) involved a significant compromise with their conscience, since, as noted earlier, the

1 From Tolstoy's *Cycle of Readings* [*Krug chtenija*], *PSS* 41:202.

2 On Jurij Chernov, see Note 44 in Chap. 1 above.

Doukhobors do not accept icons or material representations of honourable personages, biblical or otherwise.

In a moving editorial on the occasion of the unveiling of the statue in Veregin, entitled "'Dedushka' Tolstoy — what is he calling us to do?" ["Dedushka Tolstoj — k chemu on nas prizyvaet?"], *Iskra* editor Jim Popoff[3] (1987) explains Tolstoy's place in the Doukhobor understanding and emphasizes the need to continue the joint legacy of Tolstoy and their forebears; namely, a toiling and peaceful life, non-violence, and justice and brotherhood among people and nations. He writes in reference to the statues:

> These monuments to Tolstoy, as has already been stated, are not an object of worship such as an icon. But if we relate to them only superficially, like some curiosity or tourist attraction, without going into their full significance, these statues will indeed assume a less than desirable function...
>
> No — this is something we must not allow! Like any other historical monument, these statues of Tolstoy should remind us of what they represent — *fully:* of the man himself, his achievements, his hopes and ideas, of *his summons to us*, as people who acknowledge that he is right. Through the stern look expressed in these sculptures, Dedushka Tolstoy is calling upon today's generation of Doukhobors to continue the work begun by our illustrious ancestors...
>
> The world today needs this work — our relentless strivings toward the goal of love and non-violence and a just, peaceful and brotherly life for all peoples — more than at any other period in human history. Not only Tolstoy, but Providence itself is practically shouting its call to *all* of us to lay down our blind and wilful, materialistically oriented direction and devote ourselves entirely to the sacred cause.

TOLSTOY ON THE PAGES OF *ISKRA*

Further homage to Tolstoy may be seen in various Doukhobor publications, especially their twice-monthly magazine *Iskra,* from the early 1950s right up to the present day. *Iskra* is the official publication of the Union of Spiritual Communities of Christ (USCC), with about 700 subscribers. Of particular note is issue N° 1484, devoted to the sesquicentenary of Tolstoy's birth in 1978 and featuring a lead article by the chairman of the USCC, John J. Verigin Sr.[4] The article was drawn from a paper Verigin was invited to give at a Tolstoy symposium held at the University of Victoria earlier in the sesquicentenary year (see *Canadian Slavonic Papers* [1979], a special issue devoted to this conference).

The unveiling of the monuments occasioned many contributions to *Iskra* by outsiders, primarily from the Soviet Union, along with reports in local

3 Portraits of the seven *Iskra* editors from its inception in 1943 up to 2000 were featured on the cover of issue N° 1890 of 12 April 2000.

4 This article, written with the assistance of Eli and Jim Popoff, will be discussed in further detail below. It includes a photo of the exhibit provided by the USSR Ministry of Culture, the Russian Rodina Society and the USCC.

newspapers and congratulatory notes from political dignitaries.[5] While Soviet authors, predictably, emphasized the need for world peace, a contribution by Tolstoy's great-grandson, Il'ja Vladimirovich Tolstoj, was notable for its absence of political orientation.[6]

On other occasions *Iskra* has also reported on visits by Canadian Doukhobors, individually and collectively, to Yasnaya Polyana — a place which the Doukhobors evidently still hold dear and where they have been warmly welcomed by museum staff, including Il'ja Vladimirovich's son, Vladimir Il'ich Tolstoy (director of the Yasnaya Polyana Tolstoy Museum) and Dr. Galina Alexeeva (head of research at the museum).[7]

One particularly noteworthy historical account is Eli Popoff's "The meeting of a Doukhobor with Lev Nikolaevich Tolstoy," featuring an interview Popoff recorded with one of the original Doukhobor emigrants, Pavel Vasil'evich Planidin, in April 1942. First published (in Russian only) in *Iskra* in 1978 — along with a sketch by Doukhobor Ivan Kalmykov — it was later reprinted and accompanied by an English translation in 2003. The article describes Planidin's meeting with Tolstoy at Yasnaya Polyana in 1898 to discuss the question of the Doukhobor emigration, and includes some fascinating insights into Tolstoy's views on education,[8] according to Planidin's recollection of their 1898 conversation.[9] Tolstoy gave Planidin a letter appealing for government co-operation in arranging the Doukhobors' emigration, which Planidin was to deliver to the minister of internal affairs in St. Petersburg. Planidin recounted this event as follows (Popoff 2003: 44):

> And so I went, an illiterate Doukhobor, to the Minister of Internal Affairs. On my first attempt, I was not allowed into his residence, but with the help of a Molokan acquaintance who was living in Petersburg, the Minister agreed to see me. Receiving from him his letter of reply, I again went to Yasnaya Polyana. Lev Nikolaevich was satisfied with the reply and explained to me the Minister was prepared to do all in his power so that, for us, in the event of emigration, there would be no encumbrances from local authorities in regard to the reunification of the Doukhobor movement and the return of the exiles to the Doukhobor body in this event.

5 See also *Iskra*, N°s 1648, 1649, and 1652.

6 A detailed account of the celebrations and papers connected with the unveiling ceremonies in both Saskatchewan and British Columbia is presented in Tarasoff 1987. The occasion was also celebrated by Selkirk College, in Castlegar, which included speeches and a dramatic reading of Tolstoy's story *How Much Land Does a Man Need?* [*Mnogo li cheloveku zemli nuzhno?*] — see description in *Iskra*, N° 1650 (1987): 17, 26.

7 For examples of such articles, see *Iskra*, N° 1734 (1991): 29–33; also Kanigan 2003.

8 Planidin reported in particular on Tolstoy's views on the teaching of military subjects in Russian universities. Planidin quoted Tolstoy as saying: "I conclude that these departments in our universities teaching military craft are departments of insanity" (Popoff 1978/2003: 42). See also Popoff's guest essay in this volume.

9 Here is also a brief reference to a later meeting, in 1906, when Planidin was part of a delegation to Russia (headed by Pëtr V. Verigin) to investigate the possible return of the Canadian Doukhobors to Russia.

Iskra also features, from time to time, original articles and poems[10] on Tolstoy, as well as those reprinted from other sources,[11] quotations from Tolstoy's philosophical ideas, his stories for children, descriptions (often profusely illustrated) of Tolstoy seminars, stagings of his dramatic works, and exhibits.[12]

Two articles in particular are representative of the Doukhobors' linkage to and appreciation of Tolstoy: the aforementioned address by John J. Verigin Sr. (1978), entitled "Doukhobors remember Tolstoy" ["Doukhobortsy pomnjat Tolstogo"], and Larry Ewashen's (1996a) "Lev Tolstoy and the Doukhobors."[13] Though the pieces are some two decades apart, the gratitude to Tolstoy and the reasons underlying it are essentially the same.

While recognizing the creative talent of Tolstoy's genius, both authors emphasize the tremendous importance of his philosophical and spiritual teachings. "It is safe to say," writes John J. Verigin Sr. (1978: 50), "that to Doukhobors, Lev Nikolaevich Tolstoy is the most important single person outside our community in the past century of our history. Among our people he is universally regarded as a dear friend and benefactor" — a sentiment echoed by Ewashen. Both authors also point to the particular significance of Tolstoy's views on non-violence and pacifism, which served to inspire such leaders as Mahatma Gandhi and Martin Luther King Jr., both of whom the Doukhobors also hold in great respect.

Just as Tolstoy praised the Doukhobors, the depths of their beliefs, and their ideals, and brought these, along with their persecutions, to world attention, so too they honour the memory of their like-minded mentor, maintaining close ties with Yasnaya Polyana, especially (in the past decade) with its director, Vladimir Il'ich Tolstoy — great-great-grandson of Leo Tolstoy.

Iskra has featured a number of reports on this ongoing relationship. In 1998, *Iskra* editor Jim (D. I.) Popoff interviewed the Yasnaya Polyana director on the occasion of the latter's visit to the Doukhobor community in the Kootenays, British Columbia, and subsequently published a transcript, quoted in part below.

10 Perhaps one of the most fitting Doukhobor tributes to Tolstoy was Pauline Makortoff's poem — simply entitled "Lev Nikolaevitch Tolstoy" — published by *Iskra* in a booklet devoted to the 1987 Russian Canadian Heritage Festival.

11 See, e.g., the piece by Sarah Karush (2001) entitled "Church asked to forgive Tolstoy's sins," reprinted from the *Moscow Times*.

12 For a description of a particularly interesting exhibit, see Larry Ewashen 2004. As the then curator of the Doukhobor Village Museum in Castlegar, Ewashen mounted an exhibit (with the assistance of Dr. Galina Alexeeva of the Yasnaya Polyana Museum) featuring an imagined 'second trip' to Canada on the part of Sergej Tolstoy 105 years after his actual journey. This same exhibit ran at Yasnaya Polyana in 2003, celebrating the 140th anniversary of Sergej Tolstoy's birth.

13 On a similar theme ("Tolstoy and the Doukhbors today"), Ewashen (1996b) gave a banquet address at the *Lev Tolstoy and the Concept of Brotherhood* conference at the University of Ottawa. See also his historical play *The Spirit of '99* (Ewashen 2000), sponsored by the Canadian Bureau of International Education, dealing in part with Tolstoy's "pivotal role" in the Doukhobors' emigration.

ISKRA: Yesterday, you stated that the unbroken tie between Tolstoy and the Doukhobors, beginning yet with Lev Nikolaevich, has continued through all the generations, even if only through letter correspondence. We feel, however, that the meeting between our Honourary Chairman, John J. Verigin, and your father, Ilya Vladimirovich — that was at your home in Troitskoye in 1981 — this was a special historic event, which re-established a direct, personal connection...
V. I. TOLSTOY: Yes, right now you can feel a renewed impulse.
ISKRA: And now of course, it continues in your generation, and we certainly hope it will continue into the future. From our side, we will be working towards a continuing relationship.... Do you have any concluding remarks?...
V. I. TOLSTOY: All I can say is that as soon as I come home, I am going to personally get involved in implementing the projects that we've discussed here. Also, I will be looking forward to seeing the visit from your Youth Choir next year.... What I would like to see happening is for the ties between Tolstoy and the Doukhobor people, between the Tolstoy family and the Verigin family, to get broader and stronger. To make those ties not just a connection between the Doukhobors and Yasnaya Polyana, but a human, personal connection with the museum staff, with the people of Yasnaya Polyana, with their life, their work.... I feel that for me, this has been a spiritually enriching experience, and I want this to be a mutual, ongoing process.

DOUKHOBOR BAKERY CAFÉ AND COMMUNICATION CENTRE AT YASNAYA POLYANA

One of the projects referred to by Vladimir Tolstoy in the above quotation was the Doukhobors' proposal to construct a bakery/café on the outskirts of Yasnaya Polyana. The original intention was to raise $100 for each member of the Doukhobor community toward a $400,000 construction fund. An association was formed, known as Friends of Tolstoy, under the chairmanship of Alex Jmaeff. Their handsome colour brochure, sent out to potential donors, described the project.

> Canadian Doukhobors along with friends and others who share the Tolstoyan philosophy, in partnership with Yasnaya Polyana, are proposing the revitalization of a Bakery Café.
>
> Revitalization involves the construction of a facility that will house the Bakery Café, meeting rooms, a souvenir shop and other visitor amenities. The new facility will be located across the road from Yasnaya Polyana.
>
> The goal is to establish a world class Bakery Café that:
> (i) abides by International Health Organization guidelines; and
> (ii) will sustain the economic integrity of Yasnaya Polyana and area.
>
> Product from the bakery is expected to fulfill the needs of Yasnaya Polyana and the surrounding communities.

Various events were planned and executed, including exchange visits between Yasnaya Polyana museum officials and Doukhobor representatives in British

Columbia. Donors, along with the Doukhobor community, were kept up to date on the project's activities.[14]

In a moving account entitled "What Lev Nikolaevich Tolstoy means to me" Helenne Jones (2001) stressed the importance of bringing the bakery project to fruition by an appeal, through posters and letters, to Doukhobors and others, as well as to high-school and post-secondary students. One poster read "HOW THIS WILL BENEFIT YOU" and offered the following suggestions:

- Provides amenity services to support visitors
- Provides education on Tolstoy and his works
- Provides a network of academic peers
- Gives you valuable participatory experience
- Brings cultures together

While she wished her efforts could be more fruitful, Jones's personal thoughts summarize the views held by most Doukhobors at large:

> Tolstoy means a great deal to me. He is a highly important part of my history. Tolstoy was sympathetic to Doukhobor beliefs and way of life. He expressed the persecution and suffering of the Doukhobors as an atrocity: he supported Doukhobors morally and financially. With the help of Tolstoyans, British and American Quakers and the British Parliament when Queen Victoria was head of the British Commonwealth,[15] the migration to Canada was made possible. Tolstoy was an important moral thinker and a social reformer. His thoughts and spirit inspire and challenge me to this day as they do many others all over the world.

She ended her powerful plea with these words: "It is easy to forget the past, but the past is what we are and where we are" (Jones 2001: 21).

At a fundraising banquet on 24 April 2004 a change in plans was announced: "Rather than [Vladimir Il'ich] Tolstoy and his colleagues building a large new facility as originally envisaged, an existing on-site structure suitable for a Bakery Café will be renovated and equipped with funds raised by Canadian Doukhobors and friends."[16]

In its 26 January 2005 issue, *Iskra* announced that the official opening of the Bakery Café, with representation from the Canadian Doukhobor community, would take place 21 September 2005, marking the International Day of Peace (an occasion close to the Doukhobors' hearts). The programme for the opening ceremony was subsequently published in issue N° 1972 (July 2005), along with the text of a commemorative plaque:

14 See especially *Iskra*, N° 1940 (2003): 8–9; N° 1958 (2004): 20–21.

15 Technically speaking, Queen Victoria (who died in 1901) was head of the British Empire, which was replaced by the British Commonwealth of Nations in 1926.

16 *Iskra*, N° 1958: 20–21. For a description of Doukhobor-supplied equipment, see Jmaeff 2004.

> This Bakery Café was developed in partnership by the Yasnaya Polyana Administration and the Friends of Tolstoy to commemorate the centenary of the migration of the Doukhobors from Russia to Canada in 1899.
>
> It stands as testimony to the enduring gratitude of these Christian pacifists to Lev Nikolaevich Tolstoy for his moral and material support in their time of need, and to the continuing friendship between the Tolstoy family and the Doukhobor community.
>
> Formally opened in 2005, on September 21st — designated by the United Nations as the International Day of Peace — this Bakery Café is dedicated to Toil and Peaceful Life.

Although the fund-raising campaign fell short of its goal of reaching CAD$400,000, the whole undertaking is of immense significance. Not only does it pay homage to the Doukhobors' beloved benefactor, along with their willingness to help the Yasnaya Polyana Museum weather its financial difficulties, but it brings the Canadian Doukhobors back to their original roots, bridging the geographical and historical gap, fostering a new linkage with the Tolstoy family and showing fresh evidence of striving jointly to implement the common goals shared by the Doukhobors and the Tolstoy family: an unwavering quest for peace and stability in a troubled world. A report of the opening of the Bakery Café and Communication Centre (as it is now called) by Peter Rezansoff is featured in the *Iskra* (N° 1975) of 19 October 2005.[17]

According to Doukhobor Corinne Seminoff (who works as a CBC News producer in Moscow), the Bakery Café, is once again uniting the Canadian Doukhobors with Tolstoy, also serves as a bridge between them and their counterparts still living in Russia. A fitting example, no doubt, of the legacy of this historic relationship — witness the following excerpt from her article in *Iskra* (Seminoff 2005: 18):

> So there we were gathered — a small group of Doukhobors, Russian and Canadian: the ones who never left Russia and the ones who did but always longed to return. Both groups feeling the pressures of modern life and assimilation, the struggle to maintain traditions of the past, to live by the values our forefathers struggled and died for, while coping with the day to day challenges of living in today's modern world.... Our similarities were as close as our differences were wide, and all because of the man we had gathered today to thank, Leo Tolstoy.

DOUKHOBORS ON THE INTERNET

A modern attribute of the Doukhobors' Bakery Café project was its promotion, not only through *Iskra* but, even more, through the Internet. The

17 Rezansoff (2005: 21) notes that the centre "was envisioned as the Doukhobor Pasolstvo [*sic*] [embassy] at Yasnaya Polyana." A photo essay by Mike and Frances Kanigan appeared in *Iskra*, N° 1976, including a picture of a Canadian Doukhobor choir performing in front of the new centre.

Friends of Tolstoy organization quickly established a site of their own on the web, thereby establishing today's Doukhobor movement as a symbolic key link between Tolstoy and Canada as a whole. They used the Web to acquaint Canadians not only with their project but with Tolstoy and his estate in general, recruit project sponsors, and provide updates on their activities, including their visits to Yasnaya Polyana. A richly illustrated webpage authored by Vera Kanigan describes their 1999 visit under the title "Yasnaya Polyana: His legacy lives on through the action of love" (Kanigan 1999).

Since the mid-1990s the Doukhobors, both collectively and individually, have established a number of multi-page websites to tell Canadians and the world just who these people are that came to Canada from the Caucasus in 1899 (including Tolstoy's role in their emigration), and to dispel the media stereotypes which have all too often confused mainstream Doukhobors with the radical Sons of Freedom.[18] And for all their insistence on adherence to the simpler community life, some members of the Sons of Freedom have taken to the Internet themselves to tell their own story.[19]

A Google search in October 2005 turned up 587 internet pages on which both terms *Tolstoy* and *Doukhobors* appeared, including, for example, an article on the Saskatchewan Doukhobors by Lionel Hughes entitled "Tolstoy, the Bible, and everything" in the 2001 online version of *Prairies North* magazine, as well as a bibliography on "Tolstoy and the Doukhobors" drawn from resources in the library of Simon Fraser University.[20]

In April 2002, John Woodsworth of the University of Ottawa's Slavic Research Group compiled *An Annotated Guide to Canadian Doukhobors on the Web*[21] comprising more than 260 Internet references to Canadian Doukhobors as of 2002, in four main categories: (a) Doukhobor information websites, (b) Doukhbors in art and word, (c) Doukhobor bibliography, and (d) Doukhobor peripheral references, along with an introduction. A number of the pages cited (including the Hughes article above) made specific reference to Tolstoy.

Unfortunately, as might be expected, given the fluid nature of the Internet, not only did many of the links shown there from 2002 lose their validity, but the site itself has ceased to exist. The following examples of Tolstoy references (one from each of the first three categories listed above) reproduce thumbnail descriptions of now-vanished sites listed in Woodsworth's 2002 guide, including quotations from the sites in question:

18 For more on the Sons of Freedom, see Chap. 1 above (p. 13).

19 See, e.g., Soukeroff 1999. In tracing the history of the Freedomites, Soukeroff mentions Pëtr V. Verigin's close association with Tolstoy and his followers.

20 See http://digital.lib.sfu.ca/dkb-collection. Also worth noting are the active addresses of Koozma Tarasoff, Larry Ewashen, and Andrei Conovaloff. More will be said about them at the end of this chapter.

21 The site (see Woodsworth 2002) is no longer accessible.

[a] **Lawlor Island**
McNabs History, section 11–12, 11.0 Lawlor Island.
Brief description of Doukhobors' quarantine on Lawlor Island:
"Persecuted in their native Russia, the Doukhobors were en route to new homes in Western Canada with support from Leo Tolstoy and under the leadership of his son Count Sergius Tolstoy when their ship arrived at Halifax on January 28 with a possible outbreak of smallpox.... Count [Sergius] Tolstoy was interviewed by *The Halifax Herald.* Of his stay on Lawlor Island Tolstoy noted that it "was not at all to be compared with the rigors of Siberian banishment but still the three weeks spent there had been dull exceedingly."

[b] ***New York Times*, "On this day," 20 November 1910**
Obituary [of Leo Tolstoy]:
"The Count and his wife revised his biography written by Aylmer Maude" by Jeanette L. Gilder
"My wife and I have translated several of his works, have known people closely connected with him, and some ten years ago we took part in an unsuccessful 'Tolstoy' colony; besides which I went to Canada at his wish to make arrangements for the Doukhobor migration, of which I subsequently wrote the history."

[c] ***Sights of Resistance: Approaches to Canadian Visual Culture*, by Rovert Belton** (Calgary: University of Calgary Press, 2001)
Review by Heather Fraser:
"For example, in understanding a Doukhobor wool rug from 1923, we are treated to a short history of how the Russian Doukhobors came to Canada with the aid of writer Leo Tolstoy. Tolstoy's theory of art was similar to the outlook of this religious group — both were communal and non-intellectual. As the Doukhobors settled uneasily into Western Canada, their art began to exhibit a blend of traditional iconography and images of Canadian farm life."

Two interesting Tolstoy links from the Doukhobor guide, the second of which is still accessible by a new web address (at least, at the time of this publication), deal with the role of the Society of Friends (Quakers) in the Doukhobor emigration to Canada and their reaction to the publication of *Resurrection,* from which they received funding to assist in the Doukhobors' emigration. The thumbnail descriptions are reproduced below.

'Society of Friends' and Doukhobors [site no longer accessible].

Excerpt from Minutes of Canadian yearly meeting of the Society of Friends 18 August 1999, acknowledging a plaque presented by the Doukhobors in recognition of the Quakers' help during their emigration. Includes a brief description entitled "Society of Friends and Doukhobors."
"A delegation of Friends from Canada and the United States worked with Tolstoy to find a country in Europe for the Doukhobors to move to in order to escape the persecution. Country after country refused them. Even the United States considered the Doukhobors undesirable. Finally, Canadian Friends

arranged with the Canadian government to welcome them to Canada. From then on, Canadian Friends and Doukhobors have had a close association and friendship."

Types & Shadows (Journal of the Fellowship of Quakers in the Arts) Issue N° 13 (Spring 1999), at http://fqaquaker.org/wp-content/uploads/2017/04/13TypesandShadowsSpring1999.pdf.

Article: "One Hundred Years Ago," by Esther Mürer, describing Quaker reaction to Tolstoy's novel *Resurrection,* whose proceeds went to the Quakers to help finance the Doukhobors' emigration to Canada.
"*Resurrection* was censored in Russia; a full Russian version was published by the London Quaker firm Headley Bros. in 1901, and translated into many languages, the proceeds going to the Friends Doukhobor Committee. But the subject matter proved a great embarrassment to Friends. The committee minuted that the novel was 'unsuitable for general reading;' and the clerk, John Bellows, declaring that the Society of Friends ought not to accept proceeds from 'a smutty book,' refunded the money out of his own pocket. Tolstoy responded in English: '... when I wrote the book I abhorred with all my heart the lust and to express this abhorrence was one of the chief aims of the book.'"

SURVEY OF CANADIAN DOUKHOBORS TODAY

In an attempt to be more 'scientific,' as well as to provide a venue for expression from within the ranks of the Doukhobors themselves, it was decided to compile a questionnaire for a survey to be conducted by the Slavic Research Group (SRG) at the University of Ottawa. The survey was designed to determine how knowledgeable Doukhobors living in twenty-first-century Canada are about Tolstoy's role in the emigration of their forebears, as well as his literary and social activity and the key ideas in his philosophy. The questionnaire (reproduced in Appendix 5) contained not only specific questions (including multiple-choice answers) but also a strong encouragement to respondents to write additional comments or even whole letters on the subject if they so wished.

Despite a warning from an experienced Doukhobor historian not to expect too enthusiastic of a response, the results of the survey were most gratifying. The questionnaire was published as a centrefold (in both Russian and English) in *Iskra*; in addition, some 200 questionnaires were sent to individuals on the SRG's list. Altogether 146 completed forms were returned — almost all of them in English. About twenty people preferred to simply write a letter about Tolstoy, rather than responding *to* the questionnaire. A significant number of responders who filled out the form also provided additional comments.

And despite yet another Doukhobor's caution that "our people are frightened of revealing their thoughts and feelings without direction from somewhere," and "are suspicious of motives" on the part of 'investigators,' such doubts, it turned out, did not materialize, perhaps because over the past few years the SRG has demonstrated their objective treatment of the Doukhobor movement through their frequent contacts, various conferences at the University of Ottawa, and scholarly publications.[22]

The form consisted of thirty questions, which may be divided into three categories. The respondents were first asked to indicate personal information (e.g., age and level of education), as well as when and how they learnt about Tolstoy in various roles: as a human being, as a friend of the Doukhobors, as a writer and a thinker. Second, the SRG wanted to ascertain how well the Doukhobors were acquainted with Tolstoy's works — both his fiction and religious/philosophical treatises. And third, respondents were asked about their reactions to certain of Tolstoy's ideas.

In demographic terms, seventy-one (just under half) of the 146 replies received came from Doukhobors in their sixties, with another forty-four in their fifties. Only twenty-two respondents were under fifty years of age, while nine of them were seventy or over. One ninety-three-year-old Doukhobor sent in a three-page description of his friend Pavel Vasil'evich Planidin and the latter's personal meeting with Tolstoy (cf. Eli Popoff's report on this encounter cited above).

While the number of younger Doukhobor respondents was relatively small, the survey did not reveal any significant differences in their reactions from those of the more senior members of the community. As might be expected, these younger respondents did tend to have a higher level of education. A disappointment was that male respondents outnumbered their female counterparts by three to one.

DOUKHOBORS' KNOWLEDGE OF TOLSTOY'S LIFE

As to their knowledge of Tolstoy, almost all those questioned revealed their first acquaintance with the great writer took place in the family (rather than at school or through self-discovery). This is not surprising in view of the Doukhobor community's well-known attempts to preserve Tolstoy's memory. What is interesting is the depth to which this memory and sense of gratitude to 'Dedushka' Tolstoy have penetrated the hearts and minds of the community. It is evident from the responses that the *family* continued to be the

22 For example, in October 1999, the SRG, along with the Institute of Canadian Studies at the University of Ottawa, hosted a major international conference marking the Doukhobor centenary in Canada, publishing the proceedings soon thereafter (Donskov, Woodsworth, and Gaffield 2000). This was a conference in which not only scholars, but Doukhobors themselves, were invited to participate. Several other publications by the SRG have also been devoted either to the Doukhobors or their sister group, the Molokans; see Donskov 1998a; Woodsworth 1999a (with a foreword by Vladimir Il'ich Tolstoy); Donskov 2001 (a Russian and an English edition). The Tolstoy–Verigin correspondence was compiled and published in 1995 by the future initiators of the SRG (see Donskov 1995a). Three times (1995, 1998, 1999) SRG members participated in the annual Doukhobor youth festival in the Kootenays.

main bearer of this memory well into the second half of the twentieth century (judging by the age of most of our respondents).

The school is seen as acting in concert with the family, but never as the only source of such information. It is not surprising that the great majority of those polled learned about Tolstoy in their childhood or teenage years (seventy-five of them were under fifteen when they first heard about Tolstoy). Only five Doukhobors in the survey claimed to have discovered Tolstoy on their own, without any external influence.

The questionnaire results indicated no single capacity in which Tolstoy was particularly remembered by young Doukhobors of half a century ago, since many gave multiple answers to this question. There is reason to believe, however, that conversations in Doukhobor families of the period were not limited to Tolstoy's involvement in the emigration process but included reference to his work as a writer — a point that is still being investigated. Certainly, the respondents learned about his role in their emigration from a very young age and in considerable detail — including Tolstoy's and his followers' financial support, selection of the destination, and organization of the actual move. We noted with some dismay, however, that relatively little was mentioned about the personal involvement in the emigration process of Tolstoy's eldest son, Sergej L'vovich Tolstoy.

As to knowledge of Lev Nikolaevich Tolstoy beyond this role, more than a third of the respondents declared themselves to be quite familiar with the basic events of his life. When asked to specify the period of greatest familiarity, most selected, not surprisingly, his later years, some further qualifying their response to "the years of his contact with the Doukhobors." Moreover, interest in Tolstoy's life seems to remain high among today's generations of Canadian Doukhobors.

DOUKHOBORS' KNOWLEDGE OF TOLSTOY AS A WRITER

The next major group of questions touched upon the Doukhobors' knowledge of Tolstoy's *writings*, both literary and philosophical. Only four of the 146 respondents confessed to no acquaintance at all with Tolstoy as a writer. The vast majority, by contrast, traced such acquaintance to their early childhood or teenage years, demonstrating that their concept of Tolstoy was by no means limited to his assistance in the emigration of their forebears. It can also be said that almost all of them began their reading of Tolstoy with one of his major fiction works — for 60 per cent of the total sample this was *War and Peace*, in far lesser numbers *Anna Karenina* and *Resurrection*. Unexpectedly, only four respondents indicated any of his shorter works in this category: *Prisoner of the Caucasus*, for example, was mentioned only by the lone respondent from Russia,[23] who had read it in Grade 4, while the Canadian Doukhobors

23 This *Iskra* subscriber in Russia took the initiative to respond to the survey, even though it was intended primarily for Canadian Doukhobors.

overwhelmingly showed a tendency to leap directly into his major works. On the other hand, ten of the Canadian Doukhobors surveyed remembered beginning their reading of Tolstoy with one of his religious treatises.

On the whole, Doukhobors seem comparatively well acquainted with Tolstoy's writing career. Many of them have read at one time or another all three of the major novels, his autobiographical trilogy (*Childhood*, *Boyhood*, and *Youth*), along with a number of his 'stories for the people' [*narodnye rasskazy*] — *Master and Man*, *Where Love Is, There God is Also*. One respondent even included *The Death of Ivan Il'ich* in this category. Of Tolstoy's religious treatises, *The Kingdom of God is Within You* and *A Translation and Harmony of the Four Gospels* were the most frequently mentioned; some were familiar with *A Confession*. On the other hand, *The Teachings of Christ Told for Children* was noted only by a few, which is most surprising, given that at one time this was the only written material permitted in Doukhobor Sunday schools.[24] It is also interesting that eleven respondents took pride in having read *Two Wars*, Tolstoy's ardent rejection of the Spanish-American war in contrast to his full approval of the 'war' declared by the Doukhobors 'against all wars' (discussed in Chapter 5).

Naturally, there was interest in not only *what* the Doukhobors had read of Tolstoy's, but *how* they read him. As in previous parts of the questionnaire, the compilers again formulated a series of interrelated questions to explore this point in some depth. But the survey yielded few direct answers, though the overall response was positive. Under Tolstoy's 'most successful' works respondents listed the three major novels, the novella *The Death of Ivan Il'ich*, and *Master and Man*; less frequently, *A Translation and Harmony of the Four Gospels*. In the category of works most 'in harmony with Doukhobor teachings' were noted *The Kingdom of God is Within You* and the 'stories for the people.'

A number of responses indicated a critical attitude toward Tolstoy as a writer. In answer to Question 19, "Have you found in Tolstoy's works any sayings which seem to be *contradictory* to the tenets of Doukhobor doctrine?," some respondents mentioned works dealing with military action; for example, his *Sebastopol Sketches*, writings on the war in the Caucasus, battle scenes from *War and Peace* (the latter, incidentally, did not prevent Doukhobors from a high appraisal of the novel as a whole). Negative reactions were also noted in respect to *The Kreutzer Sonata* as well as, in eight instances, *A Translation and Harmony of the Four Gospels*, paradoxically listed by other respondents in the 'most successful' category.

Questions were also asked as to which of Tolstoy's works Doukhobors would recommend to their friends and acquaintances — especially children — as wholesome reading, as well as, conversely, which they would *decline* to

24 Cf. the first sample of respondents' comments below. On the importance of this work as a morally educative model for children, see Kanygina 1978.

recommend. The controversial nature of these questions was evidenced not only by the relatively low number of responses but also in the content of the responses received, which showed little agreement among the responders. While *The Kingdom of God is Within You* was unanimously favoured and *The Kreutzer Sonata* more or less rejected, *A Translation and Harmony of the Four Gospels* weighed in on both sides. *Anna Karenina* was recommendable for adults, but specifically not for young people. Strangely enough, *War and Peace,* which had been read by so many and evaluated elsewhere both positively and negatively, appeared on neither the 'recommended' nor the 'declined' list. One could infer from this that today's Doukhobors are not primarily concerned about questions either of literary merit or historical accuracy. Although this cannot be directly confirmed, as no specific question as to the educational merits of *War and Peace* was included in the survey.

On the whole, educated Canadian Doukhobors may be seen as not much different from the average educated reader of Tolstoy. Most of them became acquainted with his literary works through *War and Peace,* then proceeded to the other two major novels. Quite a few also read his stories for children and 'stories for the people'; other works are mentioned more rarely. An overall preference for his fiction over non-fiction writings is seen not only in the statistics but also in direct statements added by individual respondents.

That said, however, the survey results still indicate a remarkably high interest in Tolstoy's religious and social treatises. This and a blanket rejection of military episodes may be seen as two distinguishing characteristics of Doukhobor readers of Tolstoy as a population. In other respects, the results of the survey were more or less typical of Tolstoy's readership as a whole. Further, no significant differences among the respondents' approaches to Tolstoy as a writer could be detected, either by age, profession, or level of education.

DOUKHOBOR PERCEPTIONS OF TOLSTOY'S IDEAS

Still another group of interrelated questions concerned the Doukhobors' awareness of certain key ideas in Tolstoy's philosophy, as well as their attitudes to these ideas. One issue we were confronted with was the tendency on the part of some Doukhobors to exaggerate the influence of *their own* teachings on the great writer's views, especially in regard to their emphasis on love, peace, rejection of personal property, and non-violent resistance to evil — all of which can be traced, they say, well back into the history of their movement; that is, long before their contact with Tolstoy.[25] Significant as these points may be, their direct influence on Tolstoy's views is not something easily attestable; the evidence, by contrast, suggests more that the writer, by this time approaching seventy years old, had already come to similar ideas on his own. His contact with the Doukhobors, however, does offer a sounding board that

25 See, e.g., the third sample of respondents' comments below.

helps Tolstoy researchers better understand the specific nature of such ideas that had already developed within him. These conclusions are confirmed by the correlation of respondents' replies with their overall knowledge of Tolstoy: the more they knew about his life and writings, the more cautious they were in their evaluation of any cross-influence.

Naturally, the Doukhobor respondents gave a strong endorsement to Tolstoy's rejection of militarism, as well as, generally, to his ideas on toil and peaceful life,[26] ideas which, the survey results show, remain relevant in the twenty-first century. Many took note of Tolstoy's idea of *oproshchenie* [simplification], even though they substituted the term *simple life*. Other Tolstoyan ideas listed as 'successful' and 'relevant today' were rejection of violence, non-violent resistance to evil, the brotherhood of peoples, the need for the capacity to forgive, and, of course, *love*. Tolstoy's echo of the Bible verse "God is love"[27] was frequently repeated. Mention was also made of concepts such as equality of peoples, the advantages of a communal lifestyle, and vegetarianism. Remarkable (though in this case not surprising) was the frequent 'common-sense' response that Tolstoy's 'most successful' idea was helping the Doukhobors emigrate to Canada.

Among the 'least successful' of Tolstoy's ideas, on the other hand, were named restraint or abstinence from sexual relations, certain ideas about art and æsthetics, along with any concepts linking Tolstoy with anarchy (although how the respondents interpreted this latter term was not clearly specified). This question also revealed some differences of opinion among the Doukhobors themselves. Vegetarianism and communal living, for example, favoured by some respondents as 'successful' were soundly rejected by others. One responder, for example, declared that all Tolstoy's positive ideals would lead to a communal lifestyle in a utopian society. It should also be noted that several respondents rejected Tolstoy's ideas on æsthetics and the role of women in society as 'outmoded.'

In conclusion, it is worth highlighting several results of this survey that beg further investigation. The diametrically opposite evaluations of *A Translation and Harmony of the Four Gospels*, for example, confirm once again that Doukhobors today are not a monolithic group and do not always agree among themselves, even on questions dealing directly with their system of beliefs. It seemed strange to us that almost none of the respondents mentioned Tolstoy's constant efforts, as an ardent seeker of spiritual growth himself, to lead people back to their innate faith and desire for truth, to their natural search for God.[28] This point, after all, is one that distinguished both

26 Note the Doukhobors' motto, *Toil and Peaceful Life* [*Trud i mirnaja zhizn'*].

27 1 John 4:8, 16.

28 On the other hand, P. I. Solov'ëv (1978: 3) (anglicized, P. J. Soloveoff) wrote in *Iskra* (in Russian): "For us Doukhobors, as for many other seekers of spiritual values in the world, Tolstoy's highest essence lies in his spiritual aspect, his search for the meaning of life, his search for truth."

Tolstoy and the Doukhobors from many of their contemporaries and continues to be an important focus of interest today. It is possible, of course, that Doukhobors of the present century consider it such a natural part of their lives that they do not even think to pose such a question consciously. But it is equally possible that, in the modern Canadian context, the pressures of technology-based living, along with the relentless forces of cultural assimilation, have simply taken their toll.

While it is quite understandable that the Doukhobors are not attracted to the military scenes in *War and Peace,* as is their reluctance to readily recommend this book to children, their overall high estimation of the novel indicates an absence of dogmatic rigidity in their approach to his writings, as well as (quite possibly) a capacity to separate the 'wheat' from the 'tares.'[29] Paradoxically, for a good majority of the respondents (as noted), this particular work was their first introduction to Tolstoy as a writer. Although this may be due to the influence of its world popularity manifest in the Canadian-school context and, consequently, its greater accessibility to young Canadian readers. It is quite possible that the next generation of Canadian Doukhobors may be more inclined to get acquainted with Tolstoy through his many works written specifically for children, especially if they have children of their own and feel the need of studying Tolstoy more intently.

These and other questions raised through conducting this survey show that, if nothing else, the actuality of Tolstoy's life, writings, and ideas in the minds of at least one group of twenty-first-century thinkers, albeit one admittedly with strong associations with Tolstoy through their parentage. On the other hand, the occasionally contradictory answers to certain of the questions posed may also provoke a lively interest and further discussion among the Doukhobors themselves.

DOUKHOBORS' COMMENTS ON TOLSTOY

As mentioned earlier, survey respondents were asked to write additional comments on Tolstoy if they so desired. Many of them did so, some confessing their ignorance of Tolstoy and expressing a desire to know more about this key figure in Doukhobor history, others elaborating on their responses to specific questions in the survey — for example, listing specific sayings of Tolstoy considered to be in harmony with Doukhobor teachings. A few of the twenty or so comments received are reproduced here in full or abridged form in an effort to round out this study with a sampling of views 'from the inside.'[30]

> I wish to relate that L. Tolstoy was a major source of teaching in my family's life. During my Sunday school days we did not use the Bible (physically). I was taught in the traditional manner, orally passing on the wisdom and philosophy

29 See Jesus' parable in Matt. 13:24–30.

30 Note: The respondents are identified by their initials to preserve a degree of anonymity.

of our leaders, the two commandments, *Love thy God and thy Neighbour,* and in the latter part of my Sunday school years we were taught from a little booklet called *The Teaching of Jesus,* compiled for children, by Leo Tolstoy. The one I have in front of me right now was translated by Aylmer Maude.... My 'pot of beans' has a number of life experiences and teachings incorporated into its make-up but I can say with some certainty that L. Tolstoy's work has made a significant contribution during my formative years. — P.O.

I would like to see a scholarly article dealing with Tolstoy's influence on Peter V. Verigin and distinguishing Verigin's 'new' Doukhobor teachings [from] the older pre-Verigin teachings. — J.K.

Our parents and grandparents, being mostly illiterate peasants, knew very little about Tolstoy and his ideas or ideals. Most Doukhobors only became aware of him after their arms burning episode which led to their conflict with the Russian authorities and subsequent suffering. Our older folks referred to him as 'Dedushka' Tolstoy, their kind benefactor, who helped them move to Canada. Most of them knew little about his literary work or his social or religious beliefs. And I am not sure that Tolstoy was aware of the Doukhobor existence until their struggle against Russian militarism became widely known. I may be wrong...

There are some assumptions and opinions in the media that our Doukhobor philosophy is largely based on Tolstoy's teachings. I find this rather odd and naïve. Doukhobors, as a movement, existed long before Tolstoy was even born. I am more inclined to believe that Doukhobor teachings may have had an influence on Tolstoy's belief.

We are all individuals with our own private beliefs and opinions, which may have sometimes led to extremes in our association with one another, causing animosity and discord, but I was happy to see and feel a spirit of friendly co-operation among previously opposing factions of Doukhobors during our Centennial celebrations, which, I believe, would have gladdened the hearts of both the late Leo N. Tolstoy and Peter V. Verigin. May their memory live forever and inspire us and succeeding generations. Glory to God. — T.S.

I have no exact quotes but [Tolstoy's] philosophies about the following are compatible with the Doukhobor principles and ideals: private land ownership, rejection of military or police service, honouring the spirit of God within each being, rejection of church dogma and rituals as a control mechanism, focusing on the spiritual aspects of life through simplicity and equality, accepting all Creation as brothers and sisters, as one family, resolving conflicts through non-violent means. These are the ones that come to mind immediately but there could be others. I have not done a search but the similarities keep coming up as I explore, read and delve deeper into both life concepts...

...to date, Tolstoy's and the Doukhobors' ideas have not been wholeheartedly embraced by the world but we are slowly moving in that direction. — L.S.

[Tolstoy] was kind enough to visit [my ancestors] when they were tortured and some killed on the way to prison in Siberia for God's Truth (including my grandfather...). — N.P.

I have now read *Resurrection* and *Childhood,* and *The Gospels in Brief* and *What is Religion.* But probably the most interesting insights have come from a Tolstoy Biography written by Troyat, a French author. The Tolstoy/Verigin letters will give me yet another window to observe Tolstoy in action. This time with the Doukhobors in mind.

Of course, the diaries of both Sulerzhitsky and Sergej Tolstoy, who accompanied the Doukhobors to Canada, were a must read. Sulerzhitsky traveled on the first ship but Sergej came on the second ship which is the one my paternal and maternal grandparents sailed on. — C.C.

A pivotal point in my spiritual journey was reading [Tolstoy's] essay "God is Love," when I was about 20. I was really struggling with the traditional Christian image of a patriarchal deity in the sky. I can't recall the content of the essay (and, perhaps, the proper title), but it opened me to the spiritual nature of God.

In my recent studies for becoming a lay preacher in the United Church I was struck by how progressive Tolstoy and the Doukhobors were in their theology. — N.T.

Although I did the questionnaire, I wanted to respond again as at that time I had read only Tolstoy's major novels. Now I have also read A.N. Wilson's biography of Tolstoy, part of your [Donskov and Woodsworth 1996] *Lev Tolstoy and the Concept of Brotherhood,* [*The*] *Cossacks,* several Tolstoy short fiction[al work]s, and have deepened my knowledge of Doukhoborism by reading more books about the sect. This winter I intend to finish your collection and to read Tolstoy's *A confession* and other religious writings.

Although I have always been aware of the similarities between my parents' teachings about life and those of Tolstoy, I did not actually realize how much they are the same until I read some of the above books. To this day, I do not know when my family's words were from Doukhobor or Tolstoy philosophy. I knew that my striving to be a vegetarian and a pacifist came from both my mother and grandparents and Tolstoy. I did not realize that my father's belief that manual labour and mental work are what make a complete person was also Tolstoy's belief until I read your collection. To this day (I am 66 years old) I feel my best days are when I have done both physical and intellectual work.

Another realization about Tolstoy is his love of the soil and of nature. Of course, my predecessors loved the soil and nature too, as I do, but for some reason I never connected this love to Tolstoy, perhaps because the Doukhobor love of the soil and nature goes back millennia...

I am not particularly religious, but I must say I share his propensity for anarchy and his disapproval of icons, of ritual, of opulence, of priests, of materialism. But I must admit to living a materialistic, complex life style for which at times I feel guilty and long for a more simple, less materialistic life. Wilson makes much of Tolstoy's conflict between his ideals and his life style. Perhaps Doukhobor and Tolstoy's ideals are incompatible with life today, but they are worth striving for.

As I reread this hodgepodge of ideas, I realized how intertwined Canadian Doukhoborism, my family, and Tolstoyism are. It's not possible to tell where the influence of one on my life ends and another starts. — P.H.

Comments such as those reproduced above bear witness not only to how the Canadian Doukhobors today feel about Tolstoy in particular, but also to their ongoing attempts to preserve their ideals — as well as their identity and even their language[31] — in the face of the powerful assimilating forces associated with English-Canadian society and the materialistic aspects of its culture. Tolstoy, having experienced such struggles of his own, might not have been surprised at the titles and content of articles filling the pages of *Iskra* over the past decade — articles such as "Doukhobor faith," "Doukhobor beliefs," "Our understanding of God," "What is Doukhoborism?," and "What is a true Doukhobor?" Such questions point to the striving on the part of current members of the Doukhobor community in Canada to remind themselves of their forebears' beliefs. The reminder is especially directed at the younger generations of Doukhobors, who are increasingly entering into mixed marriages and dispersing themselves across an ever wider geographical area. It also hints at a loss of some of the characteristics dear to the hearts of Doukhobors who remember earlier times, when Tolstoy's teachings and personal support of this community was relatively contemporaneous.

In personal correspondence with Eli Popoff (2001), he wrote: "[The] situation among our Doukhobor society at present is more clearly beginning to point to accelerating degrees of assimilation into the general mainstream of Canadian society — whether this is good or bad will be only truly evaluated by history in retrospect."

Indeed, in attempting to define who they are as Doukhobors, the younger generation of community members, when faced with a world where conflicts and hostilities have reached global proportions, would do well to re-examine the ideas shared by their ancestors and Tolstoy — rejection of violence, peaceful labour, respect for every living thing, unity and brotherhood. Despite the occasional declaration to the contrary, there seems to be evidence that they are capable of this. That their parents and grandparents have largely managed to preserve these ideals — and, to some extent, their lifestyle and language — over more than a hundred years in a different cultural and linguistic environment speaks strongly in favour of their prospects in continuing this legacy in the future.

Tolstoy must have sensed this, or he would not have spent the last decade and a half of his life championing the Doukhobor cause and promoting these ideals.

The period that has elapsed since the first edition of this book in 2005, has seen the loss of two key figures in Doukhobor history: John J. Verigin Sr.

31 *Iskra*, e.g., continues to print important articles in both English and Russian, not only for the benefit of readers in Russia but also in an effort to keep the Russian language alive among Canadian Doukhobors.

(great-grandson to Pëtr Vasil'evich Verigin) — honorary chairman of the USCC, a charismatic leader of the Doukhobor movement for more than sixty years — on 26 October 2008; and Eli A. Popoff — a brilliant historian and storyteller, a unique source of Doukhobor knowledge and wisdom — on 4 July 2014.

Fascination with the Doukhobors on the part of both scholars and the Canadian public at large — including the movement's inherent relationship with Lev Nikolaevich Tolstoy — has by no means abated over this time, as evidenced by both academic and general-interest publications. Russian observers taking an ongoing interest in Canadian Doukhobors include ethnographer Svetlana Inikova, Tolstoy Museum curators Tat'jana Nikiforova and Natalija Kalinina, Yasnaya Polyana colleagues Galina Alekseeva and Tat'jana Komarova, as well as Valerij Kalmykov, who launched a new Russia-based Doukhobor website (www.doukhobor.ru) in October 2014. A Russian edition of my 1998 book *Sergej Tolstoy and the Doukhobors: A Journey to Canada* was published — together with Sergej Tolstoy's diaries and letters — by Kuchkovo Pole in Moscow in 2017.

In America, two prominent scholars continue to take an interest in the Doukhobors — Nicholas Breyfogle at Ohio State University and Josh Sanborn of Lafayette College in Pennsylvania. And Arizona-based Andrei Conovaloff regularly reports on Doukhobor activities on his Molokan website (www.molokane.org), in addition to assisting Doukhobor ethnographer Koozma Tarasoff on his 'spirit-wrestlers' site (www.spirit-wrestlers.com).

A number of Canadian scholars have been making significant contributions to the study of Doukhobor history and current affairs. These include Dr. Veronika Makarova of the University of Saskatchewan; Dr. Julie Rak of the University of Alberta; Dr. Gunter Schaarschmidt, professor emeritus at the University of Victoria; and Dr. Myler Wilkinson of Selkirk College in Castlegar.

While there have been no monographs on Tolstoy and the Doukhobors, all these individuals have written or spoken publicly on the subject of Tolstoy and his role as inspirer and mentor to the whole Doukhobor movement, their shared aspirations for world peace, their strong vocal opposition to war and military might, tolerance of others regardless of differences, and the inviolability of human beings.

A significant role in maintaining this legacy of Tolstoy's is played by the Doukhobor's monthly bilingual magazine, *Iskra*. An encouraging observation is that the magazine's editors seem to be getting younger and younger in age (which naturally attracts younger readers to its pages). The content and reception of each monthly issue bears witness to a collective willingness to work hard and in fresh ways, and to the fact that Tolstoy's original inspirational ideas, which have long dovetailed with those of the Doukhobors', are by no means lost on the upcoming generation, but are being enhanced and adapted to the conditions of life in the twenty-first century.

I wish to close this chapter by setting forth brief biographical profiles of several individuals active in the contemporary Doukhobor movement — examples with whom and whose works I am especially well acquainted. These are ethnographer Koozma J. Tarasoff, museum curator Larry A. Ewashen, former *Iskra* editor Dmitri E. (Jim) Popoff, Molokan webmaster Andrei Conovaloff, artist Jan Kabatoff, and USCC executive director John J. Verigin Jr. While these biographical sketches are chiefly based on materials provided by colleagues (and, in some cases, the subjects themselves), responsibility for their accuracy ultimately rests with the author.

KOOZMA J. TARASOFF (1932–)

This Doukhobor octogenarian has indeed worn many hats over his lifetime: ethnographer, historian, journal editor, published author, photojournalist, Internet blogger, peace activist (the list could go on). His self-description culminates in "a scholar of Spirit-wrestlers/Doukhobor studies," which for him translates into "a Tolstoyan social movement with a focus on creating a compassionate, caring world based on love and nonkilling."

Born on a Saskatchewan farm into a bilingual 'independent' Doukhobor family, he first learnt about his ancestral culture (including Tolstoy's role in it) and values through the medium of Russian. As he entered his teens, his family moved to Saskatoon (the nearest major city) so that he might pursue his post-secondary education — first at the University of Saskatchewan and eventually at the University of British Columbia. During this time, with the support of his father and other elders, he often met with first- and second-generation Canadian Doukhobors, who inspired him to become even more involved in the advancement of Doukhobor culture. This led to his founding a newsletter, which soon became a magazine known as *The Inquirer*, which published fifty issues and some 1,440 articles.

See: www.spirit-wrestlers.com/excerpts/Inquirer/history.html).

But this was only the beginning of Koozma's publishing career. He went on to author more than a dozen books and hundreds of articles, many of them superbly illustrated with his own pictures as a photojournalist. Some of these photobooks stemmed from his many travels across Canada, America, Russia/Soviet Union (which he visited thirteen times), and a number of other countries around the world, meeting with many prominent and interesting scholars and people from all walks of life, writing about Doukhobors' lives, and, most importantly, from a Doukhobor perspective.

One of his favourite subjects is Lev Nikolaevich Tolstoy.

In early November 2007, he presented a major scholarly paper entitled "Tolstoy and the Doukhobors" at the first Global Nonkilling Leadership Forum, in Hawaii, which may be read in part at the following address: www.spirit-wrestlers.com/excerpts/2007_Tolstoy_Doukhobors_Hawaii.html.

On 25 April 2010 he gave an address, on the occasion of the opening of the Doukhobor Discovery Centre in Castlegar, on Tolstoy's legacy to the world, which is available at https://tinyurl.com/LNT-legacy.

And on 13 November 2013, as a guest lecturer at the University of Ottawa, he included a major chapter on Tolstoy as part of a talk on the "Evolution of the Doukhobor Movement" — see his multimedia presentation at www.spirit-wrestlers.com/evolution.html.

Over his long lifetime, Koozma Tarasoff has amassed a huge collection of both photographic and textual documents (including more than 10,000 pages of field notes) on the Doukhobors in Canada and elsewhere. These are housed in the provincial archives of Saskatchewan and British Columbia. For Saskatchewan holdings, see http://sain.scaa.sk.ca/collections/koozma-j-tarasoff-fonds, and for British Columbia, https://search-bcarchives.royalbcmuseum.bc.ca/doukhobor-history-photograph-collection.

An overview of his scholarly work on Tolstoy and the Doukhobors, as well as his activity in the non-killing and peace movements, may be found at https://goo.gl/LT3CvQ. His Doukhobor and related blogs from 2008 to the present can be followed at www.spirit-wrestlers.com.

In sum, no serious study on Doukhobor history and culture can be undertaken without consulting Tarasoff's tremendous collection of materials and writings.

LARRY A. EWASHEN (1940–)

This long-time Doukhobor activist was born in Alberta, where he has earned both a bachelor of arts degree from the University of Alberta and a senior certificate from the Banff Centre for Arts and Creativity. He pursued post-graduate studies at the Royal Conservatory of Speech in Toronto, as well as in America at both the Actors' Studio in New York and Case Western Reserve University in Cleveland, Ohio, where he was awarded an honours master of arts degree.

On the professional film scene, his experience involved research assignments in Russia and writing assignments in New York, in addition to contract work for the Canadian Museum of Civilization (now the Canadian Museum of History). One of the films he produced and directed was *In Search of Utopia: The Doukhobors* — a major contribution to Doukhobor studies. He also composed the soundtrack for *The Herring Belt*, named best short documentary at the Cannes Film Festival in 1963.

His acting experience included many feature films and CBC Television productions; he also freelanced extensively in radio as interviewer, writer, actor, producer, and musician. Music has always been an intrinsic part of his life. As president of the Guild of Canadian Folk Artists, he conducted many workshops and performances on English, Canadian, American, and Russian folk music. He also toured extensively with his own groups and also with such well-known Canadian singers as Stompin' Tom Connors. Ewashen acted and directed in various theatres in Canada, Great Britain, and the United States. In the academic world, he founded theatre programmes at Canadore College in North Bay, Ontario, and at Toronto's Ryerson University.

In the early 1990s Ewashen was appointed museum curator of the Doukhobor Discovery Centre in Castlegar, a position he held until October 2010. During this time, which he referred to as "one of my most productive working periods," he wrote and published many Doukhobor-related articles and gave heritage workshops and lectures at various Canadian universities, along with producing films and video. His duties as curator included specific work projects and partnering with government initiatives, animating guided tours, public relations, educational programmes, documentary film assistance and research, creation of annual exhibits, general management, and organizing visits by Governors General, lieutenant-governors, and foreign ambassadors. In 2005 he was presented with a special plaque by then BC Lieutenant-Governor Iona Campagnolo, on behalf of the City of Castlegar and the Kootenay Doukhobor Historical Society.

Ewashen also served as guest curator at other museums in the province. In 2012 he was largely responsible for the official recognition of Pëtr Vasil'evich Verigin as "a person of national historic significance" by the Historic Sites and Monuments Board of Canada, along with the migration of Doukhobors to British Columbia as a "national historic event."

Now in semi-retirement, he continues many of his former activities, including participating in university seminars on Tolstoy and the Doukhobors.

DMITRI E. (JIM) POPOFF (1946–)

This former editor of the Doukhobor magazine *Iskra* was born on 7 January 1946 in Grand Forks, British Columbia, the eldest of three children born to Eli A. Popoff and his wife, Dorothy (*née* Rilkoff). During his teenage years Dmitri was active in the USCC — of which he has been a lifelong member — as well as the USCC Union of Youth. He also completed an eight-year USCC Russian-language program and began instructing hundreds of young Doukhobors in their ancestral language throughout the 1960s.

In 1965, along with eight other young Doukhobors, Popoff was invited to participate in a month-long tour of the Soviet Union; this was the first large-group visit by Canadian Doukhobors to their ancestral homeland. After marrying his wife, Lillian (*née* Popoff), in 1966, they moved to Vancouver and the following year Dmitri began an honours programme in international relations at the University of British Columbia. At that time he was instrumental in co-founding a new Vancouver-based youth group known as the Union of Young Doukhobors (UYD), which in 2018 celebrated fifty years of continuous activity.

In the 1970s, Popoff decided to withdraw from academics in order to devote his time to raising a family and promoting Doukhobor ideals among the community and the broader Canadian public — including the publication of the *UYD Newsletter* and co-founding a new Doukhobor magazine known as *Mir* (the Russian word for 'peace'), of which he served as editor/manager for its first dozen years.

At this time, in addition to publishing the magazine and several Doukhobor books, as well as operating a Doukhobor bookstore, Popoff also became more intensively involved with the USCC, serving as part-time executive assistant to Honorary Chairman John J. Verigin Sr. He was also a key member of various USCC committees, including the USCC delegation to the Expanded Kootenay Committee on Intergroup Relations, headed by then BC Assistant Deputy Attorney-General Robin Bourne. It was this committee that finally brought resolution to the seventy-five years of violent activity by the Doukhobor splinter group the Sons of Freedom.[32]

In 1978, during his second trip to the Soviet Union on behalf of Canadian Doukhobors, Popoff (along with fellow delegate William M. Rozinkin), paid an official visit to Yasnaya Polyana in honour of the sesquicentenary of Tolstoy's birth, meeting with the then museum director, Stepan Grigor'evich Bunin. Shortly thereafter, he collaborated with his father, Eli A. Popoff, on preparing a scholarly paper on Tolstoy's relationship to the Doukhobors. This paper was presented by John J. Verigin Sr. at a special three-day Tolstoy symposium organized at the University of Victoria in November 1978, in which Dmitri and his wife, Lillian, participated.[33]

In 1982 Popoff served on a four-member convening committee for the International Doukhobor Intergroup Symposium[34] in Castlegar, which made history by bringing together Doukhobors, Molokans, Mennonites, and Quakers, in addition to Lev Tolstoy's great-grandson Il'ja Vladimirovich Tolstoy. This was the first time the Doukhobors had welcomed a direct descendant of Lev Tolstoy to their communities in Canada.

Four years later Popoff (along with fellow-delegate Paul J. Seminoff) made a third trip to Russia, this time visiting sculptor Jurij Chernov to inspect progress on Chernov's latest creation — two bronze statues of Lev Tolstoy that were to go to Doukhobor historic sites in British Columbia and Saskatchewan as gifts of the Soviet Rodina Society. Their unveilings coincided with the 1987 Russian-Canadian Heritage Festival, attended by an official Soviet delegation, and including a second visit to Canada by Il'ja Vladimirovich Tolstoy.

In 1991 Popoff made his fourth trip to the Soviet Union, accompanying John J. Verigin Sr.; they participated in the largest gathering of Lev Nikolaevich

32 See summary in *Iskra*, N° 2108 (November 2016): 8–11, 28–31.

33 All these Tolstoy events of 1978 were covered in a special issue of *Iskra* (N° 1484, 29 December 1978) and in a subsequent issue of *Mir* (N° 17, May 1979). In addition, the symposium papers were published in a special edition of *Canadian Slavonic Papers*.

34 See summary in three issues of *Iskra* (N°s 2046, 2048, 2049 — September, November and December 2011).

Tolstoy's descendants in the Soviet era, and also met with the former Soviet ambassador to Canada (1973–1983), Aleksandr Nikolaevich Yakovlev (considered the 'father of perestroika') to investigate the possibility of a reverse migration of a number of Canadian Doukhobors to their ancestral homeland. During this time Dmitri held the post of secretary of the newly formed USCC committee on cultural relations with compatriots abroad, as well as secretary of the USCC migration committee; in this capacity he was part of the USCC delegation that met with Soviet leader Mikhail Sergeevich Gorbachëv in Vancouver.

Popoff's most recent trip to Russia came in 2007, when he and his wife visited his sister Elaine Podovinikoff and her husband, Alfred, at their home in Yasnaya Polyana. A prominent example of reverse migration, the couple had decided in their fifties to move to Russia indefinitely. In 2006, Elaine set up two English-language playschools in Moscow called Our Children, Our School.[35] On this occasion, Dmitri and Lillian also visited with members of the Tolstoy family.

At home in Grand Forks, Popoff served two terms as the fifth editor of *Iskra*. During his first term (1986–1992) he succeeded in increasing the magazine's circulation to its highest point ever. His second editorial term (1996–2000) covered many events celebrating the 1999 centenary of the Doukhobor's first arrival in Canada, including an interview with Tolstoy's great-great-grandson, Vladimir Il'ich Tolstoy, who visited the Canadian Doukhobors more than once during this time. Vladimir Il'ich was then serving as director of the Yasnaya Polyana estate and was subsequently appointed cultural advisor to Russian president Vladimir Putin.

After completing his second term as editor, Dmitri continued to serve as editorial consultant, contribute numerous articles for publication, and write an ongoing column about the Russian language (in particular the Doukhobor dialect). From 2008 to 2014 he assisted webmaster John J. Kalmakov in developing a brand new USCC website.

After a journalism career spanning many decades, Dmitri Popoff is now turning to writing books; the first one will focus, as he put it, on "the events, significance and meaning of the Doukhobor historical experience, from a Doukhobor perspective." He is also exploring Internet and digital technology and its potential to advance cross-cultural communication and pursue the Doukhobor (and Tolstoyan) ideals of brotherhood and peace.

ANDREI IVANOVICH CONOVALOFF (1948–)

This active researcher and webmaster was raised on an Arizona farm west of Phoenix, in a community of 'Spiritual Christians.' Whereas the Doukhobors had chosen Canada, other Spiritual Christian emigrants decided to settle in

35 See Tétrault-Farber 2014.

America, mainly in the southwestern states. Most of the Conovaloff family's neighbours had come from various ancestral Christian groups in the southern Caucasus. His grandparents' congregation came from Selim village in Kars Oblast (now in Turkey). In America, the Selimski tribes divided — the *Molokane*[36] went to San Francisco, and the *Pryguny* (Jumpers) to Arizona.[37]

It turned out that one of their neighbours was a Canadian Doukhobor, originally from Blaine Lake, Saskatchewan, who had been raised in central California and was married to the son of a 'Prygun' (Jumper) family.[38] Their children attended the same local schools as Conovaloff, though the family was shunned by nearby zealots.

By the time Conovaloff was born in 1948, there were only two significant subgroups of Spiritual Christians remaining in this part of America — the Pryguny, originally from the Kars Oblast of the Caucasus (now in Turkey), and the Maksimisty, from the Erevan area (now in Armenia). A few years later, these two groups merged into a new spiritual movement that eventually became known as Dukh-i-zhizniki (lit. 'Spirit-and-lifers'), imposing on their collective followers a 1928 Russian text, *Kniga solntse, dukh i zhizn'* [The sun, spirit and life book], in conjunction with the synodal edition of the Russian Bible.

As he was growing up, Conovaloff often wondered at the spiritual rituals and outbursts coming from these Dukh-i-zhizniki zealots, jumping 'in the Holy Spirit' (as they put it), and shouting their 'prophetic messages' in Russian. His parents could not explain them to him. Indeed, few people could offer any explanation, or even understand the new textbook themselves. But Conovaloff's first-hand observations of these radical phenomena left an indelible impression on his mind and provided a significant personal background to his later studies and research in Russian sectarian history.

It was not until his late teens that his parents explained the reasons behind their aversion to war and military service (much like the Doukhobors' aforementioned aversion). After high school they practically ordered him not only to pursue a postsecondary education, which he did at the University of California, Los Angeles, but to register as a conscientious objector with the US Selective Service. This was a new revelation to him; before his move to California, he had never realized that his grandfather, as a conscientious objector during the First World War, had spent four years in a military prison for his refusal to bear arms, or that his father had been incarcerated in a federal prison during the Second World War for the same reason.

36 The word *Molokane* is the Russian plural form of 'Molokans.' See section on "Sectarian Fëdor Zheltov and the Molokans" in Chap. 2.

37 See Conovaloff's "Taxonomy of 3 Spiritual Christian Groups: *Molokane*, *Pryguny* and *Dukh-i-zhizniki* — books, fellowship, holidays, prophets and songs," available at the address in Note 38 below.

38 See Conovaloff, http://www.molokane.org/taxonomy.

His academic experience in California did bear fruit, however. In 1972 he was awarded a degree in chemistry, followed by a successfully completed master's programme at California State University, in Fresno, specializing in business and marketing statistics. But he was still left wondering how his family had come to America, and why.

Andrei's curiosity eventually led him even deeper into the study of his ancestral ethnic and religious background. He travelled extensively along the North American west coast, from Mexico to Canada, visiting many Spiritual Christian communities of Russian origin. During the 1970s, using a university's mainframe computer, he managed to compile a comprehensive database of residents in these communities. The resulting published directory of more than 4,000 households included maps for many congregations, societies, and even cemeteries, along with a large history section and a review of a comprehensive book by A. I. Klibanov, *Istorija religioznogo sektantsva v Rossii (60-e gody XIX v. — 1917 g.)* [History of religious sectarianism in Russia (1860s–1917)], published in Moscow in 1965. The directory remained in circulation for more than a decade.

In the 1980s he began collaborating with historian Ethel Dunn[39] and her anthropologist husband, Dr. Stephen Dunn, to publish more extensive materials concerning the Russian Spiritual Christians in California. They presented him with their full English translation of Klibanov's book, which he set about promoting on a grand scale. He even remembers seeing a photo in their home of Klibanov with Doukhobor ethnographer Koozma Tarasoff. Conovaloff met Tarasoff for the first time in 1982, and Klibanov several times a decade later.

During the 1990s Conovaloff made five extensive trips to Russia, visiting a vast number of his relatives, one of whom even officiated at his marriage to a Russian Molokan girl, in 1997, in Prygun wedding style.

On his Russian trips at this time he was able to document more than a hundred communities of Spiritual Christians in the former Soviet Union, and in 1996 launched the first Molokan website (www.molokane.org). Since then, he has expanded his online activity to include assistance in hosting several Independent Doukhobor websites, including Tarasoff'sspirit-wrestlers.com. His new comprehensive portal (in both English and Russian) may be found at www.spiritualchristians.org. With a home library of hundreds of related books, he maintains regular collaboration on the subject with a number of scholars throughout the world.

His zeal in supporting not only the Molokans but also other 'Spiritual Christian' groups is seen in the following incident: When the building in Baku (Azerbaijan) known as the Molokan Centre (built ca 1913) was recently scheduled to be demolished, Conovaloff's contribution to a lobbying campaign played a major role in saving the structure and having it placed under

39 See works by Ethel Dunn in the Bibliography.

heritage protection by the government of Azerbaijan.

JAN KABATOFF (1948–)

Jan did not immediately set out to be an art student. Born in British Columbia, she moved to Alberta in 1972, where she was awarded a diploma in respiratory technology. Taking time out to raise a family, she eventually earned a bachelor of fine arts degree in 1996 from the Alberta College of Art and Design, in Calgary. With its overall postmodern atmosphere, the art college provided an ideal environment for examining not only her own Doukhobor heritage but also the role of women within the Doukhobor community, as well as the increasing loss of their cultural identity and, more broadly, the marginalization of ethnic minorities in Canada.

These explorations led her to investigate the religious beliefs that set the Doukhobors apart from the adherents of the Russian Orthodox Church and, later, from the rest of Canadian society following their emigration in 1899. Their belief that Christ resided within each person individually and therefore did not require the clergy to mediate between them and God, and that we are all brothers and sisters, was at odds with the prevailing Christian views, as was their creed of *toil and peaceful life*, which advocated living simply and peacefully, not only with all living beings but in harmony with Nature itself.

In the 1990s Kabatoff looked for ways to reflect these Doukhobor ideals of life in artistic form. Her searching culminated in a body of work that was chosen for the Alberta Biennial of Contemporary Art exhibit in 1998. Later it was featured at the Kootenay Art Gallery in Castlegar and the Grand Forks Art Gallery. During the following year, the centenary of the Doukhobor emigration to Canada, she celebrated the occasion in part by co-curating two group exhibitions involving contemporary artists of Doukhobor heritage.

From 2000 until 2011, Kabatoff lived in Canmore, Alberta, in the foothills of the Rockies. During this time she held a studio at the Banff Centre for the Arts as a self-directed artist. The Doukhobor values with which she had been brought up instilled in her a deep love of nature. Ever cognizant of the growing concerns about global warming, in 2005 she embarked on extensive research and numerous expeditions to study the changing conditions of seven glaciers on three continents.

As she explains, "I have watched the pine trees surrounding the Banff Centre succumb to the pine beetle, and learned of the unprecedented rate of glacial melt, not only in the Rockies but worldwide. I became increasingly concerned about the legacy my generation was leaving behind and the world my children were inheriting."

With the moral and financial support of both individuals and organizations — the Alberta Foundation for the Arts, the Canada Council for the Arts, the United Nations Water for Life Decade (2005–2015), Dr. Shawn Marshall of the University of Calgary Department of Earth Sciences, and Dr. Mike

Demuth of Natural Resources of Canada, in Ottawa — Kabatoff was able to bring her concerns to the public's attention. Through science she discovered that, with few exceptions, glaciers were receding at an alarming rate due to temperature fluctuations and, like the 'canary in the coal mine,' they were a most noticeable testament to the effects of climate change.

In 2009 she successfully integrated her scientific findings with data collected in situ and produced a multimedia exhibit with sound recordings of glaciers melting, along with frottage (rubbings) and mould impressions of glacier surfaces. Also included was an installation comprising some 4,000 plastic bottles containing glacier water from the Arctic. The exhibition was shown in public galleries in British Columbia, Alberta, and Newfoundland.

Since 2011 Jan Kabatoff has been residing in the West Kootenays, where she maintains an art studio. She is actively involved with the Doukhobor community, the West Kootenay EcoSociety, and the Nelson Interfaith Climate Action Collaborative.

She created the colour illustration that graced the cover of the first edition of this book and is included as the frontispiece in the present edition.

JOHN J. VERIGIN JR. (1955–)

The great-great-grandson of Pëtr V. Verigin (the first Doukhobor leader to emigrate to Canada), is currently the executive director of the official Doukhobor organization, the USCC. He was unanimously acclaimed in this position at the USCC annual general meeting in February 2009, following the passing of his father, John J. Verigin Sr., who had served as honorary chairman of the USCC for seventy years.[40]

John J. Jr. travelled a lot during the 1970s and 1980s — first through Europe, North Africa, and the Middle East, then through Asia (including Southeast Asia), and later through Central and South America. These travels at times took him through conflict zones. In 1979–80 he spent an extended period of study in Russia and Germany. In the 1980s he served as a volunteer in the peace movement both nationally and internationally; he subsequently worked for both governmental and non-governmental agencies, including a stint at the United Nations in New York. This brought him not only personal awards but also much-appreciated recognition for the USCC and the Doukhobors.

In 1990 John J. Jr. moved back to his home town of Grand Forks to devote his energies to promoting Doukhobor ideals and furthering the cause of world peace, human rights, social and economic justice, protection of the environment, as well as humanitarian assistance to those in need. A practical example of this latter goal was seen in 1992, when he collected and delivered

40 At this same meeting, USCC members voted to retire the position of honorary chairman in favour of leadership by the executive director (a capacity in which John J. Verigin Jr. had already been assisting his father in the USCC).

humanitarian aid to Russia.

In the 1990s John J. Jr. helped establish several USCC working groups, as well as the Kootenay region branch of the United Nations Association in Canada, serving on its board (including as president) for a number of years. For ten years he was a member of the board of the Canadian Peace Alliance, and for some time a board member of Selkirk College, where he was awarded an honorary diploma in peace studies. Recognition also came in the form of medals given him by both the Russian and Canadian governments.

As the hundredth anniversary of several key events in Doukhobor history approached, John J. Jr. became involved in organizing centenary celebrations, including of the Burning of Weapons (1995), the Doukhobors' emigration to Canada (1999), and the 'Community' Doukhobors' migration from Saskatchewan to British Columbia under Peter V. Verigin's leadership (2008). More than one of these celebrations involved a personal visit by Vladimir Il'ich Tolstoy, Lev Nikolaevich's great-great-grandson, who was hosted in Canada by John J. Verigin Jr., Peter V. Verigin's great-great-grandson. This was indeed a momentous occasion for both descendants of illustrious ancestors.

Since his appointment as the current de facto Doukhobor leader (though he would say their only true leader is Jesus Christ), John J. Jr. has been working assiduously to:

> deepen spiritual understanding, broaden cultural horizons, and strengthening a sense of community of membership; improving relations with other Doukhobors across Canada and in the former Soviet Union; working with other local, provincial, national and international organizations to build a better world.

PART II

GUEST ESSAYS BY THREE PROMINENT DOUKHOBORS

What Tolstoy Means to Me as an Artist

JAN KABATOFF

AFTER A FOUR-YEAR HIATUS from my ethnocultural work, Andrew Donskov's invitation to write about what Tolstoy means to me has challenged me to pause and reflect, and once again dig a little deeper into my Russian roots and Doukhobor soul. I am deeply grateful for this opportunity to speak from the heart, to explore further the Doukhobor/Tolstoy connection and to become better acquainted with an extraordinary individual.

Obviously, the significance of Leo Tolstoy on the lives of Canadian Doukhobors is immeasurable, whether each individual Doukhobor is aware of the extent of his benevolence towards our ancestors or not. His generous contribution to their migration and the symbiotic nature of their relationship, with its shared values and spiritual beliefs, have irrevocably linked us to our Russian origins with Yasnaya Polyana being as much a point of destination for a modern-day Canadian Doukhobor pilgrimage as the *peshchery* [caves] in Transcaucasia.

But what does Tolstoy mean to me personally, a hybridized, assimilated third-generation Canadian Doukhobor living a privileged and relatively safe life, whose pacifist beliefs have never been tested to the fullest extent while reaping the benefits of our ancestors?

In earlier times, tracing one's ancestry and historical trajectory back to their origins, for the purpose of understanding one's self and one's place within that history, did not seem as compelling or urgent, since tightly knit ethnic communities had a stronger sense of who they were, where they came from, and what they believed in. In the case of the Doukhobors and their identity construction, as Julie Rak concludes in her book *Negotiated Memory*, their identity was constructed as a set of reactions to the wounded ideas of home sustained in the diasporic imaginary trope "that figures home as both

Russia, and the memory of resistance to oppression in Russia"[1] And a soulful memory it is, one that has echoed through the generations in countless and diverse ways.

Growing up with a double identity — first as a Russian and second as a Canadian — invariably predisposed me to what Rak coined as a 'half-turn' to the past, to better discern how I corresponded to and/or differed from my ancestors. However, it was not until I left the Doukhobor 'fold' and had sufficiently assimilated into mainstream Canadian society (*living in the oblivion*, as some would say) that I began to examine from a broader and more contemporary perspective issues surrounding cultural identity, marginalization, and ethnicity, both from 'inside' and 'outside' the Doukhobor culture. The deeply religious, unique, and at times complex heritage inspired me to contemplate, to question, and to seek spiritual insights, to better understand some of the complexities of that heritage and the religious beliefs that shaped my destiny.

Naturally, a significant part of that history includes Leo Tolstoy. While it seems I have only just begun to examine more closely Tolstoy's philosophical views and spiritual beliefs in recent times, I feel as though I have known him all my life. The peasant life he describes in his novels, his spiritual musings, his deep sense of social responsibility — all resonate with my early beginnings in a sectarian community, and with many of the spiritual, social, and ecological views I hold today. One of my deepest connections to Tolstoy can be attributed to my grandmother, who embodied many of the ideals and Christian beliefs that defined Tolstoy after his spiritual transformation — her zealous fanaticism notwithstanding.

I grew up in a Sons of Freedom community during the 1950s, a radical sect widely known for their strong religious beliefs, anti-materialism, fierce self-determination, and at times a violent resistance to imposed assimilation.

My grandmother, Vera Pankoff, a radical among radicals, had the most lasting influence on my upbringing. It was at her knee and against her soft bosom (not to mention an occasional sting from her knitting needle) that I learnt the Russian alphabet, Doukhobor prayers, and Christian values. Growing up during a time of socio-political upheavals in the community, with RCMP raids on school-age children, I also learned to fear authority, and to feel a sense of separateness and alienation from the outside world. Paradoxically, it was those very upheavals, when my playmates were forcibly taken away to learn the Queen's English at a residential school, that set me on a solitary path of self-discovery through art.

In spite of my grandmother's radical views and anarchical behaviour, I always found something very compelling about her indomitable spirit and unwavering faith, something appealing about her humble lifestyle. To this day, the concept of living 'off the grid,' close to the land, unfettered by worldly

1 Rak 2004: xiii.

possessions and being able to 'let go' of attachments to the material world continues to tweak my imagination and ascetic tendencies. As I hurry through a cluttered world I can identify with Tolstoy's inner struggle to reconcile the opposing forces of the material world we inhabit and a spiritual ascetic ideal.

My grandparents came close to living that ideal. Looking like the peasants described in his novels, Tolstoy would have felt at home in their makeshift cozy cottage, with tarpaper siding, no electricity or indoor plumbing, and sparse furnishings. He might even have praised them for their steadfastness in refusing ownership of land and for their strong adherence to the fundamental Doukhobor precepts.

Ernest Simmons, in his book *Tolstoy*, speaks about his "maddening and uncompromising profession of religious faith, and whether one accepts or rejects his convictions, the tremendous struggle that led to them glows with an incandescent human quality compelling attention."[2] The same may be said about my grandmother and the Freedomite sect.

Perhaps it was a need on my part to make sense of, and heal, some of the wounding within a complex and unique cultural history, with its nuances and paradoxes, or an attempt at reconnecting with my community of origin in a contemporary way, that prompted me to enrol in art school in the early 1990s. Without a Doukhobor reference or visual cues to guide me, save for the absence of art or its sublimation to storytelling and song, I looked to artists of other ethnic groups for insight and inspiration — in particular, those artists utilizing a variety of media and modes of expression in speaking about post-colonialism, ethnicity, and marginalization.

As a point of departure, I began researching the origins of Doukhoborism and the split from the Russian Orthodox Church in the 1700s, with its rejection of icons and all forms of Christian symbols and imagery. I was particularly intrigued by the notion that art, or an image, could be imbued with spirituality, or be able to 'infect' a viewer with an emotion or religious feeling.

Obviously, the power of an image to evoke a feeling cannot be overstated. Haunted by images of early Doukhobor women in the familiar peasant costumes, at the plough, sifting wheat, and working together in Koozma Tarasoff's *A Pictorial History of the Doukhobors*,[3] I felt they were yearning to tell their story. It was not long before images of Doukhobor women, past and present, with their stoicism, sense of solidarity, and strong work ethic, found their way into a body of work as part of a group show entitled *Our Doukhobor Heritage — Contemporary Reflections* (1995). My aim was to honour *all* Doukhobor women — whose voices were seldom heard, but who so faithfully upheld Doukhobor traditions — and to integrate the different 'threads' that make up the Doukhobor identity into a unified whole.

2 Simmons 1973: 109.

3 Tarasoff 1969.

I chose to work with linen for its cultural and historical relevance during the early settlement years, when Doukhobors grew their own flax and produced linen textiles. In what seemed to be the mystical union of *spirit and matter*, I sensed the presence of the ancient grandmothers supporting and guiding me during the process of making four distinct wall hangings, each expressing its own theme. Not only did they succeed in telling their story to the Doukhobor community at large, but their images and voices rippled out into the world of contemporary art and ethnocultural discourse, taking their rightful place in public galleries, museums, and art collections.

It was during the production of that work that I first read Tolstoy's treatise *What is Art?*, with its harsh criticism and judgemental pronouncements on art. I cringed at his impeachment of art schools, of Impressionists and Neo-Impressionists, æsthetics, and beauty, and generally of most art that, in his mind, did not 'infect' the viewer with a feeling, or did not serve to inspire or elevate humanity towards perfection. He repeatedly stressed the need for a moral and ethical art that could be easily comprehended and accessible to all, so that it would serve a higher ideal — as a unifying force to usher in "the brotherhood of man."

> In the arts of painting and sculpture all pictures and statues in so-called genre style, depictions of animals, landscapes and caricatures with subjects comprehensible to everyone, and also all kinds of ornaments, are universal in subject matter. Such productions in painting and sculpture are very numerous, but for the most part such objects are either not considered to be art or are considered to be of low quality. In reality all such objects, if only they transmit a true feeling experienced by the artist and comprehensible to everyone (however insignificant it may seem to us to be), are works of really good Christian art.[4]

I found his didactic and moralistic statements difficult to accept, at a time when I was struggling to navigate my way through the hubris of old conditioning and outmoded authority. I was just beginning to come to terms with being an artist, after years of soul-searching and pondering art's purpose and its relevance to humanity, in the face of much suffering and impoverishment in the world. It was not that I did not share some of Tolstoy's spiritual and altruistic musings, of living an ascetic life, renouncing worldly possessions and devoting one's life to humanitarian work — while I juggled family life, art practice, and community service — or that I did not feel irritated by elitist attitudes in the art world, or the obscurity in certain works of art.

What I was searching for was a more holistic approach to creating, a way to integrate *mind*, *body*, and *spirit,* to honour the receptive side of my nature, the creative muse, the sacred and the Divine, as well as the intellect and the rational mind, in fulfilling a higher purpose. Not until Tolstoy surrenders to

4 L. N. Tolstoj 1960: 156.

the creative spark within himself, during the completion of *Resurrection* in aid of the Doukhobor fund toward their mass migration, does he speak with such passion about the *spiritual* in art. In the introduction to *Resurrection,* Rosemary Edmonds notes that "Tolstoy was so absorbed in his first full-length novel for over twenty years that distractions of any kind were almost painful. Since *War and Peace,* he told his wife, he had never been so powerfully gripped by the creative urge."[5]

Fortunately for both the Doukhobors and Tolstoy, their appeal for humanitarian assistance resurrected the creative 'urge' in him, whose long-awaited work was enthusiastically received internationally, with much monetary success. Perhaps it is in *Resurrection* that Tolstoy comes closest to integrating the different aspects of himself — the artist, the philosopher, and the humanitarian.

In my subsequent works, I continued to draw from historical sources and contemporary art theory surrounding cultural identity. In several mixed-media works, in honour of the centenary of the Doukhobor migration, I included rubbings from the gravestones of original Doukhobor immigrants, as well as excerpts from the correspondence between Tolstoy and Verigin.[6] I was particularly touched by the mutually endearing and respectful way in which the two men corresponded and impressed by the spiritual and intellectual depth of their exchange.

While they did not always agree, it is evident they shared many similar ideas and beliefs, and were instrumental in stimulating and supporting each other's spiritual and philosophical growth over the span of many years. The next large body of my work, entitled *Doukhobor Diaspora* (2000), would speak more universally about migration and loss of cultural identity — through name change, assimilation and intermarriage — as a metaphor for the passage of time and a way of life 'never to return.' Included in the body of work were a series of prints of Tolstoy's draft for *Resurrection,* screen-printed on handmade linen paper with 1930s Doukhobor-grown flax fibres. I was fascinated by the original scrawls and rewrites of a great author during the creative process, and while the text was important for its historical relevance and the imprint it left on Doukhobor history, even more importantly, it was an example of art at the service of humanity.

Even though initially I found Tolstoy's moral absolutes and dogmatic approach to art problematic, I could not help but be inspired by his impassioned plea for art to elevate humanity to a higher level of consciousness. In his paper on Tolstoy's *What* is *Art?*, critic and historian James Sloan Allen summarizes the "curmudgeonly opponent of modernism" as follows:

5 Edmonds 1966: 7.

6 Donskov 1995a; reproduced as Chap. 6 in the present volume.

> Tolstoy knows our times better than we might guess. And he urges us to grasp the importance we grant to art in the lives we live, if not in the principles we espouse, prodding us to think about art as "a great matter."[7]

Art for art's sake, rugged individualism, and the self-serving freedom cry of modernity are slowly giving way to new forms of art that emphasize interrelatedness, community, social awareness, and ecological responsibility. In *The Re-Enchantment of Art,* Suzie Gablik writes:

> The necessity for art to transform its goals and become accountable in the planetary whole is incompatible with æsthetic attitudes still predicated on the late-modernist assumption that art has no "useful" role to play in the larger scheme of things. But the fact is that many artists now conceive their roles with a different sense of purpose than current æsthetic models sanction, even though there is as yet no comprehensive theory or framework to encompass what they are doing.[8]

Whether it is Tolstoy's urging to create art with a broader 'infectious' appeal or his concerns about Nature, or a reflection of the dire conditions of our ecology, my recent work has been more focused on environmental issues and the examination of the historically divergent paths of science and natural philosophy that still inform our current views of our natural environment.

Echoes of Tolstoy's prescient insights regarding the future of humanity, his warnings about the detrimental effects of technology on Nature, about science without conscience, and about the necessity of opposing all forms of violence, are evident in the new emerging paradigm in science, art and religion. People from all spheres of life are responding to an urgent need to reframe our world view from an isolated and alienated self, from militaristic solutions and environmental abuse, to one that seeks to connect to a larger whole by acknowledging shared similarity and the interdependence of all species of life. In Tolstoy's words:

> To stand aloof, to shut oneself up in a monastery, surrounded by such angels as oneself, amounts to creating a hothouse and those conditions in which it will be easy to be good oneself, but no one else will be warm. Live in the world and be good — that is what's needed.[9]

Given Tolstoy's strong convictions, we know he is asking more of us than simply being model citizens of the world. Like the core beliefs of all religions, what we are called upon to do is to take moral responsibility for our actions and to put love and a compassionate heart into practice, locally and globally.

7 Allen 1999: 8.
8 Gablik 1991: 7.
9 Quoted in Simmons 1973: 171.

The dawning of an *interspiritual age* — as defined by Wayne Teasdale, an interreligious monk and mystic who chose to make his refuge in the heart of a major American city — is one that corresponds to many of the Doukhobor views and Tolstoy's fundamental beliefs.

> It is an age of emergence to ecological awareness; a growing sense of the rights of other species; the ideal of abandoning a militant nationalism; a deep evolving experience of community; a growing receptivity to the inner treasures of the world's religions; and an openness to the cosmos with the realization that the relationship between humans and the earth is part of the larger community of the universe.[10]

During the celebratory and reconciliatory mood of the Doukhobor centenary events in the latter half of the 1990s, I was privileged to have had the opportunity to participate in and contribute towards a new emerging paradigm of inclusivity, respect for diversity, mutuality, and collaboration with Doukhobor happenings, group art exhibitions, art projects, and women's retreats. The days of sectarianism and alienation are giving way to a socially active and practical relationship within the Doukhobor community and with the world at large.

In looking to the underlying meaning and fundamental beliefs of great thinkers, philosophers, and artists who, sometimes artfully and sometimes very forcefully and dogmatically, have expressed a response to the universal need in the collective unconscious for *interrelatedness*, for *wholeness*, and for the *sacred*, I shall always hold a special place in my heart for Tolstoy, and a deep sense of gratitude for his compassion and benevolence towards our ancestors. I continue to be inspired by his ideas on 'brotherhood' or the global family, on art with meaning and purpose, and on the need for an inner spiritual revolution. Humanity may never be unified through a universal religion, but there is an awakening to our ecological interconnectedness and a shared common belief and goal amongst a growing number, to see the preciousness of *all* life and to do whatever we can to preserve our environment. Tolstoy is part of the legacy that has brought that awakening to us.

Canmore, Alberta
21 February 2005

10 Teasdale 2000: 4.

Lev Tolstoy in My Doukhobor Family Heritage

ELI A. POPOFF

PERHAPS IT IS IMPORTANT TO STATE, at the start, that for over a century, through a chain of unique circumstances of fate and destiny, our family has possibly been more closely touched by the ever-living spirit of this world-renowned personage than many other Doukhobor families. At the same time, it is quite safe to say that in virtually every Doukhobor family there was, and is, an appreciation and feeling of sincere gratitude that 'Dedushka Tolstoy' was a friend and benefactor of the Doukhobors, who had helped them in their most dire time of need.

Tolstoy's help affected my own ancestral Popoff (historically spelt *Popov*) family very directly. In 1895, during the events leading up to the 'Burning of Arms,' my father, Aleksej Ivanovich Popov, received his conscription notice. The first group of eleven Doukhobor conscripts had already refused to serve while in actual training, and they, together with others, were now undergoing the harshest of punishments in the Ekaterinburg disciplinary battalion, which included brutal floggings, even death.

Imagine the elation that went through all of the Doukhobor settlements, including the Popov household, when word was received that, due to the intervention of a great Russian writer, the floggings at the disciplinary battalion had been stopped![1] Even though most Doukhobors at the time were not fully aware of Tolstoy's fame and world stature, their gratitude was sincere, and their reverence for Dedushka Tolstoy only grew with their increased awareness, as various historical connections unfolded in the years to come.

1 Instead, the young Doukhobor conscientious objectors would be exiled to Siberia for eighteen years, the [equivalent of a] full term of military service.

During this period of struggle and persecution the exiled Doukhobor leader, Pëtr (Peter) Vasil'evich Verigin ('the Lordly'[2]) sent his followers a letter, which they soon adopted as the psalm "My beloved Brother in our Lord Jesus Christ." At the time, the Doukhobors did not realize that parts of it had been taken directly from Tolstoy's writings. Nevertheless, this psalm was to strengthen every Doukhobor in their stand against militarism and in the suffering they endured as a result. Eventually, someone in virtually every Doukhobor household committed this psalm to memory. The young men and their families facing conscription received much inspiration from it — my father, too, memorized it at this time and recited it often throughout his lifetime.

My father was again directly affected by the benevolent actions of Tolstoy when he was serving a sentence of exile in Siberia with more than a hundred other young Doukhobors. In 1899, when the Transcaucasian Doukhobors who had remained faithful to their leader, Pëtr V. Verigin, were preparing to leave to go to Canada, the tsarist authorities gave the Siberian exiles' wives and families the choice of either joining their husbands in Siberia or joining the other Doukhobors emigrating to Canada. Understandably, most of the wives chose Siberia.

At the same time Tolstoy was providing much-needed financial help to the Doukhobors, donating a large percentage of the royalties from his new book, *Resurrection,* towards the Doukhobor emigration. He encouraged his eldest son, Sergej, and other associates to assist with the actual arrangements. He also used his influence in helping to finance and accommodate the fifty or so wives and children who had chosen to join their husbands in Siberia. Tolstoy asked a friend and colleague of his — Dr. Prokopij Nesterovich Sokol'nikov (a Yakut by birth) — to accompany them on their arduous trip to Siberia.[3]

Although my father was not married at that time, he recalled how elated all of his comrades were when their families arrived, and how much more complete the societal structure of their own 'Doukhoboria' in Siberia came to be after this event — not unlike their communities back in the Caucasus. The Doukhobor exiles in Siberia were ever grateful for all Tolstoy's efforts in bringing about this happy reunion.

It proved to be of particular importance to my father. One winter he was living with his close friends, Fëdor and Semën Usachov, as the exiled Doukhobors were building their new village of Otradnoe. Permission for settlement at this new site (vastly superior to their original place of exile) had been granted to them by the Yakut territorial governor in recognition of the Doukhobor carpenters' building him a most pleasing summer residence in the city of Yakutsk. Semën Usachov's wife, Mavrunja, who had arrived with

2 A common rendering of the Russian term *Gospodnij*, which in fact means 'belonging to the Lord.'

3 See a detailed account of this journey, from the diary of Dr. Sokol'nikov, published in *Iskra*, N°s 1945–1951 (13 August–17 December 2003).

the others, looked after the three men that winter as though they were a typical family unit.

During that period of Siberian exile my father often stayed with his cousin Masha Salykina. They had been close friends since childhood, as they both loved to sing. Masha was a great conversationalist and storyteller, and my father, too, had a similar knack. Masha and her husband, Petrunja Salykin (another of the young exiled Doukhobor conscripts), had their own rented quarters in the city of Yakutsk, where Petrunja was able to work, also by special permission from the governor. Masha Salykina was an excellent hostess and a real 'duchess' of a lady, and their home was often a meeting place for Doukhobor exiles coming to the city. It was here that the essence of the Doukhobor life-concept was discussed, and where Dedushka Tolstoy was often mentioned. They also sang their inspiring and melodious Doukhobor psalms, which helped them keep their Doukhobor consciousness alive and endure their exile in Siberia for the Doukhobor cause. In discussion, Masha would sometimes remind everyone that their suffering in Siberia was not that great in comparison to that of their ancestors, many of whom had sacrificed their very lives for their faith. This included Masha's (and my father's) own ancestor Fëdor Androsov, who had died a martyr's death in a pillory box rather than recant his Doukhobor beliefs.

During the latter years of his stay in Siberia, my father met and married my mother, Katerina Timofeevna Mokronosova. Her parents belonged to a different Russian sect and had been exiled from the Ural Mountain area. Three of Katerina's brothers and their mother (my grandmother) also came to Canada with the exiled Doukhobor group in 1905. Within the sect that my mother's family belonged to (who called themselves *Bratstvo pravednykh* [Brotherhood of the Righteous], there had also been a great reverence for Lev Tolstoy and what he stood for in his later years. In Canada, one of my mother's brothers came to have the highest regard for all of Tolstoy's life-concepts and discussed them with all who would engage him in philosophical conversation, including me in my teenage exploratory years.

With all these influences in my family background, I naturally acquired not only a keen appreciation for the essence of the Doukhobor life-concept, but also a great admiration for Tolstoy and what he stood for, and this formative process continued throughout my younger years. Shortly after my first exposure to the Russian alphabet [*azbuka*], taught to me by my father, one of my first book-reading attempts was with the well-worn, already coverless edition (from my father's meagre library) of Tolstoy's *Thoughts for Every Day* [*Na kazhdyj den'*]. Even though the depth of thought therein did not fully register upon my consciousness at that time, from then on I had an ongoing desire to follow my father's example of reading Tolstoy's works.

In my teenage years I somehow managed to get through the thousand pages of *War and Peace*, and then the shorter *Resurrection*, which gave me an appreciation for Tolstoy as a novelist. Later, the touching philosophy expressed in

The Kingdom of God is Within You alerted me to the kinship between Tolstoy's philosophy and my own faith and inspired me to delve more deeply into the essence of Doukhoborism.

There was also a more indirect Tolstoyan influence on my life. When my father and mother emigrated to Canada from their exile in Siberia in 1905, they settled in the Blaine Lake area (not far from Prince Albert in Saskatchewan) where other members of the Popov family were already living, and it was here that I was born and grew up. This particular community evolved apart from the main Doukhobor settlement in Canada (located in the Yorkton area). In contrast to the communal orientation of the latter, most Blaine Lake residents became Independent Doukhobor farmers. Before the final break in 1906, however, those who wished to remain in the mainstream moved to the Yorkton area, including the Popov family.

In spite of my mother's attraction to the communal way of life, my father, possibly because of his experience of independence during exile and unwillingness to be tied down to what he felt was an authoritarian regime, took the family back to Blaine Lake after only two years. Here he became an Independent Doukhobor farmer for the rest of his life, in contrast to the rest of the family, who joined in the en-masse Doukhobor migration from Saskatchewan to British Columbia in 1908–1910.

In the 1930s, at the initiative of the then Doukhobor leader, Peter P. Verigin (known as *Chistjakov* — 'the Cleanser'), a Doukhobor Community Centre was established in Blaine Lake, and furnished with an excellent library featuring works by Tolstoy and Tolstoyans. I delved into many of these materials, which, along with the speeches of the leader that I heard at meetings there, helped form my early Doukhobor development.

In the late 1930s and early 1940s more waves of Doukhobor families moved west, and, in 1942, possibly as a result of the influences of my teenage years, I too made the decision to join the mainstream communal Doukhobors in British Columbia. There I met and married Dorothy Rilkoff, who came from a devout Community Doukhobor family, staunchly dedicated to their faith and to the related ideals of Lev Tolstoy. My wife's background was a great factor in raising our children in a well-rounded Doukhobor Christian outlook.

In my sixty years of life and work within the structure of the USCC (Union of Spiritual Communities of Christ) — the organization that evolved in the early 1940s from the former communal structure known as the CCUB (Christian Community of Universal Brotherhood) — I have seen many significant manifestations of a continuous thread of contact with Tolstoy's family and Tolstoyan friends and followers. I have been gratified to see that these have included an active participation by three generations of my own descendants.

In further reflecting on Tolstoy's influence on my life, I must say that my closest feeling about Lev Tolstoy — as a human being, as a great writer, and as a spiritual philosopher and humanitarian — has come to me from the recollections of a highly respected Doukhobor elder — Pavel Vasil'evich Planidin, a close associate of Pëtr V. Verigin. He had had the unusual experience of visiting with Lev Tolstoy on several occasions,[4] and engaging in intimate, friendly discussions with this Russian spiritual thinker. 'Pavlusha' himself was a totally illiterate person in the formal sense of the word, yet he exhibited a very sharp mind and keen memory. For example, when I was called upon to write some of his letters for him to his relatives and his acquaintances during his latter years in Blaine Lake, I found him to be very adept at dictating his thoughts, which were always articulate and even eloquent.

When he told me of the time that Tolstoy asked him to accompany him for his usual lengthy morning walk, I was amazed at his vivid account of their conversation, and the intimate way in which Tolstoy discussed his life-concepts with him — placing Pavel on the same spiritual level as himself. Pavel's realistic telling of his experience made it seem as if I myself were hearing and feeling Tolstoy's very presence.

Pavel also told me about his trip to Russia with Pëtr V. Verigin in 1906, to appeal to Tsar Nicholas II of Russia for a guarantee of military exemption for the Doukhobors, should they decide to return to Russia en masse. Once in Moscow, they immediately enlisted Tolstoy's help to secure an audience with the tsar (Tolstoy too, after all, wanted the Doukhobors to return to Russia). Despite the writer's best efforts, however, the tsar refused to see them. The senior minister who agreed to meet with the delegation told them that the recent uprising of students in St. Petersburg and other unrest within Russia at the time made military exemptions — or, indeed, the Doukhobors' return under any circumstances whatsoever — impossible. It was this final realization that prompted Verigin to go ahead with his plans for the trek from Saskatchewan to British Columbia.

Pavel also revealed that, during this visit, Tolstoy had criticized some of the things that he had heard about Pëtr V. Verigin's position and actions among the Doukhobors in Canada. He remembered Tolstoy telling Verigin that some of the more independently minded Doukhobors had written to him from Canada, complaining that Verigin was putting on theocratic airs and allowing his followers to virtually deify him. In response, Verigin explained to Tolstoy that he certainly was not in favour of this kind of worship, but there was little he could do to change a tradition dating back more than a century to the leadership of Savelij Kapustin in the Milky Waters area. Verigin could only offer the hope that the structure of his newly envisioned CCUB, with its delegated responsibilities to various directors, would in time change people's attitude.

In listening to these recollections of Pavel Planidin, I felt both closeness to Verigin and a respect for Tolstoy's straightforwardness. The recently published

4 For an account of one of these visits, see *Iskra*, N° 1484 (1978): 20–27. See also Chap. 7 above.

collection of correspondence between the two men[5] clearly shows that Tolstoy's respect for Verigin went far beyond his remarks in his conversations with Planidin — an indication of not only his true greatness but also his humbleness toward those whom he respected as representatives of an esteemed group of people. This esteem had been earned by the Doukhobors' willingness to endure suffering and even sacrifice their lives for what they considered to be righteous ideals — ideals that happened to closely coincide with those of Tolstoy himself.

More recently, my perceptions about Tolstoy and Doukhoborism were deeply affected by reading a condensation of Tolstoy's life-concepts entitled *Ètika khristianstva* [*Ethics of Christianity*]. This book, published by the Tolstoy Institute in the city of Ekaterinburg in 1994, was presented to me in 1998 by one of the institute's directors, Aleksandr Borisovich Gramolin. It was compiled by one of Tolstoy's later secretaries, Valentin Fëdorovich Bulgakov, while Tolstoy himself was still alive, who had proofread and approved this condensed version of his life-concepts.

Upon reading this compilation, I was struck by the similarity of Tolstoy's life-concepts with those of the Doukhobors that I had intensely studied over my lifetime, including the Doukhobor psalms, hymns, and oral sayings gleaned from elders, as well as all the documents and remembered speeches and letters of our late leaders. Apart from one small chapter in the book (on anarchism, a concept which the Doukhobors have never really properly understood), literally every word and sentence only confirmed to me — as some of our Doukhobor elders were quoted as saying to outside researchers — that Dedushka Tolstoy was like a "pillar unto the heavens," whose inner spirit had made direct connection with the Eternal Spirit of Creation and who was destined to share what he knew with all of mankind.

The famous 'Open Letter' that Tolstoy sent to the Doukhobors on 15 February 1900[6] confirmed to all Doukhobors who remained faithful to their cause that they were on a righteous pathway. In this letter he explained in vivid detail the evils of private ownership of land and its connection to violence and militarism. The Communal Doukhobors used this letter to defend their stand on communal ownership when explaining it to the outside world, and it is still held in high esteem by faithful Doukhobors to this day.

The book *Ethics of Christianity* brought back to my mind one of Pavel Planidin's recollections of his conversations with Tolstoy, wherein Tolstoy admitted his amazement at hearing some of the aspects of his evolved life-concepts — which he himself had gained through intense research and study — repeated on the lips of illiterate Doukhobor peasants. The Doukhobors had acquired them from their own psalms and oral sayings that had been passed down through the centuries from their age-old wisdom.

5 See Donskov 1995a; reproduced as Chap. 6 in the present volume.

6 See Note 50 in Chap. 5 above.

As indicated, this mutual respect between Tolstoy and the Doukhobors continues to unfold to this day, manifest in their very descendants and the legacy they carry on. One final interesting note about the affection and affinity that Tolstoy felt for the Doukhobors comes from some thoughts he revealed during his very last days on earth — something that has been little known up to now.

Upon leaving home for the last time, Tolstoy wanted to hide away from the life that was no longer giving him inner peace. Initially, he sought to seclude himself from the world at the Optina Pustyn' monastery, not far from the Shamardino nunnery where his sister Marija dwelt. While he was afforded temporary lodging there, he was harshly disillusioned when he found out that even the Optina elders, with their somewhat more broad-minded religious outlook, did not wish to incur the wrath of the Russian Orthodox hierarchy by according permanent refuge to this world-famous crusader against church orthodoxy. According to a book published by the Orthodox Church in 1995, condemning the writer's supposed heresy, Tolstoy stated after his rejection by the Optina elders that he intended to go to the Doukhobors in the Caucasus.[7]

This same statement had been orally conveyed to three Doukhobors in Europe in 1932 by none other than Valentin Fëdorovich Bulgakov, Tolstoy's former secretary and compiler of the book *Ethics of Christianity.* These delegates were on their way to Russia in an effort to help Doukhobors there emigrate to Canada or Mexico, in the light of Pëtr P. Verigin's warning of the impending danger to them from the Stalin regime. Bulgakov, then living in France, tried unsuccessfully to procure Russian visas for the delegates.[8]

Upon their return to Canada, the three delegates did pass on to the Doukhobor community what Bulgakov had told them about Tolstoy, but this news was never widely circulated. While plans to buy tickets to the Caucasus are included in some detailed statements about Tolstoy's final departure from Yasnaya Polyana, there has never been any official acknowledgement — prior to the appearance of the Orthodox Church book of 1995 — of Tolstoy's intention to go to the Doukhobors.

While this revelation may be of little importance to the world at large, it is of tremendous significance to the Doukhobors, offering further dramatic evidence of Tolstoy's admiration for the Doukhobors and their life concepts, as being on the right track toward the eventual enlightenment and spiritual progression of all mankind. This fact should most certainly serve to strengthen to

7 See Kontsevich et al. 1995: 57.

8 During this time, the Doukhobors spent several months in Germany with Bulgakov and the prominent French Tolstoyan Romain Rolland, and gave a number of public performances in Berlin, including family singing (the delegates were accompanied by their grown daughters). At each of their presentations either Bulgakov or Rolland would give brief explanations of their Doukhobor history, why they were in Canada, and how Tolstoy had given them help and worldwide prominence.

an even higher degree not only the Doukhobor reverence for their 'Dedushka Tolstoy' but also our own dedication to bring about a true rebirth of the spirit of our faith in our own lives as Doukhobors, and to do whatever is necessary to keep that spirit alive for future generations.

Grand Forks, British Columbia
27 December 2004

What Lev Tolstoy Means to Me and the Doukhobors

KOOZMA J. TARASOFF

IMAGINE WHAT SOCIETY WOULD LOOK LIKE if the leaders of the world had followed Tolstoy's philosophy of love and non-resistance to evil. We would probably have avoided two devastating world wars along with the atrocious atomic bombings of Hiroshima and Nagasaki, the Korean and Vietnam blood baths, and the wars we have witnessed in the past decade. The 9/11 attacks on America would not have happened and we would be living in a much safer world than we are now.

With co-operation and a caring attitude to our neighbours, with rejection of imperialism and narrow patriotism in favour of world humanity, we would have made major inroads to solving, through good governance, the world's problems of poverty, disease, adequate housing, education for all, cultural enrichment, and clean air and water. We would have become a creative, non-killing society.

Mahatma Gandhi and Martin Luther King Jr. (both of whom were influenced by Tolstoy) would not only have received the Nobel Peace Prize, but their actions would have been accepted as standard procedure in the annals of human behaviour. Tolstoy, Gandhi, and King were truly outstanding pioneers in human development.

For me, a person of Doukhobor background who has actively studied this society for the past fifty years, Lev Tolstoy as a moral and religious reformer has been a major influence on my life. It is not an exaggeration to say that he literally saved the Doukhobors — whose philosophy and values in life he shared — from outright extinction, and so he is respected by them as a great teacher and an authority — one who not only demonstrated better than anyone else the horror and cruelty of war but scathingly denounced it as a premeditated and legalized system of wholesale murder. As for these people who are slaying each other today, I think to myself — what great friends they could be if they only took this great man's teachings to heart!

I feel truly honoured that my ancestors in Russia burnt their firearms in 1895 and gave credence to the moral dimension of opposing the institution of war. By supporting them at this time of dire need, Tolstoy made it possible for my grandparents and many other Doukhobors to come to Canada and lead a pioneering life on the Canadian prairies.

I have always been impressed by both Tolstoy's and the Doukhobors' belief in the basic goodness of man. Tolstoy reminded us that by co-operating we can create a good life instead of hating and killing people. The purpose of life is to do good, he said. Tolstoy was sure that it was man's business to establish the Kingdom of God on earth. If we want to live in an earthly paradise and avoid world catastrophe, it is up to us to pull ourselves together and act accordingly.

While some people believe that Pëtr V. Verigin, leader in exile at the time of the arms burning, was the author of all the major ideas motivating the Doukhobors to action, I have come to realize how much Verigin owed to Tolstoy — how much he adapted Tolstoy's ideas to his own ends, to attract public attention to his cause and increase the Doukhobors' prestige in the public's eyes. In return, the Doukhobors — a group of illiterate Russian peasants with practical, caring, and imaginative minds — provided the proof Tolstoy required to show the actual existence of people who supported his ideas of universal love.

In my research I have read about Tolstoy's continuing involvement with the Doukhobors and their friends during the first decade of the twentieth century — as the Doukhobors were establishing themselves in Canada. He corresponded with Pëtr V. Verigin, he invited him along with other Doukhobor delegates to his estate at Yasnaya Polyana, and kept in active contact with his own followers — outstanding intellectuals who had pledged their help to the Doukhobor cause. These included Vladimir Bonch-Bruevich, Pavel Birjukov, Vladimir Chertkov, Leopol'd Sulerzhitskij, Ivan Tregubov, and others. As a measure of their appreciation, Doukhobors bestowed upon Tolstoy the endearing name of *Dedushka* [Grandfather]. They were delighted to be associated with a figure of such world renown. In 1987, Doukhobors erected two statues of Tolstoy, one in Saskatchewan and the other in British Columbia — gifts from the Rodina Society of Russia.[1]

One thing that has particularly impressed me is Tolstoy's new concept of a universal religion, proclaiming that God is Spirit, God is Love, God is in every single individual.[2] This free-thinking and enquiring attitude brought him into conflict with the Orthodox Church, and led to his ex-communication in 1901, inasmuch as any concept that refused to accept the divinity of Christ, the sacraments, ritual worship, and the Orthodox concept of the Trinity was

1 See the beginning of Chap. 7 above

2 See especially his treatise *The Kingdom of God is Within You* (discussed in Chap. 5).

considered too close to protestantism and rationalism. "The Kingdom of God is within us," Tolstoy wrote.

And I realized it was this same free-thinking spirit that back in the 1600s had brought Doukhoborism into being in the first place, and essentially formed its original philosophical base of God as Love and God as being within us. I was interested to note how Tolstoy criticized any attempt on the part of Doukhobor leaders toward self-aggrandizement and narrow sectarianism. He said as much to Pëtr V. Verigin during the latter's visit to Yasnaya Polyana in December 1906, noting that any material excesses, as well as any pretence to divine authority, severely compromised the spirit of Doukhoborism. He criticized Verigin himself for his aristocratic style of dress and other violations of the principle of egalitarianism. Tolstoy's influence seems to have had an effect, since Verigin, partially at least, changed his image and behaviour when he returned to Canada soon thereafter.

As a researcher, I am grateful for Tolstoy's exposure of narrow sectarianism as fundamentally inconsistent with Doukhobor philosophy. Tolstoy and his rationalistic spirit deserve our thanks for reminding us of our egalitarian and international perspective. In his enduring novels and in his life, I see Tolstoy as becoming more and more cosmopolitan, seeking to understand the world as a whole, even though his masterful literary works were populated, by and large, with Russian heroes. He was a man who embraced the whole world as his own.

I see Doukhobors as now more confident than ever in looking critically at themselves, as a result of Tolstoy's free-thinking legacy, rigorously rejecting mysticism in favour of a more rational perspective on the world. The *spirit within* remains the fountain or wellspring of the spiritual basis of the Doukhobor movement. With the inspiration of *The Kingdom of God is Within You,* Doukhobors can today bravely explore the significance of this revolutionary concept in their lives. They can dispel the popular orthodox notion of God in the sky and search instead for this spirit in their hearts and minds as well as in their deeds. While Tolstoy was not the sole author of this concept, I feel he wrote about it perhaps in greater detail than any other thinker, and devoted the greatest effort to outlining a universal religion of love, manifest in moral behaviour, more relevant to the wider world. Indeed, Tolstoy and the Doukhobors together may be seen as real reformers in the history of Christendom and spirituality.

In searching for the essence of life, Lev Tolstoy discovered one law as being supreme, the Law of Love, which he saw as capable of bringing the highest degree of happiness to all humankind and each individual in particular. Like my fellow Doukhobors, like Gandhi's followers and other seekers for truth in all ages and in all parts of the world, I too am most grateful to this giant of a man as a writer, statesman, philosopher, moralist, and reformer.

Perhaps what Lev Tolstoy has meant and still means to me can be summed up best in verse, so I shall put my concluding remarks in poetic form.

Our dear Lev Nikolaevich:
Almost a century has gone by since you died.
Yet your image and aura of the spark of the inner God lives on
in the hearts and minds of many around the world.
The central thread of Love ties us together,
gives us Spirit, and serves
as a beacon to all that is decent in life.
Your thoughts urge us
to condemn the slaughter of humans, the torture,
the suffering —
all that is wrong in our civilization.
We are the ringing bells of peace, justice, equality, and the pursuit of happiness.
We are the mothers and fathers who raise our sons and daughters
not to go to war.

"Stop that nonsense!" we say.
We are the veterans who know the meaning of war:
Away with guns, soldiers and the military,
away with generals and
politicians who have a vociferous capacity
to send our youth to be cannon fodder.
We are the multitudes —
the people of the world who deserve
life, liberty and universal humanity.
Yes, we are seekers of the new life
just as you yourself were
in your search for the Green Stick.[3]

As Spirit-Wrestlers, we embrace you,
thank you, and
celebrate your wisdom
for reminding us
that life is not worth living
if we do not stretch ourselves
towards the building of a
better,
safer,
creative,
caring and
non-killing society.

Ottawa, Ontario
28 December 2004

3 According to a legend told to Tolstoy by his elder brother Nikolaj, there was a green stick (*zelënaja palochka*) — lying buried at the edge of a ravine on the Yasnaya Polyana estate — on which was carved the secret to future universal happiness.

PART III

ARCHIVAL DOCUMENTS ON TOLSTOY AND THE DOUKHOBORS

Excerpts from Sergej Tolstoy and the Doukhobors: A Journey to Canada[1]

1. "RESOLVING QUESTIONS OF EMIGRATION"

THE PLIGHT OF THE DOUKHOBOR FASTERS in 1897 was such that sending them abroad seemed to be the only way out of a truly intolerable situation; and, in fact, the question of emigration was finally decided among them at that time — a time when all advice was useless. Even the opinion of Pëtr [V.] Verigin on this matter carried no decisive weight. At the time Pëtr Verigin was writing about this issue as follows:[2]

> Personally, I am *almost* positively *against* emigration. You see, the members of our community are in need of self-improvement, and so wherever we went, we would take our weaknesses with us; and even though an individual can generally live more freely abroad, I don't think the difference would be all that great. People are the same everywhere.

Verigin further reasoned that if, nevertheless, the emigration did take place, then

> we could hire two or three American ships and go at once.... Then there is also the question as to whether there are places free in America [for us], so that the [local] population would have no objection to our settling [there].

1 Edited and with an Introduction by Andrew Donskov, compiled by Tat'jana Nikiforova (Tolstoy Museum, Moscow), translated by John Woodsworth (Ottawa: Slavic Research Group at the University of Ottawa and Moscow: L.N. Tolstoy Museum, 1998).

2 Letter from P. V. Verigin to L. N. Tolstoy of 16 August 1898, written from Obdorsk. See Letter Nº 6 in Chap. 6 above.

Such was Pëtr Verigin's opinion. Lev Tolstoy said more than once that since he himself was not being persecuted for his faith, he had no right to advise the Doukhobors either to endure or to flee persecution; but as long as the Doukhobors were turning to him for help, he felt obligated to assist them.[3] The help offered by Lev Tolstoy, the Quakers, and a number of individuals in both Russia and England really materialized:[4] first there was the personal effort of a number of individuals — the engaging of the steamships, the search for lands, relations with the Canadian government and various institutions, working together as agents, interpreters, and guides, etc.; secondly, there were the appeals for help and publicizing the plight of the Doukhobors; and, thirdly, a certain amount of financial aid was forthcoming. However, this financial aid was not very great in comparison to what the Doukhobors spent themselves on their resettlement.

This was the situation of the Doukhobor-fasters before their emigration: the 3,000 Tiflis sect members, banished from their homes, were living in low-lying and unhealthy surroundings, without land or income, eating up the little remaining money they had got from the forced sale of their property, and dying from hunger and disease. The Kars and Elizavetpol' Doukhobors stayed at home, but were under strict police surveillance (by the Caucasus police) and forbidden to leave their villages. The reservists (former soldiers) who had turned in their cards to the authorities languished in solitude in the remote indigenous villages of Baku, Erivan, and Elizavetpol' Gubernias, almost all of them suffering from intense fever. The young people who were subject to the annual conscription refused to serve; they were initially transferred to disciplinary battalions, and later, by order of the minister of internal affairs, Ivan Goremykin, exiled to Yakut Gubernia for 18 years. Pëtr Verigin, his four brothers, the Konkins, and other prominent Doukhobors were exiled to the harshest regions of Siberia (where they still are today).

The first petition for emigration was written by Pëtr Verigin to the Empress Aleksandra Fëdorovna [wife of Nicholas II] and went as follows:

> The Lord God preserve your soul, both in this life and in the time to come.
>
> Sister Aleksandra! I, a servant of Jesus Christ, living in the dispensation and prosperity of His truth, find myself since 1886 in exile from the Doukhobor community of the Caucasus. The word *dukhoborets* [spirit-wrestler] means that

3 In a letter to Verigin (Letter N° 7) of 1 November 1898, Tolstoy wrote: "I was especially happy to read your ideas on the resettlement. I share your opinion completely — namely, that it is not the place where we live that is important, or the conditions surrounding us, but our inner mental state. Ye shall know the truth and the truth shall make you free — *everywhere*, no matter where you are. You write that you are almost against resettlement, and I am too, but living in hardship and exile, you are in a position to tell the suffering people that they should keep on suffering and hold out to the end, whereas I who live in freedom and under all the best conditions find it awkward to tell people who are suffering: Keep on suffering, keep holding on." See Letter N° 7 in Chap. 6 above.

4 In England, the case of the Doukhobor emigration was being handled by the Quakers, along with Vladimir and Anna Chertkov and their assistants. Among the Tolstoyans, the participants included Pavel Birjukov, Paul Boulanger, Leopol'd Sulerzhitskij, and many others.

we in spirit and with our soul confess God — the God of the Gospel (as in the meeting with the Samaritan woman by the well).

I beg you in Christ the Lord, sister Aleksandra, to ask your husband Nicholas to spare the Christians in the Caucasus from persecution. I am appealing to you because I feel your heart is more turned towards the Lord God. The women and children are suffering the most there now. Hundreds of husbands and fathers are incarcerated, and thousands of families are scattered around indigenous mountain villages, where the residents have been encouraged by the authorities to treat them crudely; this is especially hard for Christian women. Recently they started taking women from their children and putting them in prison. Our only crime is that we are trying as much as possible to be Christians, and that in respect to certain kinds of action we tend to get confused. You have probably heard of the doctrine of vegetarianism. We share these humanitarian views and recently gave up eating meat and drinking wine and a lot of things that lead to a life of depravity and dim the brightness of man's soul, [including] not killing animals. We do not believe it is right to take a person's life under any circumstances; killing anyone, even a brigand, to us is tantamount to a decision to kill Christ. And that is the main cause. The state demands that our brethren learn to bear arms, to be well trained to murder; Christians do not agree to that and they are put in prison, beaten and punished with starvation, and their sisters and mothers are crudely treated as women. Very often we are met with mocking cries of "Where is your God? Why does he not save you?" Well, our God is in heaven and on earth and He does all according to his will (Psalms of David 113 and 134). This is all the more lamentable because all this is taking place in a Christian country. Our community in the Caucasus consists of about 20,000 people. Is it possible that such a small number could cause harm to the state structure by not being conscripted? Right now, even though they are being conscripted, it is useless, as thirty of them are now in the Ekaterinograd [Ekaterinburg] fortress in the disciplinary battalion, where they are only being tortured. We consider man to be the temple of the living God, and there is no way we can prepare ourselves to kill him, even though we ourselves be threatened with death. The best thing to do would be to settle us in some remote area where we could live peacefully and be about our work. We are willing to fulfil any state obligations in the form of taxes, but we cannot become soldiers. If the government finds it impossible to agree to this, then let them give us the right to emigrate to one of the European countries. We would gladly go to England, or better still to America, where we have a multitude of brothers in the Lord Jesus Christ.

With all my heart I pray to the Lord for the prosperity of your family.

Christ's servant Pëtr Vasil'evich Verigin

This letter apparently never reached its destination. Later petitions were written to Grand Prince Mikhail Nikolaevich and the Empress Marija Fëdorovna.[5]

5 The text of the petition addressed to the widowed Empress Marija Fëdorovna, wife of Alexander III, dated 22 September 1897, coincides in many respects with the text of that addressed to the Empress Aleksandra Fëdorovna. The petition was signed by Vasilij Popov, Ivan Abrosimov, Nikolaj Zibarov, and Vasilij Potapov, trustees of the Caucasus Doukhobor community. Among thirty-nine other petitions addressed to the royal name, on 29 October 1897 it was passed along

This last petition reached its destination, and the Doukhobors received the following response, which was delivered to Ivan Abrosimov on 24 February 1898 from the Tiflis governor's office.

> Memo N°154
> In regard to the petition addressed to Her Imperial Majesty, Empress Marija Fëdorovna, by the Doukhobor fasters, expelled in 1895 from Akhalkalak district to other districts of Tiflis Gubernia, in respect to the grouping of the Doukhobor fasters into a single settlement with exemption from military service, or to permission for all of them to emigrate, the following decree is issued:
> 1. Exemption from military service is not granted, and
> 2. The Doukhobor fasters, except, of course, for those of conscription age and those who have not completed their military service, may be allowed to go abroad under the following conditions:
> a) a valid foreign-travel passport be secured;
> b) emigrants pay their own travel costs;
> c) emigrants sign, upon departure, a guarantee that they will never come again within the borders of the Empire, on the understanding that the penalty for violation of this last point will be exile to remote regions.
> Their petition to be grouped together in a single place is not granted.

This official decree set off a tremendous movement among the Doukhobors, leading to their emigration from Russia far across the ocean to a welcoming Canada.

The new head of civil affairs in the Caucasus, Prince Golitsyn, was even convinced that emigration was the best way out of the situation in which the Doukhobors found themselves (a situation wholly created by the Caucasus authorities). However, in spite of their strong desire to emigrate, for a whole six months the Doukhobors were unable to do anything about it. Some of them thought all they had to do was to cross the Turkish border and the rest would take care of itself.

In the summer of 1898, impatient to get on with the emigration, thousands of Doukhobors (of the group of Tiflis exiles) almost unthinkingly moved on

for consideration to the chief of civil affairs in the Caucasus, Senator and Adjutant-General Prince Grigorij Sergeevich Golitsyn.

In a secret message of 22 November 1897, Prince Golitsyn wrote to the minister of internal affairs, Ivan Logginovich Goremykin, as follows:

"In passing along the said petition for Your Excellency's consideration, I am privileged to add that I myself see no impediment to granting the Doukhobor fasters permission to emigrate; indeed, I believe the granting of this request would help bring about a solution to the Doukhobor question, for the removal of such an unruly and dangerous element beyond our borders would be most desirable. Even a different outcome of this petition would not be without benefit: it is possible that foreign governments may not wish to accept anarchistic propagandists under their jurisdiction and refuse to grant the petition of the Doukhobor-fasters; or the fasters themselves, after emigrating, may have their hopes disappointed. In either case the result would undoubtedly have a sobering influence on the sick minds of the sectarians" (OR GMT, III/1, KP 3405).

Batoum to board ship for Cyprus. At that time the Quakers and others assisting the Doukhobors were actually considering the possibility of relocating them to Cyprus, but it was expected that, at first, no more than one or two hundred would go there as an experiment; the exodus of 1,100 was a complete surprise. No steamer had yet been engaged, and it was still not clear whether the British government would even permit such [mass] immigration.

It is difficult to say who was responsible for this unfortunate mistake, or whether it was an actual mistake and not just an unhappy circumstantial coincidence. In the spring of 1898, once permission for emigration had been obtained, the Doukhobors sent two emissaries to England along with their families — [Ivan] Ivin and [Pëtr] Makhortov. From there they travelled to Cyprus along with Prince Khilkov, where they were convinced that Cyprus was not suitable for resettlement: it was only a "burnt-out stump," they said, where it was impossible even to live, let alone make a living. However, the telegrams they sent to the Caucasus to this effect were a little too late — the Doukhobors had already set sail from Batoum.

At one point the English government suddenly demanded a guarantee of 150 roubles per person. The Quaker committee, however, quickly took up the cause and within a few days collected 165,000 roubles. The steamship Durand was soon engaged from the Messagers Maritimes line, and on 26th of August 1,126 Doukhobors landed on Cyprus.

Notwithstanding the considerable help afforded the Cyprus Doukhobors by the Quakers, the inhospitable climate and the unaccustomed living conditions on this sunburnt desert island meant that the Doukhobors, already weakened from their life in the Caucasus, lost more than a hundred of their number to the cruel Cyprus fever, and a great deal of money was wasted on the venture. The upshot was that [onward] emigration from Cyprus became an absolute necessity.[6]

But if Cyprus was unsuitable for resettlement, what other countries were in a position to accept such a large number of immigrants (7,500) with the limited financial resources that they had and under the non-negotiable conditions they had set: half of them to emigrate by 1 January 1899 and to a country with no military-service requirement?

In the United States there are now no longer any inexpensive, let alone gratuitous lands, that are suitable; what's more, emigration to the United States requires a considerable guarantee for each person, more than the Doukhobors can afford. In Argentina the climatic conditions are superb, there are lands available, but one cannot count on the unreliable Argentinian government and on an exemption from military service; in addition, emigration to Argentina entailed these disadvantages: the high cost of the move, the fact that neither the Russians nor the English people helping the Doukhobors

6 On the Doukhobors' life on Cyprus, see Birjukov 1908.

knew Spanish, as well as the Quakers' disinclination toward such a move. Emigration to Cape Colony[7] or Australia had to be ruled out just because of the high cost involved.

Thus emigration to Canada seemed to be the most feasible alternative. A liberal, almost independent government, exemption from military service, splendid soil, a low population density and advantageous immigration conditions — all these spoke in favour of moving to Canada. At first it seemed as though the cold Canadian climate might be unsuitable for the Doukhobors, who had been living in the Caucasus. But they had been living in very high [altitude] areas, which of course were quite cold. One would often hear them say: "Our people are used to the cold." Indeed, in the Cold Mountains where the Tiflis Doukhobors resided, not only was wheat impossible to grow, but even barley would scarcely ripen; the Kars settlements were also located on the high Armenian plateau, where there are no fruit trees; it was only the Elizavetpol' villages that were at a somewhat lower level than the others, but even they were in the mountains. Hence the Canadian climate was not all that dissimilar in temperature to that of the Doukhobor settlements in the Caucasus.

In recent times Canada, thanks to a reasonable government, the opening of Hudson's Bay Company lands to new settlement, and the increasing difficulties in immigration to the United States, is developing very quickly, and the majority of emigrants [from Europe] are heading there. Britishers, Germans, Finns, Lithuanians, Mennonites,[8] Swedes, Icelanders, Jews, Galicians etc. — all of these are finding land in Canada, along with the opportunity to live free of poverty; instances of emigration from the United States to Canada are also common.

Thus the question of where the Doukhobors should go was decided in favour of Canada — not only because emigration to other countries was practically impossible, but also because Canada offered exceptionally favourable conditions for immigration.

This solution was originally proposed by the well-known Russian emigrant P. A. Kropotkin, who, after discussing it with University of Toronto professor James Mavor, suggested this plan to the Quakers and Russians in England. The Doukhobors, having heard a great deal about [North] America and wanting to go there especially, gladly seized the opportunity. Wasting no time, the Doukhobor emissaries Ivin and Makhortov, who had just returned from Cyprus, accompanied by Dmitrij Khilkov and Aylmer Maude (an Englishman who had previously lived in Russia and was sympathetic to the Doukhobors), set out for Canada for negotiations with the Canadian government and to look for lands there. At the same time Leopol'd Sulerzhitskij went to see the

7 *Cape Colony* — a British colony in South Africa.

8 *Mennonites* — a Protestant sect named after its founder, Menno Simons (1496–1561). Occasionally the Germans who lived in two colonies in Chernigov Gubernia in Russia (from 1772) were mistakenly referred to as Mennonites.

Doukhobors [in the Caucasus], and then to Batoum, to determine how many people were prepared to leave, what financial resources they had, and, in case of favourable news from Canada, to charter a ship to transport, as a first priority, all the exiled Tiflis Doukhobors, since they were in an especially difficult position.

The emissaries' trip to Canada was successful.[9] The Canadian government agreed to an exceptional arrangement: to accept the Doukhobors that winter and to grant them privileges they would not normally grant even to 'English-speaking' immigrants — i.e., Britishers, British Colonials and Americans. They guaranteed the Doukhobors full religious freedom, exempted them from military service in any form, offered them land on the same terms as other immigrants and secured for their emissaries and all the agents involved in the emigration free passage on all Canadian railways. Since the government normally pays emigration agents and steamship companies a five-dollar (ten-rouble) commission for each adult ticket and for every two children's tickets, and since in this case the emigration agents were representatives of the Doukhobors themselves (along with the Quakers), the government agreed to put these so-called bonus payments into a general Doukhobor fund; furthermore, they offered the Doukhobors an additional one dollar per person.

One of the difficulties in conducting the whole emigration procedure was the need for quick communication with people all over the globe: the Doukhobors in the Caucasus, living in three different regions (Tiflis Gubernia, Elizavetpol' Gubernia and Kars Oblast), Sulerzhitskij in Batoum, Vladimir Chertkov and the Quakers in England, the emissaries in Canada and Lev Tolstoy in Tula Gubernia. This was one of the reasons I went to England in September,[10] where I was joined by two other Doukhobor representatives — Nikolaj Zibarov and Abrosimov. During my brief stay in England the conditions of the emigration became more defined: a telegram was received from [Aylmer] Maude in Canada to the effect that the government was prepared to accept the Doukhobors now that the Canadian Pacific Railway had agreed to transport them at half-price; the main point was settled, too — how the move of the first group of the exiled Tiflis Doukhobors would be financed. Expenses for the trip and provisions en route amounted to approximately 89,000 roubles. The Doukhobors themselves had about 45,000, the remainder would come partly from moneys collected in Russia, partly from contributions by the Purleigh colonists (a group of Englishmen who had started a land commune in Essex County[11]), and partly by the Quakers. While I was in England

9 For a detailed description of this trip, see Prince Khilkov's seven-part account in *Juzhnoe Obozrenie*, reproduced in English translation in Woodsworth (1999:121–64).

10 Sergej Tolstoy's trip to England to see about the Doukhobors' emigration is described in interesting detail in his book *Ocherki bylogo* [Sketches from the Past].

11 In the Tolstoy archives there is a copy of a letter written to the Doukhobors from the settlers of the English Brotherhood Society in Essex, dated 5 December 1897 (the following excerpt is from

I attended several Quaker committee meetings. At the time the Quakers were still favouring emigration to Cyprus and not entirely predisposed toward the move to Canada. This was evident in their readiness to take on full responsibility for the Cyprus resettlement only, while they would contribute to the Canadian emigration only to the extent that they could.

Upon my return to Russia I learnt that Sulerzhitskij, who had been in Batoum acting as an intermediary between the Doukhobors and the outside world, had been obliged by external circumstances to leave there and go to central Russia. He had already managed to charter one boat for 60,000 roubles and was looking into another for the Kars and Elizavetpol' Doukhobors, but his activity was cut short at the height of the negotiations.[12] While a number of Doukhobors did live in Batoum and they received considerable help from the British consul, a Mr. [P.] Stevens, the process required the participation of people who could represent the Doukhobors as agents, interpreters and guides, interacting not only with the Doukhobors but also with the Russian authorities, the shipowners, the ship's crew, the Canadian government and so forth.

It was then decided that Sulerzhitskij and I would go to the Caucasus, and then to Canada. Since our involvement required our securing prior permission from the Russian authorities, we headed first of all to Tiflis. Fortunately, Prince Golitsyn, the head of civil affairs in the Caucasus, saw no objection to our helping the Doukhobors in the practical procedures connected with the immigration.

On 9 November 1898[13] Leopol'd Sulerzhitskij and I set out from Yasnaya Polyana. After a day and a half's rail journey, followed by a two-day ride along the Georgian Military Road, we arrived at Tiflis. Once we had booked into a hotel there, we decided to register at once with the police, and in general to

the original English text of the letter as it appeared in *The New Order* of January 1898, p. 99, kindly supplied by Dr. M. J. de K. Holman from the Leeds Russian Archive):

> DEAR COMRADES, We know much of you not only through the public press, but through Vladimir Tchertkoff and other friends of Leo Tolstoy who in order to be near the Colony and to one another, have come to live here; but you probably never heard of us. [...] we the colonists are men and women who are trying to live by co-operation instead of competition, and to enable others to do the same. [...] And we write not so much to express our unavailing sorrow for your sufferings, nor our admiration, however great, for your endurance, but to thank you for your example; to tell you that in our temptations and our slight privations we shall think of the Doukhobortsi and that this thought will help us to hold fast to that ideal of good will for which you have sacrificed so much more than we ever can.

The letter is signed by Lewis Hone, Arthur Drover, William Hone, Maud Hone, Edward Shaw, William Sinclair, Jan Hone, Hubert Hammond, Sudbury Protheroe, Albert Hone, Arnold Eiloart, I. Wright, Evgenij Sukachev, Marsland (OR GMT, S. L. Tolstoy collection, file 12).

12 By decree N° 963 of 24 October 1898, the chief of civil affairs in the Caucasus, Prince Golitsyn, declared Sulerzhitskij's presence in the Caucasus undesirable and ordered him to leave the area immediately (OR GMT, III/I, KP 3405).

13 OS, 21 November NS; NS dates hereinafter appear in square brackets: 9 [21] November 1989.

do everything legally and openly. After that I thought I would look up my long-time friend Jurij Miljutin,[14] editor of the *Kavkaz* [Caucasus] newspaper and ask him for help and advice in dealing with the Caucasus authorities. Sulerzhitskij became concerned and was very afraid that the police would come and expel him once more from the Caucasus. We registered; no police came to the hotel. That same evening I learnt that Jurij Miljutin lived in a cottage near Ovchaly just one [coach] station from Tiflis.

On 14 [26] November I went to see Miljutin at Ovchaly. He greeted me as though we had not seen each other for but a month or two, instead of nine years. He was rather indifferent on the whole to the Doukhobor cause; while acknowledging that they had been treated rather unfairly, he said that the Doukhobors relished their suffering and so brought the persecution upon themselves, that while [Prince] Shervashidze [governor of Tiflis Gubernia, where the Cossack army attacked the Doukhobors burning their arms in 1895] had made a mistake, he always bore them good will, that the state had no choice but to persecute them since they did not recognize the state, that they were money-lovers and so forth.

He told me, among other things, about a conversation between a Doukhobor named Vorobëv and the governor. The governor asked him whether it was true that during Shervashidze's punishment [of the Doukhobors] a rumour was going around that they had seen [a vision of] Pëtr Verigin in the clouds, and therefore they had all fallen on their knees. Vorobëv answered: "Maybe someone saw Pëtr Vasil'evich [Verigin] in the clouds, but why should that be surprising? I've seen Armenians walk through the fields carrying a decorated tablet and singing, and believing that will make it rain, and you're not surprised by that!"

Miljutin is generally quite critical of the whole Caucasus administration. He doesn't think the much-touted 'Armenian national question' is a real issue — the Russians tend to blow it out of proportion; there are even less grounds for [believing in] the 'Georgian question.' Moreover, he faults the Caucasus administrators for not knowing the local languages, which places them at the mercy of interpreters. Local indigenous administrators are generally no better, seeing that they can do pretty much what they like — again, because [their overseers] do not know the local languages, they are unable to control them. As editor of *Kavkaz*, Miljutin wrote a series of articles describing this situation, but this displeased [Tsar] Alexander III and he noted somewhere in the margins: "Let the Georgians and Armenians learn Russian, and not Russians the local dialects."

Miljutin advised me: (1) to sign in at Prince Golitsyn's, (2) to get in touch with his chief of staff Mitskevich, explain our business to him and ask him to

14 *Jurij Nikolaevich Miljutin* — son of a government official of the 1860s, Nikolaj Alekseevich Miljutin, and nephew to Minister of War Dmitrij A. Miljutin.

arrange a special appointment with Golitsyn prior to Monday (his consultation day) and (3) to contact Golitsyn in advance through his adjutant Svechin — this Miljutin took it upon himself to do. All this, it turned out, was necessary to get permission for something that should not have required permission — namely, for Sulerzhitskij and me to stay in the Caucasus without being expelled, and to set about our private, purely practical business of helping the Doukhobors with their emigration.

On the morning of 15 [27] November I signed in at Prince Golitsyn's and went to see Mitskevich. Sulerzhitskij hid himself in Tiflis with his friend Julia Pashchenko,[15] as he feared that the police might be taken aback at his deliberate return to the Caucasus after being expelled and would send him away again before I had a chance to petition Golitsyn to grant us freedom of movement.

Golitsyn's chief of staff, Justin Vasil'evich Mitskevich, the son of a priest of the Western region, does not make a pleasant impression. He is devout, cunning and servile with the prince, and appears to have a significant, but less than beneficial, influence on affairs. He is now serving under his third head of civil affairs and is one of the chief instigators behind the persecution of the Doukhobors, as well as of Khilkov, Dadiani,[16] Prokopenko, and others. I tried to be as polite as I could with him, to the point of overusing the term 'Your Excellency.' Mitskevich promised to convey my request to his superior.

Sulerzhitskij did not spend the night in the hotel room but remained in hiding. He finally appeared in the morning, whereupon the hotel owner at once informed the police, and within five minutes a constable appeared, requesting him to present himself to the chief of police. A half-hour later I received a telephone call requesting me to go to Golitsyn's palace. I went at once.

The police chief met me in the reception room and told me that the head of civil affairs would most likely grant our request. In about a quarter of an hour I was taken in to see Prince Golitsyn. They say, and I later confirmed this to be true, that Prince Golitsyn is accustomed to let no visitor leave without an authoritative bellow; however, on this occasion he received me most courteously.

First of all I gave him a letter from my father,[17] asking him to allow Sulerzhitskij and me to take care of the business of the Doukhobor emigration. The letter was mistakenly addressed to "Grigorij Grigor'evich" Golitsyn (instead of "Grigorij Sergeevich"), and I very much feared that this might count against us. He, however, did not notice, or at least pretended not to notice. He

15 *Julia Grigor'evna Pashchenko* — a resident of Tiflis persecuted by the local authorities for helping the Doukhobors.

16 *Prince Georgij Aleksandrovich Dadiani* (1856–1900) — grandson of the Crown Prince Mingrelija, a veteran of the Russo-Turkish war, a colonel. Influenced by Prince D. A. Khilkov, he adopted ideas of free religion, resigned his commission, and settled with his family on a small plot of land near Nal'chik, along with others of similar persuasion.

17 L. N. Tolstoy's letter to Prince G. S. Golitsyn dated 8 November 1898. See *PSS* 71:482–83.

read my father's letter aloud (except for the salutation), and then started talking. He talked a great deal, so that I had to say very little. He said he was ready to do everything, that he would not demand the signatures of Doukhobor reservists usually required of reservists going abroad, that he would allow the Caucasus exiles to leave as well, that he hoped the Doukhobors would do well in Canada, which he himself had once visited, and that he would allow Sulerzhitskij and me to take care of the Doukhobors' emigration, even though he had received a query from the minister of internal affairs as to why Sulerzhitskij had been re-admitted [to the Caucasus],[18] but he was willing to accept responsibility for his being re-admitted, only that he should leave at once for Batoum and then set out with the first shipload of Doukhobors and never again return to Tiflis. He then began to speak about my father's influence on the Doukhobors, suggesting that he was almost wholly responsible for the latest movement among the Doukhobors. I tried to persuade him otherwise, but evidently without success.

From Golitsyn's office I returned to the hotel, where I saw Sulerzhitskij. It turned out that as soon as he had presented himself to the chief of police, the latter received a telephone call from the office of the head of civil affairs, enquiring as to Sulerzhitskij's whereabouts, to which he answered "Here." "Where?" "In my office." This was fortunate: as it turned out, Sulerzhitskij was not only not in hiding, but was even sitting in the office of the chief of police. The whole time I was talking with Prince Golitsyn, there was Sulerzhitskij, as if under arrest, sitting alone in the office of the chief of police, and he was not released until the prince gave the order. Thus it was that through cautious requests and a happy coincidence of circumstances we achieved something that no one, it seemed, had the right to deny us — namely, to stay where we wanted to, see who we wished to see and take any actions that were not prohibited by law. It is possible that if I had not registered with Golitsyn, or if he had taken offence at being addressed as "Grigorij Grigor'evich" instead of Grigorij Sergeevich, or if he had not been in the right frame of mind, we would simply have been expelled from the Caucasus.

We sent a telegram to my father at once: "Permission [granted to] both, tomorrow [we] proceed [to] Batoum."

18 A reference to a memorandum, dated 7 September 1898, addressed to G. S. Golitsyn, signed by Minister of Internal Affairs Ivan Logginovich Goremykin. It reads in part: "I consider it my duty to ask Your Excellency to recommend that the authorities under your command pay particular attention to preventing any communication between the Tolstoyan agitators and the Doukhobors living in the Caucasus, in view of their harmful influence on these people. In my opinion, therefore, it would be highly inadvisable to permit one of Count Tolstoy's most zealous followers, former art student Leopol'd Sulerzhitskij, to proceed to Batoum for closer communication with the Doukhobors. In reporting this to you, I also feel myself bound to add that there are no grounds of necessity for the efforts and participation of the local authorities in respect to the issue of where the Doukhobors should go from the Caucasus or where they are to establish themselves abroad" (OR GMT, III/ I, KP 3405).

We spent the evening at Mrs. Pashchenko's. Mrs. Pashchenko was known to the Doukhobors as *Babushka* [Grandmother]. She did a lot for them, communicating with them, writing petitions, conveying money, etc., for which the authorities had decreed she be expelled from Tiflis, even though this would have deprived her of any means of subsistence; it was only by special dispensation that she was left alone for a year until her son finished high school.

On 17 [29] November we left for Batoum. Along the way we decided to stop for about three hours in Skra,[19] where some of the exiled Doukhobors were living. We alighted from the train in Skra on a quiet moonlit night. In the darkness we heard someone ask: "Alësha, is that you?" It was a Doukhobor named Chernenkov, who had come out to meet someone else, without success, but met us instead; he recognized Sulerzhitskij and was overjoyed to see him. We went with Chernenkov to Zibarov's hut; another Doukhobor stayed behind to watch over our things. Zibarov's hut, dug out of the earth, with damp brick walls and no ceiling, was home to thirty-six people; when the Doukhobors learnt of our arrival, many more people crowded in to the place; the 'old ones' [*starichki*] came. This is what the Doukhobors call the head of the household. The Doukhobors all use diminutives in addressing each other: Alësha, Vasja, etc., and even the children address their fathers this way; it is only when they grow older and "begin to understand," as one Doukhobor later explained to me, that they start calling their father 'Parent' or 'Old one' [*Starichok*]. They call their mother 'Nanny' [*Njanja*].

They seated us in an icon-less corner[20] (of course!), under a hanging lamp. Around us were solid-looking, shaven but moustached faces with sharp features, their hair falling loosely over their foreheads, the women dressed in a kind of plaited coat and ribboned hat; blue and red are the predominant colours in their clothing. They were all glad to see Sulerzhitskij, whom most of them knew and looked upon as their saviour.

As to ships and so forth we did not learn anything new here, but all the Doukhobors were greatly impatient to leave the country as soon as possible. The exiles had already submitted their passport applications and been given permission to emigrate. The only ones refused permission were the current year's recruits; they had 'drawn their lots' (or rather, their lots had been drawn for them), and in spite of their refusal to bear arms, they, like the recruits of previous years, were supposed to set out within a few days for the Transcaspian Oblast to sign up. I do not know exactly how many of these young people there are, but it seems to me that between twenty-five and thirty Doukhobors in all have been conscripted this year.

19 Skra Station in Kutais Gubernia.

20 *Icon-less corner* — Russian Orthodox households would invariably have a corner in their home where an icon was displayed. Such outward symbols of faith were rejected by the Doukhobors.

Since the new recruits' refusal of military service represented circumstances not foreseen in the law, the conscription of this year's recruits depended exclusively on the administration's interpretation of the law. With a different interpretation the recruits might have been excused; why, then, this new cruelty — the detainment of this year's recruits?

One of the Doukhobors in Zibarov's hut was a soldier's wife from Kars. Her husband was in Yakut Oblast, and she asked for advice on how she and other wives of Yakut exiles could get there — either by convoy or at their own expense. I also met one *starichok* who was almost a hundred years old — Grisha Bokovoj,[21] a veteran of Sevastopol'. He also wanted to see 'Canadia.' They made good-natured fun of him.

Around ten o'clock the Doukhobors accompanied us back to the station and we went on to Batoum.

We arrived in Batoum on the morning of 18 [30] November and booked into the Belle-vue Hotel right at the seaside. All the ships sailing into port passed directly in front of us and we would be able to see when our ships arrived. The weather was splendid. First of all we went to see the British consul, Stevens, whose office was next door to our hotel. Here too was Matievich's shipping office, whose chief agent was an Englishman, [W. H.] Stuart, a friend of Stevens. We found them both. Stevens is gentle, pleasant in conversation — a blond, reserved Englishman. He appears to have an altruistic interest in the Doukhobors, but the emigration of the Doukhobors is good for British policy, and as a patriotic Britisher he knows this. In general, he is not opposed to doing a good deed, as long as it doesn't cost him too much; as a forty-year-old bachelor he greatly cherishes his peace and comfort; for a foreigner, he speaks Russian very well, and the Doukhobors are very trusting of him. Stuart is an Englishman of a rather inferior sort. He is kind, ready to do a good deed, but not beyond making himself a profit while doing it. The main things in life for him are money and business.

This is what we learnt about the state of affairs: at Sulerzhitskij's initiative — through Matievich's office on the one hand and through the shipping agents Westcott & Laurance in London on the other — a ship had been engaged, the *Lake Huron* (which he had chartered even before his expulsion from the Caucasus), to transport the first party of Doukhobor exiles. This was a rather old ship, built in 1883, belonging to the Beaver Line, a company which had once carried mail between Liverpool and Canada, but which got squeezed out by [newer and] better ships, and was now offering its ships for transoceanic transport of troops, cattle, emigrants and various goods.

21 *Grigorij Bokovoj* (Bokov) — a Doukhobor who served in the army from 1844 to 1855; he took part in three campaigns, as well as the battle at Inkerman on 24 October 1854. See also Note 81 in Letter N° 26 in Part IV below.

Before his expulsion Sulerzhitskij had chartered this ship through Matievich's office (that is, through Stuart) for £5,000, but during the negotiations one of the 'friends' in England, wanting to help, began to make enquiries about the charter. When the shipowners got wind of it, they decided their clients were in something of a hurry and raised the price to £5,500.

I think if the affair had been handled properly, that is, by an astute businessman in England, the same *Lake Huron* might have been engaged at less cost; it might have been possible not only to avoid the price increase, but also to save the 10 per cent commission charged by the middlemen — i.e., Westcott & Laurance and Matievich's office.

Before his departure Sulerzhitskij had left detailed instructions for Stuart regarding the conditions of hire. He had specified, for example, that the space devoted to passenger accommodations be set out exactly, and a minimum daily amount of fresh water should be agreed to; he assumed the bunks would be brought in and installed by the shipowners, but in Sulerzhitskij's absence these points were not backed up by sufficient guarantees. Thus, for example, the contract did not specify precisely what quarters on the ship would be allotted to the emigrants, but since, according to the agreement, "the whole available space in the steamer...except such as is required for the accommodation of the Master, Officers, Engineers and Crew, for the storage of bunker coals, stiffening, provisions, stores, apparel, furnishings, etc. and for the navigation and working of the steamer, is to be placed at the disposal of the charterer,"[22] the captain could, according to this condition, grant or not grant us space at his own discretion.

The main thing we found out — something that made us very upset — was that the ship had been engaged without any bunks. Hence, during the three days the *Lake Huron* was moored in Batoum, all the bunks would have to be built, all the baggage loaded and more than two thousand people embarked — an almost impossible task.

A second ship, the *Lake Superior*, belonging to the same line, had just been chartered through the same procedure for the Doukhobors from Elizavetpol' and Kars. It was newer than the *Huron* (1885), with a somewhat broader beam and a greater number of first- and second-class cabins.

On the eve of our arrival Stuart had telegraphed to England enquiring as to the date of the *Lake Huron*'s departure from Liverpool; he also asked whether in fact the *Huron* had no bunks, but received no reply, as the telegraph had broken down and was not working. This, it turns out, is a common occurrence in Batoum; besides, telegrams usually take a long time, as Batoum is linked to the outside world only by a wire through Tiflis and along the Georgian Military Road; to date there is still no telegraph line along the eastern shore of the Black Sea.

22 Cited from the original English text of the "memorandum of agreement" for the *Lake Superior*, which had identical wording (see Donskov 1998a: 373–75).

The consul and Stuart handed us all the correspondence and telegrams concerning the emigration, along with the agreement with the shipowners on the engagement of the *Huron*. From all this the following points became evident: (1) back in August all the exiles together had purchased three banker's cheques in the amount of £413.3s.4d each, for a total of £4,239.10s. Of this amount, one of the cheques was spent on transporting about a thousand people to Cyprus; the other two were sent to England for the engagement of the *Lake Huron*. This sum, however — together with 32,300 roubles from Lev Tolstoy and 9,700 from the Purleigh colony — was not sufficient for hiring the ship, and in response to a telegram from Vladimir Chertkov another 10,000 roubles had been sent to England by the Doukhobor exiles shortly before our arrival. (2) The *Lake Huron* was supposed to be bringing tea, sugar and oatmeal from England. (3) For the hire of the *Lake Superior* cheques had been sent to the London County Bank in the following amounts: £5,285.8s on 18 November (N.S.), £533.16s.6d, £105.2s.14d and £214.11s.9d, all on 24 November. Altogether the Elizavetpol' and Kars Doukhobors had sent 77,000 [roubles] (50,000 from the former and 27,000 from the latter). (4) The consul had already received permission from the Canadian government [for the Doukhobors] to disembark in Canada. (5) The Beaver Line is unwilling to go to the trouble of installing bunks on the Superior, just as with the Huron, although the Superior is bringing materials for this purpose. (6) Negotiations are underway regarding insurance for both ships. As it turned out later, this insurance was rather a waste of money. True, if the ships had sunk before arriving at Batoum, the return of funds would make sense, but the risk was not that great; but what would be the use of getting insurance money if a ship went down with the emigrants? But it is customary to have insurance. Matievich was an insurance agent, and Sulerzhitskij and I raised no objection, not realizing what was actually involved.

That same day some Doukhobors who lived in Batoum came to see us about the emigration. These included the exile Vasilij Popov, as well as Mikhail Popov from Elizavetpol'. Vasilij Popov is tall and stout, a pleasant-mannered and clever Doukhobor, not without a certain degree of Ukrainian humour (he is of Ukrainian stock). In appearance he resembles more a Poltava landowner than a fanatical Doukhobor. He was once quite wealthy, but now after four years of eating away at his possessions, he has very little left. He is one of the main Doukhobor leaders. Mikhail Popov is a gentle and clever peasant-fellow, but not outstanding. Both expressed an overwhelming impatience to leave, both for themselves and on behalf of their families. They were very happy we had come and that things were at last getting underway.

At the time the Doukhobor exiles were living in crowded quarters in Georgian villages along the Transcaucasian Railway, eating up their last remaining funds and ready to get going at the earliest opportunity. The Elizavetpol' Doukhobors by this time had already sold their possessions and were also waiting in expectation, but their situation was much better than that of the exiles — they were living at home and sustaining themselves on the bread produced from this year's fine harvest. As it turned out, the Kars Doukhobors had also sold their possessions and were waiting until they, too, could set out. Those of the two latter groups who had been exiled one by one to Baku and Erivan Gubernias had been allowed to procure a passport and go to Batoum, where they were to rejoin their families and leave together with them. The exiles numbered more than two thousand, all told. At the moment they were beginning to trickle in to Batoum; about thirty of them were already staying with a Molokan named Tret'jakov.

On 19 November [1 December] Sulerzhitskij and I decided to divide our activities: he would look after the exiles' affairs and the *Huron*, while I would see about the Kars and Elizavetpol' Doukhobors and the *Superior*; naturally we would help each other as we could. We recommended Mikhail Popov return home and we wrote the following letter to the Doukhobors in Elizavetpol' and Kars:

> Apply for your foreign passports immediately and ask that they be sent at once to the Chief of Police at Batoum. Do not get transit permits until you are advised to. Russian money is not valid in Canada; therefore collect each family's money and give it to one person who will go and stay in Batoum; this is necessary. I ask the Kars Doukhobors to draw up a list by families of those who will be going with those from Elizavetpol'. But this cannot be done before you receive an indication of how many can go with the Elizavetpol' Doukhobors.

In reading this letter, one must bear in mind that all the Doukhobors were under police surveillance and had no right to leave home without the authorities' permission; like criminals, they were given a transit permit for each trip, valid for ten days, and we feared that once these ten days had expired the authorities might not allow the Doukhobors to stay on Batoum; this fear, as it turned out later, was not justified.

20 NOVEMBER [2 DECEMBER] 1898

And so both ships have been engaged. The *Huron* is supposed to arrive around 4 [16] December; nothing is yet known as to the *Lake Superior*'s date of departure from England or its arrival, but it will not be long in coming. It is important not to lose any time and take action, especially for Sulerzhitskij and the exiles, since there is little time remaining before the Huron arrives. We have to find accommodation for 2,000 people in Batoum, work out the departure timetables and order the trains with the Transcaucasian Railway, prepare the materials for the construction of bunks on the *Huron*, get the provisions ready [for the voyage], find the wherewithal to buy the provisions, the wood and so forth for the exiles, as they no longer have any money left to speak of.

The problem of finding accommodation in Batoum was solved through the consul, Mr. P. Stevens. In August, when the first group of Doukhobor exiles left for Cyprus, they stayed in Batoum for about three weeks before departure. Initially they camped out in the open air under pouring rain, but Governor Samojlov allowed them to take shelter in army barracks that were empty at the time; however, this disposition was very quickly reversed by Prince Golitsyn, and the Doukhobors again found themselves outdoors in the pouring rain. Then the Swiss owner of a kerosene factory in Batoum, a Mr. Richner, allowed them the use of his factory, which was not in operation at the time; they stayed about two weeks there and proceeded from there directly to the ship. Mr. Stevens now got in touch once more with Mr. Richner, and since the factory was still not working, the latter offered it to the Doukhobors at no charge, with the simple provision that they would clean out the water closets [before leaving].

To order the trains and fix the departure dates, I was obliged to go to Tiflis and arrange this at the offices of the Transcaucasian Railway.

For the construction of the bunks Sulerzhitskij obtained from Stuart a plan of the *Huron*, drew up instructions on how to install the bunks and calculated the approximate amount of materials needed. He also found out the cost of wood in Batoum. We were obliged to decide primarily on alder, as there was almost nothing else or it was extremely expensive. Even the prices for alder were quite high.

As to provisions, it was decided to take one *pood* [an imperial Russian unit of weight, equal to 16.38 kg] of flour and 30 lbs[23] of cereal grains per person, about 50 *pood* of butter, about 50 *pood* of *tsibulja* [onions] and about 100 *pood* of salt; in addition, all Doukhobors were supposed to bring with them from home about 30 lbs of dried crusts each, which they had prepared during the autumn. Tea, sugar, Nestlé's milk and oatmeal was to be brought on the ship from England.

Since the Doukhobor exiles had only recently sent 10,000 roubles to England, they had very little money left, and we telegraphed Chertkov to send us 2,000 roubles by wire.

Next, Sulerzhitskij wrote and wired Aleksej Bakunin[24] (a fifth-year medical student) and Marija Sats (a doctor's assistant), who were planning to go with the Doukhobors, [requesting] that they go with him to render medical assistance to the Doukhobors during the voyage; but since there was a possibility the Russian authorities would not let them on board, he suggested they catch up with the ship at Constantinople. Then Sulerzhitskij wrote the following letter to the Doukhobors at Skra:

23 30 lbs = approx. 12.3 kg (1 Russian pound = 409.5 grams).

24 *Aleksej Il'ich Bakunin* — nephew to M. A. Bakunin (a theoretician of anarchism, organizer of the Alliance for Social Democracy), later the owner of a surgical hospital in Moscow, member of the Second State Duma.

> Dear Brethren. Apply for your transit permits for 22 November [4 December], if they are of the kind that are valid for ten days. Two hundred carpenters are needed, and they should get their tools ready — their saws and axes, and be ready to go on the first train to Batoum, which will probably be on 28 November [10 December]. The trains from Gomi and Skra will set out first, and then the remaining stations, hence it is important that the carpenters be appointed from these two stations alone. Decide ahead of time who is going to be doing the carpentry, so that when the time comes there won't be any disorder or confusion. Calculate how much money you will need before leaving Russia, that is, until 9 [21] December. Then collect all the rest of the money and give it to one person to hold, and then the person holding the money should go and stay in Batoum, since there are going to be various minor expenses and there won't be time to go and bring the money from Skra. Money will also be needed to pay for transportation to Batoum. This must be done right away. The expenses will all be recorded and [a list] will be given you. Whatever remains will be converted into English money and we'll take it with us to Canada. Get this done as quickly as possible. Your brother Lev.[25] My deepest respects to Starichok Makhortov.

21 NOVEMBER [3 DECEMBER]

Grigorij Savinov and Fëdor Borisov of the Doukhobor exiles and Aleksej Gor'kov of the Kars group arrived in Batoum. We talked over tea in our room at the Belle-vue. Savinov and Borisov, however, left in a very short time — they took Sulerzhitskij's letter to Skra; after that they were supposed to go on to Tiflis to help me arrange railway passage for their group of exiles to Batoum.

We found out that those planning to go from Elizavetpol' numbered 1,350. Since the ship only has room for 2,000 people, that means that no more than 650 can go from Kars.

22 NOVEMBER 1898 [4 DECEMBER]

As the *Superior* was supposed to leave England yesterday (21 November), and time is of the essence, I wrote to the Kars group:

> To Kazaz'janits and Fofanov at Aleksandropol'. No more than 650 Doukhobors from Kars will be able to go; exiles and those of recruiting age and their families should be given priority, and if the total is more than 650, the exiles should leave behind part of their family until the spring. Apply for your passports, and ask the authorities to send the passports to Batoum at once; do not leave before the first of the month — the fourth at the latest.

Aleksej Gor'kov took this letter to Kars Oblast.

The Kars Doukhobors, like the others, are generally impatient to leave and want as many of their people to go as possible. However, to take more than 2,000 people on ships like the *Huron* and the *Superior* would be dangerous; in

25 *Lev* — in this case a diminutive form of *Leopol'd* (Sulerzhitskij's first name).

calculating the number of places available according to the plan of the *Huron* he had drawn up, Sulerzhitskij was much afraid, right up to the last day of boarding, that there would not be room enough for all the exiles, and that some of them would have to stay behind and go on the *Superior*, which was a little larger than the *Huron*, and that those remaining would be in addition to the 2,000 projected. Hence only those in most urgent need could go from Kars; namely, those who had been exiled in the unhealthful places of Baku and Erivan Gubernias along with their families (those who had turned in their reserve cards to the authorities) and those who would be subject to conscription in 1899. Furthermore, the Kars group needed to be told as early as possible as they would have to travel five days by horse [and cart] to the Akstafa station.

23 NOVEMBER [5 DECEMBER]

Arriving at Tiflis this morning, I put in a request at the railway office for passage on special trains, as quickly as possible, with no more than thirty people to a carriage, each train to include two or three baggage-cars; in Batoum to bring the trains to Richner's factory near the goods station and to allow no less than six hours each for loading and unloading.

In my negotiations with the assistant director of operations, Mr. Mitrofanov, a very obliging individual, it turned out that 2,000 people could most conveniently be transported in four shifts on the N° 21 troop train, which is quite fast, and that the conditions I had outlined would be met, but that the Doukhobors had to pay a fourth-class fare, which was about twice the cost of the 'resettlement fare.' This was confirmed by the director, whom I also spoke to. It turned out that in August the Transcaucasian Railway had transported the Doukhobors going to Cyprus at the resettlement fare. But [the Ministry of] State Control protested, since the railway had not given them official confirmation from the administration that the Doukhobors were indeed resettlers.

From the railway office I went to see Mitskevich in the hope of getting confirmation from the administration, i. e., from Prince Golitsyn, that the Doukhobors were actually resettlers. Mitskevich was less than sympathetic, but promised to convey my request to Prince Golitsyn. In the evening, to persuade him even further, I wrote him a letter on the matter; later, as the Doukhobors Savinov and Borisov were supposed to arrive, I advised them to submit a petition to Prince Golitsyn on his consultation day — Wednesday 25 November [7 December].

24 NOVEMBER [6 DECEMBER]

At the railway office I put in a request for the transport of the second party of Elizavetpol' and Kars Doukhobors under the same conditions as for the first party; I would indicate the specific dates later. I dropped in to see Mitskevich, who informed me that Prince Golitsyn was unlikely to grant confirmation to enable the Doukhobors to travel at the resettlement fare. This evening I was at Pashchenko's, along with Grigorij Savinov and Fëdor Borisov. We wrote out for them a petition to Golitsyn, which they would submit on the morrow.

While we were writing out the petition, Mrs. Pashchenko received a visit from her son-in-law, Prokopenko, from the Nal'chik area. He too is planning on going to Canada. He showed me Khilkov's letter to Dadiani, written from Canada. Khilkov wrote about his search for land in Western Canada, near the Rocky Mountains; they only have four months of winter there, one can already feel the warm current of the Pacific Ocean, the black earth of the prairies dotted with groves of trees, the horses able to go through the whole winter on what they find on the ground, wild cherries and plums, grass more than waist-high. (These places would not be offered to the Doukhobors, who were given land further to the east, where the climate is rather more severe.)

25 NOVEMBER [7 DECEMBER]

At the railway office I negotiated the final dates for the trains and was given two documents — a timetable for the first party's trains and the tariff showing the fourth-class fare for all the stations where the Doukhobors would be boarding. All the Doukhobors would be transported by the military train which arrives in Batoum at 9 a.m. Five hundred and ninety-three people would come from Gomi on 29 November [11 December]; 553 from Skra on the 30th [12th]; 260 from Ksanki and 220 from Kaspi on 1 [13] December; also 371 from Gori and 263 from Koreli on 2 [14] December. The passenger numbers were given to me by Sulerzhitskij. Hence the dates suggested by Sulerzhitskij had been changed somewhat and the Doukhobors would be arriving a little earlier — mainly because they had to travel on four separate trains, rather than the two Sulerzhitskij had envisioned.

At eleven o'clock I went to my appointment with the head of civil affairs. The Doukhobors Grigorij Savinov and Fëdor Borisov were already waiting there on the landing at the top of the stairs. I was struck by their calm and indifference to the grandeur surrounding the prince: Cossacks in rich national costumes of the Caucasus, the grand staircase, the rugs and other such things did not impress them in the least. They had already submitted their petition and were waiting for the prince to come out. Savinov sat on a chair and was pleasantly dreaming. I told the special assignment officer that I had come on the same business as the Doukhobors. He said their petition would be conveyed to the prince. Seeing my presence was not needed, I went to the hotel. An hour later, however, Golitsyn summoned me by telephone. He said in an irritated tone of voice (I don't know why) that he could not grant the Doukhobors' petition for passage at the resettlement fare, since they were not resettlers, but emigrants, that he had done so much for them that naturally they were closer to him than any Armenians, but what could he do, and so forth.

Thus, in addition to unjustifiably high fees for the passports, the Doukhobors faced yet another major and unexpected expense.

That same evening I left for Batoum.

26 NOVEMBER [8 DECEMBER]

There were a lot of different pieces of news awaiting me in Batoum. Several telegrams had come from London regarding the ships' arrival dates, provisions, the bunks and so forth. The questions about the ships' arrival dates and the bunks had been answered. The *Huron* was supposed to arrive around 5 [17] December, the *Lake Superior* somewhat later than we were expecting — around 13 [25] December. It will be necessary to build bunks on the *Huron* and purchase wood for this; there will be lumber for the bunks on the *Superior*, but they will have to be built.

A Doukhobor had arrived in Batoum from Kars — Semën Chernov — with a message from their 'Old ones.' It turned out that a German named Herr Georg Stoeckel, together with an interpreter, had paid a visit to the Kars Doukhobors and had thrown them into some confusion. He was an agent for the Hamburg Steamship Company and proposed taking 2,200 people on his ship, offering provisions and bunks (with woollen blankets!), inviting the Doukhobors to settle in Arkansas — to the south of Kansas City — and agreed to bring two emissaries to Arkansas at his own expense to choose a place to settle. The Kars Doukhobors decided to send Semën Chernov to Lev Tolstoy for advice on this question, as well as on how the wives of Doukhobor exiles in Yakutia should go there.

That evening Herr Stoeckel himself came to see us in our hotel room and talked about the advantages of going on the Hamburg ship, suggesting that it would be no dearer than £7,500, about the splendid climate and soil in Arkansas and about the harsh climate in Canada.

27 NOVEMBER [9 DECEMBER]

I met the American consul at Stevens' office and asked him about Arkansas. He told me that it was a rather mountainous country, not too good for grain, that fruit growing and cattle raising were fine there, but that the land was rather expensive, the low-lying areas were not very healthful, and those at higher altitudes were not that good for crops. I mentioned this to Chernov and wrote a letter to my father.

28 NOVEMBER [10 DECEMBER]

Chernov has gone to see Lev Nikolaevich. He is going because he has been sent by the starichki, but has his own doubts about the usefulness of his trip.

29 NOVEMBER [11 DECEMBER]

This morning (Sunday) the first lot of 600 Doukhobors arrived from Gomi. The train was made up of several goods coaches, which had somehow been outfitted with boards for sitting and sleeping. In some carriages iron stoves had been installed, though the weather at that time was still rather warm. The train took them right to the gates of Richner's factory. The Doukhobors got themselves and their things off the train in a lively and cheerful manner. The rooms of the factory were made up partly of barns with walls of corrugated iron and doors, partly of lean-tos without walls. The first party occupied the closed barns. The baggage was stored separately. Somewhere near the seaside the Doukhobor women had gathered a quantity of wood chips, had dragged out their *kazany* [iron cauldrons], and were beginning to cook borscht and *kulesh* [a thick soup] with rice grains and onions. Everybody had brought their own bread with them.

This evening, since it was a Sunday, the Doukhobors gathered for prayer. First they sang their psalms, then one of them stepped forward and read a prayer, then psalm singing again, then a prayer, and so forth. I only remember a reference to the church, to the effect that we do not believe in stone or wooden churches, but we believe in the church of which it is said, "where two or three are gathered together in My name, there am I in the midst of them."[26] Later during the psalm singing they bowed to each other and kissed each other men with men and women with women.

The consul and I were present and removed our hats. One old man — Makhortov — came up to us and told us we needn't be shy, we could put our hats back on. Makhortov is an old fellow approaching ninety years old, he was a sailor during the Sevastopol' war, and later defended Malakh Hill. As a man of intelligence and experience he exercised a considerable influence on the starichki. Furthermore, the fact that he had not shaved his long, white, wavy beard made him stand out from the others and gave him the appearance of a Ruskin[27] or a Lev Tolstoy.

30 NOVEMBER [12 DECEMBER]

Five hundred and fifty-three Doukhobors arrived from Skra.

1 [13] DECEMBER

Two hundred and eighty-two people arrived from Kaspi and Ksanki. The factory came to life. The Doukhobors began to be noticed around town — some would be shopping for things, some worked for a day's pay on the ships. The weather started getting cloudy and colder.

2 [14] DECEMBER

The last of the exiles arrived from Koreli and Gori, 622 people. It rained the whole day; it was damp and rather cool. At Richner's factory it was cold for the people staying in the lean-tos — in the barns with no walls; it was also

26 Matt. 18:20 (Authorized Version).

27 *John Ruskin* (1819–1900) — English philosopher, writer, art critic.

difficult trying to cook — the wood was too damp to burn. And still no sign of the *Huron*!

A wire came in from the railway company office that the transport would be completed according to my telegram.

I am working on translating the lists of the Elizavetpol' Doukhobors into English; the son of the director of the South Russian Bank, an S. Muromov, has undertaken to help me. Letters have been received from Russia; one of them was from my father to both of us.[28] Among other things he wrote:

> Birjukov writes from England that he heartily approves your fund project.[29] Maude writes that they are collecting contributions in America. The Chertkovs have persuaded two doctor's assistants to accompany the Doukhobors to Canada. I wrote back that it all depended on whether they can take the rocking of the boat, since if they can't, they will be less of a help than a hindrance. What do you think about that?

3 [15] DECEMBER

I despatched telegrams and letters to the Elizavetpol' and Kars Doukhobors regarding the dates the trains would come for them; I wrote my father, in part, as follows:

> All two thousand exiles are now housed at Richner's factory; we expect the ship any day now.
>
> We curse ourselves for having made such a mistake — summoning the people too early. Although at Richner's factory things are not too bad — they are all in closed barns with floors, they are cooking in cauldrons, it's not too cold right now; but still it would have been much better if they could have spent the time at home. But we in no way imagined that the ship would not be here by now; we hurried because under the agreement it would be stopping only three days here, and for every day beyond that there would be a surcharge of £30. It has been raining here for three days now. The ship passed by Malta 30 November [11 December], and it is supposed to arrive on the 4th [16th] or the 5th [17th] .... The Doukhobors are indeed a special people: during the whole time of their trip and their stay here — and the first party has been here five days already — there has not been a single sharp word or complaint; everything is proceeding calmly and in an orderly fashion. And for two thousand people to arrive in families with their baggage, unload, settle in, feed themselves and so forth, is not an easy or simple matter.

3 [15] DECEMBER

Richner's factory is teeming with people; it seems it is so full that if another hundred people showed up, there would not be room for them. All the

28 See *PSS* 71:494.

29 Sergej Tolstoy proposed setting up a fund to help the Doukhobors independently of the Quakers.

functions of life are performed there: people cooking borscht or boiling tea in *kazany*; people washing clothes, others washing themselves, people singing psalms, others holding a conversation. The Doukhobors are slow by nature, like the Ukrainians, from which the greater part are descended, and even in a crowd they make no impression of bustling or hurrying. Many have not seen each other for a long time and are now joyfully meeting; whereupon they traditionally bow to each other three times, doffing their caps and kissing. Then a conversation invariably ensues: "How are you?" "Slava Bogu [Praise the Lord]. And how are you?" "Slava Bogu. And how is your family?" "Slava Bogu." Later: "Our family asked me to give you greetings." "Spasi Gospodi," etc. They always say *Spasi Gospodi* [May the Lord save you] in place of "Thanks" or "Thank you." After this they go on to talk about something else. Sulerzhitskij is always on the go, purchasing lumber for the bunks, firewood, provisions; he bought two large cooking cauldrons; he is seeing about passports, provisions, and so forth, but most importantly, he is busy with the doctor and medicines. The town's assistant physician makes daily visits to the factory and goes around to everyone. A great many of them are seriously ill with fever; dysentery and rashes are also widespread. Some patients are suspected of having scarlet fever, and the doctor has tried to isolate them right there at the factory in a separate room, but it was only a nominal isolation, since the Doukhobors do not at all believe in the contagiousness of scarlet fever, and visitors are always sitting by the patients' bedsides, in spite of all the warnings by Sulerzhitskij and the doctor. All the Doukhobor exiles, by their own admission, are a rather weak people, all told. Four years of living in the low-lying valleys of Georgia, eating only enough to subsist on, the crowded earthen huts they lived in, the lack of work and their fallen spirits in the face of their uncertain future — all this has had a powerful effect on them. Indeed, many of them, notwithstanding their above-average height and sound constitution, appear old, thin and weak. Almost all of them have a sallow complexion. As is known, over the past four years about a thousand out of four thousand have died, primarily children; there are virtually no children among them under four years old, since at the time of their exile they decided to abstain and not have any children until their situation improved, and this was actually carried out by almost everyone. Hence there are very few children among their numbers.

During the night one little girl died, apparently from inflammation of the lungs. It was necessary to go to the chief of police and the town's physician for permission to bury her, which was obtained not without some effort. In the evening they carried her with psalm singing to a Molokan cemetery.

The whole day it rained and became even colder. A long letter was received from [English Tolstoyan Herbert] Archer, who writes: (1) lists of the emigrants must be sent to England; (2) the Canadian government is giving the Doukhobors land, accommodations for the winter and a 'bonus' (commission payment) in the amount of five dollars plus per person, which will be used to buy provisions for them; (3) winter accommodations will be in various places along the railway lines, depending on the availability of unused buildings; (4) it would be a good idea to set up in Canada a common Doukhobor fund to receive all monies — contributions from the Quakers and other friends from England, [North] America and Russia, 'bonus' payments and so forth; (5) it would be desirable for this fund to be managed by [a committee of] several individuals responsive to the Doukhobors' needs, and some English-speaking people — local residents who are more experienced could look after buying food supplies and other monetary affairs; (6) however, one should not aspire to manage the Doukhobors' affairs, only respond to their needs.

4 [16] DECEMBER

The weather was clear and cool. The managers of the stations where the Doukhobors boarded their trains each calculated the fare to Batoum differently, so that on some invoices there was a surplus.

From Gori Station they charged the children the same full rate as the adults; however, the railway returned this money — about 150 roubles. A telegram was received: SUPERIOR PASSED GIBRALTAR 14TH AFTERNOON. That means it will arrive on the 12th [24th]. Some letters have been received from Russia, including one with an enclosed letter from Khilkov in Canada, with maps of Canada and an outline of the lots allotted the Doukhobors by the Canadian government. In describing the living conditions in that location, he wrote that they have a continental climate, that they never sow wheat there in virgin soil, but only barley, potatoes and spring rye, but that on the second ploughing wheat does beautifully; there is occasionally frost in August, which sometimes, albeit rarely, kills the wheat and as a result it yields a lesser-quality grain. This letter made us a little disenchanted with Canada.

5 [17] DECEMBER

Another girl died, about seven years old, from 'childhood disease,' say the Doukhobors, or from convulsions, but we were very much afraid it was scarlet fever.

The consul received a letter from Archer to the effect that the Canadian government is requiring the ships to dock at Halifax for a quarantine inspection, which Archer will arrange with the shipowners.

This evening it clouded over, and rain fell; we are afraid it might snow. We fell into a state of utter despair. No *Huron*; we cursed ourselves for summoning the people so early, but who would have thought that the *Huron* would be so late? We thought, according to what Stuart said, that it would arrive on the 1st or the 2nd, making the passage in twelve to thirteen days, and today is already the eighteenth day since its departure from England.

6 [18] DECEMBER

Early this morning we heard the plaintive, but the strong, deep tones of a ship's whistle, requesting to put in to port. For several days now, such whistles each morning have awakened our hopes that the Huron had finally arrived. We looked out the window, and this time, far out in the harbour we caught sight of a large three-masted steamship which was rocking to and fro in the stormy waves. The plan of the *Huron* was hanging on our wall, and we determined it was indeed she. At last! Sulerzhitskij set out at once for the ship. According to the contract, the three-day period would begin twelve hours after obtaining clearance (that is, after passing customs inspection and other formalities), during which the loading is supposed to take place; after that, if we delay the ship, a surcharge of £30 must be paid for every day of delay; if we delay it an additional three days, for the seventh day and every day thereafter the charge would be up to £60 a day. Thus, over a period of four days — the three stipulated and the fourth — a Sunday (which is not included in the count), everything must be done: building all the bunks on the ship, embark something over two thousand people and all their baggage, go through passport control, customs inspection and other formalities.

The whole day it rained with a mixture of snow. At the sight of the ship spirits rose, but what a [hard] life they were living in Richner's unheated factory! Several hundred people (who had arrived on the last train) were housed in the lean-tos — without walls. They obtained tarpaulins which they hung to protect themselves from the wind and rain, and put up boards as a barrier, but none of that was of much help.

In the evening Sulerzhitskij fell into a mood of gloom and apathy, as happens with him sometimes. Suddenly through the window we noticed the glow of a fire in the town. Sulerzhitskij always liked to put out fires. He jumped up and ran to the fire. Seeing him in some strange emotional state, I ran after him. At the site of the fire Sulerzhitskij dashed ahead, pushed a fireman aside, took his firehose and made straight for the fire. Knowing that tomorrow he would have to undertake duties that bore a heavy responsibility, I took decisive measures: I seized him by the collar, took away the hose and demanded he return to the hotel at once. I admit I actually uttered a curse. After all, it was not worth going into a fire to save some Armenian's empty barn. He looked at me in surprise, but did not show anger, and acquiesced. Back at the hotel he at once fell asleep.

7 [19] DECEMBER

No sooner had the ship been made fast to the wharf than the work began. Sulerzhitskij set about his business in earnest. Crowds of Doukhobors began carting building material through the whole town — boards, laths, etc. The carpenters' work was soon in full swing on the lower decks: the hammering, clanking and whining of saws echoed throughout the ship. According to

Sulerzhitskij's plan two-tiered bunks were laid side by side across the whole deck, without any narrow passageways between each set of bunks; this meant that extra space was available which might have otherwise been taken up with passageways; wide corridors were left lengthwise where people could walk freely; children, instead of taking up a separate bunk, would be placed between the adults, which also saved space. The work was supervised by Sulerzhitskij along with Stuart and a carpenter named Mustafa, a conscientious and serious-minded Turk.

The dead girl was buried in the Molokan cemetery without the police or the doctor; the Doukhobors carried her out when the town doctor was paying a visit to Richner's factory, but without his knowledge; the policeman didn't stop them, thinking the doctor had given his permission for the burial.

At Richner's factory there are many people ill; many have chronic fever, there were others with diarrhœa or catarrhal cough. The doctor found two people in Fëdor Rjazantsev's family with unmistakable signs of scarlet fever; in another family a little boy was recovering — his skin is peeling; there are other suspicious cases — swollen glands.

Sulerzhitskij and I wanted to isolate the scarlet-fever cases in the town hospital, which was prepared to handle cholera cases; I went to see the mayor about this, and he agreed, but the Doukhobors themselves would have none of it, afraid of being left behind in Batoum. Naturally anyone ill with scarlet fever would necessarily be left behind, since the ship's doctors would not accept them; of course, these cases could be hidden from the doctors, but we could not take such a responsibility upon ourselves. It is a most frightening prospect — that over the twenty-five-day voyage many will have had scarlet fever and a few will have to be consigned to the sea.

I again sent details about train dates to the Kars and Elizavetpol' Doukhobors, and reminding the Kars group that only 650 of them could be taken on board.

A Doukhobor named Vasilij Zybin arrived from Elizavetpol', sent by his group to see about passports. Vasilij Zybin is a tall and handsome young man, with a very pleasing appearance, though rather dull. It turned out that the Elizavetpol' governor had begun giving out passports to each adult individually, and not a single passport for a whole family, as in the case of the Tiflis Doukhobors who had gone to Cyprus or those who were now about to set out on the *Huron*. Furthermore, the governor said that he would not likely have the passports issued by the 20th — i.e., the proposed departure date. As a result of this discretionary measure on the governor's part, the Doukhobors will be obliged to spend three or four times more on passports; in addition, bureaucratic sluggishness may mean that some of them will have to stay behind and not go. I wrote out a petition to Prince Golitsyn, which Vasilij Zybin is to give him the day after tomorrow, on his consultation day, and also sent a telegram in my own name to the Elizavetpol' governor:

> As the one in charge of the Doukhobor emigration I have been informed that the head of civil affairs has given permission for the emigrants to receive external passports on the basis of one per family. This is how they were issued to those from Tiflis. It is extremely important to issue the transit permits at once and send the passports to Batoum, as the emigrants humbly request. Any delay involves considerable forfeit.

In order to comprehend the circumstances of the matter, one should bear in mind that the passports were sent to the police chief in Batoum, but were not given directly to the applicants; the Doukhobors were given only transit permits, valid for ten days. Then, upon embarkation, the police chief would check these permits against the passports, following which he would retain them. I sent a telegram with almost identical wording, also in my own name, to Prince Golitsyn.

Next I gave instructions to Vasilij Zybin on how to proceed, depending on the response he received from Prince Golitsyn and the Elizavetpol' governor, since all the train dates and the departure timetable for the Elizavetpol' Doukhobors would change according to the date the passports were issued.

Aboard the *Huron* work is proceeding day and night with feverish haste. Sulerzhitskij is not eating or sleeping. The weather has cleared.

8 [20] DECEMBER 1898

A warm sunny day. The magnificent imperial yacht *Derzhava* has been in port for several days now. The Empress Marija Fëdorovna passed through Batoum this morning. Prince Golitsyn, it appears, has come to see her off. I took advantage of the opportunity to approach him afterward. In the hotel I met some acquaintances. Adjutant Svechin conveyed my request to him, and I was granted a few minutes' 'audience.' But no sooner had I begun stammering that I had come on the matter of passports for the Elizavetpol' Doukhobors than a fountain of shouts and eloquence gushed forth; this, as I learnt, was a typical reception with Prince Golitsyn.

"Well, what do you want, mais laissez-moi tranquille,[30] this has become tiresome, after all, this emigration on the conscience of your father; the Doukhobors do not need either one of you. What about the ones who went to Cyprus? Why are you getting them to send all sorts of telegrams? And what are all these *kameral'nye* [internal office records] — they're all just commérages"[31] (a pun!), etc.

It turned out that Golitsyn had not received my telegram, but had received one from the Elizavetpol' Doukhobors, in which they had asked him to issue passports according to their internal office records — that is, by families. I had

30 French, 'but leave me in peace.'

31 French, 'gossip' — a play on words with the Russian term *kameral'nye*.

not been aware of this, though I guessed what was going on; however, for a long time I was not able to get a word in edgeways to explain.

At the hotel I became acquainted with an assistant to the Kutais governor — Samojlov, his deputy director in Batoum. He told me that in August he had let the Doukhobors going to Cyprus stay in empty army barracks, but that Prince Golitsyn had immediately reversed this permission and he had been obliged to evict them. The whole afternoon I spent aboard the ship.

The bunks will soon be ready; they are working day and night; the Doukhobors are excellent workers and with their customary teamwork everything is going ahead quickly. They have started loading the baggage into the lower hold. The winch crackles away, and the whole ship is buzzing with people like an anthill. I talked with many Doukhobors, asked them about their previous life, about the persecutions they endured, whether they were sorry to leave, and so forth. Evidently, they no longer have any doubts, and they acknowledge that emigration is a necessity. One *starichok*, repeating yet again the same line of thought which led to the emigration, told me about the last four years of his life in a Moslem village in Georgia — homeless and without employment; his son had been exiled to Yakut Gubernia; he himself had eaten up everything he had; the whole family had been ill with fever. His words were permeated with a feeling of being a victim of injustice on the part of the Russian administrators. He remembered how they had once lived; he told me of the Grand Prince Mikhail Nikolaevich, of the Turkish war, when the Doukhobors transported provisions and even weapons in their wagons, baked dried crusts for the soldiers, looked after their wounded and so on. "And now the government has forgotten all that," he said.

This evening we went to Richner's factory and saw the things the Doukhobors were taking with them to their bunks. We had to insist that they put all they could into their baggage, and take with them only what was absolutely necessary, since all that took up space; furthermore, during the rocking of the ship some items might fly around the room and cause injury. Arguments could not altogether be avoided. One pretty Doukhobor woman was most reluctant to consign her rather large trunk to the baggage hold, but Sulerzhitskij insisted, as it contained things that would not be needed on the voyage: a samovar, a tea service, homemade fabrics, etc. I might add that all Doukhobors carry with them a long clean white shirt in case of death.

9 [21] DECEMBER

A clear day. A telegram was received from Vasilij Zybin to the effect that, because of the passport delays, the Elizavetpol' group has to leave on the 13th [25th], rather than on the 11th [23rd], as planned. I accordingly wired the railway office in Tiflis about train dates. At noon [today] the *Superior* passed through the Dardanelles. The bunks on the *Huron* are ready and the baggage has been loaded. The scarlet-fever patients are feeling better.

This afternoon the Doukhobors began embarking and settling themselves in aboard ship. Earlier Sulerzhitskij had chalked on the uprights the number of places [in each section]. Who was to go where was decided by lottery, since not all places were equally good: half the places are on the lower deck (i.e., the upper hold), where there are no portholes, where light comes in only through the hatchways, and in times of strong sea-turbulence the hatchways are closed.

To find places for two thousand people is not a simple or easy task, and the boarding went on all night until early morning.

The Doukhobors are always courteous and cannot tolerate rudeness.

I once heard how Stuart, also in charge of the boarding, called out to one Doukhobor in an English accent: *Kuda lezesh', chërt!* [Where the devil are you going?]. The latter maintained his composure but answered in surprise: "You don't have to talk that way. I won't go." I heard no cursing on the part of the Doukhobors; the worst I heard was *Kakoj ty negodjashchij!* [What a good-for-nothing you are!]. They are all simple and trustworthy, and have good moral upbringing. It is especially heartwarming to see the young people with their sincere, healthy faces.

10 [22] DECEMBER

This morning I stopped by Sulerzhitskij's cabin and noticed something moving under the bed. I asked him: "What is that?" He replied: "A Doukhobor." It was a young Doukhobor of conscription age. He had run away from passport inspection and was intending to sail with his family to Canada. I admit I rebuked Leopol'd Antonovich. After all, if it were discovered that he had hidden a deserter, he would be immediately arrested and sentenced to severe punishment, and of course he would not be allowed to go with the Doukhobors. But, my rebuke notwithstanding, I secretly admired his resolve.

Passport inspection by the chief of police began in the morning. The procedure was as follows: virtually all the Doukhobors had spent the night on the ship. In the morning they were all obliged to disembark, and the police and customs officials conducted a search of the vessel. Then the police chief and his deputies, sitting at the bottom of the gangplank, called each one in turn according to their passports, took each one's transit permit, checked it against the passport, and then retained both documents.

When all two thousand plus emigrants poured on to the wharf, it seemed improbable that the ship would hold them all. But by yesterday evening they had all managed to squeeze in, even if in tight quarters. Just before the inspection Vasilij Popov addressed a few words to the chief of police on behalf of all the Doukhobors. He thanked the Russian government, the officials, and all those staying behind in Russia for everything. Popov spoke sincerely and his words were not ironic, although they involuntarily suggested an ironic interpretation.

Finally, by about noontime, the inspection was finished, the ship blew its whistle, the anchor chains clanked and the vessel cast off from the dock.

The people all stood on the upper deck and began singing their monotonous drawn-out psalms. The weather was marvellous, it was warm, sunny and calm; the sea was a deep blue. Snow-capped mountains could be seen far off in the distance. A motley crowd stood on the shore: Adzharians in their knitted hoods, fez-crowned Turks, a few Russians and some fifty Doukhobors who were staying behind in Russia or going on the next ship.

I stayed on board until the ship reached the harbour entrance, from where I returned on the pilot's launch. Several times flares went up from the ship, as is customary with English sailors when they sail off with emigrants. Sulerzhitskij, a former sailor, climbed up to the yard and waved his cap. It was all very beautiful, but I became concerned and fearful for the life of these two thousand souls. Ahead of them lay almost a month's journey, cold, disease, perhaps not enough water or water of poor quality, not enough bread and hot food (aboard ship, I would think, there would not be enough stoves or kitchen utensils), and especially the rocking, the vomiting, and all that in close, dark and poorly ventilated quarters. It is probable that some of them will die en route, even presuming a very low mortality rate. Over a month no fewer than three out of two thousand are to die. It is a pity that these good people are leaving Russia because of the stupidity and cruelty of some Shervashidze or Goremykin, and how frightening to think that even where they are going they will not be well.

A telegram was received from the head of civil affairs. The Elizavetpol' governor has been told to issue passports on the basis of one per family.

I wired Chertkov: The *Huron* has sailed with about 2,020 souls.

2. "FROM HALIFAX TO WINNIPEG"

5 [17] FEBRUARY[32]

This morning [English Tolstoyan Herbert] Archer, the captain and I went to Halifax on a small launch ordered the night before by telephone from Halifax. The transfer of the Doukhobors to the ship will proceed under the supervision of the first mate, Mr. Potter. From Halifax to Lawlor's Island is about eight kilometres. Along the way we noticed storm warnings posted at the lighthouse, but the captain is counting on reaching Saint John before the storm sets in.

Halifax, at least in its outward appearance, is nothing out of the ordinary. There are pot-holes on the streets; the snow is hardly cleared away at all; I saw

32 This chapter begins at the end of the Doukhobors' three-week quarantine on Lawlor's Island, eight km from the Canadian city of Halifax, Nova Scotia. The final leg of the sea voyage will take them southwest along the Nova Scotia coast to Saint John, New Brunswick, where they will disembark and begin their rail journey to western Canada.

several large double sleighs outfitted with buffalo rugs. People wear knitted caps in the shape of a stocking and fur coats with fur on the outside. I changed some money (two roubles to the dollar), settled my account with DeWolf who had sold us provisions, and purchased ship's biscuits for the voyage (a pound per person), nails for strengthening the bunks and something else besides. On the return trip we were accompanied by several people — reporters, three or four other gentlemen and two elderly Quakers from Philadelphia — Elkinton and Giddly. They regarded me with some curiosity, some asked me questions, a reporter took my picture. Approaching the island, we met a boat with a quite a number of people on its way back to Halifax. Thus I managed to avoid the main lot of curiosity-seekers and reporters. By the time we arrived, all the Doukhobors had already boarded the ship and taken their old places. Upon embarkation, they all had to show their cards of varying colour, which was done. Only Pëtr Zybin and his family remained in quarantine with dysentery, along with the Smorodinov family, two of whose children had acute rheumatism. Tomorrow they will be transferred to a Halifax hospital.

At two o'clock we cast off. The Quakers, Archer, and someone else are travelling with us. As soon as we reached the open sea we met two large ships, the first one towing the second with a line; the second ship was in a most sorry state rudderless, without some of its rigging and with a broken side. During our period of quarantine, the ocean had been wild with terrible storms, and many ships had greatly suffered. Now the sea is not stormy and we are sailing smoothly; the captain is not sparing the coal.

This evening the Quakers asked me to arrange a meeting with the *starichki*, which took place in the second-class dining room; I served as interpreter. Elkinton and Giddly explained who the Quakers were, and told how their ancestors came to America with William Penn to escape persecution for their faith and their refusal of military service, i.e., for the same reasons that the Doukhobors came. However, they were also persecuted in America, and during the American War of Independence five Quakers were hanged for declining to serve; even recently during the war for the abolition of slavery several Quakers were imprisoned and subjected to various restrictions. Then they offered their greetings to the Doukhobors as kindred spirits, whereupon Giddly suddenly stood up and started talking in a solemn and intermittent voice about 'the spirit that is in thee.' It was difficult for me to translate his words, as I told him; to my surprise he said that was not necessary and continued his passionate preaching. At Quaker meetings it happens that 'the Spirit descends upon one of them' and then he begins to speak with inspiration; this evidently happened with Giddly. The Doukhobors were very happy with the whole conversation, and when Giddly was preaching, they said: 'Pity we don't understand, but we can hear that he is a good and touching speaker.' There is only one point of difference with the Quakers — in the use of meat for food.

To the Quakers' question as to why the Doukhobors do not eat meat — not because of climatic conditions? — the Doukhobors replied that they do not believe it is right to deprive any living creature of life; to which the Quakers said they themselves cannot go that far in such matters, but rather leave them up to each individual to decide for themselves. As to the question of abstinence from alcohol and tobacco they expressed complete agreement.

6 [18] FEBRUARY

There was a little rocking during the night, but the morning was calm, warm and sunny. The Bay of Fundy failed to live up to our fears; it seems we have escaped the impending storm. This morning all the liquid that had frozen during our stay in quarantine thawed out and began to give off a stench; everything was assiduously washed and cleaned. I rewarded the ship's crew with the two hundred roubles they had been promised in Batoum, according to the list I had drawn up with the help of the captain and Potter.

At about three o'clock we caught sight of land — the small town of Saint John, flanked by a huge grain elevator, near which we docked.

A crowd was standing on the dock. Before disembarking, the *starichki* decided they would say a few words of greeting to the Canadians, represented by the immigration official who met us. On the dock the crowd of Canadians formed one semicircle, a crowd of Doukhobors another, and in the middle the immigration official — a Mr. [T.] Peddler — and I exchanged words of greeting. I translated the Doukhobors' words as best I could, saying that they wanted to give thanks to God for a safe arrival, and to thank the Canadian government for receiving them and giving them land. Mr. Peddler in turn welcomed the Doukhobors to Canada and said that in this country they would be free of any persecution for their faith.

Then the disembarkation began. On the other side of the dock is the railway platform from which five trains — prepared especially for the occasion — will take the Doukhobors directly to the far west. The trains will depart at two-hour intervals. A separate sixth train will take the baggage. All this has been arranged most practically and efficiently. The trains arrived and departed on schedule, and people disembarked from the ship and directly boarded the trains. A fair-sized crowd of Canadians stood by. Ladies gave out sweets to the children; many bought handcrafted wooden spoons from the Doukhobors, and for some reason had me autograph them; some came up just to shake hands according to [North] American custom, to say that they had read Tolstoy or had heard of him, and that they were very sympathetic to the arrival of the Doukhobors, etc. And I was kept running from the ship to the dock and from the dock to the railway platform to supervise the boarding, the unloading and loading. We had failed to take into account that after the first trains left there would not be as many people available to unload the baggage, with the result that the last party had to put a great deal of effort into this task. In addition, we had forgotten we had left on the ship several barrels of oatmeal. [Field nurses] Efrosin'ja Dmitrievna and Marija Aleksandrovna went on the third train; I remained until the last train. It was not until four o'clock in the morning that I went to retrieve my things from the ship, and finally said goodbye to the cabin which had been home to me for almost two months. Only two Doukhobor families remained on the ship — the Chevel'djaevs with erysipelas of the leg and the family of Semën Zybin, who was suffering the whole time with fever and its effects. Tomorrow they will be taken to hospital in Saint John. I stopped in to bid them farewell. Semën Zybin is one of those Doukhobors who turned in their military reserve cards to the authorities and consequently were sent one by one to the remote villages of the Transcaucasus. In exile he caught a severe fever, which probably led to kidney disease, and probably heart disease as well. It is strange that [Chief Public Health Inspector Dr] Montizambert did not leave him in Halifax. He had become extremely thin; his face was haggard and of a pale ashen colour and his nose had become pointed. He was fully conscious, however, bade me a hearty farewell, and said frankly that he was dying, and apparently would never get to see Canada. Naturally I tried to give him hope, even though I realized he was dying. His wife and his mother were at his side. I told one of the ship's mates about Semën Zybin and ran to catch the train before it departed. The train pulled out at four o'clock. An executive coach was attached to our train, carrying 'the CPR boss' (boss is a special American word denoting any kind of 'big cheese'). The CPR is the Canadian Pacific Railway, commonly referred to around here by its initials. This coach was also carrying our Captain Taylor, Archer, Peddler, a Mr. Whyte (another immigration official) and Elkinton, the Quaker — some of these were going to Montréal, others to Ottawa. I stopped by to see them. They were very kind and cheerful. Mr. Whyte and Mr. Peddler joked all the time, and, while getting ready for bed, threw pillows at each other, tore the blankets off each other and fooled around like children. What playful Canadian officials! I have the overall impression that Canadians are more open than the English, that they do not have that air of self-conceit (self-assurance) and the aristocratic air that characterises all English people to some degree.

7 [19] FEBRUARY

Our train rolled rapidly westward. Provisions were stored in the front carriage: milk, cheese, bread and tea. Many Doukhobors have dried crusts and other things besides. This is what we lived on. Among the passengers was the train supervisor, a Mr. MacGovern and, it seems, only one conductor. Mr. MacGovern and I made tea and distributed the provisions. The carriages are very comfortable, clean, and equipped for sleeping; there are facilities for preparing hot foods. A telegram was received on the train: Semën Zybin died during the night shortly after our departure. Another telegram from the train just in front of us informed us that Vasilij Verigin had jumped from the train while it was going but was unharmed. Vasilij Verigin is mentally ill and is subject to attacks of lunacy; he jumped off under the influence of one such attack. We have been stopping only to take on water or fuel or to change locomotives. From the windows we can see good coniferous forests. Occasionally we come across clean-looking wooden houses, mostly two-storey, as well as farm buildings or storehouses. The earth is evenly covered with a not-so-deep layer of snow. In the last carriage Peddler, Whyte, Archer, Captain Taylor, the head of the railway and the Quaker Elkinton are engaged in a lively conversation. In the evening we arrive first at Ottawa, and then at Montréal.[33] Here they get off, and the executive coach is uncoupled. Only MacGovern remains with us.

8 [20] FEBRUARY

We spent practically the whole day today riding along the shore of Lake Superior, seeing the same places we have read about in [stories by] James [Fenimore] Cooper and [Thomas] Mayne Reid. We did not see any Indians, however. The lake was frozen near the shore, but in the distance, we could see an unfrozen watery expanse with no shore in sight. The hilly shores are beautiful — sinewy, pocked with little bays, and covered with forest. Few houses.

9 [21] FEBRUARY

We continue to roll along quickly. There are few people to be seen at the stations, because the curious population has already been satisfied with the first trains passing through. The land is flat, with fewer trees. We are approaching bread country — Manitoba.

10 [22] FEBRUARY

At noon we finally arrive at Selkirk [Manitoba]. This is the last station before Winnipeg, about twenty-five miles [forty km] away. Not far from the station, in the middle of a field, stands a large building, a former railway terminal,[34] which has been adapted to house our party. Here 1,600 of the Doukhobors who came on the *Lake Superior* are to stay, while the remaining 400 (one of the five trains) has gone on further — to Winnipeg, where they are to be housed in an empty school building. In Selkirk we were met by Prince Dmitrij Khilkov, [field nurses] Mrs. [Marija Aleksandrovna] Chekhovich and Mrs. [Efrosin'ja Dmitrievna] Khir'jakova, who had come on the first trains, as well as the chief immigration agent for Manitoba and the Western territories — a Mr. [W. F.] McCreary. When everybody had got off the train and gathered in the large dining room of the immigration hall, McCreary gave a welcoming speech to the Doukhobors. The *starichki* responded with

33 There seems to be a geographical error here: trains from the east coast of Canada normally pass through Montreal first before proceeding to Ottawa.

34 It appears that a former *roundhouse* is actually being referred to here. —Trans.

expressions of gratitude, and, to McCreary's great surprise, more than a hundred of them carried out the traditional bow to the ground. The building in which the Doukhobors are now housed is a large round brick building, with the roof and ceiling resting on rails. In the centre is a vast, high-ceilinged hall; around the sides are sleeping areas, where triple-decker bunks have been constructed. The kitchen and bakery are next door. It is rather crowded, but it is warm and comfortable.

After some time, Prince Khilkov, Mrs. Chekhovich, Mrs. Khir'jakova and I left for Winnipeg. This evening I saw Sulerzhitskij. We were extremely glad to see each other; it was interesting to share our impressions, especially since the two of us had sailed under the same conditions and had had almost identical experiences. The *Huron*'s voyage, however, had been more difficult than ours. It had come through a long spell of bad weather, and ten people had died during the trip.

3. "CONCLUSION"

I shall write a few lines about my return to Russia.

I left Winnipeg at the end of March. Before my departure I visited the immigration buildings in Winnipeg and Selkirk. The Doukhobors who were still there were touching in their expression of gratitude for my contribution to their emigration and, on bidding me farewell, sang their spiritual songs for me. These songs were much more beautiful than their monotonous psalms; some of the songs were sung in a lively rhythm, and in two voices not in unison, like the psalms.

I went through Montréal and Toronto to New York. On the way I spent two days in Toronto, where I met with Professor Mavor, who has done so much for the Doukhobors. Then I stopped for several hours at Niagara to admire the falls. In New York, unfortunately, I was able to spend less than three full days. It was there that I met the handsome, pure-blooded and clever American, Ernest Crosby. Several years ago he represented the United States as an international judge in Cairo. Under the influence of my father's writings, especially *The Kingdom of God is Within You*, he left this service and adopted a world view not unlike that of Tolstoy. He came from New York to Yasnaya Polyana specifically to see my father. I too got to know him there. In New York he was very kind to me, invited me to dinner in his refined but modest house, and saw me off on the steamer. Through him I also met Henry George Jr. and [William] Lloyd Garrison Jr. They too had warm words of praise for my father.

I sailed the Atlantic from New York to Liverpool in seven days, with all the conveniences of first class, aboard the splendid steamship *Umbria*. There was no serious turbulence and I did not suffer at all from seasickness. The ship arrived at Liverpool late at night. A fast express train brought me from there to London. It was already three o'clock in the morning. I took a hansom to the hotel I had stayed at six months previously. Arriving at the hotel, I paid the coachman his fare and rang the bell. A maidservant came out and said that there were no rooms available. I began to question her, but she closed the door on me. By that time the coachman had dropped my bags on the street and departed. I was left in a rather unpleasant situation. I did not know where to go, and could neither carry my bags nor leave them to the mercies of fate. The street was deserted, with not a single passer-by in sight. I sat down on my suitcase and began meekly waiting for some way out of my dilemma. A few minutes later one of those solemn London policemen approached with measured steps and asked: "What are you doing here?"

I told him that I had just arrived from America, that the boat and the train had been late, that my hansom had left, and that they would not let me in to the hotel. Then he rang the hotel bell and when the maidservant opened the door, he enquired: "Do you have rooms available?" She replied that they had. 'Why then can you not let this gentleman have a room?' She muttered something under her breath. At that point the policeman gave her strict orders to let me have a room, and I was admitted. The next day I went to see Chertkov at Purleigh, told him about the Doukhobors' situation and my trip, and on the following day headed directly for Russia. I was in a hurry, as my mother was seriously ill.

Since I had with me my notes, letters and documents on the Doukhobors' emigration, I greatly feared that all this would be confiscated by the Russian customs agents. Therefore, before reaching the Aleksandrov border station, I asked the sleeping-car attendant to hide my rather large packet of papers and return it to me in Warsaw. The carriage in which I was riding was not detached at the Russian border; it was going to Warsaw. For a 'handsome' reward (10 marks) the attendant carried out my request and handed my papers back to me in Warsaw safe and sound.

I arrived in Moscow 4 April (1899), and went to the house in Khamovniki where our family lived at the time. My mother's health had improved.

In conclusion I should like to share my impressions of the Doukhobors. The Doukhobors by their piousness stand above the average level of both Russians and Canadians. One need not share their sense of exclusivity, their conviction that they are a special people — a community of universal brotherhood, or their worship, even the deification of their leader Pëtr Verigin, or their indifferent attitude (to the point of denial) of European culture and science. But one cannot deny their loyalty to the tenets of their faith, their perseverance in actually living their faith and their readiness to suffer for it. This they have proved by their actions. If there are among them some self-seeking people or those who depart from Doukhoborism, they are the rare exceptions. They are honest, sober, industrious, courteous and clean-living. They lack the three vices from which, it must be admitted, the Russian people suffer: drunkenness, cursing and thievishness. I am happy that I have spent almost six months with them and have come to know them. And not only do I not regret having participated in their emigration, but I am proud to have had a least a small part in bringing it about. It is a pity that these good people have left Russia, but their emigration was unavoidable. Naturally, the first years of their life in Canada will be very difficult, but their future is assured.

Moscow, 1899.

Excerpts Concerning the Doukhobors from S. A. Tolstaya's Writings

1. EXCERPTS FROM SOFIA ANDREEVNA TOLSTAYA'S MEMOIRS *MOJA ZHIZN'* [MY LIFE]

THE YEAR 1898 [PART VII]

LEV NIKOLAEVICH'S MAIN INTERESTS over the course of the winter of 1898 were his article *On Art* and the resettlement of the Doukhobors from Russia to Canada. While I was away, Lev Nikolaevich received a visit from an American[1] proposing to resettle the Doukhobors on the Hawaiian Islands. Everything he said about the locale, its beauty and facilities, was very tempting. Unfortunately, however, it was too late, since it had all been arranged by

1 *An American* — Nicholas Russel (birth name, Nikolaj Konstantinovich Sudzilovskij; 1850–1930), a radical student activist at Kiev University who fled Russia in 1874 to escape political persecution. Two years later he obtained his doctorate in medicine at the University of Bucharest. In 1887 he emigrated to America, first to San Francisco and five years later to Hawaii. He idealized the native Hawaiians and deplored their exploitation by continental Americans, especially the missionaries. He encouraged the use of Hawaiian in the local schools. After annexation of the Hawaiian territory by the United States in 1898, Russel joined the Home Rule party and was elected a territorial senator, later senate president. During the Russo-Japanese War, in 1905, Russel was persuaded by American diplomat George Kennan to go to Tokyo and preach liberal government for Russia among the Russian prisoners of war in Japanese labour camps. Always on the lookout to attract more Russian immigrants to Hawaii, upon learning of the Doukhobors' need to emigrate he wrote to and visited Tolstoy in person, urging him to facilitate their relocation there. But by this time the decision had already been made in favour of Canada. See Ronald Hayashida and David Kittelson, "The Odyssey of Nicholas Russel," *The Hawaiian Journal of History* 11 (1977): 110–24; B. S. Elepov and S. A. Pajchidze, *Geopoliticheskij kharakter rasprostranenija russkoj knigi: k postanovke voprosa* [The geopolitical nature of Russian book distribution: towards a formulation of the question] (Novosibirsk, Russia, 2001): 33.

that time for the Doukhobors to go to Canada. Only the procedure was stalled for lack of money. And on the 19th of March 1898, Lev Nikolaevich wrote his *Letter to Society* [*Pis'mo k obshchestvu*],[2] asking for help for the Doukhobors. [VII.50]

...the fact that all his [Lev Nikolaevich's] interest in life was completely swallowed up by his writing of *Resurrection* and the fate of the Doukhobors, at the expense of any participation in the life of his family, greatly distressed me. [VII.60]

At that time he wanted to finish writing and publish three stories: *Hadji Murat*, *Resurrection* and *Father Sergius*. But there were a lot of things preventing Lev Nikolaevich from carrying out this desire. He was occupied with the matter of the Doukhobors' emigration from Russia. Two Doukhobors came to see him for consultation without the police's knowledge, and this was awkward for me, since they hid them in the pavilion. I hated anything secretive and did not want to let it into my house. [VII.58]

At that time Mikhail Osipovich Men'shikov[3] was visiting us. Back then he wasn't as coarse and mercenary as he later turned out to be, and I liked his articles. Nevertheless, he strongly criticized Lev Nikolaevich for asking money from rich people to aid the Doukhobors. [VII.51]

...Lev Nikolaevich hid from me the final version of his article entitled *On Aid to the Doukhobors*, which he had earlier given me to transcribe. As usual, he redid it completely, with crossings-out everywhere, and once again I transcribed it. When Lev Nikolaevich thought that it was quite finished, it was typeset [again], but Lev Nikolaevich revised it once more around the 15th of March, and this time gave it to someone else (behind my back) to transcribe.

2 Sofia Andreevna was evidently referring to her husband's letter to the foreign press (original published in *PSS* 71:322–27), which Tolstoy actually finished on 19 March 1898. The letter was published first in Russian by V. G. Chertkov in Britain, in his periodical *Svobodnoe slovo* [Free Word], and later in English translation in the *Daily Chronicle* of 29 April 1898. In March 1898 Tolstoy had addressed a similar appeal to the Russian public, which he planned to publish in *Sankt-Peterburgskie Vedomosti* (under the editorship of Prince Èsper Èsperovich Ukhtomskij).

3 *Mikhail Osipovich Men'shikov* (1859–1919) — literary critic and essayist. In the mid-1890s he was associated with the liberal paper *Nedelja*, as well as with the journal *Knizhki nedeli*. He first wrote to Tolstoy in 1893 following his laudatory review of *The Kingdom of God is Within You*. Men'shikov's letters to Tolstoy are largely unpublished. Several of them appear in print for the first time in the current volume (see PART IV) as examples of the active involvement of both men in the Doukhobor cause.

He had been hoping that this appeal for aid to the Doukhobors [*O pomoshchi dukhoboram*] would be published in *Peterburgskie Vedomosti.*[4] I was sure that it could not be published in the form it was in, and I was right... [VII.51]

[The] departure and the whole history of the Doukhobors' resettlement has been described a number of times, and I'm not that well acquainted with the details of this event. [VII.58]

TOLSTOYANS AND THE FAMINE (1891) [V.110]

Lev Nikolaevich received frequent visits from his so-called followers Bulygin,[5] Khokhlov,[6] Alëkhin[7] and others. They were all been constantly *wandering* [*khodili*]. During the summer, a time for work, they *wandered.* Why? I could never understand this. Even now it's just the same. Being a Tolstoyan means *wandering.* Either to the Caucasus, or to their commune in the south, or back again from there. And here some of these so-called *wanderers* came to see Lev Nikolaevich.

One of them, Alëkhin, from a merchant family, had been studying chemistry for ten years at university when he quit everything, put on peasant clothes and began *wandering* with Khokhlov, who had also quit technical school, and subsequently went out of his mind.

They even lured Lev Nikolaevich, and he put a knapsack on his back and accompanied them to see the Tolstoyan Butkevich,[8] some 40 versts [approximately forty km] distant. But Butkevich was living with his father

4 *Sankt-Peterburgskie Vedomosti* (1702–1917) — a Russian newspaper, founded 16 December 1702 by order of Peter the Great under the extended title *Vedomosti o voennykh i inykh delakh, dostojnykh znanija i pamjati, sluchivshikhsja v Moskovskom Gosudarstve i vo inykh okrestnykh stranakh* [News of military and other noteworthy affairs happening in the Moscow State and other surrounding countries]. After the death of Peter the Great the paper was renamed *Sankt-Peterburgskie Vedomosti* [St. Petersburg News]. Until 1874 it was published at the Petersburg Academy of Sciences, then by the education ministry. At the turn of the twentieth century it appeared daily. In 1914 it was renamed *Petrogradskie Vedomosti* in accordance with the city's name change. It was closed at the end of 1917, following the Bolshevik revolution.

5 *Mikhail Vasil'evich Bulygin* (1863–1941) — a graduate of the Page Corps who served in the Egerskij regiment. After leaving military service in 1886, he enrolled in the Petrovsk Agricultural Academy but was expelled for his participation in student unrest in the spring of 1887. He lived in the village of Khatunka — sixteen km from Yasnaya Polyana. During the Soviet period he worked on the preparation of Tolstoy's manuscripts for publication in the academy edition of his collected works.

6 *Pëtr Galaktionovich Khokhlov* (1864–1897) — a student who was expelled from the technical academy for declaring his sympathies for Tolstoy's ideas. He later worked in the Tolstoyan land-tilling colonies in Russia.

7 *Aleksej Vasil'evich Alëkhin* (1859–1934?) — a chemist, who became acquainted with Tolstoy in December 1888. In a diary entry of 4 December 1888 Tolstoy referred to him as "a very talented scholar."

8 *Butkevich* — there were actually two Butkevich brothers: Anatolij Stepanovich Butkevich (1859–1942) and Andrej Stepanovich Butkevich (1865–1948), who lived in a village near Krapivna, forty-seven km from Yasnaya Polyana. From 13 to 16 June 1891 Tolstoy went to visit them on

and he had his own apiary — this was better. These two chaps — Alëkhin and Khokhlov — struck me at the time with their gloominess and taciturnity.

During his long travels, and even at home while in constant touch with various individuals as well as the common folk, Lev Nikolaevich began to hear more and more frequent rumours about the famine that was threatening people in many gubernias of Russia. Such talk appeared to irritate Lev Nikolaevich, and he wrote in his diary about the impression it made on him:

> *19 June 1891.*[9] Everybody's talking about the famine (all [the fields] burnt up, some places re-ploughed). Everybody's concerned about people starving, wanting to help them and rescue them. And how repulsive that is! People who don't even think about others, about the common people, all of a sudden for some reason get the burning desire to aid them.

A HUMDRUM SUMMER — THE TOLSTOYANS (1894) [VI.92]

This summer of 1894 was not memorable for any special reason. The absence of my sister [Tat'jana] Kuzminskaja's[10] family was keenly felt, especially by me. For twenty-five years we had spent every summer together, and got along fine and dandy, but then, in 1894, the annexe remained silent and empty, and my life without my sister was lonely and distressing.

We went mushroom-picking and swimming. Lev Nikolaevich got involved in hay cutting for a time, namely, on the 28th and 29th of June, and from the 1st to the 8th of July, with a large group of peasants. Tanja[11] helped him. I didn't like any aspect of this. And I was right, since, on the one hand the heat and exhaustion gave Lev Nikolaevich a stomach illness, and he had to go to bed. He wrote in his diary that on the 9th[12] he was pulling a hay-cart and this was terribly difficult for him. On the other hand, my sons Andrjusha[13] and Misha[14] returned from the hay cutting quite embarrassed. The peasants had pointed out one of their number to him, a Timofej Bazykin,[15] telling my

foot. He later described his impressions of this journey in letters to Aleksandr Dunaev and Prince Dmitrij Khilkov, written 21 June 1891.

9 *19 June 1891* — this note actually refers to 25 June 1891 (*PSS* 52:43).

10 A reference to the family of Tat'jana Andreevna Kuzminskaja (*née* Bers; 1846–1925), Sofia Andreevna's younger sister, who was married to Aleksandr Mikhajlovich Kuzminskij (1843–1917). They had two daughters: Marija Aleksandrovna (married name, Èrdeli) and Vera Aleksandrovna. The Kuzminskijs usually spent their summers at Yasnaya Polyana but in 1894 this tradition was broken.

11 *Tat'jana L'vovna Tolstaja (Tanja)* (1864–1950) — the Tolstoys' eldest daughter.

12 *On the 9th* — Tolstoy, in fact, noted on 11 July regarding the 7th: "7. I worked with the hay and it was frightfully hard" (*PSS* 52:126).

13 *Andrej L'vovich Tolstoy (Andrjusha)* (1877–1916) — fourth son of the Tolstoys.

14 *Mikhail L'vovich Tolstoy (Misha)* (1879–1944) — fifth son of the Tolstoys.

15 *Timofej Ermilovich Bazykin* (1861–1934) — a peasant of Yasnaya Polyana, the son of Aksin'ja Aleksandrovna Bazykina (see following note).

children that this was their brother, born to the peasant-woman Aksin'ja[16] and Lev Nikolaevich. This peasant bore quite a resemblance (albeit in a rough fashion) to his father, the Count.

My erstwhile jealousy was again aroused in me, along with heart-wrenchings over the children. I had a difficult talk with Lev Nikolaevich, and he wrote in his diary at the time:[17]

"A hot day… flies… buzzing... the air's sizzling hot… I was reminded of my imbalance and depravity. I was depraved, too, by my earlier debauchery and luxury, gluttony and idleness…"

Of course it was inappropriate and untimely to remind Lev Nikolaevich of his earlier sufferings after so many years of marriage, especially since he kept constantly punishing himself for his whole past and was firmly on the road to moral self-perfection, right to the end of his long life. But what was I to do? I loved him so much and passionately refused to give him up to anyone else.

At that time he made frequent trips to Demenka[18] to see the Chertkovs,[19] where we also met Ol'ga Diterikhs,[20] the future wife of our son Andrej (who by now [1911] has left her). And sitting at the feet of Chertkov's wife, Galja, was usually to be found a handsome young and likeable foreigner named Dr. Shkarvan.[21]

Lev Nikolaevich also went to see our neighbour Mikhall Vasil'evich Bulygin, who lived, according to the new convention, with someone else's wife and had fathered many fine boys who did not bear his name. I pitied this Bulygin, who had gone astray in life. He was a smart, thoroughly good and decent fellow. He had been raised in a fine aristocratic family and later studied in the Page Corps.

16 *Aksin'ja Aleksandrovna Bazykina* (*née* Sakharova; 1836–1920) — a peasant of the village of Gretsovka. Before her marriage to Ermil Nikonovich Bazykin she had a liaison with Tolstoy. She is portrayed in Tolstoy's stories *Idillija* [*The Idyll*] and *Tikhon i Malan'ja* [*Tikhon and Malania*] as well as in the novella *D'javol* [*The Devil*] in the personage of Stepanida.

17 *Diary* (19 July 1894) — Tolstoy's diary entry for this date reads: "A difficult conversation with Sonja [Sofia Andreevna]…. [T]he peasants were saying during haying that they thought Timofej was my son. That's hard on the children" (*PSS* 52:129–30).

18 *Demenka* — a village about five km from Yasnaya Polyana.

19 *Anna Konstantinovna Chertkova* (*née* Diterikhs; 1859–1927) — Tolstoyan and wife of Vladimir Grigor'evich; *Vladimir Grigor'evich Chertkov* (1854–1936) — a friend and kindred spirit of Tolstoy's, the publisher of a number of his works, and a founder of the Posrednik publishing house. At the turn of the century he was living in exile in Britain, where he founded the Svobodnoe slovo publishing house and a journal of the same name.

20 *Ol'ga Konstantinovna Diterikhs* (1872–1951) — sister to Anna Konstantinovna Chertkova. In 1899 she married the Tolstoys' son Andrej L'vovich, whom she divorced in 1906.

21 *Al'bert Shkarvan* (1869–1926) — a Slovak doctor whose pacifist beliefs led him in 1895 to renounce his commission in the Austro-Hungarian Imperial Army. He was subsequently stripped of his medical degree and sentenced to four months' imprisonment by a military court.

We also received visits from various obnoxious types such as Ozmidov,[22] a morphine addict, about whom Lev Nikolaevich said that he was "pitiful with his deformed lifestyle."

Then came Turner,[23] and for some reason Lev Nikolaevich wrote in his diary at this time:[24] "It's hard to love a Jew...." And I would add that I don't remember who this Tu[rn]er was.

At the end of June[25] Lev Nikolaevich was greatly dismayed by the news that Birjukov's place in Kostroma[26] had been raided. The same occurred with Evgenij Ivanovich Popov.[27] Several disturbed Tolstoyans came to see

22 *Nikolaj Lukich Ozmidov* (1844–1908) — an agriculturalist who became acquainted with Tolstoy in the early 1880s. He owned a dairy farm and a dairy shop in Moscow. After going bankrupt in 1882 he began earning his living copying and selling Tolstoy's banned writings. He also worked for a while in the administration of the Moscow–Kursk railway. In 1886 he and other Tolstoyans set up a farming community in the Caucasus but, following its collapse less than two years later, he returned to Moscow to reprise his former activity in promoting Tolstoy's writings. This brought him under police supervision and he spent some time in exile in Vjatka (in the Kirov district, northeast of Moscow).

23 *Charles Edward Turner* (1832–1903) — an Oxford-educated Englishman who emigrated to Russia (where he became known as Karl Ivanovich Tërner) to work as a teacher of English. He made frequent trips back to England, where he lectured on Russian literature, especially Tolstoy. He translated a number of Tolstoy's works into English. In July 1894 he visited Tolstoy to discuss the translation of *Soedinenie, perevod i issledovanie chetyrëkh Evangelij* [*A Translation and Harmony of the Four Gospels*].

24 *Diary* (11 July 1894) — On 8 July 1894, Tolstoy was visited by an American rabbi, Joseph Krauskopf (1858–1923), from Philadelphia, who had come to Russia to see about holding talks with the Russian government on offering land to Russian Jews for colonization. He presented Tolstoy with a copy of his book *Homilies: Six Lectures.* On 11 July Tolstoy noted in his diary regarding 8 July: "In the evening an American Jew came to see me. It is difficult to love a Jew. One has to try" (*PSS* 52:126). In reference to 9 July he noted, in part: "Read the whole day. Among other things, the disgusting article by the Jew that came yesterday" (126). Tolstoy's negative attitude toward Krauskopf may be explained by the fact that Krauskopf was diametrically opposed to Tolstoy's views on non-violence.

25 *The end of June* — Sofia Andreevna had originally written 'July' instead of 'June.' The raid on Evgenij Popov's office at Posrednik in Moscow occurred 18 June, the one at Birjukov's Kostroma home on the following day.

26 *Pavel Ivanovich Birjukov* (1860–1931) — a friend and follower of Tolstoy, who eventually wrote a biography of the writer. He studied in the Page Corps and then in the Naval Academy, graduating in 1884 (his training there included a round-the-world voyage). He worked closely with Tolstoy on a number of occasions, including the founding of the Posrednik publishing house, relief work for famine victims, the publication of Tolstoy's works abroad, and the drafting of *Help!* [*Pomogite!*] — an appeal for funds for the Doukhobor emigration. He actively participated in the unsuccessful move of more than a thousand Doukhobors to Cyprus (they later resettled in Canada). In the late 1920s he spent some time with the Doukhobors in Canada.

27 *Evgenij Ivanovich Popov* (1864–1938) — a Tolstoyan who took part in many agricultural communes. Tolstoy became acquainted with him in 1887.

us: Gorbunov,[28] Tregubov[29] and Bulanzhe.[30] Lev Nikolaevich wrote in his diary:[31]

"How can they not feel sufferings when they're being locked up and tortured? I feel ashamed and offended to be at liberty myself."

Nevertheless, despite the hay cutting, his illness and various disturbances, Lev Nikolaevich continued to work almost every morning at his usual activity. He could no longer restrain himself from writing. So, on the 25th of June he wrote an article *The One Thing Needful* [*Edinoe na potrebu*];[32] he continued working on his so-called *Catechism*,[33] concerning which he wrote:

"It appears everything has been clarified [*ujasnjaetsjsa*], but not yet in the form that would satisfy me."

In addition, on the 15th of July he dictated to his daughter Masha the drama *Peter the Publican*,[34] which still today remains unpublished, and I have not even been given it to read. The piece is quite unfinished. Lev Nikolaevich's articles were translated abroad, which he was glad about. But for some reason he wrote about his works in his diary of the time as follows:

28 *Nikolaj Ivanovich Gorbunov* (1861–1931) — a Tolstoyan music teacher who graduated from the Petersburg Conservatory. From 1900 to 1916 he was an actor with the Malyj Theatre in Moscow.
29 *Ivan Mikhajlovich Tregubov* (1858–1931) — a follower of Tolstoy's teachings. The son of a priest, Tregubov was a student at the Moscow Theological Academy when he broke with the Russian Orthodox Church. Meeting Tolstoy for the first time in 1891, two years later he began working at Posrednik, later assisting Chertkov in collecting materials on the persecution of sectarians by the authorities and the official church. In 1896 he collaborated with Chertkov and Birjukov in signing and promoting Tolstoy's appeal (*Help!* [*Pomogite!*]) for assistance to the Doukhobors. For this he spent four years (1887–1891) in exile in Kurland Gubernia (on the Baltic Coast) before going abroad.
30 *Pavel Aleksandrovich Bulanzhe* (Paul Boulanger; 1865–1925) — a follower of Tolstoy. In 1886 he graduated from the Faculty of Physics and Mathematics of Khar'kov University. He became acquainted with Tolstoy in 1896. In 1897, for his participation in the Doukhobor cause, which the authorities considered 'agitation,' he was sent 'under police supervision' to one of the Baltic provinces. His form of punishment, however, was altered on orders from Minister of Internal Affairs Ivan Logginovich Goremykin (see note below), and Boulanger was allowed to leave Russia without right of return except by special permission. In September 1897 Boulanger settled in England, where he published a periodical under the name of *Bratskie listy* [Brotherly Letters] in the spirit of Tolstoy's ideas. In 1900 he managed to return to Russia, where he worked in the administration of the Moscow–Kursk railway line. Later he wrote his reminiscences of Tolstoy.
31 *Diary* — from Tolstoy's diary of 25 June 1894 (*PSS* 52:121).
32 *The One Thing Needful* — Tolstoy's celebrated treatise *Edinoe na potrebu*, *PSS* 36:166–205), was actually written between 1903 and 1905 — some ten years later. The phrase, however, was one Tolstoy commonly used in his diary entries from 1894 (e.g., for 26 June 1894 — *PSS* 52:123–24).
33 *Catechism* [*Katekhizis*] — the reference here is not to Tolstoy's 1877 work *Khristianskij katekhizis* [*Christian Catechism*] (*PSS* 17:363–68), but to his later treatise *Khristianskoe uchenie* [*Christian Teaching*], which Tolstoy worked on between 1894 and 1896 (*PSS* 39:117–91).
34 *Peter the Publican* [*Pëtr Mytar'*] — Tolstoy's unfinished play (also known as *Pëtr Khlebnik*), which remained unpublished until 1918 (*PSS* 29:281–91). It is possible he had intended to dedicate it to his daughter Masha. See my article "The Life of *Peter the Publican* as edited by L. N. Tolstoy" (Donskov 1996c).

"What I engendered in agony is now running through the streets. And praised be God."

On the 15th of July a Russian lady named McGachan[35] came to Yasnaya Polyana and brought Lev Nikolaevich some books from Henry George,[36] which he was quite interested in. He wrote in his diary that he had "quite vividly realized again the crime of land ownership." He talked about this a lot with Nikolaj Nikolaevich Strakhov,[37] whose stay with us at the time had been extended on account of the cholera in Petersburg. In the evenings he would read aloud to us [his] criticism of Dostoevsky, and in the afternoons he would take walks and eagerly drink koumiss,[38] which some Bashkirs who had come from the Samara steppes were preparing for the sick Lëva.[39]

However, the koumiss did not help Lëva, but rather harmed him. He was very thin and gloomy. He said that his intestines were paralyzed and that he was going to shoot himself. I remember the suffering caused me by the painful sight of my son, so beloved, especially when he looked at his father sadly and reproachfully with his dark, agonizing eyes, when his father [told him he] didn't believe in his son's disease and unfairly reproached him for it, saying he had to get a hold of himself, not let himself go, get busy, etc. Lev Nikolaevich could never live in an atmosphere where others were suffering, especially people close to him, and deliberately — or, rather, instinctively — denied them, ran away from them. That was how it always was with me. I noted this in my diary in 1894, and in 1910 this very thing came to pass.

I was a nervous wreck, and Lev Nikolaevich couldn't stand my condition and left.

35 *Varvara Nikolaevna McGachan* (*née* Elagina; 1850–1904) — daughter of an old-time friend of Tolstoy's, Nikolaj Pavlovich Elagin, widow of an American journalist surnamed McGachan. Among the books by Henry George she brought with her was one entitled *A Perplexed Philosopher* (New York, 1894; originally published 1892), autographed by the author. In a diary entry of 9 August 1894 Tolstoy noted: "I once more read *A Perplexed Philosopher*. Marvellous. I once more became vividly aware of the sin of land ownership" (*PSS* 52:131).

36 *Henry George* (1839–1897) — American economist and journalist, a proponent of nationalization of land and a system of a "single land tax." Tolstoy became acquainted with George's book *Progress and Poverty* (1879) in February 1885. He became sympathetic to George's ideas and wrote a considerable amount about him — see, e.g., his articles *Velikij grekh* [*A Great Sin*] (1905), *Edinstvennoe vozmozhnoe reshenie zemel'nogo voprosa* [*The Only Possible Solution to the Land Question*] (1906), *Pis'mo k krest'janinu o zemle* [*Letter to a Peasant about Land*] (1905).

37 *Nikolaj Nikolaevich Strakhov* (1828–1896) — philosopher, essayist, and popular-science proponent in Russia, as well as a close friend of the Tolstoy family. Tolstoy had a very high opinion of Strakhov and trusted him with the editing of his works. For a more complete picture of the Tolstoy–Strakhov relationship, see Donskov 2000a, 2003.

38 *Koumiss* — a drink made of fermented mare's or camel's milk, known for centuries to the nomadic tribes of Central Asia. It became popular in Russia for its healing properties toward the latter part of the eighteenth century, and in 1858 the doctor Nestor Vasil'evich Postnikov founded in Samara the first Russian koumiss clinic. Tolstoy became interested in koumiss healing in the 1870s.

39 *Lev L'vovich Tolstoy (Lëva)* (1869–1945) — third son of the Tolstoys.

Back at that time he was hoping to transform me in some way. He wrote in his diary of 24 July 1894:

"How happy I would be to get Sonja to yield to me. But that is no more possible than for a goose to crawl back into its egg. [A strange comparison. —*S.T.*] She would have to do it herself, but she doesn't want to — there's no reasoning, no humility and no love."

What he actually wanted of me, I never did understand, and do not know to this day.

SERËZHA'S DEPARTURE WITH THE DOUKHOBORS — A TOLSTOY EVENING (1898) [VII.62]

After our son Serëzha's[40] divorce with his wife[41] was finalized, he agreed to accompany [a party of] Doukhobors to Canada. First of all he went to Tiflis, from where he sent a telegram saying that on the 17th [of November][42] they had secured permission and were going to Batoum [on the coast]. Then came the news that their steamer was to set sail 21 December.[43]

I was greatly distressed by Serëzha's departure and absence, but I fully realized that his broken life needed to seek out new purpose and interest.

I was alarmed, too, by the fact that he, along with his comrades and the Doukhobors, were placed in quarantine[44] on account of a spreading smallpox, which he only later wrote to us about.

For some time I had been interested in a proposed celebratory evening in Moscow on the occasion of Lev Nikolaevich's seventieth birthday.[45] [This is followed by a description of a party which turned out unsuccessfully, according to Sofia Andreevna.]

40 *Serëzha* (Sergej L'vovich Tolstoy; 1863–1947) — the Tolstoys' eldest son, who at his father's request accompanied the second boatload of Doukhobors to Canada. His experiences are described in detail in his diary of the journey, in Donskov 1998a (*Sergej Tolstoy and the Doukhobors: A Journey to Canada*).

41 Marija Konstantinovna Tolstaja (*née* Rachinskaja; 1865–1900) was Sergej Tolstoy's first wife, whom he married in 1895.

42 *17th* [of November] — upon receiving permission from the Chief of Civil Affairs in the Caucasus (Prince Grigorij Golitsyn) for himself and Tolstoyan Leopol'd Sulerzhitskij to travel to Batoum, Sergej Tolstoy sent his father a telegram: "Permission [granted to] both, tomorrow [we] proceed [to] Batoum" (Donskov 1998a: 249). Note: In the 2010 English edition of *My Life*, this date is mistakenly given as 17 December.

43 *21 December* [1898] — in fact, the *SS Lake Superior* sailed from Batoum on 22 December 1898.

44 *Quarantine* — upon arrival in Canada, the Doukhobor party escorted by Sergej Tolstoy was obliged to spend several weeks in quarantine on Lawlor's Island, near Halifax, after the death of one Doukhobor girl from smallpox during the voyage. The quarantine lasted from 16 [28] January to 4 [16] February. When the quarantine was lifted the *Lake Superior* proceeded to Saint John, New Brunswick, from where the Doukhobors were taken by a convoy of six trains to Manitoba. See excerpt from Sergej Tolstoy's diary, "From Halifax to Winnipeg," above.

45 On 28 August 1898 Tolstoy celebrated his seventieth birthday, at Yasnaya Polyana, receiving more than a hundred congratulatory telegrams on the occasion.

ON LEV NIKOLAEVICH'S ATTITUDE TO ME AND OUR SON SERËZHA — TO THE DOUKHOBORS (1900) [VIII.5]

Lev Nikolaevich was crushed by our daughter Tanja's illness. At the time (January 1900) she was in Rome. She was greatly troubled by her sinusitis, and she faced a second operation.

Lev Nikolaevich himself was healthy and treated me with kindness. On 20 January 1900 he wrote Tanja:

> In our life together it is good that I am getting along so well with Mamà — that comes first — as well as with Serëzha — [we're becoming] closer and closer and more and more loving.[46]

Our daughter Masha and her husband Kolja [Nikolaj Leonidovich Obolenskij] were staying with us then. Both of them looked pitiful and lifeless. In marrying that lazy dreamer Obolenskij, Masha lost her energy and whatever health she had left.

While travelling by railway at the time, Lev Nikolaevich was horrified to learn that workers' shifts lasted 36 hours, and that shocked him. He wrote a brief article[47] on this, which he gave to Prince Barjatinskij[48] to be published in Severnyj kur'er.

On 15 February Lev Nikolaevich wrote a letter[49] addressed to the Doukhobors who had emigrated from Russia to Canada. He encouraged them to continue living that Christian ideal for whose sake they had left Russia behind. He advised them to live peacefully, unselfishly, and not attempt to acquire personal private property, but to hold their possessions in common, on a friendly and co-operative basis.

46 *PSS* 72:287.

47 A reference to Tolstoy's article *Rabstvo nashego vremeni* [The slavery of our time] (*PSS* 34:144–99). Tolstoy did confront the problem of overly long working hours of the workers on the Kazan' railway line in December 1899, but not during his trip, as Sofia Andreevna suggests. He received information about this and on 26 December personally visited one of the freight stations. It was the impressions of this visit that immediately prompted him to write the article, which he initially entitled *Samyj deshëvyj tovar* [The very cheapest commodity] (*PSS* 90:169–75). His work on the article, which could hardly be called "brief," continued until the autumn of 1900.

48 *Prince Vladimir Vladimirovich Barjatinskij* (1874–1941) — editor of St. Petersburg paper *Severnyj Kur'er* [The Northern Courier], who had begun his journalism career with Ukhtomskij's *Sankt-Peterburgskie Vedomosti.* Barjatinskij declined to publish Tolstoy's article under threat of closure by the minister of internal affairs.

49 A reference to the letter Tolstoy sent 15 February 1900 to the Canadian Doukhobors, calling upon them to beware of falling into the temptation of personal property (*PSS* 72:305–20).

2. EXCERPTS FROM SOFIA ANDREEVNA TOLSTAYA'S DIARY

SEPTEMBER 1897

BOULANGER IS BEING SENT into exile abroad. He has been declared a threat because of his promotion of Lev Nikolaevich's ideas and because he wrote and published a letter about the plight of the Doukhobors in *Birzhevye Vedomosti*.[50] He was summoned to Petersburg to what was then known as the Third Department[51] — the police that acted on administrative orders, i.e., pretty much as they liked — and was given a severe drubbing.

Boulanger is a very bright, energetic and lively person, and they were afraid of him. But what a despotic government we have! It's as if the tsar doesn't exist, and some sort of brutish rogues like Goremykin[52] (minister of internal affairs) and Pobedonostsev[53] are taking actions which provoke resentment against the young tsar,[54] and that is a pity. [Vol. I, p. 294]

50 *Birzhevye Vedomosti* [lit. Stock Market News] (1861–1917) — a newspaper published intermittently during this period in St. Petersburg. Beginning in 1893 it came out twice a day; the morning edition, carrying mainly market information, had a small print run and was circulated only among market dealers; the evening edition, on the other hand, carried all sorts of sensational news items. At the end of October 1917, the paper was closed by order of the Petrograd City Council's Military Revolutionary Committee.

51 *Third Department* (1826–1880) — officially, the Third Department of His Imperial Majesty's Chancellery [Tret'e otdelenie sobstvennoj ego Imperatorskogo Velichestva kantseljarii] — a government organ responsible for political inquiry and investigation in Russia. Founded by Tsar Nicholas I on 3 July 1826, it was abolished on 6 August 1880, when all its functions were transferred to the Ministry of Internal Affairs and its newly formed Department of Police.

52 *Ivan Logginovich Goremykin* (1839–1917) — minister of internal affairs, 1895–99, chairman of the Council of Ministers in 1906 and 1914–16.

53 *Konstantin Petrovich Pobedonostsev* (1827–1907) — Russian statesman and tutor in legal studies to Grand Princes (later Tsars) Alexander III and Nicholas II, on whom he exercised a considerable influence. He became a senator in 1868, a member of the State Council in 1872, and from 1880 to 1905 he served as senior procurator of the Russian Orthodox Church synod. He was an outspoken supporter of tsarist autocracy resting on the church and a persistent opponent of the revolutionary movement. He retired and left public life in 1905.

The church synod is the supreme organ of authority of the Russian Orthodox Church. Founded in 1721 by Peter the Great in conjunction with his liquidation of the patriarchate, the synod constituted an ecclesiastical *college*, headed by a president and made up of representatives of the higher levels of the clergy. It was eventually accorded the title "Most Holy Ruling Synod." Its activity was in many respects under the control of government authorities. The synod's mandate included control over monasteries and church affairs, a clerical office for investigations (including investigations of heresies), and other institutions. In 1722 the office of synod president was abolished, and an "ober-procurator" (or senior procurator) was appointed from civilian ranks to oversee its affairs. Following the 1917 Revolution, the Bolshevik government, by a decree of 20 January 1918, separated the church from the state, and the schools from the church. With the restoration of the patriarchate in 1917–18 the "Most Holy Synod" was renamed the "Sacred Synod" and became a collegiate advisory board to the "Patriarch of Moscow and All the Russias."

54 A reference to Nicholas II (Nikolaj Aleksandrovich Romanov; 1868–1918), the last Russian tsar of the Romanov dysnasty, who inherited the imperial crown upon the death of his father, Alexander III. His forced abdication in March 1917 was followed shortly by his arrest. In July 1918 the tsar and his whole family were executed by the Bolsheviks at Ekaterinburg.

2 APRIL 1898

Two husky Doukhobors[55] came to see Lev Nikolaevich, each with a strong spirit and the body of a *muzhik* [i.e., peasant]. We sent them to Petersburg to see Prince Ukhtomskij[56] and Suvorin,[57] [trusting] that these two major newspaper editors could offer them some advice and help. They promised, but it is doubtful they will do anything.

Lev Nikolaevich is writing a petition for them to the tsar, asking that they be allowed to emigrate, along with all the exiled, army-recruited and imprisoned Doukhobors. All this makes me greatly fearful that we might be sent abroad too! These Doukhobors are now staying with Lev Nikolaevich, along with the young factory-worker Bulakhov,[58] who is being sent with the petition and 300 roubles to the exiled Doukhobor leader Verigin... [Vol. I, p. 369]

Lev Nikolaevich's life and interests are so particular, so personally his own, that they don't concern the children; they cannot possibly take an interest in the Doukhobor sectarians, or the rejection of art, or discussions about non-resistance. They need to have their own personal life, at their own initiative. Without any guidance from their father, without any practicable ideals, they are creating their own unruly lifestyle with card-playing, emptiness and amusements instead of serious studies or art. I don't have either the strength or the know-how to create a better life for them, were that even possible with a father who keeps rejecting everything! [Vol. I, p. 371]

3 AUGUST 1898

[Lev Nikolaevich] wants to write and publish three narratives right away: *Hadji Murat*, *Resurrection* and *Father Sergius*, and sell all these as dearly as possible in Russia and abroad and donate the whole proceeds to the Doukhobor emigration.

55 On 30 March 1898 Tolstoy was visited by two Doukhobors, Pavel Planidin and Dmitrij Chernov. They came to consult with the writer on plans for the forthcoming emigration and to ask Tolstoy to send a trustworthy emissary to Pëtr Vasil'evich Verigin in Obdorsk to keep him informed of their progress.

56 *Prince Èsper Èsperovich Ukhtomskij* (1861–1921) — Russian essayist and poet. In 1896 he was appointed acting editor of the paper *Sankt-Peterburgskie Vedomosti.*

57 *Aleksej Sergeevich Suvorin* (1834–1912) — journalist and book publisher. In 1875 he began publication of the paper *Novoe vremja.*

58 *Pëtr Alekseevich Bulakhov* — originally a peasant from Smolensk Gubernia, who later became a Moscow craftsman. He visited Tolstoy in the summer of 1897. In his diary of 7 August 1897 Tolstoy refers to him as "a man of moral and intellectual strength" [*silach nravstvennyj i umstvennyj*] (*PSS* 53:149). In early April 1898 Bulakhov left Moscow on his way to Obdorsk in Tobol'sk Gubernia to see Pëtr Vasil'evich Verigin but was detained before reaching his destination and exiled from Tobol'sk Gubernia.

This is insulting to us, to his family. He should instead be helping Il'jusha[59] and Masha;[60] they are in very bad financial straits. By the way, two Doukhobors have come here, and I am supposed to hide them in the pavilion and I find that extremely unpleasant. [Vol. I, p. 401]

26, 27 AUGUST 1898

The Doukhobors have come again; they are still waiting for something from without, some kind of favourable response from the tsar to their petition and, at the same time, help from Lev Nikolaevich. This is all turning out rather strangely and absurdly, for help from the one excludes help and participation on the part of the other... [Vol. I, p. 404]

13 SEPTEMBER 1898

This novel has put me into a heavy mood. I suddenly decided that I cannot love this work of my husband's and that I would go to Moscow, that there is less and less in common between us.... He noticed my mood and began reproaching me, saying that I don't like anything he likes or is involved in. I replied that I love his art, that I was in ecstasy from his *Father Sergius*, that I was interested in *Hadji Murat* too, had a high appreciation for *Master and Man*, and wept every time I read *Childhood*, but *Resurrection* was repulsive to me.

"But you don't like my work with the Doukhobors, either," he protested.

"I can't find any pity in my heart for people who refuse military service and thereby cause impoverished peasants to become soldiers in their place and at the same time demand a million roubles to take them out of Russia...

"I have sympathy for his efforts to help the famine victims in 1891 and 1892, and even today. I myself have worked and assisted and given money. And now, if anyone is to be helped financially, it should be only the humble peasants who are dying of starvation, and not the proud Doukhobor revolutionaries."

"I am very sad that we are not together on everything," said Lev Nikolaevich.

And what about me?! I have suffered so much from this disunity. But Lev Nikolaevich has [devoted] his whole life to people and goals foreign to me, while my whole life [has been devoted] to the family. I cannot get it into my head and heart that this work, especially since Lev Nikolaevich declined royalties [from works published after 1881] (as he wrote in the paper[61]), should now

59 *Il'ja L'vovich Tolstoy (Iljusha)* (1866–1933) — second son of the Tolstoys.

60 *Marija L'vovna Tolstaja (Masha)* (1871–1934) — second daughter of the Tolstoys.

61 On 16 September 1891 Tolstoy wrote letters to the editors of *Russkie vedomosti* and *Novoe vremja*, stating: "I hereby offer the right to publish freely and without charge, in Russia or abroad, in Russian or in translation, or to produce on stage, any of my works written since 1881, along with any of my works which have not been published in Russia and any works which may appear after this present date" (*PSS* 66:47). Tolstoy left any royalties from his works published before 1881 to his family.

be sold for an enormous sum to Marks[62] at *Niva*, and the proceeds therefrom be given not to our grandchildren who haven't got a bite to eat, and not to impoverished children, but to the Doukhobors as complete strangers, whom there is no way I can love more than my own children. But the result is that the whole world will know of Tolstoy's participation in assisting the Doukhobors, and the papers and history will write about that. And as for the children and grandchildren, they will have to get by on black bread! [Vol. I, p. 411]

5 OCTOBER 1898

[Lev Nikolaevich] has gone back to the old routine: again he is writing a work of fiction and again wants a lot of money for it. Only before, the money legitimately went to the family, while now he has thought up some kind of kindred-spirit Doukhobors, and the money will go to them, and all the papers will write about this. It would be far more natural to take pity on his own [peasant] Vlas in the country, whose children as well as cows are dying of starvation... [Vol. I, p. 416]

62 *Adol'f Fëdorovich Marks* (1838–1904) — Russian bookseller and publisher, originally from Stettin in Germany. He began his career as an independent publisher in St. Petersburg in 1870 with the launch of *Niva*, a weekly "illustrated magazine for family reading," with a print run of 200,000. Marks put out a number of various supplements to *Niva* — first, albums of art reproductions and oleographs, and later literary anthologies (beginning in 1889) and the collected works of Russian and foreign writers (beginning in 1891). Some (including Tolstoy's) were also published as separate volumes.

PART IV

ARCHIVAL LETTERS ON TOLSTOY AND THE DOUKHOBORS

ARCHIVAL LETTERS CONCERNING THE DOUKHOBORS

This section contains thirty-two archival letters concerning the Doukhobors. The correspondents, in alphabetical order, are:

Vladimir Dmitrievich Bonch-Bruevich (V. D. Bonch-Bruevich)
Vladimir Grigor'evich Chertkov (V. G. Chertkov)
Nikolaj Fëdorovich Khudjakov (N. F. Khudjakov)
Savelij Fëdorovich Khudjakov (S. F. Khudjakov)
Mikhail Osipovich Men'shikov (M. O. Men'shikov)
Ol'ga Konstantinovna Tolstaja (O. K. Tolstaja)
Sofia Andreevna Tolstaya (S. A. Tolstaya)
Lev Nikolaevich Tolstoy (L. N. Tolstoy)
Sergej L'vovich Tolstoy (S. L. Tolstoy)
Prince Èsper Èsperovich Ukhtomskij (Prince È. È. Ukhtomskij)
Pëtr Vasil'evich Verigin (P. V. Verigin)

N° 1. M. O. MEN'SHIKOV ❧ L. N. TOLSTOY
22 October 1895

I was planning on publishing the article[1] about the Doukhobors (with a few deletions to accommodate the censors). The first half had already been typeset when Gajdeburov[2] showed up (5 October) and halted it. He considered the article altogether unprintable, especially after your letter to *The Times*, as reported in the papers.

N° 2. L. N. TOLSTOY ❧ P. V. VERIGIN[3]
21 November 1895. Moscow.

Dear Brother!

Ivan Mikhajlovich Tregubov has sent me your letter to him,[4] and I was very glad to read it, glad to learn of you and to hear your voice, as it were, and understand what you are thinking about, and how you think and what you live by. I see from your letter that you live in a spiritual world and concern yourself with spiritual questions. That is vital for the good of mankind, for only in the spirit is man free, and only through the spirit is God's work done, and only in the spirit does man feel himself at one with God, since "God is spirit." The thoughts you express in your letter about the superiority of live communication over dead books greatly appealed to me, and I share them. I write books and therefore I know all the harm that they cause; I know how people who are unwilling to accept truth know how not to read or not understand anything

1 The reference is to Pavel Ivanovich Birjukov's article "Gonenie na khristian v Rossii v 1895 godu" [Persecution of Christians in Russia in 1895], to which Tolstoy wrote a preface. This article was published by Èlpidin in Geneva in 1896. See *PSS* 68:155, 173–74, 183.

2 *Vasilij Pavlovich Gajdeburov* (1866–after 1940) — editor of the liberally-oriented populist newspaper *Nedelja* and the journal *Knizhki nedeli.*

3 This and other Verigin letters below are reproduced in the entire Tolstoy–Verigin correspondence in Chap. 6 above. They are also included here in the context of other archival letters concerning the Doukhobors.

4 Letter from P. V. Verigin to Ivan Mikhajlovich Tregubov, 5 August 1895, published in Bonch-Bruevich 1901: 14–16. In 1893, Tregubov (1858–1931) left the Moscow Seminary to work at the Posrednik publishing house. Thanking Tregubov for the books sent to Obdorsk, Verigin added: "Books help a lot in working things out, but can sometimes be a big hindrance as well. Whereas our own voice of appeal will never deceive you, as long as our desires are sincere, that is, as long as the soul is fully present." Later Tregubov continued sending Tolstoy letters from Verigin and other Doukhobors.

that goes against the grain and exposes them, how they reinterpret and distort, how they have reinterpreted the Gospel. I know all that, yet all the same I think that *in our time* books are unavoidable. I say "in our time" in contrast to the gospel times, when there was no printing of books, there were [simply] no books, and the means of communicating thoughts was purely oral. Back then it was possible to get by without books, because neither did the enemies of truth have books; but now we cannot let just the enemy have this powerful tool [to use] for deceit and not use it for truth. Not to use books or letters for communicating one's thoughts and to receive thoughts of other people is tantamount to not using the power of your own voice to communicate instantly to many people what you wish to say, or not to use your hearing to understand what another person is saying out loud, but to admit that thoughts can be communicated and received only one-on-one or through whispering.

Letters and print have simply increased by thousands — by hundreds of thousands — the numbers of people capable of hearing one express one's thoughts, but the relationship between the communicator and the receiver remains the same; just as in oral conversation the listener can delve into and understand what he is hearing, or can let what is being said to him go in one ear and out the other, the same is true with print: just as it is possible for the reader to misinterpret a book he is reading, so can one who listens with his ears; just as one can — as we see — write nonsense or write too much, so is it possible to talk that way. There is a difference, but the difference is sometimes in favour of oral, sometimes written communication. The advantage of oral communication is that the listener feels the soul of the speaker, but here too is the disadvantage that quite often empty-headed chatterers — lawyers, for example — endowed with the gift of the gab, attract people not by the reasonableness of their words but by their oratorical mastery, which doesn't happen with books; another advantage of oral communication is that the person who doesn't understand can ask for clarification, and yet there is the disadvantage that people who don't understand, often on purpose, can ask unnecessary questions and break the train of thought, which also does not happen with books. The disadvantages of books are, first, that paper will tolerate anything and you can print all kinds of nonsense, at the cost of enormous efforts on the part of paper and typography workers, which would be impossible in oral communication, since people don't bother listening to nonsense; secondly, the fact that they (books) are multiplying in huge quantities and the good ones are lost in a sea of stupid, meaningless and harmful books. Nevertheless, the advantages of books are also considerable, consisting mainly in the fact that the circle of one's listeners is expanded by hundreds of thousands compared to people listening to oral communication. And this expansion of the circle of listeners is important not simply because there are a lot of them, but because among the millions of people of various nations and social status who have access to a book, 'kindred spirits' turn up all by themselves; people living tens of thousands of versts[5] from each other, people who don't even know each other, are united into one and live by a single soul and derive spiritual joy and courage from the realization that they are not alone. This is the kind of communion I now have with you and with many, many people of other nations who have never seen me, but who are closer to me than my blood sons and brothers. But the chief argument in favour of books is the fact that, given a certain degree of development in the outward standard of living, books and print in general have become people's means of communication with each other and therefore we cannot afford to neglect this means. So many harmful books have been written and circulated that this harm can be counteracted only by books. You fight fire with fire. Christ said: "What ye hear in the ear, that preach ye upon the housetops."[6] Well, this preaching upon the housetops is the printed word. The printed word is the very same language, only very far-reaching, and therefore everything said about language applies to the printed word as well: we use language to bless God and to curse people created in God's likeness; and so you can never be careful enough about what you say and hear, just as about what you print and read. I am writing all this not because I thought that you think differently (I see from your letter that you understand this the same way), but because these thoughts have come to me and I wanted to share them with you. I was especially touched by what you said in your letter to the effect that "*if we preserved what was already given to us from above, we should be perfectly happy. And whatever is necessary and lawful must inevitably be in each one* [*of us*], *and comes directly from above or from within ourselves.*" This is quite right, and that is my concept of man too. Everyone would undoubtedly know God's truth, know all they needed to know to accomplish what God wants from them in this life, as long as this truth that has been revealed to man is not clouded by false human interpretations. And for that reason, to know God's truth, man needs first of all to reject all false interpretations and all worldly temptations that would lead him to accept these interpretations, and then the truth alone will remain, the truth which is available to babes, since it is innate to the human soul. The big challenge is in throwing out the lie without throwing out some of the truth with it, as well as, in the process of explaining the truth, to avoid introducing new errors.

I thank you, dear brother, for the greetings you sent me. Write to me in Moscow, if there is nothing stopping you, at the Tolstoy house in Khamovniki Lane. Is there anything I can do for you? You will make me very happy if you give me something to do.

I embrace you as a brother.

Leo Tolstoy

5 *Versts* — a pre-revolutionary unit of linear measurement, equivalent to approximately one km.

6 Matt. 10:27.

N° 3. M. O. MEN'SHIKOV ❧ L. N. TOLSTOY
6 April 1898

My dear Lev Nikolaevich, I went directly from the train to Ukhtomskij's [office] and told him in brief everything I had heard from you about the Doukhobors, along with the draft of the petition. The prince, evidently, is himself very interested in this matter and has succeeded in arousing interest among many others. He heard from Witte's[7] report a few days ago that the Tsar himself asked: "Well, isn't there something that can be done for the Doukhobors, to use them, for example, on our eastern frontiers?" And Witte gave, it seems, a favourable response. Governor-General Dukhovskoj would *very much* like to do the very best for them in everything, settle them somewhere in a remote comer of his gubernia where they would probably not be disturbed, but he says that, as he has only just been appointed, it would be awkward for him to take the initiative in this matter. Ukhtomskij himself is against sending them to Port Arthur and Manchuria, as that will possibly become a theatre of war and there is no guarantee that the Doukhobors would be left undisturbed there. He thinks it would be best of all if the government itself funded the Doukhobors' resettlement to somewhere in Turkestan, or allowed them to emigrate to Mongolia where, as he put it, they would probably be left in peace "for more than a hundred years."

As to the draft of the petition, Ukhtomskij thinks that it is absolutely necessary to omit the reference to the [Doukhobors] exiled to the Yakutsk district. They can be interceded for after the main emigration takes place. At that point the government will have reason to change the place of exile from the Yakutsk district to Turkestan or Mongolia, but right now that would be awkward.

Ukhtomskij talked at length about how important it is to direct this petition so that it does not look as though it is coming from you, since the mere mention of your name is enough to make government officials extremely nervous. Ukhtomskij is quite embarrassed that, in spite of the prince's request, Sigma,[8] in his article on the Doukhobors, mentioned that the Doukhobors had come to see him to ask about America etc. According to Ukhtomskij, Jakov Polonskij[9] is planning to write about the Doukhobors (his reminiscences of them),

7 *Sergej Jul'evich Witte* (1849–1915) — political activist, a strong supporter of autocracy, minister of finance from 1892 to 1903.

8 *Sigma* — one of the pseudonyms of Sergej Nikolaevich Syromjatnikov (1864–1937), who also wrote under the name Sergej Normanskij. He wrote an article published in *Novoe vremja* of 5 April 1898 citing the dangers of the Doukhobors going to "America," where they would eventually be swallowed up by the dollar culture. He argued that they should be sent to China instead, where they could become teachers of Russian culture.

9 *Jakov Petrovich Polonskij* (1820–1898) — poet of conservative views. While highly critical of Tolstoy's attack on the government and the official church, Polonskij nevertheless shared Tolstoy's concern and sympathy for the persecuted Doukhobors, even writing about their plight to the senior procurator of the Holy Synod, Konstantin Pobedonostsev. See Tolstoy's letters to Polonskij in *PSS* 71:348–50, 366–67.

and that would be very significant, the prince thinks. But when Ukhtomskij remarked that you were playing a major role in this matter, Polonskij waved his hands in the air and was almost ready to change his mind. I shall go see him and ask him about this.

N° 4. M. O. MEN'SHIKOV ❧ L. N. TOLSTOY
18 May 1898

A few days ago, I. K. Diderikhs[10] came to see Ukhtomskij (at his invitation), and here is the current status of the Doukhobor situation. Count Muravёv[11] (the Minister of Foreign Affairs) has started asking the opinion of various agencies as to whether the Doukhobors could be permitted, as Ukhtomskij proposes, to emigrate to Manchuria. The answers that came back were contradictory and unclear, and Golitsyn (from the Caucasus) gave an unfavourable response. His report (compiled by the Chancellery director Mitskevich,[12] who was mixed up in the matter of taming the Doukhobors) says that the Doukhobors are an extremely dangerous element, but they should not be sent abroad, in order to avoid the appearance of persecution; it would be enough to offer to resettle individual families. Muravёv himself, who had at one time strongly sympathized with Ukhtomskij, is now decidedly opposed to his plan, for fear that the Doukhobors, once beyond the Chinese border, might gather all the enemy forces together against Russia and undermine our prestige there.

There is no hope that they will allow relocation to Cyprus, and Ukhtomskij is in a state of utter despair over this whole matter. The ministerial reaction is a form of chaos, and the Tsar wishes to alleviate the Doukhobors' plight, but without the support of the government there is no step he can take. Everybody is frightfully busy with other affairs. The most important thing is to hold their positions. According to Ukhtomskij, all the ministers have ganged up on him, accusing him of undermining the bureaucratic system. Ukhtomskij did not come to see you, wary of being labelled a Tolstoyan (which is now considered more terrifying than a socialist), but he will keep at this matter as much as he can. [...]

I have a very close friend in California, Dr. Kryshtofovich, who was formerly a member of the colonial intelligentsia around Batoum, but fled to America to escape the system in Russia. He emigrated there with his

10 *Iosif Konstantinovich Diterikhs* (also spelled Diderikhs, Ditrichs; 1861–1932) — brother to Anna Konstantinovna Chertkova. He lived in the Caucasus, but was expelled from there in 1897 for his sympathetic attitude toward the Doukhobors. He is the author of "Vospominanija o L. N. Tolstom" [Reminiscences on L. N. Tolstoy] (Diterikhs 1926).

11 *Nikolaj Valer'janovich Muravёv* (1850–1908) — minister of justice in the Russian imperial government, 1894–1904.

12 *I. Mitskevich* — director of the Office of the Chief of Civil Affairs in the Caucasus (under Prince Golitsyn).

extensive family (his children are physically giants, his wife is as meek as an angel). I wrote to him recently and asked him to think how he might be useful to the Doukhobors should they emigrate to America. This is what he wrote me:

> For the Doukhobors, of course, there is only one way out — emigration from Russia, just as for the Stundists, who will be persecuted too, in the near future. Whoever knows what they want and what is wanted of them should try with all their might to get them resettled as quickly as possible, so as not to let these splendid people simply perish. I for my part can offer the following:
>
> 1. If I am told that the Doukhobors have decided to move here, I shall enquire about the availability of government and private lands in the States of Arizona, Colorado and New Mexico. The East is densely populated, and in California it is very expensive. In Arizona there is room for agriculture, cattle raising and fruit growing.
>
> 2. The community should send two trustworthy representatives, and I shall go with them to take a look at these lands, I can help with the purchase, etc.
>
> 3. When they emigrate en masse, I shall meet them in New York and accompany them as an interpreter and doctor to the place of settlement. I can help them get oriented, find a Russian teacher who can teach some of them (the most capable ones) English, as well as a competent instructor in agriculture (to help them get started — there is a different way of doing things here, taking care of the calves, etc.). For this I am to be paid travel expenses and three dollars a day (I will have to hire a worker to take care of my farm for a dollar and a half a day, buy my meals en route, stay at hotels and lose a month's practice).
>
> I would be able to help them this way only between 1 June and 1 October.
>
> The Doukhobors should be informed that (a) they will need to pay taxes here and (b) schooling for children between 8 and 14 years is compulsory (religion is not taught in the schools).
>
> The representatives should be warned not to let themselves be taken in by Russian-speaking con-artists, beginning with Jews and ending with people 'known to the whole Russian educated public.' At the appropriate time I shall write them details about the itinerary etc.
>
> Since the Doukhobors have been living in a rather cold climate (in the mountains), it may very well be that they will prefer Canada to the western states. In Canada the population density is only 0.6 per square kilometre, an abundance of forests, water and pastureland; in short, a good deal of free space. Besides, as of this spring the Canadian railway has lowered its fares almost by half. In the Canadian province of Alberta there are rather a lot of Ukrainians, emigrants from Austrian Galicia, who speak a language fully comprehensible to a South Russian population. If necessary, I could gather some information on Canada, go there with the representatives, etc.
>
> In any case, since the well-being of the colony depends on the place of settlement, this place should be chosen very carefully, and since I have been seeking something similar for myself of late, I think the experience I have gained may be of some service to the Doukhobors as well.
>
> Here is this person's address:

Dr. Th. Krysto
Ioamosa, San Bernardino Co., Calif.
Un. St. of N. America

His name is Fëdor Fëdorovich [old style: Theodor Theodorovich] Kryshtofovich. He is a man of rare honesty and moderate independence; he is also very kind, as is their whole family. Perhaps you, Lev Nikolaevich, will write to him if you need to. I shall send his original letter to Chertkov. I think that [North] America is still the most suitable place for resettlement, if they cannot be accommodated in Russia.

N° 5. M. O. MEN'SHIKOV ☙ L. N. TOLSTOY
12 June 1898

Today they were seeing the Doukhobors[13] aboard ship. They have been comfortably settled, and everything is fine.

N° 6. M. O. MEN'SHIKOV ☙ L. N. TOLSTOY
13 June 1898

The prince showed me a letter to him written by Count Murav'ëv about the Doukhobors. Murav'ëv writes that in response to his request for his evaluation of the Doukhobors Golitsyn said that, in view of the current "stubborn and annoying" attitude of the Doukhobors to Russian authorities, it would be dangerous to resettle them in an area where our influence was desirable (i.e., in the Chinese possessions). Evaluations have been received from the ministries and, according to Ukhtomskij, it is a lost cause. Goremykin thinks the Doukhobors should not be sent anywhere, they are fine in the Caucasus.

Iosif Konstantinovich will tell you about the Ivin and Makhortov families' stay in Petersburg, as he will be coming to see you in a few days. They are now safely on their way abroad. They have been appointed spacious quarters normally reserved for merchandise, but it has been outfitted with clean, fresh bedding. It turned out that one of the first-class passengers was an Englishman who knows Russian. At my request he quickly agreed to act as an interpreter for the Doukhobors in case of need. A kitchen, boiling water, a pharmacy, etc., they have all this on board. On the 19th they will be arriving in London, where some of our friends will meet them. It is curious that the police officer took their passports, so that now they don't have any positive identification attesting to any country of origin. Since they have been deprived of the right of return, they are evidently not Russian citizens, but at the same time they are no one else's citizens either. Not a single government is now obligated to

13 A reference to the Doukhobor emissaries I. V. Ivin and P. V. Makhortov, despatched as advance scouts to Cyprus and Canada (see next letter).

defend their rights, not a single institution can make any civil arrangement on their behalf; they have all at once become a special nation unto themselves. The English agent advised me not to worry, as passports are not required in England.

I don't remember whether I wrote you about the splendid impression I had of the Doukhobors. I have finally seen real, genuine people, the kind I should like to be myself, if only it weren't so challenging. The Doukhobors seemed to me like aristocrats (in the best sense of the word) — people of fine stock, in a good state of physical and mental health, raised in a noble tradition and moral discipline. If the community of these people is forced to leave the country (where a breed of diehard conservatives, for example, is artificially supported), then that is a bad omen for the country.

N° 7. M. O. MEN'SHIKOV ❧ L. N. TOLSTOY
7 July 1898

I am sending you a new letter from that Dr. Kryshtofovich (from California) and an excerpt from his previous letter I sent you earlier (with his proposal to help the Doukhobors move to America).

Summary of Kryshtofovich's letter[14]
Appreciation for Men'shikov's knowledge both of the Doukhobors' current situation and of the various places of possible relocation.

Hawaii is unsuitable (a) because it is too warm for people accustomed to a cold climate and [due to] (b) insufficiency of arable land and water. Other disadvantages mentioned: danger of tropical fever, swarms of mosquitoes, only rainwater available for drinking, government comprised of whimsical 'adventurists,' all the good land has been bought up by large companies and the water has been reserved for irrigation of sugar plantations. The rainy side of the island sees 300 rain days per year. [Kryshtofovich's] friends Dr. Russell and his wife are both ill with fever, and he himself experienced a loss of energy during his seven months in Hawaii. Conclusion: White-skinned people should not live below the 30th parallel of latitude.

As for America itself, Kryshtofovich warns of the danger of unscrupulous people arranging (in return for a handsome fee) for the Doukhobors to settle on waste lands unsuitable for agriculture.

Now that he knows the number of potential emigrants, Kryshtofovich will make enquiries about suitable places in the USA and Canada, and advises that three representatives be sent from among the Doukhobors' own ranks and not just intellectuals.

14 The original letter is located in M. O. Men'shikov's file in the archives of the L. N. Tolstoy State Museum in Moscow.

In a postscript he tells of sending an article on "Salt-marshes and sugar-beets" to the periodical *Sel'skij Khozjain,*[15] advising on the cultivation of salt-marshes in Russia on the basis of his California experience.

NO 8. M. O. MEN'SHIKOV ❧ L. N. TOLSTOY
8 July 1898

Anna Konstantinovna [Chertkova] has asked me to find two field nurses to accompany the Doukhobors. I have contacted E. D. Khir'jakova,[16] and if she agrees, it would be hard to think of a better combination. She is a fine person.

NO 9. P. V. VERIGIN ❧ L. N. TOLSTOY
16 August 1898, Village of Obdorsk[17]

Esteemed Lev Nikolaevich!

I am taking advantage of a wayfarer to send you this letter with my heartfelt greetings and my wish that you receive all good from God. Thank God I am healthy and safe.

After a period of uninterrupted correspondence, I wrote you two or three more letters which the 'censor' has probably not sent on to your address, since I have not received any letters from you either.

So much has accumulated to talk to you about heart to heart that I shall have to restrain myself, otherwise I fear the letter will be a long one. I recently read your account in *Rus'* about the famine.[18] This chronic famine is indeed a sorry state for a people, but even sorrier is their refusal to give bread to starving people, while taking away one's daily bread is openly tolerated and even encouraged by all possible means!

Dispiritedness — or rather, the lack of development of the spirit in the life of a people — is unquestionably the root cause of all a people's ills, but the lowering or raising of a people's spirits largely depends on the material conditions of human life. When you talk of spiritual aid to a people, I presume you

15 *Sel'skij Khozjain* (1885–1917) — agricultural journal founded by writer Konstantin Masljannikov.

16 *Efrosin'ja Dmitrievna Khir'jakova* (1859–1938) — a doctor who accompanied the second boatload of Doukhobors to Canada aboard the *Lake Superior.* See the second excerpt from Sergej Tolstoy's diaries above (for 10 [22] February).

17 *Obdorsk* — a city founded in 1595 on the banks of the Lower Ob in the northwestern part of Siberia. In 1930 it was renamed Salekhard. Verigin lived in exile there from 1894 to 1902.

18 The article "Famine or not?" appeared in the newspaper *Rus'* of 2 and 3 July 1898. Here Tolstoy wrote: "If by famine is meant not enough to eat, not what people are dying from at the moment but rather what people live off of, but live poorly, dying prematurely, becoming disfigured, degenerating and failing to procreate, then such famine has existed about twenty years already for most of the centre of the black-earth [region], and is especially strong this year" (*PSS* 29:221). For running the article, the paper received a warning from the Ministry of Internal Affairs (which could be followed by suspension or closure).

mean their total liberation from outside interference by anyone offering 'aid.' Otherwise wouldn't it mean that Nature, God and life itself were unjust to every living thing, including man, holding man in a state of spiritual backwardness?

It seems to me that what has led to this sorry state of the masses is man's artificial attempt to help his fellow man — especially in respect to his spiritual development. People who have been falsely taught, wanting to protect their fellow man from the cold — not noticing that they themselves are very weak — and gradually covering his body, have piled up such a weight (on top of it) that it only serves to stifle him! This is how all educational accumulations grow in modern life. We must forsake, as much as possible, all artificially developed 'chimeras' — which themselves, as you rightly believe, live off the resources of the people — and give people room to breathe freely, and then the people will strengthen themselves and develop and advance under the influence of the universal evolution of life! All we have to do is not interfere with this movement. Because of our limited strength we of course cannot interfere with or stop this evolutionary movement, but we are retarding and disfiguring our own lives.

As an example I would cite the following: it came to people's consciousness a long time ago, as you know, that God is life (Christ's words). But some people, teachers, would have us see God in figures made by craftsmen, figures often sitting on thrones and wearing royal crowns! And this new-fangled teaching, which has held mankind for thousands of years in the chains of ignorance, etc., etc., is called education. What people in Russia are thirsting for now is not education but *liberation* in the broad sense of the word, the total liberation of the individual from being watched over by other human beings.

Cannot those who have taken upon themselves the task of educating the masses see and admit the simple fact that all their artificially worked out educational plans are a burden of oppression on the already weakened back of the working man?

Last winter the governor of Tobol'sk was here. He invited me to his quarters and was extremely kind and polite towards me. We talked for over three hours, it was over high tea, and with him were three members of his 'entourage,' who also took part in the conversation. He questioned me with some interest on how I had become acquainted with you. When I replied that I had got to know you [simply] by correspondence, they were really surprised that people could get to know each other so well through correspondence!

I attach a copy of the petition we sent to the Ministry of Internal Affairs.[19] I wanted to know your opinion, dear Lev Nikolaevich, on the matter of sending

19 The Doukhobors' application for permission to emigrate was originally addressed to the Empress Aleksandra Fëdorovna; she passed it on to the senate, from where it was sent to the commanding officer in the Caucasus, G. S. Golitsyn. Permission was forthcoming only for those who were not in exile or subject to military conscription. Later Tolstoy wrote to Russian and foreign newspapers, and on behalf of the Doukhobors to Tsar Nicholas II. A copy of Verigin's application to the Ministry of Internal Affairs is preserved in the Tolstoy archives.

the Doukhobors abroad. Personally, I am *almost* positively *against* emigration. You see, the members of our community are in need of self-improvement, and so wherever we went we would take our weaknesses with us; and even though an individual can generally live more freely abroad, I don't think the difference would be all that great. People are the same everywhere.

If it comes right down to emigration, then [I foresee the following] conditions: the government must return all the resettled Doukhobors to their families, and give a two- to three-year grace period for emigration. The community could send three or four trustworthy people to look over the place [proposed for us]. Then there is also the question as to whether there are places free in America [for us], so that the [local] population would have no objection to our settling [there]. Finally, we could hire two or three American ships and go at once.

Please write and tell me, dear Lev Nikolaevich, whether you are in touch with [any] American acquaintances regarding the emigration of the Doukhobor Community.

Aleksej Ivanovich Stepanov
Village of Zaval'naja (suburb)
City of Tobol'sk

Once he has received your letter, he will forward it to me by some traveller. If you have any papers to send me, address them to Stepanov; he is a good friend of mine — and of yours.

The police do not give me any letters at all, and do not send out any of mine. I am allowed to write — as the Governor warned me — to my parents, and my letters should not contain any 'philosophical arguments' (the Governor's expression). There is a Russian Orthodox Church mission in Obdorsk, this year two monks have come out to [run] it — one from St. Petersburg, and they have preached sermons in church over and over again about the Doukhobor community, about its evil, its danger to the State, etc. I warned the monks that if they continued doing so I would be compelled to remind them of certain unjust misrepresentations about our community. One Sunday they allowed me to speak in church. A heated debate ensued, but a lot of the people here accepted my point of view on world issues.

The priests asked about our rejection of icons. I explained that we worship God, to whom everything that exists is subject, not only the earth and everything on it, but everything in the universe too. God is *life* and is present in all that exists, and is equally present to protect man, for example, as the smallest bird or insect, and therefore, I said, God, whom we worship, is immeasurably vast and great, and it is impossible to put Him in any kind of frame, let alone to represent Him pictorially; we can feel God only in our heart and soul, and express His quality of Love to all living things around us.

There were six priests there; one of them spoke with me, but by and by they all started talking; I drew their attention to the noise they were making, and some of the people who were listening agreed with me. The priests got into such a state of excitement that one of them said: Show us your God, or Love! Some of the people even laughed at such a question. I replied: You are repeating the words of the Pharisees which were addressed to Christ; but I am sure you understand what love means, only you aren't willing to confess it, moreover, you are holding the people in darkness for the sake of material advantage.

Before this confrontation the priests had promised to ask questions and hold discussions periodically on Sundays, but this did not happen more than once. The elder priest among them made a trip to talk to the Bishop about the discussion. He recently returned, but what he came back with I have no idea.

Recently someone came to see me from my relatives. He managed to come into the apartment and was here no more than *five* minutes when the police came and arrested him. Half an hour later they sent him off in a convoy. He didn't have a passport.[20] They don't give out passports to Doukhobors. Last year too some people tried to come and visit me, but they never got here. There was another person too, Mikhajlo Androsov, I think he was at your place.[21] I find such trips quite superfluous. But my old mother is extremely concerned and doesn't even trust letters saying I am alive. Even though this person is travelling in a convoy and won't get there quickly, [at least] he'll tell her he saw me.

I don't receive any mail from those sent to the Yakutsk region, no correspondence is permitted.

In [the magazine] *God's World* there was an account of a conference of missionary priests at Kazan'. The question they raised was typical, about taking children away from sect members! Only it turned out after that that there was nowhere to put them! Any discussion of this matter is superfluous![22]

20 *Passport* — here referring to an internal identification document required for travel within the Russian empire (and later within the Soviet Union).

21 Mikhajlo Androsov, along with other Doukhobors, visited Verigin in Obdorsk in 1895. In December 1896 he tried again to see Verigin, but thirty km from Obdorsk he was arrested and sent home in a convoy. On 13 January 1897 he stopped to see Tolstoy in Khamovniki on his way through Moscow. In replying to Androsov's story of his life after his return, Tolstoy wrote him in July of the same year: "Give my greetings and love to all the brethren. I have not seen anyone except you, but all of you are closer to me than people I have spent my whole life with, because I see in your lives the manifestation of the God I live by.... More and more brethren who share our spirit are cropping up all over Russia and abroad. I believe that the kingdom of God is drawing closer. Write to me." (*PSS* 70:107).

22 The Kazan' missionary conference took place in August of 1897. Among other steps taken in the struggle with dissident sects, it was decided to petition for a law that would allow children to be taken from their parents and brought up in diocesan orphanages. Shortly thereafter this measure was applied to the children of the Molokans. After reading an account of the conference in the newspaper *Russkie vedomosti*, Tolstoy noted in his diary: "A disturbing account of a missionary conference in Kazan'" (*PSS* 53:150).

The magazine *God's World* is available in Obdorsk. I then sent a letter to the editor regarding the conference. I am sending you a copy. It is quite probable that the police did not forward it.[23]

The conference thought your writings extremely dangerous! To tell the truth, you have uncovered a lot of lies lately. The priests are especially angry at you, and with some justification, for you with your "Little Pamphlets" won't let them hide any more in their sheep's clothing, when in fact they are Wolves.

The summer here has been quite warm and relatively long. There are a lot of berries growing here: cloudberries, bilberries, bog whortleberries, *kljazhitsa,* mountain cranberries, there are a few red currants and I have spent almost the whole summer in the field gathering berries. Moreover, I have procured myself a joiner's bench and some tools, I also have a lathe and am working little by little [on that]. Come winter I thought I would start making boots, even set up a cobbler's shop, since there are no boots here and people are in great need of them. I think the disadvantage of a cobbler's trade is that you have to sit for longer periods than normal, and that is harmful. In general, I do not get regular physical exercise; but in any case I prefer work in the open air — for example, this summer I took great delight in mowing and gathering hay. Haying is also quite profitable here; they don't set up meadows, everyone mows where he wishes. There are not that many haymakers here, since almost everybody goes off fishing for a living.

Last summer there were two students here from St. Petersburg University collecting flora and fauna.

One of them very much wanted to see you, [and so] I sent a letter with him — did you receive it or not?[24]

Recently some ships passed through Obdorsk, travelling down the river to Ob Province. This is the second time they were carrying bread to exchange for foreign goods, mainly things made of iron. I don't think such trade is particularly profitable. While sending more and more crops away, Russia is going hungry herself; besides, all the soil is becoming depleted because it isn't getting enrichment in the form of crop waste, and so forth. Russians are starting to produce crops more easily, but it's sad that the producers themselves don't get to eat them, trading them instead for various foreign improvements.

Give my sincere greetings to all the Brothers
and sisters in Spirit. I wish you all the best.
Pëtr Verigin

I am sending you "A Fantasy"[25] — an idea that came together last winter. The bishop was here, and I wrote it in honour of his visit. When I met him I

23 The whereabouts of both the original sent to the magazine and the copy sent to Tolstoy are unknown.

24 See Letter N° 4 in Part I, Chap. 6, above.

25 See end of Letter N° 6 in Part I, Chap. 6, above.

presented it to him, but he didn't take it, explaining that he receives all documents through the Consistory. If possible, see if you can make a small pamphlet out of this idea; I think it will be useful for the simple folk!

N° 10. S. L. TOLSTOY ❧ L. N. TOLSTOY[26]
24–25 December 1898 — SS Lake Superior

24 December 1898 [5 January 1899]

Papà, I am now writing after twenty-four hours of sailing on the *Superior*. I am very fearful about the future. It is only when one sees what it is like to have two thousand people aboard ship where it is crowded and dirty, and that of these two thousand, unavoidably, as it were, there are many ill, several cripples, elderly, pregnant and so forth, that one begins to feel the gravity of the overall situation as well as one's own responsibility. I was in definite need of an assistant for interpreting and arranging things. But I am the only one who knows both languages and I am the only intermediary between the people and the crew on whom everything depends. The contract for hiring the ship is now in my name.

The Doukhobors, of course, are a marvellous people — rational and uncomplaining, but slow; they do not comprehend the need for some kind of organization and disciplined procedure — questions about bakers, cooks, lamps, water-closets, etc. will not be resolved as they should be for some time to come. I am not happy about myself and our ladies Khir'jakova[27] and Chekhovich[28] travelling first class while those who have chartered the ship are on the lower decks. But the captain[29] is adamant about not letting anyone into first class.

Now, having become better acquainted with the Doukhobors, I am beginning to doubt the wisdom of their emigration and whether or not one should be assisting them.[30] Assistance is a two-edged sword. Assistance is compassion and encouragement. Perhaps it was necessary for the exiles who went with Sulerzhitskij[31] to leave, but as for the others, I am still not sure. It is true that some would have gone to Yakutsk, but people live there, too, though to the limit [of their endurance], it seems, and later in time they might be returned. The others, meanwhile, would be living in their marvellous sunny mountains, in the places where they were born, and in Russia, where they are

26 Originally published in Donskov 1998a: 355–57.

27 *Efrosin'ja Dmitrievna Khir'jakova* (1859–1938) — a doctor (sometimes referred to as a field nurse) who accompanied the Doukhobors and worked among them for a time.

28 *Marija Aleksandrovna Chekhovich* — a doctor's assistant (field nurse).

29 *Captain William Taylor* — captain of the *Lake Superior*.

30 Sergej Tolstoy later became fully convinced of the wisdom of the Doukhobors' emigration.

31 *Leopol'd Antonovich Sulerzhitskij* (1872–1916) — accompanied the first boatload with the Doukhobor exiles.

needed. But Canada? They say that apples do not grow there, that there is not much hope for growing wheat, that the forest is only aspen, etc. The risk and sacrifices involved in emigration must also be weighed together with its other disadvantages.

These two days — the 22nd, when we came on board, and the 23rd — the weather has been splendid, with no rocking.

The above was written yesterday. Today, the 25th, my fears were partly justified. Yesterday the weather was no worse, but this past night there was unbearable turbulence. I too had to lie down and hence could not get anything done; I made only two tours of the ship. Down below it is frightening to see what is going on. Everything is covered with vomit, everyone is ill, everyone feels sick. They say it will be even worse on the Atlantic Ocean.

At the moment there is a respite — we are approaching Constantinople. This much I have written for everybody, but I am sending you a separate note. I shan't be able to write you again until we reach Halifax twenty days from now. Somehow these twenty days will pass!

S.T.

A separate [note] for you.

It is not that I have anything special to say, but this is not for everyone. First of all, about my current situation. I fear that in going with the Doukhobors, I have done so not just out of a desire to help them. I fear that is not the main reason. I am glad that you are pleased that I went with them, but you should really only approve if my motives are completely good. What if I went because I am unhappy with my family life, or even if one of the reasons was to win your good opinion of me? Your opinion of me is more important to me than anyone else's. Sitting in this cabin and knowing that for the next 22–25 days I shall not have contact with anyone in the outside world, I feel extremely lonely. The English on the one hand and the Doukhobors on the other. I never can feel completely at home with the Doukhobors — they are too withdrawn into their community. They trust me, they call me Sergej and even Sergunja, but I am not one of them. And I have had this great desire to see you and all those close to you; I'm so afraid I shall never see you again. And for me life without you would be a great void.

I have also been wanting to write to you for a long time about my family situation. You know that I did not marry as I should have, and since then the constant difficult, inimical and indeterminate relations with my wife[32] have constantly tormented me and made my life miserable. The torment begins as soon as I am left alone. And I don't know what I should do — make another attempt at reconciliation? — in which case I shall have to sacrifice at every

32 Sergej Tolstoy's first wife, Marija Konstantinovna (*née* Rachinskaja) had tuberculosis and lived apart from her husband with their two-year-old son, Serëzha.

step everything I consider good and everything I live by, let alone sacrifices of pride, etc., and with no assurance that I shall achieve anything at all, or remain in my current indeterminate situation? — and then thoughts come to me involuntarily about wishing for the death of another person, and she may involuntarily have such thoughts too.

And I am beginning to come to the conclusion that the best thing to do is to break completely with my wife, and for this I will be obliged to divorce her and have her place taken by another woman. Do not imagine that I have any specific intention in mind. I have nothing of the sort, but I do need to come to an internal decision, and I am more and more inclined towards this one.[33] I would very much like to know your honest opinion about this.

I very much look forward to receiving letters in either Saint John or Halifax. Both there and here I shall ask for General Delivery in my name.

S.

N^O 11. S. A. TOLSTAYA ❧ S. L. TOLSTOY

27 December 1898. Yasnaya Polyana.

Dear Serëzha. We have been reading and rereading your last letter from Batoum[34] many times. For the first time I felt a wrench in my heart and got very worried about you, even though the whole time I have been very understanding and sympathetic toward the cause you are currently involved in. We also received the telegram about your departure, and now we are constantly with you in our thoughts.

[...] What a lot of the world you are going to be seeing! Sometimes I envy you. May God help you bear any seasickness more easily; for some reason I'm frightfully afraid of it. Plus a lot of other unexpected things! Everything's up to fate and God. Sometimes I'm so fearful for you that I try not to think. Though I hope there will be letters from you, but they take so long to get here! The telegram you sent on the 22nd from Batoum got here the morning of the 25th. [...]

N^O 12. S. A. TOLSTAYA ❧ S. L. TOLSTOY

5 [17] January 1899. Yasnaya Polyana.

Dear Serëzha, the papers today [are reporting] that there is a huge storm in London, and we are all despairing for you and your fellow travellers. We too have been having a lot of storms all over and terrible winds, but no frost and almost no snow. Your letter is very bleak; I can imagine that things are pretty

33 As it turned out, Sergej Tolstoy decided not to divorce his wife. Marija Konstantinovna Tolstaja died in August 1900. Sergej Tolstoy's second marriage was to Countess Marija Nikolaevna Zubovaja, in 1906.

34 Sergej L'vovich sailed from Batoum on 22 December 1898 [3 January 1899].

challenging, difficult and complicated for you. One comfort — no efforts and no labours are ever in vain, and they will always have their reward. I remember how Papa often doubted during the famine years[35] as to whether help was really needed, were they doing the right thing? But things turned out all right in the end, and everyone was left with splendid memories.

... Papa is quite well and lively; he's enjoying writing again. He's often worried about you though, just like all of us....

Serëzha, please wire us, at least occasionally, to tell us you're alive and well. It's nice to have some first-hand news. And why won't you send me even a single letter? This is the third letter I've written you, and I'm probably the one most worried about you. If my words and my wishes can do anything for you, I would say: take care of your health, don't despair — everything will pass — don't let yourself get discouraged and keep faith in your good cause...

N° 13. S. A. TOLSTAYA ❧ S. L. TOLSTOY
10 [22] January 1899. Yasnaya Polyana.

Where are you now, dear Serëzha?

Today Papa, I, Tanja and Sasha returned to Moscow all healthy and cheery. The trip here this time was somehow especially easy...

I try not to be concerned about you, but that is impossible, and I often despair and worry about you. May God grant you a safe journey, good health and inner peace. With hugs and remembrances from everyone.

Your mother
S. Tolstaya

N° 14. S. A. TOLSTAYA ❧ S. L. TOLSTOY
23 January [4 February] 1899. Yasnaya Polyana.

At long last, dear Serëzha, we received news of your arrival in Canada. The last little while before the telegram came we had such an attack of despair that we were all walking around glumly and not sharing our thoughts with each other. We can't wait to get letters from you. The separation and the long distance are teaching us to be patient, and our hearts are getting used to the state of concern.

Everybody here is fine, everyone's healthy, lively and cheery. Papa's been having back massages, for which a medical assistant has been coming from the clinic. Papa really likes this and his back is much better. To be sure, it wasn't all that painful, since Papa was out riding all the time on [his horse] Tarpan, brought over from Yasnaya, but on the whole he hasn't looked this

35 *The famine years* — the reference is to the Russian famine of 1891–92, when Tolstoy helped organize a relief campaign for famine victims near his estate in Samara Gubernia.

well in a long time. He's continuing to work zealously on *Resurrection* — the copying is being done for him by Aleksandr Petrovich,[36] and Marusja, and Tanja, and me — we're all helping...

I'm disturbed about Lëva — he's got terribly thin again, and he's so excitable, nervous, irritable...

...Well, it seems, I've told you about everyone. Fortunately, I can say they're all just as before, just like everything else, thank God! Only you come back now hale and hearty, I'm very fearful for you.

Hugs and kisses. Don't be too harsh on my letters, I've really got out of the habit of letter-writing.

Your mother,
S. Tolstaya

N° 15. S. L. TOLSTOY ❧ S. A. TOLSTAYA
26 January [7 February] 1899. Halifax (Lawlor's Island).

Halifax, Lawlor's Island, *SS Lake Superior*
26 January [7 February] 1899

Dear Mama, I am very grateful to you for your letters, and do not think that I do not appreciate them. On the contrary, getting letters here from afar is a whole event in itself. I have received letters from Papa, Tanja,[37] Sonja, Afanasa and two from you. I have already answered some of them. Here we have been in quarantine twelve days already. I am staying on the boat, which for me personally is quite comfortable. Up until now 700 Doukhobors have been staying on the boat, 1,300 in barracks on the island.

The doctors are autocrats and tyrants — every day they subject people to new tests. There are two of them — the Chief Public Health Inspector in Canada, Dr. Montizambert, and the other, Quarantine Physician Dr. Jones. The former is gracious, albeit pedantic; the latter is pedantic but unpleasant. They gave everyone smallpox injections, and then made a second examination of everyone's arms, giving out different coloured tickets. Then they disinfected and steamed our clothing, and they are still going to be fumigating everyone's things and the whole ship with sulphur. Now they are sending people to the baths — a rather uncomfortable, coldish bathhouse, and they're giving out tickets again — yellow tickets to all those who have bathed.

When we entered the quarantine, the facilities and buildings on the island weren't yet ready. This meant that they weren't able to take everybody off the ship right away. Now another new barrack structure has been built, along with

36 *Aleksandr Petrovich Ivanov* (1836–1912) — a friend of Tolstoy's who was a copyist for some of his writings.

37 *Tat'jana L'vovna Tolstaja* (1864–1950; married name Sukhotina) — the eldest daughter of Lev Nikolaevich Tolstoy, sister to Sergej L'vovich Tolstoy.

disinfecting facilities and a bathhouse. All this time the ship has been standing idly at the wharf, and the officers have spent most of their time playing cards. It's a great loss for the shipowners, but in spite of all their difficulties, the Canadian government is holding the ship for 21 days.

We are now facing a question which hasn't yet been answered: do we first go to Saint John by sea or straight from here [Halifax] by rail? Nobody feels like boarding the ship again and travelling in the cold weather, what with the rocking and the prospect of taking three or four days to make a twenty-four hour trip. That is a possibility, since they say the weather here is usually bad at this time of year.

The day's events here include the doctors' experiments and the arrival of the *Argus* — a boat that keeps us in daily contact with Halifax and with the outside world in general. One Doukhobor woman had a baby here in quarantine. The Doukhobors here are behaving somewhat like Robinson Crusoe — they're making fires (there's free wood about) to cook borscht and kasha, they sing their less-than-pretty psalms, they carve spoons out of wood, they write letters (they've already sent off about 150 letters), and they would feel pretty good overall if the ones on the shore weren't crowded so tightly into the barracks, and the ones on the boat weren't so cold.

Besides, they're spending their money, but not earning anything. They are very reasonably submitting to the tyrant doctor, and the reaction to them here is quite favourable. Indeed, they are amazingly good, trustworthy, of course, honest, fair and especially well brought up. I have not once seen a quarrel among them and have not heard even a single swearword. I will be very sorry to leave them; some of them have become close friends. Again, what a pity their influence has been taken out of Russia.

They are really eager to read, but they have no books. Couldn't a few more Russian books be sent to Winnipeg — addressed, say, to Khilkov, along with a dozen or so English dictionaries and self-instructional English textbooks? In the future the Doukhobors will be scattered across a number of small settlements, of about 200–300 residents each. They propose to work the land together and share the harvest rather than working individually or as households.

The ladies of Halifax have been sending the Doukhobor apples and candy, along with a parcel of old Christmas cards and a book of old illustrated editions — *Chatterbox*, etc., according to the principle "if you don't want it yourself, give it away." But the Doukhobors are very pleased with this sign of welcome.

I am less busy personally at the moment, partly because there are fewer people on the ship and we're standing in port, partly because the tyrant-doctors have an interpreter — a Russian Jew named Bershtejn, who fled seventeen years ago to escape military service. However, the tyrant doctors' orders go mainly through me. I am the one who orders provisions from the city, move[s] the people about, etc. Khir'jakova and Chekhovich are still working.

However, there are not many sick. Only one little boy with pneumonia is still in danger. I am now on friendly terms with the captain. The Doukhobors have given him a splendid Persian carpet.

I am enclosing the report about us in the papers in refutation of any misleading accounts; there are, of course, no new cases of smallpox. Tell Papa that his letter had a very good effect on me. From here I plan to go (after the 21-day quarantine period is over) to Selkirk[38] (near Winnipeg) where the Doukhobors will spend the winter, and after eight or ten days there travel home[39] through New York and England. I won't be accompanying the next party — surely Papa will find somebody else? I have written to Chertkov about this. I could help whoever goes, with information and advice.

See how much I've written to you! Do share the contents of my letter with whoever is interested and write to me at General Delivery, New York. I've decided not to go to Japan, etc., as it would be too long, and I really want to go home.

Your son Sergej

N° 16. S. A. TOLSTAYA ❧ S. L. TOLSTOY
3 [15] February 1899. Moscow.

At long last, dear Serëzha, we received a letter from you today. It took from the 17th of January to the 3rd of February to get here. Now a lot more time has gone by and the quarantine has probably ended. How unexpected and bothersome that was! You've gone through a lot of suffering this past while! And you don't write anything about your health. Still, there's a lot of interesting things — that will never be erased from memory our whole lives and will be so pleasant to think back upon later, eh?

And what about our life? Here we are in Moscow, living just as before. The same hectic receptions (Sundays instead of Saturdays), and the boys scream out their gypsy songs with the guitar on the stairway and the landing. And Tanja's sitting there with Vera Sollogub, and I can barely stand all this, and so to comfort myself I go to concerts and occasionally tinkle at the piano.

We're all quite hale and hearty; Papa is quiet and kind, very busy with his writing, often talks of you. He goes round asking and collecting money from rich people for the Doukhobors, but he's never contacted or embraced or

38 *Selkirk* — a small town about forty km east of Winnipeg. Sergej L'vovich Tolstoy arrived in Selkirk on 27 February (NS), where the Doukhobors were met by Prince Dmitij Khilkov and officially welcomed to Canada by W. F. McCreary, the immigration agent for Manitoba. See entry of 10 [22] February in Sergej Tolstoy's diary in Part III above.

39 Sergej L'vovich Tolstoy spent more than a month in Canada, staying in Selkirk and Winnipeg and visiting the Doukhobor settlements in Assiniboia (now part of Saskatchewan). His journey home, which began 28 March, took him through Montreal, Toronto, New York, and London. See "Conclusion" to Sergej Tolstoy's diary in Part III above.

talked with the tsar, and we're dumbfounded and can't understand how such a worldwide rumour got started...

Your little family is well too.

It's a great pity your letter is so short — I really wanted to learn more details. You'll be telling us about your trip the whole year long, only may God grant you a safe return. But I realize you simply haven't had the time, and it's been difficult for you. Suller [Leopol'd Sulerzhitskij] is a remarkable chap!...

Now farewell, my dear energetic and long-suffering son! Hugs and kisses from all of us, and our understanding. We shall expect you alas! only at the end of March. Please write...

N° 17. S. L. TOLSTOY ❧ T. L. TOLSTAJA[40]

3 [15] February 1899. Halifax.

Halifax, 3 [15] February. Lawlor's Island (quarantine); on board *Lake Superior*

Dearest Tanja, as you see, I am continuing my stay aboard ship, in quarantine. Our twenty-one-day period finishes the day after tomorrow and we are heading for Saint John, again by boat. It is [only] a twenty-four-hour journey, but usually very stormy. For the past while storms have been raging everywhere, but for now the weather has calmed down, the moon has come out (I saw it off to starboard), so there are all the probabilities for a fair crossing. All the Doukhobors are quartered on the island, and although their accommodations are crowded, but warm, they continue to live the life of Robinson Crusoe — cooking in outdoor cauldrons, doing their laundry at the seashore, and so forth. The experiments conducted by the autocrat Dr. Montizambert and his Grand Vizier Dr. Jones are coming to an end. They have (1) inoculated everyone against smallpox, (2) checked the inoculations, (3) dry-cleaned underwear and clothing, (4) fumigated the sheepskin coats, (5) been washing everyone in a bathhouse. Everyone is healthy, more or less, with the exception of cases that are always possible — dysentery, inflammation of the lungs, erysipelas, etc. No one has died in quarantine these past three weeks, thank God; one baby boy was born. They have all had a good rest and are encouraged by the fact that the journey is almost over.

It is strange that I have been in [North] America three weeks now and have seen nothing except the quarantine island. The island is covered with fir trees, somewhat different from ours, and there are two or three trails going across it. The whole island occupies no more than two or three square kilometres. Lately we have had heavy snowstorms and severe frosts, so that the landscape, apart from the sea, looks quite Russian — like Moscow Gubernia. Only we don't have such biting winds.

40 Originally published in Donskov 1998a: 358–60.

All the residents of both the ship and the island have naturally got to know each other very well and have become fed up with each other. I must confess that the Doukhobors sometimes irritate me with their slowness and even laziness. The Kars contingent is the best, whereas those from Elizavetpol' include some (just a few) on the borderline between the Smaller and Large Parties [*Malaja partija* and *Bol'shaja partija*], and within a year some of them will be drinking, smoking and eating meat (some of them are already doing so, but are very secretive about it).

The Elizavetpol' Doukhobors always lag behind when it comes to work, and they have a noticeable tendency to live each one for himself. There is some discontent between them and the Kars contingent; it is expressed in little ways and it is hidden, but it is there. One of the difficulties I had in looking after their affairs was precisely this division of the whole lot into 675 from Kars and 1,225 from Elizavetpol' and the two do not know each other very well. The Kars people moved out of Elizavetpol' Gubernia twenty years ago, and while some still have relatives in the other contingent, there has been little communication between the contingents for these twenty years, and since then a new generation has grown up. I am writing all this, of course, because I have grown rather tired of playing the role of the Doukhobors' *leader*; they are very good people, and I don't think the autocrat Dr. Montizambert and his Grand Vizier Dr. Jones could so easily have conducted their experiments with any other group of people. I have some great friends among them, and I am, of course, very popular with them on the whole; they believe I am the one who has brought it all to pass, and that without me they would have been lost. I am called Sergej (with a Ukrainian *g*[41]), Sergunja, Serezha, and very rarely Sergej L'vovich.[42] The Kars contingent is the best. There are some who always defer to others, who always work for everybody and don't even notice that others are not doing the same.

What a pity that Papà cannot see them all as they are now, with their women, children and old ones. I often imagine how touched he would be by them.

I shall say now quite frankly that I am thinking more and more about returning to Russia; even [North] America is not that interesting to me; so, after seeing the Doukhobors to their winter quarters — Selkirk, near Winnipeg, and spending ten to fifteen days more with them in Canada, I am coming home. It will be sad for me to part from them, but I suppose I cannot live out my life with them.

Now about you. What has made you so gloomy?[43] Cheer up. Get involved in something, take a trip somewhere. I am speaking from my own experience:

41 *Ukrainian g* — soft [like German *ch*]. A feature of south Russian pronunciation.

42 *Sergej L'vovich* — this would be the customary form of address one would expect from all but one's relations or very close friends.

43 Sergej Tolstoy is referring to his sister's concern over her complicated relations with her future husband, M. S. Sukhotin.

when you see people facing death, suffering and danger close at hand, and when you become involved in other worlds, whatever sadness you may feel over unhappy relationships seems trivial. After all, regardless of anything else, you are living in a greenhouse, and even though you know about everything going on in the outside world you are not involved in it. I am very glad that I have had the opportunity to get involved (even though right now I very much want to return to the greenhouse); I feel it has changed somewhat my outlook on life — i.e., as to what is important and what is not. And that is why I wish you would put Misha Stakhovich,[44] the Kolokol'tsevs[45] and the rest, if not on the back burner, at least on the second one.

The boat has come which collects the mail, so I am hastening to finish.

Yours, S.

N° 18. S. L. TOLSTOY ❧ S. A. TOLSTAYA
23–24 February [7–8 March] 1899. Winnipeg.

My last letter to you, dear Mamà, was written from the quarantine. I have received two letters from you here, the last was dated 3 [15] February, I believe. I am writing to you no less than I have written to Papà, Tanja[46] and the others.

On 5 [17] February, after twenty-one days of quarantine, the doctor finally let us go. In the morning I went to Halifax on a small boat — it is six or seven kilometres from the island — to settle the account for the provisions purchased there. After all, the Doukhobors had to provide for themselves during the quarantine at their own expense, and we spent more than a thousand dollars on that, which was covered by a collection of fifty kopeks [25¢] per person. The provisions were bought through the shipping agent DeWolf, who delivered the provisions I ordered by boat.

Halifax is a city much like any other: snow and sleighs in the streets, people walking about in fur coats — generally a rather uninteresting scene. But I was only there for about three hours, most of that time in the agent's office. Upon my return I found that all the people had already boarded the ship, according to the arrangement made the night before. Two families with sick people, however (about 18 people all told), stayed behind in Halifax until they got better. New people — reporters, travelling salesmen, photographers, the curious — came to the island. The quarantine had been lifted, so everyone was allowed to come. We sailed at two o'clock; the weather was mild and rather grey. We were accompanied by Archer[47] and two elderly Quakers from

44 *Mikhail Aleksandrovich Stakhovich* (1861–1923) — an acquaintance of the Tolstoy family and a close friend of Sergej Tolstoy's. He was very much attracted to Tat'jana Tolstaja.

45 *Grigorij Apollonovich Kolokol'tsev* — an acquaintance of Tat'jana Tolstaja's.

46 Sergej Tolstoy's sister, Tat'jana L'vovna Tolstaja (see preceding letter).

47 *Herbert Archer* — an English Tolstoyan invited by Vladimir Chertkov to assist with the Doukhobors' emigration.

Philadelphia named Elkinton and Giddly. In the evening they held a meeting with the Doukhobor *starichki* in one of the second-class cabins, at which I served as interpreter. The Quakers talked about their teachings and about the history of the Quakers in America. There were the inevitable [references to] 'the spirit that moves thee' — along with the trembling voice. The Philadelphia Quakers are prepared to assist the Doukhobors with a loan, seeds and cattle.

We were very much dreading the crossing from Halifax to Saint John, but as it turned out, the weather was exceptionally favourable; there was hardly even any rocking, and we finally arrived at Saint John around four o'clock in the afternoon of the following day. A curious crowd had already assembled on the dock; the Canadians received the Doukhobors most warmly: ladies gave out candy to the children, and many shook hands with the Doukhobors. Before disembarking the *starichki* decided to express their thanks for the welcome, and conveyed (through me) to the government official their gratitude to God for their safe arrival, and to the Canadian government for agreeing to accept them and for what had been done for the Doukhobors. Speaking on behalf of the government, [immigration official] Mr. Peddler welcomed the Doukhobors to Canada, saying they were free to practise their beliefs here and that they would find a friendly reception. All this went rather solemnly. Then followed the disembarkation and the boarding of the trains — straight from the wharf. Five passenger trains and one baggage train came and went by turns. This continued until two o'clock in the morning. I had to do a lot of running around, making sure things were in order; I also had to introduce myself [to strangers], respond to compliments and a variety of questions and even autograph the wooden spoons which the ladies were buying from the Doukhobors.

The trains [here] are very comfortable, with sleeping accommodations. Two more families stayed behind in Saint John because of illness. One person, twenty-five-year-old Semën Zybin, who had had a fever for a long time (even back in exile in Baku Gubernia), died the following day, as we learnt by telegram — he died of complications associated with the fever — liver and kidney disease.

Several Canadian officials, the Quaker Elkinton, Archer and our captain from the *Lake Superior*, travelled with me on the last train as far as Montréal, a twenty-four-hour journey [from Saint John], where they got off. The railway journey went quickly and smoothly. On the train the Doukhobors had milk, tea, bread and cheese. On the fourth day we arrived at Selkirk — winter quarters for 1,600 people of our party. Selkirk is twenty miles [thirty-two km] east of Winnipeg. Another unloading, and the Doukhobors were finally able to settle in for the winter. The remaining four hundred went on to Winnipeg, where they were given special accomodations in an old school building. The Selkirk immigration hall stands all by itself about two miles [three km] from the actual town, which is a rather small place. It is a large round brick building, with a large dining room in the centre and sleeping quarters around the perimeter. It is crowded, but warm and comfortable. By the time our last train arrived, the others had already settled in. For three days I had been sharing the train with four hundred of the nicest Doukhobors from Kars. Now I was reunited with almost everyone, as well as with our ladies Mrs. Chekhovich and Mrs. Khir'jakova, who had come on the third train. We were met by Khilkov and McCreary (the immigration commissioner). Mr. McCreary gave a welcoming address to all the Doukhobors, who had assembled in the large dining room; the *starichki* responded, and at the end they all made a low bow. That same evening Khilkov, the ladies and I left for Winnipeg, where I am staying in a hotel. I go to the immigration hall about three times a day and make occasional trips to Selkirk. Nine hundred Doukhobors from the *Lake Huron* are housed in the immigration hall, and everything is run from here.

Suler[48] was not in Winnipeg [when we arrived]; he came the following day. We greeted each other joyfully like long-lost relatives, and eagerly shared our impressions from our ocean crossings. It had been a little more difficult for them; the weather was bad almost the whole time, and ten people died at sea.[49] Suler had organized a team of his sailors and the order and cleanliness aboard his ship were exemplary.

Now about affairs here in general.

Accommodations. The Doukhobors are being accommodated as follows: the first party — the exiles from the *Lake Huron* — are in Winnipeg, Brandon, Portage la Prairie, Dauphin and Yorkton — all these places are along the railway line, on the way to their allotments. Of our party, 1,600 are in Selkirk and almost 400 in Winnipeg. The accommodations everywhere are comfortable, though crowded. By the beginning of April (new-style) it is expected that everyone will go to the homestead sites and that these quarters will be cleared out.

Food is being bought by the government, i.e., in fact, by Mr. McCreary, out of the money allocated as a 'bonus.' He says that since the government is interested in having the quarters [currently] occupied by the Doukhobors cleared out on time and getting them settled so the government will no longer have to feed them or take care of them, he cannot allow the bonus money to be spent without his control. The Doukhobors were unhappy that the food they were getting initially (milk, cheese, syrup, etc.) was too luxurious. They were not aware that the food was being bought with the bonus money — i.e., with their money, which was a fixed amount, and so they naturally ate what they were given; everyone will eat what is set before him. Now, however, this issue has been settled and the food is being purchased more economically.

48 *Suler* — Leopol'd Antonovich Sulerzhitskij was known to his friends as Suler (Souler).

49 Three of the exiles died in Batoum, ten at sea, two in Saint John, and about eight here [in Winnipeg]. — Note by Sergej Tolstoy.

The whole running of the Doukhobors' affairs is in the hands of McCreary, even though (according to Maude's[50] agreement with the minister), this should be handled by a committee consisting of two Winnipeg residents, McCreary and Khilkov. McCreary is a very active and practical person, but he is naturally unacquainted with the Doukhobors and their needs, what they can and cannot do themselves, etc. Many little things are not being done the way the Doukhobors themselves would like. For example, they would have liked to make the harnesses for the horses themselves, while McCreary wants to buy them ready-made; they want to build their own houses, whereas McCreary has hired twenty Canadians to build their houses, and so on.

The current plan of action is the following: it is proposed to build temporary houses on the allotments for all four thousand Doukhobors and to take provisions there for the muddy season and beyond; also seeds, tools, baggage and all the people. It is proposed to get all this done by the beginning of April (new-style). Then some of the Doukhobors — between four and five hundred, it is thought — will go to work on the railway, while the remainder will be ploughing and sowing and building their houses, once the final settlement sites have been chosen, and disposing of the temporary buildings as they see fit.

Just how difficult all this is may be judged from the following tally: if we assume that each person requires three pounds of provisions a day, this means that 3x30x4,000 pounds, or 9,000 *pood*,[51] will be needed for a month. Since a team of horses can pull fifty *pood*, and the return trip from the nearest railway station takes four days, which means only seven trips a month, then to transport these 9,000 *pood* they will need approximately twenty-six (9000÷50÷7) teams of horses with sleighs, harness gear, and later [in the season], wagons. So just the hauling of one month's provisions requires twenty-six teams, and provisions will be needed for at least two months, and then seeds, ploughs, baggage and people will have to be transported in. Khilkov thinks that all this transportation will keep sixty teams of horses constantly busy. In addition, horses or oxen will be needed to haul wood to the building sites. All this, of course, is possible, but it depends above all else on the question of money, and this is where, as always, the main problem lies. The government has so far paid out $20,000 in bonus money. In July it has promised to hand over another $15,000 for the Cyprus and Kars boatloads which are still to come. Very little is left of the $20,000, and we shall have to draw an advance upon the remaining $15,000. Additional money has been promised from New York ($700) and from Philadelphia (around $3,000). Apart from this the Doukhobors themselves have money: the exiles had about 15,000 roubles

50 *Aylmer Maude* (1858–1938) — the English translator of Tolstoy's works who authored a biography of Tolstoy and participated in the Doukhobors' emigration.

51 *Pood* — an old Russian unit of weight measurement, equal to 16.38 kg.

— I don't know where they went to or are going to — and the Elizavetpol' and Kars Doukhobors have around 70,000 roubles. This much is known, as this was the amount the Doukhobors exchanged. But this is *all* of their money, and evidently we cannot count on this money as it is held by each individual as private property. Khilkov and I are very insistent that the Doukhobors lend at least 30,000 for common needs. They will probably do so when the necessity for it is explained and they are told how it will be spent. One of the difficulties in using this money is that many are unwilling to hand over their money for common use (i.e., for use by the exiles too) *as a loan*, but would rather give it away completely, and others use this as an excuse for giving only a small part of what they have; as a loan they would give more, but it is awkward for them to lend their money when others are giving it as an outright gift. This issue should be settled within a few days. The pity is that our party — from the *Lake Superior* — is made up of those from Kars and Elizavetpol', and the latter includes all sorts of people, even some from the Smaller Party.

When they were talking about money, Androsov, a member of the Kars contingent, said right away that the Kars Doukhobors were always ready to give money for common expenses to cover the exiles' portion as well as their own, since it was not the exiles' fault that they suffered more than the others; they had all left Russia for this reason. The Kars people agreed, but the Elizavetpol' contingent was divided.

A lot of *money is needed* overall. Just providing food for four thousand people costs eight to ten thousand dollars a month, sixty teams of horses are needed for transportation, and an equal number for the work. At $200 a team, that comes to $24,000. And then they still need to buy seeds, ploughs, feed for the horses, etc.

This is what has been and is being done: (1) The people are all getting fed, the exiles for almost two months now, our party for two weeks. (2) Houses have been built on the allotments for 1,500 people. (3) Somehow, provisions have been bought for the settlements. (4) Ten pair of horses and six pair of oxen have been purchased, which are in constant use in hauling. (5) Negotiations are underway with the railway company regarding work. (6) This same railway company has agreed to supply the Doukhobors with forty teams of horses for transport in return for feed.

The Canadians are generally happy about the arrival of the Doukhobors, but the opposition to the current Liberal government is attempting to find their weaker points, as well as the weaknesses of those involved in their emigration. At the moment, however, they have nothing to attack. An unexpected attack recently took place. The workers' union here decided to protest the hiring of Doukhobors for railway work as this supposedly was taking away work from local workers and lowering the wage rate. They quoted the government and McCreary as having promised not to let the Doukhobors compete in the labour market, but that is not fair, since McCreary promised this only in respect to Winnipeg and other cities. Archer was at the meeting and countered the charge. McCreary will answer in writing.

The Doukhobors are now pretty tired of being without work, and are in a hurry to get to their allotments. They are either staying at home or boldly walking the streets of Winnipeg, even managing to buy various things for themselves. People have stopped running after them. They sometimes come across Russian Jews, Galicians and Mennonites here with whom they can converse.

Winnipeg is sometimes reminiscent of a Russian city — sleigh traffic, wooden houses, wide streets. Only [here] they have electric trams and electric lighting, and a maze of telephone wires. The weather is very cold, often −25° by our thermometer. In Halifax the temperature went down to −45° R [−54° C] — even vodka would freeze. They say, though, that this winter is exceptional. Granted, the cold is easier to take here — the air is very dry. Still, I feel very sad that the Doukhobors have moved to such a cold climate.

As of today I have been here for two weeks. There have been no unusual events during this time. There have been two more deaths among our Doukhobors (making six in all since Batoum) — a little girl died of inflammation of the lungs, and an elderly woman at seventy-six; a fifth baby has been born.

On 6 March the long-awaited Deputy Minister Mr. Smart was here. He is quite straightforward in his dealings (like everyone here), and a pleasant fellow. He has given a clearer definition to the whole affair; it has been decided to spend the Cyprus and Kars boatloads' bonus money on those who came before us [on the *Lake Huron*], and to let those from the *Superior* feed themselves; the transportation issue has been moved ahead, accounts and estimates have been clarified, and so forth.

Yesterday I received letters from Tanja and Olsuf'ev.[52] I wrote several letters from Halifax to Tanja, Sonja,[53] you and Lëva.[54] I fear that some of them may not have arrived, as the mail ship *Labrador* sank and while the people were saved, the mail was lost.

I am planning to visit the homestead sites in a few days, and then head back to Russia through Toronto (where I shall meet Prof. Mavor and take a side-trip to Niagara), New York and England. Sulerzhitskij will probably arrive home about the time this letter reaches you. The Quakers have asked him to accompany the next boatload. He has left for England, and wanted to go from there to Russia through Moscow. Khir'jakova and Chekhovich have also gone, as well as Bakunin.[55]

52 At the time Tat'jana L'vovna Tolstaja was a guest on the Olsuf'evs' estate near Moscow; the Olsuf'evs were good friends of the Tolstoy family.

53 *Sof'ja Nikolaevna Tolstaja* — married to Sergej Tolstoy's brother Il'ja L'vovich.

54 *Lev L'vovich Tolstoy (Lëva)* (1866–1945) — Sergej Tolstoy's brother, a writer.

55 *Aleksej Il'ich Bakunin* — a doctor who accompanied the first boatload of Doukhobors.

Khilkov is trying to persuade me to stay, as he very much wants to leave. But I could not really take his place, since I am not abreast of things, and, while he is not an altogether tactful person, he is able to put things into the proper perspective, without getting distracted by details and trifles.

Please write to me now in England c/o V. Tchertkof,[56] Maldon, Purleigh, Essex, England.

I hope to find letters and telegrams awaiting me in New York. I have asked Suler to wire me when he arrives to let me know whether all are safe and sound. I hope you have not forgotten to mark the envelope *General Delivery.*

And so, I plan on leaving around the 17th, arriving in New York around the 24th, getting to England at the beginning of April, and returning to Moscow around the 10th or the 12th [of April] — all dates new-style.

Farewell. I don't know whether I shall be writing again; if I do, it will just be a line or two.

Sergej Tolstoy

I finished writing this letter 8 March (new-style).

N° 19. S. L. TOLSTOY ❧ S. A. TOLSTAYA[57]
26 March [7 April] 1899. RMS Umbria

As you can see,[58] dear Mamà, I am writing from the ship which is bringing me home from America. I believe my last letter was from Winnipeg after visiting the Doukhobors' homestead sites. I received Papà's letter in New York.[59] Unfortunately I had very little time there. Mr. Crosby[60] was most kind, and I dined and spent an evening with him. Unfortunately my steamship ticket was for the following day, and I was unable to stay and see Henry George Jr.[61] and [William Lloyd] Garrison Jr.,[62] who, upon learning that I was in New York, left their cards at the hotel where I was staying.

I spent two days in Toronto and saw Professor Mavor,[63] who is very kind and is interested in the Doukhobors' affairs. I cannot write much because of the rocking of the ship. Tomorrow, on the seventh day, we arrive at Liverpool, from where I shall go and see Chertkov and shall probably be

56 *Tchertkof* — one of the spelling variants of Chertkov's name in English.

57 Originally published in Donskov 1998a: 368–69.

58 The letter was written on ship's stationery, bearing the letterhead "Royal Mail Steamship *Umbria.*"

59 Letter from Lev Nikolaevich Tolstoy to Sergej Tolstoy dated 15 February 1899 (*PSS* 72:72–73).

60 *Ernest Crosby* (1856–1907) — a writer, poet, social activist and author of a number of articles on Tolstoy.

61 *Henry George Jr.* — son of the American economist Henry George (1839–1897), who proposed a single tax, on land values, replacing all other taxes. Tolstoy was an ardent supporter of this theory.

62 Son to *William Lloyd Garrison Sr.* (1805–1879) — American social activist, poet.

63 *James Mavor* — political-science professor at the University of Toronto.

seeing the Quakers regarding a loan for the Doukhobors, and then I shall head for home.

Papà has probably received my wire: SEND ALL AVAILABLE MONEY JOINT ACCOUNT HILKOF ANDROSSOF DIRECT WINNIPEG. Has he understood that: (1) the Quakers have undertaken, at their own expense, to transport the Cyprus Doukhobors to Canada, (2) Chertkov does not need money, and (3) we are not very happy that everything is in McCreary's hands, and it is desirable that Khilkov and the Doukhobors look after the money directly? Money, however, is very much needed.

Farewell for the time being. We shall see each other shortly, God willing. I enclose a newspaper clipping.

N^O 20. O. K. TOLSTAJA[64] ❧ S. L. TOLSTOY[65]
3 June 1899. Yasnaya Polyana.

...I am sending you a copy of Khilkov's letter [not extant], dear Serëzha.... Another interesting piece of news — a telegram came saying that the *Lake Huron*[66] arrived safely, but they'll be staying 21 days in quarantine, as there were several cases of smallpox. That's been written up in the papers too. Yesterday there was a letter from Dr. Sokol'nikov,[67] who was travelling with the Doukhobors. The whole lot are suffering from illness, especially the children. There are no medicines, and the conditions are very poor indeed. One little boy died on the 4th of May. Even when he was dying, his mother refused to give him bouillon. He [Sokol'nikov] is amazed at their steadfastness. They are being warmly greeted everywhere and a lot of sympathy is being expressed. It's awfully good to hear about the *Lake Huron* — I know you'll be so relieved....

N^O 21. S. L. TOLSTOY ❧ A. K. AND V. G. CHERTKOV[68]
October 1899

Dear Anna Konstantinovna and Vladimir Grigor'evich,

Your proposal that I should go to Canada — as well as the attached letters [not extant] — greatly troubled me. I think, however, that the described

64 *Ol'ga Konstantinovna Tolstaja* (*née* Diterikhs; 1872–1951) — sister to Anna Konstantinovna Chertkova. In 1899 she married the Tolstoys' son Andrej L'vovich, whom she divorced in 1906.
65 Excerpt. Almost the whole letter consists of a description of the illness and the operation that Tat'jana L'vovna Tolstaja went through in Vienna. She had serious arthritis.
66 *Lake Huron* — the steamship which carried the first boatload of Doukhobors to Canada, made a second trip to Canada in May 1899, with 2,286 Doukhobor emigrants aboard.
67 *Prokopij Nesterovich Sokol'nikov* (1867–1919) — a Yakut doctor. After graduating from the University of St. Petersburg in 1899, he returned to practise in Yakutia. At Tolstoy's request he accompanied a group of Doukhobor women from the Caucasus to join their husbands in Yakutia. He distributed contributions forwarded by Tolstoy among the Yakut Doukhobors.
68 Incomplete draft.

afflictions of the Doukhobors either have been exaggerated or apply only to certain villages. The Doukhobor exiles (Sulerzhitskij's group) along with those from Cyprus, of course, are in a worse situation than the others. The other half are probably in a better situation.

What is needed first and almost exclusively to help them is money. Right from the start of their settlement, borrowing money was an absolute necessity. However, I don't have any information as to whether the loan was finally secured. All measures ought to be taken in England and in [North] America to ensure that the loan is going ahead. I think in Russia this would be impossible. When I left, this matter did not seem to present any inconquerable difficulty, and in Canada there was an opportunity to borrow money from private individuals. If the Canadian government gives the money, it will be under the strange clause agreed upon with Maude whereby the 'bonus' becomes a loan and not an outright grant. In any case, this should be clarified. Indeed, it is possible that the Canadian government will see it otherwise — i.e., will interpret the clause in a sense more favourable to the Doukhobors.

Now I shall turn to the question of what I could do in Canada. I would be obliged to live in Winnipeg and manage current affairs as an intermediary with the government. The only thing is, I can only go for two months. How could I manage current affairs only for two months? To be effective I would have to go for a year, or at least for a long time; otherwise I don't think I could do anything useful, and for personal reasons I can't go for a long time. If there is something I could do and complete within two months and then leave — that's another matter. But I don't see anything like that, except for the loan. In any event, because of my personal affairs I could not go earlier than January and for no more than three months including travel. Besides, I don't feel I'm ready to make such a trip at the moment. Indeed, would I be helpful to the Doukhobors, do they need me?

N° 22. V. G. CHERTKOV ❧ S. L. TOLSTOY

4 [16] November 1899. Purleigh, Maldon (Essex), England.

16.11.99 (N.S.)
Dear Sergej L'vovich,

Please forgive me for taking so much time to respond to your letter. This is partly because we were all waiting for more specific information from Canada, from where we recently started receiving more satisfactory news. Finally we received today from Bonch-Bruevich a very calming letter, which we shall be sending to your father directly it is copied. From this latest information we may conclude that it is not necessary for you to go there at the present time, and since such a trip would be a very long one, we have decided not to further pursue our request that you go. Nevertheless I hasten to add that over the course of the winter there is the possibility of new and unforeseen circumstances arising, which again would make your trip there just as desirable as it seemed a few weeks ago and indeed it would be still, if circumstances had not taken quite a different turn. We hope that this will not happen, and most probably your participation will not be needed; however, it would be best if you kept yourself mentally ready to go just in case there is trouble there again, as in such a case you are the only appropriate person to ascertain the state of things on the spot and exercise your influence wherever necessary. I repeat, however, that such a necessity at this time does not seem probable, and I rejoice with you that the question of whether you should go or not has been put aside for you at least for the present, even though for myself I am sorry that such a circumstance deprives me of the great pleasure of seeing you again…[69]

Nº 23. S. F. KHUDJAKOV ❧ S. L. TOLSTOY
12 December 1899. Yorkton Station (Canada).

My dear and respected friend Sergej L'vovich!

Let me start by sending you my heartfelt greetings and best wishes for all good things from God.

I am healthy and prospering, thank God. On the 10th of May I sent you a letter, but have received no reply from you — probably it has not reached you. I sent it to the Tula address you gave me: addressed to Sergej Tolstoy c/o Lev Tolstoy. I asked you to send me some Russian books; I am very much in need of books.[70] Many of our brethren have come to Prince Albert. Everyone from the fourth boatload,[71] and many from Yorkton, including our family.

The place we have settled in is very good and clean, and the ground is even. On one side there is a forest, from which many streams flow out, with very good water. We've had an average harvest this year, what with a very rainy summer. We got twenty-five measures of wheat, and all the vegetables this year have been very good. Cattle here is not expensive, a lot cheaper than in Yorkton. A pair of good fillies costs between 150 and 200 dollars, a pair of oxen — 80 dollars, a pair of cows — 55 dollars.

Here at Prince Albert there's a lot of cattle raising and the cattle is of extremely good quality. We went out to wage-work late this year, because

69 The letter goes on to discuss the affairs of the Posrednik publishing house.

70 In the S. L. Tolstoy archives there is an account (along with others regarding the Doukhobor emigration) from N. P. Karbasnikov's bookshop in Moscow. It may be seen from this that the Doukhobors were sent copies of the Gospels, the Bible, self-instructional English textbooks, Florinskij's *Domashnjaja meditsina* [Household medicine], Fleury's *Otkrytie Ameriki* [Discovery of America], along with the writings of Pushkin, Lermontov, Cervantes, Hugo, Dickens, and many others (OR GMT, S.L. Tolstoy Fond, File 9).

71 The fourth boatload of Doukhobors, from the Kars district, numbering 2,318, arrived in Canada at the end of May 1899 on the *SS Lake Huron*, accompanied by Vladimir Bonch-Bruevich and his wife, Dr. Vera Velichkina.

during the time of any work we were settling in on our homestead. You can get good-paying work here only during the summer, and there's nothing at all in the wintertime. You could say that life has got a little better here, especially for those who have started learning a bit of English. I can ask directions on the road — which way the road is headed — and I can ask whether anyone has some cattle for sale or jobs to do.

My dear friend, Sergej L'vovich, I must say in all sincerity that I miss you very much. When you were with us, it seemed as though I were back in Russia with Russian people to whom I was very much accustomed. But now I would love to talk with Russians, but there are none around.

My dear friend, Sergej L'vovich, I beg you, write to me any news you have from Russia, I'd very much like to know. There are no Russian papers or books here — it's so boring there are no words to describe it. I'm very sorry I didn't bring any Russian books with me.

My dear friend, Sergej L'vovich, write and tell me whether you have received any letters from our [brethren] exiled to Siberia, from my brother Nikolaj Fëdorovich. And my dad, Fëdor Savel'evich, would like to know about this too. Please write.

I embrace you. Your loving friend,
Savelij Fëdorovich Khudjakov

My address in Rostan, Saskatchewan: Goreloe Village, Savelij Khudjakov.

N° 24. L. L. TOLSTOY[72] ❧ S. L. TOLSTOY
24 December 1899 [5 January 1900]. Yasnaya Polyana.

My dear friend Serëzha, the last time we saw each other we said some unpleasant things to each other, whereas in fact, now more than ever, we need to be together and feel it. One might have been against the Doukhobors' emigration — both for their sakes and ours as Russians — but now that they have made their move, one cannot help but feel for them and wish you success. Tanja [Tat'jana L'vovna] received your letter with the map some time ago. We are now waiting for news of your departure, which should be some time in the next few days.

Yesterday I received a very kind letter from Chertkov, one he owed me in return. He is now much more deeply involved in his publishing work and says that his role in the Doukhobor affair is finished.

I am writing to you first because I want to show how I feel about you, and secondly because I know when one is outside Russia it is always interesting to receive news from home. Today is Christmas Eve. Yesterday Mama

72 *Lev L'vovich Tolstoy* (Lëva; 1869–1945) — third son of the Tolstoys and younger brother to Sergej L'vovich.

and Sasha[73] and the Kolokol'tsevs' little girl arrived from Moscow. Papa has been here four days now. He is lethargic, his back aches, but then who wouldn't be lethargic in this horrible weather? Where have you been during this windy season? The Obolenskijs are here as before, and Masha is as weak as before and nobody knows whether she is pregnant or not. Yesterday Il'ja came home from Moscow, where he listened to the gypsies and played up to the Klimentova woman. Andrej still hasn't married yet and has not left his Caucasus [friends], who are threatening him over his choice.

See how much news there is to tell you. Lately I've been busy and concerned about the famine in Samara. I received a request from them, Bibikov came to see me, and I finally managed to get the letter published with [Prince] Ukhtomskij [editor of *Sankt-Peterburgskie Vedomosti*]. Contributions are already coming in and maybe I'll go there after New Year's. My piece on the community is already in press at *Novoe vremja*[74] and I expect to receive a copy in a few days.

Yesterday Adlerberg was here; he has turned out to be a fervent opponent of the community (today's Russian community, of course), which I was happy to hear. He said that the project to transform it almost passed on several occasions. I think that the liberation of the community now would be a stimulus that would raise the fallen spirits of the people.

Stadling[75] from Siberia was here too – he didn't find André. I also wrote a letter about him to *Sankt-Peterburgskie Vedomosti.*

Good-bye for now. Dora[76] sends her regards. I shall be most grateful to hear about you and the Doukhobors.

Lev

P.S. Tanja said that your son[77] is walking already, but she hasn't spoken with Manja.

N° 25. M. O. MEN'SHIKOV ❧ L. N. TOLSTOY
22 January 1900

The other day I received a letter from [Pëtr Vasil'evich] Verigin in Obdorsk — a letter requesting me to send his enclosed letter to his mother in Canada.

73 *Aleksandra L'vovna Tolstaja (Sasha)* (1884–1979) — the Tolstoys' youngest daughter.
74 *Novoe remja* (1868–1917) — a daily newspaper published in St. Petersburg. Aleksej Suvorin became its editor in 1876. In 1881 it began publishing two editions (morning and evening), and in 1884 a weekly illustrated issue was launched. It was closed by the Military Revolutionary Committee of the Petrograd City Council on 26 October [8 November] 1917.
75 *Jonas Stadling* (1847–1935) — Swedish traveller and writer, the author of several books on Russia. His article "With Tolstoy in the Russian famine" was published in the popular New York quarterly *The Century*, N° 43 (1893): 249–63.
76 *Dora Westerlund* (1878–1933) — Swedish-born wife to Lev L'vovich Tolstoy.
77 *Sergej Sergeevich Tolstoy* (1897–1974) — son of Sergej L'vovich Tolstoy and his first wife Marija Konstantinovna (Manja).

I gave it to E. D. Khir'jakova, who promised to send it via a safe route, through Sweden. In his letter to his mother Verigin writes that he awaits "with a feeling of reverence" the day he is reunited with them. Evidently he has not lost hope. He writes that this is the first letter he has written them after their emigration to Canada, and that he is healthy. In his letter to me he writes: "If you find it possible, please convey my sincere greetings to Lev Nikolaevich. I have learnt from the press that he is very ill. I have not received any letters from Moscow for a long time."

On his letter is the stamp from the Obdorsk police detachment.

N° 26. V. D. BONCH-BRUEVICH ❧ S. L. TOLSTOY
27 March 1900. Zürich.

Dear Sergej L'vovich, I just this moment received your letter which you sent 18 January and which, after going to Canada, came back to England to the Chertkovs, and at long last found me in Zürich. I am extremely sorry that I wasn't able to participate in the distribution of books, and they need books so much there. Fifteen *pood* [245 kg]! I'll write immediately to Bodjanskij and Prokopenko[78] and will ask them to send books there to the place they're needed. And we need to send them to the Northern settlement, especially since there's a proper library there which I organized. I managed the library myself while I was there (it had about 300 books), and it was running splendidly. Readers came every day, the books were being read with great enthusiasm, many discussions grew out of them. And they were read not just by children and adolescents but by adults as well. The books aimed at counteracting superstition were directly responsible for whole about-turns in attitude, they sparked debates and so forth, and I personally know several adults (Ivin,[79] Khomenov, Grisha Konygin, Misha Antifeev, Grisha Rybin and others) who, after reading these books, came and told me that they no longer believe in wood-spirits and no longer give credence to 'old wives' tales. It's true, isn't it — that, all by itself, is one great achievement of books?

The whole time I took proper notes and came up with a rather curious statistic. I lived in the village of Mikhajlovka, on the banks of the Swan River, where they built barracks for the Northerners. In the community of Voznesenie lived Alexandra Southgate — she, among other things, taught the children and also lent out books, but she didn't have very many of them and unfortunately did not keep proper records.

78 *Semën Pavlovich Prokopenko* (1865–1933) — political activist, born into a peasant family. He was a member of a number of agricultural communes. In 1899 he emigrated to Canada with the Doukhobors, but returned to Russia during the Soviet period.

79 *Ivan Ivin* (b. 1878) — a Doukhobor, who was sent as an emissary, along with Pëtr Makhortov, first to England, then to Cyprus, and finally to Canada, to find out information about possible locations where the Doukhobors might settle.

Before leaving I taught Nikola Zibarov's[80] son how to manage the library. I moved it to the community of Voznesenie, where Zibarov lives, and asked him to make sure himself that things stayed in order. Upon leaving I also asked the elders to make sure the books were preserved, and I think that will work out. I haven't yet received any information about how things are going currently, but I shall probably hear something soon. I would like very much to go on supporting this little library and I have already sent them a few books donated by my friends. Of course the books you sent will be a vital support to this library as well, if even some of them are actually received. In the Southern settlement there were also a lot of books (I once managed to get a trunkful from Russia with three *pood* [forty-nine kg] of books and divided them proportionally between the Northerners and the Southerners).

Bodjanskij wanted to set up a library, but for some reason this didn't work out — the books got scattered in various directions at random. In some of the villages there are books lying around everywhere, but in others not a single one. I don't know, perhaps your great donation will make them organize things more rationally. The Doukhobors are used to sharing everything individually, but if it is explained to them rationally in the first place, that the donator's wish is for these things to remain community property and, secondly, to simply tell them, acquaint them with the advantages of this kind of ownership in respect to, say, books, they will quickly get it and agree — at least, that's what happened in the Northern settlement.

I have been meaning to write you a letter at the request of Grandfather Bokovoj,[81] who is alive and well, and has made for his whole community sleighs, stools, ladders for storage cellars, benches and similar household accessories. He lives at Thunder Mountain in the community of Uspenie (headed by Melesha (Emel'jan) Konygin). Grandfather Bokovoj sends you his humblest greetings ("my face bowed to the ground," as he expressed it) — he wishes you all the best in the world, he remembers you, is always telling everyone about you and, as he says, prays for you — for your health, of course, along with his "righteous parents," i.e., the people he most respects. You will give him great pleasure if you write to him (his address is: Swan River, Man., To the Doukhobor [name]). Anyway, many of the Doukhobors remember you with kindness and all asked me to pay their respects to you. Indeed, Grandfather Bokovoj asked to send a special greeting to Lev Nikolaevich.

80 *Nikola Zibarov* (Nikolaj Savel'evich Zibarov) — a spokesman for the Caucasus Doukhobor community. In September 1898 Zibarov accompanied Sergej L'vovich Tolstoy to England and later went to Canada with the first boatload of Doukhobors.

81 *Grandfather Bokovoj* (Grigorij Bokov) — a Doukhobor who had served in the Russian army (1844–55) and was ninety-five years old at the time of the emigration. His cheerfulness, physical energy, and love for life (he said he was looking forward to "seeing Canada") impressed all who worked with the Doukhobors. Sergej Tolstoy made reference to Bokovoj in his diary of the trip on two occasions (see p. 271 above).

Now I have a series of requests to make — if you can manage to fulfil even one of them, I shall be most grateful.

In Canada I collected some rather significant materials on the Doukhobor life and teachings. I wrote down about 500 psalms, their rituals, customs, instances of persecution, a number of legends, etc., etc. The Chertkovs had given me access to their archives, and I found there many very interesting materials, mainly touching on the periods of the last persecutions of the Doukhobors. I am going through all this material right now and will be publishing most of it in Russia. From one of the letters from the Doukhobors in Siberia I learnt that Lev Nikolaevich sent them the diary you kept when you travelled with the Doukhobors. I should very much like to become acquainted with your diary; perhaps you would be good enough to allow me to copy excerpts therefrom.

Next I would very much like to examine in as much detail as possible the personality of Pëtr Verigin, whose strong influence on the Doukhobors is beyond doubt. I have collected his letters (I have 68 altogether), but I really want to have his correspondence with Lev Nikolaevich.[82] I dare not disturb L[ev] N[ikolaevich] but I would implore you to send me here if at all possible Vergin's letters as well as copies of the replies Lev Nikolaevich sent to him. I would be immeasurably grateful for that.

Perhaps either you or someone in Lev Nikolaevich's household have some kind of letters, explanations, etc., etc., obtained from the Doukhobors — if so, please send them to me. I shall return everything safe and sound. Perhaps Evgenij Ivanovich [Popov] has something (in Chertkov's papers I found an excerpt from a letter written by Pëtr Verigin to Evgenij Ivanovich — it would be good if he could send the whole letter).

I have just now received a letter from Canada from Vanja Khomenov of the community of Novotroitskoe (Northern settlement), a serious and entirely trustworthy person. He writes: "Dear friend, Vladimir Dmitrievich, I ask you for God's sake, don't ignore my request: send me ten roubles if possible. We are in desperate need. I myself took ill and am ill right now, and we have neither bread nor salt. You yourself know what our community is like (very unfriendly [V. B. B. notation]); for God's sake send us at least a loan. At the present time there is no bread, and by spring we shall be quite dead from hunger. You know what the roads are like here, and among the 100 people in our community there are only three lame horses and a couple of bulls. There are seven in my family. For God's sake send us a loan until autumn. Ivan Khomenov."

In another letter sent in the same envelope, Khomenov writes: "My wife bore a baby boy on the 27th of January. After the birth she was very, very

82 All currently known letters between Verigin and Tolstoy were published in *Leo Tolstoy–Peter Verigin: Correspondence* (Donskov 1995a), and reproduced in full in Chap. 6 above.

ill — she barely survived and when she took seriously ill, there was no milk in her breasts. At the time the child barely survived. The first day we fed him with bread and sugar, which we ground until it was runny, wrapped it in cheesecloth and gave it to him to suck on, but that wasn't helpful to him and his stomach began to ache. There's no cow's milk at all — there's only one cow in the community and she isn't giving milk and we haven't had any money at all," etc., etc.

I am sending these letters to Chertkov and asking him to send 10 dollars to Vanja Khomenov. Chertkov should have some money now in the Doukhobor cash fund (if he has not already sent it to Canada), since the German publisher of *Resurrection* recently paid more than three thousand deutschmarks.

I am now in the process of comparing *Resurrection* in the Marks edition and find myself cursing the censor on almost every page. What a mass distortion! Please do ask Lev Nikolaevich which version of the indictment (Chapter 10) is correct — the Marks or the London edition? There are discrepancies in expression between the two versions, so I think it is not a question of changes by Marks but simply two versions (besides, the censor deleted a large chunk of the indictment). Please let me know as soon as possible, as I am working on this bibliography at the request of Vladimir Grigor'evich [Chertkov], to be published in the next issue of *Svobodnoe slovo.*[83]

Well, all the best to you.
Yours respectfully,
V. Bonch-Bruevich

My address: Schweiz, Zürich, Sonneggstr. 6, W. Bonch-Bruevich

I am called, quite correctly, Vladimir Dmitrievich. If you send Verigin's letters, etc., send them by registered post. Give my heartfelt greetings to Lev Nikolaevich.

N° 27. N. F. KHUDJAKOV ❧ S. L. TOLSTOY

3 June 1901. City of Yakutsk.

Dear Sergej L'vovich,

I received your letter of 29 March, for which I am very glad. You asked me to write to you regarding the disagreement between the Canadian government and the Doukhobors. I think the Canadian government will never agree, nor should it, to making special laws just for the Doukhobors, since the Doukhobors will never prove that Canadian laws are part of an unjust system. Let the Doukhobors take a good look at the lives of the Canadian

83 *Svobodnoe slovo* (lit. 'Free Word') — a periodical published in England by Anna Konstantinovna Chertkova and her husband, Vladimir Grigor'evich Chertkov, which published twenty-five issues from 1898 to 1902.

people around them, and they will realize that Canadian laws do not hurt those who wish to live according to their own conscience and reasoning. After all, the Canadian government ought to know how many Doukhobor marriages and births there have been over the course of a year, or several years, not to mention deaths. Otherwise the government order would be stupid and unprincipled.

As far as land is concerned, what is the difference whether you call it mine or ours, as long as the same land belongs to the same people. The only difference would be if aboriginal or other settlers' lands were to be interspersed with the Doukhobor farms: in that case the Doukhobors could appeal to the government, and I am sure the government would not refuse.

You ask whether or not the authorities in Yakutsk are persecuting us because of our religious beliefs. The authorities are in no way interfering. Rather, as far as our outward peasant life goes, the government is actually trying to facilitate things. After the Doukhobors' arrival in Yakutsk, the government, unware of Doukhobor customs, began partially repressing us, but this did not go on for long, and soon they allowed us to go out and work at paying jobs and thereby make a living. Even if we were building the governor's residence for low wages, that was our own decision — we weren't forced into it, and the construction work was going slowly, so during the high-wage season[84] they didn't make us stay working there, but allowed us to earn independent wages through haymaking, crop harvesting and the construction of private houses in the city. This was a great help to us.

Right now, during the current spring season, all the Doukhobors have been sent out of town to worksites. Three Doukhobor settlements have been set up in the Yakutsk region — one at 20 km from Yakutsk, the second 130 km distant, and the third 350 km from the city. This year all those sent out of town received a bonus of 50 roubles for two years, an additional 6 per cent on the rouble per year.

At the moment the Irkutsk Governor-General[85] is in town. He has already visited our settlement, 20 km from the city. We asked him to release us for private jobs and increase the bonus, and he gave us a positive response. If we are not mistaken, we think he is a good man.

I'll soon send a more detailed description of our life here.

My brother Savelij writes that you sent to Canada six *pood* of books. He has given them out to the Doukhobors, and they are very grateful to you.

Please write and tell me who paid for the shipment. I would love to have some good books too, but I'm concerned that if you were the one paying for them this would be a burden on you.

84 A reference to the brief summer season, when hired workers could get higher pay.

85 *Aleksandr Dmitrievich Goremykin* (1832–1904) — appointed Irkutsk governor-general in 1889, commander-in-chief of the Irkutsk military district troops.

In a few days my family and I will be heading out to the settlement we've been assigned to. We'll be doing ploughing. Our house is almost finished.

I'll soon be writing you a detailed letter about how we live and what is going on in our community.

My heartfelt greetings to your Papa and Mama. Write me about what's happening and what happened earlier with your Papa in respect to the authorities.

Yours,
Nikolaj

My address: Yakutsk, Namogan', Prokhladnoe Village
Doukhobor Nikolaj F. Khudjakov

Nº 28. P. V. VERIGIN ❧ L. N. TOLSTOY
12 January 1903. Poterpevshee (Canada).

12th Jan. 1903. Village of Poterpevshee.[86]

To Lev Nikolaevich Tolstoy
Forgive me, dear Friend, Lev Nikolaevich, that I have not so far written you a detailed letter about my trip. On the way, of course, I could have written several letters, but I am not a very regular correspondent. Even though I very much wanted to send you a telegram once I had crossed the border, I couldn't, I was afraid I might get left behind by the train, and so I hardly stepped outside the carriage right until we reached London, where Vladimir Grigor'evich Chertkov greeted me with outstretched arms. I spent two weeks with this dear family, hardly noticing the time. Though Anna Konstantinovna is physically ill, she is cheerful and strong in spirit. Vladimir Grigor'evich went with me to Liverpool and saw me aboard ship. The crossing was quite stormy. All the passengers had to wait four days on the ship in the harbour at Saint John for medical inspection; it turned out there was one person on board with symptoms of smallpox. Three Doukhobors came to meet me in Saint John along with someone sent by the Minister from Ottawa, who told me that if I had the time free, the Minister would like to see me in Ottawa. I agreed and went to see him. I declined to talk about the matter of the Doukhobor emigration, and advised the Minister that I was still like a guest in Canada. The Minister was very kind to me. Just three days later I was with the Doukhobors. You can imagine, my dear Lev Nikolaevich, how my soul was overflowing with ecstasy and feelings of joy upon arriving at the

86 *Poterpevshee* [pronounced *po-ter-PEF-she-yeh*] — lit. 'Enduring' — the name given to one of the Doukhobor settlements in Canada.

first Doukhobor village — that was the village of Blagodarnoe.[87] The second village was the one where my mother is living; I found her extremely cheerful and quite healthy for her years.

I should now like to touch upon a more important question in the Doukhobors' life — their recent 'pilgrimage movement.' The place and time of writing this letter do not allow me to go into detail as to my own opinion on this movement or rather, on the true significance of what amounts to an accomplished fact. At the bottom of it there are three mixed feelings which prompted some fifteen hundred Doukhobors to leave the place where they were living and set out on the road without any particular direction. — Neither the representatives of the Canadian Government nor the Doukhobor people who have been looking after their liberation from their sorry plight, beginning in the Caucasus right up to now, have explained accurately or in detail what the political as well as the territorial and economic obligations of the Doukhobors would be should they decide to stay and live in Canada. This state of uncertainty has delayed the acceptance of land, and has led to one opinion among the Doukhobors that the government's conditions are too strict, and so some Doukhobors have decided they should leave the land that was offered to them, saying "Let us go in search of truth," i.e., in search of a more humane attitude toward the settlers on the Government's part. Others in this group of three 'feelings' declared that the Canadian climate is too cold and that as vegetarians they would never get used to a climate like this; "Let's go and find a milder climate," they said. According to a third opinion: "The land is fruitful here, and the climate, even though cold, is still a very healthy one; we shall prosper living here, while out there in the world — in humanity worldwide — there are many poor people, our brothers and sisters; let us go and tell everyone along the way that people must stop smoking tobacco, drinking vodka and quarrelling, put an end to military organizations and the violent oppression of people who are their brethren — people working in the mines, for example, or in other types of community labour." This was the literal explanation given me by those who belonged to the third group of the 'three feelings,' the so-called preachers of Christ's teachings.

My own personal opinion about all those fifteen hundred people, as far as I can tell, is that all these people seem very solid and reasonable [members of the community], including the women and girls, many of whom tell me they have decided not to get married but to live and work spiritually for Christ, i.e., for the equalization of human rights in community life.

That is all I know about this movement so far. As a deep-thinking psychologist, Lev Nikolaevich, you will be able to understand this phenomenon that has arisen among the Doukhobors for yourself, in general and

87 *Blagodarnoe* [*bla-go-DAR-no-yeh*] — lit. 'Grateful.'

in the particular. I shall add my own opinion: I cannot seem to distinguish this movement from the overall question of injustice in life that is vexing mankind.

The whole party was recommended by the government to turn back at Menidos, a hundred and thirty miles from the Doukhobor settlements. All the Doukhobors behaved very meekly in front of the police and there was no violence. They are now living in their own houses, they have plenty to eat, and since the day I arrived have not accepted government aid.

I might compare this movement to Abraham's actions in bringing his son as an offering to God, and when Abraham took up the knife to slay his son, God's angel stayed his hand or rather, Abraham himself came to the realization that he did not have to slay his son, and God told him to take his son, go home and live a life of praise to God.[88] I voiced this opinion to almost all the Doukhobors who were walking, having left their whole way of life behind them, and said: "Your motives of self-sacrifice for the common good of human life are legitimate and precious ones, but there is no need to let the children go hungry and cold, so for the time being why not remain with all the rest of the brethren and teach them?" Those with families took this explanation too as a revelation from God.

I embrace you and pray to God for your family's well-being.

P. Verigin

[P.S.] There will soon be a meeting to discuss acceptance of land.

N° 29. PRINCE È. È. UKHTOMSKIJ ❧ S. L. TOLSTOY

3 June 1904. City of Yakutsk.

Winnipeg, 3 June 1904
"Moskal', where have you led us?"

Dear Sergej L'vovich,

It was with unbelievable sadness that I visited the grey, repulsive wastelands to which the Doukhobors have been inexplicably and unwittingly lured. Even recently the frost has been killing off the gardens of these vegetarians, who believed that their laborious work of land-tilling would be met by some reward overseas.

Many remember you and send you their regards. Upon my return I would like very much to tell your father how poorly the celebrated English deal with unfortunate people. Their settlement in Canada is altogether a poor farce, an experiment with living beings who did not deserve to be cast overboard, as

88 See Gen. 22:12–17.

has happened. I saw Verigin and had a long talk with him. He is reconciled [to the situation].

Good-bye!
Yours, È. Ukhtomskij

N° 30. S. L. TOLSTOY ❧ PRINCE È. È. UKHTOMSKIJ
1904

My dear friend Èsper Èsperovich, I was most amazed and upset by your letter from Winnipeg. Evidently your feeling and writing were influenced by random impressions. You write about "the grey, repulsive wastelands to which the Doukhobors have been inexplicably and unwittingly lured." Undoubtedly the Armenian plateaus — in the Kars district — are further south and more fruitful than Canada, but the Cold Mountains,[89] where Nikolaj Pavlovich[90] settled the Tiflis Doukhobors with their extinction in mind, and where their barley did not ripen — could they be better than Canada? Again, "the frost has been killing off the gardens." Haven't they been sowing cucumbers three times already this year all through central Russia because each time what has come up has been killed by frost? Have the celebrated English been treating them badly? But did the celebrated (or uncelebrated) Russians treat them any better? My father once saw one Doukhobor's back all in stripes from 300 lashes of the whip administered by the Cossacks; at the same time it was found out that the women were being raped. It was determined that 1,000 of the 4,000 Tiflis Doukhobors had died just in a two-year period. I saw the Tiflis Doukhobors when they left for Canada. They were all ill or half-ill from fever which they had caught in the low unhealthy valleys where they were settled.

"Their settlement...is altogether a poor farce, an experiment with living beings who do not deserve to be cast overboard, as has happened." How many times I asked myself whether my father's participation and mine in the Doukhobor emigration was right or wrong. And with all sincerity, after going over all the circumstances of the situation, I can answer with complete conviction: Yes, the emigration was both inevitable and necessary. The Doukhobors could not simply stay and die out, subject to constant violence and devastation.

89 *Cold Mountains* — in the early 1840s the Doukhobors had been relocated to the Caucasus, to a place known as the Wet Mountains [*Mokrye gory*] or Cold Mountains [*Kholodnenskie gory*]. This is part of the Akhalkalak uplands, dotted with alpine meadows and pastureland, but ill-suited to crop farming, which was the principal occupation of the Doukhobors.

90 *Nikolaj Pavlovich Romanov* (Nicholas I; 1796–1855) — tsar of Russia 1825–1855. A reactionary, Nicholas I began his reign by crushing the Decembrist revolt of army officers (December 1825). He also accelerated the centralization of state power, founded the notorious Third Department (the imperial secret police), and introduced stricter censorship laws.

The farce was perpetrated not by those who organized the emigration but by those who drove the Doukhobors to the necessity of emigration. Neither my father nor Pëtr Verigin were in favour of it.[91]

And what is the fuss about, after all? Are the Doukhobors going hungry, are they sick or dying out? Just the opposite. They are healthy (the Canadian climate is a very healthful one), they are increasing in number (and this is the main argument for the effectiveness of the emigration) and prospering financially. They say they are even saving up money so that in time they can migrate to a warmer climate.

I know that there is a rather widespread opinion in Russia that the Doukhobors are in a state of poverty, and this is why: the [Russian] government was afraid that the Doukhobors remaining in Russia would mount a campaign to go to [North] America, and at one time the government prohibited any publication of anything from Canada it judged disadvantageous to itself. It pains our patriots to think that such a good, sober and civilized population has left the country. The liberals believed the vagabond Tverskoj,[92] who wanted to move them to California, speculating on land there; finally, people who hated [the principle of] non-violent resistance tried to reject it by any means they could. The radicals and revolutionaries are unhappy to see the departure from this part of Russia by what they considered to be a revolutionary element.

I strongly urge you, if you print anything about the Doukhobors, to learn as much as you can about their situation. Tan,[93] for example, in writing about the Doukhobors in *Russkie vedomosti*,[94] gave a fairly accurate account of their situation.

91 In a letter dated 16 August 1898, P. V. Verigin wrote to Tolstoy from Obdorsk: "Personally, I am *almost* positively *against* emigration. You see, the members of our community are in need of self-improvement, and so wherever we went we would take our weaknesses with us; and even though an individual can generally live more freely abroad, I don't think the difference would be all that great. People are the same everywhere" (Donskov 1995a: 31; reproduced in the present volume as Letter N° 6). On 1 November Tolstoy responded: "You write that you are almost against resettlement, and I am too.... And it is sad that we (Russians) are parting with those who are close to us in spirit...and it is sad too that people have not held on to the end and thereby helped other people know the truth, since nothing testifies to the truth more than the sufferings that one must bear for it" (Letter N° 7).

92 *Tverskoj* (Pëtr Alekseevich Dement'ev, a.k.a. P. A. Demens; 1852–1923?) — a Russian political emigrant, who established himself in Los Angeles (he was naturalized in America under the surname Demens). In 1899–1900 he published articles in various Russian periodicals (under the pseudonym P. A. Tverskoj), all trying to persuade the Doukhobors to move to California, where he had acquired substantial land holdings and was looking for cheap labour to settle them. Even after the Doukhobors' emigration to Canada, he persisted in his attempts to have them relocated to America.

93 *Tan* (Vladimir Germanovich Bogoraz-Tan; 1865–1936) — a writer, ethnographer and former member of the *Narodnaja volja* [People's Will] party, who visited the Doukhobors in Canada in the summer of 1903. His accounts were published in *Russkie vedomosti*. He did not meet Tolstoy in person until early in 1905.

94 *Russkie vedomosti* (1863–1918) — a Russian socio-political newspaper, initially thrice weekly and then daily (beginning in 1868). Its founder and first editor was Nikolaj Fëdorovich Pavlov.

The reasons for your being led astray are probably the following:

(1) an atypically cold spring;

(2) the Doukhobors, caught up with their current dispute with the English government, have forgotten about their persecutions in Russia and the necessity of their emigration. In such a state of mind they complained to you (among others) about their present situation.

N° 31. P. V. VERIGIN ❧ L. N. TOLSTOY[95]
3 July 1905. Otradnoe

3rd July '05. Village of Otradnoe.[96]
To Lev Nikolaevich Tolstoy
[from] Peter Verigin

Dear Friend Lev Nikolaevich, I have received your letter and it has been a very big help to me. The word 'Dear' where you are concerned has become simply the kindest word, since you, kind Lev Nikolaevich, are truly a dear person to me. Every one of your words overflows with simplicity and sincerity, and that is something dear to us all, if only people would treat each other more simply and sincerely.

Your fears for the Doukhobors' future in Canada are valid and understandable. But I cannot refuse to accept people's close participation in building material progress — since in many respects the spiritual does not depend upon us, it is something that touches each one individually. — For example, I can give someone a heifer, a horse, a hundred roubles and so on, but I can't give him a soul, and insofar as I am able to observe human life, it strikes me as an impossible task. — There is a special place for that, where the spirit of life and understanding originates. The Spirit "bloweth where it listeth"[97] and where it goes we do not know. Although Christ says: the world knoweth me not, but you know me.[98] Of course, this 'knowledge' should be interpreted as unity of the spirit.

You are aware, dear Lev Nikolaevich, that the Doukhobors came to Canada materially poor and possibly, according to your understanding, therein lies their advantage. Our material insufficiency has probably drawn their hearts closer together and led them to God — since God is manifested in the unity of human hearts.

Liberal professors from Moscow University and *zemstvo* officials also took an active role in the paper. From the 1870s on, the newspaper consistently emphasized the need for reforms which would gradually turn Russia into a constitutional monarchy. It was closed in March 1918.

95 Reproduced from Donskov 1995a: 75–77 (also in Chap. 6 above).

96 *Otradnoe* [pron. *ot-RAD-no-yeh*] — one of the Doukhobor settlements in Canada. The name literally means 'Joyful.'

97 See John 3:8.

98 See John 14:17.

It seems to me that the whole world was created and exists for good, so why should material wealth — as we deem it — serve us for evil? When someone begins to misuse his wealth or sets the acquisition of wealth as his goal in life, then that is quite a different story. The Doukhobors think a lot about the growth of the soul and it seems to me that they are even doing a lot of work in this direction, and this is their sense of good for the time being, while ahead of them stands the God of mercy — I am saying that we should become more merciful — and this is a person's goal in life.

I must say that the material conditions of our community life are basically in good order, but there is no strong growth yet. Do you think it is easy to get started in a desert place? We had to build more than sixty villages, with housing for each individual family. The climate is too cold to stay in the open air. Even in a desert place each household needs food to eat: what would you have done? — probably not just clasped your hands together and looked up to the sky expecting manna to fall, as the Israelites did.[99] The Doukhobors have a great many children, and I still notice that the children are not yet receiving enough nourishment from their mothers' milk and no wonder, since what the mothers have to eat is meagre indeed.

Would it have been rational for me to walk about the neighbourhoods, comforting the mothers who might lose their children because of malnutrition? As if the spirit which inspires our hearts and the bread which feeds our bodies did not come from the one God and Father?! Unfortunately the people up to now have made a distinction between the spiritual food and the material.

This summer in our community we have ten steam engines doing the ploughing, 25 horsepower each. It is easy for such powerful machines to pull eight ploughs each; that was the way we did it last year experimenting with just one engine. Now we hitch four [ploughs] together along with another machine called a cutter, which trails along behind and breaks up the earth, the way women cut cabbage. Such a tool is extremely useful simply because it reduces the burden on the horses, since [normally] after ploughing you have to go over it two or three more times to break it up, but this cutter is quite a heavy machine. — You probably know: it consists of twenty-inch discs or larger, very sharp, in a row of fourteen or more; with a team of four good horses, if you lower it to full depth it is too hard on the horses. That's where the steam engine has the advantage: you can lower the cutter to full depth right off, and then go over it just one more time cross-wise, and that's enough.

On the 30th of June we got a bank draft from the Yorkton bank to send to Moscow in the name of Aleksandr Nikiforovich Dunaev[100] — ten thousand

99 Ps. 78:23–24.

100 *Aleksandr Nikiforovich Dunaev* (1850–1920) — a friend of Tolstoy's who at one time shared his views; he was one of the directors of the Moscow Commercial Bank.

dollars to bring the Yakutsk brethren over. I asked Aleksandr Nikiforovich to get our Moscow Friends to arrange the tickets to be sent. Konkin too will probably be in Moscow by that time.

I told him that you, Dear Lev Nikolaevich, should not be disturbed [on this matter]; I think such affairs can be looked after by slightly younger people.

I wish your whole family complete health. And may the Lord send you, Dear Lev Nikolaevich, many more years of a healthy life.

I am keeping healthy myself. Your brother in Christ,
Peter Verigin

N° 32. N. F. KHUDJAKOV ❧ S. L. TOLSTOY

27 December 1911. Nelson, British Columbia.

27 December.
My dear friend Sergej L'vovich,

It has been many years since we last saw or wrote to each other. It may be I do not have your correct address, but I shall write and hope that I do. It is just that your kind relationship to me remains the same in my memory. Maybe you have forgotten me, as I have forgotten your address, but I hope this brief letter will remind you of me. On my way from the Yakutsk district, I stopped in Moscow, visited your dear mother's home, then went to Yasnaya Polyana, where I saw your father (now deceased), and finally came to see you and spent three days with you. After that I went to the Caucasus and from there to Canada.

My name is Nikolaj, my surname: Khudjakov. You are well acquainted with my brother Savelij, perhaps you have kept up correspondence with him. He lives far away from me, more than a thousand miles. Next spring he will be coming here along with his family. I live in British Columbia, also with my family. I won't write any news now — I'll wait for your reply to my letter.

If you wish to take up correspondence with me, just reply to my letter. After receiving your letter, I shall write you about a lot of things which, I hope, will be of great interest to you and your friends. I should especially like to tell you about how the Doukhobors are faring in Canada and living a communal lifestyle, about the conduct of Pëtr Verigin, his relationship to the Doukhobors and the Canadian government's reaction to them. Please let me know your address, as well as that of Aleksandr Nikiforovich Dunaev. We got to know each other quite well en route to Siberia, and I met him in Moscow.

I'll say good-bye for now.

Your loving
Nikolaj F. Khudjakov

My address is as follows:
Mr. N. Hudiakoff. Nelson, BC, P. O. Box 978.

APPENDICES

APPENDIX 1

Tolstoy and the Doukhobors: A Timeline

1652 PATRIARCH NIKON'S REFORMS of the Russian Orthodox Church result in a *raskol*, a schism, between those who accepted the reforms and those who did not, i.e., the 'Old Believers,' who insisted on adhering to traditional rituals and forms of worship. This paves the way for many splinter groups, including those that denied all ritual and even the priesthood itself — including a group that over time evolved into the Doukhobor movement.

1720–1740 Itinerant preacher wanders through southern Russia, proclaiming the virtues of non-violence, human equality, and a Christianity without ritual or church hierarchy — all tenets of the future Doukhobor movement.

1785–1786 According to Doukhobor legend, first use of the term *dukhobortsy* (lit., 'spirit-wrestlers'), applied pejoratively by Archbishop Ambrosius of Ekaterinoslav in reference to a group of people who wrestled *against* God, but adopted by the group in the sense of wrestling *with* God. According to ethnographer Svetlana Inikova, the word was first used by Ambrosius' predecessor, Archbishop Nikifor of Slovenia.

1791 Drafting of "Note of 1791 submitted by the Doukhobors of Ekaterinoslav Province to Governor Kakhovskij," outlining the sect's doctrinal teachings, most probably (according to Inikova) penned by a well-educated Doukhobor sympathizer.

1799 First official record of the 'Doukhobors' as a sect, in reference to the deportation of ninety of their members to Finland for protesting against violence and militarism; membership in the Doukhobor sect becomes illegal in Russia.

1802 At the encouragement of Tsar Alexander I, scattered groups of free peasants calling themselves Doukhobors are resettled in the Molochnye Vody region in Tavrida Gubernia, near the Sea of Azov, to isolate them from the general Russian populace. Other religious groups, including Mennonites, settle nearby.

1805 Savelij Kapustin (1743–1820?) takes over the Doukhobor leadership, introducing communal ownership and social structure, centred in one of the Doukhobor villages called Terpenie (lit., 'Patience').

1828 **9 September** (28/8 OS):[1] Birth of Leo Tolstoy at Yasnaya Polyana to father Nikolaj Il'ich Tolstoy (1794–1837) and mother Marija Nikolaevna Tolstaja (1790–1830; *née* Volkonskaja).

1839–1845 As the Russian population expands southward, the Doukhobors are sent farther afield, this time to the southern Caucasus, to mountainous lands now part of Georgia, Azerbajdzhan, and Armenia.

1859 **10 July** (29/6 OS): Birth of Pëtr Vasil'evich Verigin at Slavjanka, Elizavetpol' Gubernia (now in Azerbajdzhan) to father Vasilij Luk'janovich Verigin and mother Anastasija Vasil'evna Verigina (*née* Kalmakova).

1861 After the Russian peasant emancipation, Tolstoy begins devoting himself avidly to improving the lot of peasants, founding schools for their education, including one at Yasnaya Polyana.

1862 Tolstoy marries Sof'ja (Sofia) Andreevna Bers (1844–1919) and takes up permanent residence at Yasnaya Polyana.

1880 Following the completion of his two major novels (*War and Peace*, *Anna Karenina*), Tolstoy undergoes a particularly intense spiritual 'crisis,' which infuses all his subsequent writings with a more religious and philosophical point of view, beginning with *Ispoved'* [Confession] (begun in 1879, published abroad in 1884 and in Russia in 1906). He also continues vigorously advocating the virtues of a simple

1 All dates shown in bold in this timeline are NS; where appropriate, the OS equivalent is shown in parentheses.

peasant life based on manual labour and community ownership of possessions, combined with an absolute rejection of violence.

1881 Verigin is summoned by then Doukhobor leader Luker'ja Kalmykova (1841–1886) to serve in her household in the Sirotskij Dom (lit., 'Orphan House') in Goreloe, first as a secretary and then (following a compelled divorce from his wife) as a favourite to Kalmykova, with the status of an heir-apparent to the leadership succession.

1882 Publication in Kiev of a study by Orest Novitskij, *Dukhobortsy: ikh istorija i verouchenie* [Doukhobors: their history and teachings].

1884 Tolstoy assists his followers Vladimir Grigor'evich Chertkov (1854–1936) and Ivan lvanovich Gorbunov-Posadov (1864–1940) in founding the Posrednik publishing house. Chertkov would later become an active supporter of the Doukhobor cause.

1886 **27 December** (15/12 OS): Upon the death of Luker'ja Kalmykova, Verigin is recognized as leader by a majority of Doukhobors, who come to be known as the Large Party [*Bol'shaja partija*], in contrast with the Smaller Party [*Malaja partija*], headed by Kalmykova's relatives, who refused to acknowledge his leadership.

1887 **31 July** (19/7 OS): Verigin is arrested as the instigator of a violent mob action by his followers attempting to seize the Sirotskij Dom from the Kalmykov family, and is exiled to Shenkursk in Arkhangel'sk Gubernia in northwestern Russia. The Large Party is further split into (a) the *postniki* — those ready to follow Verigin's command of abstention from meat, and (b) the *mjasniki,* under Aleksej Vorob'ëv, who accept Verigin's leadership but are unwilling to become vegetarians.

1891 **30 May** (18/5 OS): Chertkov writes Tolstoy about the refusal of five Doukhobor men to perform military service.

1892 **20 December** (8/12 OS): Tolstoy is visited in Moscow by two English Quakers, John Bellows and Joseph Neave, on their way to meet the Stundists in southern Russia and the Doukhobors in the Caucasus to offer them assistance.

1893 Verigin learns of Tolstoy and his writings and begins showing a strong Tolstoyan influence in his own writings.

1894 Tolstoy learns of Verigin and the Doukhobors from a letter sent to him by one of his followers in Voronezh Gubernia, Ivan Mikhajlovich Tregubov (1858–1931).

November: Verigin is transferred from Arkhangel'sk to Obdorsk in Siberia, escorted not only by officers but also by his brother Vasilij and two other Doukhobors.

21 December (9/12 OS): While Verigin is being temporarily held in Moscow's Butyr Prison, his Doukhobor escorts (Vasilij Ob"edkov, Vasilij Verigin, Vasilij Vereshchagin) manage to meet with Tolstoy in Moscow and find a considerable commonality of views. The same day Tolstoy describes the meeting in a letter to N. N. Ivanov. Tolstoy is not allowed to meet with Pëtr Verigin.

1895 **Easter**: Eleven Doukhobors throw down their arms while training in Elizavetpol', declaring militarism to be incompatible with Christianity; they and sixty other Doukhobors are sent to disciplinary battalions and/or exile.

10–11 July (28–29/6 OS): Following Verigin's instructions, his Large Party followers (numbering some 7,000) gather in three districts of the Caucasus (notably Bogdanovka in Tiflis Gubernia) to burn all weapons in their possession--the Burning of Arms--as well as their conscription notices. Authorities treat this action as treason and respond with a persecution campaign of beatings, imprisonment and exile.

26 July (14/7 OS): Tolstoyan Prince Dmitrij Khilkov (1858–1914) writes to Tolstoy about the Burning of Arms and the persecutions, but Tolstoy rejects his suggestions for immediately publicizing the events.

17 August (5/8 OS): Verigin writes a letter to Tregubov describing the plight of the Doukhobors, along with his own views on religion and literacy.

8 September (27/8 OS): Aleksandr Mikhajlovich Bodjanskij (1842–1916), a Tolstoyan, writes to Tolstoy and fellow-Tolstoyan Pavel Ivanovich Birjukov (1860–1931) describing the Burning of Arms and the subsequent official persecution.

22 September (10/9 OS): Tolstoy writes a letter to the editor of *The Times* of London, which is printed as a foreword to Birjukov's article describing his own investigation into the persecution of the Doukhobors in the Caucasus (shortly thereafter republished in translation in France and Germany).

11 October (29/9 OS): Tolstoy sends Birjukov's article and his own afterword to Eugen Heinrich Schmitt, expressing his desire for it to be published in the leading German, Austrian, and Russian papers.

14 October (2/10 OS): In a letter, Tolstoy rejects Bodjanskij's proposal that the Doukhobors should leave Russia.

16 October (4/10 OS): Tiflis governor Prince Shervashidze, in a report to his superiors, links Doukhoborism to Tolstoyism, declaring the latter to be an even greater threat — in that it is devoid even of the basic family orientation of Doukhoborism. The link between the two is emphasized in a number of government reports and memos of the time.

6 November (25/10 OS): In a letter to Doukhobor E. I. Popov, Tolstoy asks how he can get in touch with Verigin in Obdorsk.

3 December (21/11 OS): Tolstoy initiates direct correspondence with Verigin after receiving Verigin's letter forwarded by Tregubov. His whole letter is spent defending the advantages of literacy and books.

1896 **26 March** (12/3 OS): In a letter to M. A. Schmidt, Tolstoy expresses his doubts about being able to offer any real aid to the Doukhobors, and refuses to write to the commander of the disciplinary battalion where they are being held.

11 August (30/7 OS): In a letter to V. A. Morozova, Tolstoy for the first time raises the question of offering financial help to the Doukhobors.

13 August (1/8 OS): Verigin writes his first letter to Tolstoy from exile in Obdorsk, having just received Tolstoy's first letter to him (of 3 December 1895).

12 November (31/10 OS): Tolstoy writes a letter to the commander of the disciplinary battalion, appealing for clemency for the Doukhobor soldiers in his charge.

14 December (2/12 OS): *Pomogite!*, an appeal for help, is published, signed by Pavel Birjukov, Ivan Tregubov, and Vladimir Chertkov, with a conclusion by Tolstoy. Chertkov establishes the Svobodnoe Slovo and Free Age Press publishing houses in England.

(Date unknown): Verigin advises his followers to adopt the name *Khristianskaja obshchina vsemirnogo bratstva* (Christian Community of Universal Brotherhood; CCUB).

1897 **18 January** (6/1 OS): In a letter to Tregubov, Tolstoy calls the Doukhobors "an example of non-violent organization and government which the enemies of Christianity accuse us of not having." (Compare his later letter to Tregubov of 7 November 1905.)

August: Vladimir Chertkov edits and publishes the first edition of *Christian Martyrdom in Russia: Persecution of* *the Doukhobors* (London: Free Age Press), including an English translation of Tolstoy's *Pomogite!* (republished 1899, 1900, 1905).

5 October (23/9 OS): Upon being nominated for the very first Nobel Peace Prize, in 1897, Tolstoy writes to the *Stokholm Tagblatt,* declining his candidacy and proposing the Doukhobors be awarded the prize.

(Date unknown): While visiting her son in the Caucasus, Dowager Empress Aleksandra Fëdorovna is presented with a petition by local Doukhobors and the tsar gives his permission for sect members to emigrate; following this the Doukhobors also send telegrams to Tolstoy as well as to Tolstoyans and Quakers living in England, asking for guidance and help in emigration. Chertkov and other Tolstoyans in England meet with the English Quakers and Kropotkin to discuss Doukhobor emigration.

1898 **March**: Russian anarchist and Tolstoy sympathizer Prince Pëtr Kropotkin (1842–1921) publishes an article in the British periodical *The Nineteenth Century* on the Mennonite emigrants to the Canadian prairies; Tolstoy for the first time raises the question of Doukhobor emigration "to England or America," later to Texas, Cyprus, or Manchuria or Chinese Turkestan; Kropotkin and Tolstoy prompt University of Toronto professor and political economist James Mavor (1854–1925) — who first met Tolstoy in 1889 — to make enquiries with Canadian immigration officials about the possibility of bringing Doukhobors en masse to Canada.

29 March (17/3 OS): In a letter to the paper *Sankt-Peterburgskie Vedomosti,* Tolstoy again outlines the Doukhobors' plight and appeals for public help in facilitating their emigration.

July: James Mavor contacts both Tolstoy and Canadian Interior Minister Sir Clifford Sifton (1861–1929) regarding the possibility of the Doukhobors' move to Canada.

18 August (6/8 OS): 1,126 Doukhobors depart from Batoum on the French ship *Durau* for Cyprus, where they spend an unsuccessful winter; the following May they embark for Canada.

28 August (16/8 OS): Verigin sends his Christian fairytale entitled "A Fantasy" to Tolstoy. He declares himself opposed to Doukhobor emigration, but sets a few conditions if emigration is decided upon.

29 August (17/8 OS): In a letter to Prince Dmitrij Khilkov, Tolstoy approves Canada as the best place for resettling the Doukhobors.

September: Khilkov arrives in Canada, along with Tolstoy's English translator Aylmer Maude (1858–1938) and two Doukhobor emissaries and their families: Ivan Ivin and Pëtr Makhortov. They travel through the "provisional districts" (as they were then known) of Assiniboia, Saskatchewan, and Alberta and select two suitable areas for a Doukhobor settlement — near Yorkton (Assiniboia) and Swan River (Assiniboia-Saskatchewan border). Two additional colonies are later established: Good-Spirit Lake Annex (Assiniboia) and Prince Albert (Saskatchewan). Khilkov later publishes a series of articles on his trip in *Juzhnoe obozrenie* [Southern Review] between December 1899 and March 1900.

29 September (17/9 OS): Tolstoy writes to his eldest son, Sergej L'vovich, thanking him for his willingness to help the Doukhobors.

24 October (12/10 OS): In a letter to his publisher Aleksej Suvorin (1834–1912), Tolstoy accepts the idea of allowing some royalties from his publications go to help finance the Doukhobor emigration.

6 December: An order-in-council is passed by the Canadian government, exempting Doukhobor immigrants from Canadian military service.

22 December (10/12 OS): 2,140 Doukhobors embark from the Black Sea port of Batoum on the *SS Lake Huron* for Canada, escorted by Tolstoyan actor Leopol'd Sulerzhitskij (1872–1916); they arrive at Halifax 20 January 1899 and set out by train from Saint John for the Canadian prairies.

1899

4 January (22/12/98 OS): 2,300 Doukhobors embark from Batoum on the *SS Lake Superior*, escorted by Tolstoy's eldest son, Sergej L'vovich Tolstoy (1863–1947); they arrive at Halifax 27 January, but are obliged to spend twenty-seven days in quarantine on Lawlor's Island before heading west to join the first Doukhobor contingent.

18 April (5/4 OS): Some 1,100 Doukhobors embark from Larnaca, Cyprus, en route to Canada aboard the *SS Lake Superior*, again accompanied by Sulerzhitskij. They arrive 9 May in Québec City and then take the train west.

13 May (1/5 OS): 2,286 Doukhobors embark from Batoum on the *SS Lake Huron*. On 15 May they are joined in

Constantinople by Tolstoyan Vladimir Bonch-Bruevich (1873–1955) and Dr. Vera Mikhajlovna Velichkina (later Bonch-Bruevich's wife). They arrive in Québec City in early June, but are obliged to endure a month in quarantine before setting out by rail for the west.

20 June (8/6 OS): In a letter to Khilkov, Tolstoy expresses his gratitude to the Doukhobors for what they have given him.

December: Tolstoy completes his novel *Resurrection* and directs the proceeds to go to the Doukhobors to help finance their emigration.

1900 **27 February** (15/2 OS): Tolstoy writes a long open letter "To the Doukhobors who emigrated to Canada," warning of the "temptation of private property," which many Doukhobors were falling prey to.

20 March (7/3 OS): A second letter by Tolstoy to the Canadian Doukhobors warns them against the temptation of relocating to America.

August: After spending a year with the Doukhobors in Canada, Bonch-Bruevich, now back at his home in Switzerland, publishes a preliminary outline of the Doukhobors' psalms and hymns through the Geneva branch of Chertkov's Svobodnoe Slovo publishing house, later revised and published in St. Petersburg in 1909. His wife, Dr. Velichkina, publishes an account of their journey with the Doukhobors in a series of articles in *Russkie vedomosti* (February–June 1900).

19 December (7/12 OS): Tolstoy writes an open letter to Tsar Nicholas II demanding sweeping reforms in the name of religious freedom.

1901 **9 March** (24/2 OS): In a letter to Doukhobor Ivan Konkin (P. V. Verigin's son-in-law) Tolstoy again expresses his concern that the Canadian Doukhobors are enriching themselves materially at the expense of the spiritual.

1902 **11 August** (29/7 OS): Verigin is released from Siberian exile and issued a passport for travel abroad.

October: On his way to England Verigin stops to see Tolstoy at Yasnaya Polyana.

October–December: Some 1,700 radical Canadian Doukhobors, calling themselves the "Sons of Freedom," turn their cattle loose and set out on a 'pilgrimage trek' to search for a better life, but without any clear destination. They are forcibly returned to the Doukhobor colony by the RCMP, with Verigin's help (see 12 January 1903 below).

November: Verigin stays a few days in England with the Chertkov family before heading for Canada; Chertkov presents him at a public meeting in London.

December: Verigin arrives in Canada to join the Doukhobor emigrants; he takes up residence in the Canadian-Doukhobor village of Poterpevshee.

1903 **12 January** (30/12/1902 OS): In his first letter from Canada, Verigin tells Tolstoy about how he helped calm down the Sons of Freedom pilgrimage trekkers and encouraged them to return home.

1 December (18/11 OS): Verigin sends Tolstoy $200 to contribute to the living expenses of several Doukhobors released from Siberian exile, but at the same time tries to dissuade them from coming to Canada (an attitude which surprises Tolstoy).

(Date unknown): French writer Romain Rolland (1866–1945) pens his anti-Boer War drama *Le Temps viendra*, inspired by Tolstoy's writings about the Doukhobors. In 1911 Rolland would publish a biography of Tolstoy.

1904 **20 February** (7/2 OS): Verigin sends Tolstoy $300 toward the defence of sectarians in Pavlovka (Ukraine), accused of destroying a church at Khilkov's instigation. However, he also describes the current financial plight of the Canadian Doukhobors, attaching a statement of 1903 income and expenses as evidence.

1905 **1 April** (19/3 OS): Verigin writes to Tolstoy about the Doukhobors' agricultural successes, the resulting envy on the part of their Canadian neighbours, and the conflict between the Doukhobors' communal way of life and the Canadian government's insistence on individual homesteading.

7 November (26/10 OS): In a letter to Tregubov, Tolstoy warns that "we know all too little about the Doukhobors, and they can hardly serve as an example of Christian life." (Compare his earlier letter to Tregubov of 18 January 1897.)

1906 **19–23 December** (6–10/12 OS): Verigin's second and last face-to-face meeting with Tolstoy, this time at Yasnaya Polyana, along with five other Doukhobors who had travelled with him from Canada (Ivan Makhortov, Pavel Planidin, D. N. Gridchin, Anastasija Golubëva, Marfa Dymovskaja).

1907 **January–March**: En route back to Canada, Verigin and his Doukhobor companions pay a visit to Bulgaria, then travel home through Turkey, Hungary, Austria, Switzerland, France and England. In a letter to Tolstoy of 9 March he acknowledges his great appreciation for the trip and his meeting with Tolstoy.

1908 **13 June** (31/5 OS): Verigin tells Tolstoy of the Doukhobors' purchase of land in central British Columbia and his intention to move the community there over the next few years.

1909 **2 February** (20/1 OS): Verigin, on behalf of the Doukhobor community, invites Tolstoy to come and spend his remaining days with them in Canada.

3 May (20/4 OS): Verigin's only letter to Tolstoy written from the Doukhobors' new settlement in Brilliant, British Columbia, once more including a reference to his own inner spiritual regeneration.

26 September (13/9 OS): Verigin sends Tolstoy (from Saskatchewan) a copy of his letter to the Canadian Doukhobor community describing current happenings and offering financial advice on specific points.

17 October (4/10 OS): Tolstoy's last known letter to Verigin, a brief paragraph encouraging Verigin's "striving for spiritual perfection."

(Date unknown): Publication in St. Petersburg of Tolstoyan Vladimir Bonch-Bruevich's seminal *Zhivotnaja kniga dukhobortsev* [Living book of the Doukhobors] (revision of an earlier work published in Geneva in August 1900), offering for the first time in print an extensive anthology of Doukhobor psalms, songs, and stories collected during the author's stay with the newly arrived Doukhobors in Canada.

1910 **15–17 May**: Verigin writes his last letter to Tolstoy, from Otradnoe (near Veregin, Saskatchewan), giving news of spring planting and reflecting on questions of life and immortality.

20 November (7/11 OS): Tolstoy dies at the Astapovo railway station while fleeing from his life at Yasnaya Polyana. There are various theories as to where he was headed.

1924 **29 October**: Pëtr Vasil'evich Verigin is killed in an explosion on a train at Farron, British Columbia; those responsible for the explosion remain unknown to this day.

1927 **Spring**: Pëtr V. Verigin's son, Pëtr Petrovich Verigin, arrives in Canada from the Soviet Union to take over the Doukhobor leadership.

1938 **November**: The official Doukhobor organization in Canada (the CCUB, as named by Pëtr V. Verigin in

1896) is dissolved in favour of a new body to be known as *Sojuz dukhovnykh obshchin Khrista* (Union of Spiritual Communities of Christ; USCC); Pëtr P. Verigin is appointed USCC secretary.

1939 **11 February**: Death of Pëtr Petrovich Verigin.

1940 In the absence of Pëtr P. Verigin's son, his grandson John J. Verigin Sr. becomes secretary of the USCC. He is not officially confirmed as leader until 1961, after it is established that Pëtr P. Verigin's son (Pëtr P. Verigin Jr.) died in a Soviet prison camp in 1942.

1943–1945 In 1943 the USCC publishes a Doukhobor newsletter. In 1945, the USCC's honorary chairman, John J. Verigin Sr., proposes the name *Iskra* [Spark] "to symbolize and encourage the ongoing process of spiritual revival and growth among its readers," and "the inner spiritual 'spark' which Doukhobors believe to be the manifestation of God in each human being."

1977 John J. Verigin Sr. receives the Order of Canada for his efforts at promoting world peace.

1987 **July**: The Soviet Rodina Society presents two life-size statues of Tolstoy, sculpted by Jurij Chernov, to two Canadian Doukhobor museums — one at Veregin (Saskatchewan), the other at Castlegar (British Columbia).

1989 John J. Verigin Sr. is awarded the Order of Peoples' Friendship by Soviet leader Mikhail Gorbachev.

1996 **22–24 February**: The University of Ottawa hosts a major international conference on *Lev Tolstoy and the Concept of Brotherhood* (Donskov and Woodsworth 1996). The banquet address is given by Larry Ewashen, curator of the Doukhobor Village Museum at Castlegar, British Columbia.

May: John J. Verigin Sr. is awarded the Order of British Columbia.

1999 **May:** John Woodsworth's *Russian Roots & Canadian Wings: Russian Archival Documents on the Doukhobor Emigration to Canada* is published.

22–24 October: Another international conference is held at the University of Ottawa to mark the 100th anniversary of the Doukhobors' arrival in Canada. The proceedings are published in 2000 as *The Doukhobor Centenary in Canada: A Multi-Disciplinary Perspective on Their Unity and Diversity* (Donskov, Woodsworth, and Gaffield 2000). A session is devoted to the role of Tolstoy and his followers.

(Date unknown): The Mir Centre for Peace is co-founded by Dr. Myler Wilkinson at Selkirk College in Castlegar, British Columbia, one of two major centres (along with nearby Grand Forks) of the Doukhobor community in B.C. The centre is housed in a renovated Doukhobor communal home with its original red-brick façade rebuilt for the occasion. "Its foundational vision," according to Wilkinson, is "understanding and building cultures of peace," on the principles of Tolstoy, Gandhi, and Martin Luther King Jr.

2001 **21 March**: *Iskra* publishes a Slavic Research Group questionnaire polling Doukhobors on their knowledge of and perceptions of Tolstoy as a writer and as a friend of the Doukhobors.

2003 **12 November**: Her Excellency the Right Honourable Adrienne Clarkson, Governor-General of Canada, in a speech on the occasion of the presentation of the 2003 Governor-General's Literary Awards, pays tribute to the literary legacy of Leo Tolstoy and his facilitating of the Doukhobors' emigration to Canada through the proceeds from his novel *Resurrection*.

2004 **24 April**: A fund-raising banquet is held in aid of the Doukhobors' Bakery Café project at Yasnaya Polyana.

2005 **21 September**: Official opening of the Doukhobors' Bakery Café and Communication Centre at Yasnaya Polyana.

December: Publication of the first edition of Andrew Donskov's *Leo Tolstoy and the Canadian Doukhobors: An Historic Relationship* as Volume 7 in the Canada-Russia series by Carleton University's Centre for Research on Canadian-Russian Relations.

2006 **23–28 June:** Doukhobors play a prominent role in the World Peace Forum in Vancouver.

6–9 July: The USCC hosts the largest event ever to take place at the Doukhobor Cultural Centre in Brilliant — the "Our Way Home" reunion of Vietnam-era American war resisters who ended up in Canada in the 1960s and 1970s, together with many prominent anti-war activists of that time.

2007 **19 June:** Symposium on the Doukhobors' "Being on the Land: Histories at the Confluence" — billed as a "Symposium on the people of the Kootenay and Columbia Rivers" — is held at the Mir Centre for Peace at Selkirk College, Castlegar.

2008 **March:** Andrew Donskov's *Leo Tolstoy and Russian Peasant Sectarian Writers* is published, presenting Tolstoy's selected correspondence with four peasant sectarian authors, including the Doukhobor leader Pëtr Vasil'evich Verigin.

26 October: John J. Verigin Sr. passes away. For more than sixty years he served as honorary chairman of USCC (formerly the CCUB).

2009 **21–22 February:** At the annual convention at the Doukhobor Cultural Centre in the town of Brilliant, near Castlegar, after acknowledging the passing of John J. Verigin Sr., participants decide to abolish the title of "honorary chairman" and proclaim his son John J. Verigin Jr. as USCC Executive Director (a title he still bears).

2010 **7 November:** Doukhobors hold a celebration commemorating the 100th anniversary of Tolstoy's death, under the title "The 'Green Stick': Centenary Spiritual Tribute to Lev Nikolaevich Tolstoy," in Castlegar, described as "a day of prayer, song and reflection in remembering Tolstoy's ongoing influence in the worlds of art, social justice, humanitarianism and spirituality." (Koozma Tarasoff's message to the gathering may be found at https://tinyurl.com/greenstick.)

2011 **30 November:** Alex Atamanenko, Member of Parliament (2006–2015) for British Columbia Southern Interior — a long-time champion of the Doukhobor community — introduces in the House of Commons a private member's bill (C-373) proposing "an Act to establish the Department of Peace" — something that the Doukhobors sought for decades. His bill, however, is not passed.

2012 **30 September:** Historic Sites and Monuments Board of Canada sponsors a special unveiling at the Doukhobor Discovery Centre in Castlegar, at which organizer Larry Ewashen is a featured speaker. Two plaques are officially unveiled: one declaring Peter V. Verigin as "a person of national historic significance," the other recognizing the migration of the Doukhobors from Saskatchewan to British Columbia as "an event of national historic significance."

2013 **September:** A one-semester undergraduate course, Doukhobor Culture in Canada, is introduced by the University of Saskatchewan's Department of Religion and Culture, taught by Dr. Veronika Makarova, a linguist educated at the University of St. Petersburg. According to the department's description, the course "introduces the early history of the Doukhobor religion, the settlement of Doukhobors in Saskatchewan and BC, and the subsequent development of Doukhobor communities in the 20th-21st century Canada."

2014 **4 July:** Prominent Doukhobor historian, scholar, and mentor Eli A. Popoff (b. 24 April 1921) passes away in Grand Forks. (See his guest essay "Lev Tolstoy in My Doukhobor Family Heritage" in this volume.)

2 October: Gabrielle Tétrault-Farber, a former student of Russian at the University of Ottawa turned columnist for the English-language *Moscow Times*, publishes there an article about a Doukhobor couple from Grand Forks, Elaine and Alfred Podovinikoff, who in their fifties decided to move to Russia and settle in the village of Yasnaya Polyana, close to Tolstoy's ancestral estate. Indeed, they feel an inherent connection with the writer who more than a century ago helped their ancestors emigrate to Canada.

2016 **13 December:** Koozma Tarasoff reviews a futuristic novel by retired Carleton University professor Ian Prattis, *New Planet, New World,* inspired by Tolstoy and the Doukhobors. (On Tarasoff's *Spirit-wrestlers* website, https://tinyurl.com/ianprattis.)

2017 **7 April:** Russian cultural philosopher Dr. Irina Anosova presents a paper entitled "Phenomenology of the culture of modern Canadian Doukhobors" at the sixth Canadian Conference held at the University of St. Petersburg, attended by scholars from Canada, Estonia, and a number of Russian cities. (The paper is available at https://tinyurl.com/anosova-cdc.)

October: Publication of the Russian edition of Andrew Donskov's 1998 book *Sergej Tolstoy and the Doukhobors: A Journey to Canada* by Kuchkovo Pole in Moscow.

2018 **July:** The Doukhobor journal *Iskra* — currently a monthly publication — celebrates its seventy-fifth anniversary by launching a new digital edition under co-editors Barry Verigin and Stephanie Swetlishoff.

2019 **May:** Andrew Donskov's 2008 book is re-issued in an expanded edition by the University of Ottawa Press under the title: *Leo Tolstoy in Conversation with Four Peasant Sectarian Writers: the Complete Correspondence.*

APPENDIX 2

Eli A. Popoff: A Filial Tribute

The following is an abridged version of the biographical eulogy presented by his son Dmitri (Jim), at the funeral service for Eli A. Popoff in Grand Forks, British Columbia, 9 July 2014.

Dad was born in a sod hut on a Doukhobor homestead near Blaine Lake, Saskatchewan, on April 24, 1921, the fifth of six children born to Alexey Ivanovich and Katerina Timofeyevna Popoff. His only formal education was at a one-room country school, which ended when he was thirteen — but for three of those years his teacher was Alexander Nazaroff, a Russian immigrant who later moved to the United States and gained fame for writing history books about Russia. Mr. Nazaroff also taught Russian-language classes for the children two evenings a week. He was an excellent teacher, and gave my father a very strong base in Russian grammar, and a broad understanding of Russian history and culture.

But by far the most profound influence came from Dad's parents. His father, Alexey Ivanovich Popoff, was one of the young Doukhobor men who'd been sentenced to a Russian penal battalion for refusing to serve in the tsarist army, in the great Doukhobor struggle against militarism of the 1890s. From the penal battalion he was exiled to Siberia, where he stayed for some seven years, being finally released to join his people in Canada only in 1905. Grandfather's stories of his dramatic experiences inspired his youngest son to devote his life to his Doukhobor heritage, and from a young age Dad developed a disciplined pattern of interviewing Doukhobor elders and retaining this information in his memory.

In addition to his avid curiosity and devotion, Dad's Doukhobor insights were further stimulated by the unusual mix of perspectives that he was exposed to. For one thing, his mother, Katerina, was not of Doukhobor origin, but happened to be in Siberia because *her* father had been exiled for *his* religious beliefs. There she met Grandfather Aleksey and came with him to Canada, as has been described in dramatic detail in my father's true-life book, *Annooshka's Siberian Love*. Annooshka, by the way, was Katerina's mother, but that's another story... Dad's *other* grandmother was a prominent early Sons of Freedom Doukhobor, while her son, Dad's father, Alexey, was one of the founders of the Independent Doukhobor Society of Canada, created before Dad was even born.

In his late teens, Dad encountered some health problems, and, while convalescing, he read a lot of philosophical literature, especially by Tolstoy, but also Gandhi and others, and this helped to bring about an epiphany in his life. Among other things, he became a strict vegetarian, stopped smoking cigarettes and drinking alcohol, and these changes served him well for the rest of his life.

With the onset of the Second World War, Doukhobors were struggling to retain the conscientious-objector status that had been granted to them by the Canadian government back in 1898. In 1941, at the age of twenty, Dad was chosen as one of two young Doukhobor men from the area to join a delegation to Calgary to present their case before the Selective Service Board. Referring to his own father's sacrifices in the struggle to end militarism, Dad made an impassioned presentation, and was complimented for his ardent defence of Doukhobor principles by an elder delegate, prominent Doukhobor lawyer Peter G. Makaroff.

In 1943 Dad moved to British Columbia, where, soon after, he met my mother, Dorothy Rilkoff, and they were married in March of 1945. It was a good thing that Dad had gone through his earlier epiphany, as Mother was already in the third generation of a family of strict vegetarians. Furthermore, both her paternal Rilkoff and maternal Soloveoff lineages had always been staunchly mainstream in their Doukhobor views. Dad's new father-in-law, my grandfather John J. Rilkoff, set a daunting example of USCC dedication, serving as the longest-standing chairman of the USCC executive for most of his last twenty years, until his death in 1966.

While Dad understood and empathized with the views of other Doukhobor groups, he was unwavering in his conviction that the "Community," or "orthodox," Doukhobors, as represented by the USCC organization, embodied the most authentic and balanced approach in applying Doukhobor principles to our life here in Canada. That was why he had left most of his family behind in Saskatchewan and moved to British Columbia in the first place, and he remained a USCC activist for the rest of his life.

To support his family, Dad worked with local construction firms and, shortly after marriage, my folks purchased a five-acre piece of farmland, where Dad built the small, two-room cottage in which I was born, in 1946. By 1947, with employment uncertain, my folks temporarily moved to Blaine Lake, to explore the possibility of working on the family farm, and my sister Elaine was born in nearby Hafford, Saskatchewan. Soon after, the family returned permanently to Grand Forks, where, in 1948, we moved to a ten-acre farmstead, which had a slightly larger, four-room house already on it. In 1954, my youngest sister, Natasha, was born, and that's where we all grew up.

It was a very beautiful and idyllic place to enjoy our childhood, with a wonderful neighbourhood of mostly USCC families in what was known as the Chistyakovoye community. There were many of us older baby boomers living in close proximity, and with our farm at the geographic centre, my parents were often hosting the whole neighbourhood of kids in the yard and house. As our local USCC Sunday-school teacher for many of those years, Dad was an ever-present nurturing influence in our young lives, as he was always available to take us on a hike up the mountain, or organize a picnic or an impromptu softball game. It was a common sight to see ten or more kids in the back of our 1951 red International Harvester pickup, on their way to one outing or another.

By this time Dad had already established a pattern of untiring effort on the community front, helping to set up Sunday schools and Russian-language schools, and serving many years on the USCC Union of Youth Council. From 1950 to 1952 he served as the second editor of the USCC Doukhobor periodical, *Iskra*, and in the early 1950s the first of several terms on the USCC executive committee. He also played a key role in setting up and stocking the USCC Central Library, one of the largest bilingual collections in Western Canada at the time.

In the 1950s he compiled a series of lectures on Doukhobor history and beliefs, which were extensively used in seminars and evening meetings by the youth; in 1955, the USCC published the original Russian version of his *Stories from Doukhobor History*, which has become a widely distributed Doukhobor classic.

Also in the 1950s, Dad served as secretary of the USCC land committee, which worked along with the BC Land Settlement Board and Judge Evans to expedite the resettlement of the former Doukhobor communal lands. He was also active in the local Parent Teachers Association, and in 1958 became the first Doukhobor in BC to serve in public office when he was elected to the local school board. During a decade on the board he participated in the founding of Selkirk College and provided the suggestion, taken from a fundamental Doukhobor psalm, "Be devout," that he had translated, for what was later adopted as the official slogan of Selkirk College: "Best of all, inquire."

In 1955 ten USCC members organized Interior Cement Works and Construction Co. Ltd., which, in its years of operation from 1955 to 1968, employed scores of local tradesman and construction workers, and built many local houses and bigger projects. Dad was one of the original partners and worked mostly as office manager.

Dad subsequently worked as USCC executive secretary and administrator and as a personal assistant to the late USCC honorary chairman, John J. Verigin. He helped to found, and served as the charter secretary of, the Association of Canadians of Russian Descent (ACRD) and along with its charter chairman (the late John J. Verigin), represented the ACRD at various state and multicultural functions in Ottawa, across Canada, and abroad. In the 1960s, he was also the principal Doukhobor resource person appointed to work along with Dr. Kenneth Peacock, who gathered and recorded a large volume of the traditional Doukhobor musical repertoire (much of it translated by Dad) for the National Museum in Ottawa, and published the seminal book, *Songs of the Doukhobors*.

In the last decades of his working life Dad was employed at Win Mathers Notary Public and, subsequently, with local lawyers Mellett and Geronazzo, where he was valued for his abilities and his extensive experience with legal matters, as well as his fluent bilingual skills that were often helpful in dealing with elderly clients of Russian-Canadian descent.

In between his various employments, he continued his writing and translating, authoring several books and hundreds of articles and sections of other books. His true-life account, *Tanya*, was listed by Books in British Columbia as one of the 100 most important books ever published in BC. He served over sixty years on the *Iskra* editorial board and contributed material to its pages right up to his last days. He taught night classes on Doukhobor history at Selkirk College and in the Kootenays; conducted numerous historical tours for visiting media, scholars, official guests, and tourists; was a charter member of the co-operative that restored and reactivated the Doukhobor Flour Mill in Grand Forks; was a charter director of the historical society that restored the Fructova School and established the Fructova Heritage Centre, now the site of the Boundary Museum.

Over the years, Dad came to be widely regarded as the pre-eminent Doukhobor historian and cultural resource person of his generation, and was frequently invited to speak on this area of expertise at various local, regional, national, and international venues. In 1999, which marked 100 years since the Doukhobor arrival in Canada, he was invited to give a keynote address at the University of Ottawa's Conference on the Doukhobor Centenary, where the university also presented him with the Institute of Canadian Studies Award for Outstanding Achievement in Canadian Studies. In 2001, on the occasion of his eightieth birthday, he was presented with a special certificate of appreciation, signed by the USCC honorary chairman, John J. Verigin, in recognition of his many decades of service to the USCC organization and his lifelong efforts to preserve and advance authentic Doukhobor life-concepts.

Dad was very grateful to have the opportunity to visit the land of his Doukhobor origins, where he travelled for the first of several times in 1968, accompanying the late Anna Markova, mother of the late USCC honorary chairman, during her own return visit to her homeland. In the 1990s, after more than seventy-five years of no connection with his mother's family, he was overjoyed to re-establish contact with them and even to visit with his cousins in the village of Baranchi, in the Ural area of Russia. He was always supportive of any efforts to maintain contact with our native Russian language, culture, and people, which he felt was a very important aspect of our own Doukhobor heritage, and he was gratified when my sister Natasha and her family were able to live and work for a year at Yasnaya Polyana, the famous museum-estate of the great Leo Tolstoy. Later, when my sister Elaine and her family established a successful English-language preschool in Moscow, and built a home at Yasnaya Polyana, my parents were very thrilled to be able to visit with them there.

Aside from these and other delegations to Russia, my parents had one other rare travel opportunity when, in 1978, they joined John and Laura Verigin and six other Doukhobor participants in a special delegation of the Canadian Council of Christians and Jews (led by Dr. Richard Jones, council president), which conducted an ecumenical tour to London, Rome, and Jerusalem, during which (among many other highlights) they were hosted by Prince Philip at Windsor Castle.

One of the aspects of his Doukhobor heritage that Dad appreciated the most was singing, and he and Mom enjoyed their participation in various choirs, particularly their three decades in the USCC Friendship Choir, and their performances at various expos. In addition, both Dad and Mom have enjoyed meeting and hosting people, and, with Mom's exceptional gifts in the Doukhobor culinary arts, our parents have over the years hosted countless friends and hundreds of guests from over thirty different countries, including ambassadors and other officials, authors, media journalists, scholars, cultural icons, youth groups, and all types of ecumenical and religious representatives, as well as prominent social activists in the fields of human justice, non-violence, and peace. But their favourite gatherings were always with family, whether immediate or extended, and their home became a Mecca for relatives near and far.

Dad continued to provide an inspiring example to his last days. This April, right up to his ninety-third birthday, Dad was still walking at least a mile a day. But by early May his health took a sudden downturn. After a week's stay in the hospital, he made one last heroic effort at community involvement when he kept his promise to his grandson, Vanya, that he would participate in a three-generational festival appearance with Vanya's Bratstvo Choir. This was his last public appearance — and fittingly so, for one who had helped organize the first USCC Union of Youth Festival in 1948 and had participated at all sixty-seven annual festivals since!

Dad re-entered the hospital on June 9, and passed away on July 4, 2014, quietly in his sleep, in the same dignified and peaceful demeanour that he maintained throughout his life.

May he rest in peace and enjoy eternal consciousness in God's heavenly Kingdom. He will live on in our hearts forever.

(A few months after Eli Popoff's passing, the mayor and council of the City of Grand Forks bestowed the Freedom of the City on Eli and Dorothy Popoff. A special provision was passed by council to allow for the first-ever such granting posthumously. This was only the third occasion on which this honour was granted to a married couple, and only the second time that the recipients were of Doukhobor origin — USCC Honorary Chairman John J. Verigin was made a Freeman of Grand Forks during the Doukhobor centennial year of 1999.)

APPENDIX 3

Chronology of Tolstoy's Letters on the Doukhobors (1891–1910)

THIS SECTION COMPRISES a tabular listing of Tolstoy's letters (all drawn from the Jubilee Edition [*Polnoe sobranie sochinenie*] of his works) either written to Doukhobors or where Doukhobors are mentioned.

Please note the column conventions in the following table:

- **Index:** This is the number assigned to a given letter for reference throughout the volume. It also indicates either the exact or the approximate date the letter was written according the *New Style* (NS/Gregorian) calendar. Where more than one letter is deemed to be written on a given date, the letters 'a', 'b', 'c' etc. are added according to the order of appearance in the *Jubilee Edition (JE=PSS)*.
- **Date shown in *Jubilee Edition:*** This is the exact (or approximate) date either shown on the original letter or determined by the *JE* compilers, according to the *Old Style* (OS/Julian) calendar. If Tolstoy also indicated the New Style variant in the original, that is included following a forward slash (/).
- **Volume and page of the *Jubilee Edition*:** The bold-face number preceding the colon indicates the volume number; the numbers following the colon represent the page in that volume.
- **Letter number in *Jubilee Edition*:** This is the number assigned to the letter in the given volume of the *JE*. A dagger (†) indicates that the *JE* includes only a brief summary, rather than the full text of the letter, whose whereabouts may be unknown. The letter *P* in this column

indicates attention should be paid to the *JE* editor's *Primechanie* (annotation) – either the general note or a numbered footnote.

- **Addressee**: As indicated in the *JE*. Letters Tolstoy wrote in a language other than Russian are designated by a bracketed initial following the name: [E] = English; [F] = French; [G] = German.
- **In response to addressee's Letter of...**: This column indicates: (a) the date of the Letter to which Tolstoy is replying and/or (b) (if asterisked [*]) the date of a subsequent reply to Tolstoy's letter. All dates are indicated in *OS* to facilitate comparison with the date of Tolstoy's letter. If the *JE* shows a NS date (in addition to or in place of the OS) it is included here following a forward slash (/). A dash in this column (–) means no letter from the addressee (either preceding or following Tolstoy's) is indicated in the *JE*.

Index	Date shown in J.E.: O.S. or O.S./N.S.	J.E. volume: page	J.E. N°†	Addressee§	In response to the addressee's letter of*
1891–05–20	8 May 1891	**87:** 88	*291.P*	V. G. Chertkov	29 Apr. | *18 May
1892–04–16	3–4? Apr. 1892	**66:** 197–198	*235*	I. B. Fajnerman	*date unknown*
1892–05–07	25 Apr. 1892	**66:** 206–208	*256*	D. A. Khilkov	29 Mar.
1892–09–26	14 Sep. 1892	**66:** 257–258	*339*	D. A. Khilkov	*30 Nov.
1892–12–20	8? Dec. 1892	**66:** 281–282	*386*	D. A. Khilkov	—
1894–12–21	9 Dec. 1894	**67:** 279–280	*288*	N. N. Ivanov	5 Dec.
1894–12– 23	11 Dec. 1894	**67:** 281–282	*290*	M. V. Alekhin	—
1895–04–08	27 Mar. 1895	**68:** 55–66	*60*	E. H. Schmitt [G]	17/29 Mar.
1895–06–20	8 May 1895	**87:** 328	*401.P*	V. G. Chertkov	*12 Jun.
1895–08–10	29 July 1895	**68:** 131–132	*129*	D. A. Khilkov	14 Jul.
1895–08–14	2 Aug. 1895	**39:** 209–15	—	*Foreign newspapers* [unsent]	—
1895–08–31	19 Aug. 1895	**68:** 142	*138*	F. A. Zheltov	6 Aug.
1895–09–16a	4 Sep. 1895	**68:** 154–155	*151*	M. V. Alekhin	30 Aug.
1895–09–16b	4 Sep. 1895	**68:** 157–158	*154*	L. L. Tolstoy	—
1895–09–22	10 Sep. 1895	**68:** 173	*160*	*English newspaper editor*	—
1895–09–27	mid-Sep. 1895	**68:** 177–179	*165*	E. H. Schmitt [G]	29 Aug/10 Sep.

† A dagger indicates that the *Jubilee Edition (J.E.)* does not include the full text of the letter. *P* = See *Primechanie* (Note).

§Letters written by Tolstoy in a language other than Russian are indicated as follows: [E] = English; [F] = French; [G] = German.

*An asterisk designates the date of a subsequent reply by the addressee to Tolstoy's letter (Old Style or Old Style/New Style).

Index	Date shown in J.E.: O.S. or O.S./N.S.	J.E. volume: page	J.E. N° †	Addressee§	In response to the addressee's letter of*
1895–09–30	18/30 Sep. 1895	**68:** 182–183	*169*	J. Kenworthy [E]	*26 Sep/8 Oct.
1895–10–11	29 Sep. 1895	**68:** 189–191	*176*	E. H. Schmitt [G]	—
1895–10–14	2 Oct. 1895	**68:** 193–196	*179*	A. M. Bodjanskij	15& 16 Sep.
1895–10–17a	5 Oct. 1895	**68:** 202–203	*182*	A. M. Bodjanskij	21? Sep.
1895–10–17b	5 Oct. 1895	**68:** 203–204	*183*	M. O. Men'shikov	—
1895–10–17c	5 Oct. 1895	**68:** 206–207	*185*	N. N. Strakhov	*9 Oct.
1895–10–18	5–6 Oct. 1895	**68:** 211–212	*189*	J. Bellows [E]	*date unknown*
1895–10–19	7 Oct. 1895	**87:** 331–333	*403*	V. G. Chertkov	19–24 Sep.
1895–10–20	8/20 Oct. 1895	**68:** 213	*191*	E. H. Schmitt [G]	29 Sep./11 Oct.
1895–10–29	16–17 Oct. 1895	**68:** 218–219	*197*	I. I. Khudjakov	1 Oct.
1895–10–31	19 Oct. 1895	**68:** 229–230	*199*	L. L. Tolstoy	8 Oct.
1895–11–02	21 Oct. 1895	**68:** 233	*203*	J. Marshall	—
1895–11–06a	24–25 Oct. 1895	**68:** 233–234	*204*	E. I. Popov	—
1895–11–06b	25 Oct. 1895	**87:** 337–338	*405*	V. G. Chertkov	13, 14, 20 Oct.
1895–11–21	9 Nov. 1895	**68:** 21–5252	*222*	K. K. Bool'	15 Sep.
1895–11–26	14 Nov. 1895	**68:** 252–253	*224*	E. I. Popov	29 Oct.
1895–12–03	21 Nov. 1895	**68:** 262–265	*229*	P. V. Verigin	—
1895–12–12	30 Nov. 1895	**68:** 267–269	*232*	E. I. Popov	21 Nov.

Index	Date shown in J.E.: O.S. or O.S./N.S.	J.E. volume: page	J.E. N° †	Addressee§	In response to the addressee's letter of*
1895–12–13	1 Dec. 1895	**87:** 341–342	*406*	V. G. Chertkov	23 Oct., 18 & 21 Nov.
1895–12–30a	18 Dec. 1895	**68:** 281	*245*	L. L. Tolstoy	—
1895–12–30b	18/30 Dec. 1895	**68:** 283–284	*247*	E. H. Schmitt [G]	16/28 Nov.
1896–01–17	5 Jan. 1896?	**69:** 11	*1*	K. T. Soldatenkov	—
1896–02–25	13 Feb. 1896	**87:** 356	*412*	V. G. Chertkov	9 & 10 Feb.
1896–03–05	22 Feb. 1896	**69:** 45–46	*32*	D. P. Makovitskij	—
1896–03–10a	27 Feb. 1896	**69:** 46–47	*35*	J. Kenworthy	6/18 Feb.
1896–03–10b	27 Feb. 1896	**69:** 48–49	*38*	E. H. Schmitt [G]	20 Jan./1 Feb.
1896–03–24	12 Mar. 1896	**69:** 57–58	*49*	M. A. Schmidt	4 & 7 Mar.
1896–03–27	12…15 Mar. 1896	**69:** 59–60	*51*	E. I. Popov	9 Mar. | *18 Mar.
1896–04–01	20 Mar. 1896	**69:** 71–72	*58*	D. A. Khilkov	—
1896–04–24	11… 12 Apr. 1896	**69:** 81–82	*67*	I. M. Tregubov	3 Apr.
1896–05–14	2 May 1896	**69:** 95–97	*76*	A. A. Shkarvan	21 Apr.
1896–08–11	30 July 1896	**69:** 119–120	*96*	V. A. Morozova	—
1896–08–15	July… Aug. 1896	**69:** 140–141	*104*	D. A. Khilkov	11 Jun.
1896–10–13	1 Oct. 1896	**69:** 158–160	*132*	A. G. Makeev	*14 Oct.
1896–10–26	14 Oct. 1896	**69:** 168–172	*138*	P. V. Verigin	1 Aug.
1896–10–31	19 Oct. 1896	**69:** 180–181	*146*	T. F. Gotojtsev	—

Index	Date shown in J.E.: O.S. or O.S./N.S.	J.E. volume: page	J.E. N°[†]	Addressee[§]	In response to the addressee's letter of[*]
1896–11–03	22 Oct. 1896	**69:** 184–185	*149*	*Irkutsk disciplinary battalion commander*	—
1896–11–12a	31 Oct. 1896	**69:** 190–192	*159*	*Ekaterinograd disciplinary battalion commander*	—
1896–11–12b	late Oct. 1896	**69:** 193–194	*161*	V. I. Ob"edkov & I. I. Ponomarёv	6 Sep.
1896–11–12c	31 Oct. 1896	**84:** 268–269	*667*	S. A. Tolstaya	31 Oct.
1896–11–14	30 Oct.–2 Nov. 1896	**87:** 376–378	*424*	V. G. Chertkov	26 Oct.
1896–11–23a	11 Nov. 1896	**69:** 201–203	*170*	D. Zanini [F]	7/19 Oct.
1896–11–23b	11 Nov. 1896	**87:** 381–382	*426*	V. G. Chertkov	31 Oct.
1896–11–24a	12 Nov. 1896	**69:** 203–204	*172*	T. M. Bondarev	23 Aug.
1896–11–24b	12 Nov. 1896	**84:** 271–272	*669*	S. A. Tolstaya	9 Nov.
1896–11–29	17 Nov. 1896	**69:** 207–208	*179*	I. M. Tregubov	12 Nov.
1896–12–06	24 Nov. 1896	**69:** 212–213	*184*	E. H. Schmitt [G]	—
1896–12–07a	25 Nov. 1896	**69:** 213–215	*185*	J. Van der Veer [G]	date unknown
1896–12–07b	25 Nov. 1896	**87:** 383–384	*427*	V. G. Chertkov	16 & 17 Nov.
1896–12–14	2 Dec. 1896	**87:** 387	*428*	V. G. Chertkov	28 Nov.
1896–12–16	4 Dec. 1896	**69:** 217–218	*190*	V. I. Ikskul' fon Gil'debrandt	*16 Dec.
1896–12–18a	6 Dec. 1896	**69:** 219–220	*191*	D. Zanini (F]	—

Index	**Date shown in J.E.: O.S. or O.S./N.S.**	**J.E. volume: page**	**J.E. N°** †	**Addressee**§	**In response to the addressee's letter of***
1896–12–18b	6 Dec. 1896	**69:** 220–221	*192*	F. Fénéon [F]	—
1896–12–29	17 Dec. 1896	**69:** 222–223	*195*	P. V. Velikanov	date unknown
1897–01–18	6 Jan. 1897	**70:** 12–13	*3*	I. M. Tregubov	—
1897–01–19	early Jan. 1897	**70:** 13–14	*4*	L. I. Veselitskaja	date unknown
1897–01–23	11 Jan. 1897	**70:** 14–15	*5*	P. I. Birjukov	31 Dec.
1897–02–08	27 Jan. 1897	**88:** 7	*434*	V. G. Chertkov	—
1897–02–24	12 Feb. 1897	**70:** 19–20	*16*	D. A. Khilkov	—
1897–03–02	18 Feb. 1897	**70:** 24–25	*24*	S. Byrdin	30 Jan.
1897–03–03	19 Feb. 1897	**70:** 28	*27*	N. M. Danilevskaja	19 Feb.
1897–03–06a	22 Feb. 1897	**70:** 30	*30*	P. A. Bulanzhe	17 Feb.
1897–03–06b	22 Feb. 1897	**70:** 32–33	*32*	I. M. Tregubov	—
1897–03–10	26 Feb. 1897	**70:** 37–38	*38*	P. N. Gastev	12 Feb.
1897–03–12	26–28? Feb. 1897	**70:** 40–41	*42*	I. M. Tregubov	24 Feb.
1897–03–14	2 Mar. 1897	**70:** 44–45	*46*	E. H. Schmitt [G]	9/21 Feb.
1897–03–18	6 Mar. 1897	**70:** 48–49	*50.P7*	P. I. Birjukov	—
1897–03–23a	11 Mar. 1897	**70:** 54	*55*	A. M. Bodjanskij	—
1897–03–23b	11 Mar. 1897	**88:** 16–18	*441*	V. G. Chertkov & A. K. Chertkova	2 & 6 Mar.
1897–03–30	18 Mar. 1897	**70:** 59–60	*62.P4*	T. L. Tolstaja	—

Index	Date shown in J.E.: O.S. or O.S./N.S.	J.E. volume: page	J.E. N° †	Addressee§	In response to the addressee's letter of*
1897–04–08	27 Mar. 1897	**70:** 61–62	*65*	J. Van der Veer [G]	17 Mar.
1897–04–26	13 Apr. 1897	**70:** 67–68	*71.P7*	P. I. Birjukov	—
1897–05–19	7 May 1897	**70:** 71–72	*79.P*	I. M. Tregubov	—
1897–05–22	10 May 1897	**70:** 72–75	*81*	Emperor Nicholas II	—
1897–05–30a	18 May 1897	**70:** 85–86	*97*	A. S. Suvorin	—
1897–05–30b	18 May 1897	**70:** 86	*98*	*Birzhevye Vedomosti*	—
1897–05–30c	18 May 1897	**70:** 87	*99*	*Sankt-Peterburgskie Vedomosti*	—
1897–06–11a	30 May 1897	**70:** 89–90	*105*	A. V. Jushko	8 May
1897–06–11b	30 May 1897	**70:** 91	*106*	P. A. Bulanzhe	20 May
1897–07–01	19 June 1897	**88:** 30–32	*451.P5*	V. G. Chertkov	7/19 Jun.
1897–07–02a	20 June 1897	**70:** 99–100	*116*	E. P. Nakashidze	1 Mar, 11 & 13 Apr., 9 May
1897–07–02b	20? June 1897	**70:** 100–101	*119*	*Caucasus Doukhobors*	—
1897–07–02c	20? June 1897	**70:** 101	*120*	P. A. Bulanzhe	—
1897–07–24	12 July 1897	**88:** 38–40	*455*	V. G. Chertkov & A. K. Chertkova	15/27Jun. 14 & 16 Jun.[?]
1897–07–26	14 July 1897	**70:** 103–104	*126*	P. I. Birjukov	26 Jun.
1897–07–28a	15–16? July 1897	**70:** 105–106	*129*	P. A. Bulanzhe	—
1897–07–28b	16 July 1897	**70:** 106–107	*130*	M. Androsov	14 Jul.
1897–08–25a	13? Aug. 1897	**70:** 114–115	*140*	P. I. Birjukov	*date unknown*

Index	Date shown in J.E.: O.S. or O.S./N.S.	J.E. volume: page	J.E. N° †	Addressee§	In response to the addressee's letter of*
1897–08–25b	13/25 Aug. 1897	**70:** 118–119	*142*	L. Bähler & J. Van der Veer [G]	25 Jul./6 Aug.
1897–08–27	15 Aug. 1897	**70:** 120	*143*	K. T. Soldatenkov	—
1897–09–02	20–21? Aug. 1897	**70:** 126–127	*150*	*Caucasus Doukhobors*	—
1897–09–15	3 Sep. 1897	**70:** 130	*154*	P. A. Bulanzhe	31 Aug.
1897–09–24	12? Sep. 1897	**70:** 134	*160*	A. Maude	10/22Sep.
1897–09–27a	14–15? Sep. 1897	**70:** 135	*161*	I. P. Nakashidze	5 Sep.
1897–09–27b	14–15? Sep. 1897	**84:** 290–291	*686*	S. A. Tolstaya	—
1897–10–03	21 Sep. 1897	**84:** 291–292	*687*	S. A. Tolstaya	*date unknown*
1897–10–05	23 Sep./[5] Oct. 1897	**70:** 148–149	*175*	*Stockholm Tagblatt* [F]	—
1897–10–08	26 Sep. 1897	**70:** 157	*179*	A. N. Dunaev	*2 Oct.
1897–10–29	17 Oct. 1897	**70:** 170–171	*199*	W. Gum [E]	*date unknown*
1897–12–19	7 Dec. 1897	**70:** 210–211	*246*	M. V. Alekhin	*date unknown*
1898–01–06	25 Dec. 1897	**70:** 220–221	*261*	*Caucasus Doukhobors*	—
1898–01–12	31 Dec. 1897	**70:** 223–225	*266*	G. P. Men'shenin	10 Dec.
1898–01–13	1? Jan. 1898	**71:** 251	*1*	P. A. Bulanzhe	23 Dec.
1898–01–21a	9 Jan. 1898	**71:** 254	*5*	P. I. Birjukov	1 Jan.
1898–01–21b	9 Jan. 1898	**71:** 254–255	*6*	I. M. Tregubov	3 Jan.
1898–01–22	10 Jan. 1898	**71:** 255–256	*8*	P. A. Bulanzhe	3 Jan.

Index	Date shown in J.E.: O.S. or O.S./N.S.	J.E. volume: page	J.E. N° †	Addressee§	In response to the addressee's letter of*
1898-01-30	18 Jan. 1898	**71:** 259	*13*	I. M. Tregubov	26 Dec.
1898-02-02	21? Jan. 1898	**88:** 76	*482*	V. G. Chertkov	—
1898-02-15	2–3? Feb. 1898	**71:** 269–270	*28*	I. M. Tregubov	19 Jan.
1898-02-26	14 Feb. 1898	**71:** 278–279	*38*	A. V. Zhirkevich	6 Feb.
1898-03-09a	25 Feb. 1898	**71:** 286	*47*	I. K. Diterikhs	20 Feb.
1898-03-09b	25 Feb. 1898	**71:** 289–290	*51*	A. V. Zhirkevich	19 Feb.
1898-03-09c	25 Feb. 1898	**71:** 291	*53*	S. O. Krasovskij	24 Feb.
1898-03-20	8 Mar. 1898	**71:** 301–302	*62*	P. I. Birjukov	*date unknown*
1898-03-21	11/23 Mar. 1898	**71:** 306–310	*67*	G. Gibson [E]	10/22 Feb.
1898-03-29a	17 Mar. 1898	**71:** 314–317	*71*	*Sankt-Peterburgskie vedomosti*	—
1898-03-29b	17 Mar. 1898	**71:** 317–318	*72*	È. È. Ukhtomskij	—
1898-03-29c	17 Mar. 1898	**71:** 318	*73*	I. P. Nakashidze	*21 Mar.
1898-03-29d	17 Mar. 1898	**71:** 319	*74*	M. O. Men'shikov	—
1898-03-30	18? Mar. 1898	**71:** 319–320	*78*	L. F. Annenkova	17 Mar.
1898-03-31a	19 Mar. 1898	**71:** 320–321	*80*	D. A. Litoshenko	8 Mar.
1898-03-31b	19 Mar. 1898	**71:** 322–327	*81*	*Various foreign newspapers*	—
1898-03-31c	19 Mar. 1898	**71:** 327–328	*82*	*Caucasus Doukhobors*	—
1898-04-01	20 Mar. 1898	**71:** 330–331	*85*	I. M. Tregubov	16 Mar.

Index	Date shown in J.E.: O.S. or O.S./N.S.	J.E. volume: page	J.E. N° †	Addressee§	In response to the addressee's letter of*
1898–04–02	21 Mar. 1898	**71:** 332–333	*87*	F. Fortey [E]	24 Feb./8 Mar. 1/13 & 3/15 Mar.
1898–04–05a	24 Mar. 1898	**71:** 335	*91*	V. F. Mevius	16 Mar.
1898–04–05b	24 Mar. 1898	**71:** 335–336	*92*	*Ust'–Notor Assessor*	—
1898–04–05c	24 Mar. 1898	**71:** 336–337	*93*	N. E. Fedoseev	10? Dec.
1898–04–05d	24 Mar. 1898	**71:** 338	*95*	S. P. Khlystov	14 Mar.
1898–04–05e	24 Mar. 1898	**71:** 338	*96*	I. M. Tregubov	*date unknown*
1898–04–10a	29 Mar. 1898	**71:** 341–343	*102*	P. A. Bulanzhe	—
1898–04–10b	29 Mar. 1898	**71:** 343–344	*103*	È. È. Ukhtomskij	—
1898–04–10c	29 Mar. 1898	**88:** 88–89	*493*	V. G. Chertkov	22 Mar./3 Apr.
1898–04–11	30 Mar. 1898	**71:** 344–345	*105*	È. È. Ukhtomskij	—
1898–04–14	2 Apr. 1898	**71:** 345–347	*107*	Emperor Nicholas II	—
1898–04–16	4 Apr. 1898	**88:** 90–91	*494*	V. G. Chertkov	—
1898–04–17a	5 Apr. 1898	**88:** 92	*495*	V. G. Chertkov	31 Mar./12 Apr.
1898–04–17b	5 Apr. 1898	**88:** 345	*2†*	T. L. Tolstaja-Sukhotina	—
1898–04–18a	6 Apr. 1898	**88:** 93–94	*496*	V. G. Chertkov	—
1898–04–18b	6 Apr. 1898	**88:** 94–95	*497*	V. G. Chertkov	*date unknown*
1898–04–19	7 Apr. 1898	**71:** 348–349	*112*	Ja. P. Polonskij	*14 Apr.

Index	Date shown in J.E.: O.S. or O.S./N.S.	J.E. volume: page	J.E. N°[†]	Addressee[§]	In response to the addressee's letter of[*]
1898–04–22	10 Apr. 1898	**71:** 351	*114*	A. V. Zhirkevich	21 Mar.
1898–04~24	12? Apr. 1898	**71:** 356	*119*	F. Kh. Grauberger	19 Mar.
1898–05–02	19–20? Apr. 1898	**71:** 357–358	*121*	P. I. Birjukov	—
1898–05–13	1 May 1898	**71:** 359–361	*124*	P. I. Birjukov	—
1898–05–16	4 May 1898	**88:** 96–98	*498*	V. G. Chertkov	2/14 Apr., 20 Apr./2 May
1898–05–27	15 May 1898	**71:** 362–364	*135*	P. I. Birjukov	27 Apr./9 May
1898–06–03	21–22? May 1898	**71:** 367–368	*139*	P. A. Bulanzhe	15 May
1898–06–21	9 June 1898	**71:** 374–375	*153*	N. E. Fedoseev	28 May
1898–07–06a	24 June 1898	**71:** 385	*165*	P. V. Verigin	—
1898–07–06b	24 June 1898	**71:** 386	*166*	V. A. Potapov	9 & 22 Jun.
1898–07–06c	24 June 1898	**71:** 387–388	*167*	A. N. Dunaev	19 May
1898–07–06d	24 June 1898	**71:** 388–389	*168*	E. I. Mansurova	16 May
1898–07–06e	24 June 1898	**88:** 100–101	*502*	V. G. Chertkov	—
1898–07–08	26 June 1898	**71:** 392–393	*170*	N. F. Khudjakov	8 Apr.
1898–07–09	27 June 1898	**71:** 395–396	*173*	P. I. Birjukov	—
1898–07–12a	30 June/11 July 1898	**71:** 396–397	*176*	C. F. Willard [E]	*date unknown*
1898–07–12b	30 June/11 July 1898	**71:** 397–398	*177*	E. Crosby [E]	—
1898–07–18a	6 July 1898	**71:** 400	*180*	M. O. Men'shikov	29 Jun.

Index	Date shown in J.E.: O.S. or O.S./N.S.	J.E. volume: page	J.E. N° †	Addressee§	In response to the addressee's letter of*
1898–07–18b	6 July 1898	**88:** 104–105	*505*	V. G. Chertkov & A. K. Chertkova	14/26 Jun.
1898–07–25a	13 July 1898	**71:** 403	*186*	Ju. G. Pashchenko	23 May
1898–07–25b	13 July 1898	**71:** 403–304	*187*	V. A. Potapov & F. I. Borisov	27 Jun.
1898–07–25c	13 July 1898	**71:** 404	*188*	L. A. Sulerzhitskij	6 Jul.
1898–07–25d	13 July 1898	**71:** 405–406	*189*	P. A. Bulanzhe	31 May/12 Jun., 3/15 Jun.
1898–07–26a	14 July 1898	**71:** 408–409	*193*	G. S. Golitsyn	*21 Jul.
1898–07–26b	14 July 1898	**88:** 105–107	*506*	V. G. Chertkov	8/20 Jul.
1898–07–28a	16? July 1898	**71:** 409–410	*195*	A. N. Dunaev	—
1898–07–28b	16 July 1898	**84:** 325	*722*	S. A. Tolstaya	—
1898–08–02a	21 July 1898	**71:** 413	*201*	L. A. Sulerzhitskij	—
1898–08–02b	2 July 1898	**71:** 414	*202*	A. N. Dunaev	—
1898–08–02c	21 July 1898	**88:** 110–111	*509*	V. G. Chertkov	*date unknown*
1898–08–12	Late July? 1898	**71:** 415	*205*	L. A. Sulerzhitskij	*9 Aug
1898–08–16	4/16 Aug. 1898	**71:** 415–416	*206*	J. Mavor [E]	*date unknown*
1898–08–17a	5 Aug. 1898	**71:** 417–418	*208*	L. I. Brodskij	—
1898–08–17b	5 Aug. 1898	**71:** 419–420	*209*	V. A. Morozova	—
1898–08–17c	5 Aug. 1898	**71:** 420–421	*210*	S. T. Morozov	—
1898–08–17d	5 Aug. 1898	**71:** 421–422	*211*	A. M. Sibirjakova	—

Index	Date shown in J.E.: O.S. or O.S./N.S.	J.E. volume: page	J.E. N° †	Addressee§	In response to the addressee's letter of*
1898–08–17e	5 Aug. 1898	**71:** 423–424	*212*	K. T. Soldatenkov	—
1898–08–19	7 Aug. 1898	**71:** 424	*213*	G. S. Golitsyn	—
1898–08–24a	7–12? Aug. 1898	**71:** 424	*215*	L. A. Sulerzhitskij	—
1898–08–24b	12 Aug. 1898	**88:** 112–114	*510*	V. G. Chertkov	*20 Aug./1 Sep.
1898–08–24c	12? Aug.1898	**88:** 115	*511*	V. G. Chertkov [E]	—
1898–08–29a	14–17? Aug. 1898	**71:** 425	*217*	A. M. Bodjanskij	8 Aug.
1898–08–29b	17 Aug. 1898	**71:** 426	*218*	D. A. Khilkov	6/18 Aug.
1898–09–03	20–22? Aug. 1898	**71:** 430	*223*	*New York paper "Sunday World"*	19/31 Aug.
1898–09–04	20–23 Aug. 1898	**71:** 431	*224*	O. K. Klodt	28 Jul.
1898–09–08a	27 Aug. 1898	**71:** 433–434	*229*	*Caucasus Doukhobors*	—
1898–09–08b	27 Aug. 1898	**88:** 116–117	*513*	V. G. Chertkov	—
1898–09–10a	29...30 Aug. 1898	**88:** 118–119	*514*	V. G. Chertkov	—
1898–09–10b	29 Aug. 1898	**88:** 119	*515*	V. G. Chertkov [E]	—
1898–09–11	30 Aug. 1898	**88:** 120	*516*	V. G. Chertkov [E]	—
1898–09–12	30–31 Aug. 1898	**71:** 435	*233*	*Messagerie Maritime agent*	—
1898–09–13	1 Sep. 1898	**88:** 120–121	*517*	V. G. Chertkov	—
1898–09–14	2? Sep. 1898	**88:** 121–122	*518*	V. G. Chertkov	—
1898–09–15a	3 Sep. 1898	**88:** 122	*519*	V. G. Chertkov [E]	20 Aug./1 Sep.

Index	**Date shown in J.E.: O.S. or O.S./N.S.**	**J.E. volume: page**	**J.E. N° †**	**Addressee§**	**In response to the addressee's letter of***
1898–09–15b	3? Sep. 1898	**88:** 122–123	*520*	V. G. Chertkov	20 Aug./1 Sep.
1898–09–21	9 Sep. 1898	**71:** 436–437	*241*	A. M. Bodjanskij	17 Aug.
1898–09–23	11 Sep. 1898	**88:** 123–125	*521*	V. G. Chertkov	3/15, 8/20 Sep.
1898–09–29a	9–17? Sep. 1898	**71:** 439	*246*	S. L. Tolstoy	—
1898–09–29b	9–17? Sep. 1898	**71:** 440	*247*	V. F. Orlov	29 Aug.
1898–09–29c	12–17? Sep. 1898	**71:** 440	*248*	L. A. Sulerzhitskij	*date unknown*
1898–09–29d	17 Sep. 1898	**71:** 441–442	*249*	P. I. Khlebnikov	*6 oct.
1898–09–29e	17 Sep. 1898	**71:** 442–443	*250*	L. A. Shanjavskaja	*11 Oct.
1898–09–30a	18 Sep. 1898	**71:** 444	*251*	P. I. Birjukov	4 Sep.
1898–09–30b	18 Sep. 1898	**71:** 445–446	*252*	K. M. Mazurin?	—
1898–09–30c	18 Sep. 1898	**71:** 446–447	*253*	A. V. Morozov	*23 Sep.
1898–09–30d	18 Sep. 1898	**71:** 447–448	*254*	A. M. Sibirjakova	*7 Oct.
1898–09–30e	18 Sep. 1898	**71:** 448–449	*255*	P. M. Tret'jakov	*28 Sep.
1898–10–06a	24 Sep. 1898	**71:** 450–451	*258*	P. D. Botkin?	—
1898–10–06b	24 Sep. 1898	**71:** 451–452	*259*	M. G. Komissarov	*29 Sep.
1898–10–06c	24 Sep. 1898	**71:** 452–453	*260*	*unknown addressee*	—
1898–10–07	25 Sep. 1898	**71:** 453	*261*	V. A. Maklakov	22 Sep.
1898–10–12a	30 Sep. 1898	**71:** 456	*265*	M. G. Komissarov	29 Sep.

Index	Date shown in J.E.: O.S. or O.S./N.S.	J.E. volume: page	J.E. N°[†]	Addressee[§]	In response to the addressee's letter of*
1898–10–12b	30 Sep. 1898	**71:** 456–457	*266*	P. I. Kharitonenko	*26 Oct.
1898–10–12c	30 Sep. 1898	**71:** 457–458	*267*	P. I. Birjukov	25 Sep.
1898–10–12d	30 Sep. 1898	**71:** 458–459	*268*	L. A. Sulerzhitskij	16, 19, 22 Sep.
1898–10–12e	30 Sep. 1898	**88:** 127–128	*523*	V. G. Chertkov	18/30 Sep.
1898–10–18a	6 Oct. 1898	**71:** 460–461	*271*	Ju. I. Bazanova	—
1898–10–18b	6 Oct. 1898	**71:** 461–462	*272*	E. I. Nekrasov	—
1898–10–18c	6 Oct. 1898	**71:** 462–463	*273*	S. I. Prokhorov	*26 Oct.
1898–10–21	9 Oct. 1898	**88:** 129–131	*524*	V. G. Chertkov	1/13 Oct.
1898–10–24a	12 Oct. 1898	**71:** 463–464	*276*	A. N. Konshin	*5 Nov.
1898–10–24b	12 Oct. 1898	**71:** 464–465	*277*	S. V. Perlov	—
1898–10–24c	12 Oct. 1898	**71:** 465–466	*278*	K. S. Popov	—
1898–10–24d	12 Oct. 1898	**71:** 467–468	*280*	A. S. Suvorin	7 Oct.
1898–10–24e	12 Oct. 1898	**88:** 132	*525*	V. G. Chertkov [E]	1/13 & 3/15 Oct.
1898–10–27	15 Oct. 1898	**88:** 133–134	*526*	V. G. Chertkov	6–7/18–19 Oct.
1898–10–28a	16? Oct. 1898	**71:** 468–469	*283*	P. I. Birjukov	23 Sep./5 Oct., 29 Sep./11 Oct.
1898–10–28b	16 Oct. 1898	**71:** 470	*284*	D. A. Litoshenko	*date unknown*
1898–10–28c	16 Oct. 1898	**71:** 471	*285*	A. M. Sibirjakova	7 Oct.

Index	Date shown in J.E.: O.S. or O.S./N.S.	J.E. volume: page	J.E. N°[†]	Addressee[$]	In response to the addressee's letter of[*]
1898–10–28d	16 Oct. 1898	**88:** 135–136	*527*	V. G. Chertkov	—
1898–11–01a	20 Oct. 1898	**71:** 471–472	*288*	L. A. Sulerzhitskij	12 Oct.
1898–11–01b	20 Oct. 1898	**88:** 136–138	*528*	V. G. Chertkov	—
1898–11–06	25 Oct. 1898	**71:** 476	*294*	P. V. Velikanov	*date unknown*
1898–11–10a	29 Oct. 1898	**71:** 477	*295*	A. V. Zhirkevich	9 Oct.
1898–11–10b	29 Oct. 1898	**88:** 138–139	*529*	V. G. Chertkov & A. K. Chertkova [F]	20 Oct./1 Nov.
1898–11–11	30 Oct. 1898	**84:** 330–331	*730*	S. A. Tolstaya	—
1898–11–12	31 Oct. 1898	**88:** 139	*530*	V. G. Chertkov	—
1898–11–13a	1 Nov. 1898	**71:** 478–479	*301*	P. V. Verigin	*date unknown*
1898–11–13b	1 Nov. 1898	**88:** 139–140	*531*	V. G. Chertkov & A. K. Chertkova	27 Oct./8 Nov.
1898–11–20	8 Nov. 1898	**71:** 482–483	*308*	G. S. Golitsyn	—
1898–11–24	12? Nov. 1898	**71:** 483–484	*309*	È. È. Ukhtomskij	8/20 Oct.
1898–11–27	15 Nov. 1898	**71:** 486	*312*	I. M. Tregubov	10 Oct.
1898–11–29	17? Nov. 1898	**71:** 487–489	*314*	E. Crosby [E]	—
1898–11–30	18 Nov. 1898	**84:** 335–336	*735*	S. A. Tolstaya	—
1898–12–05	23? Nov. 1898	**88:** 141–142	*532*	V. G. Chertkov & A. K. Chertkova	16/28 Nov.
1898–12–06	24 Nov. 1898	**71:** 493	*322*	A. M. Khirjakov	21 Nov.
1898–12–07	25 Nov. 1898	**71:** 494	*323*	S. L. Tolstoy & L. A. Sulerzhitskij	17 Nov.

Index	**Date shown in J.E.: O.S. or O.S./N.S.**	**J.E. volume: page**	**J.E. N°** †	**Addressee**§	**In response to the addressee's letter of***
1898–12–11	late Nov. 1898	**71:** 495	*326*	A. M. Bodjanskij	24 Oct.
1898–12–16	4 Dec. 1898	**71:** 496	*329*	S. L. Tolstoy	*date unknown*
1898–12–17a	5 Dec. 1898	**71:** 497–498	*331*	T. L. Tolstaja & M. L. Obolenskaja	—
1898–12–17b	5 Dec. 1898	**71:** 498–499	*332*	S. L. Tolstoy	28 Nov.
1898–12–17c	5? Dec. 1898	**71:** 500–502	*333*	P. V. Verigin	*date unknown*
1898–12–17d	5? Dec. 1898	**71:** 502–503	*334*	V. N. Skripitsyn	—
1898–12–17e	5? Dec. 1898	**71:** 503–504	*335*	D. A. Khilkov	13/25 Nov.
1898–12–17f	5? Dec. 1898	**71:** 504–505	*336*	A. Maude	*date unknown*
1898–12–17g	5 Dec. 1898	**88:** 143–144	*533*	V. G. Chertkov	—
1898–12–19	7 Dec. 1898	**71:** 506	*337*	S. O. Poljakov	5 Dec. | *12 Dec.
1898–12–22	9–10? Dec. 1898	**71:** 507–508	*338*	T. L. Tolstaja & M. L. Obolenskaja	—
1898–12–23	11? Dec. 1898	**71:** 510–511	*341*	V. I. Skorokhodov	27 Nov.
1898–12–24a	12 Dec. 1898	**71:** 512–513	*345*	A. Maude	28 Nov./10 Dec.
1898–12–24b	12? Dec. 1898	**71:** 513–514	*346*	H. Archer	29 Nov./11 Dec., 1/13 + 3/15 Dec.
1898–12–24c	12 Dec. 1898	**88:** 145	*535*	V. G. Chertkov	7/19 Dec.
1898–12–28a	16 Dec. 1898	**71:** 515–516	*347*	P. I. Birjukov	27 Nov./9 Dec., 1/13 Dec.
1898–12–28b	16 Dec. 1898	**71:** 516–517	*348*	A. Järnefelt	14 Dec.

Index	Date shown in J.E.: O.S. or O.S./N.S.	J.E. volume: page	J.E. N° †	Addressee§	In response to the addressee's letter of*
1898–12–28c	16 Dec. 1898	**71:** 517–518	*349*	A. P. Shcherbak	25 Nov.
1898–12–28d	16 Dec. 1898	**88:** 146	*536*	V. G. Chertkov	9/21 Dec.
1899–01–12	end Dec. 1898	**71:** 522	*355*	P. I. Birjukov	27 Nov./9 Dec.
1899–01–14	2/14 Feb. 1899	**72:** 3–4	*1*	E. Sinet [F]	13/25 Dec.
1899–01–16	4? Jan. 1899	**72:** 6–7	2	S. L. Tolstoy	25 Dec.
1899–01–21	7–9? Jan. 1899	**72:** 9–13	3	*Swedish intelligentsia*	*date unknown*
1899–01–24a	12 Jan. 1899	**72:** 22	*8*	D. A. Khilkov	19/31 Dec.
1899–01–24b	12 Jan. 1899	**72:** 27–28	*10*	A. Maude	28 Dec./9 Jan., 1/13+2/14 Jan.
1899–01–24c	12 Jan. 1899	**88:** 149–150	*538*	V. G. Chertkov & A. K. Chertkova	19/31 Dec., 20 Dec./1 Jan.
1899–02–03	22 Jan. 1899	**88:** 345	*4*†	V. G. Chertkov	—
1899–02–04	23 Jan. 1899	**88:** 150–151	*539*	V. G. Chertkov	—
1899–02–05a	24? Jan. 1899	**72:** 49	*24*	P. I. Birjukov	8/20 Jan.
1899–02–05b	24 Jan. 1899	**88:** 151–153	*540*	V. G. Chertkov	—
1899–02–13	early Feb. 1899	**72:** 52	*29*	A. M. Bodjanskij	—
1899–02–17	5 Feb. 1899	**88:** 153–154	*541*	V. G. Chertkov	—
1899–02–24a	12?/24? Feb. 1899	**72:** 55	32	*unknown addressee* [E]	—
1899–02–24b	11–12? Feb. 1899	**84:** 340	*740*	S. A. Tolstaya	—

Index	Date shown in J.E.: O.S. or O.S./N.S.	J.E. volume: page	J.E. N° †	Addressee§	In response to the addressee's letter of*
1899–02–25a	13 Feb. 1899	**72:** 55	*34*	*Pavlovka sectarians*	—
1899–02–25b	13? Feb. 1899	**72:** 56	*35*	*Pavlovka sectarians?*	*date unknown*
1899–02–26	12...19 Feb. 1899	**88:** 155–156	*542*	V. G. Chertkov	*date unknown*
1899–02–27a	12–15? Feb. 1899	**72:** 59–60	*38*	P. A. Bulanzhe	*date unknown*
1899–02–27b	12–15? Feb. 1899	**72:** 62	*39*	I. K. Diterikhs	21 Jan.
1899–02–27c	12–15? Feb. 1899	**72:** 63–64	*40*	D. A. Khilkov	8/20 Jan.
1899–02–27d	15 Feb. 1899	**72:** 67	*41*	A. St-John [E]	26 Jan./7 Feb.
1899–02–27e	15 Feb. 1899	**72:** 69–70	*42*	N. Potapov & I. Verigin	26 Jan./7 Feb.
1899–02–27f	15 Feb. 1899	**72:** 72–73	*43*	S. L. Tolstoy	*date unknown*
1899–02–27g	15 Feb. 1899	**84:** 341	*741*	S. A. Tolstaya	*date unknown*
1899–02–27h	15 Feb. 1899	**88:** 156–157	*543*	V. G. Chertkov	*date unknown*
1899–02–27i	15 Feb. 1899	**90:** 308–309	*128*	E. Crosby [E]	*date unknown*
1899–03–11	26? Feb. 1899	**72:** 77	*50*	M. L. Obolenskaja	*28 Feb.
1899–03–14a	2 Mar. 1899	**72:** 85	*56*	A. F. Marks	—
1899–03–14b	2? Mar. 1899	**88:** 159	*545*	V. G. Chertkov	—
1899–03–15	3 Mar. 1899	**72:** 87–88	*58*	A. F. Marks	2 Mar.
1899–03–21	9 Mar. 1899	**88:** 160–161	*548*	V. G. Chertkov	1/13 Feb.
1899–03–26a	12–14 Mar. 1899	**88:** 162–163	*550*	A. K. Chertkova	12/24 Mar.

Index	Date shown in J.E.: O.S. or O.S./N.S.	J.E. volume: page	J.E. N°[†]	Addressee[§]	In response to the addressee's letter of*
1899–03–26b	14 Mar. 1899	**90:** 310	*129*	S. M. Martynova	—
1899–03–28	16? Mar. 1899	**72:** 98	*71*	M. A. Stakhovich	—
1899–04–03	22 Mar. 1899	**72:** 100–101	*73*	A. D. Goremykin	—
1899–04–0Sa	24 Mar. 1899	**72:** 102	*74*	*Yakut Doukhobor exiles*	*8 Jun.
1899–04–0Sb	24 Mar. 1899	**72:** 565	*74a*	M. V. Pikhtin	—
1899–04–08	27 Mar. 1899	**72:** 105–106	*75*	A. F. Marks	*date unknown*
1899–04–09	28 Mar. 1899	**88:** 163–164	*551*	V. G. Chertkov [F]	—
1899–04–16	4 Apr. 1899	**88:** 164	*552*	V. G. Chertkov	1/13 Apr.
1899–05–17a	5 May 1899	**88:** 166	*554*	V. G. Chertkov	27 Apr./9 May
1899–05–17b	5 May 1899	**88:** 167	*556*	V. G. Chertkov [F]	—
1899–05–19	7 May 1899	**72:** 119–120	*95*	P. N. Sokol'nikov	25 Apr.
1899–05–26	14 May 1899	**88:** 168	*558*	V. G. Chertkov	—
1899–06–08a	27 May 1899	**72:** 124–125	*107*	P. A. Demens	29 Apr./11 May
1899–06–08b	27 May 1899	**72:** 128	*110*	F. P. Sergeev	27 Apr.
1899–06–08c	27 May 1899	**72:** 130	*111*	P. Stevens	8 May
1899–06–08d	27 May 1899	**72:** 130	*112*	L. A. Sulerzhitskij	—
1899–06–20	8 June 1899	**72:** 138–139	*123*	D. A. Khilkov	12/24 May | *16/28 Jul.
1899–07–21	9 July 1899	**88:** 175–176	*569*	V. G. Chertkov	*date unknown*

Index	**Date shown in J.E.: O.S. or O.S./N.S.**	**J.E. volume: page**	**J.E. N° †**	**Addressee§**	**In response to the addressee's letter of***
1899–07–31	19? July 1899	**90:** 312–313	*133*	A. N. Dunaev	—
1899–08–07	26 July 1899	**72:** 161–162	*151*	*Foreign newspaper editors*	—
1899–08–13a	1 Aug. 1899	**72:** 163–164	*153*	P. I. Birjukov	—
1899–08–13b	1 Aug. 1899	**72:** 171	*155*	A. V. Morozov	*25 Aug.
1899–08–20a	8?/20? Aug. 1899	**72:** 547	*13†*	[W. F.] McCreary	*29 Sep./11 Oct.
1899–08–20b	8 Aug. 1899	**88:** 178–179	*572*	V. G. Chertkov	31 Jul./12 Aug.
1899–09–09a	28 Aug. 1899	**72:** 567–568	*162a*	D. A. Khilkov	25 & 28 Jul.
1899–09–09b	28 Aug. 1899	**88:** 180–181	*573*	V. G. Chertkov	—
1899–09–12	late Aug. 1899	**72:** 548	*18†*	S. G. Barskij	*12 Sep.
1899–10–08	26 Sep. 1899	**72:** 189	*174*	*"Narodnaja pol'za" publishers*	18 Sep.
1899–10–09a	27 Sep. 1899	**72:** 193–194	*177*	A. N. Konshin	*26 Oct./7 Nov.
1899–10–09b	27 Sep. 1899	**72:** 197–198	*179*	A. D. Obolenskij	—
1899–10–17	5 Oct. 1899	**72:** 203	*181*	L. A. Sulerzhitskij	—
1899–10–18a	6 Oct. 1899	**88:** 182–183	*575*	V. G. Chertkov	30 Sep./12 Oct.
1899–10–20	8 Oct. 1899	**72:** 208	*185*	V. M. Velichkina	25–28 Aug./6–9 Sep. | *17/29 Nov.
1899–11–11	30 Oct. 1899	**72:** 226	*194*	I. M. Tregubov	—
1899–11–13a	1?/13? Nov. 1899	**72:** 231–232	*198*	A. St-John [E]	—

Index	Date shown in J.E.: O.S. or O.S./N.S.	J.E. volume: page	J.E. N° †	Addressee§	In response to the addressee's letter of*
1899–11–13b	1?/13? Nov. 1899	**72:** 233	*199*	W. [F]. McCreary [E)	—
1899–11–18a	6? Nov. 1899	**72:** 234	*201*	V. O. Bonch–Bruevich	9/21 Oct.
1899–11–18b	6 Nov. 1899	**72:** 238	*202*	*Canadian Doukhobors*	—
1899–11–18c	6 Nov. 1899	**88:** 184	*577*	V. G. Chertkov	—
1899–11–19	7? Nov. 1899	**72:** 240	*206*	P. I. Birjukov	—
1899–12–27	15 Dec. 1899	**88:** 184–185	*578*	V. G. Chertkov	29 Nov./11 Dec., 8/20 Dec.
1900–01–14	2 Jan. 1900	**88:** 188	*581*	V. G. Chertkov	4/16 Dec.
1900–01–19	7 Jan. 1900	**72:** 284	*232*	*Pavlovka sectarians*	—
1900–02–17	5 Feb. 1900	**72:** 299–300	*243*	E. Sinet [F]	26 Dec./7 Jan.
1900–02–27	15/27 Feb. 1900	**72:** 305–316	*246*	*Canadian Doukhobors*	—
1900–03–20a	7/[20] Mar. 1900	**72:** 328	*257*	*Canadian Doukhobors*	—
1900–03–20b	7 Mar. 1900	**88:** 192	*583*	V. G. Chertkov	—
1900–03–20c	7 Mar. 1900	**88:** 192	*584*	V. G. Chertkov	25 Feb./9 Mar.
1900–03–25a	12 Mar. 1900	**72:** 332	*260*	F. M. Dzjube	3 Mar.
1900–03–25b	12? Mar. 1900	**72:** 333	*261*	*Vladikavkaz Prison director*	*26 Apr.
1900–04–17a	1–3? Apr. 1900	**88:** 194	*586*	V. G. Chertkov & A. K. Chertkova	3/16 Apr.
1900–04–17b	3? Apr.1900	**88:** 194	*587*	V. G. Chertkov	—

Index	Date shown in J.E.: O.S. or O.S./N.S.	J.E. volume: page	J.E. N° †	Addressee§	In response to the addressee's letter of*
1900–04–19	24 Mar.–6? Apr. 1900	**72:** 342	*269*	P. N. Sokol'nikov	*15 Jul.
1900–05–15	02 May 1900	**72:** 353–354	*278*	D. A. Khilkov	—
1900–05–19	06 May 1900	**72:** 360–361	*284*	S. N. Tolstoy	—
1900–05–20	07 May 1900	**88:** 195	*588*	V. G. Chertkov	19 Apr./2 May, 29 Apr./12 May
1900–06–21	08 Jun 1900	**72:** 373–374	*304*	F. M. Dzjube	16 May
1900–07–03a	20 Jun 1900	**72:** 387–388	*315*	A. Järnefelt	8/21 Jun.
1900–07–03b	20 June 1900	**72:** 391	*317*	S. P. Chizhov	12 Jun.
1900–07–03c	20 June/[3] July 1900	**72:** 394–395	*320*	E. Sinet [F]	11/24 May
1900–07–24	11 July 1900	**72:** 407–408	*327*	M. L. Obolenskaja	*13 Jul.
1900–08–15	2 Aug. 1900	**72:** 430	*345*	E. E. Egorov	31 May
1900–08–16	3 Aug. 1900	**72:** 436–437	*350*	I. M. Tregubov	—
1900–09–07	25 Aug. 1900	**72:** 443–444	*356*	P. Sergeev	—
1900–10–11	28 Sep. 1900	**72:** 461	*375*	P. I. Birjukov	—
1900–10–15a	2 Oct. 1900	**72:** 465–466	*382*	A. M. Bodjanskij	8/21 Aug.
1900–10–15b	2 Oct. 1900	**72:** 470	*386*	I. P. Nakashidze	—

Index	Date shown in J.E.: O.S. or O.S./N.S.	J.E. volume: page	J.E. N° †	Addressee§	In response to the addressee's letter of*
1900–11–18	5 Nov. 1900	**72:** 497	*414*	P. N. Sokol'nikov	—
1900–12–06	23 Nov. 1900	**72:** 505–506	*419*	A. Maude	15/28 Nov.
1900–12–18	5 Dec. 1900	**72:** 507–508	*421*	E. I. Popov	30 Nov.
1900–12–19a	6 Dec. 1900	**72:** 510	*423*	A. M. Bodjanskij	—
1900–12–19b	6 Dec. 1900	**72:** 511	*424*	A. Maude	*13/26 Dec.
1900–12–20	7 Dec. 1900	**72:** 514–520	*426*	Emperor Nicholas II	—
1901–01–14	early Jan. 1901	**73:** 360	*1†*	H. Archer	13/26 Dec.
1901–01–31	18 Jan. 1901	**73:** 17–18	*7*	V. Potapov & I. Ponomarëv	18/31 Dec.
1901–02–01	19 Jan. 1901	**88:** 220–221	*611*	V. G. Chertkov	13/26 Jan.
1901–02–02a	20 Jan. 1901	**73:** 19–20	*11*	P. V. Verigin	—
1901–02–02b	20? Jan. 1901	**73:** 21	*12*	M. O. Men'shikov	—
1901–02–10	28? Jan. 1901	**73:** 29	*20*	M. O. Men'shikov	—
1901–02–14	1 Feb. 1901	**73:** 32	*26*	V. V. Stasov	27 Jan.
1901–03–09	24 Feb. 1901	**73:** 42	*38*	I. E. Konkin	1 Oct.
1901–03–20	7 Mar. 1901	**73:** 47	*44*	P. P. Gnedich	—
1901–03–21	early Mar. 1901	**73:** 48–49	*47*	A. Maude	24 Feb./9 Mar.
1901–04–04	22 Mar. 1901	**73:** 54–55	*55*	A. Maude	17/30 Mar.
1901–05–28	mid-May 1901	**73:** 361	*14†*	N. Struve	27 Apr./10 May

Index	Date shown in J.E.: O.S. or O.S./N.S.	J.E. volume: page	J.E. N° †	Addressee§	In response to the addressee's letter of*
1901–06–12	30 May 1901	**73:** 85–86	*99*	*Canadian Doukhobors*	*date unknown*
1902–01–05	23 Dec. 1901	**73:** 172–173	*190*	A. Maude	28 Nov./11 Dec.
1902–01–30	17 Jan. 1902	**73:** 198–199	*205*	P. V. Verigin	1 Feb. 1899
1902–02–18a	5 Feb. 1902	**73:** 364	*50†*	S. Makhortov	7/20 Nov.
1902–02–18b	5 Feb. 1902	**73:** 364	*51†*	O. F. Novokshonov	4 Dec.
1902–05–05	19–22 Apr. 1902	**88:** 260–261	*651*	V. G. Chertkov	13/26 + 14/27 Apr.
1902–05–28	mid-May 1902	**73:** 365	*65†*	A. Maude	3/16 May
1902–09–02	20 Aug. 1902	**73:** 282–283	*319*	I. M. Tregubov	18/31 Jul.
1902–10–07	24 Sep./7 Oct. 1902	**73:** 298	*344*	E. [H]. Schmitt [G]	11/24 Sep.
1902–11–13	31 Oct. 1902	**73:** 315	*367*	S. L. Tolstoy	—
1902–11–21	8? Nov. 1902	**88:** 279–280	*670*	V. G. Chertkov & A. K. Chertkova	26 Oct./8 Nov., 3/16 Nov.
1902–11–23	10? Nov. 1902	**73:** 317–318	*372*	A. Shkarvan	3/16 Oct.
1902–11–24a	11 Nov. 1902	**73:** 318–319	*373*	P. I. Birjukov	24 Oct./6 Nov.
1902–11–24b	11 Nov. 1902	**73:** 322–323	*376*	Grand Prince Nikolaj Mikhajlovich	3 Oct.
1902–12–04	21 Nov. 1902	**73:** 331–332	*390*	T. L. Sukhotina	*date unknown*
1902–12–07	24 Nov. 1902	**73:** 332	*392*	F. Kh. Grauberger	17 Nov.
1902–12–13	30 Nov./13 Dec. 1902	**73:** 334–335	*396*	J. Mavor [E]	*date unknown*
1903–02–26	9–13? Feb. 1903	**74:** 37–38	*40*	P. V. Verigin	30 Dec./12 Jan.

Index	**Date shown in J.E.: O.S. or O.S./N.S.**	**J.E. volume: page**	**J.E. N° †**	**Addressee§**	**In response to the addressee's letter of***
1903–05–19	6/19 May 1903	**74:** 115–116	*141*	A. Maude	25 Apr./8 May
1903–09–06	24 Aug. 1903	**88:** 305	*699*	V. G. Chertkov	—
1903–10–13	30 Sep. 1903	**74:** 192	*255*	P. I. & P. N. Birjukov	22 Sep.
1903–10–26	13/26 Oct. 1903	**74:** 205–206	*275*	E. James [El	16/29 Sep.
1903–11–04	22 Oct. 1903	**74:** 209	*281*	A. Ja. Ostrogorskij	—
1903–11–06a	24 Oct./6 Nov. 1903	**74:** 211–212	*284*	P. V. Verigin	*18 Nov./1 Dec.
1903–11–06b	24 Oct. 1903	**74:** 213	*286*	A. Maude	—
1903–11–06c	24 Oct. 1903	**74:** 214	*287*	Grand Prince Nikolaj Mikhajlovich	—
1903–11–25	12 Nov. 1903	**74:** 230	*307*	A. Maude	—
1903–11–28	15 Nov. 1903	**74:** 232–233	*310*	Grand Prince Nikolaj Mikhajlovich	31 Oct.
1903–12–02	19 Nov. 1903	**74:** 269	*19†*	O. F. Novokshonov	*28 Nov.
1903–12–26	13 Dec. 1903	**74:** 258	*342*	O. F. Novokshonov	—
1903–12–29	15–16? Dec. 1903	**74:** 270	*22†*	O. F. Novokshonov	*16 Dec.
1904–01–15a	2 Jan. 1904	**75:** 3	*1*	O. F. Novokshonov et al.	*date unknown*
1904–01–15b	2 Jan.1904	**75:** 4–6	*3*	P. V. Verigin	1 Dec.
1904–01–15c	12 Jan. 1904	**75:** 8	*6*	G. S. Golitsyn	—
1904–02–02	20 Jan.1904	**75:** 18	*18*	F. Kh. Grauberger	18? Dec.
1904–02–04	22 Jan. 1904	**75:** 28	*29*	I. M. Sergeev	18 Dec.

Index	Date shown in J.E.: O.S. or O.S./N.S.	J.E. volume: page	J.E. N° †	Addressee§	In response to the addressee's letter of*
1904–03–16	3/[16] Mar. 1904	**75:** 56–57	*69*	P. V. Verigin	7/20 Feb.
1904–03–17	4 Mar. 1904	**75:** 58	*70*	I. E. Konkin	2 Feb.
1904–04–28	15 Apr. 1904	**75:** 73	*92*	A. Maude	22 Mar./5 Apr.
1904–06–14a	1 June 1904	**75:** 109	*144*	P. Orlov & S. Usachëv	? Apr.
1904–06–14b	1 June 1904	**75:** 110–111	*148.P*	I. M. Tregubov	19 May
1904–06–14c	1 June 1904	**75:** 116–117	*155*	Grand Prince Nikolaj Mikhajlovich	16 May
1904–06–23	10 June 1904	**88:** 336–337	*722*	V. G. Chertkov	27 May/9 Jun.
1905–02–25	12 Feb. 1905	**75:** 221	*313*	P. P. Rajskij	3 Feb.
1905–03–11	8 Mar. 1905	**89:** 13	*737*	A. K. Chertkova	—
1905–06–10	28 May 1905	**75:** 245	*351*	P. V. Verigin	l Apr.
1905–06–20	7 June 1905	**75:** 251–252	*359*	A. Maude	30 May/12 Jun.
1905–11–08	26 Oct. 1905	**76:** 46–47	*68*	I. M. Tregubov	22 Oct.
1906–02–13	late Jan. 1906	**76:** 279	*74†*	P. Molchanov	13 Jan.
1906–03–11	26 Feb. 1906	**76:** 109–110	*152*	I. I. Gorbunov–Posadov	—
1906–09–15	2 Sept. 1906	**76:** 290	*184†*	A. Kanevskij	23 Jul.
1906–12–08	25 Nov. 1906	**76:** 242	*324*	I. I. Gorbunov–Posadov	24 Nov.
1906–12–13	30 Nov. 1906	**76:** 249	*336*	P. V. Verigin	24 Nov.
1907–01–14	early Jan. 1907	**77:** 288	*1†*	I. K. Diterikhs	27 Dec.

Index	Date shown in J.E.: O.S. or O.S./N.S.	J.E. volume: page	J.E. N° †	Addressee§	In response to the addressee's letter of*
1907–04–24	11 April 1907	**77:** 80	*85*	*Canadian Doukhobors*	28 Mar.
1907–05–19a	6 May 1907	**77:** 96–98	*109*	N. G. Sutkovoj	28, 30 Apr.
1907–05–19b	6 May 1907	**77:** 98–99	*110*	L. Maertz [E]	12/25 Apr.
1907–05–30a	17 May 1907	**77:** 107	*118*	P. P. Kartushin	2 May
1907–05–30b	17 May 1907	**77:** 107–108	*119*	A. I. Kudrin	*date unknown*
1907–05–30c	17 May 1907	**77:** 109	*121*	V. A. Makaseev	21 Apr./4 May
1907–07–14a	early July 1907	**77:** 299	*114*†	Ja. Ja. Melekh	27 Jun.
1907–07–14b	early July 1907	**77:** 299	*115*†	I. E. Nikiforov	29 Jun.
1907–07–20	7 July 1907	**77:** 149	*171*	P. A. Kuznetsov	5 Apr.
1907–08–14	early Aug. 1907	**77:** 303	*150*†	I. I. Sopran'kov	29 Jul.
1907–08–23	10 Aug. 1907	**77:** 176	*201*	P. V. Verigin	*2/15 Sep.
1907–09–15	2 Sep. 1907	**77:** 183	*211*	A. M. Bodjanskij	23 Aug.
1907–10–24	11 Oct. 1907	**77:** 286	*14*†	A. M. Bodjanskij	early Oct.
1907–10–31	18 Oct. 1907	**77:** 228	*268*	P. A. Stolypin	*23 Oct.
1907–11–02	20 Oct. 1907	**77:** 226–229	*269*	A. M. Khir'jakov	—
1907–11–15	2 Nov. 1907	**89:** 75–78	*794*	V. G. Chertkov	*14/27 Nov.
1907–12–28a	15 Dec. 1907	**77:** 263	*321*	D. A. Olsuf'ev	*28 Dec.
1907–12–28b	15 Dec. 1907	**77:** 264	*323*	N. G. Sutkovoj	6 Dec.

Index	Date shown in J.E.: O.S. or O.S./N.S.	J.E. volume: page	J.E. N° †	Addressee[§]	In response to the addressee's letter of*
1908–01–13	31 Dec. 1907	**77:** 278	*338*	D. A. Olsuf'ev	28 Dec.
1908–02–09a	27 Jan. 1908	**78:** 38–39	*26*	I. M. Tregubov	24 Jan.
1908–02–09b	27 Jan. 1908	**78:** 317	*27*†	V. Ju. Ustinova	24 Jan.
1908–02–10	28 Jan. 1908	**78:** 40	*28*	B. Sakhatov	24 Dec.
1908–02–11	29 Jan. 1908	**78:** 317	*32*†	A. I. Bejlin	12 Jan.
1908–02–12	30 Jan. 1908	**78:** 318	*37*†	Lifshits–Brodskaja	12 Jan.
1908–02–23	10 Feb. 1908	**78:** 56–57	*44*	O. K. Tolstaja	1/14 Feb.
1908–02–24	11 Feb. 1908	**78:** 60–61	*47*	M. Varzin (M. Zamjatin)	17 Jan.
1908–05–15	2 May 1908	**78:** 338	*236*†	E. Popov	6 Apr.
1908–07–08	25 June 1908	**78:** 347	*321*†	E. Popov	6/19 Jun.
1908–09–24	11 Sep. 1908	**78:** 357	*410*†	V. M. Anderson	26 Aug.
1908–11–06	24 Oct. 1908	**78:** 366	*493*†	I. Kosenko	20 Oct.
1908–11–13	31 Oct. 1908	**78:** 368	*521*†	M. Varzin	5/18 Oct.
1908–11–14	early Nov. 1908	**78:** 369	*532*†	N. N. Barabanov	29 Oct.
1909–01–27	14 Jan. 1909	**79:** 252	*33*†	P. V. Jablonskij–Sokolovskij	19 Dec.
1909–02–11	29 Jan. 1909	**79:** 253	*44*†	P. E. Eremeev	28 Jan.
1909–02–16	3 Feb. 1909	**79:** 257	*86*†	P. A. Tokarev	29 Jan.
1909–02–17	4 Feb. 1909	**79:** 258	*95*†	I. V. Pavljukovskij	20 Jan.

Index	Date shown in J.E.: O.S. or O.S./N.S.	J.E. volume: page	J.E. N° †	Addressee§	In response to the addressee's letter of*
1909–03–24	11 Mar. 1909	**79:** 266	*169*†	A. D. Shevtsov	28 Feb.
1909–03–31	18 Mar. 1909	**79:** 122	*134*	P. V. Verigin	2 Feb.
1909–05–07	24 Apr. 1909	**79:** 170	*197*	P. V. Jablonskij-Sokolovskij	25 Mar.
1909–05–23	10 May 1909	**79:** 278	*267*†	I. V. Toporov	5 May
1909–06–18	5 June 1909	**79:** 282	*305*†	M. Foks	20 May
1909–07–07	24 June 1909	**79:** 284	*323*†	N. Derjabin	21 Jun.
1909–07–14	1 July 1909	**80:** 274	*4*†	P. V. Planidin	7/20 Jun.
1909–07–23	10 July 1909	**80:** 276	*27*†	Gabrielov	5 Jul.
1909–10–17	4 Oct. 1909	**80:** 124–125	*171*	P. V. Verigin	13/26 Sep.
1909–10–20	7 Oct. 1909	**80:** 128–129	*179*	E. S. Makarov	3 Oct.
1909–10–21	8 Oct. 1909	**80:** 290	*172*†	F. Zalovskij	2 Oct.
1910–01–05	23 Dec. 1909	**80:** 303	*296*†	M. P. Lokhov	18 Dec.
1910–01–21	8 Jan. 1910	**81:** 25–26	*22*	A. T. Dzjuba	29 Dec.
1910–03–18	5 Mar. 1910	**81:** 286	*195*†	V. I. Zasosov	*date unknown*
1910–04–10	28 Mar. 1910	**81:** 292	*261*†	F. Malov & P. Verigin	*date unknown*
1910–04–18	5 Apr. 1910	**81:** 295	*286*†	A. Timofeevskij	*date unknown*
1910–05–27	14 May 1910	**82:** 237	*35*†	V. Solověv	*date unknown*
1910–06–24	11 June 1910	**82:** 244	*104*†	N. Logunov	*date unknown*

Index	**Date shown in J.E.: O.S. or O.S./N.S.**	**J.E. volume: page**	**J.E. N° †**	**Addressee§**	**In response to the addressee's letter of***
1910–07–28	15 July 1910	**82:** 252	*172*†	V. V. Popov	*date unknown*
1910–09–26	13 Sep. 1910	**82:** 264	*280*†	M. Egoshin	*date unknown*
1910–11–05	23 Oct. 1910	**82:** 275	*379*†	G. I. Semin	*date unknown*

APPENDIX 4

List of Sergej Tolstoy's Publications

1. *Delo Pyrkina* [The Pyrkin case]. *Knizhki «Nedeli»*, May 1894. (Published under the pseudonym S. Brodinskij.)
2. "Karpenter È. Sovremennaja nauka" [E. Carpenter. Modern science]. *Severnyj vestnik*, N° 3 (1898). Uncredited. Foreword by L. N. Tolstoy.
3. "O sostave krest'janskogo soslovija" [On the make-up of the peasant class]. Moscow: Izd. zhurnala «Russkaja mysl'», 1904. 78 pp.
4. "Lev Tolstoj o poèzii F. I. Tjutcheva" [Lev Tolstoy on the poetry of F. I. Tiutchev]. *Tolstovskij ezhegodnik* [Tolstoy Annual], 1912.
5. *Jasnaja Poljana: Putevoditel' i opisanie* [Yasnaya Polyana: a descriptive guide]. 1916.
6. "L. Tolstoj i P. Chajkovskij" [L. Tolstoy and P. Tchaikovsky]. *Trudy Gosudarstvennogo instituta muzykal'noj nauki.* Moscow, 1925.
7. *Fëdor Tolstoy — Amerikanets* [Fëdor Tolstoy — an American]. Moscow: Gosudarstvennaja Akademija Khudozhestvennykh nauk, 1926. Reprint, Moscow: «Sovremennik», 1990.
8. *Mat' i ded L. N. Tolstogo. Ocherki zhizni, dnevniki i pis'ma po neizdannym materialam* [L. N. Tolstoy's mother and grandfather. Biographical sketches, diaries, notes and letters, from unpublished materials]. Moscow: Federatsija, 1928.
9. "Les Derniers jours de ma mère. Fragment inédit d'un journal intime." *Europe*, N° 67 (1928).
10. "Kvartet «Kljuch» v romane «Vojna i mir»" [The 'Key' quartet in the novel *War and Peace*]. *Zven'ja*, N° 2 (Moscow), 1933. (Written together with I. V. Il'inskij.)

11. "Otrazhenie zhizni v «Anne Kareninoj»" [Reflection of life in *Anna Karenina*]. *Literaturnoe nasledstvo* [Moscow], vol. 37/38, N° 2, 1939.
12. "Istorija pisanija i pervoj postanovki «Plodov prosveshchenija»" [History of the writing and the first production of *The Fruits of Enlightenment*]. *Teatr*, N° 11 (1940).
13. *Ocherki bylogo* [Sketches of the past]. Moscow: Goslitizdat, 1949, 1956. Reprinted as part of the *Serija literaturnykh memuarov* [Literary Memoirs Series]. Tula, Russia: Priokskoe knizhnoe izdatel'stvo, 1965, 1966, 1968, 1975.
14. "Nikolaj Nikolaevich Strakhov." *Jasnopoljanskij sbornik*. Tula, Russia, 1982, 1984. Prepared by N. P. Puzin.
15. "Olsuf'evy «Devich'epol'skie»" [The 'Maiden-Field' Olsuf'evs]. *Jasnopoljanskij sbornik*. Tula, Russia,1986. Prepared by T. G. Nikiforova.

APPENDIX 5

Questionnaire for Doukhobors on L. N. Tolstoy

The English version of the questionnaire included here is an adaptation of the bilingual questionnaire first published in *Iskra*, N° 1905, 21 March 2001.

1. What is your age? _______
   - sex? _______
   - education? _______
   - profession? _______

2. How did you become acquainted with Leo Tolstoy?
   - school _______
   - discovered for yourself _______
   - at home _______
   - some other way _______

3. In what capacity did you first learn about Leo Tolstoy?
   - as a writer _______
   - as a social activist (helping famine & persecution victims) _______
   - as a thinker or life-teacher _______
   - as a friend of the Doukhobors _______

4. How old were you when you first learnt about Tolstoy's participation in the Doukhobor emigration to Canada? _______

5. How did you first hear of this?
    - school _______
    - discovered for yourself _______
    - at home _______
    - some other way _______

6. What aspects of Tolstoy's help to the Doukhobors did you learn about then?
    - search and choice of destination _______
    - financial help _______
    - contact with those helping the Doukhobors in Canada _______
    - role in organizing the emigration process _______
    - role of Leo Tolstoy's son Sergej in the emigration process _______
    - role of Tolstoyan L. A. Sulerzhitsky in the emigration process _______

7. Were there any personal links between your ancestors who emigrated to Canada and Leo Tolstoy? (Use a separate sheet if necessary.)

____

8. How familiar are you with any biographical details of Leo Tolstoy?
    - fairly well _______
    - a little _______
    - no information at all _______

9. Are there periods in Leo Tolstoy's life you are more familiar with than others? If so, which, specifically?

____

10. Are there periods in Leo Tolstoy's life which interest you more than others? If so, which, specifically?

____

11. How familiar are you with Leo Tolstoy's literary works?
    - fairly well _______
    - a little _______
    - no information at all _______

12. How old were you when you learn about Tolstoy as a writer? _______

13. How did you learn about Tolstoy as a writer? (Use a separate sheet if necessary.)

____

14. What literary works of Tolstoy's did you become acquainted with first?

---

15. What fiction works by Tolstoy have you read?

---

16. What religious or social tracts?

---

17. Which works by Tolstoy seem the most successful to you?

---

18. Have you found in Tolstoy's works any sayings which seem to be **in harmony with** Doukhobor teachings? (If so, please identify the work and/or write out some examples on a separate sheet.)

---

19. Have you found in Tolstoy's works any sayings which seem to be **contradictory to** the tenets Doukhobor doctrine? (If so, please identify the work and/or write out some examples on a separate sheet.)

---

20. Have you found any sayings which seem to be the **result of Doukhobor influence** on Leo Tolstoy? (If so, please identify the work and/or write out some examples on a separate sheet)

---

21. Which of Tolstoy's fiction or non-fiction works would you recommend to your fellow Doukhobors and their children as reading beneficial to the soul?

---

22. Which of his works would you **not** recommend for such a purpose?

---

23. Which of Tolstoy's ideas seem to you to be the **most** successful? (Use a separate sheet if necessary.)

---

24. Which of Tolstoy's ideas seem to you to be the **least** successful? (Use a separate sheet if necessary.)

---

25. Which of Tolstoy's ideas seem to you feel are still relevant today? (Use a separate sheet if necessary.)

---

26. Which of Tolstoy's ideas seem to you consider obsolete? (Use a separate sheet if necessary.)

---

27. Do you think that in other areas of his activity Tolstoy …

- contradicted his basic calling?
always _______ sometimes _______
- acted in accord with his basic calling?
always _______ sometimes _______
- subjected these forms of his activity to the interests of his basic calling?
always _______ sometimes _______

28. Are you familiar with our publications such as …

- *Leo Tolstoy—Peter Verigin: Correspondence*? _______
- *Sergej Tolstoy and the Doukhobors: A Journey to Canada*? _______
- *The Doukhobor Centenary in Canada*? _______

29. Do you have any information about the Doukhobors' relationship to Leo Tolstoy (or those associated with him) which you would like to share with us? (Use a separate sheet if necessary.)

---

30. Please write out any further comments on a separate sheet.

Please return the completed questionnaire to this address:
Dr Andrew Donskov, Head
Slavic Research Group
University of Ottawa
Ottawa K1N 6NS

BIBLIOGRAPHY

Abramov, Ja. V. 1884. *Dukhobortsy.* Moscow.

Abrams, Irwin. 2001. *The Nobel Peace Prize and the Laureates: An Illustrated Biographical History, 1901–2001.* New York: Science History Publications.

Afanas'ev, A. N. 1913. *Narodnye russkie legendy.* Moscow.

Afanas'ev, E. S. 1976. "O nekotorykh osobennostjakh tvorcheskogo metoda L. N. Tolstogo pozdnego perioda." *Russkaja literatura,* N° 4: 159–66.

Alexeeva (Alekseeva), Galina. 1995. "Literature on the Doukhobors contained in Lev N. Tolstoy's private library in the village of Yasnaya Polyana." *Canadian Ethnic Studies,* vol. 27, N° 3: 234–44.

—, 1998. "Leo Tolstoy and James Mavor." *Tolstoy Studies Journal,* vol. 10, 80–89.

—, 2000. "James Mavor and the Doukhobors." In Donskov, Woodsworth, and Gaffield, 149–57.

Allen, James Sloan. 1998. "Tolstoy's prophecy: 'What is art?' today." *The New Criterion,* vol. 12, N° 4: 15–21.

Alston, Charlotte. 2014a. "A Great Host of Sympathisers: The Doukhobor Emigration and its International Supporters 1895–1905." *Journal of Modern European History,* vol. 12, N° 2 (April): 200–15.

—, 2014b. *Tolstoy and his Disciples. The History of a Radical International Movement.* London: I.B. Tauris.

Anderson, Jennifer. 1997. "Leo Tolstoy, Peter Kropotkin and James Mavor on the Doukhobors." Master's thesis, Carleton University.

Anderson, V. M. 1908. "Dukhoborchestvo (Obshchina Vsemirnago Bratstva) i svjaz' ego s tolstovstvom." In *Staroobrjadchestvo i sektantstvo: istoricheskij ocherk russkago religioznago raznomyslija,* 371–409. St. Petersburg.

Anosova, Irina A. 2006. "Canada — second homeland of the Doukhobors: integration and cultural localization/Kanada — vtoraja Rodina Dukhobortsev: filosofija ljubvi kak put' kul'turnoj integratsii." *Mir Rossii,* vol. 25, N° 4: 198–99. Available at http://www.spirit-wrestlers.com/excerpts/Inquirer/Anosova.html.

—, 2016. "Phenomenologija kul'tury sovremennykh dukhobortsev Kanady (k voprosu o dialektike professii i konfessii)..." In *Professional'naja Kul'tura Spetsialista v XXI veke. Trudy nauchno prakticheskoj konferentsii.* St. Petersburg. Available at https://tinyurl.com/anosova-cdc.

Anuchin, D. N. 1913. "Iz vospominanij." In *Russkie vedomosti. Sbornik,* 84–85. Moscow.

Armytage, W. H. G. 1961. *Heavens Below: Utopian Experiments in England, 1560–1960.* Toronto: University of Toronto Press, and London: Routledge and Kegan Paul.

Arkhiv S.L. Tolstogo. Moscow: Gosudarstvennyj muzej im. L.N. Tolstogo.

Arkhiv S.A. Tolstoj. Moscow: Gosudarstvennyj muzej im. L.N. Tolstogo.

Ashkinazi, M.O. [Michel Delines, pseud.]. 1909. "Tolstoï et les Doukhobors." In *Bibliothèque universelle et revue Suisse.* Lausanne-Genève, ser. 4, vol. 53, 5–31.

Assistant Prosecutor of Elisavetpol' Regional Court. 1898. Representation to the Prosecutor of Elisavetpol' Regional Court, 10 February. Document #1898-03-12b in Woodsworth 1997. English translation in Woodsworth 1999a: 90–97.

Avakumovic, Ivan. 1978. "Tolstoy and the Doukhobors." Paper delivered at the Tolstoy Symposium, University of Victoria.

Ballou, Adin. 1846. *Christian Non-resistance.* Philadelphia: J.M. M'Kim.

Bazanov, V. 1973. "Vokrug narodnykh rasskazov L.N. Tolstogo." In *Ot fol'klora k narodnoj knige*, 297–321. Leningrad: Khudozhestvennaja literatura.

Bekker, M. 1935. "L. Tolstoj i nachinajushchie pisateli iz naroda." *Literaturnaja ucheba*, N° 10: 130–45.

Bellows, Amanda. 2014. *Serfs and Slaves in the Post-Emancipation Imagination 1861–1915.* Washington, DC: American Councils for International Education.

Berlin, Isaiah. 1967. "Tolstoy and enlightenment." In *Tolstoy*, edited by Ralph Matlaw. Englewood Cliffs, NJ: Prentice-Hall.

Bienstock, J.-W. (V. L. Binshtok). 1899. "Léon Tolstoy sur les Doukhobors." *Revue blanche* [Paris], vol.18 (January), 79–80.

—, ed. and trans. 1902. *Tolstoï et les doukhobors: faits historiques réunis et traduits du russe.* Bibliothèque sociologique, N° 32. Paris: Stock.

Billington, James. 1966. *The Icon and the Axe: An Interpretive History of Russian Culture.* New York: Vintage Books. See esp. "The sectarian tradition," 174–80.

Birjukov, P. I. 1896. "Gonenie na khristian v Rossii v 1895 g." Carouge-Genève: Èlpidin.

—, 1897. *Pomogite! Obrashchenie k obshchestvu po povodu gonenij na kavkazskikh dukhoborov.* Izd. Vladimira Chertkova 3. Sostavili P. Birjukov, I. Tregubov, V. Chertkov. Posleslovie L. N. Tolstogo. London: Tchertkoff, 1897. English translation in *Essays, Letters, Miscellanies*, by L. N. Tolstoy, vol. 1, 304–09. New York: Scribner's, 1911; and in *Patriotism: Slavery of our Times*, edited by Nathan Dole, 304–09. New York: Crowell, 1928.

—, 1908. *Dukhobortsy: sbornik statej, vospominanij, pisem* i *drugikh dokumentov.* Izd. Posrednika 689. St. Petersburg: Kushnerev.

—, (Paul Birukoff) 1911. "The Dukhobor movement." In *The Life of Tolstoy*, 131–35. London: Cassell and Co.

—, 1923. *Biografija L'va Nikolaevicha Tolstogo.* Vol. 3, 241–42, 257–59, 299–303; vol. 4, 15–20, 72. Moscow: Gosizdat.

—, 1938. "Gonenie na khristian v Rossii v 1895 g." In *Letopisi Gosudarstvennogo literaturnogo muzeja. Kniga 2: L. N. Tolstoj*, 6–11. Moscow: Gos. lit. muzej.

Birjukov, P. I., and V. G. Chertkov 1897. *Polozhenie dukhoborov na Kavkaze v 1896 godu, i neobkhodimye sredstva oblegchenija ikh uchasti.* Croydon, UK: Izd. Vladimira Chertkova.

Birkhead, Alice. 1966. "The reformer of the East." In *Heroes of Modern Europe*, 216–27. Freeport, NY: Books for Libraries Press. Reprint of 1913 publication.

Black, J. Laurence. 2000. "Imperial Russia at the turn of the twentieth century: volatile cross-currents in the Doukhobor homeland." In Donskov, Woodsworth, and Gaffield, 49–54.

—, 2001. *The Peasant Kingdom: Canada in the 19th-Century Russian Imagination.* Ottawa: Penumbra Press.

—, 2003. *Everything You Want To Know About Canadian-Russian Relations: Catalogue of Research Holdings.* Compiled by Lindsay Kent. Ottawa: Carleton University Centre for Research on Canadian-Russian Relations.

Blum, J. 1961. *Lord and Peasant in Russia from the Ninth to the Nineteenth Century.* Princeton, NJ: Princeton University Press.

Bolshakoff, Serge. 1950. *Russian Nonconformity.* Philadelphia: Westminster Press.

Bonch-Bruevich, V. O., ed. 1900. *Spisok psalmov, pisem, razskazov i drugikh rukopisej po izsledovaniju uchenija, zhizni i pereselenija v Kanadu zakavkazskikh dukhobortsev, s prilozheniem bibliograficheskago ukazatelja literatury po dukhoborcheskomu voprosu.* Geneva: Ukrainskaja tipografija.

—, ed. 1901. *Pis'ma dukhoborcheskogo rukovoditelja Petra Vasil'evicha Verigina.* Materialy k istorii i izucheniju russkogo sektantstva 1. Christchurch, UK: Svobodnoe Slovo.

—, 1905. "K istorii russkago dukhoborchestva." *Obrazovanie* [St. Petersburg], N° 9: 27–56; N° 10: 145–203; N° 11/12: 52–80.

—, 1908. *Baptisty, Beguny, Dukhobortsy, L. Tolstoj o skopchestve, Pavlovtsy, Pomortsy, Staroobrjadtsy, Skoptsy, Shtundisty.* St. Petersburg.

—, 1918. *Dukhobortsy v kanadskikh prerijakh.* Petrograd: Izd. Zhizn' i znanie. See esp. Chap. 1, 10–12.

—, 1934. "Ko vsem dukhobortsam." *Kanadskij gudok* [Winnipeg], N° 153 (9 May).

—, comp. 1909. *Zhivotnaja kniga dukhobortsev.* St. Petersburg. 2nd ed. Reprint, Winnipeg: Union of Doukhobors of Canada, 1954. Also published in English translation as *Book of Life of the Doukhobors.* Saskatoon: Doukhobor Societies of Saskatchewan, 1978.

Bondarev, Timofej (Bondareff, Timothé), and L. N. Tolstoj (Tolstoï). 1890. *Léon Tolstoï et Timothé Bondareff. Le travail.* Traduit du russe par V. Tseytline et A. Pagès. Paris, 1890. Translated in English (from the French) by Mary Cruger as *Labour: the divine command. Made known, augmented and edited by Count Lyof Tolstoy* [at head of title: *The suppressed book of the peasant Bondareff*]. Toronto, 1890.

Bondarev, Timofej. 1906. *Torzhestvo zemledel'tsa, ili trudoljubie* i *tunejadstvo.* Moscow: Posrednik.

Borisova, I. 1994. *Neizvestnyj Tolstoj. V arkhivakh Rossii i SShA.* Moscow: Tekhna-2.

Breyfogle, Nicholas. 1995. "Building Doukhoboriia: religious culture, social identity and Russian colonization in Transcaucasia, 1845–1895." *Canadian Ethnic Studies,* vol. 27, N° 3: 24–51.

—, 2000. "Rethinking the origins of the Doukhobor arms-burning: 1886–1893." In Donskov, Woodsworth, and Gaffield, 55–82.

—, 2005. *Heretics and Colonizers: Forging Russia's Empire in the South Caucasus.* Ithaca, NY: Cornell University Press.

Brock, Peter. 1964–65. "Vasya Pozdnyakov's Dukhobor narrative." *Slavonic & East European Review,* vol. 43, N° 100 (December), 152–76; N° 101 (June): 400–14. Reprinted as *Vasya Pozdnyakov's Dukhobor Narrative.* New York: School of International Affairs, Columbia University, n.d.

—, ed. 1972. "Russian sectarian pacifism: The Tolstoyans." *Pacifism in Europe to 1914,* 442–70. Princeton, NJ: Princeton University Press.

—, 1991. *Freedom from War: Nonsectarian Pacifism, 1814–1914.* Toronto: University of Toronto Press.

—, 1992. *A Brief History of Pacifism from Jesus to Tolstoy.* Toronto.

—, 2003. "'A light shining in darkness.' Tolstoï and the imprisonment of conscientious objectors in imperial Russia." *Slavonic & East European Review,* vol. 81, N° 4: 683–97.

Brock, Peter, and John Keep, eds. 2001. *Life in a Penal Battalion of the Imperial Russian Army: The Tolstoyan N.T. Iziumchenko's Story.* Translated by John L. H. Keep. York, UK: William Sessions Ltd.

Bruford, W. H. 1947. "The Peasant." *Chekhov and his Russia.* London: Kegan Paul: 38–75.

Bulanzhe, P. A. (Paul Boulanger). 1954. Correspondence. In *PSS* 70:86–87; *PSS* 71:115–16.

Bulgakov, V. F. 1917. *Khristianskaja ètika. Sistematicheskie ocherki mirovozzrenija L.N. Tolstogo.* Reprint, Ekaterinburg: TOO Al'fa, 1994. Also appears in Eli A. Popoff's English translation as "Christian Ethics," in four parts. *Iskra*, 1 April–1 July 2011.

Bumgardner, April. 2001. "The Doukhobors: History, Ideology and the Tolstoy-Verigin Relationship." Mphil dissertation, University of Glasgow.

Burlakova, T. T., ed. 2002. *Tolstovskij sbornik 2002. Aktual'nye problemy izuchenija nasledija L.N. Tolstogo.* Tula, Russia: Izd. TPGU im. L.N. Tolstogo.

Burlakova, Tamara. 1995. "Leopold Sulerzhitsky and the voyage of the Doukhobors to Canada." In Tarasoff and Robert Klymasz, 101–09.

Busch, R. L. 1977. "Nature and natural man in early Tolstoï." *Canadian Slavonic Papers*, vol. 19, N° 1: 16–32.

Butkievich, T. B., and V. M. Skvortsov 1897. "Tolstovstvo kak sekta." *Missionerskoe obozrenie* [St. Petersburg], t. 2, kn. 1, 807–43.

Buyniak, V. O. 1969. "Aylmer Maude on the practical application of the non-resistance doctrine and its implication in establishment of Tolstoyan and Doukhobor colonies." *Canadian Ethnic Studies*, vol. 1: N° 2 (December), 87–94.

—, 1978. "Tolstoy and the Doukhobors." *Chelsea Journal* [Saskatoon], vol. 4, N° 3: 151–55.

Bychkov, S. P. 1947. "Tolstoj i problema naroda. 50–60-e gody." In *Istoriko-literaturnyj sbornik*, 384–452. Moscow.

Camfield, G. P. 1990. "The Pavlovtsy of Khar'kov Province, 1886–1905: Harmless sectarians or dangerous rebels?" *Slavonic & East European Review*, vol. 68, N° 4: 692–717.

Canadian Slavonic Papers. 1979. Vol. 21, N° 3. "Tolstoy Symposium" issue.

Chertkov, V. G. 1897. *Christian Martyrdom in Russia: Persecution of the Spirit-Wrestlers (or Doukhobortsi) in the Caucasus.* Concluding chapter and letter by L.N. Tolstoy. London: Brotherhood Publishing Co., 1897. Reprint, Toronto: G.N. Morang.

—, 1900. *Christian Martyrdom in Russia: Persecution of the Doukhobors.* 2nd ed. Concluding chapter and letter by L. N. Tolstoy; account of the emigration to Cyprus and Canada. London: Free Age Press.

—, ed. 1918. *Lev Tolstoj i russkie tsari.*

Chertkov, V. G., and A. K. Chertkova. 1902. *Dukhobortsy v distsiplinarnom batal'one.* Svobodnoe Slovo 53; Materialy k istorii i izucheniju russkago sektantstva 4. Christchurch, UK: Tchertkoff.

Chesterton, Gilbert K. 1968. "Tolstoy and the cult of simplicity." In *Varied Types*, 125–46. Freeport, NY: Books for Libraries Press. Reprint of 1903 publication.

Christian, Reginald F. 1988. "The road to Yasnaya Polyana: some pilgrims from Britain and their reminiscences." *Slavonic & East European Review*, vol. 66, N° 4: 526–52.

Chulos, Chris J. 2003. *Converging worlds: Religion and community in peasant Russia, 1861–1917.* DeKalb: Northern Illinois University Press.

Cockerell, Sydney. 1940. "Count Leo Tolstoy." In *Friends of a Lifetime*, edited Viola Meynell, 78–86. London: Cape.

Coneybeare, Frederick C. 1921. "The Dukhobortsy." In *Russian Dissenters*, edited by F. C. Coneybeare, 267–87. Cambridge, MA: Harvard University Press.

Conovaloff, Andrei. n.d. *Spiritual Christians Around the World/Dukhovnye khristiane mira*. http://www.molokane.org.

Diterikhs, I. K. 1926. "Vospominanija o L.N. Tolstom." In *Tolstoj i o Tolstom*, edited by N. N. Gusev. Moskva: Tolstovskij muzej.

Dole, Nathan H. 1911. "The Doukhobors." In *The Life of Count Lyof N. Tolstoï*, edited by N. H. Dole, 352–59. New York: Crowell.

Dolgov, N. 1917. "Poslednjaja ispoved' L.N. Tolstogo: ego zapreshchennaja p'esa «I svet vo t'me svetit»." *Solntse Rossii*, N° 377: 9–12.

Donskov, Andrew. 1972. *The changing image of the peasant in nineteenth-century Russian drama*. Helsinki: Annales Academiæ Scientiarum Fennicæ.

—, 1979. "The peasant in Tolstoy's thought and writings." *Canadian Slavonic Papers*, vol. 21, N° 2: 183–96.

—, 1983. "L.N. Tolstoï as an editor of literature by peasant writers." In *Crisis and Commitment: Studies in German and Russian Literature in Honour of J.W. Dyck*, edited by John Whiton and Harry Loewen, 41–47. Waterloo, ON: University of Waterloo Press.

—, 1988. *Essays on L.N. Tolstoj's dramatic art*. Wiesbaden: Otto Harrassowitz.

—, 1989. "The stylistic nature of L.N. Tolstoj's *The Wisdom of Children*." *Russian Literature* vol. 26, 355–72.

—, ed. 1995a. *L.N. Tolstoj — P. V. Verigin: perepiska*. St. Petersburg: Izd. Dmitrij Bulanin; published in English as *Leo Tolstoy — Peter Verigin: Correspondence*. Translated by John Woodsworth. Ottawa: Legas, 1995.

—, 1995b. "On the censorship of Tolstoy's early 'Stories for the people': an unpublished *Doklad tsenzora P.E. Astafeva*." *Russian Language Journal*, vol. 49, N°s 162–164, 223–39.

—, 1995c. "On the Doukhobors: from imperial Russian archival files." *Canadian Ethnic Studies*, vol. 27, N° 3: 252–61.

—, 1996a. "Tolstoj i Novikov i russkoe krest'janstvo." In *L.N. Tolstoj i M.P. Novikov: perepiska*, edited by A. Donskov, 1–26. Munich: Verlag Otto Sagner.

—, 1996b. "L.N. Tolstoj i krest'janskij myslitel' T.M. Bondarev." In *L.N. Tolstoj i T. M. Bondarev: perepiska*, edited by A. Donskov, 1–15. Munich: Verlag Otto Sagne.

—, 1996c. "The life of *Peter the Publican* as edited by L.N. Tolstoy." *Russian Language Journal*, N°s 165–167, 241–62.

—, 1996d. "«Zhitie Petra Mytarja» v obrabotke L.N. Tolstogo." *Russkaja rech'*, N° 4: 6–9.

—, 1996e. "Sozhzhenie ognestrel'nogo oruzhija (1895 g.) i ego posledstvija." *Novyj zhurnal*, N° 197: 272–87.

—, 1997. "Pis'ma Bondareva k L.N. Tolstomu." *Russkaja literatura*, N° 1: 163–81.

—, ed. 1998a. *Sergej Tolstoy and the Doukhobors: A Journey to Canada*. Compiled by Tat'jana Nikiforova, English translation by John Woodsworth. Ottawa: Slavic Research Group at the University of Ottawa; Moscow: L.N. Tolstoy State Museum.

—, 1998b. "Tolstoj, Tolstoyans and the Doukhobors. From imperial Russian archival files." *Russian Literature*, vol. 43, N° 4: 431–44.

—, ed. 1999. *L.N. Tolstoj i F.A. Zheltov: Perepiska*. Compiled by L. Gladkova. Ottawa: Slavic Research Group at the University of Ottawa; Moscow: L.N. Tolstoy State Museum. (See Dunn 2001 for the English edition.)

—, ed. 2000a. *L. N. Tolstoj i S.A. Tolstaja: Perepiska s N.N. Strakhovym/The Tolstoys' correspondence with N.N. Strakhov.* Compiled by L. D. Gromova and T. G. Nikiforova. Ottawa: Slavic Research Group at the University of Ottawa; Moscow: L.N. Tolstoy State Museum.

— (Donskov, A. A.). 2000b. "Zapiski S.L. Tolstogo o ego puteshestvii s dukhoborami v Kanadu." In Shcherbakova and Mozharova, 307–20.

—, ed. 2003. *L.N. Tolstoj — N.N. Strakhov: Polnoe sobranie perepiski/Leo Tolstoy & Nikolaj Strakhov: Complete correspondence.* 2 vols. Compiled by L. D. Gromova and T. G. Nikiforova. Ottawa: Slavic Research Group at the University of Ottawa; Moscow: L.N. Tolstoy State Museum.

—, 2004. "Leo Tolstoy and Mikhail Novikov: selected letters." *Tolstoy Studies Journal,* 16: 55–76.

—, 2005. "Verigin, Peter Vasil'evich." In *Dictionary of Canadian Biography,* vol. 15, edited by Ramsay Cook and Jean Hammelin, 1032–36. Toronto: University of Toronto Press. Available at http://www.biographi.ca/en/bio/verigin_peter_vasil_evich_15E.html.

—, 2007. "Tolstoj i kanadskie dukhobortsy segodnja." In *Lev Tolstoj i mirovaja literatura. Materialy IV mezhdunarodnoj nauchnoj konferentsii,* edited by G. Alekseeva, 137–49. Tula, Russia: Izd. Jasnaja Poljana.

—, 2008. *Leo Tolstoy and Russian Peasant Sectarian Writers.* Ottawa: Slavic Research Group at the University of Ottawa.

—, ed. 2012. *V. F. Bulgakov. Kak prozhita zhizn': vospominanija poslednego sekretarja L.N. Tolstogo.* Compiled by Liudmila Gladkova, John Woodsworth, and Arkadi Klioutchanski. Moscow: Kuchkovo pole.

—, ed. 2014a. *V. F. Bulgakov. V spore s Tolstym: Na vesakh zhizni.* Compiled by Liudmila Gladkova and Arkadi Klioutchanski. Moscow: Kuchkovo pole.

—, 2014b. "Die Duchoborzen in Kanada." In *Tolstoy als theologisher Denker und Kirchenkritiker,* edited by Martin George, Jens Herlth, Christian Münch, and Ulrich Schmid, 719–30. Göttingen: Vandenhoeck & Ruprecht, 2014.

—, 2014c. "Pis'ma kanadskikh dukhobortsev k V.F. Bulgakovu." In *V.F. Bulgakov: V spore s Tolstym: na vesakh zhizni,* edited by A. Donskov, compiled by Liudmila Gladkova and Arkadi Klioutchanski, 301–18. Moscow: Kuchkovo pole.

—, ed. 2016. *S.L. Tolstoj: puteshestvie s dukhoborami v Kanadu: dnevniki i perepiska.* Russian translation of Donskov 1998a. Moscow: Kuchkovo Pole, 2016.

—, 2017. *Tolstoy and Tolstaya: A Portrait of a Life in Letters.* Ottawa: University of Ottawa Press.

—, 2019. *Leo Tolstoy in Conversation with Four Peasant Sectarian Writers.* Ottawa: University of Ottawa Press.

Donskov, Andrew, Galina Galagan, and Lidija Gromova. 2002. *Edinenie ljudej v tvorchestve L.N. Tolstogo/The Unity of People in Leo Tolstoy's Works.* Ottawa: Slavic Research Group at the University of Ottawa; St. Petersburg: Institute of Russian Literature, and Moscow: Institute of World Literature.

Donskov, Andrew, and John Woodsworth, eds. 1996. *Lev Tolstoy and the Concept of Brotherhood.* Proceedings of a conference held at the University of Ottawa 22–24 February 1996. Ottawa: Legas.

Donskov Andrew, John Woodsworth, and Chad Gaffield. 2000. *The Doukhobor Centenary in Canada: A Muiti-Disciplinary Perspective on Their Unity and Diversity.* Proceedings of a conference held at the University of Ottawa 22–24 October

1999. Ottawa: Slavic Research Group and the Institute of Canadian Studies at the University of Ottawa.

Druzhkina, V. 1927. "Opyt krest'janskogo romana u L. Tolstogo." *Na literaturnom postu*, N° 14: 22–28.

Dukhobortsy: istoriko-genealogicheskij arkhiv. Posted by Valery Kalmakov on the website: http://www.doukhobor.ru/literatura/.

"Dukhoborchestvo — russkaja sekta." 1913. In *Polnyj pravoslavnyj bogoslovskij entsiklopedicheskij slovar'* 1, 777–79. St. Petersburg, Izd. P.P. Sojkina. Reprint, London: Variorum, 1971.

Dunn, Ethel. 1970. "Canadian and Soviet Doukhobors: an examination of the mechanisms of culture change." *Canadian Slavic Studies*, vol. 4, N° 2 (Summer): 300–26.

—, 1976. "American Molokans and Canadian Doukhobors: economic position and ethnic identity." In *Ethnicity in the Americas*, edited by Frances Henry, 97–114. The Hague: Mouton.

—, 1995. "Spiritual and economic renewal among Molokans and Doukhobors." *Canadian Ethnic Studies* 27 (3): 164–180.

—, ed. 2001. *A Molokan's Search for Truth: The Correspondence of Leo Tolstoy and Fedor Zheltov*. English edition edited by Ethel Dunn, translated by John Woodsworth. Berkeley, CA: Highgate Road Social Science Research Station; and Ottawa: Slavic Research Group at the University of Ottawa. English translation of Donskov 1999.

Edmonds, Rosemary. 1966. Introduction to *Resurrection* by Leo Tolstoy. London: Penguin.

Edgerton, William. 1968. "The artist turned prophet: Leo Tolstoj after 1880." In *American Contributions to the Sixth International Congress of Slavists*, edited by William Harkins, 61–85. The Hague: Mouton.

—, ed. and trans. 1993. *Memoirs of Peasant Tolstoyans in Soviet Russia*. Bloomington: Indiana University Press. See esp. 182–84.

Elkinton, Joseph. 1903. *The Doukhobors: Their History in Russia, Their Migration to Canada*. Philadelphia: Ferris & Leach.

Emerson, Caryl. 1996. "What is infection and what is expression in *What Is Art?*" In Donskov and Woodsworth, 102–15.

Ershova, O. E. 2001. "D.A. Khilkov — pravoslavnyj opponent L.N. Tolstogo (po materialam perepiski)." In *Tolstovskij ezhegodnik*, edited by Vitalij Remizov, 288–30. Moscow: Gos. Muzej L.N. Tolstogo.

Ètkind, Aleksandr. 1995. "Russkie skoptsy: opyt istorii." *Zvezda*, N° 4: 131–63.

Evnin, F. I. 1954. "'Mysl' narodnaja' v *Anne Kareninoj* (*Anna Karenina* i okonchatel'nyj perekhod Tolstogo na pozitsii patriarkhal'nogo krest'janstva)." In *Izvestija AN SSSR, otd. lit-ry i jazyka* t. 13, vyp. 1, 66–81.

Ewashen, Larry A. 1985. *Peter V. Verigin: 1859–1924. An Appreciation*. Creston, BC: Great West Publishing.

—, 1992. "Embellishments and fanciful notions not needed" (review of S. G. Stupnikoff, *Historical saga of the Doukhobor faith 1750–1900s*). *Kamsack Times* [Kamsack, SK], 10 December, 8.

—, 1996a. "Lev." *Iskra*, N° 1817: 29–32.

—, 1996b. "Tolstoy and the Doukhbors today." In Donskov and Woodsworth, 225–28.

—, 2000. *The Spirit of '99*. Castlegar, BC: Crossroads Publishers.

—, 2001a. "A brief history of Peter, the Lordly, Verigin."

—, 2001b. "The Doukhobor immigration: Leo Tolstoy's project." *Iskra*, N° 1903: 7–10.

—, 2004. "Sergei L'vovich Tolstoy — the Second Coming." *Iskra*, N° 1958: 49–50.

—, 2010. "Tolstoy and the Doukhobors." Paper presented at the *Tolstoy Forum*, Simon Fraser University, 22 September.

Ewashen, Larry A., and Koozma J. Tarasoff. 1994. *In Search of Utopia: The Doukhobors.* Castlegar, BC: Spirit Wrestlers Associates.

Faminov, Peter. 1995. "A view from within: Tolstoy and his *Resurrection*." In Tarasoff and Klymasz, 21–23.

Fanger, D. 1968. "The peasant in literature." In Vucinich, 231–63.

Fedoseev, N. E. 1939. "N.E. Fedoseev — L.N. Tolstomu." *Literaturnoe nasledstvo*, N°s 37–38: 286–88. Reprinted from *Listok Svobodnago slova* [Christchurch, UK], N° 1 (1898): 6. Republished in *Stat'i i pis'ma*, by N. E. Fedoseev, 263–64. Moscow: Gospolitizdat, 1958.

Fersen, Nikolaj. 1979. "Tolstoj i shèkery." In *Transactions of the Association of Russian-American Scholars in the USA*, vol. 12, 162–72.

Field, Daniel. 1976. *Rebels in the Name of the Tsar.* Boston: Houghton Mifflin.

—, 1987. "Peasants and propagandists in the Russian movement To the People of 1874." *Journal of Modern History*, vol. 59 (September), 415–38.

Fodor, Alexander. 1986. "Changes in the evaluation of V. Čertkov's impact on the Tolstojs." *Russian Language Journal*, vol. 40, N° 136–37,181–98.

—, 1989. *The Quest for a Non-Violent Russia: The Partnership of Leo Tolstoy and Vladimir Chertkov.* Lanham, MD: University Press of America.

Frank, Stephen P. 1987. "Popular justice, community and culture among the Russian peasantry, 1870–1900." *Russian Review*, vol. 46, N° 3: 239–65.

Frantz, Charles E. 1961. "Historical continuities in an immigrant Russian sect: Doukhobor ideology and political organization." *Canadian Slavonic Papers*, vol. 5, 31–53.

Freeze, Gregory L. 1983. *The Parish Clergy in Nineteenth-Century Russia: Crisis, Reform, Counter-Reform.* Princeton, NJ: Princeton University Press.

Friends of Tolstoy. n.d. Friends of Tolstoy Centennial Project. Previously available at http://www.tolstoy.bc.ca.

Frierson, Cathy A. 1987. "Crime and punishment in the Russian village: concepts of criminality at the end of the nineteenth century." *Slavic Review*, vol. 46, N° 1: 55–69.

—, 1987. "*Razdel*: the peasant family divided." *Russian Review*, vol. 46 (January), 35–51.

—, 1990. "The peasant family division and the commune." In *Land Commune and Peasant Community in Russia: Communal Forms in Imperial and Early Soviet Society*, edited by Roger Bartlett, 303–20. Basingstoke, UK: Macmillan.

—, 1993. *Peasant Icons: Representation of Rural People in Late Nineteenth-Century Russia.* Oxford: Oxford University Press.

Friesen, John W. 1995. "The changing public image of Doukhobors in Canada." *Canadian Ethnic Studies*, vol. 27, N° 3: 131–40.

Friesen, John, and Michael Verigin. 1989. *The Community Doukhobors: A People in Transition.* Ottawa: Borealis.

Gablik, Suzie. 1991. *The Re-Enchantment of Art.* New York: Thames & Hudson.

Galagan, G. Ja. 1981. *L. N. Tolstoj. Khudozhestvenno-èticheskie iskanija.* Leningrad: Nauka.

—, 1996. "The idea of world renewal" (trans. John Woodsworth). In Donskov and Woodsworth, 33–35.

Gale, D. T., and Paul M. Koroscil. 1977. "Doukhobor settlements: experiments in idealism." *Canadian Ethnic Studies*, vol. 9, N° 2: 53–71.

Garrison, William Lloyd. 1838. "Declaration of sentiments adopted by the peace convention held in Boston, Sept. 18, 19, and 20, 1838." Previously available at http://www.wfu.edu/~zulick/340/peacedeclaration.html.

Gashkene-Chervinskene, E. 1960. "Drama L.N. Tolstogo «I svet vo t'me svetit»." *Uchenye zapiski Vil'njusskogo gosudarstvennogo universiteta im. V. Kapsukasa*, N° 31, vyp. 2: 109–29.

Gastev, Petr. 1912. "Vospominanija o Vasilii Kirilloviche Sjutaeve." *Vegetarianskoe obozrenie*, N° 1: 24–28; N° 2: 66–72.

Gladkova, L. V. 1994a. "M.P. Novikov: Ja vinovat v ego smerti." *Oktjabr'*, vol. 9, 155–90.

—, 1994b. "M.P. Novikov. Ukhod L. N. Tolstogo. Stolypinskaja reforma. Pis'mo k I. V. Stalinu." In Borisova, 318–47.

—, 1994c. "Pis'ma L.N. Tolstogo v kopiroval'nykh knigakh." In Borisova, 153–63.

—, 2000. "Ob istinnom iskusstve (po perepiske L.N. Tolstogo s pisatelem-krest'janinom F.F. Tishchenko)." *Oktjabr'*, vol. 9: 173–77.

—, 2004. *Mikhail Novikov. Iz perezhitogo.* Moscow: Èntsiklopedija sël i dereven'.

Gladwin, Jessie L. (1898) 1965. Letter to L.N. Tolstoy [Russian translation]. *Literaturnoe nasledstvo* 75, kn. 1, 474.

Golinenko, O. A. 1994. "Voprosy L.N. Tolstogo dukhoboru." In Borisova, 194–205.

Golitsyn G. S. 1897. "O sovremennom polozhenii Zakavazskogo dukhoborchestva i o prinjatykh Glavnym Nachal'stvom merakh presechenija vrednogo protivopravitel'stvennogo dvizhenija sredi posledovatelej ètoj sekty." 13 July 1897. GARF [State Archives of the Russian Federation]: Delo 1043, L. 513–61. Document #1897-07-13b in Woodsworth 1997. Excerpts published in Donskov 1998b.

—, 1898. Letter to Minister of Internal Affairs I.L. Goremykin, 1 August 1898. GARF: Delo 1053, L. 612–15. Document #1898-08-ola in Woodsworth 1997. (English translation in Woodsworth 1999a: 98–103.)

Gosudarstvennyj arkhiv Rossijskoj federatsii, Departament politsii.

Grebenschikov, V. I. 1978. "Golos naroda u L.N. Tolstogo i Solzhenitsyna." *Lev Tolstoj. Zapiski russkoj akademicheskoj gruppy v SShA* t. 11, 154–64.

Greenwood, John 1975. *Quaker Encounters: Friends and Relief.* Vol. 1. York, UK: William Sessions Ltd, 1975. See esp. Chap. 8, "Friends and Russia in the late nineteenth century — the great famines, and the Mennonite and Doukhobor migrations," 95–148.

Grinkova, N. P. 1960. "Lev Tolstoj i narodnyj jazyk." *Russkij jazyk v shkole*, N° 6: 49–53.

Grodetskaja, A. G. 2000a. *Otvety predanija «Zhitija svjatykh» v dukhovnom poiske L'va Tolstogo.* St. Petersburg: Nauka.

—, 2000b. "«Semejnoe» i «khrest'janskoe» v «Anne Kareninoj»." In Shcherbakova and Morozova, 212–27.

Gromova-Opul'skaja, L. D. 1979. *Lev Nikolaevich Tolstoj: materialy k biografii s 1886 po 1892 god.* Moscow: Nauka, 1979.

—, 1995. "Dialog uchitelej zhizni." In Donkov 1995a ("Two Teachers of Life: A Dialogue"), 1–7.

—, 1996. "The philosophy and æsthetics of brotherhood in Tolstoy's fiction." In Donskov and Woodsworth, 5–22.

—, 1998. *Lev Nikolaevich Tolstoj: materialy k biografii s 1892 po 1899 god.* Moscow: Nasledie.

—, 2000. "The idea of 'universal brotherhood' and unity: Lev Tolstoy and Pëtr Verigin." In Donskov, Woodsworth, and Gaffield, 158–70.

Guffee, Ruth Meyer. 1980. "The Yasnaya Polyana school 1859–62: Its place in Leo Tolstoy's development as writer and thinker." PhD dissertation, Yale University.

Gusev, N. N. 1907. "Pavlovtsy (iz istorii religiozno-obshchestvennykh dvizhenij russkago krest'janstva)." *Russkaja mysl'* [Moscow], t. 28: N° 7: 40–71; N° 8: 1–19.

Gustafson, Richard F. 1986. *Leo Tolstoy, Resident and Stranger. A Study in Fiction and Theology.* Princeton, NJ: Princeton University Press.

Hanzen-Lëve, A. A. 1997. "Russkoe sektantstvo i ego otrazhenie v literature russkogo modernizma." In *Russkaja literatura i religija*, edited by R. Grjube'l and V. Odinokov, 153–226. Novosibirsk, Russia: Nauka.

Haugh, Richard S. 1978. "The correspondence between Count Lev Tolstoy and the American Shakers: introduction and texts." In *Transactions of the Association of Russian-American Scholars in the USA*, vol. 11: 231–40.

Hawthorn, Harry B., ed. 1955. *The Doukhobors of British Columbia.* Vancouver: University of British Columbia and J. M. Dent and Sons.

Heier, Edmund. 1962. "A note on the Pashkovites and L.N. Tolstoy." *Canadian Slavonic Papers*, vol. 5, N° 3: 114–21.

—, 1970. *Religious Schism in the Russian Aristocracy 1860–190: Radstockism and Pashkovism.* The Hague: Nijhoff.

—, 1979. "Hadji Murat in the light of Tolstoy's moral and æsthetic theories." *Canadian Slavonic Papers*, vol. 21, N° 3: 324–36.

Hingley, R. 1967. "Peasants." In *Russian Writers and Society, 1825–1904*, 111–42. London: World University Library.

Holman, Michael J. de K. 1978. "The Purleigh colony: Tolstoyan togetherness in the late 1890s." In *New Essays on Tolstoy*, edited by Malcolm Jones, 194–222. Cambridge: Cambridge University Press.

—, 1988. "Translating Tolstoy for the Free Age Press: Vladimir Chertkov and his English manager Arthur Fifield." *Slavonic & East European Review*, vol. 66, N° 2: 184–97.

—, 2000. "British Tolstoyans, *The New Order* and the Doukhobors in the late 1890s: solidarity in word and deed." In Donskov, Woodsworth, and Gaffield, 131–48.

Horvath, Maria. 1970–1973. *A Doukhobor Bibliography. Based on Material Available in The University of British Columbia Library.* Vancouver: UBC Library.

Hughes, Lionel. 2001. "Tolstoy, the Bible, and everything." *Prairies North.* Previously available at http://www.prairiesnorth.com/summerol/doukhobor.html.

Ianela, Frank 1965. "The Dukhobors in Russia." Master's thesis, Northem Illinois University.

Inikova, Svetlana. 1999a. *Doukhobor Incantations Through the Centuries.* Translated and edited by Koozma Tarasoff. Ottawa: Legas.

—, 1999b. *The History of the Doukhobors in the Archives of Vladimir D. Bonch-Bruevich (1886–1950s).* Translated and edited by Koozma Tarasoff. Ottawa: Legas.

—, 2000a. "Rol' «tolstovstva» i tolstovtsev v dvizhenii kavkazskikh dukhobortsev 1890-kh godov." In *XXVI Mezhdunarodnye tolstovskie chtenija*, part 2, 50–63. Tula, Russia.

—, 2000b. "Spiritual origins and the beginnings of Doukhobor history." In Donskov, Woodsworth, and Gaffield, 1–21.

—, 2002. "Uchenie L.N. Tolstogo i syny svobody v Kanade." *Religiovedenie*, N° 3.

Ishchuk, G. N. 1958. "L.N. Tolstoj i nachalo «Posrednika»." *Uchenye zapiski Marijskogo ped. instituta*, t. 21, 122–56.

Iskra. 1943–. Journal of the Union of Spiritual Communities of Christ [Brilliant and Grand Forks, BC]. Available at http://www.iskra.ca.

"Istorija dukhoborcheskago obshchenija." n.d.. Doklad Departamenta Obshchikh Del MVD, Otd. V. See Document #1906-12-09a in Woodsworth 1997 (pp. C5, D9).

Istorija dukhoborcheskogo obshchenija. n.d. (Summarized in Woodsworth 1997, Document #1906-12-09a, pp. C5, D9.)

Jaenen, J. C. 1971. *The Doukhobors in Canada: Select Bibliography.* Ottawa: University of Ottawa, Department of History.

Jahn, Gary. 1972. "L.N. Tolstoj's 'Stories for the people' on the theme of brotherly love." PhD thesis, University of Wisconsin.

—, 1996. "Brother or other: Tolstoy's equivocal surrender to the concept of brotherhood." In Donskov and Woodsworth, 71–87.

James, Edward Holton. 1903. "Life among the Doukhobors." *The Co-operator* [Burley, WA], vol. 6, N° 196 (September), 111. (Translated into Russian by L. N. Tolstoy, and sent to *Obrazovanie,* but not published.)

Janzen, William. 1990. *The Experience of Mennonite, Hutterite and Doukhobor Communities in Canada.* Toronto: University of Toronto Press.

Jmaeff, Alex. 2004. "Friends of Tolstoy Bakery/Café Yasnaya Polyana update." *Iskra,* N° 1965: 22.

Jones, Helenne. 2001. "What Lev Nicholayevich Tolstoy means to me." *Iskra,* N° 1902: 20–21.

Kalmakoff, Jonathan. n.d. Doukhobor Genealogy Website. Available at http://www.doukhobor.org

Kanigan, Francis. 2003. "Visiting Yasnaya Polyana." *Iskra,* N° 1935: 21–24.

Kanigan, Vera 1999. "Yasnaya Polyana: his legacy lives on through the action of love." Previously available at http://www.tolstoy.ca/visit.htm.

Kanygina, V. 1978. "Uchenie Khrista dlja detej." *Iskra,* N° 1484: 28–31.

Karush, Sarah. 2001. "Church asked to forgive Tolstoy's sins." *Iskra,* N° 1905: 42.

Kashirin, Aleksandr. 2002. Ètika tolstovstva. Avtoreferat. Moscow.

"K istorii dukhoborov v Kanade." 1945. In *Jubilejnyj sbornik Mezhdunarodnogo kooperativnogo obshchestva 1919–1944,* 73–81. Detroit: Izd. MKO goroda Detroita.

Klibanov, A. I. 1969. *Religioznoe sektantstvo i sovremennost' (sotsiologicheskie i istoricheskie ocherki).* Moscow.

—, 1985. *History of religious sectarianism in Russia (1860s–1917).* Translated by Ethel Dunn, edited by Stephen P. Dunn. New York: Pergamon Press. See esp. 125–40.

Kline, George L. 1968. "The anarchist critique: Bakunin and Tolstoy." In *Religious and Anti-Religious Thought in Russia,* 11–34. Chicago: University of Chicago Press.

Klioutchanski, Arkadi 2000. "L'immigration des Doukhobors : une fenêtre sur le Canada en rétrospective." In Donskov, Woodsworth, and Gaffield, 171–84.

Kolesnikoff, James. 2000. "Understanding violent behaviour: the 'Sons of Freedom' case." In Donskov, Woodsworth, and Gaffield, 114–28.

Kolesnikoff, Nina, and James Kolesnikoff. 1978. "Leo Tolstoy and the Doukhobors." In *Canadian contributions to the VIII International Congress of Slavists (Zagreb-Ljubljana 1978),* edited by Z. Folejewski et al., 37–44. Ottawa: Canadian Association of Slavists.

Kolstø, Pål. 1991. "Leo Tolstoy, a church critic influenced by Orthodox thought." In *Church, Nation and State in Russia and Ukraine,* edited by Geoffrey A. Hosking, 148–67. London: MacMillan.

—, 2001. "A mass for a heretic? The controversy over Lev Tolstoy's burial." *Slavic Review*, vol. 60, N° 1: 75–96.

"Kommentarij neizvestnogo avtora o dukhoborakh, vyselivshikhsja v Kanadu i ob otnoshenii k nim L. N. Tolstogo." 1900. Unpublished manuscript, 18 May. (Document #1900-2TD-d in Woodsworth 1997.)

Kontsevich, I. M., et al. 1995. *Dukhovnaja tragedija L'va Tolstogo*. Moscow: Otchij dom.

Kopotilov, M. P. 1928. "Lev Nikolaevich Tolstoj i dukhobortsy (po dokumentam Muzeja Tobol'skogo Severa)." *Bjulleten' Obshchestva izuchenija kraja pri Muzee Tobol'skogo Severa* [Tobol'sk], N° 3 (4): 13–15.

Kosachova, Natalia 1983. "The Doukhobors." In *Russian Canadians: Their Past and Present*, edited by Tamara F. Jeletzky, 11–47. Ottawa: Borealis.

Kosovanov, A. 1958. *Timofej Bondarev i Lev Tolstoj*. Abakan: Khakasskoe knizhnoe izdatel'stvo.

Krajneva, I. 1980. "K izucheniju krest'janskogo voprosa v rannem tvorchestve L.N. Tolstogo: Iz arkhivnykh istochnikov." *Russkaja literatura*, N° 2: 164–72.

Kranikhfel'd, V. P. 1911. "Poreformennoe krest'janstvo v belletristike. *Velikaja Reforma: Russkoe obshchestvo i krest'janskij vopros v proshlom* i *nastojashchem*, 303–43. Moscow: Izd. Sytina, t. 6.

—, 1912. "Ot velikogo barina k velikomu muzhiku." *V mire idej i obrazov*. St. Petersburg: Prosveshchenie.

Kuropatkin, A. N. 1896. *Soobrazhenija nachal'nika zakaspijskoj oblasti po voprosu o pereselenii v Zakaspijskuju oblast' dukhoborov-postnikov*. Ashkhabad.

L.N. Tolstoy Archives n.d. Moscow: Gosudarstv. muzej L.N. Tolstogo.

Laliberté, G.-Raymond. 1962. "Origines idéologiques des Doukhobors au Canada." Master's thesis, Université de Montréal.

Lampert, E. 1966. "On Tolstoi, prophet and teacher." *Slavic Review*, vol. 25, N° 4: 604–14.

Lane, Christel. 1978. "The Old Russian sects." In *Christian Religion in the Soviet Union*, 91–11 2. New York: State University of New York Press.

Lapshinoff, Steve. 1993. *Names of Doukhobor Immigrants to Canada in 1899*. Crescent Lake, BC: self-published.

Latimer, Robert S. 1909. "The Dukhobors and Count Leo Tolstoy." In *Under Three Tsars: Liberty of Conscience in Russia 1856–1909*, 192–203. London: Morgan & Scott.

Lavretskij, V. L. 1929. "L.N. Tolstoj i krepostnoe pravo." In *Tolstoj, L.N. Polikushka*, 98–119. Moscow: Gosizdat.

Library and Archives Canada. "Doukhobors." Available at https://www.bac-lac.gc.ca/eng/discover/immigration/history-ethnic-cultural/Pages/doukhobor.aspx.

Lindstrom, Thais. 1957. "From chapbooks to classics: the story of the *Intermediary*." *American Slavic & East European Review*, vol. 2, 190–201.

Maevskij (Maevsky), V. A. 1952. "Tolstoj i dukhobory." In *Tragedija bogoiskatel'stva L'va Tolstogo*, 147–76. Buenos Aires: Talleres Graficos "Salguero."

Makovitskij, D. P. 1979–81. *U Tolstogo, 1904–1910: Jasnopoljanskie zapiski*. Literaturnoe nasledstvo 90. Edited by S. A. Makashin. Kn. 1–4. Moscow: Nauka.

Malov (Maloff), P. N. 1948. *Dukhobortsy, ikh istorija, zhizn'* i *bor'ba. K 50-letiju prebyvanija dukhobortsev v Kanade* t. 1. Thrums, BC.

Mandelker, Amy. 1996. "Tolstoy's eucharistic æsthetics." In Donskov and Woodsworth, 116–27.

Marlin, Marguerite. 2009. "Soviet-Canadian Doukhobor correspondence: building global civil society in a cold-war political climate." Master's thesis, Carleton University.

Maroger, D. 1976. "Le tolstoïsme (1895–1910 et 1965–1976)." In *Cahier II: Les littératures de langues européennes au tournant du siècle. Lectures d'aujourd'hui*, 7–24. Ottawa: Carleton University.

"Materialy dlja pomeshchenija vo frantsuzskikh gazetakh stat'i o dukhoborakh" p. t. "Une évolution dans l'histoire d'une secte Russe (Le Tolstoïsme des Doukhobors)." 1902. Unpublished manuscript, 1902. Document #1900-2DA-b in Woodsworth 1997.

Maude, Aylmer F. 1901. "The Doukhobors: a Russian exodus." In *Tolstoy and His Problems*, 262–326. London: Richard.

—, 1904. *A Peculiar People: The Doukhobors*. New York: Funk & Wagnalls; and London: A. Constable, 1905. Reprint, New York: AMS Press, 1970.

—, 1953. *The Life of Tolstoy*. Vol. 2, *Later Years*. The World's Classics 384. London: Oxford University Press.

Mavor, James F. 1923. "The Doukhobors." In *My Windows on the Street of the World*, vol. 2: 1–37. London and Toronto: Dent; New York: Dutton.

—, n.d. The James Mavor papers. Ms group 29, subgroup B. Ottawa: Public Archives of Canada.

Mayes, Hubert G. 1999. "'Resurrection': Tolstoy and Canada's Doukhobors." *The Beaver*, vol. 79, N° 5 (October/November): 39–44.

McIntosh, Jack. 1995a. "Rarely cited 'gems' in the Doukhobor bibliography." *Canadian Ethnic Studies*, vol. 27, N° 3: 262–69.

—, 1995b. "Update 1973–1993: excerpts from the Doukhobor bibliography. Expanded and updated edition." In Tarasoff and Robert Klymasz, 187–217.

McLaren, John. 1995. "Wrestling spirits: the strange case of Peter Verigin II." *Canadian Ethnic Studies*, vol. 27, N° 3: 95–130.

McLean, Hugh. 1994. "Tolstoy and Jesus." In *Christianity and the Eastern Slavs: Russian Culture in Modern Times*, edited by Robert P. Hughes and Irina Paperno, 103–23. Berkeley: University of California Press.

—, 1997. "Rousseau's God and Tolstoy's." *Tolstoy Studies Journal*, vol. 9: 25–35.

Mealing, F. Mark 1977. "A study in Doukhobor hymnody and folklife." Unpublished doctoral dissertation, University of Michigan.

—, 1995. *Doukhobor Life: A Survey of Doukhobor Religion, History and Folklore*. Castlegar, BC: Kootenay Doukhobor Historical Society.

Mel'gunov, S. P. 1919. *Iz istorii religiozno-obshchestvennykh dvizhenij v Rossii XIX v. Staroobrjadchestvo. Religioznye gonenija. Sektantstvo*, 203–10. Moscow: Zadruga.

Melent'ev, Ju. S. 1987. "L.N. Tolstoj v dukhovnom mire sovremennika." *Iskra*, N° 1647: 4–8.

Meleshko, E. D. 1999. *Filosofija neprotivlenija L.N. Tolstogo*. Tula, Russia: Izd. TPGU im. L.N. Tolstogo.

Metzele, Josef. 1996. "The concept of 'brotherly love' in Tolstoy's late prose." In Donskov and Woodsworth, 152–68.

Miljukov, Paul 1972. "The development of Russian sectarianism." Part 1. In *Religion and the Church (Outlines of Russian Culture)*, edited by Michael Karpovich, translated by Valentine Ughet and Eleanor Davis. New York: A. S. Bames.

Minokin, M. V. 1950. "Problema krest'janstva v tvorchestve L.N. Tolstogo (80–90-e gody XIX veka)." Moscow: Moskovskij Gos. Ped. Institut.
Mir. 1977. "An interview with George Woodcock." *Mir*, N° 15 (May): 3–14, 62.
Mir Centre for Peace. n.d. Website, http://selkirk.ca/mir-centre-for-peace.
Missionerskoe obozrenie (*MR*). 1896–1901. Periodical.
Moher, Frank. 1997. *Tolstoy's Wife*. Gabriola Island, BC: Single Lane, 1997.
Moon, David. 2001. *The Abolition of Serfdom in Russia. 1762–1907.* Harlow, UK: Longman.
Morozov, V. S. 1917. *Vospominanija o Tolstom uchenika Jasnopoljanskoj shkoly Vasilija Stepanovicha Morozova*. Moscow: Posrednik.
MR — See *Missionerskoe obozrenie*.
Muratov, M. V. 1934. *L.N. Tolstoj i V.G. Chertkov po ikh perepiske*. Moscow: Gos. Tolstovskij Muzej.
Mürer, Esther. 1999. "One hundred years ago." *Types & Shadows (Journal of the Fellowship of Quakers in the Arts)*, N° 13 (Spring). Available at http://fqa.quaker.org/types/t13-hundred.html.
Myshkovskaja, L. M. 1935. "Narodnye rasskazy Tolstogo." *Literaturnaja uchëba*, vol. 9: 31–45.
—, 1958. "Narodnye rasskazy." In *Masterstvo L.N. Tolstogo*, 369–89. Moscow: Sovetskij pisatel'.
Nikitina, Nina. 2000. "Tolstoï o dukhobortsakh — ljudjakh XXV stoletija." *Iskra* N° 1889 (2000): 8–11, and N° 1890: 40–45.
Novikov, M. P. 1904. "Golos krest'janina." *Svobodnoe slovo*, N° 10: 1–43.
Novitskij, O. 1982. *Dukhobortsy, ikh istorija i verouchenie*. 2nd ed. Kiev.
Oliver, Edmund. 1932. *Peter Verigin*. Transactions of the Royal Society of Canada, section 2, 97–123.
Otchizna. 1978. "L.N. Tolstoj i kanadskie dukhobory." *Iskra*, N° 1484: 31–40, reprinted from *Otchizna*, N° 9.
Ovsjaniko-Kulikovskij, D. N. 1905. *Tolstoj kak khudozhnik*. St. Petersburg.
Palmieri, Aurelio. 1915. "The Russian Doukhobors and their religious teachings." *Harvard Theological Review*, vol. 8, N° 1 (January): 62–81.
Perris, G. H. 1898. *Leo Tolstoy, the Grand Mujik*. London: T. Fisher Unwin.
Perry, Shirley. 2000. "The importance of song in Doukhobor life." In Donskov, Woodsworth, and Gaffield, 342–56.
Pevey, Martha. 1983. "The Dukhobor emigration crisis of 1899 from three perspectives." Master's thesis, Columbus, Ohio.
Philipp, F. H. 1959. *Tolstoj und der Protestantismus*. Giessen, Germany: Schmitz.
Philipson, Morris. 1967. *The Count Who Wished He Were a Peasant*. New York: Pantheon Books.
Polnyj pravoslavnyj bogoslovskij èntsiklopedicheskij slovar'. 1913. Vol. l. Moscow: Izd. P.P. Sojkina.
Popoff, Eli A. 1975. *Tanya*. Grand Forks, BC: Mir Publications.
—, 1978. "Vstrecha dukhobortsa s L. N. Tolstym." *Iskra*, N° 1484: 20–28. Reprinted with English translation, "The meeting of a Doukhobor with Lev Nikolaevich Tolstoy." *Iskra*, N° 1935 (2003): 36–44.
—, 1982. *An Historical Exposition on the Origin and Evolvement of the Basic Tenets of the Doukhobor Life-Conception*. Grand Forks, BC: P.O.P. Press.
—, 1991. *Katya. A Canadian Doukhobor.* Leningrad: TITUL/ LenArt.
—, 1992. *Stories from Doukhobor History.* Grand Forks, BC: Iskra Publications.

—, 2000. "The Doukhobors: the 'enigma' and the reality." In Donskov, Woodsworth, and Gaffield, 22–46.

—, 2001. Personal correspondence, 12 March.

—, 2003. See Popoff, Eli A. 1978.

—, n.d. "Doukhobor poetry, and Doukhobor poets in Canada." Unpublished manuscript.

Popoff, Jim (Popov, D. I.). 1987–88. "What were the main historical reasons and causes for the rise of the splinter movement known as the Sons of Freedom?" Series of articles. *Iskra*.

—, 1987. "Dedushka Tolstoj — k chemu on nas prizyvaet?" *Iskra*, N° 1647: 2–3.

—, 1998. "Interv'ju s V.I. Tolstym." *Iskra*, N° 1855: 5–10, 34–38. Translated in English as "Interview with V.I. Tolstoy." *Iskra*, N° 1856: 7–13, 49–51.

Popov, Evgenij Ivanovich. 1898. *Zhizn' i smert' Evdokima Nikiticha Drozhzhina, 1866–1894*. 2nd ed. Purleigh, UK.

—, 1909. "L. N. Tolstoj i dukhobory." In *Mezhdunarodnyj tolstovskij al'manakh*, edited by P. Sergeenko, 250–56. Moscow: Kniga. Reprinted in *Dukhobortsy, ikh istorija, zhizn' i bor'ba. K 50-letiju prebyvanija dukhobortsev v Kanade*, by P. N. Malov (Maloff), t. l. Thrums, BC.

Popovskij (Popovsky), Mark. 1983. *Russkie muzhiki rasskazyvajut*. London: Overseas Publication Interchange.

Porakishvili, Z. I. 1970. *Dukhobory v Gruzii*. Tbilisi.

Pozdnjakov, V. N. 1914. "Pravda o dukhoborakh v Zakavkaz'e i v Sibiri." *Ezhemesjachnyj zhurnal literatury, nauki i obshchestvennoj zhizni*, N° 7.

Prokhanov, I. S. 1992. *V kotle Rossii, 1869–1933. Avtobiografija Ivana Stepanovicha Prokhanova s izlozheniem glavnykh faktov dvizhenija Evangel'skikh khristian v Rossii*. Izdanie 1-e. Chicago.

Prugavin, A. S. 1881. "Znachenie sektantstva v russkoj narodnoj zhizni." In *Russkaja mysl'*, kn. 1, 301–63. Moscow.

—, 1906a. *Golodajushchee krest'janstvo: ocherki golodovki 1898–99 gg.* Moscow: Posrednik.

—, 1906b. *Religioznye otshchepentsy. Ocherki sovremennago sektantstva*. Moscow: Posrednik.

—, 1911a. "Lev Tolstoj i samarskie molokane." In *O L've Tolstom i o tolstovtsakh*, 35–71. Izd. 2-e. Moscow.

—, 1911b. "Rol' tolstovstva v dukhoborcheskom dvizhenii (Po otchetam g. ober-prokurora sv. Sinoda)." *O L've Tolstom i o tolstovtsakh*. Izd. 2-e. Moscow, 1911: 201–20.

PSS (*Polnoe sobranie sochienij*)—see L. N. Tolstoj 1928–58.

Rak, Julie. 2004. *Negotiated Memory: Doukhobor Autobiographical Discourse*. Vancouver and Toronto: UBC Press.

Rasporich, A. W. 1987. "Utopia, sect, and millennium in Western Canada, 1870–1940." *Prairie Forum*, vol. 12, N° 2: 217–43.

Remizov, Vitalij, and Liudmila Gladkova, eds. 2011. *S.A. Tolstaja: «Moja zhizn'»*. Moscow: Gos. muzej L.N. Tolstogo.

Rezansoff, Peter 2005. "Bakery Café and Communication Centre opens at Yasnaya Polyana." *Iskra*, N° 1975: 19–21.

Rimvydas Silbajoris's *Tolstoy's Aesthetics and his Art* (1990).

Rozanov, V. V. 1990. *Religija i kul'tura*. Tom 1. Moscow.

Sampson, R. V. 1973. *Tolstoy: the discovery of peace*. London: Heinemann.

Sanborn, Josh. 1995. "Pacifist politics and peasant politics: 1895–99." *Canadian Ethnic Studies*, vol. 27, N° 3: 52–71.

— (Joshua A.). 2000. "Non-violent protest and the Russian state: the Doukhobors in 1895 and 1937." In Donskov, Woodsworth, and Gaffield, 83–102.

Seminoff (Semenoff), Corinne. 2005. "A bridge to bake for." *Iskra*, N° 1976: 13–19.

Semjakin, G. 1897. Letter to the Director of the Department of Police, A.P. Solomon, 21 July. GARF [State Archives of the Russian Federation]: Delo 1053, L. 564. Document #1897-07-19c in Woodsworth 1997.

Shcherbakova, M. I., and M. A. Mozharova, ed. 2000a. *Mir filologii.* Moscow: Nasledie.

—, 2000b. "«Brat'ja» (Sektanty I.S. i A.S. Prokhanovy)." In Shcherbakova and Mozharova, 320–29.

Sherriff, Peggy. 1959. "The Doukhobors: A selected bibliography." Diploma thesis, University of London.

Shesterikov S. 1928. "Zametka Leskova o Sjutaeve." In *Lev Nikolaevich Tolstoj. Jubilejnyj sbornik*, edited by N. N. Gusev, 329–31. Moscow and Leningrad: Gosizdat (Khudozhdestvennoj literatury).

Shklovskij, V. B. 1963. "O dukhoborakh i o «Voskresenii»." In *Lev Tolstoj*, 701–10. Zhizn' zamechatel'nykh ljudej 6 [363]. Moscow: Molodaja gvardija. Appears in English as "About the Dukhobors and *Resurrection*" in *Lev Tolstoy* by Victor Shklovsky, translated by Olga Shartse, 643–52. Moscow: Progress.

Sidorov, N. P. 1911. "Krepostnye krest'jane v russkoj belletristike." *Velikaja Reforma: Russkoe obshchestvo i krest'janskij vopros v proshlom i nastojashchem*, t. 3. Moscow: Izd. Sytina.

Signori, Dolores A., comp. 1989. *Guide to the Papers of James Mavor.* Toronto: Thomas Fisher Rare Book Library. Pertinent material in Vol. 1 (n.d.), Box 17, File 27, and Vol. 3 (1899), Box 1A, File 48.

Silbajoris, Rimvydas. 1996. "The brotherhood and solitude of death in Tolstoy." In Donskov and Woodsworth, 88–101.

Simmons, Ernest J. 1960. *Leo Tolstoy*. vol. 2. New York: Vintage Books. See esp. 111, 227, 231, 236, 250–51, 275, 277, 384.

—, 1973. *Tolstoy.* London and Boston: Routledge and Kegan Paul.

Simon Fraser University Library. n.d. "Tolstoy and the Doukhobors." Bibliography of resources available in the Simon Fraser University Library. Available at https://databases.lib.sfu.ca/record/61245145880003610/Doukhobor-Collection-of-Simon-Fraser-University.

Simpson, Mark. 1981. "L.N. Tolstoy and the famine of 1891–1892." *Melboume Slavonic Studies*, vol. 15, 41–53.

Siniavski, André. 1990. "Vassili Sioutaev et les autres rationalistes à la recherche de la vérité." In *Ivan le Simple*, translated by Antonina Roubichon-Stretz, 376–93. Paris: Albin Michel.

"Sjutaev and Bondarev." 1913. *Tolstovskij ezhegodnik.* St. Petersburg and Moscow: Izd. Tolstovskogo muzeja v Sankt-Peterburge i Tolstovskogo obshchestva v Moskve, 1–44.

Skvortsov, V. M. 1896. *Zapiska o dukhobortsakh na Kavkaze.* GARF [State Archives of the Russian Federation]: Delo 1053, L. 1–22r. Document #1896-02-a in Woodsworth 1997. Published in Donskov 1998b.

—, 1899. Report to Senior Procurator of the Holy Synod, K. P. Pobedonostsev, 6 February 1899. GARF: Delo 1053, L. 635–36. Document #1899-02-04d in Woodsworth 1997. English translation in Woodsworth 1999a: 112–14.

— (E. Ja.) 1900. "Razocharovanija golodajushchikh v Amerike dukhobor i farisejskoe poslanie k nim grafa L. N. Tolstogo." *Missionerskoe obozrenie* [St. Petersburg], t. 2, kn. 11 (November), 521–42.

—, 1901. *Dukhobory v Amerike i graf L. N. Tolstoj.* St. Petersburg: Izd. Missionerskoe obozrenie.

—, 1904. "Dukhoborcheskaja sekta." In *Missionerskij Sputnik*, 447–61. St. Petersburg: Komarov.

—, 1912. *Dukhobory v Amerike* i *tolstovtsy.* St. Petersburg: Izd. V.M. Skvortsova.

—, n.d. "Dva slova o kanadskikh dukhoborakh." *Missionerskoe obozrenie*, 703–04.

Slivitskaja, Ol'ga 1988. *«Vojna i mir» L.N. Tolstogo — problemy chelovecheskogo obshchenija.* Leningrad.

Society of Friends, 1999. Minutes of Canadian yearly meeting of the Religious Society of Friends, fourth-day morning, 18 August. Previously available at http://www.quaker.ca/minutes/99minutes18Morn.html#M36.

Solov'ëv, Èduard 1987. "L.N. Tolstoj — èto chestnaja sovest' vremeni." *Iskra*, N° 1649: 4–6, 25–30; also printed in *Golos rodiny* [Moscow], N° 36 [2596] (1987): 10–11, with cover illustration.

Solov'ëv, P. I. 1978. "Velikij Tolstoj." *Iskra*, N° 1484: 2–5.

Soukeroff, William 1999. "The origin of the Freedomite movement." Previously available at http://www.doukhobor.org/Soukeroff.htm.

Sreznevskij, V. I. 1920. "O lichnom èlemente v drame L. N. Tolstogo «I svet vo t'me svetit»." *Birjuch petrogradskikh gosudarstvennykh akademicheskikh teatrov* 2, 144–58.

Steinitz, Hugo, ed. 1902. *Pis'ma L. N. Tolstogo k dukhobortsam.* Berlin.

Stepnjak-Kravchinskij, S. M. 1962. "Gonenija na dukhobortsev. S zakljucheniem grafa L.N. Tolstogo." Publ. i vstup. stat'ja M. I. Perper. *Literaturnoe nasledstvo* t. 69, kn. 2: 307–10.

Stoochnoff, John P. 1961. *Doukhobors As They Are.* Toronto: Ryerson.

Stupnikoff, S. G. 1992. *Historical Saga of the Doukhobor Faith 1750–1900s.* Saskatoon.

Subbotnik Information Exchange. n.d. Available at http://www.russianaz.org/molokane/subbotniki/.

Sukhorev, V. A. 1944. *Dokumenty po istorii dukhobortsev i kratkoe izlozhenie ikh veroispovedanija.* North Kildonan (MB).

Sulerzhitskij, Leopol'd Antonovich. 1905. *V Ameriku s dukhoborami.* Moscow: Kushnerev. Translated by Michael Kalmakoff as *To America with the Doukhobors.* Regina: Canadian Plains Research Centre, 1982.

Sushkov, Boris. 1991. "Zemnoe Evangelie." (In L. N. Tolstoj 1991: 3–22.)

Szalasznyj, Kathlyn. 1977. "The Doukhobor homestead crisis 1896–1907." Master's thesis, University of Saskatchewan.

Taliashvili, G. A. 1967. "Lev Tolstoj i Gruzija." In *Russko-gruzinskie literaturnye vzaimootnoshenija (XVIII–XIX vv.)*, 342–439. Tbilisi: Izd. Ganatleba.

Tarasoff, Koozma J. 1963. "In search of brotherhood: the history of the Doukhobors." Unpublished 3-volume manuscript. Vancouver.

—, 1969. *A Pictorial History of the Doukhobors.* Saskatoon: Modern Press.

—, 1982 *Plakun Trava: The Doukhobors.* Grand Forks, BC: Mir Publications.

—, 1987. "An international happening in Western Canada: the unveiling of two Leo Tolstoy statues." *Iskra*, N° 1648: 23–25, 41–43.

—, 1988. "Mysli u pamjatnika L'vu Tolstomu" (trans. È. Solov'ëv). *Golos rodiny* [Moscow], N° 1 (2613), Jan., 13.

—, ed. 1995. *From Russia with Love: The Doukhobors.* Special issue of *Canadian Ethnic Studies*, vol. 27, N° 3.

—, comp. and ed. 1998. *Spirit-Wrestlers' Voices.* Ottawa: Legas.

—, 2002. *Spirit Wrestlers: Doukhobor Pioneers' Strategies for Living.* Book and CD-ROM. Ottawa: Legas & Spirit-Wrestlers Publishing.

—, 2007. "Tolstoy and the Doukhobors." Paper presented at the First Global Nonkilling Leadership Forum, Hawaii, 1–4 November.

—, n.d. *Spirit Wrestlers.* Website: www.spirit-wrestlers.com.

Tarasoff, Koozma J., and Robert Klymasz, eds. 1995. *Spirit Wrestlers: Centennial Papers in Honour of Canada's Doukhobor Heritage.* Canadian Centre for Folk Culture Studies 67. Hull, QC: Canadian Museum of Civilization.

Tarasov, N. P., comp. 1959. *L.N. Tolstoj i krest'jane: iz dokumentov Gosudarstvennogo arkhiva Tul'skoj oblasti.* Tula, Russia.

Tarasova, Irina. 1995. "Doukhobor materials in the collections of the museum of religious history in St Petersburg." In Tarasoff and Robert Klymasz, 217–33.

Teasdale, Wayne. 2000. *The Mystic Heart.* Novato, CA: New World Library.

Terletskij, V. I. 1911. "Sekta dukhoborov." In *Russkie sektanty, ikh uchenie, kul't i sposoby propagandy*, edited by M. A. Kal'nev, 12. Odessa.

Tétrault-Farber, Gabrielle. 2014. "Tolstoy's Canadian Doukhobors return to Russia over 100 years after fleeing." *Moscow Times*, 2 October. Available at https://tinyurl.com/podovinikoff.

Timofeev, P. P. 1957. "Krest'janskaja problema v rannem tvorchestve. L.N. Tolstogo." In *Uch. zap. Minskogo ped. in-ta*, vyp. 8, 71–85.

Tolstaja, A. L. 1953. *Otets.* New York: Izd. imeni Chekhova. See esp. vol. 2, 148–53, 201–11.

Tolstaja, S. A. (Sofia Andreevna). 1916. "Moja zhizn'." (Unpublished in Russian until 2011—see Remizov and Gladkova 2011.)

—, 1936. *Pis'ma k L.N. Tolstomu 1862–1910.* Edited by P. S. Popov. Moscow: Academia.

—, 1978. *Dnevniki.* 2 vols. Edited by S. I. Mashinskij. Moscow.

— (Sofia Andreevna Tolstaya). 2010. *My Life.* Translated by J. Woodsworth and A. Klioutchanski, edited by A. Donskov. Ottawa: University of Ottawa Press.

Tolstoj, I. V. 1987. "Ne oruzhiem, no siloj dukha." *Iskra*, N° 1652: 6–7, 41.

Tolstoj, L. N. (Leo Tolstoy). 1895. "Posleslovie k stat'e o gonenii na dukhoborov (1895)." In *Lev Tolstoj*, kn. 1, 475–76. *Literaturnoe nasledstvo* 69. Moscow.

—, 1898a. *Dve vojny. Listki svobodnogo slova*, N° 1. (Also *PSS* 31:97–101.)

—, 1898b. *Emigration of the Doukhobortsi.* London: Kegan Paul.

—, 1898c. "Pis'ma N.E. Fedoseevu (2). 24 marta, 9 ijunja 1898." (Also *PSS* 71:336–37; 374–75.) Also published with introduction and commentary by N. Pokrovskaja and K. Shokhor-Trotskij in *L.N. Tolstoj II, V: Neizdannaja perepiska*, 277–89. Literaturnoe nasledstvo 37–38. Moscow: Akademija Nauk, 1939. Reprint, Vaduz: Kraus Reprint Ltd., 1963.

—, 1899. "Po povodu kongressa o mire: Pis'mo k shvedam." (Also *PSS* 90:60–66.)

—, 1900. "Pis'mo k pereselivshimsja v Kanadu dukhoboram (15/27 fevralja 1900 g.)." *Svobodnaja mysl'* [Genève], N° 5–6 (May–June), 77–80. Reprinted with French and English translations in Robert Minden, *Separate From the World*. Vancouver: National Film Board of Canada, 1979. Another English translation published in *The Complete Works of Count Tolstoy*, translated and edited by Leo Wiener, vol. 12, *Fables for Children; Natural Science Stories; Popular Education; Decembrists; Moral Tales*, 345–52. Boston: Dana Estes & Co, 1905.

—, 1902. *Pis'ma k dukhoborstam*. Published in German as *L. N. Tolstoï: Sendschreiben an die Duchoborzen*. Izvestnejshaja russkaja biblioteka 35. Berlin: Izd. Hugo Steinitz.

—, 1905. "Konets veka. O predstojashchem perevorote." Also *PSS* 36. Moscow, 1936: 241. Published in English as "The end of the age. An essay on the approaching revolution," in *Government is Violence: Essays on Anarchism and Pacifism*, by Lev Tolstoy, 28. London: Phoenix Press, 1990.

—, 1905. "Appeal in behalf of the Dukhobors." In *The Complete Works of Count Tolstoy*, translated and edited by Leo Wiener, vol. 12, *Fables for Children; Natural Science Stories; Popular Education; Decembrists; Moral Tales*, 338–42. Boston: Dana Estes & Co.

—, 1911a. "The emigration of the Doukhobors." In *Essays, Letters, Miscellanies*, vol. 1, 310–16. New York: Scribner's.

—, 1911b. "Nobel's bequest: a letter addressed to a Swedish editor." In *Essays, Letters, Miscellanies*, vol. 1, 1–7. New York: Scribner's.

—, 1912–13. *Polnoe sobranie sochinenij* (ed. and annot. P. I. Birjukov). 20 vols. Moscow: Izd. Sytina. Distinct from following entry.

—, 1913a. "E.I. Popovu." In L.N. Tolstoj. *Polnoe sobranie sochinenij v 24 tt.* (ed. and annot. P. I. Birjukov), t. 22, 162–63. Moscow: Izd. Sytina.

—, 1913b. "Pis'ma L.N. Tolstogo k kn. G.S. Golitsynu." *Tolstovskij ezhegodnik* [St. Petersburg], otd. 2, 150–52.

—, 1913c. *Polnoe sobranie sochinenij v 24 tt.* (ed. and annot. P. I. Birjukov). Moscow: Izd. Sytina.

—, 1928–58. *Polnoe sobranie sochinenij. Jubilejnoe izdanie* [*PSS*; Jubilee Edition]. 90 vols. Moscow: Goslitizdat, 1928–58. See esp. vols. 68–72.

—, 1960. *What is Art?* Indianapolis: Bobs-Merill, 1960.

—, 1978. *Tolstoy's Letters, Volume II: 1880–1910* (selected, ed., and trans., R. F. Christian). London: University of London and Athlone Press.

—, 1979. *The Teachings of Jesus: Compiled for Children*. Grand Forks, BC: Union of Spiritual Communities of Christ.

—, 1987. "The inevitable revolution." In *Writings on Civil Disobedience and Nonviolence*, 385–415. Philadelphia: New Society.

—, 1991. *Evangelie dlja detej*. Tula, Russia.

Tolstoj, Sergej L'vovich 1949. "Moe uchastie v èmigratsii dukhoborov v Kanadu. P.A. Kropotkin." In *Ocherki bylogo*, 193–212. Moscow: Izd. Khudozhestvennoj literatury.

Tolstoj, Vladimir 1995. "Nasha vera, vechno novaja i zhivaja." *Voskresenie*, N° 2: 16–24.

Tolstoy, A. 1960. "Tolstoy and the Russian peasant." *Russian Review*, vol. 19 (April), 150–56.

Tracie, Carl, 2002. "Doukhobor communal settlement in 1917." Paper delivered at the annual meeting of the Canadian Historical Association, Toronto.

Treadgold, Donald W. 1968. "The Peasant and religion." In Vucinich, 72–108.

Uspenskij, I. N. 1953. "Lev Tolstoj i russkoe krest'janstvo." In *Izvestija Akademii Nauk SSSR (Otdelenie literatury i jazyka)*, t. 12, vyp. 4, 297–314.

Vanek, Anthony L., and Regna Darnell. 1971. "Canadian Doukhobor Russian in Grand Forks (BC): some social aspects." In *Linguistic Diversity in Canadian Society*, edited by Regna Darnell, 267–90. Edmonton, AB, and Champagne, IL: Linguistic Research.

Vejksan, V. A. 1959. *L.N. Tolstoj — narodnyj uchitel'*. Moscow: Uchpedgiz.

Velikanova, Natal'ja, and Robert Vittaker (Whittaker), eds. 2004. *L.N. Tolstoj i SShA. Perepiska*. Moscow: IMLI RAN.

Verigin, Grigory. 1935. *Ne v sile Bog, a v pravde*. Paris: Dreyfus & Charpentier. Excerpt (Chap. 8) available in an English translation by Galina Alexeyeva (Alekseeva) and Larry Ewashen at http://www.doukhobor.org/Grigory-Verigin.html.

Verigin, John J. (Ivan Ivanovich) Sr. 1978. "Dukhobortsy pomnjat Tolstogo." *Iskra*, N° 1484: 50–63.

Verigin, Pëtr Vasil'evich. 1901. *Pis'ma dukhborcheskago rukovoditelja Petra Vasil'evicha Verigina*. Izd. Svobodnago slova 47. Edited by Vladimir Bonch-Bruevich, preface by V. G. Chertkov and Anna Chertkova. Christchurch, UK: Tchertkoff.

Vucinich, Wayne S., ed. 1968. *The Peasant in Nineteenth-Century Russia*. Stanford, CA: Stanford University Press.

Wasiolek, Edward. 1978. *Tolstoy's Major Fiction*. Chicago and London: University of Chicago Press.

Weisbein, Nicolas. 1960. "Tolstoï et les Doukhobors." Pièce N° 2 in "Notes et documents." In *L'évolution religieuse de Tolstoï*, edited by N. Weisbein, 476–81. Paris: Librairie des Cinq Continents.

Wilkinson, Myler. 1992. "Tolstoy and the Doukhobors." Paper delivered at the Institute of World Literature, Russian Academy of Sciences, Moscow, May.

—, 2007. "Being on the land: Histories at the confluence." Symposium on the people of the Kootenay and Columbia Rivers. Selkirk, BC: Mir Press. Also available at https://tinyurl.com/beingontheland.

—, 2014. "Tolstoy at the Mir Centre for Peace — The Long Tradition." *Peace and Conflict Monitor*. Last modified 18 July. Available at http://www.monitor.upeace.org/archive.cfm?id_article=1058.

Woodcock, George 1989. "Russian writers and the Doukhobors." *Canadian Literature*, N° 120: 110–14.

—, 1995. "James Mavor, Peter Kropotkin, Lev Tolstoy and the Doukhobors." In Tarasoff and Klymasz, 95–101.

Woodcock, George, and Ivan Avakumovic. 1968. *The Doukhobors*. Toronto: Oxford University Press.

Woodsworth, John. 1995. "Attitude and character transformation as revealed in the correspondence of Tolstoy and Verigin." *Canadian Ethnic Studies*, vol. 27, N° 3: 245–51.

—, comp. 1997. *The Doukhobors 1895–1943*. CRCR Document Series 8. 2nd ed. (rev.). Ottawa: Centre for Research on Canadian-Russian Relations, Carleton University.

—, 1998. "Recent and current studies on the Doukhobors at Ottawa universities." In *Spirit-Wrestlers' Voices*, edited and compiled by Koozma J. Tarasoff, 313–26. Ottawa: Legas.

—, comp., trans., and annot. 1999a. *Russian Roots & Canadian Wings: Russian Archival Documents on the Doukhobor Emigration to Canada*. Ottawa: Penumbra Press.

—, 1999b. "Novye perspektivy na istoriju dukhobortsev." *Iskra*, N° 1878: 13–16. Translated in English as "New perspectives on the history of the Doukhbors." *Iskra*, N° 1879: 71–75.

—, 2002. "Canadian Doukhobors on the Web: An Annotated Guide." Previously available at http://www.canada.uottawa.ca/doukhobor.htm.

—, 2003. "Tri mezhdunarodnye konferentsii v Rossii, posvjashchennye 175-letiju goda rozhdenija L.N. Tolstogo/Report on three international conferences in Russia celebrating the 175th anniversary of Tolstoy's birth." Part 1, *Iskra*, N° 1949: 5–8; Part 2: *Iskra* N° 1950: 56–69. (Available in Russian and English at http://kanadacha.ca/academic/aug2003engl.html.)

—, 2005. "Lev Nikolaevich Tolstoy and the Canadian Doukhobors." Talk given at Principia College, Elsah, Illinois, 4 October.

Worobec, Christine 1991. *Peasant Russia: Family and Community in the Post-Emancipation Period.* Princeton, NJ: Princeton University Press. See esp. 151–74.

Wright, J. F. C. 1940. *Slava Bohu.* New York.

Young, Pauline. 1932. *The Pilgrims of Russian-Town: The Community of Spiritual Christian Jumpers in America.* New York: Russell & Russell. Revised, 1967.

Zajdenshnur, È. E. 1951. "Narodnaja pesnja i poslovitsa v tvorchestve L.N. Tolstogo." In *L.N. Tolstoj: Sbornik statej i materialov*, 511–76. Moscow: Akademija Nauk.

Zhdanov, V. A., ed. 1955. *Opisanie rukopisej khudozhestvennykh proizvedenij L.N. Tolstogo.* Moscow: Akademija Nauk SSSR.

Ziolkowski, Margaret. 1988. "Anti-hagiography: Tolstoy's assault on orthodoxy." In *Hagiography and Modern Russian Literature*, 218–46. Princeton, NJ: Princeton University Press.

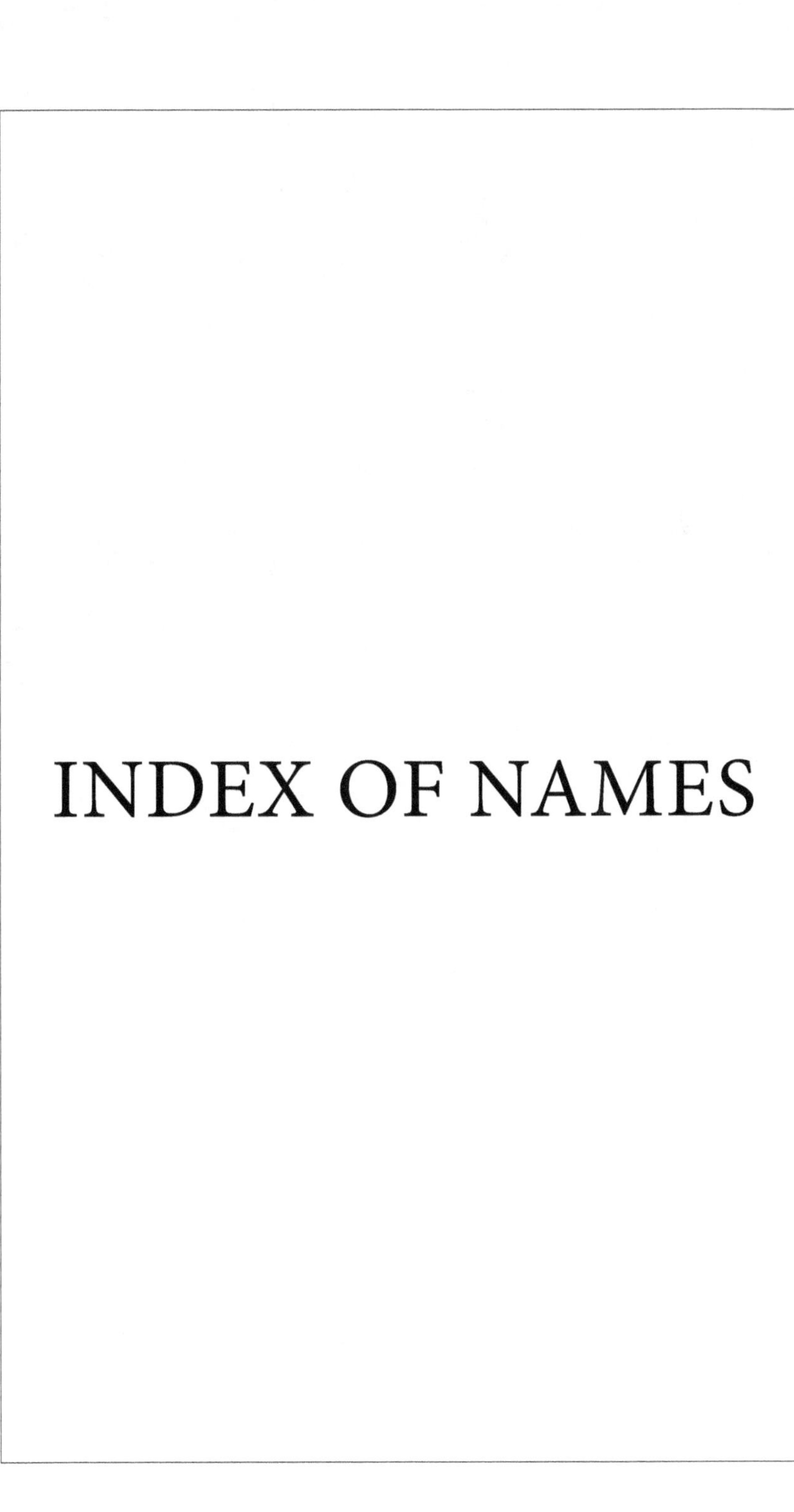

INDEX OF NAMES

Note: This index covers all texts in Part I and Part II, as well as the Doukhobor Timeline and the filial tribute to Eli A. Popoff in the Appendices.

L

M

N

O

T

www.ingramcontent.com/pod-product-compliance
Lightning Source LLC
Chambersburg PA
CBHW071532120726
47907CB00014B/1531

* 9 7 8 0 7 7 6 6 2 8 5 0 9 *